AN INTRODUCTION TO THE

THEORY OF STATISTICS

AN INTRODUCTION TO THE
THEORY OF STATISTICS

G. UDNY YULE, M.A., F.R.S.
Formerly Reader in Statistics, University of Cambridge

and

M. G. KENDALL, M.A., Sc.D.
Formerly Professor of Statistics, University of London

FOURTEENTH EDITION
REVISED AND ENLARGED
Fifth Impression

1968
HAFNER PUBLISHING COMPANY
NEW YORK

First edition	.. 1911	*Eleventh edition*	.. 1937
Second edition	.. 1912	*Twelfth edition*	.. 1939
Third edition	.. 1916	*Thirteenth edition*	.. 1944
Fourth edition	.. 1917	*(Five impressions)*	
Fifth edition	.. 1919	*Fourteenth edition*	.. 1950
Sixth edition	.. 1922	*Second impression*	.. 1953
Seventh edition	.. 1924	*Third impression*	.. 1958
Eighth edition	.. 1927	*Fourth impression*	.. 1965
Ninth edition	.. 1929		
Tenth edition	.. 1932	*Fifth impression*	.. 1968
(Two impressions)			

Printed in Great Britain by J. W. Arrowsmith Ltd., Winterstoke Road, Bristol 3

PREFACE TO THE FOURTEENTH EDITION

THE FIRST edition of this book, by Mr. Udny Yule, was based on the courses given during his tenure of the Newmarch lectureship in Statistics at University College London. It appeared in 1911 and ran to ten editions by 1935, at which stage Mr. Yule felt that a complete revision was necessary and asked me to undertake it. The eleventh edition, under our joint names, appeared in 1937. Two further editions and several reprints have subsequently been necessary, and translations have appeared in Portuguese and Spanish.

This fourteenth edition is again a substantial revision. Although fewer than fifteen years have passed since the last revision, so much has happened in the statistical world in the meantime that Mr. Yule and I both felt that the usefulness of the book would be increased by some further changes. Most of the alterations are additions, but the treatment of the theory of attributes, which in earlier editions occupied five chapters, has been condensed into three to make room for the new material.

The major additions fall into two groups. Chapters 21–23 expand the former treatment of small-sample theory and give an introduction to the practical problems of sampling. Chapters 25–27 give an account of index numbers and the elementary theory of time-series. Chapter 13 on practical problems of correlation has also been rewritten. Additions have been made in the remaining chapters to keep the treatment abreast of new discoveries, some of the examples have been modernised and some further exercises added.

Mr. Yule's original object was to make this book a systematic introductory course on statistical methods suited to those who possess only a limited knowledge of mathematics. I have never lost sight of this object. The amendments in this edition are not due to any alteration in our design; they are necessitated by the development of our subject. Although I assume responsibility for the new material, the general plan of the revision was agreed between Mr. Yule and myself and once again I have been able to draw on his experience and advice. A bald acknowledgment of this kind completely fails to express the extent of my indebtedness to him.

v

The tables of " Student's " t are reproduced by permission of the late W. S. Gosset and the proprietors of *Metron* ; those of the F- and z-distributions by permission of Professor R. A. Fisher and Messrs Oliver and Boyd to whom my grateful thanks are due. I shall be indebted to any reader who calls my attention to errors or obscurities.

M.G.K.

LONDON,
March, 1950

NOTE TO SECOND IMPRESSION

George Udny Yule died on June 26th, 1951 in his eighty-first year. Among his many and varied contributions to the advancement of statistics this book has a high place. I shall try to carry it forward in the spirit in which he originally conceived it.

This printing is the same as the fourteenth edition except for the correction of a few minor misprints.

M.G.K.

LONDON,
March, 1953

NOTE TO THIRD IMPRESSION

As the study of statistics develops—and it has grown very substantially over the past few years—a book such as this has to contend with numerous competitors. I am gratified to note that it appears to be maintaining its place, not only in Great Britain but in many other countries of the world. This is, in my opinion, chiefly due to the basic soundness of Udny Yule's original approach to the subject. At all events, new generations of students continue to use the book, and another large impression of this edition has been demanded long before I expected it. As in the previous impression, only minor amendments have been required to remove a few misprints and ambiguities and to bring some of the references up to date.

M.G.K.

LONDON,
November, 1957

NOTE TO FOURTH IMPRESSION

To satisfy the continued and world-wide demand for this textbook, the fourteenth edition has been once again reprinted with minor amendments and up-dating of references.

M. G. K.

LONDON,
July, 1964

CONTENTS

(1) Normal curve. (2) areas under the normal curve. (3) Significance points of χ^2. (4) t-table. (5) Significance points of the variance-ratio F. (6) Significance points of the distribution of z.

NOTES ON NOTATION AND ON TABLES FOR FACILITATING STATISTICAL WORK

A. Notation

The reader is assumed to be familiar with the commoner mathematical signs, e.g. those for addition and multiplication. We shall also employ the following symbols, all of which are in general use—

The factorial sign

The symbol $n!$, read " factorial n," means the number

$$1 \times 2 \times 3 \times \ldots \times (n-2) \times (n-1) \times n$$

Factorial n is by some writers expressed by the symbol $\lfloor n$, but this notation appears to be falling out of use in favour of $n!$, probably owing to the greater ease with which the latter form can be printed and type-written.

The combinatorial sign

The symbol $^{n}C_{r}$ means the number of ways in which r things can be chosen from n things, e.g., $^{52}C_{13}$ is the number of ways in which a hand of cards can be dealt from an ordinary pack of 52 cards.

In most textbooks on algebra it is shown that

$$^{n}C_{r} = \frac{n!}{r!(n-r)!} = {}^{n}C_{(n-r)}$$

A more modern symbol is

$$\binom{n}{r} = {}^{n}C_{r} = \binom{n}{n-r}$$

and we shall use this form occasionally.

The summation sign

The sum of n numbers $x_1, x_2, \ldots x_n$ is written $\sum\limits_{r=1}^{r=n} (x_r)$, read " sum x_r from one to n," i.e.

$$\sum_{r=1}^{r=n} (x_r) = x_1 + x_2 + x_3 + \ldots + x_{(n-1)} + x_n$$

Where no ambiguity is likely to arise, the suffix r and the limits written above and below Σ are omitted, e.g. the above sum would be written simply $\Sigma(x)$, it being understood from the context that the summation extends over the n values.

Many writers use the Roman letter S instead of Σ.

The Greek alphabet

As the letters of the Greek alphabet will often be used as symbols, we give for convenience the names of those letters.

Small letter	Capital letter	Name	Small letter	Capital letter	Name
α	A	alpha	ν	N	nu
β	B	beta	ξ	Ξ	xi
γ	Γ	gamma	o	O	omicron
δ	Δ	delta	π	Π	pi
ϵ	E	epsilon	ρ	P	rho
ζ	Z	zeta	σ, s	Σ	sigma
η	H	eta	τ	T	tau
θ	Θ	theta	υ	Υ	upsilon
ι	I	iota	ϕ	Φ	phi
κ	K	kappa	χ	X	chi (*pron.* ki)
λ	Λ	lambda	ψ	Ψ	psi
μ	M	mu	ω	Ω	omega

B. Calculating Tables

For heavy arithmetical work a calculating machine is invaluable ; but owing to their cost machines are, as a rule, beyond the reach of the student.

For a great deal of simple work, especially work not intended for publication, the student will find a slide rule exceedingly useful : particulars and prices will be found in any instrument-maker's catalogue. For greater exactness in multiplying or dividing, logarithms are almost essential.

The student will derive invaluable aid from Barlow's *Tables of Squares, Cubes, Square-roots, Cube-roots, and Reciprocals of all Integral Numbers up to* 10,000 (E. & F. N. Spon, London and New York), which are useful over a wide range of statistical work.

C. Special Tables of Functions useful in Statistical Work

The tables at the end of this book will cover most of the student's ordinary requirements. The more advanced student will find it useful to have *Tables for Statisticians and Biometricians* (Cambridge University Press)—particularly Part I. Research workers will wish to have Fisher and Yates' *Statistical Tables for Biological, Agricultural and Medical Research* (Oliver and Boyd).

D. References to the Text

Each section in the book is distinguished by a number in heavy type consisting of the number of the chapter in which the section occurs prefixed to the number of the section in that chapter and separated from it by a period ; e.g., **7.13** means the thirteenth section of Chapter **7**, and **10.1** refers to the first section of Chapter 10. The Introduction, which precedes Chapter 1, is for this purpose regarded as Chapter 0, e.g., **0.26** refers to the twenty-sixth section of the Introduction. References to sections are given simply by the number of the sections, e.g., " We saw in **8.3** " means " We saw in the third section of Chapter 8."

Similarly, equations, tables, examples, exercises, diagrams and references are distinguished first of all with the number of the chapter in which they occur and then, separated by a period, with their serial number within the chapter, e.g., " Table 6.7 " refers to the seventh table in Chapter 6, and " Equation (17.8) " refers to the eighth equation of Chapter 17. These figures are in ordinary type.

This simple notation saves a good deal of unnecessary wording. To facilitate quickness of reference we sometimes give pages as well.

A distinction is drawn between *examples*, which are given in the text for purposes of illustration, and *exercises*, which are set at the end of the chapter for the student to work out for himself.

INTRODUCTION

Number and measurement

0.1 Western civilisation is pervaded by ideas of number and measurement. Even the events of our everyday life are inextricably bound up with them. We have only to picture a race which cannot count or measure trying to run the Bank of England or control the milk market, or even understand the sporting columns of the daily press, to realise how deeply rooted numbers are in the complex activities of the modern world.

0.2 Science itself is particularly indebted to numerical expression. As organised knowledge has increased, the necessity for precision has become greater, and in the formulation of precise statements number and measurement have played a leading part. The desire for quantitative expression was first felt in the physical sciences, but it has now spread into nearly all branches of knowledge. The movement is by no means complete, however, and may be seen at work to-day. As a significant instance we may note that courageous attempts are being made to subject the process of thought itself—that last stronghold of the contentious and the mysterious—to quantitative inquiry.

0.3 Many people, in fact, have been led by their enthusiasm for numerical data to regard knowledge of a non-quantitative kind as hardly deserving the name " knowledge " at all. Towards the close of the nineteenth century it was possible for Lord Kelvin to say : " When you can measure what you are speaking about and express it in numbers you know something about it ; but when you cannot measure it, when you cannot express it in numbers, your knowledge is of a meagre and unsatisfactory kind." This remark has often been quoted with an approval which it does not altogether deserve—it does not, for example, do justice to the work of Darwin and Pasteur, to name only two of Kelvin's contemporaries. But there can be no denying that it expresses a point of view which many people will endorse.

Numerical data

0.4 The desire for precision, in fact, leads investigators of all kinds, from the atomic physicist to the business man, to express the facts about that part of the universe which interests them in a quantitative way. Numerical data have come into being not only in the laboratory and the study, but in the counting-house, the sales department, the Board Room and the legislative assembly. It is difficult to see how our society could be

organised without them.   Where the Jews and the Romans were content
with occasional censuses for military or fiscal purposes,[1] the progressive
modern state finds itself under the necessity of keeping a close and quantitative eye on all that goes on within or without its frontier.   A country
which does not do so may be fairly regarded as backward.   In a typical
phrase, Anatole France summed up this point of view when he said of the
Chinese: "Tant qu'ils ne se seront pas comptés, ils ne compteront pas"—
if they don't count they won't count.

Statistics concerned with numerical data

0.5   There are certain features of numerical data, no matter in what
branch of knowledge they originate, which may call for a special type of
scientific method to treat them and elucidate them.   This is known as
" Statistical method," or more briefly, as " Statistics."   It does not,
however, embrace the study of numerical data of every kind, and before
we attempt a formal definition of its nature and scope, it is necessary to
give some words of explanation.

Effects and causes

0.6   One of the principal aims of Science is to trace, amidst the tangled
complex of the external world, the operation of what are called " laws "—
to interpret a multiplicity of natural phenomena in terms of a few fundamental principles.   A knowledge of the operation of these laws enables us
to talk of " cause " and " effect."   The metaphysical problems associated
with these words need not detain us, but since in the sequel we shall often
use them, it is proper to explain that we adopt them as a convenient way
of expressing serviceable and familiar ideas.   We shall be dealing with
the everyday world, where " law " and " cause " have significant and
important connotations.

0.7   With this convention, we may say that any physical event, and
in particular that described by quantitative data, is produced by the
operation of one or more causes.   The number of causes which produce any
particular effect may be, and usually is, extremely large.   For instance,
the height of a man is causally linked with his race, his ancestry, his
habitation, his diet during youth, his age, his occupation, and at any given
moment even with his position and the time of day.

0.8   Experiment, the great weapon of scientific inquiry, derives its power
from the ability of the experimenter to replace such complex systems of
causation by simple systems in which only one causal circumstance is

---

[1] David (II Samuel, 24) numbered the people of Israel and called down a plague by
doing so.   He counted 800,000 valiant men who drew the sword, and though the text
is not entirely clear it seems likely that Divine disapproval was directed against the
militaristic purpose of the census, not the census itself.   We are told later that 70,000
men died of the resulting pestilence, so it looks as if there was no ban on counting *dead*
men.

allowed to vary at a time. This is perhaps an ideal, but it is one which is closely approached with the technique of modern laboratory practice.

0.9 Let us, however, turn for a moment to social science, as the parent of the methods termed " statistical," and consider its characteristics as compared, say, with physics or chemistry. One characteristic stands out so markedly that attention has been repeatedly directed to it by " statistical " writers as the source of the peculiar difficulties of their science—*the observer of social facts cannot experiment, but must deal with circumstances as they occur, apart from his control.* The simplification open to the experimenter being impossible, the observer has, in general, to deal with highly complicated cases of multiple causation—cases in which a given result may be due to any one of a number of alternative causes or to a number of different causes acting conjointly.

0.10 A little consideration will show that this is also characteristic of observations in other fields. The meteorologist, for example, is in almost precisely the same position as the student of social science. He can experiment on minor points, but the records of the barometer, thermometer and rain gauge have to be treated as they stand. With the biologist, matters are somewhat better. He can and does apply experimental methods to a very large extent, but frequently cannot approximate closely to the experimental ideal ; the internal circumstances of animals and plants too easily evade complete control. Hence a large field (notably the study of variation and heredity) is left in which methods of experiment have to be supplemented by other methods. The physicist and chemist, finally, stand at the other extremity of the scale. Theirs are the sciences in which experiment has been brought to its greatest perfection. But even so, there is still scope for the application of statistical treatment in these sciences. The methods available for eliminating the effect of disturbing circumstances, though continually improved, are not, and cannot be, absolutely perfect. The observer himself, as well as the observing instrument, is a source of error ; the effects of changes of temperature, or of moisture, or pressure, and draughts, vibration, etc., cannot be completely eliminated.

0.11 It is with data affected by numerous causes that Statistics is mainly concerned. Experiment seeks to disentangle a complex of causes by removing all but one of them, or rather by concentrating on the study of one and reducing the others, as far as circumstances permit, to a comparatively small residuum. Statistics, denied this resource, must accept for analysis data subject to the influence of a host of causes, and must try to discover from the data themselves which causes are the important ones and how much of the observed effect is due to the operation of each.

Definitions

0.12 In the light of the foregoing discussion we may accordingly give the following definitions—

By *Statistics* we mean quantitative data affected to a marked extent by a multiplicity of causes.

By *Statistical Methods* we mean methods specially adapted to the elucidation of quantitative data affected by a multiplicity of causes.

By *Theory of Statistics* or, more briefly, *Statistics* we mean the exposition of statistical methods.

(It will be observed that the same word may be used both for the science and for the raw material on which it works. This dual use gives rise to no confusion in practice, but the distinction is worth bearing in mind.)

Use of " statistic "

0.13 This is perhaps the appropriate place to remark that there has recently come into use the singular form " statistic." This is the name given to a particular kind of estimate compiled from observations, usually according to some algebraical formula. In this book we shall not meet the term until we reach the theory of sampling (Chapter 18) and shall there use it in a restricted sense.

History of the word " statistics "

0.14 In their present meaning the words " statistics," " statistician " and " statistical " are barely a century old. They have, however, been in use longer than that, and it is instructive to consider the process by which they have reached their present meaning.

0.15 The words " statist," " statistics," " statistical," appear to be all derived, more or less indirectly, from the Latin *status*, in the sense, acquired in mediaeval Latin, of a political *State*.

0.16 The first term is, however, of much earlier date than the two others. The word " statist " is found, for instance, in *Hamlet* (1602)[1], *Cymbeline* (1610 or 1611),[2] and in *Paradise Regained* (1671).[3] The earliest occurrence of the word " statistics " yet noted is in *The Elements of Universal Erudition*, by Baron J. F. von Bielfeld, translated by W. Hooper, M.D. (3 vols., London, 1770). One of its chapters is entitled *Statistics*, and contains a definition of the subject as " The science that teaches us what is the political arrangement of all the modern states of the known world." [4] " Statistics " occurs again with a rather wider definition in the preface to *A Political Survey of the Present State of Europe*, by E. A. W. Zimmermann,[5]

---

[1] Act 5, sc.2.   [2] Act 2, sc. 4.   [3] Bk. 4.

[4] We cite from Dr W. F. Willcox, *Quarterly Publications of the American Statistical Association*, vol. 14, 1914, p. 287.

[5] Zimmermann's work appears to have been written in English, though he was a German and Professor of Natural Philosophy at Brunswick.

issued in 1787. " It is about forty years ago," says Zimmermann, " that that branch of political knowledge, which has for its object the actual and relative power of the several modern states, the power arising from their natural advantages, the industry and civilisation of their inhabitants, and the wisdom of their governments, has been formed, chiefly by German writers, into a separate science. . . . By the more convenient form it has now received . . . this science, distinguished by the new-coined name of *statistics*, is become a favourite study in Germany " (p. ii) ; and the adjective is also given (p. v) : " To the several articles contained in this work, some respectable *statistical* writers have added a view of the principal epochas of the history of each country."

0.17 Within the next few years the words were adopted by several writers, notably by Sir John Sinclair, the editor and organiser of the first *Statistical Account of Scotland*,[1] to whom, indeed, their introduction has been frequently ascribed. In the circular letter to the Clergy of the Church of Scotland, issued in May 1790,[2] he states that in Germany " ' Statistical Inquiries,' as they are called, have been carried to a very great extent," and adds an explanatory footnote to the phrase " Statistical Inquiries "— "or inquiries respecting the population, the political circumstances, the productions of a country, and other matters of state." In the " History of the Origin and Progress "[3] of the work, he tells us, " Many people were at first surprised at my using the new words, *Statistics* and *Statistical,* as it was supposed that some term in our own language might have expressed the same meaning. But in the course of a very extensive tour, through the northern parts of Europe, which I happened to take in 1786, I found that in Germany they were engaged in a species of political inquiry, to which they had given the name of *Statistics* ;[4] . . . as I thought that a new word might attract more public attention, I resolved on adopting it, and I hope that it is now completely naturalised and incorporated with our language." This hope was certainly justified, but the meaning of the word underwent rapid development during the half-century or so following its introduction.

0.18 " Statistics " (statistik), as the term was used by German writers of the eighteenth century, by Zimmermann and by Sir John Sinclair, meant simply the exposition of the noteworthy characteristics of a state, the mode of exposition being—almost inevitably at that time—preponderantly verbal. The conciseness and definite character of numerical

---

[1] Twenty-one vols., 1791-99.
[2] *Statistical Account*, vol. 20, Appendix to " The History of the Origin and Progress . . . " given at the end of the volume.
[3] *Loc, cit., p.* xiii.
[4] The *Abriss der Staatswissenschaft der Europäischen Reiche* (1749) of Gottfried Achenwall, Professor of Politics at Göttingen, is the volume in which the word " statistik " appears to be first employed, but the adjective " statisticus " occurs at a somewhat earlier date in works written in Latin.

data were recognised at a comparatively early period—more particularly by English writers—but trustworthy figures were scarce. After the commencement of the nineteenth century, however, the growth of official data was continuous, and numerical statements, accordingly, began more and more to displace the verbal descriptions of earlier days. " Statistics " thus insensibly acquired a narrower signification, viz. the exposition of the characteristics of a State by *numerical* methods. It is difficult to say at what epoch the word came definitely to bear this quantitative meaning, but the transition appears to have been only half accomplished even after the foundation of the Royal Statistical Society in 1834. The articles in the first volume of the *Journal*, issued in 1838-39, are for the most part of a numerical character, but the official definition has no reference to method. " Statistics," we read, " may be said, in the words of the prospectus of this Society, to be the ascertaining and bringing together of those facts which are calculated to illustrate the condition and prospects of society." It is, however, admitted that " the statist commonly prefers to employ figures and tabular exhibitions."

0.19 Once the first change of meaning was accomplished, further changes followed. From the name of a science, the word was transferred to those series of figures on which it operated, so that one spoke of vital statistics, shipping statistics, and so on. It was then applied to the similar numerical data which occurred in other sciences, such as anthropology and meteorology. By the end of the nineteenth century we find " statistics of mental characteristics in man," " statistics of children under the headings bright-average-dull," and even " an examination of the characteristics of the Virgilian hexameter with statistics." The development of the meaning of the adjective " statistical " and the noun " statistician " was naturally similar.

0.20 Perhaps the most abstract use of the word occurs in the theory of thermodynamics, wherein one speaks of *entropy* as *proportional to the logarithm of the statistical probability of the universe*—a definition which no statesman would be unwilling to admit to lie completely outside his purview. But it is unnecessary to multiply instances to show that the word " statistics " is now entirely divorced from " matters of State."

The theory of statistics

0.21 The *theory* of statistics as a distinct branch of scientific method is of comparatively recent growth. Its roots may be traced in the work of Laplace and Gauss on the theory of errors of observation, but the study itself did not begin to flourish until the last quarter of the nineteenth century. Under the influence of Galton and Karl Pearson remarkable progress was made, and the foundations of the subject were laid in the next thirty years—as it has turned out, very securely. The subject has not, however, yet reached a stage whereat a cut-and-dried exposition of its methods can be given. Research, particularly into the mathematical theory of statistics, is rapidly proceeding, and fresh discoveries are being made with a rapidity which makes it difficult to keep pace with them. It may, however, help the student to appreciate the work of later chapters if we sketch in brief general terms the field of statistical theory as it now exists.

The collection of data

0.22   The first question which the statistician has to consider is the collection and assembling of his data. In many fields, such as economics and sociology, he cannot prepare the data himself but has to get what he can from such sources as official statistics, which are usually prepared with an object differing from his own. Such information is therefore rarely all that one could wish. Investigator A, studying the sugar market, finds that the official figures run cane and beet sugar together. Investigator B, wanting to compare prices over a period of years, finds that during the war period 1939-1945 there is a gap in the information. Investigator C, wishing to study poverty, has to content himself with indirect figures such as those of wage levels and unemployment. But however incomplete the data may be, and however tangentially pertinent to his inquiry, the investigator must take what he can get and be thankful.

0.23   In other cases, and particularly in meteorology, biology and psychology, he can produce his own data or borrow those of other investigators similarly engaged. He does not merely take his figures from some source or other ; he is instrumental in their production, and within limits can control their nature so as to bring them to bear directly on his inquiry.

It might be thought that the only qualities required for such work are an ability to count or measure and a reasonable care   But this is not so. Once outside the laboratory the investigator is beset with a swarm of practical difficulties. We might illustrate the point by referring to the troubles of an investigator who wished to find out how many dairy cows there were in a certain parish. He took the simplest course and went to all the farms in the parish and asked the occupier how many cows he had. Farmer A said that he had fifteen, but had sold eight and was waiting for the buyer to come and fetch them. Farmer B had " about twenty." Farmer C obviously could not be bothered and said the first figure which came into his head ; and so on. It is clear that the result of such an inquiry would be to give a quite illusory figure. One of the duties of the practising statistician is to design his inquiries so as to minimise this kind of error.

0.24   A full discussion of such matters lies outside the scope of this book, but we have given them more than a passing mention in order to introduce one very necessary caution.

The reliability of data must always be examined before any attempt is made to base conclusions on them. This is true of all data, but particularly so of numerical data, which do not carry their quality written large upon them. It is a waste of time to apply the refined theoretical methods of statistics to data which are suspect from the beginning.

The treatment of data

0.25 Having obtained his data and satisfied himself that they are reliable enough to permit him to proceed, the statistician must then " lick them into shape." He must decide on some form of arrangement and presentation, reduce them to a convenient scale of units, and so on ; in short, he must work on his raw material until it is ready for the application of his prepared tools.

0.26 The only process of treatment to which attention need be called is that of condensation. The mind is incapable of grasping the significance of a large mass of figures. If, therefore, the quantity of data available is of any size, some process of condensation is necessary to enable the mind to appreciate the picture which the data represent.

Suppose, for instance, we are discussing the stature of a thousand men, and have as data the height of each man to the nearest inch. Our raw material then consists of a thousand sets of figures ranging from four feet to seven feet, or thereabouts. Only the supermind could look over these figures and grasp their essentials. Nor would the position be met by rearranging the figures in order of magnitude. To get a clear picture of the situation some condensation is necessary, and in this case it can be carried out easily by grouping together all the men whose heights lie in a certain range, say of three inches. Our total range of three feet is then replaced by twelve sub-ranges, each of three inches, and we may summarise the data by giving the numbers of men who fall into the twelve sub-ranges. In short, we have replaced our original thousand figures by twelve.

0.27 It will be clear that in so doing we have sacrificed a certain amount of information. Twelve figures cannot possibly tell us as much as a thousand. It may very well be, however, that the information in the twelve is all that we require ; the lost information may be irrelevant to the inquiry. Such a case would happen if we wanted to know, to an inch or so, what was the height exhibited by the greatest number of men.

0.28 The process of condensation thus sacrifices information but gives us instead a very necessary clarity and adaptability for manipulation. How far the process is carried in any particular case will depend on how far the disadvantages of the sacrifice are offset by the advantages of the clarity.

Summarising and descriptive statistics

0.29 The process of summarising which we have just described may be carried a great deal further, and leads to a branch of theory which has very important practical applications.

The reader is probably familiar already with the idea of an " *average value*," and with its use in compressing into a single number the results of a series of observations. Such quantities are, in fact, the result of summarising to the greatest possible.extent ; they are summaries in which the statistician has distilled the information of a diffuse mass of figures into a single drop, so to speak.

0.30 There is a wide demand for such summarising numbers, and a good deal of this book will be devoted to considering them from one aspect or another. They give a convenient bird's-eye view of what is sometimes a complex and confusing whole. Special sciences have evolved special quantities of this type to meet their own needs. For instance, the economist has invented various kinds of index numbers to express in a short-hand way complicated changes in prices; and the psychologist has devised coefficients to express the reactions of an individual mind to a sequence of tests.

0.31 The remarks we made in **0.27** and **0.28** apply here with additional force. It must never be forgotten that in summarising we omit. Part of the statistician's task is to see that we do not omit too much.

0.32 The problem of describing a complicated set of data in as few terms as possible is facilitated by the use of mathematical functions. Suppose, for instance, that in the thousand men of **0.26** we assumed that the number of men (y) of height x inches varied as the square of x— frankly a most improbable result, but one which will serve for the purposes of illustration. Then we may describe the data completely by an equation of the form—

$$y = ax^2$$

where a is a constant to be determined from the data. Knowing a we can find the number of men of any given height.

0.33 In this case it rather looks as if we have condensed all the information into a single number a without losing any of it. But that is not so. What we have done is to replace the set of a thousand figures by an assumption about their nature. We have lost none of the information because we assumed, in using the equation, that the information was of a type known to us already.

0.34 It is found in practice that many sets of data may be very conveniently expressed by mathematical functions. The question as to which functions are the most suitable for purposes of description leads to some interesting theory, some of which will be dealt with later and some of which is of an advanced character lying outside the scope of an Introduction to the Theory of Statistics. Such functions are particularly helpful in the theory of sampling.

Analysis of data

0.35 When the statistician has arranged and compressed his data into a suitable form, or decided on the functions and evaluated the quantities which he has chosen to describe them, the first stage of his inquiry is finished. It may be that he would wish to take it no further ; for instance, if he is preparing an index number for the economist he may wish to hand over the number to that person without comment, for him to make such use of it as he thinks fit. More frequently, however, he has prepared the data for his own use as a statistician. He then proceeds to the next stage, that of analysis and elucidation of the causal system which gave rise to them.

0.36 The methods for such purposes are very numerous. In this brief review we need only point out the importance of the investigation of *relationship*, the theory of which bulks very large in statistical literature. If two events are related there is usually, though not always, some causal nexus between them. The problems of the investigation of relationship between phenomena lead to the theory of dependence, contingency and correlation, and the formulation of various coefficients to measure the extent to which one set of events depends upon another.

Sampling

0.37 When we wish to discuss the properties of an aggregate we may be prevented by practical or theoretical reasons from examining every single member of it. For example, in considering the stature of the male inhabitants of the United Kingdom we cannot measure every man, because of the time and trouble involved ; and in considering the scores of a roulette wheel we cannot examine every score, because the number is practically infinite and observations can be continued as long as the wheel lasts.

0.38 We do not despair, nevertheless, of being able to gain some knowledge of the aggregate. Where we cannot take the whole we do the best we can and try to obtain a selection of members. This selection is called a *sample*.

0.39 It is clear that a sample will not tell us everything about the parent aggregate from which it is derived. Nevertheless, most people have a feeling, and we shall see later in this book that under certain conditions the feeling is a justifiable one that the sample will give us some information about the parent. Values calculated from the sample may be taken to be estimates of values in the parent, to a degree of approximation which becomes closer as the sample gets larger; and even where the sample is small we can sometimes draw inferences of a general nature about the parent.

0.40 We are rarely, if ever, able to reason from the sample to the parent with the categorical certainty of a mathematical proof. Our inferences will usually be expressed in terms of probabilities. Moreover, we shall find it much easier to reject a hypothesis than to accept it. Our inferences will generally be not of the type "the hypothesis H is true," or even "the hypothesis H is probably true," but of the type "hypotheses A, B and C are probably untrue, but we see no reason to doubt hypothesis H."

For example, suppose we take a sample of a thousand men from the population of the United Kingdom and find their average height to be 5 ft 8 in. What can we say about the average height of the population as a whole ? We cannot give it with any certainty. We cannot even say, with certainty, that it lies within, say, one inch of 5 ft 8 in. What we can say, assuming that the sampling technique is sound, will be something to the effect that a hypothesis which supposes that the mean of the whole population is greater than 5 ft 9 in. or less than 5 ft 7 in. is *probably* incorrect, but that the data are consistent with the supposition that the mean lies between those limits.

0.41 The theory of sampling is thus closely bound up with the theory of probability. The many problems which arise in this connection are among the most interesting and at times the most difficult which science and philosophy can offer. It is only fair to warn the student that there still exists an important difference of opinion among scientific men about the validity of certain types of statistical inference. In this book we have, so far as we could, avoided these contentious matters, but the advanced student will have to be prepared to face them sooner or later.

The popular attitude towards statistics

0.42 Finally, to conclude this introduction we may, perhaps, refer to the popular mistrust of statistics and statistical methods.

The layman's attitude towards statistics is admirably summed up in the remark that mankind is divided into two parts, those who say that figures can prove anything and those who assert that they can prove nothing. It must be admitted that this attitude is not unreasonable. From the advertisement hoarding, from the electioneering platform, from the partisan press, and from a dozen other sources, the man in the street is bombarded with tendentious figures put forward to support some *ex parte* statement. Sometimes such figures are justifiably used to form a basis for the arguments which are built upon them ; more often they give a specious picture of the truth, which may be due to ignorance or inadvertence, but has also been known to be occasioned by a deliberate wish to mislead. The layman is well aware of this fact. His attitude in distrusting all arguments based on figures is that of a reasonable man, who has not the training to distinguish for himself the true from the false, and is therefore inclined to suspect everything.

0.43 We are not concerned here with the vindication of statistics in the public view   We have alluded to the matter in order to remind the student that statistical methods are most dangerous tools in the hands of the inexpert.   Few subjects have a wider application ; no subject requires such care in that application.   Statistics is one of those sciences whose adepts must exercise the self-restraint of an artist.

CHAPTER ONE

THEORY OF ATTRIBUTES

BASIC IDEAS

Attributes and variables

1.1 The methods of statistics, as defined in the Introduction, deal with quantitative data alone. The quantitative character may, however, arise in two different ways.

In the first place, the observer may note only the *presence* or *absence* of some attribute in a series of objects or individuals and count how many do or do not possess it. Thus, in a given *population*,[1] (a useful general term for the aggregate of objects under discussion, the extent and nature of which should always be kept in mind) we may count, if we are dealing with human beings, the number of blind and seeing, or of Europeans and non-Europeans ; if it is a population of coin-tosses, the number of heads and tails ; if a population of pea-plants, the number of talls and dwarfs. The quantitative character, in such cases, arises solely in the counting.

In the second place, the observer may note or measure the actual magnitude of some variable character for each of the objects or individuals observed. He may record, for instance, the ages of persons at death, the prices of different samples of a commodity, the statures of men, the numbers of petals in flowers. The observations in these cases are quantitative *ab initio*.

1.2 The methods applicable to the former kind of observations, which may be termed "statistics of attributes", are also applicable to the latter, or "statistics of variables." A record of statures of men, for example, may be treated by simply counting all measurements as *tall* that exceed a certain limit, neglecting the magnitude of any excess, and stating the numbers of *tall* and *short* (or more strictly not-tall) on the basis of this classification. Similarly, the methods that are specially adapted to the treatment of statistics of variables, making use of each value recorded, are available to a greater extent than might at first sight seem possible for dealing with statistics of attributes. For example, we may treat the presence or absence of the attributes as corresponding to the changes of a variable which can only possess two values, say 0 and 1. Or, we may assume that we have really to do with a variable character which has been

---

[1] In the present edition we have substituted this less technical and more usual term for the logical term "universe" used in preceding editions.

crudely classified, as suggested above, and we may be able, by auxiliary hypotheses as to the nature of this variable, to draw further conclusions. But the methods and principles developed for the case in which the observer only notes the presence or absence of attributes are the simplest and most fundamental, and are best considered first. This and the next two chapters are accordingly devoted to the Theory of Attributes.

Classification with reference to attributes

1.3 The objects or individuals that possess the attribute, and those that do not possess it, may be said to be members of two distinct " classes," the observer " classifying " the population observed. In the simplest case, where attention is paid to one attribute alone, only two complementary classes are formed. If several attributes are noted, the process of classification may, however, be continued indefinitely. Those that do and do not possess the first attribute may be reclassified according as they do or do not possess the second, the members of each of the sub-classes so formed according as they do or do not possess the third, and so on, every class being divided into two at each step. Thus the members of the population of any district may be classified into males and females ; the members of each sex into sane and insane ; the insane males, sane males, insane females and sane females into blind and seeing. If we were dealing with a number of peas (*Pisum sativum*) of different varieties, they might be classified as tall or dwarf, with green seeds or yellow seeds, with wrinkled seeds or round seeds, so that we should have eight classes— tall with round green seeds, tall with round yellow seeds, tall with wrinkled green seeds, tall with wrinkled yellow seeds, and four similar classes of dwarf plants.

1.4 It may be noticed that the fact of classification does not necessarily imply the existence of either a natural or a clearly defined boundary between the two classes. The boundary may be wholly arbitrary, e.g., where prices are classified as above or below some special value, barometer readings as above or below some particular height. The division may also be vague and uncertain : sanity and insanity, sight and blindness, pass into each other by such fine gradations that judgments may differ as to the class in which a given individual should be entered. The possibility of uncertainties of this kind should always be borne in mind in considering statistics of attributes : whatever the nature of classification, however, natural or artificial, definite or uncertain, the final judgment must be decisive ; any one object or individual must be held either to possess the given attribute or not.

Dichotomy

1.5 A classification of the simple kind considered, in which each class is divided into two sub-classes and no more, has been termed by logicians *classification*, or, to use the more strictly applicable term, *division by* *dichotomy* (cutting in two). The classifications of most statistics are not dichotomous, for most usually a class is divided into more than two sub-classes, but dichotomy is the fundamental case. In Chapter 3 the relation of dichotomy to more elaborate (*manifold*, instead of twofold or dichotomous) processes of classification, and the methods applicable to some such cases, are dealt with briefly.

1.6 For theoretical purposes it is necessary to have some simple notation for the classes formed, and for the numbers of observations assigned to each.

The capitals A, B, C, . . . will be used to denote the several attributes. An object or individual possessing the attribute A will be termed simply A. The class, all the members of which possess the attribute A, will be termed *the class A*. It is convenient to use single symbols also to denote the *absence* of the attributes A, B, C, . . . We shall employ the Greek letters α, β, γ, . . . Thus if A represents the attribute *blindness*, α represents *sight*, i.e., non-blindness ; if B stands for *deafness*, β stands for *hearing*. Generally " α " is equivalent to " not-A," or *an object or individual not possessing the attribute A ; the class α is equivalent to the class none of the members of which possesses the attribute A*.

1.7 Combinations of attributes will be represented by juxtapositions of letters. Thus if, as above, A represents *blindness*, B *deafness*, AB represents the combination *blindness and deafness*. If the presence and absence of these attributes be noted, the four classes so formed, viz. AB $A\beta$, αB, $\alpha\beta$, include respectively the *blind and deaf*, the *blind but not deaf*, the *deaf but not blind*, and the *neither blind nor deaf*. If a third attribute be noted, e.g. insanity, denoted say by C, the class ABC includes those who are at once *deaf, blind and insane*, $AB\gamma$ those who are *deaf and blind but not insane*, and so on.

Any letter or combination of letters like A, AB, αB, $AB\gamma$, by means of which we specify the characters of the members of a class, may be termed a *class symbol*.

Class-frequencies

1.8 The number of observations assigned to any class is termed, for brevity, the " frequency " of the class, or the " class-frequency." Class-frequencies will be denoted by enclosing the corresponding class-symbols in brackets. Thus, (A) denotes the number of A's, i.e., objects possessing attribute A ; $(\alpha\beta C)$ denotes the number of $\alpha\beta C$'s, i.e. objects possessing attribute C but neither A nor B ; and so on for any number of attributes.

Order of classes and class-frequencies

1.9 The classes obtained by noting, say, n attributes fall into natural groups according to the numbers of attributes used to specify the respective classes, and these natural groups should be borne in mind in tabulating the class-frequencies. A class specified by r attributes may be spoken of as a class of the rth order and its frequency as a frequency of the rth order. Thus AB, AC, BC are classes of the second order ; (A), $(A\beta)$, (αBC), $(AB\gamma D)$, class-frequencies of the first, second, third and fourth orders respectively.

1.10 Class frequencies should, in tabulating, be arranged so that frequencies of the same order and frequencies belonging to the same aggregate are kept together. Thus the frequencies for the case of three attributes should be grouped as given below, the whole number of observations denoted by the letter N being reckoned as a frequency of order zero, since no attributes are specified.

$$
\left.
\begin{array}{llll}
\text{Order 0} & N \\
\text{Order 1} & (A) & (B) & (C) \\
 & (\alpha) & (\beta) & (\gamma) \\
\text{Order 2} & (AB) & (AC) & (BC) \\
 & (A\beta) & (A\gamma) & (B\gamma) \\
 & (\alpha B) & (\alpha C) & (\beta C) \\
 & (\alpha\beta) & (\alpha\gamma) & (\beta\gamma) \\
\text{Order 3} & \quad (ABC) & (\alpha BC) \\
 & \quad (AB\gamma) & (\alpha B\gamma) \\
 & \quad (A\beta C) & (\alpha\beta C) \\
 & \quad (A\beta\gamma) & (\alpha\beta\gamma)
\end{array}
\right\} \quad . \quad . \quad (1.1)
$$

The total number of class-frequencies

1.11 In such a complete table for the case of three attributes, twenty-seven distinct frequencies are given : 1 of order zero, 6 of the first order, 12 of the second and 8 of the third.

In general, for n attributes, there are 3^n distinct class-frequencies, if we count N as a frequency of order 0. To demonstrate this, let us consider the number of classes of different orders.

Of order 0 there is one class N.

Of order 1 there are $2n$ classes, for classes of this order contain only one symbol, and each of the n attributes contributes two symbols, one of the type A and one of the type α.

Of order 2 there are $\dfrac{n(n-1)}{2} \times 2^2$ classes, for each class contains two symbols, two attributes can be chosen from n in $\dfrac{n(n-1)}{2}$ ways, and each pair gives rise to 2^2 different frequencies of the types (AB), $(A\beta)$, (αB) and $(\alpha\beta)$.

Similarly, it may be seen that of order r there are

$$
\frac{n(n-1) \ . \ . \ . \ (n-r+1)}{r!} \times 2^r
$$

classes.

Hence, the total number of class-frequencies is

$$1+n.2+\frac{n(n-1)}{2}.2^2+ \ . \ . \ . \ +\frac{n(n-1) \ . \ . \ . \ (n-r+1)}{r!}\times 2^r+ \ . \ . \ .$$

and this is the binomial expansion of $(1+2)^n=3^n$.

It is clear that if n is at all large the number of class-frequencies will be very great. For instance if $n=6$, the number is 729.

1.12 Fortunately, however, the class-frequencies are not independent of one another, and it is not necessary, in order to specify the data completely, to give every class-frequency.

In the first place, let us note the simple result that *any class-frequency can always be expressed in terms of class-frequencies of higher order.* For the whole number of observations must clearly be equal to the number of A's added to the number of α's, i.e.

$$N=(A)+(\alpha) \qquad . \qquad . \qquad . \qquad . \quad (1.2)$$

Similarly, the number of A's is equal to the number of A's which are B's added to the number of A's which are β's, i.e.

$$(A)=(AB)+(A\beta) \qquad . \qquad . \qquad . \qquad . \quad (1.3)$$

Similarly,

$$(AB)=(ABC)+(AB\gamma) \qquad . \qquad . \qquad . \quad (1.4)$$

and so on.

Ultimate class-frequencies

1.13 It follows at once from the result we have just given that every class-frequency can be expressed in terms of the frequencies of the highest order, i.e., of order n. For any frequency can be analysed into higher frequencies, and the process need stop only when we have reached the frequencies of the highest order. For example, with three attributes;

$$(A)=(AB)+(A\beta)$$
$$=(ABC)+(AB\gamma)+(A\beta C)+(A\beta\gamma)$$

The classes specified by n attributes, i.e. those of the highest order, are termed the ultimate class-frequencies.

Our result may then be expressed in the form : *Every class-frequency can be expressed as the sum of certain of the ultimate class-frequencies.* To specify the data completely it is, therefore, only necessary to give the ultimate class-frequencies.

Example 1.1—(See F. Warner and others, " Report on the Scientific Study of the Mental and Physical Conditions of Childhood," Parkes Museum, 1895.) A number of school-children were examined for the presence or absence of certain defects of which three chief descriptions were noted : A, development defects ; B, nerve signs ; C, low nutrition.

Given the following ultimate frequencies, find the frequencies of the classes defined by the presence of the defects, i.e. those involving the Roman letters A, B, C but not the Greek letters α, β, γ, including the whole number of observations N—

(ABC)	57	(αBC)	78
$(AB\gamma)$	281	$(\alpha B\gamma)$	670
$(A\beta C)$	86	$(\alpha\beta C)$	65
$(A\beta\gamma)$	453	$(\alpha\beta\gamma)$	8310

The whole number of observations N is equal to the grand total : $N=10{,}000$.

The frequency of any first-order class, e.g. (A), is given by the total of the four third-order frequencies the class-symbols for which contain the same letter—

$$(ABC)+(AB\gamma)+(A\beta C)+(A\beta\gamma)=(A)=877$$

Similarly, the frequency of any second-order class, e.g. (AB), is given by the total of the two third-order frequencies the class-symbols for which both contain the same pair of letters—

$$(ABC)+(AB\gamma)=(AB)=338$$

The complete results are—

N	10,000	(AB)	338
(A)	877	(AC)	143
(B)	1,086	(BC)	135
(C)	286	(ABC)	57

The number of ultimate class-frequencies

1.14   The class-frequencies of highest order each contain n symbols. Now each letter corresponding to a particular attribute may be written in two ways : A or α, B or β, etc.   Hence the total number of possible symbols is

$$2\times2\times2\times2\times2\times2\times2\times \ \ldots \ =2^n$$

and this is the number of ultimate class-frequencies.

Hence the 3^n frequencies may all be expressed in terms of the 2^n ultimate frequencies.   For example, if $n=6$, the 729 frequencies can be written in terms of 64 ultimate class-frequencies, which specify the data completely.

The ultimate frequencies are, however, not the only set which specify the whole of the data.   In fact. any set will serve the purpose provided that (a) they are 2^n in number, and (b) they are algebraically independent ; that is to say, when they are written symbolically no one can be expressed in terms of some or all of the others.

We may call such a set of frequencies a *fundamental* set.

Positive attributes

1.15 The attributes denoted by capitals ABC . . . may be termed positive attributes, and their *contraries*, denoted by Greek letters, negative attributes. If a class-symbol includes only capital letters, the class may be termed a positive class ; if only Greek letters, a negative class. Thus the classes A, AB, ABC are positive classes ; the classes α, $\alpha\beta$, $\alpha\beta\gamma$, negative classes.

If we make a certain dichotomy with regard to a definite attribute A—such as male sex, blindness or blue eyes—it may be of practical importance to note a possible distinction in the nature of the class not-A. The complementary class may, in fact, either be equally definite—female sex, ability to see—or it may be a mere heterogeneous remainder, as in our last instance—not-blue-eyed, the not-blue-eyed being brown-eyed, grey-eyed, or even possessing no eyes at all.

Logically, this distinction is difficult to maintain, but practically it is of some importance. The statistical data in official returns are almost always classified according to positive and clearly defined attributes. For example, we are given the numbers of persons dying from typhoid, not the numbers who did *not* die of typhoid ; the number of acres under grass, not the number of acres *not* under grass.

1.16 The positive class-frequencies form a fundamental set in the sense of **1.14** ; that is to say, they specify the data completely. They are algebraically independent ; no one positive class-frequency can be expressed wholly in terms of the others. Their number is, moreover, 2^n, as may be readily seen from the fact that if the Greek letters are struck out of the symbols for the ultimate classes, they become the symbols for the positive classes, with the exception of $\alpha\beta\gamma$ . . . for which N must be substituted.

Example 1.2.—Given the positive class-frequencies of Example 1.1, to find all the class-frequencies.

The data are—

$$N=10{,}000 ; \quad (A)=877 ; \quad (B)=1086 ; \quad (C)=286 ; \quad (AB)=338 ;$$
$$(AC)=143 ; \quad (BC)=135 ; \quad (ABC)=57.$$

We have—

$$(AB)=(AB\gamma)+(ABC)$$

or

$$338=(AB\gamma)+57$$

i.e.

$$(AB\gamma)=281$$

Similarly, from (AC) and (BC) we find—

$$(A\beta C)=86$$
$$(\alpha BC)=78$$

This gives us the three ultimate class-frequencies which contain only one Greek letter. For the others,

$$(\alpha\beta C) = (\beta C) - (A\beta C)$$
$$= (C) - (BC) - (A\beta C)$$
$$= 286 - 135 - 86$$
$$= 65$$

Similarly, we have—

$$(A\beta\gamma) = 453$$
$$(\alpha B\gamma) = 670$$

Finally,

$$(\alpha\beta\gamma) = (\beta\gamma) - (A\beta\gamma)$$
$$= (\gamma) - (B\gamma) - (A\beta\gamma)$$
$$= N - (C) - \{(B) - (BC)\} - (A\beta\gamma)$$
$$= 10,000 - 286 - 951 - 453$$
$$= 8310$$

We can now calculate any class-frequency by expressing it in terms of the ultimate class-frequencies, e.g.

$$(\alpha\gamma) = (\alpha B\gamma) + (\alpha\beta\gamma)$$
$$= 670 + 8310$$
$$= 8980$$

1.17 The data encountered in practice are rarely dichotomised according to more than three or four variables, and the student should experience little difficulty in expressing any class-frequency in terms of the known class-frequencies, either directly, or by first finding the ultimate class-frequencies and then expressing the desired frequency in terms of them.

It is, however, interesting to note the general result that the class symbols can be treated as operators and multiplied together like algebraical quantities. Let us write $A.N$ for the operation of dichotomising N according to A, and write

$$A . N = (A)$$

which is the symbolic way of saying that if we dichotomise N according to A we get a class-frequency equal to (A). We can similarly put

$$\alpha . N = (\alpha)$$

Adding these two, and putting $A.N + \alpha.N$ equal to $(A + \alpha).N$, we have—

$$(A + \alpha) . N = N$$

so that we may take

$$A + \alpha = 1$$

In any symbolic expression we can therefore replace the operators A or α by $1 - \alpha$, $1 - A$, respectively.

Furthermore, since $(AB) = A . (B) = B . (A)$, we may take the symbol

$AB \cdot N$ to be the dichotomy of N according to both A and B, and equate it to (AB). A little reflection will show that the operative symbols therefore obey the ordinary laws of algebra and in particular may be multiplied together.

For example, we have—

$$\begin{aligned}(\alpha\beta)=\alpha\beta \cdot N &=(1-A)(1-B) \cdot N\\ &=(1-A-B+AB) \cdot N\\ &=N-(A)-(B)+(AB) \, . \qquad . \qquad . \qquad (1.5)\end{aligned}$$

And, similarly,

$$\begin{aligned}(\alpha\beta\gamma)=\alpha\beta\gamma \cdot N\\ &=(1-A)(1-B)(1-C) \cdot N\\ &=(1-A-B-C+AB+BC+AC-ABC) \cdot N\\ &=N-(A)-(B)-(C)+(AB)+(AC)+(BC)-(ABC) \, . \qquad . \qquad (1.6)\end{aligned}$$

Similar results could, of course, be obtained by step-by-step substitution ; for instance,

$$\begin{aligned}(\alpha\beta)&=(\alpha)-(\alpha B)\\ &=N-(A)-(B)+(AB)\end{aligned}$$

Consistence

1.18 Any class-frequencies which have been or might have been observed within one and the same population may be said to be *consistent* with one another. They conform with one another, and do not in any way conflict.

The conditions of consistence are some of them simple, but others are by no means of an intuitive character. Suppose, for instance, the following data are given—

N	1000	(AB)	42
(A)	525	(AC)	147
(B)	312	(BC)	86
(C)	470	(ABC)	25

—there is nothing obviously wrong with the figures. Yet they are certainly inconsistent. They might have been observed at different times, in different places or on different material, but they cannot have been observed in one and the same population. They imply, in fact, a negative value for $(\alpha\beta\gamma)$—

$$\begin{aligned}(\alpha\beta\gamma)&=1000-525-312-470+42+147+86-25\\ &=1000-1307+275-25\\ &=-57\end{aligned}$$

Clearly no class-frequency can be negative. If the figures, consequently, are alleged to be the result of an actual inquiry in a definite population, there must have been some miscount or misprint.

Condition for consistence

1.19 It is, in fact, the necessary and sufficient condition for the consistence of a set of independent class-frequencies that no ultimate class-frequency be negative. It is necessary for the obvious reason that no class-frequency occurring by counting real attributes can be negative; it is sufficient because, given any non-negative set of 2^n numbers, we can always imagine a real population with n dichotomies which should have these numbers for its ultimate class-frequencies, and it is impossible for this real population to give inconsistent results.

Hence to test the consistence of a set of 2^n algebraically independent class-frequencies we need only calculate the ultimate class-frequencies and ascertain whether any one is negative. If it is, the data are inconsistent. If no ultimate frequency is negative, the data are consistent.

1.20 For data given by a heterogeneous collection of class-frequencies, consistence is best tested by actually calculating the ultimate frequencies. We saw in **1.15**, however, that the positive class-frequencies hold a peculiar position in that many data encountered in practice are given entirely in terms of them alone. It may be useful to consider the consistence conditions for this type of material.

If two attributes are noted there are four ultimate frequencies (AB), $(A\beta)$, (αB), $(\alpha\beta)$. Expressing them in terms of positive classes we find the following conditions—

$$
\left.
\begin{aligned}
(AB) &\geqslant 0 \\
(AB) &\geqslant (A)+(B)-N \\
(AB) &\leqslant (A) \\
(AB) &\leqslant (B)
\end{aligned}
\right\} \qquad . \qquad . \qquad . \qquad (1.7)
$$

The third and fourth merely express the fact that the number of members which are both A and B must not be greater than the number of A's or B's separately. The second inequality is perhaps not so obvious.

1.21 For three attributes the conditions that the eight ultimate frequencies are not negative will be found to lead to the following—

$$
\left.
\begin{aligned}
(ABC) &\geqslant 0 \\
(ABC) &\geqslant (AB)+(AC)-(A) \\
(ABC) &\geqslant (AB)+(BC)-(B) \\
(ABC) &\geqslant (AC)+(BC)-(C)
\end{aligned}
\right\} \qquad . \qquad . \qquad (1.8)
$$

$$
\left.
\begin{aligned}
(ABC) &\leqslant (AB) \\
(ABC) &\leqslant (AC) \\
(ABC) &\leqslant (BC) \\
(ABC) &\leqslant (AB)+(AC)+(BC)-(A)-(B)-(C)+N
\end{aligned}
\right\} \qquad . \qquad (1.9)
$$

These are not of a new form. They can all be derived from inequalities (1.7) by " specifying the population "; that is to say, by considering one of the inequalities as holding in a sub-population. For instance, from the condition $(AB) \leqslant (A)$ we have in the population of γ's $(AB\gamma) \leqslant (A\gamma)$ which is equivalent to

$$(AB)-(ABC) \leqslant (A)-(AC)$$

or the second equality of (1.8).

1.22 If we express the condition that the lower limits to (ABC) given by (1.8) must be not greater than the upper limits given by (1.9) we obtain 16 further inequalities. All but four of them are of the type already found, but there are four new ones—

$$\left.\begin{array}{l}(AB)+(AC)+(BC) \geqslant (A)+(B)+(C)-N \\ (AB)+(AC)-(BC) \leqslant (A) \\ (AB)-(AC)+(BC) \leqslant (B) \\ -(AB)+(AC)+(BC) \leqslant (C)\end{array}\right\} \qquad (1.10)$$

Incomplete data

1.23 We can now take up the question of the inferences which may be drawn from data which, though giving us a certain amount of information in the shape of class-frequencies, yet are insufficient to enable us to calculate all the class-frequencies.

The form of the consistence conditions shows that a knowledge of certain class-frequencies allows us to assign limits to others, even though we may not be able to find the actual values of those others. The following will serve as illustrations of the statistical uses of the conditions—

Example 1.3.—Given that $(A)=(B)=(C)=\frac{1}{2}N$ and 80 per cent of the A's are B's, 75 per cent of A's are C's, find the limits to the percentage of B's that are C's.

The data are : $\qquad \dfrac{2(AB)}{N}=0{\cdot}8 \qquad \dfrac{2(AC)}{N}=0{\cdot}75$

and the conditions (1.10) give—

$$\begin{array}{lllll}(a) & 2(BC)/N \geqslant 1 & -0{\cdot}8 & -0{\cdot}75 \\ (b) & \geqslant 0{\cdot}8+0{\cdot}75 & -1 \\ (c) & \leqslant 1 & -0{\cdot}8 & +0{\cdot}75 \\ (d) & \leqslant 1 & +0{\cdot}8 & -0{\cdot}75\end{array}$$

(a) gives a negative limit and (d) a limit greater than unity ; hence they may be disregarded. From (b) and (c) we have—

$$\frac{2(BC)}{N} \geqslant 0{\cdot}55 \qquad \frac{2(BC)}{N} \leqslant 0{\cdot}95$$

—that is to say, not less than 55 per cent nor more than 95 per cent of the B's can be C's.

Example 1.4.—If a report gives the following frequencies as actually observed, show that there must be a misprint or mistake of some sort, and that possibly the misprint consists in the dropping of a 1 before the 85 given as the frequency (BC)—

$$N \ 1000$$

(A)	510	(AB)	189
(B)	490	(AC)	140
(C)	427	(BC)	85

From (1.10) we have—

$$(BC) \geqslant 510 + 490 + 427 - 1000 - 189 - 140$$
$$\geqslant 98$$

But $85 < 98$, therefore it cannot be the correct value of (BC).
If we read 185 for 85 all the conditions are fulfilled.

Example 1.5.—In a certain set of 1000 observations $(A) = 45$, $(B) = 23$, $(C) = 14$. Show that whatever the percentages of B's that are A's and of C's that are A's, it cannot be inferred that any B's are C's.
The first two conditions of (1.10) give the lower limit of (BC) which is required. We find —

$$\frac{(BC)}{N} \geqslant -\frac{(AB)}{N} - \frac{(AC)}{N} - 0 \cdot 918$$

$$\frac{(BC)}{N} \geqslant -\frac{(AB)}{N} + \frac{(AC)}{N} - 0 \cdot 045$$

The first limit is clearly negative. The second must also be negative, since $(AB)/N$ cannot exceed $0 \cdot 023$ nor $(AC)/N$, $0 \cdot 014$. Hence we cannot conclude that there is any limit to (BC) greater than 0. This result is indeed immediately obvious when we consider that, even if all the B's were A's, and of the remaining 22 A's 14 were C's, there would still be 8 A's that were neither B's nor C's.

1.24 The student should note the result of the last example, as it illustrates the sort of result at which one may often arrive by applying the conditions (1.10) to practical statistics. For given values of N, (A), (B), (C), (AB) and (AC), it will often happen that *any* value of (BC) not less than zero will satisfy the conditions (1.10), and hence no true inference of a lower limit is possible. The argument of the type " So many A's are B's and so many B's are C's that we must expect some A's to be C's " must be used with caution.

1.25 Where the data are not given in terms of the positive or of the ultimate class-frequencies, and cannot readily be thrown into such a form, the device illustrated in the following example is often useful—

Example 1.6.—Among the adult population of a certain town 50 per cent of the population are male, 60 per cent are wage-earners and 50 per cent are 45 years of age or over. 10 per cent of the males are not wage-earners and 40 per cent of the males are under 45. Can we infer anything about what percentage of the population of 45 or over are wage-earners?

Denoting the attributes male, wage-earner and 45 years old or more by A, B and C, respectively, and letting $N=100$ for convenience, we have—

$$(A)=50$$
$$(B)=60$$
$$(C)=50$$
$$(A\beta)= 5$$
$$(A\gamma)=20$$

We require the limits, if any, of (BC).

Let us note first of all that we are given 6 class-frequencies (including N). If we knew two more, independent of these 6, the problem would be completely determinate, for we should have 2^3 class-frequencies.

Let us therefore put

$$(\alpha\beta\gamma)=x$$
$$(ABC)=y$$

We can then solve for the ultimate class-frequencies and get

$$(AB\gamma)=45-y$$
$$(A\beta C)=30-y$$
$$(\alpha BC)= x-15$$
$$(A\beta\gamma)= y-25$$
$$(\alpha B\gamma)=30-x$$
$$(\alpha\beta C)=35-x$$

The condition that these must be non-negative gives us conditions on x and y. In fact, from (αBC) and $(\alpha B\gamma)$ we get

$$15 \leqslant x \leqslant 30$$

and from $(A\beta C)$ and $(A\beta\gamma)$,

$$25 \leqslant y \leqslant 30$$

the conditions from the other frequencies being included in these limits to x and y.

Now
$$(BC)=(ABC)+(\alpha BC)$$
$$=y+x-15$$

and hence, from the limits to x and y,

$$25 \leqslant (BC) \leqslant 45$$

Consequently, the percentage of the population 45 years old or more (50 per cent of the total population) who are wage-earners lies between 50 and 90 per cent.

It is worth while examining whether these limits are the narrowest possible which can be assigned with the available data ; and it is easy to see that they are. For if $x=15$ and $y=25$, $(BC)=25$; and if $x=30$ and $y=30$, $(BC)=45$. There is nothing in the conditions of the problem to prevent x and y, and hence (BC), from reaching the limiting values, and thus no narrowing of the limits is possible.

SUMMARY

1. A collection of individuals may be divided into two classes according to whether they do or do not possess a particular attribute. This process is called dichotomy.

2. Continued dichotomy according to n attributes gives rise to 3^n classes.

3. The frequencies in these classes can be expressed in terms of the 2^n ultimate class frequencies, or of the 2^n positive class frequencies.

4. Given 2^n independent class-frequencies, all the class-frequencies may be calculated by simple arithmetical processes.

5. The necessary and sufficient condition for the consistence of a set of independent class-frequencies relating to a particular population is that no ultimate class-frequency which may be calculated from them is negative.

6. In view of the practical importance of the positive class-frequencies, the form of the consistence conditions is expressed solely in terms of such frequencies.

7. The conditions may be applied to the examination of inaccurate or incomplete data. For the latter they may allow us to assign limits to an unknown class-frequency.

EXERCISES

1.1 The following are the numbers of boys observed with certain classes of defects amongst a number of school-children. A denotes development defects ; B, nerve signs ; C, low nutrition.

(ABC)	149	(αBC)	204
$(AB\gamma)$	738	$(\alpha B\gamma)$	1,762
$(A\beta C)$	225	$(\alpha\beta C)$	171
$(A\beta\gamma)$	1,196	$(\alpha\beta\gamma)$	21,842

Find the frequencies of the *positive* classes.

1.2 The following are the frequencies of the positive classes for the girls in the same investigation—

N	23,713	(AB)	587
(A)	1,618	(AC)	428
(B)	2,015	(BC)	335
(C)	770	(ABC)	156

Find the frequencies of the ultimate classes.

1.3 (Figures from *Census, England and Wales*, 1891, vol. 3) Convert the census statement as below into a statement in terms of (*a*) the positive, (*b*) the ultimate class-frequencies. A =blindness, B =deaf-mutism, C = mental derangement.

N	29,002,525	$(AB\gamma)$	82
(A)	23,467	$(A\beta C)$	380
(B)	14,192	(aBC)	500
(C)	97,383	(ABC)	25

1.4 Show that if A occurs in a larger proportion of the cases where B is than where B is not, then B will occur in a larger proportion of the cases where A is than where A is not : i.e. given $(AB)/(B)>(A\beta)/(\beta)$, show that $(AB)/(A) > (\alpha B)/(\alpha)$.

1.5 Given that
$$(A)=(\alpha)=(B)=(\beta)=\tfrac{1}{2}N$$
show that
$$(AB)=(\alpha\beta), \quad (A\beta)=(\alpha B)$$

1.6 Given that
$$(A)=(\alpha)=(B)=(\beta)=(C)=(\gamma)=\tfrac{1}{2}N$$
and also that
$$(ABC)=(\alpha\beta\gamma)$$
show that
$$2(ABC)=(AB)+(AC)+(BC)-\tfrac{1}{2}N$$

1.7 Measurements are made on a thousand husbands and a thousand wives. If the measurements of the husbands exceed the measurements of the wives in 800 cases for one measurement, in 700 cases for another, and in 660 cases for both measurements, in how many cases will both measurements on the wife exceed the measurements on the husband ?

1.8 100 children took three examinations. 40 passed the first, 39 passed the second and 48 passed the third. 10 passed all three, 21 failed all three, 9 passed the first two and failed the third, 19 failed the first two and passed the third. Find how many children passed at least two examinations.

Show that for the question asked certain of the given frequencies are not necessary. Which are they ?

Show further that the data are not sufficient to permit of the determination of the ultimate class-frequencies.

1.9   (Lewis Carroll, *A Tangled Tale*, 1881)   In a very hotly fought battle 70 per cent at least of the combatants lost an eye, 75 per cent at least lost an ear, 80 per cent at least lost an arm and 85 per cent at least lost a leg.   How many at least must have lost all four ?

1.10   Show that for n attributes A, B, C, ... M,

$$(ABC \ldots M) \geqslant \{(A)+(B)+(C)+ \ldots +(M)\} -(n-1)N$$

where N is the total frequency ;   and hence generalise the result of Exercise 1.9.

1.11   In a free vote in the House of Commons, 600 members voted.   300 Government members representing English constituencies (including Welsh) voted in favour of the motion.   25 Opposition members representing Scottish constituencies voted against the motion.   The Government majority among those who voted was 96.   135 of the members voting represented Scottish constituencies.   18 Government members voted against the motion.   102 Scottish members voted in favour of the motion.   The motion was carried by 310 votes.   Analyse the voting according to the nationality of the constituencies and party.

1.12   In a war between White and Red forces there are more Red soldiers than White ;   there are more armed Whites than unarmed Reds ;   there are fewer armed Reds with ammunition than unarmed Whites without ammunition.   Show that there are more armed Reds without ammunition than unarmed Whites with ammunition

1.13.   If, in an urban district 817 per thousand of the women between 20 and 25 years of age were returned as " occupied " at a census, and 263 per thousand as married or widowed, what is the lowest proportion per thousand of the married or widowed that must have been occupied ?

1.14   If, in a series of houses actually invaded by smallpox, 70 per cent of the inhabitants are attacked and 85 per cent have been vaccinated, what is the lowest percentage of the vaccinated that must have been attacked ?

1.15   Given that 50 per cent of the inmates of an institution are men, 60 per cent are " aged " (over 60), 80 per cent non-able-bodied, 35 per cent aged men, 45 per cent non-able-bodied men, and 42 per cent non-able-bodied and aged, find the greatest and least possible proportions of non-able-bodied aged men.

1.16   The following are the proportions per 10,000 of boys observed for certain classes of defects amongst a number of school-children. $A =$ development defects, $B =$ nerve signs, $D =$ mental dullness.

$$N = 10,000 \qquad (D) = 789$$
$$(A) = 877 \qquad (AB) = 338$$
$$(B) = 1{,}086 \qquad (BD) = 455$$

Show that some dull boys do not exhibit development defects, and state how many at least do not do so.

1.17 The following are the corresponding figures for girls—

$$N = 10,000 \qquad (D) = 689$$
$$(A) = 682 \qquad (AB) = 248$$
$$(B) = 850 \qquad (BD) = 363$$

Show that some defectively developed girls are not dull, and state how many at least must be so.

1.18 Take the syllogism " All A's are B's, all B's are C's, therefore all A's are C's," express the premises in terms of the notation of the preceding chapter, and deduce the conclusion by the use of the general conditions of consistence.

1.19 Do the same for the syllogism " All A's are B's, no B's are C's, therefore no A's are C's."

1.20 Given that $(A)=(B)=(C)=\frac{1}{2}N$, and that $(AB)/N=(AC)/N=p$, find what must be the greatest and least values of p in order that we may infer that $(BC)/N$ exceeds any given value, say q.

1.21 Show that if

$$\frac{(A)}{N}=x \qquad \frac{(B)}{N}=2x \qquad \frac{(C)}{N}=3x$$

and

$$\frac{(AB)}{N}=\frac{(AC)}{N}=\frac{(BC)}{N}=y$$

the value of neither x nor y can exceed $\frac{1}{4}$.

1.22 A market investigator returns the following data. Of 1000 people consulted, 811 liked chocolates, 752 liked toffee and 418 liked boiled sweets ; 570 liked chocolates and toffee, 356 liked chocolates and boiled sweets and 348 liked toffee and boiled sweets ; 297 liked all three. Show that this information as it stands must be incorrect.

1.23 50 per cent of the imports of barley into a country come from the Dominions ; 80 per cent of the total imports go to brewing ; 75 per cent of the imports are grown in the Northern Hemisphere ; 80 per cent of Northern-grown barley goes to brewing ; 100 per cent of foreign Southern-grown barley goes to stock-feeding. Show that the foreign Northern-grown barley which goes to brewing cannot be less than 30 per cent nor more than 50 per cent of the total imports.

(It is assumed that brewing and stock-feeding are the only two uses to which imported barley is put.)

1.24   A penny is tossed three times and the results, heads and tails, noted. The process is continued until there are 100 sets of threes.   In 69 cases heads fell first, in 49 cases heads fell second, and in 53 cases heads fell third.   In 33 cases heads fell both first and second, and in 21 cases heads fell both second and third.   Show that there must have been at least 5 occasions on which heads fell three times, and that there could not have been more than 15 occasions on which tails fell three times, though there need not have been any.

CHAPTER TWO

ASSOCIATION OF ATTRIBUTES

Independence

2.1 If there is no sort of relationship of any kind between two attributes A and B, we expect to find the same proportion of A's amongst the B's as amongst the not-B's. We may anticipate, for instance, the same proportion of abnormally wet seasons in leap years as in ordinary years, the same proportion of male to total births when the moon is waxing as when it is waning, the same proportion of heads whether a coin be tossed with the right hand or the left.

Two such unrelated attributes may be termed *independent*, and we have accordingly as the *criterion of independence* for A and B—

$$\frac{(AB)}{(B)} = \frac{(A\beta)}{(\beta)} \qquad \cdot \qquad \cdot \qquad \cdot \qquad \cdot \qquad (2.1)$$

If this relation holds good, the corresponding relations

$$\frac{(\alpha B)}{(B)} = \frac{(\alpha\beta)}{(\beta)}$$

$$\frac{(AB)}{(A)} = \frac{(\alpha B)}{(\alpha)}$$

$$\frac{(A\beta)}{(A)} = \frac{(\alpha\beta)}{(\alpha)}$$

must also hold. For it follows at once from (2.1) that

$$\frac{(B)-(AB)}{(B)} = \frac{(\beta)-(A\beta)}{(\beta)}$$

that is,

$$\frac{(\alpha B)}{(B)} = \frac{(\alpha\beta)}{(\beta)}$$

and the other two identities may be similarly deduced.

The student may find it easier to grasp the nature of the relations stated if the frequencies are supposed grouped into a table with two rows and two columns, thus—

Attribute	B	β	Total
A	(AB)	$(A\beta)$	(A)
α	(αB)	$(\alpha\beta)$	(α)
Total	(B)	(β)	N

Equation (2.1) states a certain equality for the columns ; if this holds good, the corresponding equation

$$\frac{(AB)}{(A)}=\frac{(\alpha B)}{(\alpha)}$$

must hold for the rows, and so on.

Forms of the criterion of independence

2.2 The criterion may, however, be put into a somewhat different and theoretically more convenient form. The equation (2.1) expresses (AB) in terms of (B), (β) and a second-order frequency $(A\beta)$; eliminating this second-order frequency we have—

$$\frac{(AB)}{(B)}=\frac{(AB)+(A\beta)}{(B)+(\beta)}=\frac{(A)}{N}$$

i.e. in words, " the proportion of A's amongst the B's is the same as in the population at large." The student should learn to recognise this equation at sight in any of the forms—

$$\frac{(AB)}{(B)}=\frac{(A)}{N} \qquad (a)$$

$$\frac{(AB)}{(A)}=\frac{(B)}{N} \qquad (b)$$

$$(AB)=\frac{(A)(B)}{N} \qquad (c)$$

$$\frac{(AB)}{N}=\frac{(A)}{N}\cdot\frac{(B)}{N} \qquad (d)$$

$$\qquad\qquad . \qquad . \qquad . \qquad (2.2)$$

The equation (d) gives the important fundamental rule : *If the attributes A and B are independent, the proportion of AB's in the population is equal to the proportion of A's multiplied by the proportion of B's.*

The advantage of the forms (2.2) over the form (2.1) is that they give expressions for the second-order frequency in terms of the frequencies of the first order and the whole number of observations alone ; the form (2.1) does not.

Example 2.1.—If there are 144 A's and 384 B's in 1024 observations, how many AB's will there be, A and B being independent ?

$$\frac{144 \times 384}{1024} = 54$$

There will therefore be 54 AB's.

Example 2.2.—If the A's are 60 per cent, the B's 35 per cent, of the whole number of observations, what must be the percentage of AB's in order that we may conclude that A and B are independent ?

$$\frac{60 \times 35}{100} = 21$$

and therefore there must be 21 per cent (more or less closely, cf. **2.8** and **2.9** below) of AB's in the population to justify the conclusion that A and B are independent.

2.3 It follows from **2.1** that if the relation (2.2) holds for any one of the four second-order frequencies, e.g. (AB), similar relations must hold for the remaining three. Thus we have directly from (**2.1**)—

$$\frac{(A\beta)}{(\beta)} = \frac{(AB) + (A\beta)}{(B) + (\beta)} = \frac{(A)}{N}$$

giving

$$(A\beta) = \frac{(A)(\beta)}{N}$$

and so on.   This is seen at once to be true on consideration of the fourfold table on page 20.   For if (AB) takes the value $(A)(B)/N$, $(A\beta)$ must take the value $(A)(\beta)/N$ to keep the total of the row equal to (A), and so on for the other rows and columns.   The fourfold table in the case of independence must in fact have the form—

Attribute	B	β	Total
A	$(A)(B)/N$	$(A)(\beta)/N$	(A)
α	$(\alpha)(B)/N$	$(\alpha)(\beta)/N$	(α)
Total	(B)	(β)	N

Example 2.3.—In Example 2.1 above, what would be the number of $\alpha\beta$'s, A and B being independent ?

$$(\alpha) = 1024 - 144 = 880$$
$$(\beta) = 1024 - 384 = 640$$
$$\therefore \quad (\alpha\beta) = \frac{880 \times 640}{1024} = 550$$

2.4 Finally, the criterion of independence may be expressed in yet a third form viz. in terms of the second-order frequencies alone. If A and B are independent, it follows at once from the preceding section that

$$(AB)(\alpha\beta) = \frac{(A)(B)(\alpha)(\beta)}{N^2}$$

And evidently $(\alpha B)(A\beta)$ is equal to the same fraction.

Therefore

$$
\left.
\begin{array}{ll}
(AB)(\alpha\beta) = (\alpha B)(A\beta) & (a) \\[4pt]
\dfrac{(AB)}{(\alpha B)} = \dfrac{(A\beta)}{(\alpha\beta)} & (b) \\[10pt]
\dfrac{(AB)}{(A\beta)} = \dfrac{(\alpha B)}{(\alpha\beta)} & (c)
\end{array}
\right\} \qquad \cdot \qquad \cdot \qquad \cdot \quad (2.3)
$$

The equation (b) may be read : " The ratio of A's to α's amongst the B's is equal to the ratio of A's to α's amongst the β's," and (c) similarly.

This form of criterion is a convenient one if all the four second-order frequencies are given, enabling one to recognise almost at a glance whether or not the two attributes are independent.

Example 2.4.—If the second-order frequencies have the following values, are A and B independent or not ?

$$(AB) = 110 \qquad (\alpha B) = 90 \qquad (A\beta) = 290 \qquad (\alpha\beta) = 510$$

Clearly

$$(AB)(\alpha\beta) > (\alpha B)(A\beta)$$

so A and B are not independent.

Association

2.5 Suppose now that A and B are not independent, but related in some way or other, however complicated.

Then if

$$(AB) > \frac{(A)(B)}{N}$$

A and B are said to be *positively associated*, or sometimes simply *associated*. If, on the other hand,

$$(AB) < \frac{(A)(B)}{N}$$

A and B are said to be *negatively associated* or, more briefly, *disassociated*.

The student should carefully note that in statistics the word " association " has a technical meaning different from the one current in ordinary speech. In common language one speaks of A and B as being " associated " if they appear together in a number of cases. But in statistics A and B are associated only if they appear together in a greater number of cases than is to be expected if they are independent. Thus, if we consider means of land transport as dichotomised into road and rail travel, we may say, in the customary use of the term, that road transport is associated with speed.   But it does not follow that the two are statistically associated, because rail transport may equally be associated with speed and, in fact, the attribute speed may be independent of the means of travel in these two manners.

Association, therefore, cannot be inferred from the mere fact that *some* A's are B's, however great the proportion ; this principle is fundamental and should always be borne in mind.

Complete association and disassociation

2.6 We have now to consider in what circumstances we may regard the association of two attributes as *complete*. Two courses are open to us. Either we may say that for complete association all A's must be B's *and* all B's must be A's, in which case it must follow that the A's and the B's occur in the population in equal numbers ; or we may adopt a rather wider meaning and say that all A's are B's *or* all B's are A's, according to whether the A's or the B's are in the minority.   Similarly, complete disassociation may be taken either as the case when no A's are B's *and* no α's are β's, or more widely as the case when either of these statements is true.

We shall adopt the wider definition in the sequel.   Thus two attributes are *completely associated* if one of them cannot occur without the other, though the other may occur without the one.

Measurement of intensity of association

2.7 It follows from the foregoing that if two attributes are completely associated, (AB) must be equal to (A) or (B), whichever is the smaller. If they are completely disassociated, (AB) must be equal to zero or to $(A)+(B)-N$ whichever is the greater. (AB) must in general lie between these two limits.   We may thus regard the divergence of (AB) from the " independence " value $(A)(B)/N$ towards the limiting value in either direction as indicating the *intensity* of association or disassociation, so that we may speak of attributes as being *more* or *less*, *highly* or *slightly*, associated.   This conception of degrees of association quantitatively expressible is important, and we return in a later section to consider the formulae which may be used to measure such degrees.

Sampling fluctuations

2.8 When the association is very slight, i.e. where (AB) differs from $(A)(B)/N$ by only a few units or by a small proportion, it may be that such association is not really significant of any definite relationship.   To give an illustration, suppose that a coin is tossed a number of times, and the tosses noted in pairs ; then 100 pairs may give such results as the following (taken from an actual record)—

First toss heads and second heads	·	·	·	26
,,	,,	,,	tails	·	·	·	18
First toss tails and second heads	·	·	·	27
,,	,,	,,	tails	·	·	·	29

If we use A to denote " heads " in the first toss, B " heads " in the second, we have from the above $(A)=44$, $(B)=53$. Hence $(A)(B)/N=\dfrac{44\times53}{100}=23\cdot32$, while actually (AB) is 26. Hence there is a positive association, in the given record, between the result of the first throw and the result of the second. But it is fairly certain, from the nature of the case, that such association cannot indicate any real connection between the results of the two throws ; it must therefore be due merely to such a complex system of causes, impossible to analyse, as leads, for example, to differences between small samples drawn from the same material. The conclusion is confirmed by the fact that, of a number of such records, some give a positive association (like the above), but others a negative association.

2.9 An event due, like the above occurrence of positive association, to an extremely complex system of causes of the general nature of which we are aware, but of the detailed operation of which we are ignorant, is sometimes said to be due to *chance*, or better to the *chances* or *fluctuations of sampling*.

A little consideration will suggest that such associations due to the fluctuations of sampling must be met with in all classes of statistics. To quote, for instance, from **2.1**, two illustrations there given of independent attributes, we know that in any *actual* record we should not be likely to find *exactly* the same proportion of abnormally wet seasons in leap years as in ordinary years, or *exactly* the same proportion of male births when the moon is waxing as when it is waning. But so long as the divergence from independence is not well marked we must regard such attributes as practically independent, or dependence as at least unproved.

The discussion of the question, how great the divergence must be before we can consider it as " well marked," must be postponed to the chapters dealing with the theory of sampling. At present the attention of the student can only be directed to the existence of the difficulty, and to the serious risk of interpreting a " chance association " as physically significant.

The choice of a suitable form for testing association

2.10 The definition of **2.5** suggests that we are to test the existence or the intensity of association between two attributes by a comparison of the actual value of (AB) with its independence value (as it may be termed) $(A)(B)/N$. The procedure is from the theoretical standpoint perhaps the most natural, but it is more usual, and is simplest and best in practice, to compare *proportions*, e.g. the proportion of A's amongst the B's with the proportion amongst the β's. Such proportions are usually expressed in the form of percentages or proportions per thousand.

It will be evident from **2.1** and **2.2** that a large number of such comparisons are available for the purpose, and the question arises, therefore, which is the best comparison to adopt?

2.11 Two principles should decide this point : (1) of any two comparisons, that is the better which brings out the more clearly the degree of association ; (2) of any two comparisons, that is the better which illustrates the more important aspect of the problem under discussion.

The first condition at once suggests that comparisons of the form

$$\frac{(AB)}{(B)} > \frac{(A\beta)}{(\beta)} \qquad . \qquad . \qquad . \qquad . \quad (2.4)$$

are better than comparisons of the form

$$\frac{(AB)}{(B)} > \frac{(A)}{N} \qquad . \qquad . \qquad . \qquad . \quad (2.5)$$

For it is evident that if most of the objects or individuals in the population are B's, i.e. if $(B)/N$ approaches unity, $(AB)/(B)$ will necessarily approach $(A)/N$ even though the difference between $(AB)/(B)$ and $(A\beta)/(\beta)$ is considerable. The second form of comparison may therefore be misleading.

Setting aside, then, comparisons of the general form (2.5), the question remains whether to apply the comparison of the form (2.4) to the rows or the columns of the table, if the data are tabulated as on page 21. This question must be decided with reference to the second principle, i.e. with regard to the more important aspect of the problem under discussion, the exact question to be answered, or the hypothesis to be tested, as illustrated by the examples below. Where no *definite* question has to be answered or hypothesis tested both pairs of proportions may be tabulated.

Example 2.5.—Association between inoculation against cholera and exemption from attack. (Data from Greenwood and Yule, *Proc. Roy. Soc. Med.*, 1915, **8**, 221, Table III).

	Not attacked	Attacked	Total
Inoculated . .	276	3	279
Not inoculated . .	473	66	539
Total . . .	749	69	818

Here the important question is, How far does inoculation protect from attack ? The most natural comparison is therefore—

Percentage of inoculated who were not attacked · · 98·9
,, not inoculated ,, ,, · · 87·8

Or we might tabulate the complementary proportions—

Percentage of inoculated who were attacked · · 1·1
,, not inoculated ,, ,, · · 12·2

Either comparison brings out simply and clearly the fact that *inoculation* and *exemption from attack* are *positively associated* (*inoculation* and *attack* negatively associated).

We are making above a comparison by rows in the notation of the table on page 21, comparing $(AB)/(A)$ with $(\alpha B)/(\alpha)$, or $(A\beta)/(A)$ with $(\alpha\beta)/(\alpha)$. A comparison by columns, e.g. $(AB)/(B)$ with $(A\beta)/(\beta)$, would serve equally to indicate whether there was any appreciable association, but would not answer directly the particular question we have in mind—

Percentage of not-attacked who were inoculated · · 36·8
,, attacked ,, ,, · · 4·3

Example 2.6.—Eye-colour of father and son (material due to Galton, as given by Pearson, *Phil. Trans.*, A, 1900, **195**, 138 ; the classes 1, 2 and 3 of the memoir treated as " light ").

Fathers with light eyes and sons with light eyes (AB) · · 471
,, ,, ,, ,, not light ,, $(A\beta)$ · · 151
,, not light ,, ,, light ,, (αB) · · 148
,, ,, ,, ,, not light ,, $(\alpha\beta)$ · · 230

Required to find whether the colour of the son's eyes is associated with that of the father's. In cases of this kind the father is reckoned once for each son ; e.g. a family in which the father was light-eyed, two sons light-eyed and one not, would be reckoned as giving two to the class AB and one to the class $A\beta$.

The best comparison here is—

Percentage of light-eyed amongst the sons of light-eyed fathers · · · } 76 per cent

Percentage of light-eyed amongst the sons of not-light-eyed fathers · · · } 39 ,,

But the following is equally valid—

Percentage of light-eyed amongst the fathers of light-eyed sons · · } 76 per cent

Percentage of light-eyed amongst the fathers of not-light-eyed sons · · } 40 ,,

The reason why the former comparison is preferable is that we usually wish to estimate the character of offspring from that of the parents, and not *vice versa*. Both modes of statement, however, indicate equally clearly that there is considerable resemblance between father and son.

Example 2.7—Association between inoculation against cholera and exemption from attack, five separate epidemics (cf. Example 2.5, data from Tables IX, X, XXVIII, XXIX, XXXI of the paper there cited.)

	Not attacked	Attacked	Total
Inoculated · · ·	192	4	196
Not inoculated · · ·	113	34	147
Total · · ·	305	38	343

	Not attacked	Attacked	Total
Inoculated · · ·	5,751	27	5,778
Not inoculated · · ·	6,351	198	6,549
Total · · ·	12,102	225	12,327

	Not attacked	Attacked	Total
Inoculated · · ·	4,087	5	4,092
Not inoculated · · ·	113,856	1,144	115,000
Total · · ·	117,943	1,149	119,092

	Not attacked	Attacked	Total
Inoculated · · ·	8,332	8	8,340
Not inoculated · · ·	84,444	556	85,000
Total · · ·	92,776	564	93,340

	Not attacked	Attacked	Total
Inoculated · · ·	4,870	5	4,875
Not inoculated · · ·	153,096	904	154,000
Total · · ·	157,966	909	158,875

With the table of Example 2.5 the above give data for six separate epidemics, in all of which the same method of inoculation appears to have been used : the data refer to natives only, and the numbers of observations are sufficiently large to reduce " fluctuations of sampling " within reasonably narrow limits. The proportions not attacked are as follows—

Proportion not attacked

	Not inoculated	Inoculated	Difference
1 · · ·	0·8776	0·9892	0·1116
2 · · ·	0·7687	0·9796	0·2109
3 · · ·	0·9698	0·9953	0·0255
4 · · ·	0·9901	0·9988	0·0087
5 · · ·	0·9935	0·9990	0·0055
6 · · ·	0·9941	0·9990	0·0049

In each case *inoculation* and *exemption from attack* are positively associated, but it will be seen that the several proportions, and the differences between them, vary considerably. Evidently in a very mild epidemic this difference can only be small, and the question arises how far the data for the separate epidemics can be said to be consistent in their indication of the " efficiency " of the inoculation. This is not a simple question to answer : the more advanced student is referred to the discussion in the original.

The symbols $(AB)_0$ and δ

2.12 The values that the four second-order frequencies take in the case of independence, viz.

$$\frac{(A)(B)}{N}, \quad \frac{(\alpha)(B)}{N}, \quad \frac{(A)(\beta)}{N}, \quad \frac{(\alpha)(\beta)}{N}$$

are of such great theoretical importance, and of so much use as reference-values for comparing with the actual values of the frequencies (AB), (αB), $(A\beta)$ and $(\alpha\beta)$, that it is often desirable to employ single symbols to denote them. We shall use the symbols

$$(AB)_0 = \frac{(A)(B)}{N} \qquad (\alpha\beta)_0 = \frac{(\alpha)(\beta)}{N}$$

$$(\alpha B)_0 = \frac{(\alpha)(B)}{N} \qquad (A\beta)_0 = \frac{(A)(\beta)}{N}$$

If δ denote the excess of (AB) over $(AB)_0$, then, in order to keep the totals of rows and columns constant, the general table (cf. the table for the case of independence on page 21) must be of the form—

Attribute	B	β	Total
A	$(AB)_0 + \delta$	$(A\beta)_0 - \delta$	(A)
α	$(\alpha B)_0 - \delta$	$(\alpha\beta)_0 + \delta$	(α)
Total	(B)	(β)	N

Therefore, quite generally we have—

$$(AB) - (AB)_0 = (\alpha\beta) - (\alpha\beta)_0 = (A\beta)_0 - (A\beta) = (\alpha B)_0 - (\alpha B) = \delta$$

2.13 The value of this common difference δ may be expressed in a form that is useful to note. We have by definition—

$$\delta=(AB)-(AB)_0=(AB)-\frac{(A)(B)}{N}$$

Bring the terms on the right to a common denominator, and express all the frequencies of the numerator in terms of those of the second order ; then we have—

$$\delta=\frac{1}{N}\left\{\begin{array}{c}(AB)[(AB)+(\alpha B)+(A\beta)+(\alpha\beta)]\\-[(AB)+(A\beta)][(AB)+(\alpha B)]\end{array}\right\}$$

$$=\frac{1}{N}\{(AB)(\alpha\beta)-(\alpha B)(A\beta)\}$$

That is to say, the common difference is equal to 1/Nth of the difference of the " cross-products " $(AB)(\alpha\beta)$ and $(\alpha B)(A\beta)$.

It is evident that the difference of the cross-products may be very large if N be large, although δ is really very small. In using the difference of the cross-products to test mentally the sign of the association in a case where all the four second-order frequencies are given, this should be remembered ; the difference should be compared with N, or it will be liable to suggest a higher degree of association than actually exists.

Example 2.8—The following data were observed for hybrids of *Datura* (Bateson and Saunders, Report to the Evolution Committee of the Royal Society, 1902)—

Flowers violet, fruits prickly (AB)	·	·	47
,,	,, smooth $(A\beta)$	·	·	12
Flowers white,	,, 'prickly (αB)	·	·	21
,,	,, smooth $(\alpha\beta)$	·	·	3

Investigate the association between colour of flower and character of fruit.

Since $3\times47=141$, $12\times21=252$ i.e. $(AB)(\alpha\beta) < (\alpha B)(A\beta)$, there is clearly a negative association ; $252-141=111$, and at first sight this considerable difference is apt to suggest a considerable disassociation. But $\delta=111/83=1\cdot3$ only, and forms a small proportion of the frequency, so that in point of fact the disassociation is small, so small that no stress can be laid on it as indicating anything but a fluctuation of sampling. Working out the percentages we have—

Percentage of violet-flowered plants with prickly fruits · · · · · } 80 per cent

Percentage of white-flowered plants with prickly fruits · · · · · } 87 ,,

Coefficient of association

2.14 In the previous examples we have judged the association by comparing the class-frequencies with those which would exist if the data were given by independent attributes, and we can form a rough idea of the strength of the association by examining the extent of the difference. This is sufficient for almost all practical purposes, although, if the data are likely to be affected seriously by fluctuations of random sampling, some test of the significance of the difference is also necessary. Apart from this question, however, it is sometimes convenient to measure the intensities of the associations by means of a coefficient.

It is clearly convenient if such a coefficient can be devised as to be zero if the attributes are independent, $+1$ if they are completely associated and -1 if they are completely disassociated.

2.15 Many such coefficients may be devised, but perhaps the simplest possible (though not necessarily the most advantageous) is the expression—

$$Q = \frac{(AB)(\alpha\beta) - (A\beta)(\alpha B)}{(AB)(\alpha\beta) + (A\beta)(\alpha B)}$$

$$= \frac{N\delta}{(AB)(\alpha\beta) + (A\beta)(\alpha B)}$$

where δ is the symbol used in **2.12** and **2.13** for the difference $(AB) - (AB)_0$. It is evident that Q is zero when the attributes are independent, for then δ is zero : it takes the value $+1$ when there is complete association, for then the second term in both numerator and denominator of the first form of the expression is zero : similarly it is -1 where there is complete disassociation, for then the first term in both numerator and denominator is zero. Q may accordingly be termed a *coefficient of association*. As illustrations of the values it will take in certain cases, the association between light eye-colour in father and in son (Example 2.6) is $+0\cdot66$; between colour of flower and prickliness of fruit in *Datura* (Example 2.8), $-0\cdot28$: a disassociation which, however, as already stated, is probably of no practical significance and due to mere fluctuations of sampling.

The student should note that if all the terms containing A are multiplied by a constant, the value of Q is unaltered. Similarly for α, B and β. Hence Q is independent of the relative proportions of A's and α's in the data. This property is important, and renders such a measure of association specially adapted to cases in which the proportions are arbitrary (e.g. experiments).

2.16 Another coefficient which has the same property is the *coefficient of colligation*.

$$Y = \frac{1 - \sqrt{\dfrac{(A\beta)(\alpha B)}{(AB)(\alpha\beta)}}}{1 + \sqrt{\dfrac{(A\beta)(\alpha B)}{(AB)(\alpha\beta)}}} \qquad . \qquad . \qquad . \qquad (2.6)$$

It is easy to show that

$$Q = \frac{2Y}{1 + Y^2} \qquad . \qquad . \qquad . \qquad (2.7)$$

Association in sub-populations

2.17 Up to this point we have considered association between two attributes in a population without regard to whether any information existed about other attributes in the population. If, however, such information does exist and, say, we can find the frequency-classes of attributes C, D, etc., the question arises, What are the associations of A and B in the sub-populations C, γ, CD, etc.?

Thus, if $A =$ standard of health and $B =$ consumption of food, the foregoing discussion would enable us to examine whether health and food-consumption were associated in any particular population, say the population of Great Britain. But we might want to go further than this and examine the association between A and B among males, or among the poorer classes, and compare it with the association among females or among the well-to-do classes, respectively. Defining $C =$ males and $D =$ poor, this amounts to examining the associations of A and B in the populations C, γ, D and δ.

2.18 Associations of this kind are of the utmost importance in statistical practice. As instances of the ways in which they arise let us consider the following two illustrations—

(1) Suppose that we have established, in the manner of foregoing sections, a positive association between inoculation and exemption from smallpox in a population of persons. It is natural to infer that this association is due to some causal relation between the two attributes and may be expected to recur in the future ; in short, that smallpox is prevented by vaccination.

This rather hasty conclusion might, however, meet an opponent who argues in this way : vaccination is accepted among the well-to-do classes, but is looked on with suspicion by the lower classes. For this and other reasons most of the unvaccinated persons are drawn from the lower classes. But these are precisely the people whom, from the unhygienic conditions under which they live, one would expect to be exposed to infection and who, moreover, being malnourished, would be more likely to contract disease when they were infected. Hence the comparative exemption of the vaccinated persons is not due to the fact that they have been vaccinated, but to the fact that they belong to the well-to-do classes. It is, as it were, an accident that these people also happen to be from a class which favours vaccination.

Denoting *vaccination* by *A*, *exemption from attack* by *B* and *hygienic conditions* by *C*, this argument amounts to saying that the observed association between *A* and *B* is not of itself causally direct, but is due to the associations of both *A* and *B* with *C*.

Now it is clear that this objection could not be lodged if the hygienic conditions among all the members of the population were the same. If, therefore, we examine the association of *A* and *B* in the sub-population *C* and still find an association, the supposed argument will be refuted. We are thus led to a consideration of the association in that sub-population.

(2) As a second example, suppose that an association is noted between the presence of an attribute in the father and the presence in the son, and also between the presence in the grandfather and the presence in the grandson. The question which arises here is : Does the resemblance between grandfather and grandson arise from a kind of hereditary transmission which may, in the common phrase, " skip a generation," or is it merely due to the fact that the grandfather is like the father and the father is like the son ?

Denoting the presence of the attribute in the son, father and grandfather by *A*, *B* and *C*, the question is : Is the association between *A* and *C* due to associations between *A* and *B*, and *B* and *C* ?

If the association between *A* and *C* is observed among all the cases in which the father possesses the attribute or all those in which he does not, and is still sensible, clearly the association between *A* and *C* cannot be due to associations between *A* and *B*, *B* and *C* ; hence, as before, to resolve the question we are led to consider the association between *A* and *C* in the sub-populations *B* and β.

2.19 Generally, ambiguity of the type to which we have just referred arises from the fact that the population under discussion contains not merely objects possessing the third attribute alone, but a mixture of objects with and without it. To meet the requirements of the discussion we have to consider the associations in sub-populations wherein this attribute is entirely absent or entirely present. By this means we can go deeper into the nature of the underlying causes and eliminate certain possible explanations of the type : an association between *A* and *B* does not mean that the two are directly related, but only that each is associated with a third attribute *C*.

Partial associations

2.20 The associations between *A* and *B* in sub-populations are called *partial associations*, to distinguish them from the *total* associations between *A* and *B* in the population at large.

As for total association, A and B are said to be positively associated in the population of C's if

$$(ABC) > \frac{(AC)(BC)}{(C)} \qquad \cdot \qquad \cdot \qquad \cdot \qquad \cdot \quad (2.8)$$

and negatively associated in the converse case.

Similarly they are positively associated in the population of CD's if

$$(ABCD) > \frac{(ACD)(BCD)}{(CD)} \qquad \cdot \qquad \cdot \qquad \cdot \quad (2.9)$$

and so on. These formulae are derived from the formula for total association by specifying the population in which the partial association exists.

Alternative forms of the conditions for partial association

2.21 As in the case of total association, the above forms can be written in many ways, adapted to the nature of the data and of the question which is to be answered. The partial association is most conveniently tested by comparisons of percentages or proportions in the manner of **2.2,** and we may quote the four most convenient comparisons in the case of three attributes—

$$\frac{(ABC)}{(BC)} > \frac{(AC)}{(C)} \quad \cdot \quad (a) \qquad \frac{(ABC)}{(AC)} > \frac{(BC)}{(C)} \quad \cdot \quad (b)$$

$$\left. \frac{(ABC)}{(BC)} > \frac{(A\beta C)}{(\beta C)} \quad \cdot \quad (c) \qquad \frac{(ABC)}{(AC)} > \frac{(\alpha BC)}{(\alpha C)} \quad \cdot \quad (d) \right\} \quad (2.10)$$

Similar formulae may be written down for the cases of four or more attributes, and the methods of this chapter are applicable to such cases. For the sake of simplicity we shall, however, confine ourselves to three attributes hereafter.

Example 2.9.—The following are the proportions per 10,000 of boys observed with certain classes of defects amongst a number of school-children. (A) denotes the number with development defects, (B) the number with nerve signs (D) the number of the " dull."

N	10,000	(AB)	338
(A)	877	(AD)	338
(B)	1,086	(BD)	455
(D)	789	(ABD)	153

The *Report* (referred to in Example 1.1) from which the figures are drawn concludes that " the connecting link between defects of body and mental dullness is the coincident defect of brain which may be known by observation of abnormal nerve signs." Discuss this conclusion.

The phrase " connecting link " is a little vague, but it may mean that the mental defects indicated by nerve signs B may give rise to development defects A, and also to mental dullness D; A and D being thus common effects of the same cause B (or another attribute necessarily indicated by B) and not directly influencing each other. The case is thus similar to that of the first illustration of **2.18** (liability to smallpox and to non-vaccination being held to be common effects of the same circumstances), and may be similarly treated by investigation of the partial associations between A and D for the populations B and β. As the ratios $(A)/N$, $(B)/N$, $(D)/N$ are small, comparisons of the form (2.10), (a) and (b) above, may be used.

The following figures illustrate, then, the association between A and D for the whole population, the B-population and the β-population—

For the entire material—

$$\text{Proportion of the dull} = (D)/N \quad \cdot \quad \cdot \quad = \frac{789}{10,000} = 7 \cdot 9 \text{ per cent}$$

$$\left.\begin{array}{l} \text{,,} \qquad \text{,, defectively developed who} \\ \text{were dull} = (AD)/(A) \qquad \cdot \qquad \cdot \qquad \cdot \end{array}\right\} = \frac{338}{877} = 38 \cdot 5 \quad \text{,,}$$

For those exhibiting nerve signs—

$$\text{Proportion of the dull} = (BD)/(B) \quad \cdot \quad \cdot \quad = \frac{455}{1,086} = 41 \cdot 9 \text{ per cent}$$

$$\left.\begin{array}{l} \text{,,} \qquad \text{,, defectively developed who} \\ \text{were dull} = (ABD)/(AB) \qquad \cdot \qquad \cdot \qquad \cdot \end{array}\right\} = \frac{153}{338} = 45 \cdot 3 \quad \text{,,}$$

For those not exhibiting nerve signs—

$$\text{Proportion of the dull} = (\beta D)/(\beta) \quad \cdot \quad \cdot \quad = \frac{334}{8,914} = 3 \cdot 7 \quad \text{,,}$$

$$\left.\begin{array}{l} \text{,,} \qquad \text{,, defectively developed who} \\ \text{were dull} = (A\beta D)/(A\beta) \qquad \cdot \qquad \cdot \qquad \cdot \end{array}\right\} = \frac{185}{539} = 34 \cdot 3 \quad \text{,,}$$

The results are extremely striking; the association between A and D is high both for the material as a whole (the population at large) and for those not exhibiting nerve signs (the β-population), but it is *small* for those who do exhibit nerve signs (the B-population).

This result does not appear to be in accord with the conclusion of the *Report*, as we have interpreted it, for the association between A and D in the β-population should in that case have been low instead of high.

Notation for partial associations

2.22 We now introduce a notation which is analogous to that used for total associations. It will be remembered that in **2.13** we wrote—

$$(AB)_0 = \frac{(A)(B)}{N}$$

$$\delta = (AB) - (AB)_0$$

We now write—

$$(AB.C)_0 = \frac{(AC)(BC)}{(C)}, \quad (AB.CD)_0 = \frac{(ACD)(BCD)}{(CD)} \quad \left.\right\} \quad \cdot \quad (2.11)$$
$$\delta_{AB.C} = (ABC) - (AB.C)_0, \quad \delta_{AB.CD} = (ABCD) - (AB.CD)_0, \text{ etc.} \left.\right\}$$

The δ-numbers measure the divergence of the actual frequencies from those which would exist if the attributes were independent in the sub-population under discussion.

It is also possible to generalise the coefficient of association Q by defining partial coefficients of the type

$$Q_{AB.C} = \frac{(ABC)(\alpha\beta C) - (A\beta C)(\alpha BC)}{(ABC)(\alpha\beta C) + (A\beta C)(\alpha BC)} \quad \left.\right\}$$
$$= \frac{(C)\delta_{AB.C}}{(ABC)(\alpha\beta C) + (A\beta C)(\alpha BC)} \left.\right\} \quad \cdot \quad \cdot \quad (2.12)$$

The student will notice that the formulae for the δ-numbers and for the Q numbers are obtained from the expressions for total association by specifying the population in which the partial association is to be considered. They need not therefore be memorised.

Number of partial associations

2.23 For three attributes A, B, C there are three total associations, namely, those of A with B, B with C and C with A ; and six partial associations, namely, those of A and B in C and γ, B and C in A and α, and C and A in B and β.

For four attributes there are fifty-four associations ; for we can choose two attributes from four in six ways, and there are nine associations for each pair (one total, four partials in the sub-populations specified by one attribute, and four partials in the sub-populations specified by two).

We state without proof that for n attributes there are $\frac{n(n-1)}{2}3^{n-2}$ associations. Of these, $\frac{n(n-1)}{2}$ are total and the remainder partial. For $n > 4$ this number is so large as to be almost unmanageable. For instance, if $n=5$ it is 270, and if $n=6$ it is 1215.

The large number of partial associations which exists might be thought to occasion some difficulty. We may, however, reassure ourselves by two considerations.

In the first place, it is rarely necessary to investigate in any practical instance all the partial associations which are theoretically possible. For instance, in Example 2.9 the total and partial associations between A and D were alone investigated ; those between A and B, B and D were not essential for answering the question which was asked.

Relations between partial associations

2.24 In the second place, a theoretical discussion of the partial associations is assisted by the following result : The $\dfrac{n(n-1)}{2}3^{n-2}$ associations are all expressible in terms of $2^n-(n+1)$ algebraically independent associations, together with the class-frequencies N, (A), (B), (C), etc.

In fact, we saw in Chapter 1 that all the class-frequencies can be expressed in terms of the positive class-frequencies, which are 2^n in number in the case of n attributes. Hence the frequencies N, (A), (B), (C), etc., of which there are $(n+1)$, together with the $2^n-(n+1)$ other positive frequencies, completely determine the data, and hence determine the associations, which are expressed in terms of the data. Hence the number of algebraically independent associations which can be derived is only $2^n-(n+1)$.

2.25 In practice the existence of these relations is of little or no value. The formal relations between the ratios and the δ-numbers which express the associations are, in fact, so complex that lengthy algebraic manipulation is necessary to express those which are not known in terms of those which are. It is usually better to evaluate the class-frequencies and calculate the desired results directly from them.

2.26 There is, however, one result which has important theoretical consequences.

We have, by definition,

$$\delta_{AB.C}=(ABC)-\frac{(AC)(BC)}{(C)}$$

$$\delta_{AB.\gamma}=(AB\gamma)-\frac{(A\gamma)(B\gamma)}{(\gamma)}$$

Hence,

$$\delta_{AB.C}+\delta_{AB.\gamma}=(AB)-\frac{1}{(C)(\gamma)}\left\{(AC)(BC)(\gamma)+(A\gamma)(B\gamma)(C)\right\}$$

$$=(AB)-\frac{1}{(C)(\gamma)}\left\{N(AC)(BC)-(A)(C)(BC)-(B)(C)(AC)\right.$$
$$\left.+(A)(B)(C)\right\}$$

$$=(AB)-\frac{(A)(B)}{N}-\frac{N}{(C)(\gamma)}\left\{(AC)-\frac{(A)(C)}{N}\right\}\left\{(BC)-\frac{(B)(C)}{N}\right\}$$

$$=\delta_{AB}-\frac{N}{(C)(\gamma)}\delta_{AC}\delta_{BC} \qquad . \qquad . \qquad . \qquad . \ (2.13)$$

This gives us the sum of the δ-numbers for the partial associations of A and B in C and γ in terms of the total associations between A, B and C.

Now suppose that A and B are independent in C and γ. Then we have—

$$\delta_{AB.c} = \delta_{AB.\gamma} = 0$$

and

$$\delta_{AB} = \frac{N}{(C)(\gamma)} \delta_{AC} \delta_{BC}$$

δ_{AB} is not zero unless one or both of δ_{AC}, δ_{BC} are zero.

Hence, if A and B are independent within the populations of C's and not-C's, they will nevertheless·be associated in the population at large unless C is independent of A or B or both.

Illusory associations

2.27 This peculiar result indicates that, although a set of attributes independent of A and B will not affect the association between them, the existence of an attribute C with which they are both associated may give an association in the population at large which is illusory in the sense that it does not correspond to any real relationship between them. If the associations between A and C, B and C are of the same sign, the resulting association between A and B will be positive ; if of opposite signs, negative.

The cases which we discussed at the beginning of this chapter are instances in point. In the first illustration we saw that it was possible to argue that the positive associations between *vaccination* and *hygienic conditions*, *exemption from attack* and *hygienic conditions*, led to an illusory association between *vaccination* and *exemption from attack*. Similarly, the question was raised whether the positive association between *grandfather* and *grandchild* may not be due to the positive associations between *grandfather* and *father*, and *father* and *child*.

2.28 Misleading associations may easily arise through the mingling of records which a careful worker would keep distinct.

Take the following case, for example. Suppose there have been 200 patients in a hospital, 100 males and 100 females, suffering from some disease. Suppose, further, that the death-rate for males (the case mortality) has been 30 per cent, for females 60 per cent. A new treatment is tried on 80 per cent of the males and 40 per cent of the females, and the results published without distinction of sex. The three attributes, with the relations of which we are here concerned, are *death*, *treatment* and *male sex*. The data show that more males were treated than females, and more females died than males ; therefore the first attribute is associated negatively, the second positively, with the third. It follows that there will be an illusory negative association between the first two—*death* and *treatment*.

If the treatment were completely inefficient we should, in fact, have the following results—

	Males	Females	Total
Treated and died · . .	24	24	48
,, and did not die . .	56	16	72
Not treated and died . .	6	36	42
,, and did not die .	14	24	38

i.e. of the treated, only $48/120=40$ per cent died, while of those not treated $42/80=52\cdot5$ per cent died. If this result were stated without any reference to the fact of the mixture of the sexes, to the different proportions of the two that were treated and to the different death-rates under normal treatment, then some value in the new treatment would appear to be suggested. To make a fair return, either the results for the two sexes should be stated separately, or the same proportion of the two sexes must receive the experimental treatment. Further, care would have to be taken in such a case to see that there was no selection (perhaps unconscious) of the less severe cases for treatment, thus introducing another source of fallacy (*death* positively associated with *severity*, *treatment* negatively associated with *severity*, giving rise to illusory negative association between *treatment* and *death*).

2.29 Illusory associations may also arise in a different way through the personality of the observer or observers. If the observer's attention fluctuates, he may be more likely to notice the presence of A when he notices the presence of B, and *vice versa* ; in such a case A and B (so far as the record goes) will both be associated with the observer's attention C, and consequently an illusory association will be created. Again, if the attributes are not well defined, one observer may be more generous than another in deciding when to record the presence of A and also the presence of B, and even one observer may fluctuate in the generosity of his marking. In this case the recording of A and the recording of B will both be associated with the generosity of the observer in recording their presence, C, and an illusory association between A and B will consequently arise, as before.

Determination of sign of association when the data are incomplete

2.30 It is important to notice that, though we cannot actually determine the partial associations unless the third-order frequency (ABC) is given, we can make some conjecture as to their signs from the values of the second-order frequencies.

In **2.26** we have—

$$\delta_{AB.C}+\delta_{AB.\gamma}=(AB)-\frac{(AC)(BC)}{(C)}-\frac{(A\gamma)(B\gamma)}{(\gamma)} \qquad . \qquad . \quad (2.14)$$

Hence, if the expression on the right is positive, one at least of $\delta_{AB.C}$, $\delta_{AB.\gamma}$, is positive, i.e. A and B are positively associated either in C or γ or both. Similarly, if the expression is negative, A and B are negatively associated either in C or in γ or in both. Finally, if the expression is zero, A and B are either independent in both C and γ, or positively associated in one and negatively in the other.

The expression may be thrown into a form more convenient when percentages are given. Dividing through by (B) we have—

$$\frac{\delta_{AB.C}+\delta_{AB.\gamma}}{(B)}=\frac{(AB)}{(B)}-\frac{(AC)}{(C)}\frac{(BC)}{(B)}-\frac{(A\gamma)}{(\gamma)}\frac{(B\gamma)}{(B)} \qquad \cdot \quad (2.15)$$

The following example illustrates the method.

Example 2.10 (Figures compiled from the *Registrar-General's Decennial Supplement*, 1931, *Part IIa*—1938). The following are the mean annual death-rates for occupied (including retired) males of 16 years of age and over for England and Wales during the three years 1930-1932.

	Death rate per thousand
Occupied and retired males over 16	14·63
Farmers over 16	19·68
Anglican clergy over 16	27·81
Coal hewers and getters over 16	14·69

At first sight it appears that coal hewing is about the average in healthiness (as measured by death rate) and that farmers and clergy are decidedly unhealthy. These conclusions are quite wrong.

The following are the proportions of the occupations 65 years old or more at the census date 1931—

	Proportion per thousand 65 years of age or more
Occupied and retired males	86·8
Farmers	172·1
Anglican clergy	279·4
Coal hewers and getters	68·6

For the whole class of occupied and retired males the death rates for the groups 16-65 years and 65 years and over were 7·93 per thousand and 85·10 per thousand.

If A denote *death*, B the given *occupation*, C *old age*, we have to apply the principles of equation (2.15), calculate what would be the death-rate for each occupation on the supposition that the rates for occupied and retired males in general (7·93 and 85·10) apply to each of the separate age-groups (16–65, 65 and over), and see whether the total death-rate so calculated exceeds or falls short of the actual death-rate. If it exceeds the actual rate the occupation must on the whole be healthy ; in the contrary case, unhealthy. Thus we have the following calculated death rates—

Farmers	$7·93 \times ·8279 + 85·10 \times ·1721 = 21·20$
Anglican clergy	$7·93 \times ·7206 + 85·10 \times ·2794 = 29·48$
Coal hewers and getters	$7·93 \times ·9314 + 85·10 \times ·0686 = 13·21$

The calculated rate for farmers and clergy largely exceeds the actual rate ; these occupations then must, on the whole, be healthy. On the other hand the rate for coal hewers and getters falls short of the actual rate and this occupation is relatively unhealthy. The true facts are masked in the death-rates for the occupations taken irrespective of age by the various proportions of young and old engaged in the occupations.

It is evident that age-distributions vary so largely from one occupation to another that total death-rates are liable to be very misleading. Similar fallacies are liable to occur in comparisons of local death-rates, owing to variations not only in the relative proportions of the old, but also in the relative proportions of the two sexes.

It is hardly necessary to observe that as *age* is a variable quantity, the above procedure for calculating the comparative death-rates is extremely rough. The death-rate of those engaged in any occupation depends not only on the mere proportions over and under 65, but on the relative numbers at every single year of age. The simpler procedure brings out, however, better than a more complex one, the nature of the fallacy involved in assuming that crude death-rates are measures of healthiness.

Complete independence

2.31 The particular case in which all the $2^n - (n+1)$ given associations are zero is worth some special investigation.

It follows, in the first place, that all other possible associations must be zero, i.e. that a state of *complete independence*, as we may term it, exists. Suppose, for instance, that we are given—

$$(AB) = \frac{(A)(B)}{N} \qquad (AC) = \frac{(A)(C)}{N}$$

$$(BC) = \frac{(B)(C)}{N} \qquad (ABC) = \frac{(AC)(BC)}{(C)} = \frac{(A)(B)(C)}{N^2}$$

Then it follows at once that we have also—

$$(ABC) = \frac{(AB)(BC)}{(B)} = \frac{(AB)(AC)}{(A)}$$

i.e. A and C are independent in the population of B's, and B and C in the population of A's, Again,

$$(AB\gamma) = (AB) - (ABC) = \frac{(A)(B)}{N} - \frac{(A)(B)(C)}{N^2}$$

$$= \frac{(A)(B)(\gamma)}{N^2} = \frac{(A\gamma)(B\gamma)}{(\gamma)}$$

Therefore A and B are independent in the population of γ's. Similarly, it may be shown that A and C are independent in the population of β's, B and C in the population of α's.

In the next place it is evident from the above that relations of the general form (to write the equation symmetrically)

$$\frac{(ABC)}{N}=\frac{(A)}{N}\cdot\frac{(B)}{N}\cdot\frac{(C)}{N} \qquad . \qquad . \qquad . \qquad . \quad (2.16)$$

must hold for every class-frequency. This relation is the general form of the equation of independence (2.2) (*d*).

2.32 It must be noted, however, that (2.16) is not a *criterion* for the *complete independence* of A, B and C in the sense that the equation

$$\frac{(AB)}{N}=\frac{(A)}{N}\cdot\frac{(B)}{N}$$

is a criterion for the complete independence of A and B. If we are given N, (A) and (B), and the last relation quoted holds good, we know that similar relations must hold for $(A\beta)$, (αB) and $(\alpha\beta)$. If N, (A), (B) and (C) be given, however, and the equation (2.16) holds good, we can draw no conclusion without further information ; the data are insufficient. There are *eight* algebraically independent class-frequencies in the case of three attributes, while N, (A), (B), (C) are only four : the equation (2.16) must therefore be shown to hold good for *four* frequencies of the third order before the conclusion can be drawn that it holds good for the remainder, i.e. that a state of complete independence subsists. The direct verification of this result is left for the student.

Quite generally, if N, (A), (B), (C), . . . be given, the relation

$$\frac{(ABC \; . \; . \; . \;)}{N}=\frac{(A)}{N}\cdot\frac{(B)}{N}\cdot\frac{(C)}{N} \qquad . \qquad . \qquad . \quad (2.17)$$

must be shown to hold good for $2^n-(n+1)$ of the *n*th order classes before it may be assumed to hold good for the remainder. It is only because

$$2^n-(n+1)=1$$

when $n=2$ that the relation

$$\frac{(AB)}{N}=\frac{(A)}{N}\cdot\frac{(B)}{N}$$

may be treated as a *criterion* for the independence of A and B. *If* all the *n* ($n > 2$) attributes are completely independent, the relation (2.17) holds good ; but it does not follow that if the relation (2.17) holds good they are all independent.

SUMMARY

1. Two attributes are independent if the proportion of A's among the B's is the same as the proportion among the not-B's.

2. This definition can be expressed symbolically in numerous forms, in

terms of either first-order or second-order frequencies. The form in which the data are given, and the question which is to be answered, determine which form is to be employed in any particular case.

3. Attributes which are not independent are said to be positively associated if

$$(AB) > \frac{(A)(B)}{N}$$

and negatively associated if

$$(AB) < \frac{(A)(B)}{N}$$

4. The statistical meaning of the word " association " is different from the meaning ascribed to it in ordinary language.

5. Before association may be said to indicate a definite relation between the attributes, it is necessary to be satisfied that the divergence from independence is not due to fluctuations of sampling.

6. The divergence of the actual frequency from the " independence " frequency is denoted by the symbol δ, and hence

$$\delta = (AB) - \frac{(A)(B)}{N}$$

7. The coefficient of association is defined by

$$Q = \frac{N\delta}{(AB)(\alpha\beta) + (A\beta)(\alpha B)}$$

It is zero if the attributes are independent, $+1$ if they are completely associated and -1 if they are completely disassociated. There are, however, other forms of coefficient more advantageous in certain cases.

8. The association of A and B in sub-populations of the type C, γ, CD, CDE, etc. is called a partial association.

9. If

$$(\overset{\bullet}{A}BC) > \frac{(AC)(BC)}{(C)}$$

A and B are positively associated in C ; and if

$$(ABC) < \frac{(AC)(BC)}{(C)}$$

A and B are negatively associated in C.

10. There are $\frac{n(n-1)}{2}3^{n-2}$ associations in a population characterised by n attributes, $\frac{n(n-1)}{2}$ of which are total and the remainder partial.

11. All the associations are expressible in terms of N, (A), (B), (C), etc., and $2^n - (n+1)$ algebraically independent associations. These relations have, however, only a theoretical value.

12. If A and B are independent within the population of C's they will nevertheless be associated within the population at large, unless C is independent of either A or B or both.

13. In interpreting an association between A and B it must be remembered that this may arise owing to associations of A with C and B with C. To resolve this point it is necessary to consider the partial associations of A and B in C and γ.

14. Complete independence of n attributes occurs if $2^n - (n+1)$ algebraically independent associations and hence all associations are zero. In this case

$$\frac{(ABC \ldots)}{N} = \frac{(A)}{N} \frac{(B)}{N} \frac{(C)}{N} \ldots$$

but this last condition is not sufficient for complete independence.

EXERCISES

2.1 At the census of England and Wales in 1901 there were (to the nearest 1,000) 15,729,000 males and 16,799,000 females ; 3,497 males were returned as deaf-mutes from childhood, and 3,072 females.

State proportions exhibiting the association between deaf-mutism from childhood and sex. How many of each sex for the same total number would have been deaf-mutes if there had been no association ?

2.2 Show, as briefly as possible, whether A and B are independent, positively associated or negatively associated in each of the following cases—

(a) $N = 5,000$ $(A) = 2,350$ $(B) = 3,100$ $(AB) = 1,600$
(b) $(A) = 490$ $(AB) = 294$ $(\alpha) = 570$ $(\alpha B) = 380$
(c) $(AB) = 256$ $(\alpha B) = 768$ $(A\beta) = 48$ $(\alpha\beta) = 144$

2.3 (Figures derived from Darwin's *Cross- and Self-fertilisation of Plants*.) The table below gives the numbers of plants of certain species that were above or below the average height, stating separately those that were derived from cross-fertilised and from self-fertilised parentage. Investigate the association between height and cross-fertilisation of parentage, and draw attention to any special points you notice.

Species	Parentage cross-fertilised. Height—		Parentage self-fertilised. Height—	
	Above average	Below average	Above average	Below average
Ipomæa purpurea. . . .	63	10	18	55
Petunia violacea	61	16	13	64
Reseda lutea	25	7	11	21
Reseda odorata	39	16	25	30
Lobelia fulgens	17	17	12	22

2.4 (Figures from same source as Example 2.6; classes 7 and 8 of the memoir treated as " dark.") Investigate the association between darkness of eye-colour in father and son from the following data—

Fathers with dark eyes and sons with dark eyes	(AB)	.	50
,, ,, ,, not-dark eyes	$(A\beta)$	.	79
Fathers with not-dark eyes and sons with dark eyes	(αB)	.	89
,, ,, ,, not-dark eyes	$(\alpha\beta)$	.	782

Also tabulate for comparison the frequencies that would have been observed had there been no heredity, i.e. the values of $(AB)_0$, $(A\beta)_0$, etc.

2.5 (Figures from same source as above.) Investigate the association between eye-colour of husband and eye-colour of wife ("assortative mating") from the data given below.

Husbands with light eyes and wives with light eyes	(AB)	.	309
,, ,, ,, not-light eyes	$(A\beta)$	.	214
Husbands with not-light eyes and wives with light eyes	(αB)	.	132
,, ,, ,, not-light eyes	$(\alpha\beta)$	.	119

Also tabulate for comparison the frequencies that would have been observed had there been strict independence between eye-colour of husband and eye-colour of wife, i.e., the values of $(AB)_0$, etc., as in Exercise 2.4.

2.6 (Figures from the *Census of England and Wales*, 1891, vol. 3: the data cannot be regarded as trustworthy.) The figures given below show the number of males in successive age-groups, together with the number of the blind (A), of the mentally deranged (B) and the blind mentally deranged (AB). Trace the association between blindness and mental derangement from childhood to old age, tabulating the proportions of insane amongst the whole population and amongst the blind, and also the association coefficient Q of **2.15**. Give a short verbal statement of your results.

	5–	15–	25–	35–	45–	55	65–	75 and upwards
N	3,304,230	2,712,521	2,089,010	1,611,077	1,191,789	770,124	444,896	161,692
(A)	844	1,184	1,165	1,501	1,752	1,905	1,932	1,701
(B)	2,820	6,225	8,482	9,214	8,187	5,799	3,412	1,098
(AB)	17	19	19	31	32	34	22	9

2.7 Show that if

$$(AB)_1 \quad (\alpha B)_1 \quad (A\beta)_1 \quad (\alpha\beta)_1$$
$$(AB)_2 \quad (\alpha B)_2 \quad (A\beta)_2 \quad (\alpha\beta)_2$$

be two aggregates corresponding to the same values of (A), (B), (α) and (β),

$$(AB)_1 - (AB)_2 = (\alpha B)_2 - (\alpha B)_1 = (A\beta)_2 - (A\beta)_1 = (\alpha\beta)_1 - (\alpha\beta)_2$$

2.8 Show that if
$$\delta = (AB) - (AB)_0$$
$$(AB)^2 + (\alpha\beta)^2 - (\alpha B)^2 - (A\beta)^2 = [(A) - (\alpha)][(B) - (\beta)] + 2N\delta$$

2.9 The existence of association may be tested either by comparison of proportions (e.g. $(AB)/(B)$ with $(A\beta)/(\beta)$), as in **2.10** and **2.11**, or by the value of δ as in **2.12** and **2.13**. Show that

$$\delta = \frac{(B)(\beta)}{N}\left\{\frac{(AB)}{(B)} - \frac{(A\beta)}{(\beta)}\right\}$$
$$= \frac{(A)(\alpha)}{N}\left\{\frac{(AB)}{(A)} - \frac{(\alpha B)}{(\alpha)}\right\}$$

2.10 Spence and Charles, in *An Investigation into the Health and Nutrition of Certain of the Children of Newcastle-on-Tyne between the Ages of One and Five Years* (City and Council of Newcastle-on-Tyne, February 1934), compared two groups of children, one belonging to the professional classes, 125 in number, and the other belonging to the labouring classes, 124 in number. They found the following results—

	Poor Children Per cent	Well-to-do Children Per cent
Below normal weight . . .	55	13
Above normal weight . . .	11	48

Find the coefficient of association between the weight of the children and their social status.

2.11 (Data from the *Report on the Spahlinger Experiments in Northern Ireland*, 1931–1934, H.M. Stationery Office, 1935.) In experiments on the immunisation of cattle from tuberculosis the following results were secured—

Treatment	Cattle		Total
	Died of tuberculosis or very seriously affected	Unaffected or only slightly affected	
Inoculated with vaccine . .	6	13	19
Not inoculated or inoculated with control media	8	3	11
Total . .	14	16	30

(The cattle were first inoculated with protective vaccine and then deliberately infected with serious quantities of tubercle germs.)

Find the coefficient of association between inoculation and exemption from serious tuberculosis.

2.12 Criticise the following argument : " Nearly all the A's are B's, and therefore A and B must be associated," and state what suppressed premises would justify it in the following cases—

" 99 per cent of the people who drink beer die before reaching 100 years of age. Therefore drinking beer is bad for longevity."

" 99 per cent of the members who voted for the Army Estimates were military officers. Therefore it was unfair to suppose that the voting was unbiased."

" In every country where the sale of contraceptives is tolerated by the Government the birth-rate is declining. Therefore contraception must exert an influence on the birth-rate."

2.13 Write down in the form of the table of **2.1** the frequency groups when (1) all A's are B's ; (2) all B's are A's ; (3) all A's are B's and all B's are A's ; and the three similar tables when A and B are completely disassociated.

2.14 Take the following figures for girls corresponding to those for boys in Example 2.9, page 33, and discuss them similarly, but not necessarily using exactly the same comparisons, to see whether the conclusion that " the connecting link between defects of body and mental dullness is the coincident defect of brain which may be known by observation of abnormal nerve signs " seems to hold good.

A, development defects ; B, nerve signs ; D, mental dullness.

N	10,000	(AB)	248
(A)	682	(AD)	307
(B)	850	(BD)	363
(D)	689	(ABD)	128

2.15 (Material from *Census of England and Wales*, 1891, vol. 3.) The following figures give the numbers of those suffering from single or combined infirmities : (1) for all males ; (2) for males of 55 years of age and over.

A, blindness ; B, mental derangement ; C, deaf-mutism.

	(1) All Males	(2) Males 55–		(1) All Males	(2) Males 55–
N	14,053,000	1,377,000	(AB)	183	65
(A)	12,281	5,538	(AC)	51	14
(B)	45,392	10,309	(BC)	299	47
(C)	7,707	746	(ABC)	11	3

Tabulate proportions per thousand, exhibiting the total association between blindness and mental derangement, and the partial association between the same two infirmities among deaf-mutes : (1) for males in general ; (2) for those of 55 years of age and over. Give a short verbal statement of the results.

2.16 (Material from same source as in Example 2.10).

The death-rate from cancer for occupied and retired males in general (over 16) is 2·004 per thousand per annum, and for farmers 2·633.

The death-rates from cancer for occupied males under and over 45 respectively are 0·184 and 4·960 respectively. Of the farmers, 53·22 per cent are over 45.

Would you say that farmers were peculiarly liable to cancer ?

2.17 A population of males over 15 years of age consists of 7 per cent over 65 years of age and 93 per cent under. The death-rates are 12 per thousand per annum in the younger class and 110 in the older, or 18·86 in the whole population. The death-rate of males (over 15) engaged in a certain industry is 26·7 per thousand.

If the industry be not unhealthy, what must be the approximate proportion of those over 65 engaged in it (neglecting minor differences of age distribution) ?

2.18 Show that if A and B are independent, while A and C, B and C are associated, A and B must be disassociated either in the population of C's, the population of γ's, or both.

2.19 As an illustration of Exercise 2.18, show that if the following were actual data, there would be a slight disassociation between the eye-colours of husband and wife (father and mother) for the parents either of light-eyed sons or not-light-eyed sons, or both, although there is a slight positive association for parents at large.

A light eye-colour in husband, B in wife, C in son—

N	1,000	(AB)	358
(A)	622	(AC)	471
(B)	558	(BC)	419
(C)	617		

2.20 Show that if $(ABC)=(\alpha\beta\gamma)$, $(\alpha BC)=(A\beta\gamma)$, and so on (the case of "complete equality of contrary frequencies" of Exercise 1.6, page 15), A, B and C are completely independent if A and B, A and C, B and C are independent pair and pair.

2.21 If, in the same case of complete equality of contraries,

$$(AB)-N/4=\delta_1$$
$$(AC)-N/4=\delta_2$$
$$(BC)-N/4=\delta_3$$

show that

$$2\left[(ABC)-\frac{(AC)(BC)}{(C)}\right]=2\left[(AB\gamma)-\frac{(A\gamma)(B\gamma)}{(\gamma)}\right]=\delta_1-\frac{4\delta_2\delta_3}{N}$$

so that the partial associations between A and B in the populations C and γ are positive or negative according as

$$\delta_1 \lessgtr \frac{4\delta_2\delta_3}{N}$$

2.22   In the straight contests of a general election (contests in which one Conservative opposed one Socialist and there were no other candidates) 66 per cent of the winning candidates (according to the returns) spent more money than their opponents.   Given that 63 per cent of the winners were Conservatives, and that the Conservative expenditure exceeded the Socialist in 80 per cent of the contests, find the percentages of elections won by Conservatives (1) when they spent more and (2) when they spent less than their opponents, and hence say whether you consider the above figures evidence of the influence of expenditure on election results or no. (Note that if the one candidate in a contest be a *Conservative-winner-who spends more than his opponent*, the other must necessarily be a *Socialist-loser-who spends less*—and so forth.   Hence the case is one of complete equality of contraries.)

2.23   Given that $(A)/N=(B)/N=(C)/N=x$, and that $(AB)/N=(AC)/N=y$, find the major and minor limits to y that enable one to infer positive association between B and C, i.e. $(BC)/N > x^2$.

Draw a diagram on squared paper to illustrate your answer, taking x and y as co-ordinates, and shading the limits within which y must lie in order to permit of the above inference.   Point out the peculiarities in the case of inferring a positive association from two negative associations.

2.24   Discuss similarly the more complex case $(A)/N=x$, $(B)/N=2x$, $(C)/N=3x$—

(1) for inferring positive association between B and C given $(AB)/N=(AC)/N=y$.
(2) for inferring positive association between A and C given $(AB)/N=(BC)/N=y$.
(3) for inferring positive association between A and B given $(AC)/N=(BC)/N=y$.

2.25   Draw a graph of the curve $y=2x/(1+x^2)$ for the range $-1 \leqslant x \leqslant 1$ and hence discuss the relationship between the coefficient of association Q and the coefficient of colligation Y.   Hence show, graphically or otherwise, that the maximum difference between the two occurs when Q is ± 0.786 approximately.

MANIFOLD CLASSIFICATION

Manifold classification

3.1 Instead of dividing the population under consideration into two parts by a simple dichotomy, we may also divide it into a number of parts by a similar process. For instance, we can extend the dichotomy of the population of men into " those with blue eyes " and " those not with blue eyes " to a threefold division : " those with blue eyes " " those with brown eyes," and " those with neither blue nor brown eyes " ; or into a fourfold division by adding a fresh category, " those with grey eyes " ; and so on.

Generally, our population may be divided first according to s heads, $A_1, A_2, \ldots A_s$; each of the classes so obtained into t heads, $B_1, B_2, \ldots B_t$; each of these into u heads, $C_1, C_2, \ldots C_u$; and so on.

This is called *manifold classification.*

3.2 The general theory of manifold classification for n attributes is rather complicated, but its fundamental principles are very similar to those which apply to dichotomy. A straightforward extension of the methods of Chapter 1 will give the following results, which we are content to announce without a formal proof—

(*a*) There are $s \times t \times u \times \ldots$ ultimate classes.

(*b*) The total number of classes, including N and the ultimate classes, is $(s+1)(t+1)(u+1) \ldots$

(*c*) The data are consistent if, and only if, every ultimate class-frequency is not negative.

(*d*) The data are completely specified by $s \times t \times u \times \ldots$ algebraically independent class-frequencies. Even if all these are not given, it may be possible to set limits to the other class-frequencies.

For example, if the population of the United Kingdom is classified geographically according to habitation in England, Wales, Scotland and Northern Ireland ; by eye-colour into blue, brown, grey, green and the remainder ; and by hair-colour into black, fair, red and the remainder ; there will be 150 classes altogether, expressible in terms of 80 independent class-frequencies.

3.3 Data so completely specified are very rare, and an elaborate discussion of the general case would hardly be justified by its practical value. For the remainder of this chapter, therefore, we shall be concerned solely with the case of two characteristics, A and B.

Contingency tables

3.4 Let us suppose that the classification of the A's is s-fold and that of the B's is t-fold. Then there will be st classes of the type A_mB_n.

Generalising slightly the notation of previous chapters, let the frequency of individuals A_m be denoted by (A_m) and of individuals A_mB_n by (A_mB_n). The data can then be set out in the form of a table of t rows and s columns as follows—

TABLE 3.1

Attribute	A_1	A_2	—	—	A_{s-1}	A_s	Totals
B_1	(A_1B_1)	(A_2B_1)	—	—	$(A_{s-1}B_1)$	(A_sB_1)	(B_1)
B_2	(A_1B_2)	(A_2B_2)	—	—	$(A_{s-1}B_2)$	(A_sB_2)	(B_2)
—	—	—	—	—	—	—	—
B_t	(A_1B_t)	(A_2B_t)	—	—	$(A_{s-1}B_t)$	(A_sB_t)	(B_t)
Totals	(A_1)	(A_2)	—	—	(A_{s-1})	(A_s)	N

In this table the frequency of the class A_mB_n is entered in the compartment common to the mth column and the nth row; the totals at the ends of rows and at the feet of columns give the first order frequencies, i.e. the numbers of A_m's and B_n's; and finally, the grand total in the bottom right-hand corner gives the whole number of observations.

Such a table is called a *contingency table*. It is a generalised form of the fourfold (2×2-fold) table in **2.1**.

Example 3.1—In Table 3.2 below the classification is 3×4-fold: the eye-colours are classed under the three heads "blue," "grey or green" and "brown," while the hair-colours are classed under four heads, "fair," "brown," "black" and "red." Taking the first row,

TABLE 3.2—Hair- and eye-colours of 6800 males in Baden
(Ammon, *Zur Anthropologie der Badener*)

Attribute	Hair-colour				Total
	Fair	Brown	Black	Red	
Eye-colour					
Blue.	1768	807	189	47·	2811
Grey or Green	946	1387	746	53	3132
Brown	115	438	288	16	857
Total	2829	2632	1223	116	6800

the table tells us that there were 2811 men with blue eyes noted, of whom 1768 had fair hair, 807 brown hair, 189 black hair and 47 red hair. Similarly, from the first column, there were 2829 men with fair hair, of whom 1768 had blue eyes, 946 grey or green eyes and 115 brown eyes.

Association in contingency tables

3.5 For the purpose of discussing the nature of the relation between the A's and the B's, any such table may be treated on the principles of the preceding chapter by reducing it in different ways to a 2×2-fold form. It then becomes possible to trace the association between any one or more of the A's and any one or more of the B's, either in the population at large or in populations limited by the omission of one or more of the A's, of the B's, or of both.

If, for example, we desire to trace the association between a lack of pigmentation in eyes and in hair, rows 1 and 2 may be pooled together as representing the least pigmentation of the eyes, and columns 2, 3 and 4 may be pooled together as representing hair with a more or less marked degree of pigmentation. We then have—

Proportion of light-eyed with fair hair . . . $\Big\}$ 2714/5943 = 46 per cent

Proportion of brown-eyed with fair hair . . . $\Big\}$ 115/857 = 13 „

The association is therefore well marked. For comparison we may trace the corresponding association between the most marked degree of pigmentation in eyes and hair, i.e. brown eyes and black hair. Here we must add together rows 1 and 2 as before, and pool columns 1, 2 and 4—the column for red being really misplaced, as red represents a comparatively slight degree of pigmentation. The figures are—

Proportion of brown-eyed with black hair . . . $\Big\}$ 288/857 = 34 per cent

Proportion of light-eyed with black hair . . . $\Big\}$ 935/5943 = 16 „

The association is again positive and well marked, but the difference between the two percentages is rather less than in the last case.

3.6 The mode of treatment adopted in the preceding two paragraphs rests on first principles and, if fully carried out, gives us all the information possible about the associations of the two attributes. At the same time it is laborious if s and t are at all large. Moreover, in practical work we are often concerned, not with the associations of individual A's with individual B's, but with finding the answer to a general question of the type : Are the A's *on the whole* distinctly dependent on the B's, and if so, is this dependence very close, or the reverse ? In fact, what we want is a coefficient which will summarise the general nature of the dependence. We will proceed to discuss two such coefficients.

Coefficients of contingency

3.7 If the A's and B's be completely independent in the population at large, we must have for all values of m and n—

$$(A_m B_n) = \frac{(A_m)(B_n)}{N} = (A_m B_n)_0 \qquad . \qquad . \qquad (3.1)$$

If, however, A and B are not completely independent, $(A_m B_n)$ and $(A_m B_n)_0$ will not be identical for all values of m and n. Let the difference be given by

$$\delta_{mn} = (A_m B_n) - (A_m B_n)_0 \qquad . \qquad . \qquad (3.2)$$

Let us note in passing the following properties of these quantities—

(1) In the first place, δ_{mn} is not equal to δ_{nm}.

(2) In the second place, the δ's are not all algebraically independent. We have, in fact, for any particular m—

$$\delta_{m1} + \delta_{m2} + \delta_{m3} + \ldots + \delta_{mn} + \ldots + \delta_{mt}$$

$$= (A_m B_1) - \frac{(A_m)(B_1)}{N} + (A_m B_2) - \frac{(A_m)(B_2)}{N} \ldots + (A_m B_t) - \frac{(A_m)(B_t)}{N}$$

$$= (A_m) - \frac{(A_m)}{N} \{(B_1) + (B_2) + \ldots + (B_t)\}$$

$$= 0 \qquad . \qquad . \qquad . \qquad . \qquad . \qquad . \qquad . \qquad . \qquad (3.3)$$

A similar relation is true for any particular n.

Now there are st δ-quantities. In virtue of the relationship we have just proved, for any particular m only $(t-1)$ of the t-quantities δ_{mn} are independent. Similarly, for any n only $(s-1)$ are independent. Hence the total number of independent δ's is $(s-1)(t-1)$.

3.8 These δ-quantities indicate the extent of the associations, and we expect a summarising coefficient to be built up from them in some way. It would, however, be useless to add them together, for in virtue of the relation of the preceding paragraph the sum is zero. We wish to construct a coefficient which shall be independent of the signs of the δ-numbers. We therefore define

$$\chi^2 = \Sigma \left(\frac{\delta^2_{mn}}{(A_m B_n)_0} \right) \qquad . \qquad . \qquad (3.4)$$

and call χ^2 the " square contingency."

We then write—

$$\phi^2 = \frac{\chi^2}{N} \qquad . \qquad . \qquad . \qquad . \quad (3.5)$$

and call ϕ^2 the   mean-square contingency."

Clearly χ^2 and ϕ^2, being the sums of squares, cannot be negative. They vanish if, and only if, every δ-number vanishes, in which case A and B are independent.

Pearson's coefficient of mean-square contingency

3.9   The quantity ϕ^2 is not quite suitable in itself to form a coefficient, because its limits vary in different cases.   Karl Pearson therefore proposed the coefficient C, defined by

$$C = \sqrt{\frac{\chi^2}{N + \chi^2}} = \sqrt{\frac{\phi^2}{1 + \phi^2}} \qquad . \qquad . \qquad . \quad (3.6)$$

This is called the *coefficient of mean-square contingency*.   In general, no sign should be attached to the root, for the coefficient merely shows whether two characters are or are not independent ; but in certain cases a conventional sign may be used.   Thus, in Table 3.2 slight pigmentation of eyes and hair appear to go together, and the contingency may be regarded as positive.   If *slight* pigmentation of eyes had been associated with *marked* pigmentation of hair, the contingency might have been regarded as negative.

3.10   The coefficient C has one serious disadvantage. Although, as may be seen from its definition, it increases with ϕ^2 towards a limit 1, it never reaches that limit.   In fact, the maximum value which it can attain depends on s and t, and reaches unity only for an infinite number of classes. This may be briefly illustrated as follows.   Replacing δ_{mn} in equation (3.4) by its value in terms of $(A_m B_n)$ and $(A_m B_n)_0$, we have—

$$\chi^2 = \Sigma \left\{ \frac{(A_m B_n)^2}{(A_m B_n)_0} \right\} - N \qquad . \qquad . \qquad . \quad (3.7)$$

and therefore, denoting the summation by S,

$$C = \sqrt{\frac{S - N}{S}} \qquad . \qquad . \qquad . \quad (3.8)$$

Now suppose we have to deal with a $t \times t$-fold classification in which $(A_m) = (B_m)$ for all values of m ; and suppose, further, that the association between A_m and B_m is perfect, so that $(A_m B_m) = (A_m) = (B_m)$ for all values of m, the remaining frequencies of the second order being zero ; all the frequency is then concentrated in the diagonal compartments of the table, and each contributes N to the summation S. The total value of S is accordingly tN, and the value of C—

$$C = \sqrt{\frac{t-1}{t}}$$

This is the greatest possible value of C for a symmetrical $t \times t$-fold classification, and therefore, in such a table, for—

$$
\begin{array}{llll}
t = & 2, & C \text{ cannot exceed} & 0 \cdot 707 \\
t = & 3 & ,, \qquad ,, & 0 \cdot 816 \\
t = & 4 & ,, \qquad ,, & 0 \cdot 866 \\
t = & 5 & ,, \qquad ,, & 0 \cdot 894 \\
t = & 6 & ,, \qquad ,, & 0 \cdot 913 \\
t = & 7 & ,, \qquad ,, & 0 \cdot 926 \\
t = & 8 & ,, \qquad ,, & 0 \cdot 935 \\
t = & 9 & ,, \qquad ,, & 0 \cdot 943 \\
t = & 10 & ,, \qquad ,, & 0 \cdot 949 \\
\end{array}
$$

3.11 Hence, coefficients calculated from different systems of classification are not, strictly speaking, comparable. This is clearly undesirable. Two coefficients calculated from the same data classified in two different groupings ought not to be very different.

It is as well, therefore, to restrict the use of the C-coefficient to 5×5 or finer groupings. At the same time, the classification must not be made too fine, or the value of the coefficient is largely affected by causal irregularities arising from sampling fluctuations.[1]

Tschuprow's coefficient

3.12 To remedy the defect to which we have just referred, Tschuprow proposed the coefficient T, defined by

$$T^2 = \frac{\phi^2}{\sqrt{(s-1)(t-1)}} \qquad . \qquad . \qquad . \quad (3.9)$$

This coefficient varies between 0 and 1 in the desired manner when $s = t$. We have

$$C^2 = \frac{\phi^2}{1 + \phi^2}$$

$$= \frac{T^2 \sqrt{\{(s-1)(t-1)\}}}{1 + T^2 \sqrt{\{(s-1)(t-1)\}}} \qquad . \qquad . \quad (3.10)$$

and conversely,

$$T^2 = \frac{C^2}{(1 - C^2)\sqrt{\{(s-1)(t-1)\}}} \qquad . \qquad . \quad (3.11)$$

---

[1] Karl Pearson discussed a " correction " to be made to C calculated from coarsely grouped data. The use of such corrections depends to some extent on assumptions about the population, and may be regarded as attempts to bring the value of C closer to a putative coefficient of correlation (cf. **10.20**).

Calculation of C and T

3.13 The calculation of C and T is simplified by the use of equation (3.8), which enables us to replace the calculation of the δ's by calculations based on frequencies of types (A_m), (B_n) and (A_mB_n). All these quantities are contained in the contingency tables. The following example will illustrate the method—

Example 3.2—Consider the data of Table 3.2. (The classification is only 3×4-fold and is therefore rather crude for calculating C, but it will serve as an illustration of the form of the arithmetic.)

We require first of all the quantities $(A_mB_n)_0$, i.e. the "independence" values. These are calculated directly from their definition

$$(A_mB_n)_0 = \frac{(A_m)(B_n)}{N}$$

and thus the value for the compartment in the mth column and nth row is the product of the total frequencies in that column and row divided by the whole frequency, e.g. $(A_1B_1)_0 = 2829 \times 2811 / 6800 = 1169$, and so on.

It is convenient to tabulate the frequencies so obtained in a second contingency table, as in Table 3.3.

TABLE 3.3—Independence values of the frequencies for Table 3.2

Attribute		Hair-colour			
		Fair	Brown	Black	Red
Eye-colour					
Blue.		1169	1088	506	48·0
Grey or Green		1303	1212	563	53·4
Brown		357	332	154	14·6

We now calculate the quantities $\dfrac{(A_mB_n)^2}{(A_mB_n)_0}$

$$
\begin{array}{ll}
(1768)^2/1169 & 2673\cdot9 \\
(946)^2/1303 & 686\cdot8 \\
(115)^2/357 & 37\cdot0 \\
(807)^2/1088 & 598\cdot6 \\
(1387)^2/1212 & 1587\cdot3 \\
(438)^2/332 & 577\cdot8 \\
(189)^2/506 & 70\cdot6 \\
(746)^2/563 & 988\cdot5 \\
(288)^2/154 & 538\cdot6 \\
(47)^2/48\cdot0 & 46\cdot0 \\
(53)^2/53\cdot4 & 52\cdot6 \\
(16)^2/14\cdot6 & 17\cdot5 \\
\end{array}
$$

$$\text{Total} = S = 7875.2$$

From equation (3.8)

$$C = \sqrt{\frac{S-N}{S}} = \sqrt{\frac{1075 \cdot 2}{7875 \cdot 2}}$$

$$= \sqrt{0 \cdot 1365} = 0 \cdot 37$$

and

$$T^2 = \frac{C^2}{(1 - C^2)\sqrt{(s-1)(t-1)}}$$

$$= \frac{0 \cdot 1365}{0 \cdot 8635\sqrt{6}}$$

$$T = \sqrt{0 \cdot 0645}$$

$$= \quad 0 \cdot 25$$

The squares in such work may conveniently be taken from Barlow's *Tables of Squares, Cubes, etc.*, or logarithms may be used throughout—five-figure logarithms are quite sufficient.

It will be seen that T is less than C. This is not always true. Whichever coefficient we use, however, the contingency between pigmentation of hair and eye is evident.

3.14 While such coefficients of contingency are a great convenience in many forms of work, their use should not lead to a neglect of the more detailed treatment of **3.5**. Whether the coefficients be calculated or no, every table should always be examined with care to see if it exhibits any apparently significant peculiarities in the distribution of frequency, e.g. in the associations subsisting between A_m and B_n in limited populations. A good deal of caution must be used in order not to be misled by casual irregularities due to paucity of observations in some compartments of the table, but important points that would otherwise be overlooked will often be revealed by such a detailed examination.

3.15 Suppose, for example, that any four adjacent frequencies, say

$$(A_m B_n) \qquad (A_{m+1} B_n)$$
$$(A_m B_{n+1}) \qquad (A_{m+1} B_{n+1})$$

are extracted from the general contingency table. If these are considered as a table exhibiting the association between A_m and B_n in a population limited to $A_m A_{m+1} B_n B_{n+1}$ alone, the association is positive, negative or zero according as $(A_m B_n)/(A_{m+1} B_n)$ is greater than, less than, or equal to the ratio $(A_m B_{n+1})/(A_{m+1} B_{n+1})$. The whole of the contingency table can be analysed into a series of elementary groups of four frequencies like the above, each one overlapping its neighbours, so that an $s \times t$-fold table contains $(s-1)(t-1)$ such "tetrads," and the associations in them all can be very quickly determined by simply tabulating the ratios like

$(A_mB_n)/(A_{m+1}B_n)$, $(A_mB_{n+1})/(A_{m+1}B_{n+1})$, etc., or perhaps better, the proportions $(A_mB_n)/\{(A_mB_n)+(A_{m+1}B_n)\}$, etc., for every pair of columns or of rows, as may be most convenient. Taking the figures of Table 3.2 as an illustration, and working from the rows, the proportions run as follows—

For rows 1 and 2		For rows 2 and 3	
1768 /2714	0·651	946 /1061	0·892
807 /2194	0·368	1387 /1825	0·760
189 /935	0·202	746 /1034	0·721
47 /100	0·470	53 /69	0·768

In both cases the first three ratios form descending series, but the fourth ratio is greater than the second. The signs of the associations in the six tetrads are, accordingly,

$$+ \quad + \quad -$$
$$+ \quad + \quad -$$

The negative sign in the two tetrads on the right is striking, the more so as other tables for hair- and eye-colour, arranged in the same way, exhibit just the same characteristic. But the peculiarity will be removed at once if the fourth column be placed immediately after the first : if this be done, i.e. if " red " be placed between " fair " and " brown " instead of at the end of the colour-series, the sign of the association in all the elementary tetrads will be the same. The colours will then run fair, red, brown, black, and this would seem to be the more natural order, considering the depth of the pigmentation.

Isotropic contingency tables

3.16 A distribution of frequency of such a kind that the association in every elementary tetrad is of the same sign, possesses several useful and interesting properties, as shown in the following theorems. It will be termed an *isotropic* distribution.

(1) *In an isotropic distribution the sign of the association is the same not only for every elementary tetrad of adjacent frequencies, but for every set of four frequencies in the compartments common to two rows and two columns,* e.g. (A_mB_n), $(A_{m+p}B_n)$, (A_mB_{n+q}), $(A_{m+p}B_{n+q})$.

For suppose that the sign of association in the elementary tetrads is positive, so that

$$(A_mB_n)(A_{m+1}B_{n+1}) > (A_{m+1}B_n)(A_mB_{n+1})$$

and similarly,

$$(A_{m+1}B_n)(A_{m+2}B_{n+1}) > (A_{m+2}B_n)(A_{m+1}B_{n+1})$$

Then multiplying up and cancelling, we have—

$$(A_mB_n)(A_{m+2}B_{n+1}) > (A_{m+2}B_n)(A_mB_{n+1})$$

That is to say, the association is still positive though the two columns A_m and A_{m+2} are no longer adjacent.

(2) *An isotropic distribution remains isotropic in whatever way it may be condensed by grouping together adjacent rows or columns.*

Thus from the first and third inequalities above we have, adding—

$$(A_m B_n)[(A_{m+1}B_{n+1}) + (A_{m+2}B_{n+1})] > (A_m B_{n+1})[(A_{m+1}B_n) + (A_{m+2}B_n)]$$

that is to say, the sign of the elementary association is unaffected by throwing the $(m+1)$th and $(m+2)$th columns into one.

(3) As the extreme case of the preceding theorem, we may suppose both rows and columns grouped and regrouped until only a 2×2-fold table is left ; we then have the theorem—

If an isotropic distribution be reduced to a fourfold distribution in any way whatever by addition of adjacent rows and columns, the sign of the association in such fourfold table is the same as in the elementary tetrads of the original table.

The case of complete independence is a special case of isotropy. For if

$$(A_m B_n) = (A_m)(B_n)/N$$

for all values of m and n, the association is evidently zero for every tetrad. Therefore the distribution remains independent in whatever way the table be grouped, or in whatever way the population be limited by the omission of rows or columns. The expression " complete independence " is therefore justified.

From the work of the preceding section we may say that Table 3.2 is not isotropic as it stands, but may be regarded as a disarrangement of an isotropic distribution. It is best to rearrange such a table in isotropic order, as otherwise different reductions to fourfold form may lead to associations of different sign, though of course they need not necessarily do so.

3.17 The following will serve as an illustration of a table that is not isotropic and cannot be rendered isotropic by any rearrangement of the order of rows and columns—

TABLE 3.4—Showing the frequencies of different combinations of
eye-colours in father and son
1. Blue   2. Blue-green, grey   3. Dark grey, hazel   4. Brown
(Data of Galton, from Karl Pearson, *Phil. Trans.*, A, 1900, **195**, 138 ; classification condensed.)

Son's Eye-colour	Father's Eye-colour				Total
	1	2	3	4	
1	194	70	41	30	335
2	83	124	41	36	284
3	25	34	55	23	137
4	56	36	43	109	244
Total	358	264	180	198	1000

The following are the ratios of the frequency in column m to the sum of the frequencies in columns m and $m+1$—

COLUMNS

1 and 2	2 and 3	3 and 4
0·735	0·631	0·577
0·401	0·752	0·532
0·424	0·382	0·705
0·609	0·456	0·283

The order in which the ratios run is different for each pair of columns, and it is accordingly impossible to make the table isotropic. The distribution of signs of association in the several tetrads is—

+	−	+
−	+	−
−	−	+

The distribution is a curious one, the associations in tetrads round the diagonal of the whole table being so markedly positive, and those in the immediately adjacent tetrads equally markedly negative. Neglecting the other signs, this is the effect that would be produced by taking an isotropic distribution and then increasing the frequencies in the diagonal compartments by a sufficient percentage. Comparison of the given table with others from the same source shows that the peculiarity is common to the great majority of the tables, and accordingly its origin demands explanation. Were such a table treated by the method of the contingency coefficient, or a similar summary method. alone, the peculiarity might not be remarked.

Complete independence in contingency tables

3.18 It may be noted that in the case of complete independence the distribution of frequency in every row is similar to the distribution in the row of totals, and the distribution in every column similar to that in the column of totals ; for in, say, the column A_n the frequencies are given by the relations—

$$(A_n B_1) = \frac{(A_n)}{N}(B_1), \qquad (A_n B_2) = \frac{(A_n)}{N}(B_2), \qquad (A_n B_3) = \frac{(A_n)}{N}(B_3)$$

and so on. This property is of special importance in the theory of variables.

Homogeneous and heterogeneous classification

3.19 The classifications both of this and of the preceding chapters have one important characteristic in common, viz. that they are, so to speak, " homogeneous "—the principle of division being the same for all the sub-classes of any one class. Thus A's and α's are both subdivided into B's and β's, A_1's, A_2's, . . . A_s's into B_1's, B_2's, . . . B_t's, and so on. Clearly this is necessary in order to render possible those comparisons on which the discussions of associations and contingencies depend. If we only know that amongst the A's there is a certain percentage of B's, and amongst the α's a certain percentage of C's, there are no data for any conclusion.

Many classifications are, however, essentially of a heterogeneous character, e.g. biological classifications into orders, general and species ; the classifications of the causes of death in vital statistics and of occupations in the census. To take the last case as an illustration, the 1931 census of England and Wales divides occupations into 32 classes. Some of these are not further subdivided—e.g. " Fishermen ". Others are subdivided into further general classes ; e.g. Class 1 is divided into (1) Employers, (2) Furnacemen, (3) Foundry Workers, (4) Smiths, (5) Metal Machinists, (6) Fitters and (7) Other Workers. These sub-heads are necessarily peculiar to the class under which they occur and their number is arbitrary and variable, and different for each main heading ; but so long as the classification remains purely heterogeneous, however complex it may become, there is no opportunity for any discussion of causation within the limits of the matter so derived. *It is only when a homogeneous division is in some way introduced that we can begin to speak of associations and contingencies.*

3.20 This may be done in various ways according to the nature of the case. Thus the relative frequencies of different botanical families, genera or species may be discussed in connection with the topographical characters of their habitats—desert, marsh or heath—and we may observe statistical associations between given genera and situations of a given topographical type. The causes of death may be classified according to sex, or age, or occupation, and it then becomes possible to discuss the association of a given cause of death with one or other of the two sexes, with a given age-group or with a given occupation. Again, the classifications of deaths and of occupations are repeated at successive intervals of time ; and if they have remained strictly the same, it is also possible to discuss the association of a given occupation or a given cause of death with the earlier or later year of observation—i.e. to see whether the numbers of those engaged in the given occupation or succumbing to the given cause of death have increased or decreased. But in such circumstances the greatest care must be taken to see that the necessary condition as to the identity of the classifications at the two periods is fulfilled, and unfortunately it very seldom is fulfilled. All practical schemes of classification are subject to alteration and improvement from time to time, and these alterations, however desirable in themselves, render a certain number of comparisons impossible. Even where a classification has remained verbally the same, it is not necessarily really the same ; thus in the case of the causes of death, improved methods of diagnosis may transfer many deaths from one heading to another without any change in the incidence of the disease, and so bring about a virtual change in the classification. In any case, heterogeneous classification should be regarded only as a partial process, incomplete until a homogeneous division is introduced either directly or indirectly, e.g. by repetition.

Manifold classification as a series of dichotomies

3.21 From a theoretical point of view, manifold classification can be regarded as compounded of a series of dichotomies. Take, for example, a case we have already considered, that of the classification of a population of men according to the eye-colours blue, grey, brown and green. We could have produced this fourfold division by three dichotomies. In fact, dividing the population first into those with blue eyes and those with not-blue eyes we get two classes. Then dividing again into those with brown eyes and those with not-brown eyes we get four classes. This operation on the class of blue-eyed men, however, results in one zero class, because there are no men with blue eyes which are at the same time brown, and one class which is, in fact, the class of blue-eyed men. Virtually, therefore, we have three classes : those with blue eyes, those with brown eyes, and the remainder. If we now dichotomise each of these into those with grey eyes and those with not-grey eyes, we shall again get, neglecting the zero classes, the four classes of the manifold classification.

3.22 It follows from this that any manifold classification can be regarded as produced by a succession of divisions in which, at each stage, each individual could fall into one of two alternatives, A or not-A.

Put in another way, this means that the possible answers to an unambiguous question can be reduced to a succession of answers of either " yes " or " no." For instance, suppose the question is, " How old are you, in years? " We can replace this question by the succession of questions, " Are you one year old ? " " Are you two years old ? " . . . " Are you 120 years old ? " An answer of " 47 " to the first-mentioned question can then be expressed as an answer of " No " to the first 46 of these questions, " Yes " to the 47th and " No " to the rest.

Similarly, an answer to the question, " What is your name ? " can be reduced to the questions, " Is the first letter of your name A ? " " Is the first letter B ? " . . . " Is the second letter A ? " and so on. Replies to a more general question can be reduced to the same form by a convenient classification ; e.g. the replies to the question, " Are you in favour of war?" can be classified in the four forms " Favourable without qualification," " Favourable with some qualification." " Unfavourable without qualification," " Unfavourable with some qualification," and the answers to the questions can be reduced to answers " yes " or " no " to the questions, "Are you, without qualification, in favour of war ? " and so on.

Recording classified information on punched cards

3.23 The information about an individual, considered as a member of a population, is information whether he does or does not fall into the alternative classes which, as we have just seen, compose the most general homogeneous classification of the population. If we imagine each individual filling in a questionnaire about himself, the totality of answers may, by suitably expressing the questions, be expressed as a number of " yes's " and " no's," and these replies express all the information about the individual.

This simple fact allows us to record the data in a most convenient way. Each individual is allotted a card, which is divided into a number of cells. Each cell corresponds to one of the dichotomies or simple questions the answers to which constitute the information. If the answer is " Yes," a hole is punched in the cell; if the answer is " No," the cell is left untouched.

The card of any individual will thus be like a complicated bus ticket, with holes punched in various places. The punching is usually performed either by hand with a ticket collector's punch, or with a machine similar in principle to the typewriter. The totality of punched cards forms a miniature of our population—each individual has a card on which is recorded the whole of the information about him.

The use of this system lies in the fact that punched cards are easily handled and sorted by machinery. If, for example, we want to know a particular class-frequency, we can adjust certain electrical, pneumatic or mechanical stops, and the machine will segregate all the cards in the class and count them for us.

3.24 A similar device has been applied to the sorting of data by hand. A card is prepared with a row of circular holes punched all the way round near its edge but so that no hole is open to the edge. Each hole corresponds to a dichotomy or a simple question. When preparing the card, if the individual falls into the A class, or the answer to the question is " Yes," a piece is clipped out of the card so that the hole is now open to the edge. If the individual falls into the not-A class, or the answer to the question is " No," the hole is left alone.

To separate the A's from the not-A's, or the " yes " cards from the " no " cards, they are arranged in a vertical plane so that corresponding cells are similarly placed. A skewer is then inserted in the appropriate hole and lifted. The not-A cards are lifted out, whilst the A cards fall away, since the piece of card between the hole and the edge has been cut away. By repeating the operation with the skewer in the appropriate holes we can isolate the cards in any given class. These can then be counted and the size of the class-frequency determined.

3.25 The labour of punching cards and the expense of machinery is justified only when the number of individuals is large and the number of ultimate classes is also large. This arises, for example, in the taking of a census of population.

Numerically defined attributes

3.26 The attributes we have instanced in the foregoing pages have usually been of a qualitative kind. The methods described are, however, applicable to data classified on a numerical basis. Consider, for example, the following table—

TABLE 3.5—Families deficient in room space
Their number in 95 crowded London wards
(Census of 1931, *Housing Report*, p. xxxii)

Families deficient by	Standard room requirement (rooms)							Totals
	2	3	4	5	6	7	8	
1 room	12,999	18,198	7,724	2,170	164	19	....	41,274
2 rooms	....	3,054	4,479	1,448	221	15	1	9,218
3 rooms	....	....	310	508	106	4	1	929
4 rooms	....	....	....	10	21	4	....	35
Totals	12,999	21,252	12,513	4,136	512	42	2	51,456

The distinction between successive rows and columns is not quite of the kind of Table 3.2. In the latter, for instance, we drew a line between black hair and brown, a line which could be drawn by anybody who was not colour-blind, although there may be border-line cases of mixed colours which would present difficulty. But in Table 3.5 above the line is drawn by counting—a much more precise operation. Moreover, the rows and columns have a certain natural order given by the numerical sequence. It would seem absurd to put the column which is headed " two rooms " between those headed " three rooms " and " four rooms," but in Table 3.2 there is no *a priori* reason for putting " black " between " brown " and " red."

3.27 We might also have a contingency table in which the attributes were measurable quantities, and the rows and columns of the table determined by ranges of those quantities. This, again, is slightly different from the case of the previous paragraph, for these ranges are to a large extent arbitrary, whereas in Table 3.5 the indivisible nature of the room compels us to count in units of at least one room.

3.28 Finally, we may have a table which is given by one qualitative attribute and one quantitative attribute. Consider, for example, the following—

TABLE 3.6—Weight and mentality in a selection of criminals

(Data from M. H. Whiting, "On the Association of Temperature, Pulse and Respiration with Physique and Intelligence in Criminals," *Biometrika*, 1912, **11**, 1)

Mentality	Weight (lb)					Totals
	90–120	120–130	130–140	140–150	150 upward	
Normal	21	51	94	106	124	396
Weak	15	18	34	15	15	97
Totals	36	69	128	121	139	493

3.29 The methods of the previous chapters are applicable also to such tables. Numerically measurable quantities may, however, be treated by other methods, to which we shall come in due course. We mention the point here in order to remove any possible idea that the theory of attributes is concerned solely with qualitative classification, and is not appropriate to the more precise data given by a numerically assessable attribute.

SUMMARY

1. The division of a population according to an attribute A into a number of heads is called manifold classification. This is an extension of the idea of dichotomy, in which the population is divided into two parts only.

2. Manifold classification according to two attributes A and B gives rise to a contingency table.

3. Association in a contingency table may be examined by reducing it in a number of ways to a 2×2 table.

4. We define

$$\delta_{mn} = (A_m B_n) - (A_m B_n)_0$$

The " square contingency " is given by—

$$\chi^2 = \Sigma \left\{ \frac{\delta^2_{mn}}{(A_m B_n)_0} \right\} = \Sigma \left\{ \frac{(A_m B_n)^2}{(A_m B_n)_0} \right\} - N$$

The " mean-square contingency " by—

$$\phi^2 = \frac{\chi^2}{N}$$

5. Pearson's " coefficient of mean-square contingency " is defined by—

$$C = \sqrt{\frac{\chi^2}{N+\chi^2}} = \sqrt{\frac{\phi^2}{1+\phi^2}}$$

6. Tschuprow's " coefficient of contingency " is defined by—

$$T^2 = \frac{\phi^2}{\sqrt{(s-1)(t-1)}} =$$

7. Certain types of table, known as isotropic contingency tables, possess special features of some importance.

8. Any manifold classification may be regarded as a succession of dichotomies. This fact is the basis of the use of punched cards for recording and analysing statistical data.

9. Manifold classification may arise not only from an attribute which is specified under heads of a qualitative kind, but also from a quantitative attribute specified by counting or measurement.

EXERCISES

3.1 (Data from Karl Pearson, " On the Inheritance of the Mental and Moral Characters in Man," *Jour. of the Anthrop. Inst.*, vol. 33, and *Biometrika*, vol. 3.) Find the coefficient of contingency (coefficient of mean-square contingency) for the two tables below, showing the resemblance between brothers for athletic capacity and between sisters for temper. Show that neither table is even remotely isotropic. (As stated in **3.11**, the coefficient of contingency should not as a rule be used for tables smaller than 5×5-fold : these small tables are given to illustrate the method, while avoiding lengthy arithmetic.)

A. Athletic capacity

Second Brother	First Brother			Total
	Athletic	Betwixt	Non-athletic	
Athletic . . .	906	20	140	1066
Betwixt . . .	20	76	9	105
Non-athletic . .	140	9	370	519
Total . . .	1066	105	519	1690

B. Temper

| Second Sister | First Sister Good- | | | Total |
	Quick	natured	Sullen	
Quick . . .	198	177	77	452
Good-natured . .	177	996	165	1338
Sullen . . .	77	165	120	362
Total . . .	452	1338	362	2152

3.2   Calculate T and C for the following table, and trace the association between the progress of building and the urban character of the district—

Houses in England and Wales

(*Census of* 1901. *Summary Table X,* 000's omitted)

	Inhabited	Unin-habited	Building	Total
Adm. County of London . .	571	40	5	616
Other urban districts . .	4064	285	45	4394
Rural districts . . .	1625	124	12	1761
Total for England and Wales	6260	449	62	6771

3.3   Show that for a given s and t, C and T are equal for two values of ϕ^2, one of which is zero ; that for ϕ^2 between these values $C > T$; and that for ϕ^2 greater than the higher value $T > C$.

3.4   Find whether the following contingency table is isotropic, and if it is not, ascertain whether it can be arranged in an isotropic form—

	A_1	A_2	A_3	A_4	A_5	Totals
B_1	90	43	17	27	16	193
B_2	235	88	44	60	40	467
B_3	300	103	54	71	48	576
Totals	625	234	115	158	104	1236

3.5 Calculate C and T for the table of the previous example.

3.6 Show that in a positively isotropic contingency table,

$$\frac{\delta_{11}}{(A_1B_1)_0} > \frac{\delta_{1s}}{(A_1B_s)_0} \text{ and is} > \frac{\delta_{r1}}{(A_rB_1)_0}$$

3.7 1,000 subjects of English, French, German, Italian and Spanish nationality were asked to name their preferences among the music of those five nationalities. The results were as follows (1=English, 2=French, 3=German, 4=Italian, 5=Spanish)—

Nationality of subject	Nationality of music preferred					Totals
	1	2	3	4	5	
1	32	16	75	47	30	200
2	10	67	42	41	40	200
3	12	23	107	36	22	200
4	16	20	44	76	44	200
5	8	53	30	43	66	200
Totals	78	179	298	243	202	1000

Discuss the association between the nationality of the subject and the nationality of the music preferred.

3.8 In Table 3.6 calculate C and T, and discuss the light thrown by this table on the association between physique and intelligence in the criminals of the data.

3.9 Show that for a 2×2 contingency table in which the frequencies are $(A_1B_1)=a$, $(A_2B_1)=b$, $(A_1B_2)=c$ and $(A_2B_2)=d$,

$$\chi^2 = \frac{(a+b+c+d)\ (ad-bc)^2}{(a+b)(c+d)(b+d)(a+c)}$$

and hence find C and T in terms of a, b, c, d.

3.10 In a paper discussing whether laterality of hand is associated with laterality of eye (measured by astigmatism, acuity of vision, etc.) T. L. Woo obtained the following results (*Biometrika*, vol. 20A, pp. 79-148)—

Manual laterality as determined by a balancing test	Ocular laterality for general astigmatism			Totals
	" Left-eyed "	Ambiocular	" Right-eyed "	
Left-handed .	34	62	28	124
Ambidextrous .	27	28	20	75
Right-handed .	57	105	52	214
Totals . .	118	195	100	413

Show that laterality of eye is only slightly associated with laterality of hand.

CHAPTER FOUR

FREQUENCY-DISTRIBUTIONS

Variables

4.1 As we emphasised at the close of the last chapter, the methods of the theory of attributes are applicable to all observations, whether qualitative or quantitative. We have now to proceed to the consideration of special processes adapted to the treatment of quantitative data, but not as a rule available for the discussion of purely qualitative observations (though there are some important exceptions to this statement, as suggested in **1.2**).

A measurable quantity which can vary from one individual to another is called a *variable*,[1] and this section of our work may be termed the *theory of variables*.

As common examples of variables which are subject to statistical treatment we may cite birth- and death-rates, prices, wages, barometer readings, rainfall records, and measurements or enumerations (e.g. of glands, spines or petals) on animals or plants.

Quantities which can take any numerical value within a certain range are called *continuous variables*. Such, for example, are birth-rates and barometric readings. Quantities which can take only discrete values are called *discontinuous variables*. This class, for instance, would include data of the number of petals on flowers or the number of rooms in a house.

Frequency-distributions

4.2 If some hundreds or thousands of values of a variable have been noted merely in the arbitrary order in which they occur, the mind cannot properly grasp the significance of the record. We must condense the data by some method of ranking or classification before their characteristics can be comprehended.

One way of doing this would be to dichotomise the data by classifying the individuals as A's or not-A's, according as the value of the variable exceeded or fell short of some given value. But this is too crude, and the sacrifice of information is too great. A manifold classification, however, avoids the crudity of the dichotomous form, since the classes may be made as numerous as we please. Moreover, numerical measurements lend themselves with peculiar readiness to a manifold classification,

---

[1] It is also called a *variate*. We shall use the two terms as synonymous.

for the class limits can be conveniently and precisely defined by assigned values of the variable.

4.3 For convenience, the values of the variable chosen to define the successive classes should be equidistant, so that the numbers of observations in different classes are comparable.

The interval chosen for classifying is called the *class-interval*, and the frequency in a particular class-interval is called a *class-frequency.*

Thus, for measurements of stature, the class-interval might be 1 inch, or 2 centimetres, and the class-frequencies would be the numbers of individuals whose statures fell within each successive inch or each successive 2 centimetres of the scale ; returns of birth- or death-rates might be grouped to the nearest unit per thousand of the population ; returns of wages might be classified to the nearest shilling, or, if it is desired to obtain a more condensed table, to the nearest five or ten shillings. Discontinuous variables to a great extent determine their own class-intervals, which must either be equal in width to the unit amount of variation, or equal to some multiple of it. For example, in enumerations of the number of rooms in a house we naturally take our class-interval to be one room ; in enumerations of the petals on a flower we may take one petal or, if the range of variation is very great, say five petals or more.

4.4 The manner in which the class-frequencies are distributed over the class-intervals is spoken of as the *frequency-distribution* of the variable.

A few illustrations will make clearer the nature of such frequency-distributions, and the service which they render in summarising a long and complex record.

TABLE 4.1—Showing the number of local government areas in England with specified birth-rates per thousand of population

(Material from the Registrar-General's Statistical Review of England and Wales for 1933)

Birth-rate	Number of districts with birth-rate between limits stated	Birth-rate	Number of districts with birth-rate between limits stated
1·5– 2·5	1	13·5–14·5	271
2·5– 3·5	2	14·5–15·5	190
3·5– 4·5	2	15·5–16·5	127
4·5– 5·5	3	16·5–17·5	89
5·5– 6·5	7	17·5–18·5	78
6·5– 7·5	9	18·5–19·5	37
7·5– 8·5	14	19·5–20·5	21
8·5– 9·5	41	20·5–21·5	17
9·5–10·5	83	21·5–22·5	4
10·5–11·5	131	22·5–23·5	4
11·5–12·5	192	23·5–24·5	2
12·5–13·5	242	Total	1567

(a) Table 4.1. In this illustration the birth-rates per thousand of the population in 1933 of 1,567 local government areas of England have been classified to the nearest unit ; i.e. the number of districts has been counted in which the birth-rate was between 1·5 per thousand and 2·5, between 2·5 and 3·5, and so on. The frequency-distribution is shown by the table.

Although a glance through the original returns, which are spread amongst many other figures over 42 pages, fails to convey any definite impression, a brief inspection of the above table brings out a number of important points. Thus, we see that the birth-rates range, in round numbers, from 2 to 24 per thousand ; that the birth-rates in some 75 per cent of the districts lie within the narrow limits 10·5 to 16·5, the rates most frequent being near 14 ; and so on. It may be remarked that some of the areas are very small, with no more than 10 or 20 births, and these account mainly for the extremely divergent rates.

(b) Table 4.2. The numbers of stigmatic rays on a number of Shirley poppies were counted. As the range of variation is not great, the unit is taken as the class-interval. The frequency-distribution is given by the following table—

TABLE 4.2—Showing the frequencies of seed capsules on certain Shirley poppies with different numbers of stigmatic rays

(Cited from G. Udny Yule, *Biometrika*, 1902, **2**, 89)

Number of stigmatic rays	Number of capsules with said number of stigmatic rays	Number of stigmatic rays	Number of capsules with said number of stigmatic rays
6	3	14	302
7	11	15	234
8	38	16	128
9	106	17	50
10	152	18	19
11	238	19	3
12	305	20	1
13	315		
		Total	1905

The numbers of rays range from 6 to 20, the most usual numbers being 12, 13 or 14.

(c) Table 4.3. 206 screws were taken as they came off the lathe which was turning them. Their lengths, which should have been 1 inch, were measured. The following table shows the screws classified by the number of thousandths of an inch by which they exceeded or fell short of 1 inch in length—

TABLE 4.3—Showing the frequencies of screws classified according to the extent to which they varied in length from the standard of 1 inch

Difference in length from 1 inch (Thousandths of an inch)	Number of screws	Difference in length from 1 inch (Thousandths of an inch)	Number of screws
−6 to −5	1	+1 to +2	34
−5 to −4	4	+2 to +3	25
−4 to −3	11	+3 to +4	16
−3 to −2	22	+4 to +5	8
−2 to −1	25	+5 to +6	1
−1 to 0	27		
0 to +1	32	Total	206

It will be seen that the maximum frequency, i.e. **34**, occurs for screws from 0·001 to 0·002 inch in excess of the standard. About 80 per cent lie in the range three-thousandths of an inch on either side of the standard.

4.5 Expanding slightly the brief description we have given, tables setting out frequency-distributions are formed in the following way—

(1) The magnitude of the class-interval is first fixed. In Tables 4.1, 4.2 and 4.3 one unit was chosen.

(2) The position or origin of the intervals must then be determined ; e.g. in Table 4.1 we must decide whether to take as intervals 9–10, 10–11, 11–12, etc., or 9·5–10·5, 10·5–11·5, 11·5–12·5, etc.

(3) This choice having been made, the complete scale of intervals is fixed and the observations are classified accordingly.

(4) The process of classification being finished, a table is drawn up on the general lines of Tables 4.1–4.3, showing the total number of observations in each class-interval.

It is necessary to make a few remarks about each of these heads.

Magnitude of class-interval

4.6 As already remarked, in cases where the variation proceeds by discrete steps of considerable magnitude as compared with the range of variation, there is very little choice as regards the magnitude of the class-interval. The unit will in general have to serve. But if the variation be continuous, or at least takes place by discrete steps which are small in comparison with the whole range of variation, there is no such natural class-interval, and its choice is a matter for judgment.

The two conditions which guide the choice are these : (a) We desire to be able to treat all the values assigned to any one class, without serious error, as if they were equal to the mid-value of the class-interval, e.g. as if the birth-rate of every district in the first class of Table 4.1 were exactly 2·0, the birth-rate of every district in the second class 3·0, and so on ; (b) for convenience and brevity we desire to make the interval as large as possible, subject to the first condition. These conditions will generally be fulfilled if the interval be so chosen that the whole number of classes lies between 15 and 25. A number of classes less than, say, ten leads in general to very appreciable inaccuracy, and a number over, say, thirty makes a somewhat unwieldy table. A preliminary inspection of the record should accordingly be made and the highest and lowest values be picked out. Dividing the difference between these by, say, twenty-five, we have an approximate value for the interval. The actual value should be the nearest integer or simple fraction.

Position of intervals

4.7 The position or starting-point of the intervals is, as a rule, more or less a matter of indifference. It can therefore be chosen as is most convenient for the particular case under discussion, e.g. so that the limits of the intervals are integers, or, as in Table 4.1, so that the mid-values are integers. It may also be chosen so that no limits correspond exactly to any recorded value of the variate, in order to obviate any difficulty in deciding to which class a particular individual should be assigned (cf. **4.9**).

The location of the intervals is, however, important when the values of the variate tend for some reason to cluster round particular values. Such a case arises, for instance, in age returns, owing to the tendency to state a round number where the true age is unknown, or a reluctance to admit one's real age.[1] It is also common wherever there is some doubt as to the final digit in reading a scale, and scope is given to the idiosyncrasies of the observer.

Table 4.4 shows results for four observers as illustrations, the frequencies being reduced for comparability to a total of 1,000. Column A is based on measures by G. U. Yule, on drawings, to the nearest tenth of a milli-metre. It is recognised, of course, that measures cannot really be made to such a degree of precision ; but the measurer believed that he was making them carefully, and as they were made with a Zeiss scale, in which the divisions are ruled on the under side of a piece of plate-glass, readings were unaffected by parallax. Nevertheless, it will be seen that the zeros, and also 2, 8 and 9, were heavily over-emphasised—an odd selection of preferences! On the whole, the centre of the millimetre was neglected and measures piled up at the two ends.

The data for columns B, C and D are all drawn from the same published report, and refer to sundry head measurements taken on the living subject.

---

[1] This effect is practically the same for men as for women. Cf. Table I in the Appendix to the paper cited in the heading to Table 4.4 above.

On the basis of a statement in the introduction to the report, it was possible to compile the data separately for the three assistants (B, C, D) who had done the actual measuring. It will be seen that B was rather good : there is a relatively slight excess at 0 and 5, but otherwise his measurements are fairly uniformly distributed. C was decidedly not good, rounding off nearly one measurement in two to the nearest centimetre or half-centimetre. D was simply outrageously bad—so bad that it might have been better not to publish his measurements. Nearly 57 per cent of his measurements were made only to the nearest centimetre or half-centimetre—a quite inadequate degree of precision for head measurements often only a few centimetres in magnitude.

TABLE 4.4—Frequency-distributions of final digits in measurements by four observers

(G. U. Yule, " On Reading a Scale," *J. Roy. Stat. Soc.*, 1927, **90**, 570)

Final digit	Frequency of final digit per 1,000 for observer			
	A	B	C	D
0	158	122	251	358
1	97	98	37	49
2	125	98	80	90
3	73	90	72	63
4	76	100	55	37
5	71	112	222	211
6	90	98	71	62
7	56	99	75	70
8	126	101	72	44
9	129	81	65	16
Total	1001	999	1000	1000
Actual ob-⎱ servations ⎰	1258	3000	1000	1000

When there is any possibility of clustering of variate values it is as well to subject the data to a close examination before finally fixing on the method of classification. On the whole, the intervals should be arranged as far as possible so that the values round which the clustering occurs fall towards the interval mid-values. This procedure avoids sensible error in the assumption that the interval mid-value is approximately representative of the values of the class.

Classification

4.8 The scale of intervals having been fixed, the observations may be classified. If the number of observations is not large, it will be sufficient to mark the limits of successive intervals in a column down the left-hand side of a sheet of paper, and transfer the entries of the original record to this sheet by marking a 1 on the line corresponding to any class for each entry assigned thereto. It saves time in subsequent totalling if each fifth entry in a class is marked by a diagonal across the preceding four, or by leaving a space.

The disadvantage in this process is that it offers no facilities for checking : if a repetition of the classification leads to a different result, there is no means of tracing the error. If the number of observations is at all considerable and accuracy is essential, it is accordingly better to enter the values observed on cards, one to each observation. These are then dealt out into packs according to their classes and the whole work checked by running through the pack corresponding to each class, and verifying that no cards have been wrongly sorted.

4.9 In some cases difficulties may arise in classifying, owing to the occurrence of observed values corresponding to class-limits. Thus, in compiling Table 4.1 some districts will have been noted with birth-rates entered in the Registrar-General's returns as $16 \cdot 5$, $17 \cdot 5$ or $18 \cdot 5$, any one of which might at first sight have been apparently assigned indifferently to either of two adjacent classes. In such a case, however, where the original figures for numbers of births and population are available, the difficulty may be readily surmounted by working out the rate to another place of decimals : if the rate stated to be $16 \cdot 5$ proves to be $16 \cdot 502$, it will be sorted to the class $16 \cdot 5$–$17 \cdot 5$; if $16 \cdot 498$, to the class $15 \cdot 5$–$16 \cdot 5$. Birth-rates that work out to half-units exactly do not occur in this example, and so there is no real difficulty.

In the case of Table 4.3, again, there is little difficulty in knowing the class to which an individual should be assigned.

Difficulties of this type may, in fact, always be avoided if they are borne in mind in fixing the class-intervals, by fixing the intervals to a further place of decimals or a smaller fraction than the values in the original record. Thus, if statures are measured to the nearest centimetre, the class-intervals may be taken as $150 \cdot 5$–$151 \cdot 5$, $151 \cdot 5$–$152 \cdot 5$, etc.; if to the nearest eighth of an inch, the intervals may be $59\frac{15}{16}$–$60\frac{15}{16}$, $60\frac{15}{16}$–$61\frac{15}{16}$, and so on.

If the difficulty is not evaded in any of these ways, it is usual to assign one-half of an intermediate observation to each adjacent class, with the result that half-units occur in the class-frequencies (cf. Table 4.9, p. 86). The procedure is rough, but probably good enough for practical purposes ; strict precision is usually unattainable, for in point of fact the odd way in which different individuals read a scale, for example, renders it impossible to assign exact limits to intervals.

Tabulation

4.10 As regards the actual drafting of the final table there is little to be said, except that care should be taken to express the class-limits clearly and, if necessary, to say how the difficulty of intermediate values has been met or evaded. The class-limits are perhaps best given as in

Tables 4.1 and 4.3, but may be more briefly indicated by the mid-values of the class-intervals. Thus, Table 4.1 might have been given in the form—

Birth-rate per 1,000 to the nearest unit	Number of districts with said birth-rate
2	1
3	2
4	2
etc.	etc.

It is also permissible to write the table in the form—

Interval	Frequency
1·5–	1
2·5–	2
3·5–	2
etc.	etc.

it being understood that the closing point of any interval is the starting point of the following interval. Cf. Table 4.11 below.

It should be noticed that the method of defining class-intervals adopted in Table 4.3 leaves the class-limits uncertain unless the degree of accuracy of the measurements is also given. Thus, in a table giving frequencies of men in certain height-ranges of 1 inch in width, say " 57 and less than 58," etc., if measurements were taken to the nearest eighth of an inch, the class-limits are really $56\frac{15}{16}$–$57\frac{15}{16}$, $57\frac{15}{16}$–$58\frac{15}{16}$, etc.; if they were only taken to the nearest quarter of an inch, the limits are $56\frac{7}{8}$–$57\frac{7}{8}$, $57\frac{7}{8}$–$58\frac{7}{8}$, etc. With such a form of tabulation a statement as to the number of significant figures in the original record is therefore essential. It is better, perhaps, to state the true class-limits and avoid ambiguity.

4.11 The rule that class-intervals should be all equal is one that is very frequently broken in official statistical publications, principally in order to condense an otherwise unwieldy table, thus not only saving space in printing but also considerable expense in compilation, or possibly, in the case of confidential figures, to avoid giving a class which would contain only one or two observations, the identity of which might be guessed. It would hardly be legitimate, for example, to give a return of incomes relating to a limited district in such a form that the income of the two or three wealthiest men in the district would be clear to any intelligent reader with local knowledge.

If the class-intervals be made unequal, the application of many statistical methods is rendered awkward, or even impossible. Further, the relative values of the frequencies are misleading, so that the table is not perspicuous. Thus, consider the first two columns of Table 4.5, showing the number of persons liable to sur-tax and super-tax classified according to their annual income. On running the eye down the column headed " Number of Persons," the attention is at once caught by the three irregularities at the classes " £3,000 and not exceeding £4,000," " £8,000 and not exceeding £10,000," and " £10,000 and not exceeding £15,000." But these have no real significance ; they are merely due to changes in the magnitude of the class-interval at those points. A further change occurs at the £30,000 and at the £50,000 mark, although the attention is not directed thereto by any marked irregularity in the frequencies.

TABLE 4.5—The numbers of persons in the United Kingdom liable to sur-tax and super-tax in the year beginning 5th April 1931

Classified according to the magnitudes of their annual incomes

(From the Statistical Abstract for the United Kingdom for the Years 1913 and 1919-32, Cmd. 4489)

Annual income (£000)	Number of persons	Frequency per £500 interval
2 and not exceeding 2·5	23,988	23,988
2·5 ,, ,, 3	15,781	15,781
3 ,, ,, 4	17,979	8,989
4 ,, ,, 5	9,755	4,877
5 ,, ,, 6	5,921	2,960
6 ,, ,, 7	3,729	1,864
7 ,, ,, 8	2,546	1,273
8 ,, ,, 10	3,193	798
10 ,, ,, 15	3,616	362
15 ,. ,, 20	1,328	133
20 ,, ,, 25	679	68
25 ,, ,, 30	378	38
30 ,, ,, 40	372	19
40 ,, ,, 50	192	10
50 ,, ,, 75	182	4
75 ,, ,, 100	57	1
100 and over	94	?
Total number of persons	89,790	—

To make the class-frequencies really comparable *inter se* they must first be reduced to a common interval as basis, say £500, by dividing the third and subsequent numbers by 2, the eighth by 4, and so on. This gives the mean frequencies tabulated in the third column of Table 4.5. The reduction is, however, impossible in the case of the last class, for we are told only the number of persons with an income of £100,000 and upwards. Such an indefinite class is in many respects a great inconvenience, and should always be avoided in work not subjected to the necessary limitations of official publications.

4.12 The general rule that intervals should be equal must not be held to bar the analysis by smaller equal intervals of some portion of the range over which the frequency varies very rapidly. In Table 4.11, page 89, for example, giving the numbers of deaths from scarlet fever at successive ages, it is desirable to give the numbers of deaths in each year for the first five years, so as to bring out the rapid rise to the maximum in the third year of life.

Graphical representation : frequency-polygon and histogram

4.13 It is often convenient to represent the frequency-distribution by means of a diagram which conveys to the eye the general run of the observations. The following short table, giving the distribution of head-breadths for 1,000 men, will serve as an example—

TABLE 4.6—Showing the frequency-distribution of head-breadths for students at Cambridge

Measurements taken to the nearest tenth of an inch

(Cited from W. R. Macdonell, *Biometrika*, 1902, **1**, 220)

Head-breadth in inches	Number of men with said head-breadth	Head-breadth in inches	Number of men with said head-breadth
5·5	3	6·3	99
5·6	12	6·4	37
5·7	43	6·5	15
5·8	80	6·6	12
5·9	131	6·7	3
6·0	236	6·8	2
6·1	185		
6·2	142	Total	1000

Taking a piece of squared paper ruled, say, in inches and tenths, mark off along a horizontal base-line a scale representing class-intervals ; a half-inch to the class-interval would be suitable. Then choose a vertical scale for the class-frequencies, say 50 observations per interval to the inch, and mark off, on the verticals or *ordinates* through the points marked 5·5, 5·6, 5·7, . . . at the centres of the class-intervals on the base-line, heights representing on this scale the class-frequencies 3, 12, 43, . . . The diagram may then be completed in one of two ways : (1) as a *frequency-polygon*, by joining up the marks on the verticals by straight lines, the last points at each end being joined down to the base at the centre of the next class-interval (fig. 4.1) ; or (2) as a column diagram or *histogram*, short horizontals being drawn through the marks on the verticals (fig. 4.2), which now form the central axes of a series of rectangles representing the class-frequencies.

4.14 The student should note that in any such diagram, of either form, a certain *area* represents a given number of observations. On the scales suggested, 1 inch on the horizontal represents 2 intervals, and 1 inch on the vertical represents 50 observations per interval : 1 square inch therefore represents $50 \times 2 = 100$ observations. The diagrams are, however, conventional : in both cases the whole area of the figure is proportional to the total number of observations, but the area over every interval is not correct in the case of the frequency-polygon, and the frequency of every fraction of any interval is not the same, as suggested by the histogram. The area shown by the frequency-polygon over any interval with an ordinate y_2 (fig. 4.3) is only correct if the tops of the three successive ordinates y_1, y_2, y_3 lie on a line, i.e. if $y_2 = \frac{1}{2}(y_1 + y_3)$, the areas of the two little triangles shaded in the figure being equal. If y_2 fall short of this value, the area shown by the polygon is too great ; if y_2 exceed it,

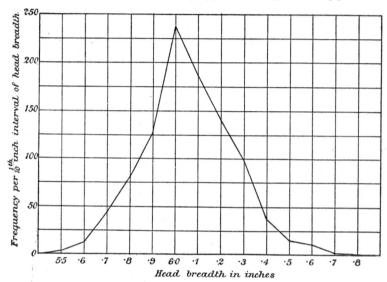

Fig. 4.1.—Frequency-polygon for head-breadths of 1,000 Cambridge students
(Table 4.6)

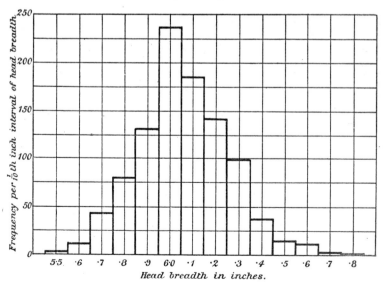

Fig. 4.2.—Histogram for the same data as fig. 4.1

the area shown by the polygon is too small ; and if, for this reason, the frequency-polygon tends to become very misleading at any part of the range, it is better to use the histogram.

4.15   The histogram may also be used when the class-intervals are unequal.   The construction of the previous section is easily adapted to such cases.   All that is necessary is to describe an area equal, on the scale adopted, to the frequency in a particular interval ; this is done, as before, by erecting at the centre of the interval an ordinate equal in length to the total frequency divided by the width of the interval.

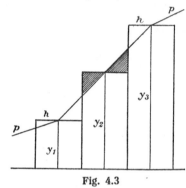

Fig. 4.3

An example of this kind of construction is given in fig. 4.11 (Table 4.11).   The frequencies of deaths for ages over 5 years are given in 5-yearly periods, whereas those for ages under 5 years are given in 1-yearly periods. On the scale indicated, therefore, the height of the cell of the histogram corresponding to the ages 2–3 years is 89, the class-frequency ; that of the cell corresponding to the ages 5–10 is 42·6, i.e. 213 divided by 5.   Hence the areas of the two cells are, to the scale adopted, 89 and 213, respectively, so that the areas accurately represent the frequencies.

Frequency-curves

4.16   If the class-intervals be made smaller, and at the same time the number of observations increased so that the class-frequencies may remain finite, the polygon and the histogram will approach more and

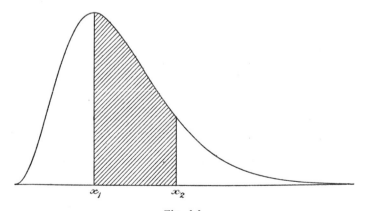

Fig. 4.4

more closely to a smooth curve. Such an ideal limit to the polygon or the histogram is called a *frequency-curve*. It is a concept of supreme importance in statistical theory.

In the frequency-curve the area between any two ordinates whatever is proportional to the number of observations falling between the corresponding values of the variable. Thus, the number of observations falling between the values of the variable x_1 and x_2 in fig. 4.4 will be proportional to the area of the shaded strip in the figure ; the number of observed values greater than x_2 will be given by the area of the curve to the right of the ordinate at x_2 ; and so on.

4.17 When we come to consider the theory of sampling we shall regard the frequency curve as representing a population from which the actual data are a specimen. The frequency-polygon and the histogram will then be approximations to the curve, but will diverge from it to some extent owing to fluctuations of sampling. For the present we must defer a closer inquiry into this subject. We may remark, however, that when the number of observations is considerable—say a thousand at least—the run of the class-frequencies is usually sufficiently smooth to give a good notion of the form of the " ideal " distribution.

Some common types of frequency-distribution

4.18 The forms presented by smoothly running sets of data are almost endless in their variety, but among them we may notice a comparatively small number of simple types. Such types also form a set into which more complex distributions may often be analysed. For elementary

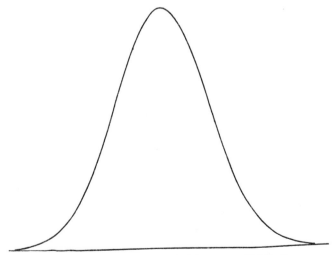

Fig. 4.5.—An ideal symmetrical frequency-distribution

purposes it is sufficient to consider four fundamental simple types, which we shall call the symmetrical distribution, the moderately asymmetrical or skew distribution,[1] the extremely asymmetrical or J-shaped distribution and the U-shaped distribution. In the following sections we give some examples of each of these types, together with a few more complex distributions.

The symmetrical distribution

4.19 In this type the class-frequencies decrease to zero symmetrically on either side of a central maximum. Fig. 4.5 illustrates the ideal form of the distribution.

Being a special case of the more general type described under the second heading, this form of distribution is comparatively rare. It

TABLE 4.7—The frequency-distributions of statures for adult males born in England Scotland, Wales and Ireland

As measurements are stated to have been taken to the nearest ⅛th of an inch, the class-intervals are here presumably 56 15/16–57 15/16, 57 15/16–58 15/16, and so on (cf. 4.9). (See fig. 4.6.)

(Final Report of the Anthropometric Committee to the British Association.) (*Report*, 1883, p. 256.)

| Height without shoes, inches | Number of men within said limits of height Place of birth— | | | | Total |
	England	Scotland	Wales	Ireland	
57–	1	—	1	—	2
58–	3	1	—	—	4
59–	12	—	1	1	14
60–	39	2	—	—	41
61–	70	2	9	2	83
62–	128	9	30	2	169
63–	320	19	48	7	394
64–	524	47	83	15	669
65–	740	109	108	33	990
66–	881	139	145	58	1,223
67–	918	210	128	73	1,329
68–	886	210	72	62	1,230
69–	753	218	52	40	1,063
70–	473	115	33	25	646
71–	254	102	21	15	392
72–	117	69	6	10	202
73–	48	26	2	3	79
74–	16	15	1	—	32
75–	9	6	1	—	16
76–	1	4	—	—	5
77–	1	1	—	—	2
Total	6,194	1,304	741	346	8,585

[1] These two types, from their shape, are frequently referred to as "humped," "cocked hat," "single peaked," and so on.

occurs in the case of biometric, more especially anthropometric, measurements, from which the following illustration is drawn, and is important in much theoretical work. Table 4.7 shows the frequency-distribution of statures for adult males born in the British Isles, from data published by a British Association Committee in 1883, the figures being given separately for persons born in England, Scotland, Wales and Ireland, and totalled in the last column. These frequency-distributions are approximately of the symmetrical type. The frequency-polygon for the totals given by the last column of the table is shown in fig. 4.6. The student will notice that an error of $\frac{1}{16}$ inch, scarcely appreciable in the diagram on its reduced scale, is neglected in the scale shown on the base-line, the intervals being treated as if they were 57–58, 58–59, etc. Diagrams should be drawn for comparison showing, to a good open scale, the separate distributions for England, Scotland, Wales and Ireland.

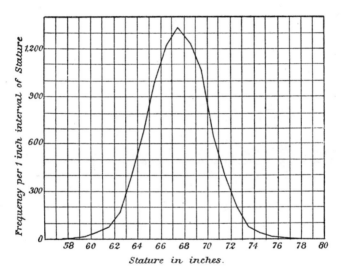

Fig. 4.6.—Frequency-distribution of stature for 8,585 adult males born in the British Isles (Table 4.7)

The moderately asymmetrical (skew) distribution

4.20 In this case the class-frequencies decrease with markedly greater rapidity on one side of the maximum than on the other, as in fig. 4.7 (*a*) or (*b*). This is the most common of all smooth forms of frequency-distribution, illustrations occurring in statistics from almost every source. The distribution of birth-rates given in Table 4.1 is slightly asymmetrical.

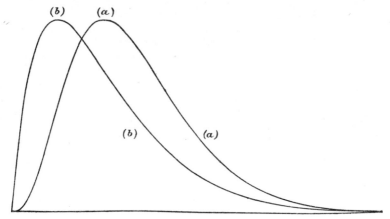

Fig. 4.7.—Ideal distributions of the moderately asymmetrical form

The distribution of Australian marriages given in Table 4.8 (fig. 4.8) is rather more asymmetrical and is of the type (a) of fig. 4.7. The frequency attains its maximum for ages between 24 and 27 and then tails off slowly. We have not drawn the tail of the curve, which is very close to the x-axis, for values of the variate above 58·5.

Table 4.9 and fig. 4.9 give a biological illustration, viz. the distribution of fecundity (ratio of yearling foals produced to coverings) in mares.

TABLE 4.8.—Numbers of marriages contracted in Australia, 1907-14

Arranged according to the age of bridegroom in 3-year groups

(From S. J. Pretorius, " Skew Bivariate Frequency Surfaces," *Biometrika*, 1930, **22**, 210)   (See fig. 4.8)

Age of bridegroom (Central value of 3-year range, in years)	Number of marriages	Age of bridegroom (Central value of 3-year range, in years)	Number of marriages
16·5	294	55·5	1,655
19·5	10,995	58·5	1,100
22·5	61,001	61·5	810
25·5	73,054	64·5	649
28·5	56,501	67·5	487
31·5	33,478	70·5	326
34·5	20,569	73·5	211
37·5	14,281	76·5	119
40·5	9,320	79·5	73
43·5	6,236	82·5	27
46·5	4,770	85·5	14
49·5	3,620	88·5	5
52·5	2,190		
		Total	301,785

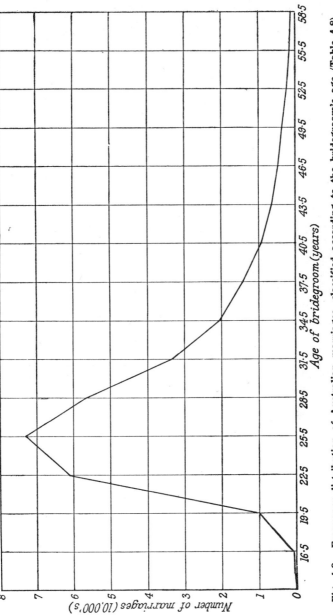

Fig. 4.8.—Frequency-distribution of Australian marriages, classified according to the bridegroom's age (Table 4.8)

The student should notice the difficulty of classification in this case : the class-interval chosen throughout the middle of the range is 1 /15th, but the last interval is " 29 /30–1." This is not a whole interval, but it is more than a half, for all the cases of complete fecundity are reckoned into the class. In the diagram (fig. 4.9) it has been reckoned as a whole class, and this gives a smooth distribution.

To take an illustration from meteorology, the distribution of barometer heights at any one station over a period of time is, in general, asymmetrical, the most frequent heights lying towards the upper end of the range for stations in England and Wales. Table 4.10 and fig. 4.10 show the distribution for daily observations at Greenwich during the years 1848-1926 inclusive.

The distributions of Tables 4.8–4.10 all follow more or less the type of fig. 4.7 (*a*), the frequency tailing off, at the steeper end of the distribution, in such a way as to suggest that the ideal curve is tangential to the base. Cases of greater asymmetry, suggesting an ideal curve that meets the base (at one end) at a finite angle, even a right angle, as in fig. 4.7 (*b*), are less frequent, but occur occasionally. The distribution of deaths from scarlet fever, according to age, affords one such example of a more asymmetrical kind. The actual figures for this case are given in Table 4.11 and illustrated by fig. 4.11 ; and it will be seen that the frequency of deaths reaches a maximum for children aged " 2 and under 3," the number rising very rapidly to the maximum, and thence falling so slowly

TABLE 4.9.—The frequency-distribution of fecundity, i.e. the ratio of the number of yearling foals produced to the number of coverings, for brood-mares (racehorses) covered eight times at least

(See fig. 4.9)

(Pearson, Lee and Moore, *Phil. Trans.*, A, 1899, **192**, 303)

Fecundity	Number of mares with fecundity between the given limits	Fecundity	Number of mares with fecundity between the given limits
1 /30– 3 /30	2	17 /30–19 /30	315
3 /30– 5 /30	7·5	19 /30–21 /30	337
5 /30– 7 /30	11·5	21 /30–23 /30	293·5
7 /30– 9 /30	21·5	23 /30–25 /30	204
9 /30–11 /30	55	25 /30–27 /30	127
11 /30–13 /30	104·5	27 /30–29 /30	49
13 /30–15 /30	182	29 /30–1	19
15 /30–17 /30	271·5		
		Total	2000·0

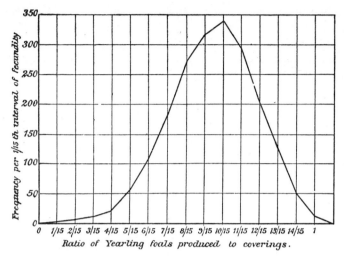

Fig. 4.9.—Frequency-distribution of fecundity for brood-mares (Table 4.9)

that there is still an appreciable frequency for persons over 50 years of age.

Asymmetrical curves are also said to be "skew." In Chapter 7 we shall consider skewness at some length and discuss various ways of measuring it. In particular we shall find that skewness has a sign, and we may explain at this stage that the skewness is said to be positive if the longer tail of the curve lies to the right, or negative if it lies to the left ; e.g. the curve of fig. 4.8 has positive skewness, whilst those of figs. 4.9 and 4.10 have negative skewness.

The extremely asymmetrical, or J-shaped, distribution

4.21 In this type the class-frequencies run up to a maximum at one end of the range, as in fig. 4.12.

This may be regarded as a limiting form of the previous distribution, and, in fact, the two cannot always be distinguished by elementary methods if the original data are not available. If, for instance, the frequencies of Table 4.11 had been given by five-year intervals only, they would have run 322, 213, 70, 27, etc., thus suggesting that the maximum number of deaths occurred at the beginning of life, i.e. that the distribution was J-shaped. It is only the analysis of deaths in the earlier years by one-year intervals which shows that the frequencies reach a maximum in the third year and that therefore the distribution is of the moderately asymmetrical type. In practical cases no hard-and-fast rule can be drawn between the moderately and extremely asymmetrical types, any more than between the asymmetrical and the symmetrical types.

TABLE 4.10.—Barometric heights at Greenwich on alternate days from 1848 to 1926

(See fig. 4.10)

(Data from S. J. Pretorius, "Skew Bivariate Frequency Surfaces," *Biometrika*, 1930, **22**, 154)

Barometric height (Central value in inches)	Number of days	Barometric height (Central value in inches)	Number of days
28·35	1	29·65	3176
28·45	4	29·75	3700
28·55	12	29·85	3921
28·65	43	29·95	3749
28·75	60	30·05	2951
28·85	81	30·15	1951
28·95	189	30·25	1148
29·05	282	30·35	563
29·15	542	30·45	258
29·25	813	30·55	73
29·35	1233	30·65	13
29·45	1752	30·75	7
29·55	2333		
		Total	28,855

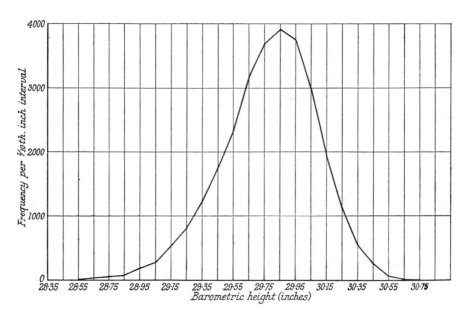

Fig. 4.10.—Barometric height at Greenwich on alternate days from 1848-1926
(Table 4.10)

TABLE 4.11.—The number of deaths from scarlet fever at different ages in England and Wales in 1933

(See fig. 4.11)

(Data from Registrar-General's Statistical Review of England and Wales for 1933, Tables, Part I, Medical)

Age in years	Number of deaths	Number per year
0–	16	16
1–	69	69
2–	89	89
3–	74	74
4–	74	74
5–	213	42·6
10–	70	14·0
15–	27	5·4
20–	26	5·2
25–	17	3·4
30–	12	2·4
35–	11	2·2
40–	10	2·0
45–	6	1·2
50–	7	1·4
55–	5	1·0
60–	—	—
65–	1	0·2
70–	1	0·2
75—	1	0·2
80–	—	—
Total	729	—

4.22 In economic statistics this form of distribution is particularly characteristic of the distribution of wealth in the population at large, as illustrated by income tax and house valuation returns, and the curve to which it gives rise has been called the " Pareto line," after Vilfredo Pareto who directed the attention of economists to it.

Such distributions may, of course, be a very extreme case of the last type. It is difficult to say. But if the maximum is not absolutely at the lower end of the range, it is very close thereto.

Official returns do not usually give the necessary analysis of the frequencies at the lower end of the range to enable the exact position of the maximum to be determined ; and for this reason the data on which Table 4.12 is founded, though of course very unreliable, are of some interest. It will be seen from the table and fig. 4.13 that with the given classification the distribution appears clearly assignable to the present type, the number of estates between zero and £100 in annual value being more than six times as great as the number between £100 and £200 in annual value, and the frequency continuously falling as the value increases. A close analysis of the first class suggests, however, that the greatest frequency does not occur actually at zero, but that there is a true maximum frequency for estates of about £1 15/- in annual value. The distribution might therefore be more correctly assigned to the second type, but the position of the greatest frequency indicates a degree of skewness which is high even compared with the skewness of fig. 4.11.

The type is more frequent in other classes of material than was at one time thought. Distributions of deaths of centenarians afford an example, and so, curiously enough, do deaths of infants unless the class-interval is exceedingly fine—a matter of hours. The distribution may be obtained by compiling the frequencies of the numbers of genera with 1, 2, 3, . . . species in any biological group. Table 4.13 shows such a distribution for the Chrysomelid beetles. Yule has also shown that it is characteristic of the numbers of words used once, twice, thrice, etc., in a given work and has used it in investigations into literary vocabularies.

The U-shaped distribution

4.23 This type exhibits a maximum frequency at the ends of the range and a minimum towards the centre, as in fig. 4.14.

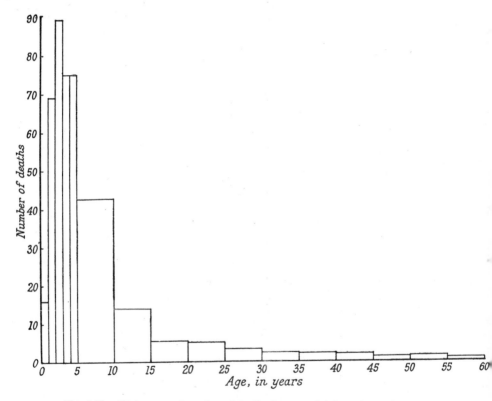

Fig. 4.11.—Histogram of number of deaths from scarlet fever for various ages
(Table 4.11)

This is a rare but interesting form of distribution, as it stands in some-what marked contrast to the preceding forms. Table 4.14 and fig. 4.15 illustrate an example based on a considerable number of observations, viz. the distribution of degrees of cloudiness, or estimated percentage of the sky covered by cloud, at Greenwich in July.

For the purposes of the illustration we regard cloudiness as a variate varying from complete overcastness to clear sky, the range being divided into eleven *equal* parts.

It will be seen that a sky completely or almost completely overcast at the time of observation is the most common, a practically clear sky comes next, and the intermediates are more rare.

The remarks we made about the extreme end of the J-shaped dis-tribution also apply to the U-shaped distribution. In particular cases it

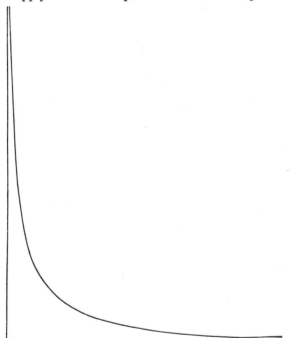

Fig. 4.12.—An ideal distribution of the extremely asymmetrical form

may be that the grouping is too coarse to reveal the true character of the frequency at the maxima, and if the data were more complete we might discover that the two arms of the U in fact were bent over.

Truncated forms

4.24 The four types we have been considering sometimes occur in an incomplete form. Certain limitations on the range of the variate may result in a kind of truncation at one end or the other. Consider, for example, Table 4.15, p. 96.   In obtaining these figures, twelve dice were thrown and the occurrence of a 6 was called a success.   At one throw there could thus be any number of successes from 0 to 12.   The dice were thrown 4096 times.

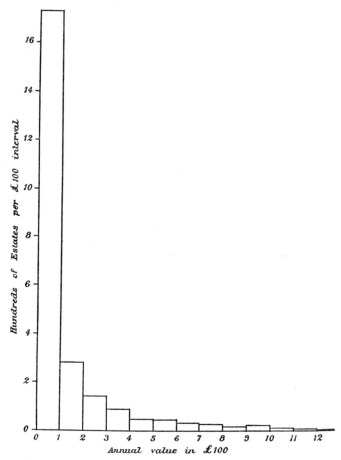

Fig. 4.13.—Frequency-distribution of the annual values of certain estates in England in 1715 ; 2,476 estates (Table 4.12)

Fig. 4.16 gives the frequency-polygon for this distribution.   We can picture it as a slightly skew distribution which has been cut off on the left owing to the inadmissibility of negative values of the variate.   Discontinuous variates not infrequently give rise to this effect of truncation.

Complex distributions

4.25   Table 4.16 gives the number of male deaths within certain age-limits for England and Wales in the years 1930–32.

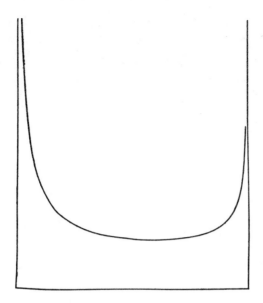

Fig. 4.14.—An ideal distribution of the U-shaped form

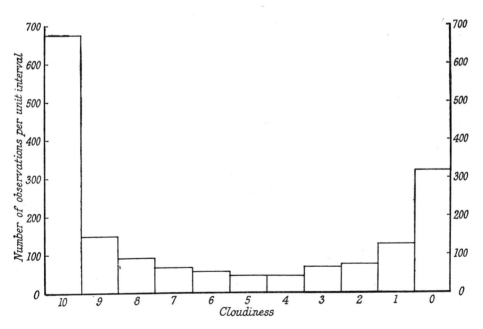

Fig. 4.15.—Cloudiness at Greenwich in July ; 1,715 observations (Table 4.14)

The histogram for these data is given in fig. 4.17. It will be seen that the distribution has three maxima, one for each of the 0–5, the 20–25 and the 70-75 age–groups.

Without looking too closely into this mortality curve we can see that the high frequency at the beginning is undoubtedly due to the heavy infantile death-rate. We can, if we choose, regard the distribution as

TABLE 4.12.—The numbers and annual values of the estates of those who had taken part in the Jacobite rising of 1715

(See fig. 4.13)

(Compiled from Cosin's " *Names of the Roman Catholics, Nonjurors, and others who Refused to take the Oaths to his late Majesty King George, etc.*"; London, 1745. Figures of very doubtful absolute value. See a note in Southey's " *Commonplace Book*," vol. 1, p. 573, quoted from the Memoirs of T. Hollis)

Annual value in £100	Number of estates	Annual value in £100	Number of estates
0– 1	1726·5	17–18	1
1– 2	280	—	—
2– 3	140·5	20–21	4
3– 4	87	21–22	1
4– 5	46·5	22–23	1
5– 6	42·5	23–24	1
6– 7	29·5	—	—
7– 8	25·5	27–28	2
8– 9	18·5	—	—
9–10	21	31–32	1
10–11	11·5	—	—
11–12	9·5	39–40	1
12–13	4	—	—
13–14	3·5	45–46	1
14–15	8	—	—
15–16	3	48–49	1
16–17	5		
		Total	2,476

made up by the superposition of three others : a J-shaped distribution for the lower years, a small one-humped distribution with its maximum about the period 20-25 years, and a skew distribution for the higher ages. This is an example of the fact we have already mentioned, that a complex distribution can sometimes be analysed into simpler types. In this particular case the analysis is likely to be of real service in actuarial work and in investigations into the causes of death.

4.26 Finally, we give an example of a pseudo-frequency-distribution of a type occasionally resorted to when the data can be classified according to a characteristic which, though not strictly speaking measurable, can nevertheless be graduated in an ordered sequence. Such a case arises fairly often in psychological work.

A list of 100 words was read out to each of 11 subjects. Subsequently, at 15-minute intervals, four fresh lists were read out which contained 25 of the words in the original and 25 new words, the four taken together accounting for the whole of the original 100. The subject had to say whether these individual words were in the original list or not, and to state whether he was certain, fairly sure, doubtful but inclined one way or the other, or merely doubtful. The various phases of belief were then allotted numbers, and ran from −3 (certainty that a word was not in the original) through 0 (doubt, without inclination one way or the other) to +3 (certainty that a word was in the original). The tabulation on p. 97 sets out the results for words in the original list (data reproduced by permission from the records of the Department of Psychology, University of St. Andrews).

TABLE 4.13.—Chrysomelidæ (beetles). Numbers of genera with 1, 2, 3, . . . species

(Compiled by Dr. J. C. Willis, F.R.S. ; cited from G. U. Yule, " A Mathematical Theory of Evolution based on the Conclusions of Dr. J. C. Willis," *Phil. Trans.*, B, 1924, **213**, 85)

Species	Genera	Species	Genera	Species	Genera
1	215	32	1	74	1
2	90	33	1	76	1
3	38	34	1	77	1
4	35	35	1	79	1
5	21	36	3	83	1
6	16	37	1	84	3
7	15	38	1	87	2
8	14	39	2	89	1
9	5	40	2	92	2
10	15	41	1	93	1
11	8	43	4	110	1
12	9	44	1	114	1
13	5	45	1	115	1
14	6	46	1	128	1
15	8	49	2	132	1
16	6	50	4	133	1
17	6	52	1	146	1
18	3	53	1	163	1
19	4	56	1	196	1
20	3	58	1	217	1
21	4	59	1	227	1
22	4	62	1	264	1
23	5	63	3	327	1
24	4	65	1	399	1
25	2	66	1	417	1
26	3	67	1	681	1
27	1	69	1		
28	3	71	1		
29	3	72	1	Total	627
30	3	73	1		

TABLE 4.14.—The frequencies of estimated intensities of cloudiness at Greenwich during the years 1890-1904 (excluding 1901) for the month of July

(See fig. 4.15)

(Data from Gertrude E. Pearse, *Biometrika*, 1928, **20A**, 336)

Degrees of cloudiness	Frequency	Degrees of cloudiness	Frequency
10	676	4	45
9	148	3	68
8	90	2	74
7	65	1	129
6	55	0	320
5	45		
		Total	1,715

TABLE 4.15.—Twelve dice thrown 4,096 times, a throw of 6 points reckoned as a success

(See fig. 4.16)

(Weldon's data ; cited by F. Y. Edgeworth, *Encyclopedia Britannica*, 11th ed., **22**, 39)

Number of successes .	0	1	2	3	4	5	6	7 and over	Total
Number of throws .	447	1,145	1,181	796	380	115	24	8	4,096

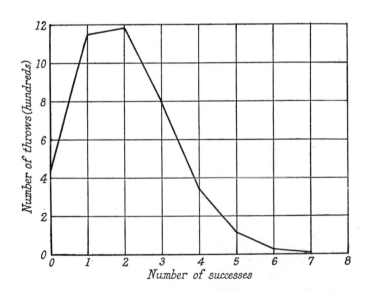

Fig. 4.16.—Frequency polygon of successes with dice throwing (Table 4.15)

TABLE 4.16.—The number of male deaths in England and Wales for 1930-32
Classified by ages at death

(See fig. 4.17)

(Data from Registrar-General's Statistical Review of England and Wales, 1933, Text)

Age at death (years)	Number of deaths	Age at death (years)	Number of deaths
0– 5	97,290	55– 60	56,639
5–10	11,532	60– 65	68,103
10–15	7,305	65– 70	80,690
15–20	13,062	70– 75	84,041
20–25	16,741	75– 80	72,180
25–30	16,126	80– 85	45,094
30–35	15,673	85– 90	19,913
35–40	18,345	90– 95	5,145
40–45	23,778	95–100	767
45–50	33,158	100 and over	48
50–55	43,812		
		Total	'729,442

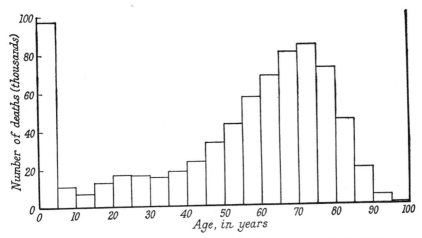

Fig. 4.17.—Histogram of number of deaths at various ages (Table 4.16)

Words in the original list were classified as—

In			Possibly either in or out	Out		
Certain	Fairly sure	Doubtful		Doubtful	Fairly sure	Certain
+3	+2	+1	0	−1	−2	−3
540	117	63	39	63	87	191

These results are very curious, and are borne out by other data of a similar kind. In particular we see that there were more cases of certainty about something which was not true than of doubt without inclination.

In this example we are clearly making some assumption in allotting numbers to various degrees of belief; but it would be impossible to measure belief on a scale, and we have to do the best we can. The numbers attached to the variate in such cases are not measures, but convenient ordinals, like the numbers attached to kings of the same name. For this reason a frequency diagram of such data can only give a very general idea of their true nature.

SUMMARY

1. Data in which the individuals are specified by the numerical values of a variable, or variate, may with convenience be arranged in a table which gives the frequency lying within successive, preferably equal, ranges of the variable. Such an arrangement is called a frequency-distribution.

2. The frequency-distribution can be represented diagrammatically by means of a frequency-polygon or a histogram.

3. The histogram is particularly appropriate to cases in which the frequency changes rapidly or the class-intervals are not all of the same width.

4. As the width of the class-intervals becomes smaller, the frequency-polygon or the histogram may be imagined to approach a smooth curve, which is called the frequency-curve.

5. A large number of frequency distributions occurring in practice fall into four types : the symmetrical, the moderately asymmetrical or skew, the extremely asymmetrical or J-shaped and the U-shaped types. Certain other distributions can be analysed into constituents each of which belongs to one of these types.

EXERCISES

4.1 If the diagram fig. 4.6 is redrawn to scales of 300 observations per interval to the inch and 4 inches of stature to the inch, what is the scale of observations to the square inch ?

If the scales are 100 observations per interval to the centimetre and 2 inches of stature to the centimetre, what is the scale of observations to the square centimetre ?

4.2 If fig. 4.10 is redrawn to scales of 900 days to the inch and 0·3 inch of barometric height to the inch, what is the scale of observations to the square inch ?

If the scales are 400 days to the centimetre and 0·1 inch of barometric height to the centimetre, what is the scale of observations to the square centimetre ?

4.3 If a frequency-polygon be drawn to represent the data of Table 4.1, what number of observations will the polygon show between birth-rates of 16·5 and 17·5 per thousand, instead of the true number 89 ?

4.4 If a frequency-polygon be drawn to represent the data of Table 4.6, what number of observations will the polygon show between head-breadths 5·95 and 6·05, instead of the true number 236 ?

4.5 Draw frequency-polygons or histograms, as the case seems to require, for the following distributions, and assign them to the four types we have enumerated in **4.18**—

(a) Size of firms in the food, drink and tobacco trades of Great Britain

The table shows the number of firms employing on an average certain numbers of persons—

(Final Report of the Fourth Census of Production, 1930, Part III)

Size of firm (average numbers employed)	11–24	25–49	50–99	100–199	200–299	300–399	400–499	500–749	750–999	1000–1,499	1,500 and over	Total
Number of firms	2,245	1,449	771	439	164	75	36	54	31	23	29	5,316

(b) The percentages of deaf-mutes among children of parents one of whom at least was a deaf-mute, for marriages producing five children or more

(Compiled from material in " *Marriages of the Deaf in America*," ed. E. A. Fay, Volta Bureau, Washington, 1898)

Percentage of deaf-mutes	Number of families	Percentage of deaf-mutes	Number of families
0–20	220	60– 80	5·5
20–40	20·5	80–100	15
40–60	12		
		Total	273

(c) Yield of grain in pounds from plots of $\frac{1}{500}$th acre in a wheat field

(Mercer and Hall, " The Experimental Error of Field Trials," *Journ. Agr. Science*, **4**, 1911, 107)

Yield of grain in pounds per $\frac{1}{500}$th acre (Central value of range)	2·8	3·0	3·2	3·4	3·6	3·8	4·0	4·2	4·4	4·6	4·8	5·0	5·2	Total
Number of plots .	4	15	20	47	63	78	88	69	59	35	10	8	4	500

(d) The frequencies of different numbers of petals for three series of ranunculus bulbosus

(H. de Vries, *Ber. deutsch. bot. Ges.*, Bd. 12, 1894, *q.v.* for details)

Number of petals	Frequency		
	Series A	Series B	Series C
5	312	345	133
6	17	24	55
7	4	7	23
8	2	—	7
9	2	2	2
10	—	—	2
11	—	2	—
Total	337	380	222

4.6 A number of perfectly spherical balls, all of the same material, give a symmetrical distribution when classified according to their diameters. Show that, if they are classified according to their weights, their frequency-distribution will be positively skew towards the higher weights.

Table to Exercise 4.6

The frequency-distribution of weights for adult males born in England, Scotland, Wales and Ireland (loc. cit., Table 4.7)

Weights were taken to the nearest pound, consequently the true class-intervals are $89 \cdot 5$–$99 \cdot 5$, $99 \cdot 5$–$109 \cdot 5$, etc.

Weight in lb	Number of men within given limits of weight. Place of birth—				Total
	England	Scotland	Wales	Ireland	
90–	2	—	—	—	2
100–	26	1	2	5	34
110–	133	8	10	1	152
120–	338	22	23	7	390
130–	694	63	68	42	867
140–	1,240	173	153	57	1,623
150–	1,075	255	178	51	1,559
160–	881	275	134	36	1,326
170–	492	168	102	25	787
180–	304	125	34	13	476
190–	174	67	14	8	263
200–	75	24	7	1	107
210–	62	14	8	1	85
220–	33	7	1	—	41
230–	10	4	2	—	16
240–	9	2	—	—	11
250–	3	4	1	—	8
260–	1	—	—	—	1
270–	—	—	—	—	—
280–	—	—	1	—	1
Total	5,552	1,212	738	247	7,749

In the light of this result compare the distributions of Table 4.7 with the distributions of the table on the previous page.

4.7 Toss a coin six times and note the number of heads. Repeat the experiment 100 times or more, and draw a frequency-polygon of your results classified according to the number of heads at each throw.

4.8 Find the frequency-distribution of 200 bars of a waltz by Strauss classified according to the number of notes in the principal melody in the treble clef of each bar, and compare it with a similar distribution from modern waltzes.

4.9 Examine qualitatively the effect on the distribution of Table 4.8 of an allowance for the fact that minors tend to overstate their age when marrying.

4.10 The distribution of a herd of cows classified according to the quantity of milk produced by each cow per week is symmetrical. The distribution of the same herd classified according to the amount of butter-fat produced by each cow per week is negatively skew towards the lower quantities. Suggest a possible explanation for this fact.

CHAPTER FIVE

AVERAGES AND OTHER MEASURES OF LOCATION

The principal characteristics of frequency-distributions

5.1 The condensation of data into a frequency-distribution is a first and necessary step in rendering a long series of observations comprehensible. But for practical purposes it is not enough, particularly when we want to compare two or more different series. As a next step we wish to be able to define quantitatively the characteristics of a frequency-distribution in as few numbers as possible.

5.2 It might seem at first sight that very difficult cases of comparison of two distributions could arise in which, for example, we had to contrast a symmetrical distribution with a J-shaped distribution. In practice, however, we rarely have to deal with such a case. Distributions drawn from similar material are usually of similar form—as, for instance, when we wish to compare the distributions of stature in two races of man, or the birth-rates in English registration districts in two successive decades, or the numbers of wealthy people in two different countries. The practical use of the various statistical quantities which we shall discuss in this and the next two chapters is based on this fact.

5.3 There are two fundamental characteristics in which similar frequency-distributions may differ—

(1) They may differ markedly in position, i.e. in the value of the variate round which they centre, as in fig. 5.1, A.

(2) They may differ in the extent to which the observations are dispersed about the central value. Figs. 5.1, B and C, show cases in which distributions differ in dispersion only, and in both dispersion and position, respectively.

To these two characteristics we may add a third group of less importance, comprising differences in skewness, peakedness, and so on.

Measures of the first character, i.e. position or location, are generally known as *averages*. Measures of the second are termed *measures of dispersion*. Measures of the properties in the third group have each their appropriate name, which we shall give when we come to consider them in detail.

The present chapter deals only with averages. Chapter 6 deals with measures of dispersion, whilst Chapter 7 deals with the remaining quantities.

Dimensions of an average

5.4 In whatever way an average is defined, it may be as well to note it is merely a certain value of the variable, and is therefore necessarily of the same *dimensions* as the variable : i.e. if the variable be a length, its average is a length ; if the variable be a percentage, its average is a percentage ; and so on. But there are several different ways of approximately defining the position of a frequency-distribution—that is, there

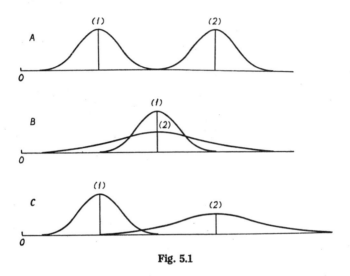

Fig. 5.1

are several different forms of average, and the question therefore arises, By what criteria are we to judge the relative merits of different forms ? What are, in fact, the desirable properties for an average to possess ?

Desiderata for a satisfactory average

5.5 (*a*) In the first place, it almost goes without saying that an average should be rigidly defined, and not left to the mere estimation of the observer. An average that was merely estimated would depend too largely on the observer as well as the data.

(*b*) An average should be based on all the observations made. If not, it is not really a characteristic of the whole distribution.

(*c*) It is desirable that the average should possess some simple and obvious properties to render its general nature readily comprehensible : an average should not be of too abstract a mathematical character.

(*d*) It is, of course, desirable that an average should be calculated with reasonable ease and rapidity. Other things being equal, the easier calculated is the better of two forms of average. At the same time great weight must not be attached to mere ease of calculation, to the neglect of other factors.

(*e*) It is desirable that the average should be as little affected as may be possible by what we have termed *fluctuations of sampling*. If different samples be drawn from the same material, however carefully they may be taken, the averages of the different samples will rarely be quite the same, but one form of average may show much greater differences than another. Of the two forms, the more stable is the better. The full discussion of this condition must, however, be postponed to a later section of this work (Chap. 18).

(*f*) Finally, by far the most important desideratum is this, that the measure chosen shall lend itself readily to algebraical treatment. If, e.g., two or more series of observations on similar material are given, the average of the combined series should be readily expressed in terms of the averages of the component series ; if a variable may be expressed as the sum of two or more others the average of the whole should be readily expressed in terms of the averages of its parts. A measure for which simple relations of this kind cannot be readily determined is likely to prove of somewhat limited application.

5.6 There are three forms of average in common use, the *arithmetic mean*, the *median* and the *mode*, the first named being by far the most widely used in general statistical work. To these may be added the *geometric mean* and the *harmonic mean*, more rarely used, but of service in special cases. We will consider these in the order named.

The arithmetic mean

5.7 The arithmetic mean of a series of values of a variable X_1, X_2, X_3, . . . X_N, N in number, is the quotient of the sum of the values by their number. That is to say, if M be the arithmetic mean,

$$M = \frac{1}{N}(X_1 + X_2 + X_3 + \ . \ . \ . \ + X_N)$$

The arithmetic mean is also denoted by placing a bar over the variate symbol, so that we may also write—

$$\bar{X} = \frac{1}{N}(X_1 + X_2 + \ . \ . \ . \ + X_N)$$

To express these formulæ more briefly by the use of the summation symbol Σ,

$$\bar{X} = M = \frac{1}{N}\Sigma(X) \qquad . \qquad . \qquad . \qquad . \qquad . \qquad (5.1)$$

The word *mean* or *average* alone, without qualification, is very generally used to denote this particular form of average ; that is to say, when anyone speaks of " the mean " or " the average " of a series of observations, it may, as a rule, be assumed that the arithmetic mean is meant.

5.8 It is evident that the arithmetic mean fulfils the conditions laid down in (*a*) and (*b*) of **5.5**, for it is rigidly defined and based on all the observations made. Further, it fulfils condition (*c*), for its general nature is readily comprehensible. If the wages-bill for N workmen is $£P$, the arithmetic mean wage, P/N pounds, is the amount that each would receive if the whole sum available were divided equally between them : conversely, if we are told that the mean wage is $£M$, we know this means that the wages-bill is NM pounds. Similarly, if N families possess a total of C children, the mean number of children per family is C/N—the number that each family would possess if the children were shared uniformly. Conversely, if the mean number of children per family is M, the total number of children in N families is NM. The arithmetic mean expresses, in fact, a simple relation between the whole and its parts.

The mean is also satisfactory as regards conditions (*e*) and (*f*), but we shall have to defer proof of this statement for the present.

Calculation of the arithmetic mean

5.9 As regards condition (*d*), simplicity of calculation, the mean takes a high place. In the cases just cited, it will be noted that the mean is actually determined without even the necessity of determining or noting all the individual values of the variable : to get the mean wage we need not know the wages of every hand, but only the wages-bill ; to get the mean number of children per family we need not know the number in each family, but only the total. If this total is not given, but we have to deal with a moderate number of observations—so few (say 30 or 40) that it is hardly worth while compiling the frequency-distribution—the arithmetic mean is calculated directly as suggested by the definition, i.e. all the values observed are added together and the total divided by the number of observations.

5.10 But if the number of observations be large, the process of adding together all the values of the variate may be prohibitively lengthy. It may be shortened considerably by forming the frequency-table and treating all the values in each class as if they were identical with the mid-value of the class-interval, a process which in general gives an approximation that is quite sufficiently exact for practical purposes if the class-interval has been taken moderately small. In this process each class-frequency is multiplied by the mid-value of the interval, the products added together, and the total divided by the number of observations. If f denote the frequency of any class, X the mid-value of the corresponding class-interval, the value of the mean so obtained may be written—

$$M = \frac{1}{N}\Sigma(fX) \qquad . \qquad . \qquad . \qquad . \qquad . \qquad (5.2)$$

5.11 But this procedure is still further abbreviated in practice by the following artifices : (1) The class-interval is treated as the unit of measurement throughout the arithmetic ; (2) the difference between the mean and the mid-value of some arbitrarily chosen class-interval is computed instead of the absolute value of the mean.

If A be the arbitrarily chosen value and

$$X = A + \xi \qquad . \qquad . \qquad . \qquad . \qquad (5.3)$$

then

$$\Sigma(fX) = \Sigma(fA) + \Sigma(f\xi)$$

or, since A is a constant,

$$M = A + \frac{1}{N}\Sigma(f\xi) \qquad . \qquad . \qquad . \qquad . \qquad (5.4)$$

The calculation of $\Sigma(fX)$ is therefore replaced by the calculation of $\Sigma(f\xi)$. The advantage of this is that the class-frequencies need only be multiplied by small integral numbers ; for A being the mid-value of a class-interval, and X the mid-value of another, and the class-interval being treated as a unit, the ξ's must be a series of integers proceeding from zero at the arbitrary origin A. To keep the values of ξ as small as possible, A should be chosen near the middle of the range.

It may be mentioned here that $\frac{1}{N}\Sigma(\xi)$, or $\frac{1}{N}\Sigma(f\xi)$ for the grouped distribution, is sometimes termed the *first moment* of the distribution about the arbitrary origin A.

Example 5.1.—As an example, let us find the arithmetic mean of the heights in the "total" column of Table 4.7. In this case the class-interval is a unit (1 inch), so the value of $M - A$ is given directly by dividing $\Sigma(f\xi)$ by N. The student must notice that, measures having been made to the nearest eighth of an inch, the mid-values of the intervals are $57\frac{7}{16}$, $58\frac{7}{16}$. etc., and not $57\cdot5$, $58\cdot5$, etc.

Calculation of the arithmetic mean stature of male adults in the British Isles from the figures of Table 4.7, p. 82

(1) Height, inches	(2) Frequency f	(3) Deviation from arbitrary value A ξ	(4) Product $f\xi$
57–	2	−10	− 20
58–	4	− 9	− 36
59–	14	− 8	− 112
60–	41	− 7	− 287
61–	83	− 6	− 498
62–	169	− 5	− 845
63–	394	− 4	−1576
64–	669	− 3	−2007
65–	990	− 2	−1980
66–	1223	− 1	−1223
67–	1329	0	−8584
68–	1230	+ 1	1230
69–	1063	+ 2	2126
70–	646	+ 3	1938
71–	392	+ 4	1568
72–	202	+ 5	1010
73–	79	+ 6	474
74–	32	+ 7	224
75–	16	+ 8	128
76–	5	+ 9	45
77–	2	+10	20
Total	8585	—	+8763

$$\Sigma(f\xi) = +8{,}763 - 8{,}584 = +179$$
$$M - A = +\frac{179}{8{,}585} = +0 \cdot 02 \text{ class-intervals or inches.}$$
$$\therefore\ M = 67\tfrac{7}{16} + 0 \cdot 02 = 67 \cdot 46 \text{ inches.}$$

5.12 As calculations of the mean constantly have to be made, the student should familiarise himself with the process we have just illustrated, and note that a check can always be effected on the arithmetic in the following way—

Since
$$f(\xi+1) = f\xi + f$$
$$\Sigma\{f(\xi+1)\} = \Sigma(f\xi) + \Sigma(f)$$
$$\Sigma\{f(\xi+1)\} - \Sigma(f\xi) = \Sigma(f)$$
$$= \text{Total frequency}$$

Hence, if we tabulate the values of $f(\xi+1)$ as well as those of $f\xi$ and find their totals, the difference must, if the arithmetic is correct, be equal to the total frequency.

5.13   It will be evident that a classification by unequal intervals is, at best, a hindrance in the calculation of the mean, and the use of an indefinite interval at the end of the distribution renders exact calculation impossible.   The following example illustrates the calculation for unequal class-intervals and the arithmetical check to which we have just referred.

Example 5.2.—Data from Table 4.11, page 89.   What is the average age at death from scarlet fever ?

Here there is a change of the class-interval at the five-year point.   We take a year to be the unit, and the centre of the interval 5–10 years as an arbitrary origin, which means that $A = 7 \cdot 5$ years.

Calculation of the arithmetic mean age of persons dying from scarlet fever in the United Kingdom in 1933 (Table 4.11, p. 89)

Age Years	Frequency f	Deviation from A ξ	$f\xi$	$f(\xi+1)$
0–	16	−7	− 112	− 96
1–	69	−6	− 414	− 345
2–	89	−5	− 445	− 356
3–	74	−4	-- 296	− 222
4–	74	−3	− 222	− 148
5–	213	0	−1489	−1167
				213
10–	70	5	350	420
15–	27	10	270	297
20–	26	15	390	416
25–	17	20	340	357
30–	12	25	300	312
35–	11	30	330	341
40–	10	35	350	360
45–	6	40	240	246
50–	7	45	315	322
55–	5	50	250	255
60–	—	55	—	—
65–	1	60	60	61
70–	1	65	65	66
75–	1	70	70	71
Total	729	—	+3330	+3737

Hence,
$$\Sigma(f\xi) = 3330 - 1489 = 1841$$
and
$$\Sigma \{f(\xi+1)\} = 3737 - 1167 = 2570$$
and the difference $2570 - 1841 = 729$, as it should.

Hence,
$$M - A = \frac{1841}{729} = 2 \cdot 525 \text{ years}$$
and
$$M = 7 \cdot 5 + 2 \cdot 525 = 10 \cdot 025 \text{ years}$$

5.14 We return again below, in **5.16** (*c*), to the question of the errors caused by the assumption that all values within the same interval may be treated as approximately the mid-value of the interval. It is sufficient to say here that the error is in general very small and of uncertain sign for a distribution of the symmetrical or only moderately asymmetrical type, provided, of course, the class-interval is not large. In the case of the " J-shaped " or extremely asymmetrical distribution, however, the error is evidently of definite sign, for in all the intervals the frequency is piled up at the limit lying towards the greatest frequency, i.e. the lower end of the range in the case of the illustrations given in Chapter 4, and is not evenly distributed over the interval. In distributions of such a type the intervals must be made very small indeed to secure an approximately accurate value for the mean. The student should test for himself the effect of different groupings in two or three different cases, so as to get some idea of the degree of inaccuracy to be expected.

5.15 If a diagram has been drawn representing the frequency-distribution, the position of the mean may conveniently be indicated by a vertical through the corresponding point on the base. In a moderately asymmetrical distribution the mean lies on the side of the greatest frequency towards the longer " tail " of the distribution : *M* in fig. 5.2 shows the

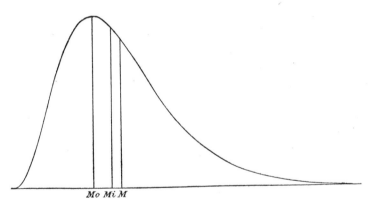

Mo Mi M

Fig. 5.2.—Mean *M*, median *Mi* and mode *Mo* of the ideal moderately asymmetrical distribution

position of the mean in an ideal distribution. In a symmetrical distribution the mean coincides with the centre of symmetry. The student should mark the position of the mean in the diagram of every frequency-distribution that he draws, and so accustom himself to thinking of the mean not as an abstraction, but always in relation to the frequency-distribution of the variable concerned.

Properties of the arithmetic mean

5.16   The following are important properties of the arithmetic mean, and the examples illustrate the facility of its algebraic treatment—

(*a*) The sum of the deviations from the mean, taken with their proper signs, is zero.

This follows at once from equation (5.4) : for if M and A are identical, evidently $\Sigma(f\xi)$ must be zero.

(*b*) If a series of N observations of a variable X consist of, say, two component series, the mean of the whole series can be readily expressed in terms of the means of the two components.   For if we denote the values in the first series by X_1 and in the second series by X_2,

$$\Sigma(X) = \Sigma(X_1) + \Sigma(X_2)$$

that is, if there be N_1 observations in the first series and N_2 in the second, and the means of the two series be M_1, M_2, respectively,

$$NM = N_1 M_1 + N_2 M_2 \qquad . \qquad . \qquad . \qquad . \quad (5.5)$$

For example, we find from the data of Table 4.7,
Mean stature of the 346 men born in Ireland $= 67 \cdot 78$ inches
,,   ,,   ,,   741 ,,   ,,   Wales $= 66 \cdot 62$,,

Hence the mean stature of the 1087 men born in the two countries is given by the equation

$$1087 M = (346 \times 67 \cdot 78) + (741 \times 66 \cdot 62)$$

that is, $M = 66 \cdot 99$ inches.

It is evident that the form of the relation (5.5) is quite general : if there are r series of observations $X_1, X_2, \ldots X_r$, the mean M of the whole series is related to the means $M_1, M_2, \ldots M_r$ of the component series by the equation

$$NM = N_1 M_1 + N_2 M_2 + \ldots + N_r M_r \, . \qquad . \quad (5.6)$$

For the convenient checking of arithmetic, it is useful to note that, if the same arbitrary origin A for the deviations ξ be taken in each case, we must have, denoting the component series by the subscripts $1, 2, \ldots r$ as before,

$$\Sigma(f\xi) = \Sigma(f_1\xi_1) + \Sigma(f_2\xi_2) + \ldots + \Sigma(f_r\xi_r) \, . \qquad . \quad (5.7)$$

The agreement of these totals accordingly checks the work.

As an important corollary to the general relation (5.6), it may be noted that the approximate value for the mean obtained from any frequency-distribution is the same whether we assume (1) that all the values in any class are identical with the mid-value of the class-interval, or (2) that the mean of the values in the class is identical with the mid-value of the class-interval.

(c) The mean of all the sums or differences of corresponding observations in two series (of equal numbers of observations) is equal to the sum or difference of the means of the two series.

This follows almost at once. For if

$$X = X_1 \pm X_2$$
$$\Sigma(X) = \Sigma(X_1) \pm \Sigma(X_2)$$

That is, if M, M_1, M_2 be the respective means,

$$M = M_1 \pm M_2 \qquad . \qquad . \qquad . \qquad . \qquad . \qquad (5.8)$$

Evidently the form of this result is again quite general, so that if

$$X = X_1 \pm X_2 \pm \ldots \pm X_r$$
$$M = M_1 \pm M_2 \pm \ldots \pm M_r \qquad . \qquad . \qquad . \qquad (5.9)$$

As a useful illustration of equation (5.8), consider the case of measurements of any kind that are subject (as indeed all measures must be) to greater or less errors. The actual measurement X in any such case is the algebraic sum of the true measurement X_1 and an error X_2. The mean of the actual measurements M is therefore the sum of the true mean M_1, and the arithmetic mean of the errors M_2. If, and only if, the latter be zero, will the observed mean be identical with the true mean. Errors of grouping (5.14) are a case in point.

The Median

5.17 The median may be defined as the middlemost or central value of the variable when the values are ranged in order of magnitude, or as the value such that greater and smaller values occur with equal frequency. In the case of a frequency-curve, the median may be defined as that value of the variable the vertical through which divides the area of the curve into two equal parts, as the vertical through Mi in fig. 5.2.

The median, like the mean, fulfils the conditions (b) and (c) of **5.5**, seeing that it is based on all the observations made, and that it possesses the simple property of being the central or middlemost value, so that its nature is obvious.

5.18 But the definition does not necessarily lead in all cases to a determinate value. If there be an odd number of different values of X observed, say $2n+1$, the $(n+1)$th in order of magnitude is the only value fulfilling the definition. But if there be an even number, say $2n$ different values, any value between the nth and $(n+1)$th fulfils the conditions. In such a case it appears to be usual to take the mean of the nth and $(n+1)$th values as the median, but this is a convention supplementary to the definition.

5.19 It should also be noted that in the case of a discontinuous variable the second form of the definition in general breaks down : if we range the values in order there is always a middlemost value (provided the number of observations be odd), but there is not, as a rule, any value such that greater and less values occur with equal frequency. Thus, in Table 4.2 we see that 45 per cent of the poppy capsules had 12 or fewer stigmatic rays, 55 per cent had 13 or more ; similarly, 61 per cent had 13 or fewer rays, 39 per cent had 14 or more. There is no number of rays such that the frequencies in excess and defect are equal. In the case of the butter-cups of Exercise 4.5 (*d*), page 100, there is no number of petals that even remotely fulfils the required condition. An analogous difficulty may arise, it may be remarked, even in the case of an odd number of observations of a continuous variable if the number of observations be small and several of the observed values identical.

The median is therefore a form of average of most uncertain meaning in cases of strictly discontinuous variation, for it may be exceeded by 5, 10, 15 or 20 per cent only of the observed values, instead of by 50 per cent : its use in such cases is to be deprecated, and is perhaps best avoided in any case, whether the variation be continuous or discontinuous, in which small series of observations have to be dealt with.

Determination of the median

5.20 When all the values of the variate are given and the total frequency is small, the median can be determined by inspection as the middlemost value or, if there is no such value, as the mean of the two middlemost values. When the distribution is given as a frequency-distribution, however, a certain amount of approximation is necessary, as in the case of the calculation of the mean.

For the frequency-distribution of a continuous variable a sufficiently approximate value of the median can be obtained by interpolation. If the total frequency is large it is sufficient to assume that the values in each class are uniformly distributed throughout the interval.

Example 5.3.—Let us determine the median of the distribution whose mean we found in Example 5.1. The work may be indicated thus—

Half the total number of observations (8585) .	= 4292·5
Total frequency under $66\frac{15}{16}$ inches . .	= 3589
Difference	= 703·5
Frequency in next interval	= 1329

Hence we take the median to be—

$$66\tfrac{15}{16} + \frac{703 \cdot 5}{1329} \times 1$$

$$= 67 \cdot 47 \text{ inches}$$

The difference between the median and mean in this case is therefore only about one-hundredth of an inch.

Example 5.4.—To find the median of the distribution of Example 5.2.

Half the total number of observations . .	$= 364 \cdot 5$
Total frequency under 5 years . . .	$= 322$
Difference	$= 42 \cdot 5$
Frequency in next interval	$= 213$

Hence we take the median to be—

$$5 + \frac{42 \cdot 5}{213} \times 5$$

$$= 6 \text{ years}$$

Here the median is very far from coinciding with the mean.

Graphical determination of the median

5.21 Graphical interpolation may, if desired, be substituted for arithmetical interpolation. Taking the figures of Example 5.1, we see that the number of men with height less than $65\tfrac{15}{16}$ is 2366, less than $66\tfrac{15}{16}$ is 3589, less than $67\tfrac{15}{16}$ is 4918, and less than $68\tfrac{15}{16}$ is 6148.

Plot the numbers of men with height not exceeding each value of X to the corresponding value of X on squared paper, to a good large scale, as in fig. 5.3, and draw a smooth curve through the points thus obtained, preferably with the aid of one of the " curves," splines or flexible curves sold by instrument-makers for the purpose. The point at which the smooth curve so obtained cuts the horizontal line corresponding to a total frequency $N/2 = 4292 \cdot 5$ gives the median. In general the curve is so flat that the value obtained by this graphical method does not differ appreciably from that calculated arithmetically (the arithmetical process assuming that the curve is a straight line between the points on either side of the median) ; if the curvature is considerable, the graphical value —assuming, of course, careful and accurate draughtsmanship—is to be preferred to the arithmetical value, as it does not involve the crude assumption that the frequency is *uniformly* distributed over the interval in which the median lies.

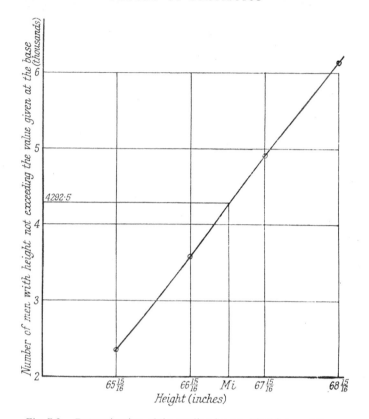

Fig. 5.3.—Determination of the median by graphical interpolation

Comparison of the mean and the median

5.22 If we adopt the convention that the median of an even number of observations is midway between the two central values, both the mean and the median satisfy the first three of the desiderata we enumerated in 5.5 ; that is to say, they are rigidly defined, based on all the observations, and are readily comprehensible. In the remaining three, however, they differ considerably.

5.23 As regards ease of calculation, the median has distinct advantages over the mean.

Whether the stability of the median under fluctuations of sampling is greater than that of the mean depends to some extent on the form of the distribution which is being sampled. In general, the mean is the more stable, but cases occur in which the median is preferable (cf. **5.24** (*d*) below, and Chap. 18).

When, however, the ease of algebraical treatment of the two forms of average is compared, the superiority lies wholly on the side of the mean.

As was shown in **5.16,** when several series of observations are combined into a single series, the mean of the resultant distribution can be simply expressed in terms of the means of the components. Expression of the median of the resultant distribution in terms of the medians of the components is, however, not merely complex and difficult, but usually impossible : the value of the resultant median depends on the forms of the component distributions, and not on their medians alone. If two symmetrical distributions of the same form and with the same numbers of observations, but with different medians, be combined, the resultant median must evidently (from symmetry) coincide with the resultant mean, i.e. lie half-way between the means of the components. But if the two components be asymmetrical, or (whatever their form) if the degrees of dispersion or numbers of observations in the two series be different, the resultant median will not coincide with the resultant mean, nor with any other simply assignable value. It is impossible, therefore, to give any theorem for medians analogous to equations (5.5) and (5.6) for means. It is equally impossible to give any theorem analogous to equations (5.8) and (5.9) of **5.16.** The median of the sum or difference of pairs of corresponding observations in two series is not, in general, equal to the sum or difference of the medians of the two series ; the median value of a measurement subject to error is not necessarily identical with the true median, even if the median error be zero, i.e. if positive and negative errors be equally frequent.

5.24 These limitations render the applications of the median in any work in which theoretical considerations are necessary comparatively circumscribed. On the other hand, the median may have an advantage over the mean for special reasons.

(*a*) It is very readily calculated ; a factor to which, however, as already stated, too much weight ought not to be attached.

(*b*) It is readily obtained, without the necessity of measuring all the objects to be observed, in any case in which the objects can be arranged in order of magnitude. If, for instance, a number of men be ranked in order of stature, the stature of the middlemost is the median, and he alone need be measured. (On the other hand, it is useless in the cases cited at the end of **5.8** ; the median wage cannot be found from the total of the wages-bill, and the total of the wages-bill is not known when the median is given.)

(*c*) It is sometimes useful as a makeshift, when the observations are so given that the calculation of the mean is impossible, owing, e.g., to a final indefinite class.

(*d*) The median *may* sometimes be preferable to the mean, owing to its being less affected by abnormally large or small values of the variable. The stature of a giant would have no more influence on the median stature of a number of men than the stature of any other man whose height is only just greater than the median. If a number of men enjoy incomes closely clustering round a median of £500 a year, the median will be no more affected by the addition to the group of a man with an income of £50,000 than by the addition of a man with an income of £5,000, or even £600. If observations of any kind are liable to present occasional *greatly* outlying values of this sort (whether real, or due to errors or blunders), the median will be more stable and less affected by fluctuations of sampling than the arithmetic mean (cf. Chap. 18).

(*e*) It may be added that the median is, in a certain sense, a particularly real and natural form of average, for the object or individual that is the median object or individual on any one system of measuring the character with which we are concerned will remain the median on any other method of measurement which leaves the objects in the same relative order. Thus a batch of eggs representing eggs of the median price, when prices are reckoned at so much per dozen, will remain a batch representing the median price when prices are reckoned at so many eggs to the shilling.

The mode

5.25   The mode is the value of the variable corresponding to the maximum of the ideal curve which gives the closest possible fit to the actual distribution. It represents the value which is most frequent or typical, the value which is, in fact, the fashion (*la mode*).[1] The mode is sometimes denoted by writing the sign $\smile$ over the variate symbol, e.g. $\breve{X}$ means the mode of the values $X_1, X_2, \ldots X_N$.

There is evidently something anticipatory about this definition, for we have not yet defined what we mean by " closest possible fit." For the present the student must content himself with intuitive ideas on this head. Nor have we given a method of finding the curve of closest fit, which would be a necessary preliminary to ascertaining the mode.

5.26   It is, in fact, difficult to determine the mode for such distributions as arise in practice, particularly by elementary methods. It is no use giving merely the mid-value of the class-interval into which the greatest frequency falls, for this is entirely dependent on the choice of the scale of class-intervals. It is no use making the class-intervals very small to avoid error on that account, for the class-frequencies will then become small and the distribution irregular. What we want to arrive at is the mid-value of the interval for which the frequency would be a maximum, if the intervals could be made indefinitely small, and at the same time the number of observations be so increased that the class-frequencies

---

[1] Unless we state expressly to the contrary, we shall be thinking of single-humped distributions in talking of " the " mode. When the distribution is of the complicated form of fig. 4.17 there may be more than one mode. Such distributions are therefore sometimes called multimodal. The mean and the median are still unique for such distributions.

should run smoothly. As the observations cannot, in a practical case, be indefinitely increased, it is evident that some process of smoothing out the irregularities that occur in the actual distribution must be adopted, in order to ascertain the approximate value of the mode. But there is only one smoothing process that is really satisfactory, in so far as every observation can be taken into account in the determination, and that is the method of fitting an ideal frequency-curve of given equation to the actual figures. The value of the variable corresponding to the maximum of the fitted curve is then taken as the mode, in accordance with our definition. The determination of the mode by this—the only strictly satisfactory—method must, however, be left to the more advanced student. The methods of curve-fitting which we shall discuss in Chapter 15 are not appropriate to the fitting of frequency-curves, but we give an approximate method which is of use in certain cases in **25.21.**

Empirical relation between mean, median and mode

5.27 For a symmetrical distribution, mean, median and mode coincide, as will be evident on a little consideration. For other distributions, as a rule, they do not. Fig. 5.2 shows the position of the three in a moderately skew distribution.

There is an approximate relation between mean, median and mode which appears to hold good with surprising closeness for moderately asymmetrical distributions, approaching the ideal type of fig. 4.7, and it is one that should be borne in mind as giving—roughly, at all events— the relative values of these three averages for a great many cases with which the student will have to deal. It is expressed by the equation

$$\text{Mode} = \text{Mean} - 3(\text{Mean} - \text{Median})$$

That is to say, the median lies one-third of the distance mean to mode from the mean towards the mode. The student will find it easy to remember this relation if he notes that mean, median and mode occur in the same order (or the reverse order) as in the dictionary, and that the median is nearer to the mean, also as in the dictionary.

The following table gives the true mode and the mode calculated in accordance with the above formula for certain skew distributions of the type of fig. 4.10—

Comparison of the approximate and true modes in the case of five distributions of the height of the barometer for daily observations at the stations named

(Distributions given by Karl Pearson and Alice Lee, *Phil. Trans.*, A. 1897, **190**, 423)

Station	Mean	Median	Approximate Mode	True Mode
Southampton .	29·981	30·000	30·038	30·039
Londonderry .	29·891	29·915	29·963	29·960
Carmarthen .	29·952	29·974	30·018	30·013
Glasgow . .	29·886	29·906	29·946	29·967
Dundee .	29·870	29·890	29·930	29·951

It will be seen that the true and approximate values are extremely close, except in the case of Dundee and Glasgow, where the divergence reaches two-hundredths of an inch.

5.28 Summing up the preceding paragraphs, we may say that the mean is the form of average to use for all general purposes ; it is simply calculated, its value is nearly always determinate, its algebraic treatment is particularly easy, and in most cases it is rather less affected than the median by errors of sampling. The median is, it is true, somewhat more easily calculated from a given frequency-distribution than is the mean ; it is sometimes a useful makeshift, and in a certain class of cases it is more and not less stable than the mean ; but its use is undesirable in cases of discontinuous variation, its value may be indeterminate, and its algebraic treatment is difficult and often impossible. The mode, finally, is a form of average hardly suitable for elementary use, owing to the difficulty of its determination, but at the same time it represents an important value of the variable. The arithmetic mean should invariably be employed unless there is some very definite reason for the choice of another form of average, and the elementary student will do very well if he limits himself to its use. Objection is sometimes taken to the use of the mean in the case of asymmetrical frequency-distributions, on the ground that the mean is not the mode, and that its value is consequently misleading. But no one in the least degree familiar with the manifold forms taken by frequency-distributions would regard the two as in general identical ; and while the importance of the mode is a good reason for stating its value in addition to that of the mean, it cannot replace the latter. The objection, it may be noted, would apply with almost equal force to the median, for, as we have seen (**5.27**), the difference between mode and median is usually about two-thirds of the difference between mode and mean.

The geometric mean

5.29 The geometric mean G of a series of values $X_1, X_2, X_3. \ldots X_N$ is defined by the relation

$$G = (X_1 X_2 X_3 \ldots X_N)^{1/N} \qquad . \qquad . \qquad . \quad (5.10)$$

The definition may also be expressed in terms of logarithms—

$$\log G = \frac{1}{N} \Sigma (\log X) \qquad . \qquad . \qquad . \quad (5.11)$$

that is to say, the logarithm of the geometric mean of a series of values is the arithmetic mean of their logarithms.

The geometric mean of a given series of quantities is always less than their arithmetic mean ; the student will find a proof in most textbooks of algebra. The magnitude of the difference depends largely on the amount of dispersion of the variable in proportion to the magnitude of the mean (cf. Exercise 6.12, p. 150). The geometric mean is necessarily zero, it should be noticed, if even a single value of X is zero, and it may become imaginary if negative values occur.

Calculation of the geometric mean

5.30 From equation (5.11) it will be evident that the calculation of the geometric mean is exactly the same as that of the arithmetic mean except that instead of adding the values of the variable we add the logarithms of those values. If there are many values we can draw up a frequency table for the logarithms and proceed as in Examples 5.1 and 5.2.

Properties of the geometric mean

5.31 The geometric mean is rigidly defined and takes account of all the observations. It is also fairly easily calculated, though not so easily as the arithmetic mean. It has, however, no simple and obvious properties which render its general nature readily comprehensible. This, coupled with its rather abstract mathematical character, has prevented it from coming into general use as a representative average.

5.32 At the same time, as the following examples show, the geometric mean possesses some important properties, and is readily treated algebraically in certain cases.

(a) If the series of observations X consist of r component series, there being N_1 observations in the first, N_2 in the second, and so on, the geometric mean G of the whole series can be readily expressed in terms of the geometric means G_1, G_2, etc., of the component series. For evidently we have at once (as in **5.16** (b))—

$$N\log G = N_1\log G_1 + N_2\log G_2 + \ldots + N_r\log G_r \qquad (5.12)$$

(b) The geometric mean of the ratios of corresponding observations in two series is equal to the ratio of their geometric means. For if

$$X = X_1/X_2$$
$$\log X = \log X_1 - \log X_2$$

then summing for all pairs of X_1's and X_2's—

$$G = G_1/G_2 \qquad . \qquad . \qquad . \qquad . \qquad . \qquad . \qquad (5.13)$$

(c) Similarly, if a variable X is given as the product of any number of others, i.e. if

$$X = X_1 X_2 X_3 \ldots X_r$$

$X_1, X_2, \ldots X_r$, denoting corresponding observations in r different series, the geometric mean G of X is expressed in terms of the geometric means $G_1, G_2, \ldots G_r$ of $X_1, X_2, \ldots X_r$, by the relation

$$G = G_1 G_2 G_3 \ldots G_r \qquad . \qquad . \qquad . \qquad . \quad (5.14)$$

That is to say, the geometric mean of the product is the product of the geometric means.

5.33 The geometric mean finds applications in several cases where we have to deal with a quantity whose changes tend to be directly proportional to the quantity itself, e.g. populations; or where we are dealing with an average of ratios, as in index-numbers of prices. Suppose, for instance, we wish to estimate the numbers of a population midway between two epochs (say two census years) at which the population is known. If nothing is known concerning the increase of the population save that the numbers recorded at the first census were P_0 and at the second census n years later P_n, the most reasonable assumption to make is that the percentage increase in each year has been the same, so that the populations in successive years form a geometric series, $P_0 r$ being the population a year after the first census, $P_0 r^2$ two years after the first census, and so on, so that

$$P_n = P_0 r^n \qquad . \qquad . \qquad . \qquad . \qquad . \quad (5.15)$$

The population midway between the two censuses is therefore

$$P_{n/2} = P_0 r^{n/2} = (P_0 P_n)^{\frac{1}{2}} . \qquad . \qquad . \qquad . \quad (5.16)$$

i.e. the geometric mean of the numbers given by the two censuses. This result must, however, be used with discretion. The rate of increase of population is not necessarily, or even usually, constant over any considerable period of time particularly where immigration or emigration are serious factors.

We shall have more to say about the geometric mean in Chapter 25, which deals with index-numbers.

The harmonic mean

5.34 The harmonic mean of a series of quantities is the reciprocal of the arithmetic mean of their reciprocals; that is, if H be the harmonic mean,

$$\frac{1}{H} = \frac{1}{N} \Sigma \left(\frac{1}{X} \right) \qquad . \qquad . \qquad . \qquad . \quad (5.17)$$

The following illustration will serve to show the method of calculation—

Example 5.5.—The table gives the number of litters of mice, in certain breeding experiments, with given numbers (X) in the litter.   (Data from A. D. Darbishire, *Biometrika*, 1903, **3**, 30.)

Number in litter X	Number of litters f	f/X
1	7	7·000
2	11	5·500
3	16	5·333
4	17	4·250
5	26	5·200
6	31	5·167
7	11	1·571
8	1	0·125
9	1	0·111
—	121	34·257

$$\text{Whence} \quad \frac{1}{H} = \frac{34\cdot257}{121} = 0\cdot2831$$

$$H = 3\cdot532$$

The arithmetic mean is 4·587, more than a unit greater.

Reciprocal character of arithmetic and harmonic means

5.35   Prices may be stated in two different ways which are reciprocally related, the resulting arithmetic mean of the one being the harmonic mean of the other.   Supposing we had 100 returns of retail prices of eggs, 50 returns showing six eggs to the shilling, 30 seven to the shilling, and 20 five to the shilling ;   then the mean number per shilling would be 6·1, equivalent to a price of 1·967d. per egg.   But if the prices had been quoted in the form usual for other commodities, we should have had 50 returns showing a price of 2d. per egg, 30 showing a price of 1·714d. and 20 a price of 2·4d. :   arithmetic mean 1·994d., a slightly greater value than the harmonic mean of 1·967.

The harmonic mean of a series of quantities is always lower than the geometric mean of the same quantities, and *a fortiori*, lower than the arithmetic mean, the amount of difference depending largely on the magnitude of the dispersion relatively to the magnitude of the mean (cf. Exercise 6.13, p. 150).

SUMMARY

1. Measures of the location or position of a frequency-distribution are called averages.

2. There are three types of average in general use, the mean (arithmetic, geometric and harmonic), the median and the mode.

3. The arithmetic mean of N values $X_1, X_2, \ldots X_N$ is given by

$$M = \frac{1}{N}\Sigma(X)$$

The geometric mean is given by

$$G = (X_1 \ldots X_N)^{1/N}$$

or

$$\log G = \frac{1}{N}\Sigma(\log X)$$

The harmonic mean is given by

$$\frac{1}{H} = \frac{1}{N}\Sigma\left(\frac{1}{X}\right)$$

4. The median is the central value of the variable when the values are ranged in order of magnitude ; if the number of values is even, the median is conventionally taken to be the arithmetic mean of the two central values.

5. The mode is the value of the variate corresponding to the maximum of the ideal curve which gives the closest possible fit to the actual distribution.

6. For distributions of moderate skewness there is an empirical relationship between the mean, the median and the mode expressed by the equation

$$\text{Mode} = \text{Mean} - 3(\text{Mean} - \text{Median})$$

EXERCISES

5.1   Verify the following means and medians from the data of Table 4.7, page 82—

	England	Scotland	Wales	Ireland
Stature in inches for adult males in				
Mean . .	67·31	68·55	66·62	67·78
Median . .	67·35	68·48	66·56	67·69

In the calculation of the means use the same arbitrary origin as in Example 5.1 and check your work by the method of **5.16** (*b*).

5.2   The mean of 13 numbers is 10, and the mean of 42 other numbers is 16.   Find the mean of the 55 numbers taken together.

5.3   Find the mean weight of adult males in the United Kingdom from the data in the last column of Exercise 4.6, page 100.   Find the median weight, and hence find the approximate mode by the relation of **5.27**.

5.4 Similarly, find the mean, median and approximate value of the mode for the distribution of fecundity in race-horses, Table **4.9**, page 86.

5.5 Using a graphical method, find the median income subject to sur- or super-tax in the financial year 1931 from the data of Table **4.5**, page 77.

5.6 Find the arithmetic mean of the first n natural numbers and show that it coincides with the median.

5.7 (Data from *Agricultural Statistics, England and Wales*, Part 2, 1932.) The figures in columns 1 and 2 of the small table below show the index-numbers of prices of certain commodities in the harvest years 1926 and 1931, the years 1911–13 being taken as 100. In column 3 have been added the ratios of the index-numbers in 1931 to those in 1926, the latter being taken as 100.

Find the average ratio of prices in 1931 to those in 1926—

    (1) From the arithmetic mean of the ratios in column 3.
    (2) From the ratio of the arithmetic means of columns 1 and 2.
    (3) From the ratio of the geometric means of columns 1 and 2.
    (4) From the geometric mean of the ratios of column 3.
Note that, by **5.32**, the last two methods must give the same result.

Commodity	Index-number of price in		Ratios
	1926	1931	'31 / '26
	(1)	(2)	(3)
1. Wheat	157	79	50·3
2. Fat cattle	131	118	90·1
3. Milk	163	139	85·3
4. Eggs	149	110	73·8
5. Fruit	165	132	80·0
6. Vegetables	135	158	117·0

5.8 Find the arithmetic and geometric means of the series 1, 2, 4, 8, 16, . . . 2^n. Find also the harmonic mean.

5.9 Supposing the frequencies of values 0, 1, 2, . . . of a variable to be given by the terms of the binomial series

$$q^n, \quad nq^{n-1}p, \quad \frac{n(n-1)}{1.2}q^{n-2}p^2, \quad \ldots$$

where $p+q=1$, find the mean.

5.10 Show that, in finding the arithmetic mean of a set of readings on a thermometer, it does not matter whether we measure temperature in Centigrade or Fahrenheit degrees, but that in finding the geometric mean it does matter.

5.11   (Data from Census of 1901.)   The table below shows the population
of the rural sanitary districts of Essex, the urban sanitary districts (other
than the borough of West Ham), and the borough of West Ham, at the
censuses of 1891 and 1901.   Estimate the total population of the county
at a date midway between the two censuses, (1) on the assumption that
the percentage rate of increase was constant for the county as a whole ;
(2) on the assumption that the percentage rate of increase was constant
in each group of districts and the borough of West Ham.

Essex	Population	
	1891	1901
Rural districts . . .	232,867	240,776
West Ham . . .	204,903	267,358
Other urban districts .	345,604	575,864
Total	783,374	1,083,998

5.12   (Data from *Agricultural Statistics*, Part 2, 1932.)   The following
statement shows the monthly average prices of eggs in England and Wales
in 1932, as compiled from returns from certain markets for National Mark
Specials and English Ordinaries, First Quality, per 120—

Month	N.M. Specials	English Ordinaries, First Quality
	s. d.	s. d.
January . . .	18 11	15 2
February . . .	15 0	12 11
March	11 11	10 0
April	10 10	·9 2
May	10 9	8 9
June	12 0	10 0
July	14 2	12 6
August	15 6	13 9
September . . .	18 10	16 3
October . . .	20 9	18 9
November . . .	24 1	21 8
December . . .	21 2	16 10
Mean for year	16 2	13 10

What would have been the mean price for the year in each case if the
wholesale prices had been recorded as retail prices sometimes are, i.e. at
so many eggs per shilling ?   State your answer in the form of the equivalent
price per 120, and obtain it in the shortest way by taking the harmonic
mean of the above prices.

CHAPTER SIX

MEASURES OF DISPERSION

Range

6.1 We can now turn to a consideration of measures of the dispersion of variate values about the central values we have discussed in the last chapter.

The simplest possible measure of dispersion is the *range*, i.e. the difference between the greatest and least values observed. The extreme ease with which this measure may be calculated and its very obvious interpretation have led to its use in many industrial problems. There are, however, objections to the use of the range in fields where speed of calculation and simplicity of interpretation are not of paramount importance.

In fact, the range is subject to fluctuations of considerable magnitude from sample to sample. There are seldom real upper or lower limits to the values which a variable can take, large or small values being only more or less infrequent. The occurrence of one of these infrequent values may have quite a disproportionate effect on the range. Suppose, for example, we consider the data of Exercise 4.6, page 100 showing the frequency-distributions of weights of adult males in several parts of the United Kingdom. In Wales one individual was observed with a weight of over 280 lb, the next heaviest being under 260 lb. The addition of this one exceptional man to 737 others has increased the range by some 30 lb, or about 20 per cent.

Moreover, the range takes no account of the form of the distribution within the range. We might get the same value for the range from a symmetrical and a J-shaped frequency-curve. Clearly we could not regard two such distributions as exhibiting the same dispersion.

6.2 In modern statistics the range finds its chief use in Quality Control, that is to say, the control of the average quality of a manufactured product. For instance, when a machine is turning out large numbers of a particular component, it is customary to examine a small sample of four or five taken at, say, half-hourly intervals to see whether the process is remaining constant within limits of error and is not altering by tool-wear or some such systematic change. The series of values of mean and range of the samples can easily be found by comparatively inexpert operators and are often sufficient to enable an adequate check to be kept on the process.

6.3 A measure of dispersion should obey conditions similar to those we laid down for measures of location in the last chapter (**5.5**).   That is to say, it should be based on all the observations, should be readily comprehensible, fairly easily calculated, affected as little as possible by fluctuations of sampling, and amenable to algebraical treatment.

There are three measures of dispersion in general use, the *standard deviation*, the *mean deviation* and the *quartile deviation* or *semi-interquartile range*.   We will consider them in that order.

The standard deviation

6.4 The standard deviation is the square root of the arithmetic mean of the squares of all deviations, deviations being measured from the arithmetic mean of the observations.   If the standard deviation be denoted by σ, and a deviation from the arithmetic mean by x, then the standard deviation is given by the equation

$$\sigma^2 = \frac{1}{N}\Sigma(x^2) \qquad . \qquad . \qquad . \qquad . \qquad . \quad (6.1)$$

To square all the deviations may seem at first sight an artificial procedure, but it must be remembered that it would be useless to take the mere sum of the deviations, in order to obtain a measure of dispersion, since this sum is necessarily zero if deviations be taken from the mean.   In order to obtain some quantity that shall vary with the dispersion, it is necessary to average the deviations by a process that treats them as if they were all of the same sign, and *squaring* is the simplest process for eliminating signs which leads to results of algebraical convenience.

Root-mean-square deviation

6.5 The standard deviation is a particular case of a more general quantity, known as the root-mean-square deviation, which has theoretical importance.

Let A be any arbitrary value of X, and let ξ (as in **5.11**) denote the deviation of X from A ; i.e. let

$$\xi = X - A$$

Then we may define the root-mean-square deviation s from the origin A by the equation

$$s^2 = \frac{1}{N}\Sigma(\xi^2) \qquad . \qquad . \qquad . \qquad . \quad (6.2)$$

The standard deviation is the value of the root-mean-square deviation taken from the mean.

6.6 The quantities σ^2 and s^2, i.e. the squares of the standard and root-mean-square deviations, are sufficiently important in much theoretical work to have special names.

The square of the standard deviation, σ^2, is called the *variance*.

The quantity $\frac{1}{N}\Sigma(\xi^2)$, i.e. s^2, is called the *second moment* about the value A. We have already seen (**5.11**) that the quantity $\frac{1}{N}\Sigma(\xi)$ is called the first moment about A, and in the next chapter we shall consider moments of higher orders.

Thus, the variance is the second moment about the mean.

Relation between standard and root-mean-square deviations

6.7 There is a very simple relation between the standard deviation and the root-mean-square deviation from any other origin. Let

$$M - A = d \qquad . \qquad . \qquad . \qquad . \quad (6.3)$$

so that

$$\xi = x + d$$

Then

$$\xi^2 = x^2 + 2xd + d^2$$

$$\Sigma(\xi^2) = \Sigma(x^2) + 2d\Sigma(x) + Nd^2$$

But the sum of the deviations from the mean is zero, therefore the second term vanishes, and accordingly

$$s^2 = \sigma^2 + d^2 \qquad . \qquad . \qquad . \quad (6.4)$$

Hence the root-mean-square deviation is least when deviations are measured from the mean, i.e. the standard deviation is the least possible root-mean-square deviation.

6.8 If σ and d are the two sides of a right-angled triangle, s is the hypotenuse. If, then, MH be the vertical through the mean of a frequency distribution (fig. 6.1), and MS be set off equal to the standard deviation (on the same scale by which the variable X is plotted along the base), SA will be the root-mean-square deviation from the point A. This construction gives a concrete idea of the way in which the root-mean-square deviation depends on the origin from which deviations are measured. It will be seen that for small values of d the difference of s and σ will be very minute, since A will lie very nearly on the circle drawn through M with centre S and radius SM : slight errors in the mean due to approximations in calculation will not, therefore, appreciably affect the value of the standard deviation.

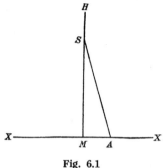

Fig. 6.1

Calculation of the standard deviation

6.9 If we have to deal with relatively few, say thirty or forty, ungrouped observations, the method of calculating the standard deviation is perfectly straightforward. It is illustrated by the figures below giving the minimum wage-rates for agricultural labourers in England and Wales at the beginning of 1936.

First of all the mean is ascertained. Then we find the values of x by subtracting the mean from all values of the variable. Each difference is squared and the total, $\Sigma(x^2)$, obtained. This total divided by the total frequency is the square of the standard deviation.

In practice, we can simplify the arithmetic by working from an arbitrary value A instead of from the mean. Such a value is usually known as the " working mean." When we have found the mean-square deviation s^2 about A we can easily find the value of σ^2 from equation (6.4).

Example 6.1—*Calculation of Standard Deviation* for a short series of observations (49) ungrouped. Minimum weekly rates of wages for ordinary adult male agricultural workers in England and Wales as at 1st January 1936.

By inspection of the table opposite we see that the mean is in the neighbourhood of 32 shillings. We therefore take this as the working mean A. The column headed " Difference " is the excess of the value of the variable over this value. The column headed " (Difference)^2 " is the square of the excess. We find

$$\frac{1}{N}\Sigma(\xi) = \frac{-79}{49} = -1\cdot612 \text{ pence}$$

Hence the mean = 32 shillings $-1\cdot612$ pence

= 31 shillings $10\cdot4$ pence approximately.

Area	Wage rates	Difference ξ (pence)	(Difference)^2 ξ^2
	s. d.		
Bedford and Huntingdon shires .	31 6	− 6	36
Berkshire	31 0	−12	144
Bucks	32 0	—	—
Cambridgeshire . . .	31 6	− 6	36
Cheshire	32 6	6	36
Cornwall	32 0	—	—
Cumberland	32 6	6	36
Derbyshire	36 0	48	2,304
Dorset	31 6	− 6	36
Durham	29 0	−36	1,296
Essex	31 0	−12	144
Gloucester	31 0	−12	144
Hampshire	31 0	−12	144
Hereford	31 0	−12	144
Hertford	32 0	—	—
Kent	33 0	12	144
Lancashire (South) . .	32 9	9	81
,, (Rest) . . .	36 6	54	2,916
Leicester	33 0	12	144
Lincs (Holland) . . .	34 0	24	576
,, (Kesteven and Lindsey) .	31 0	−12	144
Middlesex	33 8	20	400
Monmouth	32 0	—	—
Norfolk	31 6	− 6	36
Northants	31 6	− 6	36
Northumberland . . .	31 6	− 6	36
Notts	32 0	—	—
Oxfordshire	31 6	− 6	36
Rutland	31 6	− 6	36
Shropshire	32 0	—	—
Somerset	32 6	6	36
Staffs	31 6	− 6	36
Suffolk	31 0	−12	144
Surrey	32 3	3	9
Sussex	32 0	—	—
Warwickshire	30 0	−24	576
Westmorland	31 0	−12	144
Wiltshire	31 0	−12	144
Worcester	31 0	−12	144
Yorks, E. Riding . .	33 6	18	324
,, N. Riding . .	33 0	12	144
,, W. Riding . .	33 9	21	441
Anglesey and Caernarvon .	31 0	−12	144
Carmarthen . . .	31 6	− 6	36
Denbigh and Flint . . .	30 6	−18	324
Glamorgan . . .	33 6	18	324
Merioneth and Montgomery .	28 6	−42	1,764
Pembroke and Cardigan .	31 0	−12	144
Radnor and Brecon . .	30 0	−24	576
Totals	—	−79	14,539

Also

$$\frac{1}{N}\Sigma(\xi^2) = \frac{14,539}{49} = 296 \cdot 714 = s^2$$

$$\sigma^2 = s^2 - d^2 = 296 \cdot 714 - (1 \cdot 612)^2$$

$$= 294 \cdot 112$$

$$\sigma = 17 \cdot 15 \text{ pence approximately.}$$

We would direct the student's attention to the necessity for checking his work at each stage before proceeding to the next. If he neglects this warning he is likely to learn by bitter experience how essential it was. For instance, in the above work it would be well to check the value of the mean by summing the wage rates and dividing by 49. We get in this way—

$$\text{Mean} = \frac{1561\text{s. } 5\text{d.}}{49} = 31\text{s. } 10 \cdot 4\text{d.}$$

which checks with the mean found from the working mean. Secondly, the squares of differences should be checked before they are added, and if the addition is made without a machine, a check should be carried out by summing first from bottom to top and then from top to bottom, to avoid repeating errors. A further systematic check is given in **6.11** below.

6.10 If we have to deal with a grouped frequency-distribution the same artifices and approximations are used as in the calculation of the mean (**5.10** and **5.11**). The mid-value of one of the class-intervals is chosen as the arbitrary origin A from which to measure the deviations ξ, the class-interval is treated as a unit throughout the arithmetic, and all the observations within any one class-interval are treated as if they were identical with the mid-value of the interval. If, as before, we denote the frequency in any one interval by f, these f observations contribute $f\xi^2$ to the sum of the squares of deviations, and we have—

$$s^2 = \frac{1}{N}\Sigma(f\,\xi^2)$$

The standard deviation is then calculated from equation (6.4).

6.11 As the arithmetic in calculating the standard deviation is often extensive, it is as well to use some check similar to that of **5.12**. In this case we have—

$$(\xi+1)^2 = \xi^2 + 2\xi + 1$$

$$f\,(\xi+1)^2 = f\,\xi^2 + 2f\,\xi + f$$

$$\therefore \quad \Sigma\{f\,(\xi+1)^2\} = \Sigma(f\,\xi^2) + 2\Sigma(f\,\xi) + N$$

Hence, if we calculate $\Sigma\{f(\xi+1)^2\}$ as well as $\Sigma(f\xi^2)$, the above equation gives us a simple check on the accuracy of our work. The following examples illustrate the method—

Example 6.2.—Calculation of the standard deviation of stature of male adults in the British Isles from the figures of Table 4.7, page 82.

(1) Height inches	(2) Frequency f	(3) Deviation from value A ξ	(4) Product $f\xi$	(5) $f(\xi+1)$	(6) Product $f\xi^2$	(7) $f(\xi+1)^2$
57–	2	−10	− 20	− 18	200	162
58–	4	− 9	− 36	− 32	324	256
59–	14	− 8	− 112	− 98	896	686
60–	41	− 7	− 287	− 246	2,009	1,476
61–	83	− 6	− 498	− 415	2,988	2,075
62–	169	− 5	− 845	− 676	4,225	2,704
63–	394	− 4	− 1,576	− 1,182	6,304	3,546
64–	669	− 3	− 2,007	− 1,338	6,021	2,676
65–	990	− 2	− 1,980	− 990	3,960	990
66–	1,223	− 1	− 1,223	− 4,995	1,223	—
67–	1,329	0	− 8,584	1,329	—	1,329
68–	1,230	+ 1	1,230	2,460	1,230	4,920
69–	1,063	+ 2	2,126	3,189	4,252	9,567
70–	646	+ 3	1,938	2,584	5,814	10,336
71–	392	+ 4	1,568	1,960	6,272	9,800
72–	202	+ 5	1,010	1,212	5,050	7,272
73–	79	+ 6	474	553	2,844	3,871
74–	32	+ 7	224	256	1,568	2,048
75–	16	+ 8	128	144	1,024	1,296
76–	5	+ 9	45	50	405	500
77–	2	+10	20	22	200	242
Total	8,585	—	8,763	13,759	56,809	65,752

$$\Sigma(f\xi) = 8,763 - 8,584 = 179$$
$$\Sigma\{f(\xi+1)\} = 13,759 - 4,995 = 8,764$$

This is an example we have already considered when calculating the mean, and the work of the first four columns is the same as that of Example 5.1, page 107.

As a check on $\Sigma(f\xi)$ we have—

$$\Sigma\{f(\xi+1)\} - \Sigma(f\xi) = 8764 - 179$$
$$= 8585$$
$$= N$$

As a check on $\Sigma(f\xi^2)$ we have—

$$\Sigma\{f(\xi+1)^2\} - \Sigma(f\xi^2) - 2\Sigma(f\xi) = 65{,}752 - 56{,}809 - 358$$
$$= 8{,}585$$
$$= N$$

From previous work, $M - A = d = +0 \cdot 0209$ class-intervals or inches.

$$\frac{\Sigma(f\xi^2)}{N} = \frac{56{,}809}{8{,}585} = 6 \cdot 6172$$

$$\sigma^2 = 6 \cdot 6172 - (0 \cdot 0209)^2$$
$$= 6 \cdot 6168$$
$$\therefore \sigma = 2 \cdot 57 \text{ class-intervals or inches.}$$

Example 6.3.—Let us find the mean and standard déviation of the distribution of Australian marriages given in Table 4.8, page 84.

Calculation of standard deviation of age of bridegroom in a distribution of Australian marriages.

Age of bridegroom (central value) Years	Frequency f	ξ	$f\xi$	$f(\xi+1)$	$f\xi^2$	$f(\xi+1)^2$
16·5	294	−4	− 1,176	− 882	4,704	2,646
19·5	10,995	−3	− 32,985	− 21,990	98,955	43,980
22·5	61,001	−2	− 122,002	− 61,001	244,004	61,001
25·5	73,054	−1	− 73,054	—	73,054	—
28·5	56,501	0	—	56,501	—	56,501
31·5	33,478	1	33,478	66,956	33,478	133,912
34·5	20,569	2	41,138	61,707	82,276	185,121
37·5	14,281	3	42,843	57,124	128,529	228,496
40·5	9,320	4	37,280	46,600	149,120	233,000
43·5	6,236	5	31,180	37,416	155,900	224,496
46·5	4,770	6	28,620	33,390	171,720	233,730
49·5	3,620	7	25,340	28,960	177,380	231,680
52·5	2,190	8	17,520	19,710	140,160	177,390
55·5	1,655	9	14,895	16,550	134,055	165,500
58·5	1,100	10	11,000	12,100	110,000	133,100
61·5	810	11	8,910	9,720	98,010	116,640
64·5	649	12	7,788	8,437	93,456	109,681
67·5	487	13	6,331	6,818	82,303	95,452
70·5	326	14	4,564	4,890	63,896	73,350
73·5	211	15	3,165	3,376	47,475	54,016
76·5	119	16	1,904	2,023	30,464	34,391
79·5	73	17	1,241	1,314	21,097	23,652
82·5	27	18	486	513	8,748	9,747
85·5	14	19	266	280	5,054	5,600
88·5	5	20	100	105	2,000	2,205
Total	301,785	—	88,832	390,617	2,155,838	2,635,287

We take a working mean $A = 28 \cdot 5$.

As a check on $\Sigma(f\xi)$ we have—

$$\Sigma\{f(\xi+1)\} - \Sigma(f\xi) = 390,617 - 88,832$$
$$= 301,785$$
$$= N$$

As a check on $\Sigma(f\xi^2)$ we have—

$$\Sigma\{f(\xi+1)^2\} - \Sigma(f\xi^2) - 2\Sigma(f\xi) = 2,635,287 - 2,155,838 - 177,664$$
$$= 301,785$$
$$= N$$

Then

$$M - A = d = \frac{88,832}{301,785} = 0 \cdot 29436 \text{ interval}$$

$$= 0 \cdot 88308 \text{ year}$$

Hence,

$$M = 29 \cdot 383 \text{ years}$$

We have—

$$s^2 = \frac{2,155,838}{301,785} = 7 \cdot 143622 \text{ intervals}^2$$

$$\sigma^2 = s^2 - d^2 \text{ intervals}^2$$
$$= 7 \cdot 056974 \text{ intervals}^2$$
$$\sigma = 2 \cdot 6565 \text{ intervals}$$
$$= 7 \cdot 969, \text{ or } 8 \text{ years approximately.}$$

Sheppard's correction for grouping

6.12 The student must remember that the treatment of all the values of a variable in a class-interval as if they were concentrated at the centre of that interval is an approximation, although, for distributions of symmetrical or moderately skew type and class-intervals not greater than about one-twentieth of the range, the approximation may be a very close one.

It has been shown that if

(a) the distribution of frequency is continuous, and

(b) the frequency tapers off to zero in both directions,

the variance obtained from grouped data may with advantage be corrected for the grouping effect by subtracting from it one-twelfth of the square of the class-interval; i.e. if the class-interval be h units in width, σ^2 the corrected value of the variance and σ_1^2 the value obtained from the grouped data—

$$\sigma^2 = \sigma_1^2 - \frac{h^2}{12} \qquad \qquad . \qquad . \qquad . \qquad . \qquad . \qquad (6.5)$$

The proof of this formula lies outside the scope of this book. We may emphasise condition (*b*). The Sheppard correction is not applicable to J- or U-shaped distributions, or even to the skew form of fig. 4.7 (*b*), page 84.

Furthermore, unless the total frequency is fairly large, the Sheppard correction is likely to be of secondary importance compared with fluctuations of sampling (see **19.13**). We suggest that, as a general rule, the correction should not be made unless the frequency is at least 1,000, or the grouping coarser than that given by intervals of about one-twentieth of the range. We give in Exercise 6.15 a result which will convey the general magnitude of the correction for the finer grouping.

Example 6.4.—In Example 6.2 we have—

$$\sigma_1{}^2 = 6 \cdot 6168$$

Here $h^2 = 1$, and $h^2/12 = 0 \cdot 0833$

$\therefore$ corrected value of $\sigma^2 = \sigma_1{}^2 - h^2/12$

$$= 6 \cdot 6168 - 0 \cdot 0833$$

$$= 6 \cdot 5335$$

and σ corrected $= 2 \cdot 56$, differing from the uncorrected value by $0 \cdot 01$.

Example 6.5.—In Example 6.3 we have—

$$\sigma^2 (\text{uncorrected}) = 7 \cdot 056974 \text{ intervals}^2$$

Here σ^2 is expressed in terms of h^2, and hence to correct it we subtract $\frac{1}{12}$, giving

$$\sigma^2 \text{ (corrected)} = 6.973641$$

$$\sigma = 2 \cdot 6408 \text{ intervals}$$

$$= 7 \cdot 922 \text{ years}$$

as against an uncorrected value of $7 \cdot 969$ years.

Spread of observations and standard deviation

6.13 It is a useful empirical rule to remember that a range of six times the standard deviation usually includes 99 per cent or more of all the observations in the case of distributions of the symmetrical or moderately asymmetrical type. Thus in Example 6.2 the standard deviation is $2 \cdot 57$ in., six times this is $15 \cdot 42$ in., and a range from, say, 60 in. to $75 \cdot 4$ in. includes all but some 36 out of 8,585 individuals, i.e. about $99 \cdot 6$ per cent. This rough rule serves to give a more definite and concrete meaning to the standard deviation, and also to check arithmetical work to some extent—sufficiently, that is to say, to guard against very gross blunders. It must not be expected to hold for short series of observations :

in Example 6.1, for instance, the actual range is a good deal less than six times the standard deviation.

Properties of the standard deviation

6.14 The standard deviation is the measure of dispersion which it is most easy to treat by algebraical methods, resembling in this respect the arithmetic mean amongst measures of position. The majority of illustrations of its treatment must be postponed to a later stage, but the work of **6.9** has already served as one example. We showed in **5.16** that if a series of observations of which the mean is M consists of two component series, of which the means are M_1 and M_2 respectively,

$$NM = N_1 M_1 + N_2 M_2$$

N_1 and N_2 being the numbers of observations in the two component series, and $N = N_1 + N_2$ the number in the entire series. Similarly, the standard deviation σ of the whole series may be expressed in terms of the standard deviations σ_1 and σ_2 of the components and their respective means. Let

$$M_1 - M = d_1$$
$$M_2 - M = d_2$$

Then the mean-square deviations of the component series about the mean M are, by equation (6.4), $\sigma_1{}^2 + d_1{}^2$ and $\sigma_2{}^2 + d_2{}^2$ respectively. Therefore, for the whole series

$$N\sigma^2 = N_1(\sigma_1{}^2 + d_1{}^2) + N_2(\sigma_2{}^2 + d_2{}^2) \qquad . \qquad . \quad (6.6)$$

If the numbers of observations in the component series be equal and the means be coincident, we have as a special case—

$$\sigma^2 = \tfrac{1}{2}(\sigma_1{}^2 + \sigma_2{}^2) \qquad . \qquad . \qquad . \qquad . \qquad . \quad (6.7)$$

so that in this case the variance (**6.6**) of the whole series is the arithmetic mean of the variances of its components.

It is evident that the form of the relation (6.6) is quite general : if a series of observations consists of r component series with standard deviations σ_1, σ_2, . . . σ_r, and means diverging from the general mean of the whole series by d_1, d_2, . . . d_r, the standard deviation σ of the whole series is given (using m to denote any subscript) by the equation

$$N\sigma^2 = \Sigma(N_m \sigma_m{}^2) + \Sigma(N_m d_m{}^2) \qquad . \qquad . \quad (6.8)$$

Again, as in **5.16**, it is convenient to note, for the checking of arithmetic, that if the same arbitrary origin be used for the calculation of the standard deviations in a number of component distributions, we must have—

$$\Sigma(f\,\xi^2) = \Sigma(f_1\xi_1{}^2) + \Sigma(f_2\xi_2{}^2) + \ldots + \Sigma(f_r\xi_r{}^2) \qquad . \qquad . \quad (6.9)$$

6.15 As another useful illustration, let us find the standard deviation of the first N natural numbers. The mean in this case is evidently $(N+1)/2$. Further, as is shown in any elementary algebra, the sum of the squares of the first N natural numbers is

$$\frac{N(N+1)(2N+1)}{6}$$

Applying equation (6.4) we have that the standard deviation σ is given by

$$\sigma^2 = \tfrac{1}{6}(N+1)(2N+1) - \tfrac{1}{4}(N+1)^2$$

that is,

$$\sigma^2 = \tfrac{1}{12}(N^2 - 1) \qquad . \qquad . \qquad . \qquad . \qquad . \quad (6.10)$$

This result is of service if the relative merit of, or the relative intensity of some character in, the different individuals of a series is recorded not by means of measurements, e.g. marks awarded on some system of examination, but merely by means of the respective positions when ranked in order as regards the character, in the same way as boys are numbered in a class. With N individuals there are always N *ranks*, as they are termed, whatever the character, and the standard deviation is therefore always that given by equation (6.10).

Another useful result follows at once from equation (6.10), namely, the standard deviation of a frequency-distribution in which all values of X within a range $\pm l/2$ on either side of the mean are equally frequent, values outside these limits not occurring, so that the frequency-distribution may be represented by a rectangle. The base l may be supposed divided into a very large number N of equal elements, and the standard deviation reduces to that of the first N natural numbers when N is made indefinitely large. The single unit then becomes negligible compared with N, and consequently

$$\sigma^2 = \frac{l^2}{12} \qquad . \qquad . \qquad . \qquad . \qquad . \qquad . \quad (6.11)$$

6.16 It will be seen from the preceding paragraphs that the standard deviation possesses the majority at least of the properties which are desirable in a measure of dispersion as in an average (**5.5**). It is rigidly defined ; it is based on all the observations made ; it is calculated with reasonable ease ; it lends itself readily to algebraical treatment ; and we may add, though the student will have to take the statement on trust for the present, that it is, as a rule, the measure least affected by fluctuations of sampling. On the other hand, it may be said that its general nature is not very readily comprehended, and that the process of squaring deviations and then taking the square root of the mean seems a little involved. The student will, however, soon surmount this feeling after a little practice in the calculation and use of the constant, and will realise, as he advances further, the advantages that it possesses. Such root-mean-square quantities, it may be added, frequently occur in other branches of science. The standard deviation should always be used as the measure of dispersion, unless there is some very definite reason for preferring another measure, just as the arithmetic mean should be used as the measure of position.

Note on nomenclature

6.17 A great deal of confusion has been introduced into statistical literature by the many different expressions which have been used for the standard deviation and simple derivatives of it. It used to be almost a case of *tot homines quot nomina*, and as the student may meet these expressions elsewhere, we give a short list of them. The term " standard deviation " is now almost universally accepted, and in this book we shall use no other.

" Mean error " (Gauss), " mean square error " and " error of mean square " (Airy) have all been used to denote the standard deviation.

The standard deviation is not to be confused with the " standard error." We shall use this term in a special sense, that of the standard deviation of simple sampling (cf. **17.8**).

The standard deviation multiplied by the square root of 2 is also known as " the modulus." The student will see the reason for this multiplication later. The reciprocal of the modulus is called the " precision."

There is also a quantity known as the " probable error," which is defined as being $0 \cdot 67449$ times the standard deviation (cf. **17.9**). These last four quantities are particularly important in the theory of errors of observation and the theory of sampling.

Finally, we may remark that since we shall use the expression " standard deviation " very frequently, we shall sometimes use the abbreviation " s.d." or simply the symbol σ.

Mean deviation

6.18 We have already remarked that it would be useless to take the sum of deviations from the mean as a measure of dispersion because such sum is identically zero. We therefore remove the signs of the deviations by squaring to reach the standard deviation.

It is also possible to overcome this difficulty by adding the sum of deviations taken regardless of sign. The arithmetic mean of these " absolute " deviations is called the *mean deviation*.

If we write $|\xi|$ to denote the deviation from an arbitrary value A taken as positive whatever its actual sign, the mean deviation is thus defined as

$$\text{m.d.} = \frac{1}{N}\Sigma(|\xi|) \qquad . \qquad . \qquad . \qquad . \qquad . \quad (6.12)$$

(The expression $|\xi|$ is read "mod ξ"—an abbreviation for "the modulus of ξ").

6.19 Just as the root-mean-square deviation is least when deviations are measured from the arithmetic mean, so the mean deviation is least when deviations are measured from the median. For suppose that, for some origin exceeded by m values out of N, the mean deviation has a value Δ. Let the origin be displaced by an amount c until it is just exceeded by $m-1$ of the values only, i.e. until it coincides with the mth value from the upper end of the series. By this displacement of the origin the sum of deviations in excess of the origin is reduced by mc, while the sum of deviations in defect of the mean is increased by $(N-m)c$. The new mean deviation is therefore

$$\Delta + \frac{(N-m)c - mc}{N}$$

$$= \Delta + \frac{1}{N}(N - 2m)c$$

The new mean deviation is accordingly less than the old so long as

$$m > \tfrac{1}{2}N$$

That is to say, if N be even, the mean deviation is constant for all origins within the range between the $N/2$th and the $(N/2+1)$th observations, and this value is the least ; if N be odd, the mean deviation is lowest when the origin coincides with the $(N+1)/2$th observation. The mean deviation is therefore a minimum when deviations are measured from the median or, if the latter be indeterminate, from an origin within the range in which it lies.

Calculation of the mean deviation

6.20 The mean deviation is perhaps most easily calculated about the mean, which is always determinate, except in the case of distributions with an indeterminate final class. As, however, it is a minimum about the median, we sometimes require to know the value about that point. The following examples will make the method of calculation clear.

Example 6.6.—Let us find the mean deviation about the mean and about the median in the ungrouped data of Example 6.1.

The data were arranged in alphabetical order of the county wage areas, which makes it a little difficult to ascertain the median by inspection. On rearranging in order of magnitude, we find that the median is the value 31s. 6d.

The deviations from the median value are, then, in order of magnitude

$$-36, \; -30, \; -18, \; -18, \; -12, \; -6 \; (12 \text{ times}), \; 0 \; (10 \text{ times}),$$
$$6 \; (7 \text{ times}), \; 9, \; 12, \; 12, \; 12, \; 15, \; 18, \; 18, \; 18, \; 24, \; 24, \; 26, \; 27,$$
$$30, \; 54, \; 60$$

The sum of the negative deviations $= -186$

The sum of the positive deviations $= \quad 401$

Hence the sum of absolute deviations $= \quad 587$

Hence m.d. $= \dfrac{587}{49} = 12$ pence approximately.

To find the m.d. about the mean, 31s. 10·4d., we note that the 27 negative or zero deviations from the median would be increased by 4·4 pence on transferring to the mean, and the 22 positive deviations decreased by 4·4 pence. The net effect on the total absolute deviations is then an increase of $(27 - 22) \times 4 \cdot 4$ pence $= 22$ pence.

Hence the m.d. about the mean is—

$$\frac{587}{49} + \frac{22}{49}$$

$$= 12 \cdot 43 \text{ pence}$$

Example 6.7.—Let us find the mean deviation of heights about the mean in the data of Example 6.2.

In the case of a grouped frequency-distribution the sum of deviations should first be calculated from the centre of the class-interval in which the mean (or median) lies and then reduced to the mean (or median) as origin.

In this case the mean lies in the interval 67-. We found when calculating it that the negative deviations totalled -8584 and the positive deviations 8763. Hence the sum of absolute deviations from the centre of the interval is 17,347—the unit of measurement being the class-interval.

To reduce to the mean as origin we note that if the number of observations below the mean is N_1 and above the mean N_2, and $M - A = d$ as before, we have to add $N_1 d$ to the sum when found and subtract $N_2 d$. In this case $d = 0 \cdot 02$ class-interval, $N_1 = 4,918$ and $N_2 = 3,667$.

Hence we must add

$$(4{,}918-3{,}667)\times 0\cdot 2=+25 \text{ intervals}$$

i.e.   the total of deviations $=17{,}372$

and

$$\text{m.d.}=\frac{17{,}372}{8{,}585}=2\cdot 02 \text{ intervals or inches.}$$

The mean deviation from the median should be found in a similar way, the calculation being assisted if the class-interval in which the median lies is taken as origin.

6.21   As in the case of the standard deviation, the above calculations assume for certain purposes that all the values of the variable can be treated as if they were concentrated at the centres of class-intervals.   This gives sufficient accuracy for all practical purposes if the class-intervals are reasonably narrow.   It has not been found possible to give any simple correction, such as Sheppard's correction, for errors of grouping in the mean deviation, but we give at the end of this chapter an Exercise (6.11) as to the correction to be applied if the values in each interval are treated as if they were evenly distributed over the interval instead of being concentrated at its centre.

Empirical relation between mean and standard deviations for symmetrical or moderately skew distributions

6.22   It is a useful rule for the student to remember that for symmetrical or moderately skew distributions the mean deviation is about four-fifths of the standard deviation.   Thus, for the distribution of male statures of Examples 6.2 and 6.7, we have—

$$\frac{\text{m.d.}}{\text{s.d.}}=\frac{2\cdot 02}{2\cdot 57}=0\cdot 79$$

For the short series of observations of Example 6.1—

$$\frac{\text{m.d.}}{\text{s.d.}}=\frac{12\cdot 43}{17\cdot 15}=0\cdot 72$$

Quartiles

6.23   A natural extension of the idea of the median consists in ascertaining the variate values Q_1 and Q_3, such that one-quarter of the observations lies below Q_1 and one-quarter above Q_3.   In this case clearly one-quarter lies between Q_1 and Mi, the median, and one-quarter between Mi and Q_3.

Q_1 is termed the *lower quartile* and Q_3 the *upper quartile*.   The quartiles and the median thus divide the observed values of the variable into four classes of equal frequency.

We saw that if the number of observations was even, there was an indeterminacy in the position of the median which required the additional convention that in such cases the median would be taken to be mid-way between the two central values. Similar indeterminacies may arise in fixing the quartiles unless the number of observations is one less than a multiple of four. Such cases are treated in an analogous way by supplementary conventions, which will be clear from the following examples.

Example 6.8.—To determine the quartiles of the data of Example 6.1.

Here there are 49 observations, and so the 25th gives the median. We regard half the 25th observation as falling below the median and half above. The lower quartile must divide into two equal parts the $24\frac{1}{2}$ observations falling below the median. The observations other than the median are—

28 /6, 29 /-, 30 /-, 30 /-, 30 /6, 31 /- (12 times), 31 /6 (7 times).

The lower quartile must divide the $24\frac{1}{2}$ observations into two sets of $12\frac{1}{4}$. The 12th and the 13th values are both, as it happens, 31 /-, and Q_1 being between the two is thus 31 /- also.

The 24 observations between the median and the highest value are—

31 /6 (twice), 32 /- (7 times), 32 /3, 32 /6 (3 times), 32 /9, 33 /- (3 times), 33 /6, 33 /6, 33 /8, 33 /9, 34 /-, 36 /-, 36 /6.

The 12th and 13th observations are both 32 /6, and hence this is the value of Q_3.

If the 12th and 13th observations had been, say, 32 /6 and 33 /-, we might have taken Q_3 to be 32 /6 but regarded $\frac{1}{4}$ of the 12th observation as lying above that value.

Example 6.9.—To determine the quartiles of the distribution of Example 6.2.

Data of this kind are treated by simple arithmetical interpolation or graphical interpolation on the lines of **5.20** or **5.21**.

The quartiles are to divide the distribution into four equal parts. We have, therefore

$$\frac{8585}{4} = 2146 \cdot 25$$

To the interval 65– are   1,376 individuals

Difference $= 770 \cdot 25$

Hence, Q_1 is $\dfrac{770 \cdot 25}{990}$ in. from the beginning of the interval, which is $64\frac{15}{16}$.

$$\therefore \quad Q_1 = 65 \cdot 71$$

Similarly, from the interval 70– onwards are 1,374 individuals. Difference from $2146 \cdot 25 = 772 \cdot 25$.

Hence,

$$Q_3 = 69\tfrac{15}{16} - \frac{772 \cdot 25}{1063}$$

$$= 69 \cdot 21 \text{ inches}$$

It is left to the student to check the values by graphical interpolation.

Quartile deviation

6.24 If Mi be the value of the median, in a symmetrical distribution

$$Mi - Q_1 = Q_3 - Mi$$

and the difference may be taken as a measure of dispersion. But as no distribution is rigidly symmetrical, it is usual to take as the measure

$$Q = \frac{Q_3 - Q_1}{2}$$

and $\dot{Q}$ is termed the quartile deviation, or better, the semi-interquartile range—it is not a measure of the deviation from any particular average.

Thus, from the values calculated in Example 6.8 we have—

$$Q = \frac{32/6 - 31/-}{2} = \frac{18d.}{2} = 9 \text{ pence}$$

and from Example 6.9 we have—

$$Q = \frac{69 \cdot 21 - 65 \cdot 71}{2} = 1 \cdot 75 \text{ inches}$$

Empirical relation between quartile and standard deviations

6.25 For symmetrical and moderately skew distributions the semi-interquartile range is usually about two-thirds of the standard deviation.

Thus, for the height distribution of Examples 6.2 and 6.9,

$$\frac{Q}{\sigma} = \frac{1 \cdot 75}{2 \cdot 57} = 0 \cdot 68$$

For the wage statistics of Examples 6.1 and 6.8,

$$\frac{Q}{\sigma} = \frac{9}{17 \cdot 15} = 0 \cdot 52$$

which is considerably lower. We should, however, hardly have expected the comparatively few observations comprised in these data to conform at all closely to the empirical relation.

6.26 It follows from this relation that a range of 6 times the standard deviation corresponds to a range of 9 times the semi-interquartile range (and 7·5 times the mean deviation). Within these ranges we expect to find at least 99 per cent of the observations in symmetrical or moderately skew distributions.

Comparison of the three measures of dispersion

6.27 The semi-interquartile range has two advantages over the standard deviation and the mean deviation ; it is calculated with great ease, and it has a clear and simple meaning.

In almost all other respects the advantage lies with the standard deviation. The semi-interquartile range has no simple algebraical properties, and its behaviour under fluctuations of sampling is difficult to decide. In all but the most elementary statistical work these are overwhelming disadvantages, and the use of the semi-interquartile range is not to be recommended unless the calculation of the standard deviation has been rendered difficult or impossible, e.g. owing to the employment of irregular class-frequencies or of an indefinite terminal class.

Absolute measures of dispersion

6.28 The three measures of dispersion we have been discussing have all been expressed in terms of the units of the variate ; e.g. the standard deviation of height-frequencies was found in inches, and the mean deviation of wage-frequencies in pence. It is thus impossible to compare dispersions in different populations unless they happen to be measured in the same units.

For this reason some. statisticians have recommended the use of " absolute " measures of dispersion, which shall be pure numbers and not expressible in some particular scale of units. Such measures would permit of comparison between populations of very different natures.

It is easy to construct several coefficients of the kind required. The standard deviation and the mean deviation have the dimensions of the variate, and it is only necessary to divide them by another factor which has the same dimensions ; e.g.

$$\frac{\text{Mean deviation}}{\text{Mean}}, \quad \frac{\text{Mean deviation}}{\text{Mode}} \quad \text{and} \quad \frac{\text{Standard deviation}}{\text{Mean}}$$

are all of the required type.

Coefficient of variation

6.29 The last-mentioned in the foregoing paragraph in a modified form is the only coefficient which has come into general use. We define the *coefficient of variation, v,* as

$$v = 100\frac{\sigma}{M} \qquad . \qquad . \qquad . \qquad . \qquad . \quad (6.13)$$

This coefficient is obviously rather unreliable if the mean is near to zero ; but provided the nature of the ratio is kept in mind the coefficient may be useful in comparing the variation of materials which emanate from populations of the same type.

Reduction of frequency-distribution to absolute scale

6.30 Comparability of form may, however, be reached in a different way ; that is to say, by regarding σ itself as a unit and expressing other measures in terms of it. Thus, in the height distribution of Example 6.2, $\sigma = 2 \cdot 57$ inches, or 1 inch $= 0 \cdot 389\ \sigma$. Hence the intervals are $0 \cdot 389\ \sigma$ in width, and run : $57 \times 0 \cdot 389\ \sigma-$, $58 \times 0 \cdot 389\ \sigma-$, etc. ; i.e. $22 \cdot 173\ \sigma-$, $22 \cdot 562\ \sigma-$, etc.

A distribution expressed in this way has unit standard deviation, for

$$\frac{1}{N}\Sigma\left(\frac{x}{\sigma}\right)^2 = \frac{1}{\sigma^2 N}\Sigma(x^2) = \frac{\sigma^2}{\sigma^2}$$
$$= 1$$

The distribution reduced to the scale of σ may thus be regarded as expressed in " absolute " units, and two distributions expressed in this way may readily be compared as regards form, but not as regards dispersion, for this has been made the same in the two cases.

Deciles and percentiles

6.31 We may conclude this chapter by describing briefly methods which have been much used in the past in lieu of the methods described in this and the preceding chapter.

Instead of dividing the total frequency into 4 parts by quartiles, we may divide it into 100 parts by what are called *percentiles*. Or we may divide into 10 parts by *deciles*. The theory of these quantities is precisely analogous to that of the quartiles : there may, for instance, be certain indeterminacies in their exact definition which are removed by supplementary conventions ; they can be obtained by arithmetical or graphical interpolation ; and they have simple and obvious meanings.

Quantities such as quartiles, deciles, etc., which divide the total frequency into a number of parts, are called *quantiles* or *grades*, and when we speak of the grade of an individual we mean thereby the proportion of the total frequency which lies below it. Conventionally, half the individual is regarded as lying above, and half below, the point determined by the variate value which it bears.

The distribution curve

6.32 The grades or quantiles may conveniently be found by a graphical method which is an extension of that of **5.21**. Against the variate-value as abscissa we graph as ordinate the *cumulated* frequency up to and including the corresponding variate-value. This is called the *distribution curve*. By reading off the ordinate corresponding to a given variate we can find, approximately at least, the number of members of the population bearing that or a lower value. Similarly, by reading off the variate corresponding to a given ordinate we can find the quartiles, just as we found the median in **5.21**. In figure 6.2 we show the distribution curve for the data of Example 6.2, with the lines corresponding to the median and the quartiles. Figure 5.3 is really an enlarged version of part of this curve.

A somewhat similar form of graph (with the percentiles as abscissa and the variate as ordinate) was formerly in use and was known as Galton's ogive. The curve was not, however, always shaped like an ogive. The distribution curve appears to provide a more natural method of representation and a better name. The mathematical reader will recognise it as the graph of the integral of the frequency curve.

6.33 An extension of the method of quantiles to the treatment of non-measurable characters has also become of some importance. For example, the capacity of the different boys in a class as regards some school subject cannot be directly measured, but it may not be very difficult for the master to arrange them in order of merit as regards this character : if the boys are then " numbered up " in order, the number of each boy, or his

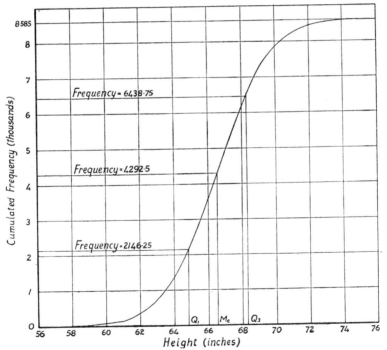

Fig. 6.2.—**Distribution curve for stature**
(Same data as fig. 4.6, p. 83)

rank, serves as some sort of index to his capacity. It should be noted that rank in this sense is not quite the same as grade ; if a boy is tenth, say, from the bottom in a class of a hundred his grade is 9·5, but the method is in principle the same as that of grades or quantiles. The method of ranks, grades or quantiles in such a case may be a very serviceable auxiliary, though, of course, it is better if possible to obtain a numerical measure. But if, in the case of a measurable character, the quantiles are used not merely as constants illustrative of certain aspects of the frequency-distribution, but entirely to replace the table giving the frequency-distribution, serious inconvenience may be caused, as the application of other methods to the data is barred. Given the table showing the frequency-distribution, the reader can calculate not only the quantiles, but any form of average or measure of dispersion that has yet been proposed, to a sufficiently high degree of approximation. But given only certain quantiles such as the percentiles, or at least so few of them as the nine deciles, he cannot pass back to the frequency-distribution, and thence to other constants, with any degree of accuracy. In all cases of published work, therefore, the figures of the frequency-distribution should be given ; they are absolutely fundamental.

Gini's mean difference

6.34   The Italian statistician Corrado Gini has proposed a measure of dispersion which at first sight seems to have certain advantages over the standard deviation. It is the mean of the differences (taken regardless of sign) of each possible pair of variate values exhibited by the population ; e.g., if the frequency of the value x_j is f_j, the coefficient of mean difference is

$$\Delta_1 = \frac{1}{N(N-1)} \sum_{j=1}^{n} \sum_{k=1}^{n} \left\{ |x_j - x_k| \, f_j f_k \right\} \qquad . \qquad . \qquad . \quad (6.14)$$

or, if we regard each member as taken with itself, contributing nothing to the sum in (6.14) but increasing the number of pairs of values to N^2 instead of $N(N-1)$, we have the coefficient of mean difference with repetition—

$$\Delta'_1 = \frac{1}{N^2} \sum_{j=1}^{n} \sum_{k=1}^{n} \left\{ |x_j - x_k| \, f_j f_k \right\} \qquad . \qquad . \qquad . \quad (6.15)$$

6.35   These coefficients are more difficult to calculate than the standard deviation or the mean deviation, but they have a theoretical attraction in that they depend on the differences of values between themselves and not on the spread about some arbitrary point such as the mean or the median. They thus measure, in a sense, the intrinsic spread of the population independently of an origin of location.

A similar property, however, is possessed by the standard deviation. Suppose that, in equation (6.15), we sought to obviate the difficulties of using absolute values by defining a new coefficient E by the similar expression.

$$E^2 = \frac{1}{N^2} \sum_{j=1}^{n} \sum_{k=1}^{n} \left\{ (x_j - x_k)^2 f_j f_k \right\} \qquad . \qquad . \quad (6.16)$$

Since

$$(x_j - x_k)^2 = x_j^2 + x_k^2 - 2x_j x_k$$

and

$$\sum_{j=1}^{n} \sum_{k=1}^{n} \left(x_j^2 f_j f_k \right) = \left(\sum_{j=1}^{n} x_j^2 f_j \right) \left(\sum_{k=1}^{n} f_k \right)$$

$$= N \sum_{j=1}^{n} (x_j^2 f_j)$$

$$= N^2 s^2$$

we find

$$E^2 = \frac{1}{N^2} \left\{ N^2 s^2 + N^2 s^2 - 2N^2 d^2 \right\}$$

$$= 2(s^2 - d^2)$$

$$= 2\sigma^2 \qquad . \qquad . \qquad . \qquad . \qquad . \qquad . \quad (6.17)$$

so that E is merely the standard deviation multiplied by $\sqrt{2}$. This relation shows that, apart from the constant $\sqrt{2}$, the standard deviation may be regarded as the root-mean-square of all possible pairs of differences of the variate values. Such being the case, the mean difference of Gini loses most of its relative theoretical attraction, and as it is more difficult to calculate the balance of advantage remains with the standard deviation.

SUMMARY

1. The standard deviation σ is defined by

$$\sigma^2 = \frac{1}{N} \Sigma(x^2)$$

where x is the deviation from the arithmetic mean. σ^2 is called the " variance."

2. The root-mean-square deviation s about a point A is defined by

$$s^2 = \frac{1}{N} \Sigma(\xi^2)$$

where ξ is the deviation from A.

3. If $M - A = d$, then

$$s^2 = \sigma^2 + d^2.$$

4. For grouped data the variance should be corrected by subtracting $\dfrac{h^2}{12}$, where h is the width of the class-interval, provided that (a) the frequency is continuous, and (b) that it tapers off to zero in both directions.

5. The s.d. is the minimum root-mean-square deviation.

6. The mean deviation is defined as

$$\text{m.d.} = \frac{1}{N}\Sigma(\ |\ \xi\ |\ ).$$

7. The m.d. is a minimum about the median.

8. The quartiles are the values of the variate which divide the total frequency into 4 equal parts ; similarly, the deciles divide it into 10 equal parts and the percentiles into 100 equal parts.

9. The quartile deviation, or semi-interquartile range, is defined as

$$Q = \frac{Q_3 - Q_1}{2}$$

10. For symmetrical or moderately skew distributions,
$$\text{m.d.} = 0 \cdot 8\sigma \text{ and } Q = 0 \cdot 67\sigma \text{ approximately.}$$

11. For the majority of such distributions 99 per cent of the total frequency lies within a range of 6σ, $7 \cdot 5$ m.d. or $9Q$.

EXERCISES

6.1 Verify the following for the data of Table 4.7, page 82 (in continuation of the work of Exercise 5.1)—

	Stature in inches for adult males born in			
	England	Scotland	Wales	Ireland
Standard deviation (uncorrected) .	2·56	2·50	2·35	2·17
Mean deviation	2·05	1·95	1·82	1·69
Quartile deviation	1·78	1·56	1·46	1·35
Mean deviation /standard deviation .	0·80	0·78	0·78	0·78
Quartile deviation /standard deviation	0·69	0·62	0·62	0·62
Lower quartile.	65·55	66·92	65·06	66·39
Upper ,, ...	69·10	70·04	67·98	69·10

6.2 Find the standard deviation, mean deviation, quartiles and semi-interquartile range for the data in the last column of the table of Exercise 4.6, page 100 (in continuation of the work of Exercise 5.3).

Compare the ratios of mean and quartile deviations to the standard deviation with those stated in **6.22** and **6.25** to be usual for moderately skew distributions.

6.3 Using, or extending if necessary, your diagram for Exercise 5.5, page 123, find the median and upper quartile for incomes subject to sur- or super-tax.

Find also the 9th decile (the value exceeded by 10 per cent of incomes only).

6.4 Find the quartiles of the distribution of Australian marriages given in Example 6.3, and find the semi-interquartile range.

6.5 Find directly the standard deviation of the natural numbers from 1 to 10, and hence verify equation (6.10).

6.6 Show that, for any distribution, the standard deviation is not less than the mean deviation about the mean.

6.7 Show that, for a J-shaped distribution with the maximum frequency towards the lower values of the variate, the median is nearer to Q_1 than to Q_3.

6.8. Find the mean and standard deviation of the following numbers (1) without further grouping, (2) grouping the numbers by fives (40–, 45–, 50–, etc.), (3) grouping by tens (40–, 50–, etc.)—

40, 43, 43, 46, 46, 46, 54, 56, 59, 62, 64, 64, 66, 66, 67, 67, 68, 68, 69, 69, 69, 71, 75, 75, 76, 76, 78, 80, 82, 82, 82, 82, 82, 83, 84, 86, 88, 90, 90, 91, 91, 92, 95, 102, 127.

6.9 Apply Sheppard's correction to the standard deviations calculated in Exercises 6.1 and 6.2 above.

6.10 (Continuing Exercise 5.9, p. 123.) Supposing the frequencies of values 0, 1, 2, 3, . . . of a variable to be given by the terms of the binomial series.

$$q^n, \quad nq^{n-1}p, \quad \frac{n(n-1)}{1.2}q^{n-2}p^2, \quad \cdots$$

where $p+q=1$, find the standard deviation.

6.11 (Cf. the remarks at the end of **6.21**.) The sum of the deviations (without regard to sign) about the centre of the class-interval containing the mean (or median), in a grouped frequency-distribution, is found to be S. Find the correction to be applied to this sum, in order to reduce it to the mean (or median) as origin, on the assumption that the observations are evenly distributed over each class-interval. Take the number of observations below the interval containing the mean (or median) to be n_1, in that interval n_2 and above it n_3, and the distance of the mean (or median) from the arbitrary origin to be d.

6.12   Show that if deviations are small compared with the mean, so that $(x/M)^3$ and higher powers of x/M may be neglected, we have approximately the relation

$$G = M\left(1 - \tfrac{1}{2}\frac{\sigma^2}{M^2}\right)$$

where G is the geometric mean, M the arithmetic mean and σ the standard deviation: and consequently to the same degree of approximation $M^2 - G^2 = \sigma^2$.

6.13   Similarly, show that if deviations are small compared with the mean, we have approximately

$$H = M\left(1 - \frac{\sigma^2}{M^2}\right)$$

H being the harmonic mean.

6.14   Find the coefficients of variation of the height distributions of Exercise 6.1 (using the uncorrected values of the s.d. as given).

6.15   Show that if a range of six times the standard deviation covers at least 18 class-intervals, Sheppard's correction will make a difference of less than 0·5 per cent in the uncorrected value of the standard deviation.

CHAPTER SEVEN

MOMENTS AND MEASURES OF SKEWNESS AND KURTOSIS

Moments

7.1 In considering the calculation of the mean and the root-mean-square deviation we have defined, in passing, the quantities $\frac{1}{N}\Sigma(f\,\xi)$ and $\frac{1}{N}\Sigma(f\,\xi^2)$ as the first and second moments about the value A, ξ being as before the value $X-A$, i.e. the excess of the variate value X over the value A. The first moment about the mean is zero, and the second moment about the mean is the variance (**6.6**).

In generalisation of these definitions we now define the nth moment about A as $\mu_n{}'$, where

$$\mu_n{}' = \frac{1}{N}\Sigma(f\,\xi^n) \qquad . \qquad . \qquad . \qquad . \qquad . \qquad . \qquad (7.1)$$

The moments about the mean, which are of particular importance, we write without dashes so that

$$\mu_n = \frac{1}{N}\Sigma(fx^n) \qquad . \qquad . \qquad . \qquad . \qquad . \qquad . \qquad (7.2)$$

From these definitions we have—

$$\mu_0{}' = \mu_0 = \frac{1}{N}\Sigma(f) = 1 \qquad \text{since } \xi^0 \text{ and } x^0 = 1$$

$$\mu_1{}' = \frac{1}{N}\Sigma(f\,\xi) = M - A = d$$

$$\mu_1 = 0$$

$$\mu_2{}' = \frac{1}{N}\Sigma(f\,\xi^2) = \sigma^2 + d^2$$

$$\mu_2 = \sigma^2$$

These results we have already seen.

7.2 The word "moment" derives from Statics, and we may direct the attention of the student who is familiar with moments of forces to the fact that the sum $\Sigma(f\,\xi^n)$ is divided by N in the definition above. This amounts to a slight departure from the Statical practice, and some writers refer to what we have called "moments" as "moment-coefficients" in order to keep this fact in mind. In Statistics, however, no confusion is likely to arise from the use of the briefer form "moments."

Moments about the mean in terms of moments about any point

7.3 We have, by definition,

$$\xi = X - A = (X-M)+(M-A)$$
$$=x+d$$

Hence,
$$f\,\xi^n = f\,(x+d)^n$$

and
$$\Sigma(f\,\xi^n) = \Sigma\,\{f\,(x+d)^n\}$$

Now, by the binomial theorem,
$$(x+d)^n = x^n + {}^nC_1 dx^{n-1} + {}^nC_2 d^2 x^{n-2} + \ldots + d^n$$

Hence,
$$\Sigma(f\,\xi^n) = \Sigma(fx^n) + {}^nC_1 d\Sigma(fx^{n-1}) + {}^nC_2 d^2\Sigma(fx^{n-2}) + \ldots + d^n\Sigma(f)$$

Dividing by N we get—

$$\mu_n' = \mu_n + {}^nC_1 d\mu_{n-1} + {}^nC_2 d^2\mu_{n-2} + \ldots + d^n \qquad . \qquad . \quad (7.3)$$

Similarly,
$$\Sigma(fx^n) = \Sigma\,\{f\,(\xi-d)^n\}$$

and
$$\mu_n = \mu_n' - {}^nC_1 d\mu'_{n-1} + {}^nC_2 d^2\mu'_{n-2} - \ldots + (-1)^n d^n \qquad . \quad (7.4)$$

These useful relations express the moments about the mean in terms of those about an arbitrary point A, and *vice versa*.

In particular we have—

If $n=1$,

$$\mu_1' = \mu_1 + d = d \qquad\qquad\qquad \text{from (7.3)}$$
$$\mu_1 = \mu_1' - d = 0 \qquad\qquad\qquad \text{from (7.4)}$$

which are simply the relation $M - A = d$ in another form.

If $n=2$,

$$\mu_2' = \mu_2 + 2d\mu_1 + d^2 \qquad\qquad\qquad \text{from (7.3)}$$
$$= \mu_2 + d^2 = \sigma^2 + d^2$$
$$\mu_2 = \mu_2' - 2d\mu_1' + d^2 \qquad\qquad\qquad \text{from (7.4)}$$
$$= \mu_2' - 2d^2 + d^2$$
$$= \mu_2' - d^2$$

These are the relation $\mu_2' = \sigma^2 + d^2$.

If $n=3$,

$$\mu_3'=\mu_3+3d\mu_2+3d^2\mu_1+d^3 \qquad \text{from (7.3)}$$
$$=\mu_3+3d\mu_2+d^3 \qquad . \qquad . \qquad . \qquad . \qquad (7.5)$$
$$\mu_3 =\mu_3'-3d\mu_2'+3d^2\mu_1'-d^3 \qquad \text{from (7.4)}$$
$$=\mu_3'-3d\mu_2'+2d^3 \qquad . \qquad . \qquad . \qquad (7.6)$$

If $n=4$,

$$\mu_4'=\mu_4+4d\mu_3+6d^2\mu_2+4d^3\mu_1+d^4 \qquad \text{from (7.3)}$$
$$=\mu_4+4d\mu_3+6d^2\mu_2+d^4 \qquad . \qquad . \qquad . \qquad (7.7)$$
$$\mu_4=\mu_4'-4d\mu_3'+6d^2\mu_2'-4d^3\mu_1'+d^4 \qquad \text{from (7.4)}$$
$$=\mu_4'-4d\mu_3'+6d^2\mu_2'-3d^4 \qquad . \qquad . \qquad . \qquad (7.8)$$

Calculation of moments

7.4 The calculation of moments of the third and higher orders is similar to that of the first and second. For grouped data we regard the observations as concentrated at the mid-points of the intervals; we choose a convenient arbitrary origin A, find the moments about it and use the relations (7.3) and (7.4) above to find the moments about the mean; we use a check on the arithmetic similar to that of **6.11**; and we have under certain conditions certain Sheppard corrections for grouping.

In practice we rarely require to ascertain moments higher than the fourth. Indeed, moments of higher orders, though important in theory, are so extremely sensitive to sampling fluctuations that values calculated for moderate numbers of observations are quite unreliable and hardly ever repay the labour of computation.

7.5 There are various checks in use for the arithmetic of calculation. We shall use a generalisation of the simple identities of **5.12** and **6.11** In fact, we have

$$(\xi+1)^3=\xi^3+3\xi^2+3\xi+1$$

and hence,

$$\Sigma\{f(\xi+1)^3\} =\Sigma(f\xi^3)+3\Sigma(f\xi^2)+3\Sigma(f\xi)+N$$

Similarly,

$$\Sigma\{f(\xi+1)^4\} =\Sigma(f\xi^4)+4\Sigma(f\xi^3)+6\Sigma(f\xi^2)+4\Sigma(f\xi)+N$$

and so on.

Thus, in calculating $\Sigma(f\xi^n)$ we also find $\Sigma\{f(\xi+1)^n\}$, and this, together with the sums of lower orders, will give us a ready check on the work.

Example 7.1.—Continuing our work on the height distribution of Table 4.7, page 82, let us find the third and fourth moments of the distribution about the mean.

In almost all practical work we require the first and second moments as a matter of course. It is therefore best to proceed systematically in

Calculation of first four moments of the distribution of heights of Table 4.7, p. 82

Height inches	f	ξ	$f\xi$	$f(\xi+1)$	$f\xi^2$	$f(\xi+1)^2$	$f\xi^3$	$f(\xi+1)^3$	$f\xi^4$	$f(\xi+1)^4$
57–	2	–10	–20	–18	200	162	–2,000	–1,458	20,000	13,122
58–	4	–9	–36	–32	324	256	–2,916	–2,048	26,244	16,384
59–	14	–8	–112	–98	896	686	–7,168	–4,802	57,344	33,614
60–	41	–7	–287	–246	2,009	1,476	–14,063	–8,856	98,441	53,136
61–	83	–6	–498	–415	2,988	2,075	–17,928	–10,375	107,568	51,875
62–	169	–5	–845	–676	4,225	2,704	–21,125	–10,816	105,625	43,264
63–	394	–4	–1,576	–1,182	6,304	3,546	–25,216	–10,638	100,864	31,914
64–	669	–3	–2,007	–1,338	6,021	2,676	–18,063	–5,352	54,189	10,704
65–	990	–2	–1,980	–990	3,960	990	–7,920	–990	15,840	990
66–	1,223	–1	–1,223	–4,995	1,223	—	–1,223	–55,335	1,223	—
67–	1,329	0	–8,584	1,329	—	1,329	–117,622	1,329	—	1,329
68–	1,230	1	1,230	2,460	1,230	4,920	1,230	9,840	1,230	19,680
69–	1,063	2	2,126	3,189	4,252	9,567	8,504	28,701	17,008	86,103
70–	646	3	1,938	2,584	5,814	10,336	17,442	41,344	52,326	165,376
71–	392	4	1,568	1,960	6,272	9,800	25,088	49,000	100,352	245,000
72–	202	5	1,010	1,212	5,050	7,272	25,250	43,632	126,250	261,792
73–	79	6	474	553	2,844	3,871	17,064	27,097	102,384	189,679
74–	32	7	224	256	1,568	2,048	10,976	16,384	76,832	131,072
75–	16	8	128	144	1,024	1,296	8,192	11,664	65,536	104,976
76–	5	9	45	50	405	500	3,645	5,000	32,805	50,000
77–	2	10	20	22	200	242	2,000	2,662	20,000	29,282
Total	8,585	—	8,763	13,759	56,809	65,752	119,391	236,653	1,182,061	1,539,292

the computation of the various moments by setting out the arithmetic in tabular form as on opposite page.

From this table we have—

$$\Sigma(f\xi) = \quad 8{,}763 - 8{,}584 = \qquad 179$$
$$\Sigma(f\xi^2) \qquad\qquad = \quad 56{,}809$$
$$\Sigma(f\xi^3) = 119{,}391 - 117{,}622 = \quad 1{,}769$$
$$\Sigma(f\xi^4) \qquad\qquad = 1{,}182{,}061$$

As a check on $\Sigma(f\xi^3)$ we have—

$$\Sigma(f\xi^3) + 3\Sigma(f\xi^2) + 3\Sigma(f\xi) + N$$
$$= 1{,}769 + 170{,}427 + 537 + 8{,}585$$
$$= 181{,}318$$
$$= \Sigma\{f(\xi+1)^3\}$$

As a check on $\Sigma(f\xi^4)$ we have—

$$\Sigma(f\xi^4) + 4\Sigma(f\xi^3) + 6\Sigma(f\xi^2) + 4\Sigma(f\xi) + N$$
$$= 1{,}182{,}061 + 7{,}076 + 340{,}854 + 716 + 8{,}585$$
$$= 1{,}539{,}292$$
$$= \Sigma\{f(\xi+1)^4\}$$

We have then—

$$d = \mu_1' = \frac{1}{N}\Sigma(f\xi) = \frac{179}{8{,}585} = \quad 0\cdot020{,}850{,}32$$

$$\mu_2' = \frac{56{,}809}{8{,}585} \qquad = \quad 6\cdot617{,}239{,}37$$

$$\mu_3' = \frac{1{,}769}{8{,}585} \qquad = \quad 0\cdot206{,}057{,}08$$

$$\mu_4' = \frac{1{,}182{,}061}{8{,}585} \qquad = 137\cdot689{,}108{,}91$$

$$\mu_2 = \mu_2' - d^2$$
$$= 6\cdot616{,}805$$

From equation (7.6)—

$$\mu_3 = \mu_3' - 3d\mu_2' + 2d^3$$
$$= 0\cdot206{,}057{,}08 - 0\cdot413{,}914{,}67 + 0\cdot000{,}018{,}13$$
$$= -0\cdot207{,}839$$

From equation (7.8)—

$$\mu_4 = \mu_4' - 4d\mu_3' + 6d^2\mu_2' - 3d^4$$
$$= 137\cdot689{,}108{,}91 - 0\cdot017{,}184{,}24 + 0\cdot017{,}260{,}51 - 0\cdot000{,}000{,}57$$
$$= 137\cdot689{,}185$$

which gives us μ_2, μ_3, μ_4 in units based on class-intervals, i.e. inches.

Calculation of the first four moments of the distribution of marriages of Table 4.8, p. 84

Mid-value of intervals Years	f	ξ	$f\xi$	$f(\xi+1)$	$f\xi^2$	$f(\xi+1)^2$	$f\xi^3$	$f(\xi+1)^3$	$f\xi^4$	$f(\xi+1)^4$
16·5	294	4	—1,176	—882	4,704	2,646	—18,816	—7,938	75,264	23,814
19·5	10,995	3	—32,985	—21,990	98,955	43,980	—296,865	—87,960	890,595	175,920
22·5	61,001	2	—122,002	—61,001	244,004	61,001	—488,008	—61,001	976,016	61,001
25·5	73,054	1	—73,054	—83,873	73,054	—	—73,054	—156,899	73,054	—
28·5	56,501	0	—229,217	56,501	—	56,501	—876,743	56,501	—	56,501
31·5	33,478	1	33,478	66,956	33,478	133,912	33,478	267,824	33,478	535,648
34·5	20,569	2	41,138	61,707	82,276	185,121	164,552	555,363	329,104	1,666,089
37·5	14,281	3	42,843	57,124	128,529	228,496	385,587	913,984	1,156,761	3,655,936
40·5	9,320	4	37,280	46,600	149,120	233,000	596,480	1,165,000	2,385,920	5,825,000
43·5	6,236	5	31,180	37,416	155,900	224,496	779,500	1,346,976	3,897,500	8,081,856
46·5	4,770	6	28,620	33,390	171,720	233,730	1,030,320	1,636,110	6,181,920	11,452,770
49·5	3,620	7	25,340	28,960	177,380	231,680	1,241,660	1,853,440	8,691,620	14,827,520
52·5	2,190	8	17,520	19,710	140,160	177,390	1,121,280	1,596,510	8,970,240	14,368,590
55·5	1,655	9	14,895	16,550	134,055	165,500	1,206,495	1,655,000	10,858,455	16,550,000
58·5	1,100	10	11,000	12,100	110,000	133,100	1,100,000	1,464,100	11,000,000	16,105,100
61·5	810	11	8,910	9,720	98,010	116,640	1,078,110	1,399,680	11,859,210	16,796,160
64·5	649	12	7,788	8,437	93,456	109,681	1,121,472	1,425,853	13,457,664	18,536,089
67·5	487	13	6,331	6,818	82,303	95,452	1,069,939	1,336,328	13,909,207	18,708,592
70·5	326	14	4,564	4,890	63,896	73,350	894,544	1,100,250	12,523,616	16,503,750
73·5	211	15	3,165	3,376	47,475	54,016	712,125	864,256	10,681,875	13,828,096
76·5	119	16	1,904	2,023	30,464	34,391	487,424	584,647	7,798,784	9,938,999
79·5	73	17	1,241	1,314	21,097	23,652	358,649	425,736	6,097,033	7,663,248
82·5	27	18	486	513	8,748	9,747	157,464	185,193	2,834,352	3,518,667
85·5	14	19	266	280	5,054	5,600	96,026	112,000	1,824,494	2,240,000
88·5	5	20	100	105	2,000	2,205	40,000	46,305	800,000	972,405
Totals	301,785	—	318,049	474,490	2,155,838	2,635,287	13,675,105	19,991,056	137,306,162	202,091,751

Example 7.2.—To find the moments about the mean of the distribution of Australian marriages of Table 4.8, page 84.

Until the last stage we work in class-intervals of 3 years. As in Example 6.3, page 132, we take a working mean at 28·5 years.

From this table we have—

$$\Sigma(f\,\xi) = \quad 318,049 - 229,217 = \quad 88,832$$
$$\Sigma(f\,\xi^2) \qquad\qquad\qquad = \quad 2,155,838$$
$$\Sigma(f\,\xi^3) = 13,675,105 - 876,743 = \ 12,798,362$$
$$\Sigma(f\,\xi^4) \qquad\qquad\qquad = 137,306,162$$

As a check on $\Sigma(f\,\xi)$ we have—

$$\Sigma(f\,\xi) + N = 88,832 + 301,785 = 390,617$$
$$= \Sigma\{f\,(\xi+1)\}$$

Similarly, for $\Sigma(f\,\xi^2)$—

$$\Sigma(f\,\xi^2) + 2\Sigma(f\,\xi) + N = 2,155,838 + 177,664 + 301,785$$
$$= 2,635,287$$
$$= \Sigma\{f\,(\xi+1)^2\}$$

As a check on $\Sigma(f\,\xi^3)$—

$$\Sigma(f\,\xi^3) + 3\Sigma(f\,\xi^2) + 3\Sigma(f\,\xi) + N$$
$$= 12,798,362 + 6,467,514 + 266,496 + 301,785$$
$$= 19,834,157$$
$$= \Sigma\{f\,(\xi+1)^3\}$$

As a check on $\Sigma(f\,\xi^4)$—

$$\Sigma(f\,\xi^4) + 4\Sigma(f\,\xi^3) + 6\Sigma(f\,\xi^2) + 4\Sigma(f\,\xi) + N$$
$$= 137,306,162 + 51,193,448 + 12,935,028 + 355,328 + 301,785$$
$$= 202,091,751$$
$$= \Sigma\{f\,(\xi+1)^4\}$$

Hence, about the working mean—

$$d = \mu_1' = \frac{88,832}{301,785} = \ 0\cdot294,355,253$$

$$\mu_2' = \frac{2,155,838}{301,785} = \ 7\cdot143,622,115$$

$$\mu_3' = \frac{12,798,362}{301,785} = 42\cdot408,873,867$$

$$\mu_4' = \frac{137,306,162}{301,785} = 454\cdot980,075,219$$

For moments about the mean—

$$\mu_2 = \mu_2' - d^2 = 7 \cdot 056{,}977$$

$$\mu_3 = \mu_3' - 3d\mu_2' + 2d^3 = 36 \cdot 151{,}595$$

$$\mu_4 = \mu_4' - 4d\mu_3' + 6d^2\mu_2' - 3d^4 = 408 \cdot 738{,}210$$

These are expressed in class-intervals, which are units of three years. If, as we rarely do, we wish to express the results in other units, say one year, we must multiply the first moment by 3, the second by 3^2, the third by 3^3, the fourth by 3^4, and so on ; e.g.

$$\mu_2 = 7 \cdot 056{,}977 \times 9 = 63 \cdot 512{,}79$$

In this and the preceding example we have retained more digits than are probably necessary, but the student will find it as well to retain several more than appear to be required, since subsequent work involving multiplication or addition may otherwise throw doubt on the final figures.

7.6 It will be evident that the labour involved in calculating the third and fourth moments is very considerable. Calculating machines or tables of powers are a great help, and certain tables for the specific purpose of computing moments will be found in *Tables for Statisticians and Biometricians, Part I.* The student should familiarise himself with the methods given in the two examples above, since, although we shall not use them to any great extent in this book, moments are important in more advanced theory.

Sheppard corrections for moments

7.7 As in the case of the second moment, the effect due to grouping at mid-points of intervals may be corrected for by formulæ due to W. F. Sheppard, from whom they derive their name. The formulæ for the second, third and fourth moments are as follows—

$$\left. \begin{aligned} \mu_2 \text{ (corrected)} &= \mu_2 - \frac{h^2}{12} \\ \mu_3 \text{ (corrected)} &= \mu_3 \\ \mu_4 \text{ (corrected)} &= \mu_4 - \tfrac{1}{2}h^2\mu_2 + \frac{7}{240}h^4 \end{aligned} \right\} \qquad \cdot \quad \cdot \quad (7.9)$$

where h is the width of the class-interval. If we are working in class-intervals as units, h is taken to be unity.

The use of these formulæ is restricted to the cases which we mentioned in **6.12**, i.e. those in which (a) the frequency-distribution is continuous, and (b) the distribution tapers off to zero in both directions.

Example 7.3.—In Example 7.1 we found—

$$\mu_2 = \quad 6 \cdot 616,805$$
$$\mu_3 = -0 \cdot 207,839$$
$$\mu_4 = 137 \cdot 689,185$$

Applying the above corrections, h being 1—

$$\mu_2 \text{ (corr.)} = \quad 6 \cdot 616,805 - 0 \cdot 083,333$$
$$= \quad 6 \cdot 533,472$$
$$\mu_3 \text{ (corr.)} = -0 \cdot 207,839$$
$$\mu_4 \text{ (corr.)} = 137 \cdot 689,185 - 3 \cdot 308.402 + 0 \cdot 029,167$$
$$= 134 \cdot 409\ 950$$

Example 7.4.—In Example 7.2 we have, in units of 3 years—

$$\mu_2 = \quad 7 \cdot 056,977$$
$$\mu_3 = \quad 36 \cdot 151,595$$
$$\mu_4 = 408 \cdot 738,21$$

Thus—

$$\mu_2 \text{ (corr.)} = \quad 7 \cdot 056,977 - 0 \cdot 083,333$$
$$= \quad 6 \cdot 973,644$$
$$\mu_3 \text{ (corr.)} = 36 \cdot 151,595$$
$$\mu_4 \text{ (corr.)} = 408 \cdot 738,210 - 3 \cdot 528,489 + 0 \cdot 029,167$$
$$= 405 \cdot 238,888$$

In units of one year the corrected moments are given by multiplying by 9, 27 and 81 as before.

β- and γ-coefficients

7.8 Certain quantities calculated from the moments about the mean are of particular importance in statistical work. We define—

$$\beta_1 = \frac{\mu_3{}^2}{\mu_2{}^3} \qquad \qquad \qquad . \quad (7.10)$$

$$\beta_2 = \frac{\mu_4}{\mu_2{}^2} \qquad \qquad \qquad . \quad (7.11)$$

and two further quantities—

$$\gamma_1 = +\sqrt{\beta_1} \qquad \qquad \qquad . \quad (7.12)$$

$$\gamma_2 = \beta_2 - 3 = \frac{\mu_4 - 3\mu_2{}^2}{\mu_2{}^2} \qquad . \quad (7.13)$$

The reason for the introduction of these arbitrary-looking quantities will appear in the sequel.[1]

---

[1] In general, Karl Pearson defined

$$\beta_{2n+1} = \frac{\mu_3\mu_{2n+3}}{\mu_{2n+3}}$$

$$\beta_{2n} = \frac{\mu_{2n+3}}{\mu_{2n+1}}$$

It is to be noted that these four coefficients are all pure numbers and, as such, are independent of the scale of measurement of the variable ; for since μ_n has the dimensions of (variable)^n, $\mu_3{}^2$ has the dimensions (variable)^6 and so has $\mu_2{}^3$, and hence their quotient has dimension zero, i.e. is a pure number ; and similarly for the quotient of μ_4 and $\mu_2{}^2$.

Example 7.5.—Let us calculate β_1 and β_2 for the distribution of Example 7.1.

We have, using the corrected values of Example 7.3—

$$\beta_1 = \frac{\mu_3{}^2}{\mu_2{}^3}$$

$$= \frac{(-0\cdot207839)^2}{(6\cdot533472)^3}$$

$$= \frac{0\cdot043197}{278\cdot889} = 0\cdot000155$$

$$\beta_2 = \frac{\mu_4}{\mu_2{}^2}$$

$$= \frac{134\cdot40995}{42\cdot68662}$$

$$= 3\cdot149$$

Example 7.6.—Similarly, in the data of Example 7.2, using corrected values—

$$\beta_1 = \frac{(36\cdot151595)^2}{(6\cdot973644)^3}$$

$$= 3\cdot854$$

$$\beta_2 = \frac{405\cdot238888}{(6\cdot973644)^2}$$

$$= 8\cdot333$$

It should be noted in this last example that, since the coefficients are pure numbers, it does not matter whether we work in units of three years or of one year.

Measures of skewness

7.9 The departure of a frequency-distribution from symmetry has a certain interest, and several measures have been devised to permit of the measurement of this skewness. Such measures should (*a*) be pure numbers, so as to be independent of the units in which the variable is measured, and (*b*) be zero when the distribution is symmetrical.

7.10 Three such measures deserve mention. In the first place, we can define

$$\text{Skewness} = \frac{(Q_3 - Mi) - (Mi - Q_1)}{2Q} = \frac{Q_1 + Q_3 - 2Mi}{2Q} \qquad . \qquad . \quad (7.14)$$

This can be put in the form—

$$\text{Skewness} = \frac{(Q_3 - Mi) - (Mi - Q_1)}{(Q_3 - Mi) + (Mi - Q_1)} \quad . \quad . \quad . \quad (7.15)$$

i.e. the skewness is taken to be the difference of the quartile deviations from the median divided by their sum. It is clearly a pure number, for both numerator and denominator have the same dimensions, and it is zero when the distribution is symmetrical. It varies from -1 to $+1$.[1]

This is a rather rough-and-ready measure which might, however, be useful if we were using the semi-interquartile range as a measure of dispersion and were unable or unwilling to calculate the standard deviation.

7.11 The most common measure of skewness is Pearson's, defined by

$$\text{Skewness} = \frac{\text{Mean} - \text{Mode}}{\text{Standard deviation}} = \frac{M - Mo}{\sigma} \quad . \quad . \quad (7.16)$$

This evidently is a pure number and is zero for symmetrical distributions.

7.12 The calculation of this coefficient of skewness is subject to the inconvenience of determining the position of the mode. We may circumvent this difficulty in several ways. In the first place, for distributions which are obviously not too skew we may use the empirical relation of **5.27**. We then have—

$$\text{Skewness} = \frac{3(\text{Mean} - \text{Median})}{\text{Standard deviation}} \quad . \quad . \quad . \quad (7.17)$$

Secondly, for a large class of curves to which the moderately skew humped curve is a close approximation, the skewness of equation (7.16) is given exactly by

$$\text{Skewness} = \frac{\sqrt{\beta_1}(\beta_2 + 3)}{2(5\beta_2 - 6\beta_1 - 9)} \quad . \quad . \quad . \quad (7.18)$$

We may, therefore, take this to be an approximation to the value given by equation (7.16).

It should be noted that the measures (7.14) and (7.16) are positive if the longer tail of the distribution lies toward the higher values of the variate (the right) and negative in the contrary case. This accords with the anticipatory remarks of **4.20**. The measure (7.18) is to be regarded as without sign.

---

[1] In the 10th and previous editions of this book the measure $\text{Skewness} = \frac{Q_1 + Q_3 - 2Mi}{Q}$ was suggested, i.e. twice the measure (7.14). The above form has the advantage that its limits are -1 and $+1$.

Limits of the measures of skewness

7.13 We have already remarked that the measure given by equation (7.14) lies between −1 and +1. There is no limit in theory to the measure (7.16) or its approximation (7.18), and this is a slight drawback. But in practice the value given by equation (7.16) is rarely very high, and for moderately skew single-humped curves is usually less than unity.

It has been shown that the quantity $\dfrac{\text{Mean}-\text{Median}}{\text{Standard deviation}}$ lies between the limits −1 and +1, and the measure (7.17) therefore lies between −3 and +3. In practice it rarely approaches these limits.

Example 7.7.—Let us once again consider the height distribution of Table 4.7, which has been already discussed in this chapter (Examples 7.1, 7.3 and 7.5).

We have—

Mean (Example 5.1, p. 106)	$=67\cdot46$ inches
S.d. (corrected, Example 6.4, p. 134)	$= 2\cdot56$ inches
Median (Example 5.3, p. 112)	$=67\cdot47$ inches
Q_1 (Example 6.9, p. 141)	$=65\cdot71$ inches
Q_3 (*ibid.*)	$=69\cdot21$ inches
Q (*ibid.*)	$= 1\cdot75$ inches
β_1 (corrected, Example 7.5, p. 160)	$= 0\cdot000155$
β_2 (*ibid.*)	$= 3\cdot149$

The measure of skewness (7.14) is, then,

$$\text{Sk} = \frac{Q_1+Q_3-2Mi}{2Q}$$
$$= \frac{65\cdot71+69\cdot21-(2\times67\cdot47)}{2\times1\cdot75}$$
$$= -0\cdot006$$

We can clearly place no reliance on this figure. The median and quartiles were obtained by methods of approximation which we cannot expect to give accuracy to the second decimal place. We can only conclude, therefore, that so far as the measure (7.14) is concerned, there is no significant skewness.

The measure (7.18) gives—

$$\text{Sk} = \frac{0\cdot0124\times6\cdot149}{2(15\cdot745-0\cdot001-9)}$$
$$= \frac{0\cdot0124\times6\cdot149}{2\times6\cdot744}$$
$$= 0\cdot006$$

Here again the skewness is extremely small, and is, in fact, almost equal to the value given by (7.14).

If we take the measure (7.17) we get—

$$Sk = \frac{3(M-Mi)}{\sigma}$$

$$= \frac{-0\cdot03}{2\cdot56}$$

$$= -0\cdot012$$

This value is suspect because we have determined the mean and the median only to the second decimal place, but clearly the value is small.

We conclude that there is only very slight skewness. At this stage we cannot say whether such small skewness is significant, but it is at least probably attributable to sampling fluctuations.

Example 7.8.—For the marriage data of Examples 7.2, 7.4 and 7.6 it will be found that, using the working mean as origin—

$$\text{Mean} = 0\cdot2944$$
$$\text{Median} = -0\cdot4018$$
$$Q_1 = -1\cdot4568$$
$$Q_3 = 1\cdot2316$$

and

$$\sigma \text{ (corrected) (Ex. 6.5)} = 2\cdot6408$$
$$\beta_1 = 3\cdot854$$
$$\beta_2 = 8\cdot333$$

The measure (7.14) is—

$$Sk = \frac{(Q_3-Mi)-(Mi-Q_1)}{(Q_3-Mi)+(Mi-Q_1)}$$

$$= \frac{1\cdot6334-1\cdot0550}{1\cdot6334+1\cdot0550}$$

$$= \frac{0\cdot5784}{2\cdot6884}$$

$$= 0\cdot22$$

The measure (7.18) is—

$$Sk = \frac{\sqrt{3\cdot854}(11\cdot333)}{2(41\cdot665-23\cdot124-9)}$$

$$= \frac{1\cdot963\times11\cdot333}{2\times9\cdot541}$$

$$= 1\cdot17$$

The two are very different, as we might expect, but both indicate strong positive skewness. As a matter of interest we may compare the value (7.17), which gives

$$Sk = \frac{3\times0\cdot6962}{2\cdot6408}$$

$$= 0\cdot79$$

Kurtosis

7.14 The coefficient β_2 or its derivative γ_2 is used to measure a property of the single-humped distribution known as kurtosis ($\kappa\upsilon\rho\tau\acute{o}s$, humped).

We take as the standard value of β_2 the number 3, for reasons which will appear when we study the so-called " normal " curve (**8.24**). This curve is approximately of the shape given in fig. 4.5, page 81. Curves with values of β_2 less than 3 are called platykurtic ($\pi\lambda\alpha\tau\acute{v}s$, broad, $+$ $\kappa\upsilon\rho\tau\acute{o}s$). Curves with values greater than 3 are called leptokurtic[1] ($\lambda\epsilon\pi\tau\acute{o}s$, narrow, $+\kappa\upsilon\rho\tau\acute{o}s$). " Student " gives an amusing mnemonic for these names : Platykurtic curves, like the platypus, are squat with short tails. Leptokurtic curves are high with long tails like the kangaroo— noted for " lepping " !

Example 7.9.—In the height distribution of Examples 7.1, 7.3, 7.5 and 7.7—

$$\beta_2 = 3 \cdot 149$$
$$\gamma_2 = \beta_2 - 3 = 0 \cdot 149$$

Hence the curve is slightly leptokurtic.

On the other hand, in the marriage distribution of Examples 7.2, 7.4, 7.6 and 7.8—

$$\beta_2 = 8 \cdot 333$$
$$\gamma_2 = 5 \cdot 333$$

and the curve is very leptokurtic.

Cumulants

7.15 We may conclude this chapter by referring briefly to a set of quantities similar to moments which have some theoretical and practical importance. These are the cumulants.[2]

The cumulants are defined by a rather complicated mathematical expression which we shall not here reproduce. For present purposes it is sufficient to note that the first four cumulants may be expressed as simple functions of the first four moments. In fact we have—

$$\left. \begin{array}{l} \kappa_1 = \mu_1' \\ \kappa_2 = \mu_2' - \mu_1'^2 \\ \kappa_3 = \mu_3' - 3\mu_1'\mu_2' + 2\mu_1'^3 \\ \kappa_4 = \mu_4' - 4\mu_1'\mu_3' - 3\mu_2'^2 + 12\mu_1'^2\mu_2' - 6\mu_1'^4 \end{array} \right\} \qquad . \qquad . \quad (7.19)$$

---

[1] These terms are due to Karl Pearson and appear to have been given for the first time in *Biometrika*, 1905, **4**, 169. By a slip *leptokurtosis* is there inadvertently applied to distributions for which $\beta_2 < 3$.

It has often been stated that platykurtic curves are relatively more flat-topped and leptokurtic curves more peaked than the " normal " curve. This is the origin of the name and of " Student's " mnemonic, and the assertion was made in the 13th and earlier editions of this book. It is, however, very difficult to justify in general.

[2] These quantities were introduced into statistics by T. N. Thiele under the name of semi-invariants, the forms " seminvariant " and " half-invariant " also occurring in earlier literature. The word " cumulant " is preferable and is now in general use, there being other families of quantities which also have the seminvariant property in the algebraical sense.

In particular, about the mean,

$$
\left.
\begin{aligned}
\kappa_1 &= 0 \\
\kappa_2 &= \mu_2 \\
\kappa_3 &= \mu_3 \\
\kappa_4 &= \mu_4 - 3\mu_2{}^2
\end{aligned}
\right\} \qquad . \qquad . \qquad . \qquad . \quad (7.20)
$$

7.16 These relations are used in the calculation of the cumulants, the moments being first ascertained in the manner of the earlier sections of this chapter. For instance, the first four cumulants of the height distribution which has served us as an example are, about the mean,

$$
\begin{aligned}
\kappa_1 &= 0 \\
\kappa_2 &= 6 \cdot 616805 \\
\kappa_3 &= -0 \cdot 207839 \\
\kappa_4 &= 137 \cdot 689185 - 3 \times (6 \cdot 616805)^2 = 6 \cdot 34286
\end{aligned}
$$

if we take uncorrected values of the moments.

7.17 The cumulants have several remarkable properties. In the first place, all cumulants except the first are independent of the origin of calculation. The moments vary according to the point about which they are calculated, which makes it necessary to specify the origin A in speaking of them. The cumulants, on the other hand, do not, so that it is unnecessary to specify any value A in giving their values; the sole exception to this rule is the first cumulant, which is the same as the first moment.

Secondly, if the scale of measurement of the variate is altered by multiplying all values by a constant a, the nth cumulant is multiplied by a^n. Thus, in the height distribution, if we change our scale to centimetres instead of inches, and so multiply all values of the variate by $2 \cdot 54$, the cumulants in the previous section are to be multiplied by $2 \cdot 54$, $2 \cdot 54^2$, $2 \cdot 54^3$, $2 \cdot 54^4$, respectively.

We shall also see in the next chapter that the cumulants take simple values for certain theoretical frequency-distributions of importance.

SUMMARY

1. The nth moment about the point A is defined as

$$
\mu_n' = \frac{1}{N} \Sigma(f \, \xi^n)
$$

where $\xi = X - A$, and X is the value of the variate.

2. The nth moment about the mean is written μ_n.

3.
$$\mu_n = \mu_n' - {}^nC_1 d\mu'_{n-1} + {}^nC_2 d^2 \mu'_{n-2} - \ldots + (-1)^n d^n$$

where

$$d = M - A$$

and in particular

$$\mu_3 = \mu_3' - 3d\mu_2' + 2d^3$$
$$\mu_4 = \mu_4' - 4d\mu_3' + 6d^2\mu_2' - 3d^4$$

4. Sheppard's corrections for the moments are—

$$\mu_2 \text{ (corrected)} = \mu_2 - \frac{h^2}{12}$$

$$\mu_3 \text{ (corrected)} = \mu_3$$

$$\mu_4 \text{ (corrected)} = \mu_4 - \tfrac{1}{2}h^2\mu_2 + \frac{7}{240}h_4$$

5.
$$\beta_1 = \frac{\mu_3^2}{\mu_2^3} \qquad \beta_2 = \frac{\mu_4}{\mu_2^2}$$

$$\gamma_1 = \sqrt{\beta_1} = \frac{\mu_3}{\mu_2^{3/2}} \qquad \gamma_2 = \beta_2 - 3 = \frac{\mu_4 - 3\mu_2^2}{\mu_2^2}$$

6. Pearson's measure of skewness is given by

$$Sk = \frac{\text{Mean} - \text{Mode}}{\text{Standard deviation}}$$

which, for a large class of curves, is equal to

$$\frac{\sqrt{\beta_1}(\beta_2 + 3)}{2(5\beta_2 - 6\beta_1 - 9)}$$

7. If the standard deviation is not known, a rough measure of skewness is obtained by taking

$$Sk = \frac{Q_1 + Q_3 - 2Mi}{2Q}$$

8. Distributions for which $\beta_2 > 3$ are said to be leptokurtic; those for which $\beta_2 < 3$ are platykurtic.

9. The first four cumulants, in terms of the moments about the mean, are—

$$\kappa_1 = 0$$
$$\kappa_2 = \mu_2$$
$$\kappa_3 = \mu_3$$
$$\kappa_4 = \mu_4 - 3\mu_2^2$$

10. The cumulants are independent of the origin of calculation, except the first, which is equal to the mean.

EXERCISES

7.1 Find the first four moments about the mean of the distribution of males in the United Kingdom according to weight given in Exercise 4.6., page 100. (Correct your values for grouping.)

Hence find β_1 and β_2 and measure the kurtosis of the distribution.

7.2 For the same distribution find the three measures of skewness, approximating to the mode by the empirical relation of **5.27**.

7.3 Find the first four moments about the mean, the values of β_1, β_2, and the three measures of skewness for the following distribution (see table below). (Apply Sheppard's corrections.)

7.4 In the data of Example 7.1, group the individuals by intervals of three inches (57–, 60–, etc.) and calculate the first four moments about the mean. Compare your results with those of Example 7.1, (a) before Sheppard's corrections are applied, and (b) after Sheppard's corrections are applied.

7.5 Find the third and fourth moments about the mean of the binomial series—

$$q^n, \qquad nq^{n-1}p, \qquad \frac{n(n-1)}{1.2}q^{n-2}q^2, \ldots \text{ where } p+q=1$$

(continuing the work of Exercise 6.10, page 149).

Data for Exercise 7.3—4912 Cows classified according to their yield of milk
(Data from J. F. Tocher, " An Investigation of the Milk Yield of Dairy Cows,"
Biometrika, 1928, **20B**, 105.)

Yield of milk (gallons per week) (Central value of interval)	Number of cows	Yield of milk (gallons per week) (Central value of interval)	Number of cows
8	1	23	214
9	5	24	153
10	13	25	112
11	33	26	58
12	71	27	35
13	151	28	13
14	236	29	15
15	339	30	4
16	499	31	5
17	552	32	2
18	585	33	1
19	586	34	1
20	496		
21	448	Total	4,912
22	284		

7.6 The first four moments of a distribution about the value 4 are $-1 \cdot 5$, 17, -30 and 108 ; find the moments about the mean and the origin.

7.7 Show that for a symmetrical distribution all moments about the mean of odd order are zero.

7.8 Show that for any distribution $\beta_2 > 1$.

7.9 Calculate the second, third and fourth cumulants of the distribution of Australian marriages of Example 7.2, (a) from the moments about the mean, using equation (7.20), and (b) from the moments about the value $28 \cdot 5$, using equation (7.19) ; and hence verify that the values of the cumulants are independent of the origin of calculation. (Use uncorrected values of the moments.)

7.10 Show that

$$d = \kappa_1$$

$$\sigma = \sqrt{\kappa_2}$$

$$\gamma_1 = \frac{\kappa_3}{\sigma^3}$$

$$\gamma_2 = \frac{\kappa_4}{\kappa_2{}^2}$$

CHAPTER EIGHT

THREE IMPORTANT THEORETICAL DISTRIBUTIONS
THE BINOMIAL, THE NORMAL AND THE POISSON

Theoretical distributions

8.1 In the examples of frequency-distributions which we have given in Chapter 4 and subsequent chapters we have been careful to take data from observation and experiment. It is possible, however, starting with certain general hypotheses, to deduce mathematically what the frequency-distributions of certain populations should be. Such distributions we shall call theoretical.

8.2 There are three theoretical distributions which, from their historical interest as well as their intrinsic importance, occupy a position in the forefront of statistical theory. They are, in the order of their discovery, the Binomial (due to James Bernoulli, *circa* 1700), the Normal (due to Demoivre, but more often associated with the names of Laplace and Gauss, who discussed it at the close of the eighteenth and the beginning of the nineteenth centuries), and the Poisson (due to S. D. Poisson, who published it in 1837).

These three are, so to speak, the classical distributions. Certain others were discovered during the nineteenth century, but it was not until the end of the century that there began the second period of statistical discovery which has since given us a wealth of theoretical distributions. Even this latest crop depends to some extent on the properties of the first three, and particularly of the Normal Distribution The three therefore form, historically and logically, the starting-point of the theory of particular distributions, and in this chapter we propose to give an account of their main properties.

The binomial distribution

8.3 If we may regard an ideal coin as a uniform, homogeneous circular disc, there is nothing which can make it tend to fall more often on the one side than on the other ; we may expect, therefore, that in any long series of throws the coin will fall with either face uppermost an approximately equal number of times, or with, say, heads uppermost approximately half the times. Similarly, if we may regard the ideal die as a perfect homogeneous cube, it will tend, in any long series of throws, to fall with each of its six faces uppermost an approximately equal number of times, or with any given face uppermost one-sixth of the whole number of times. These results are sometimes expressed by saying that the chance of throwing heads (or tails) with a coin is 1/2, and the chance of throwing six (or any other face) with a die is 1/6. To avoid speaking of such particular instances as coins or dice we shall in future, using terms which have become conventional, refer to an event the chance of success of which is p and the chance of failure q. Obviously $p+q=1$.

8.4 We will now assume that the events in a number of trials are all independent, i.e. that the chances p and q are the same for each event and remain constant throughout the trials. The case corresponds to the tossing of perfect coins or the throwing of perfect dice.

Suppose now we take a number of sets of n trials and count the number of successes in each set; for example, we might toss a coin ten times for each set, and observe the number of heads in each set of ten. In general, there will be some sets with no successes, some with one success, some with two successes, and so on. Hence, if we classify the sets according to the number of successes which they contain we shall get a frequency-distribution. Table 4.15, page 96, gives such a distribution for some dice-throwing experiments. We shall now see how, on the assumption of independence of successive events to which we have just referred, the nature of this distribution may be theoretically determined.

8.5 For the case of single events we expect in N trials to get Np successes and Nq failures.

Suppose now we take N pairs of events, i.e. two to the set. There will be Nq cases in which the first event is a failure, and, in virtue of the independence of the events, among these Nq there will be $Nq \times q$ failures, and $Nq \times p$ successes, of the second event on the average. Similarly, of the Np cases in which the first event was a success, the second event will, on the average, be a success in $Np \times p$ and a failure in $Np \times q$ cases. Hence there will be Nq^2 cases in which both events are failures, $2Npq$ cases with one success and one failure, and Np^2 cases in which both are successes.

If we now take N sets of three events, we see that, of the Nq^2 cases in which the first two events were failures, $Nq^2 \times q$ will give a third failure and $Nq^2 \times p$ one success; of the $2Npq$ cases, $2Npq^2$ will give two failures and a success and $2Np^2q$ one failure and two successes; and of the Np^2 cases, Np^2q will give one failure and two successes and Np^3 will give three successes. Hence the number of sets with 3 failures, 2 failures and 1 success, 1 failure and 2 successes, and 3 successes are, respectively,

$$Nq^3, \qquad 3Nq^2p, \qquad 3Nqp^2, \qquad Np^3$$

8.6 From these results it is evident that the frequencies of 0, 1, 2, . . . successes are given

for *one* event by the binomial expansion of $N(q+p)$

for *two* events   ,,   ,,   ,, $N(q+p)^2$

for *three* events ,,   ,,   ,, $N(q+p)^3$

In general, for n events the frequencies of successes in N sets are given by the successive terms in the binomial expansion of $N(q+p)^n$, i.e.

$$N\left\{q^n+nq^{n-1}p+\frac{n(n-1)}{1.2}q^{n-2}p^2+\frac{n(n-1)(n-2)}{1.2.3}q^{n-3}p^3+\ldots\right\}$$

This is the so-called *binomial distribution*.

Example 8.1.—If we take 100 sets of 10 tosses of a perfect coin, in how many cases should we expect to get 7 heads and 3 tails ?

Here $$p=\tfrac{1}{2}, \qquad q=\tfrac{1}{2}$$

Hence, the numbers of successes 0, 1, . . . 10 are the terms in $100(\tfrac{1}{2}+\tfrac{1}{2})^{10}$,

i.e. $$100\left\{\left(\frac{1}{2}\right)^{10}+10.\ \frac{1}{2}\ ^9\left(\frac{1}{2}\right)+\frac{10.9}{1.2}\left(\frac{1}{2}\right)^8\left(\frac{1}{2}\right)^2+\ldots\right\}$$

The term giving 7 successes and 3 failures is—

$$100\times{}^{10}C_7(\tfrac{1}{2})^7(\tfrac{1}{2})^3$$

$$=100.\frac{10.9.8}{1.2.3}\cdot\frac{1}{2^{10}}$$

$$=\frac{3000}{256}$$

$$=12 \text{ approximately.}$$

Example 8.2.—In the previous example, in how many cases should we expect to get 7 heads at least ? As before, the numbers of successes are the terms in

$$\frac{100}{2^{10}}\left\{1+10+\frac{10.9}{1.2}+\ \ldots\ \right\}$$

We require the *sum* of terms with 7, 8, 9, 10 successes. Our expected number is, then,

$$\frac{100}{2^{10}}\{{}^{10}C_7+{}^{10}C_8+{}^{10}C_9+{}^{10}C_{10}\}$$

$$=\frac{100}{2^{10}}\left\{\frac{10.9.8}{1.2.3}+\frac{10.9}{1.2}+\frac{10}{1}+1\right\}$$

$$=\frac{100}{2^{10}}\{176\}$$

$$=\frac{1100}{64}$$

$$=17 \text{ approximately.}$$

General form of the binomial distribution

8.7 The form of the binomial distribution depends (1) on the values of p and q, (2) on the value of the exponent n.

If p and q are equal the distribution is evidently symmetrical, for p and q may be interchanged without altering the value of any term, and consequently terms equidistant from the two ends of the series are equal.

If, on the other hand, p and q are unequal, the distribution is skew. The following table shows the calculated distributions for $n=20$ and values of p, proceeding by 0·1, from 0·1 to 0·5. When $p=0·1$, cases of two successes are the most frequent, but cases of one success almost equally frequent : even nine successes may, however, occur about once in 10,000 trials. As p is increased, the position of the maximum frequency gradually advances, and the two tails of the distribution become more nearly equal, until $p=0·5$, when the distribution is symmetrical. Of course, if the table were continued, the distribution for $p=0·6$ would be similar to that for $q=0·6$, but reversed end for end, and so on.

TABLE 8.1—Terms of the binomial series 10,000 $(q+p)^{20}$ for values of p from 0·1 to 0·5

(Figures given to the nearest unit)

Number of successes	$p=0·1$ $q=0·9$	$p=0·2$ $q=0·8$	$p=0·3$ $q=0·7$	$p=0·4$ $q=0·6$	$p=0·5$ $q=0·5$
0	1,216	115	8	—	—
1	2,702	576	68	5	—
2	2,852	1,369	278	31	2
3	1,901	2,054	716	123	11
4	898	2,182	1,304	350	46
5	319	1,746	1,789	746	148
6	89	1,091	1,916	1,244	370
7	20	545	1,643	1,659	739
8	4	222	1,144	1,797	1,201
9	1	74	654	1,597	1,602
10	—	20	308	1,171	1,762
11	—	5	120	710	1,602
12	—	1	39	355	1,201
13	—	—	10	146	739
14	—	—	2	49	370
15	—	—	—	13	148
16	—	—	—	3	46
17	—	—	—	—	11
18	—	—	—	—	2
19	—	—	—	—	—
20	—	—	—	—	—

8.8 If $p=q$, the effect of increasing n is to raise the mean and increase the dispersion.   If p is not equal to q, however, not only does an increase in n raise the mean and increase the dispersion, but it also lessens the asymmetry ; the greater n, for the same values of p and q, the less the asymmetry. Thus, if we compare the first distribution of the above table with that given by $n=100$, we have the following—

TABLE 8.2—Terms of the binomial series 10,000 $(0\cdot9+0\cdot1)^{100}$

(Figures given to the nearest unit)

Number of successes	Frequency	Number of successes	Frequency	Number of successes	Frequency
0	—	8	1,148	16	193
1	3	9	1,304	17	106
2	16	10	1,319	18	54
3	59	11	1,199	19	26
4	159	12	988	20	12
5	339	13	743	21	5
6	596	14	513	22	2
7	889	15	327	23	1

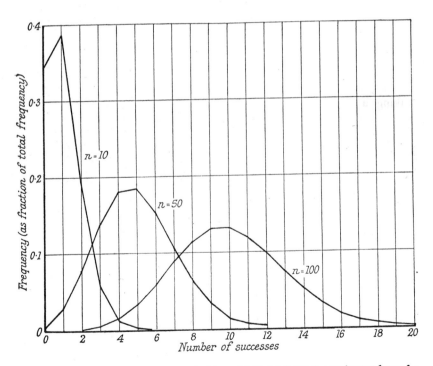

Fig. 8.1.—Frequency-polygons of the binomial $(0\cdot9+0\cdot1)^{n}$ for various values of n

The maximum frequencies now occur for 9 and 10 successes, and the two " tails " are much more nearly equal. If, on the other hand, n is reduced to 2, the distribution is—

Number of successes	Frequency
0	8,100
1	1,800
2	100

and the maximum frequency is at one end of the range.

The tendency towards symmetry may be seen from fig. 8.1, in which the binomial $(0 \cdot 9 + 0 \cdot 1)^n$ has been drawn for various values of n. See also **8.12** below.

Constants of the binomial distribution

8.9 We proceed to find the lower moments of the distribution $N(q+p)^n$.

Taking an arbitrary origin at 0 successes, we have the successive deviations ξ as 0, 1, 2, . . . n, and hence,

$$\mu_1' = (q^n \times 0) + ({}^nC_1 q^{n-1} p \times 1) + ({}^nC_2 q^{n-2} p^2 \times 2) + \ . \ . \ . + (p^n \times n)$$
$$= p\{nq^{n-1} + n(n-1)q^{n-2}p + \ . \ . \ . + np^{n-1}\}$$
$$= np\{q^{n-1} + (n-1)q^{n-2}p + \ . \ . \ . + p^{n-1}\}$$
$$= np(q+p)^{n-1}$$

Now, $q+p=1$

Hence, $\mu_1' = np$

That is, the mean M is np.

We have, further,

$$\mu_2' = (q^n \times 0) + ({}^nC_1 q^{n-1}p \times 1) + ({}^nC_2 q^{n-2}p^2 \times 2^2) + \ . \ . \ . + (p^n \times n^2)$$

$$= np\left\{q^{n-1} + 2(n-1)q^{n-2}p + \frac{3(n-1)(n-2)}{2}q^{n-3}p^2 + \ . \ . \ . + np^{n-1}\right\}$$

The expression in brackets is the first moment of the binomial $(q+p)^{n-1}$ about origin -1, and hence is equal to $(n-1)p+1$.

Hence,

$$\mu_2' = np\{(n-1)p+1\}$$

It may also be shown in a similar way (but we omit the proof) that

$$\mu_3' = np\{(n-1)(n-2)p^2 + 3(n-1)p + 1\}$$
$$\mu_4' = np\{(n-1)(n-2)(n-3)p^3 + 6(n-1)(n-2)p^2 + 7(n-1)p + 1\}$$

8.10 From these results we may find the moments about the mean We have—

$$\mu_2=\mu_2{}'-d^2$$
$$=np\{(n-1)p+1\}-n^2p^2$$
$$=np(1-p)$$
$$=npq$$

Hence we have the important result that—

$$\sigma=\sqrt{npq} \qquad . \qquad . \qquad . \qquad . \qquad . \qquad (8.1)$$

8.11 Similarly, it will be found that—

$$\mu_3=npq(q-p) \quad . \qquad . \qquad . \qquad . \qquad . \qquad (8.2)$$
$$\mu_4=3p^2q^2n^2+pqn(1-6pq) \qquad . \qquad . \qquad (8.3)$$

Hence,

$$\beta_1=\frac{\mu_3{}^2}{\mu_2{}^3}=\frac{(q-p)^2}{npq} \qquad . \qquad . \qquad . \qquad (8.4)$$

$$\beta_2=\frac{\mu_4}{\mu_2{}^2}=3+\frac{1-6pq}{pqn} \qquad . \qquad . \qquad (8.5)$$

8.12 Thus the binomial distribution has mean np and standard deviation $\sqrt{npq}$. It is instructive to note that β_1 and (β_2-3) are both of order $\frac{1}{n}$ Hence, as n becomes larger, the distribution tends to symmetry and zero kurtosis.

The values of β_1 and β_2 for some values of p and q and ranges of n are shown in Tables 8.3, 8.4 and 8.5.

From an inspection of these tables it will be seen that even for an extremely small value of p the binomial tends to zero β_1 and zero kurtosis for values of n well within practical limits. For the symmetrical binomial $p=q=0\cdot5$, β_1 is of course zero, and β_2 rapidly approaches 3.

TABLE 8.3.—Values of β_1 and β_2 for the binomial with $p=0\cdot02$, $q=0\cdot98$
(From M. Greenwood, *Biometrika*, 1913, 9, 69.)

n	β_1	β_2
100	0·4702	3·4502
200	0·2351	3·2251
300	0·1567	3·1501
400	0·1176	3·1126
500	0·0940	3·0900
600	0·0784	3·0750
700	0·0672	3·0643
800	0·0588	3·0563
900	0·0522	3·0500
1,000	0·0470	3·0450

TABLE 8.4.—Values of β_1 and β_2 for the binomial with $p=0\cdot1$, $q=0\cdot9$

n	β_1	β_2
100	$0\cdot0711$	$3\cdot0511$
200	$0\cdot0356$	$3\cdot0256$
1,000	$0\cdot0771$	$3\cdot0051$

TABLE 8.5.—Values of β_2 for the binomial with $p=0\cdot5$, $q=0\cdot5$

n	β_2
4	$2\cdot5$
6	$2\cdot6667$
8	$2\cdot75$
10	$2\cdot8$
50	$2\cdot96$
100	$2\cdot98$
1,000	$2\cdot998$

Mechanical representation of the binomial distribution

8.13 There is an interesting mechanical method of constructing a representation of the binomial series. The apparatus, which is illustrated in fig. 8.2, consists of a funnel opening into a space—say a $\frac{1}{4}$ inch in depth —between a sheet of glass and a back-board. This space is broken up by

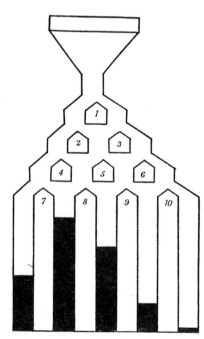

successive rows of wedges like 1, 2 3, 4 5 6, etc., which will divide up into streams any granular material such as shot or mustard seed which is poured through the funnel when the apparatus is held at a slope. At the foot these wedges are replaced by vertical strips, in the spaces between which the material can collect. Consider the stream of material that comes from the funnel and meets the wedge 1. This wedge is set so as to throw q parts of the stream to the left and p parts to the right (of the observer). The wedges 2 and 3 are set so as to divide the resultant streams in the same proportions. Thus wedge 2 throws q^2 parts of the original material to the left and qp to the right, wedge 3 throws pq parts of the original material to the left and p^2 to the right. The streams passing these wedges are therefore in the ratio of $q^2 : 2qp : p^2$. The next row of wedges is again set so as to divide these streams in the

Fig. 8.2.—The Pearson-Galton binomial apparatus

same proportions as before and the four streams that result will bear the proportions $q^3 : 3q^2p : 3qp^2 : p^3$. The final set, at the heads of the vertical strips, will give the streams proportions $q^4 : 4q^3p : 6q^2p^2 : 4qp^3 : p^4$, and these streams will accumulate between the strips and give a representation of the binomial by a kind of histogram, as shown. Of course as many rows of wedges may be provided as may be desired.

This kind of apparatus was originally devised by Galton in a form that gave roughly the symmetrical binomial, a stream of shot being allowed to fall through rows of nails, and the resultant streams being collected in partitioned spaces. The apparatus was generalised by Karl Pearson, who used rows of wedges fixed to movable slides, so that they could be adjusted to give any ratio of $q : p$.

8.14 It must not be forgotten that although we have spoken in **8.12** of the skewness and kurtosis of the binomial distribution, it is essentially discontinuous. This is a serious limitation.

Consider, for example, the frequency-distribution of the number of male births in batches of 10,000 births, the mean number being, say, 5,100. The distribution will be given by the terms of the series $(0 \cdot 49 + 0 \cdot 51)^{10,000}$, and the standard deviation is, in round numbers, 50 births. The distribution will therefore extend to some 150 births or more on either side of the mean number, and in order to obtain it we should have to calculate some 300 terms of a binomial series with an exponent of 10,000 ! This would not only be practically impossible without the use of certain methods of approximation, but it would give the distribution in quite unnecessary detail : as a matter of practice, we should not have compiled a frequency-distribution by single male births, but should certainly have grouped our observations, taking probably 10 births as the class-interval. We want, therefore, to replace the binomial polygon by some continuous curve, having approximately the same ordinates, the curve being such that the area between any two ordinates y_1 and y_2 will give the frequency of observations between the corresponding values of the variable x_1 and x_2.

Limiting form of the binomial for large n

8.15 When n becomes large, each term of the binomial becomes small. We are, however, concerned with the sum of the terms falling within certain ranges, and these will not be small in general.

Let us consider first of all the case when p and q are equal. The terms of the series are—

$$N(\tfrac{1}{2})^n \left\{ 1 + n + \frac{n(n-1)}{1 \cdot 2} + \frac{n(n-1)(n-2)}{1 \cdot 2 \cdot 3} + \cdots \right\}$$

The frequency of m successes is

$$N(\tfrac{1}{2})^n \frac{n!}{m! \, (n-m)!}$$

and the frequency of $m+1$ successes is derived from this by multiplying it by $(n-m)/(m+1)$. The latter frequency is therefore greater than the former so long as

$$n-m>m+1$$

or

$$m<\frac{n-1}{2}$$

Suppose, for simplicity, that n is even, say equal to $2k$; then the frequency of k successes is the greatest, and its value is

$$y_0=N(\tfrac{1}{2})^{2k}\frac{(2k)\,!}{k\,!\,k\,!} \qquad . \qquad . \qquad . \qquad (8.6)$$

The polygon tails off symmetrically on either side of this greatest ordinate. Consider the frequency of $k+x$ successes; the value is

$$y_x=N(\tfrac{1}{2})^{2k}\frac{(2k)\,!}{(k+x)\,!\,(k-x)\,!} \qquad . \qquad . \qquad . \qquad (8.7)$$

and therefore

$$\frac{y_x}{y_0}=\frac{(k)(k-1)(k-2)\,\ldots\,(k-x+1)}{(k+1)(k+2)(k+3)\,\ldots\,(k+x)}$$

$$=\frac{\left(1-\frac{1}{k}\right)\left(1-\frac{2}{k}\right)\left(1-\frac{3}{k}\right)\,\ldots\,\left(1-\frac{x-1}{k}\right)}{\left(1+\frac{1}{k}\right)\left(1+\frac{2}{k}\right)\left(1+\frac{3}{k}\right)\,\ldots\,\left(1+\frac{x-1}{k}\right)\left(1+\frac{x}{k}\right)} \qquad (8.8)$$

Now let us approximate by assuming that k is very large, and indeed large compared with x, so that $(x/k)^2$ may be neglected compared with (x/k). This assumption does not involve any difficulty, for we need not consider values of x much greater than three times the standard deviation or $3\sqrt{k/2}$, and the ratio of this to k is $3/\sqrt{2k}$, which is necessarily small if k be large. On this assumption we may apply the logarithmic series

$$\log_e(1+\delta)=\delta-\frac{\delta^2}{2}+\frac{\delta^3}{3}-\frac{\delta^4}{4}+\,\ldots$$

to every bracket in the fraction (8.8), and neglect all terms beyond the first. To this degree of approximation,

$$\log_e\frac{y_x}{y_0}=-\frac{2}{k}(1+2+3+\,\ldots\,+\overline{x-1})-\frac{x}{k}$$

$$=-\frac{x(x-1)}{k}-\frac{x}{k}$$

$$=-\frac{x^2}{k}$$

Therefore, finally

$$y_x = y_0 e^{-\frac{x^2}{k}} = y_0 e^{-\frac{x^2}{2\sigma^2}} \qquad \cdot \qquad \cdot \qquad \cdot \qquad (8.9)$$

where, in the last expression, the constant k has been replaced by the standard deviation σ, for $\sigma^2 = k/2$.

8.16 The case when p is not equal to q may be treated in a somewhat similar way but is slightly more complicated.

As before the frequency of m successes is

$$N \times {}^{n}C_{m} q^{n-m} p^{m}$$

$$= N \frac{n!}{m!\,(n-m)!} q^{n-m} p^{m}$$

The frequency of $(m+1)$ successes is derived by multiplying this expression by $\dfrac{n-m}{m+1} \cdot \dfrac{p}{q}$, and hence is greater than the former if

$$\frac{n-m}{m+1} \cdot \frac{p}{q} > 1$$

or

$$m < np - q$$

Let us assume that np is a whole number. Since n is going to tend to infinity, this really imposes no limitation on our work.

The maximum frequency is, then,

$$y_0 = N \frac{n!}{(np)!\,(nq)!} q^{nq} p^{np} \qquad \cdot \qquad \cdot \qquad (8.10)$$

The frequency of $pn + x$ successes is

$$y_x = N \frac{n!}{(np+x)!\,(nq-x)!} q^{nq-x} p^{np+x} \qquad \cdot \qquad \cdot \qquad (8.11)$$

Hence,

$$\frac{y_x}{y_0} = \frac{np!\,nq!}{(np+x)!\,(nq-x)!} q^{-x} p^{x} \qquad \cdot \qquad \cdot \qquad (8.12)$$

Now, by an important theorem due to James Stirling (1730), if n be large, we have approximately

$$n! = \sqrt{2n\pi}\, n^{n} e^{-n}$$

Applying this formula here—

$$\frac{y_x}{y_0} = \frac{\sqrt{2n p \pi}\,(np)^{np} e^{-np} \sqrt{2nq\pi}\,(nq)^{nq} e^{-nq p^x}}{\sqrt{2(np+x)\pi}\,(np+x)^{np+x} e^{-np-x} \sqrt{2(nq-x)\pi}\,(nq-x)^{nq-x} e^{-nq+x} q^x}$$

which reduces to

$$\frac{y_x}{y_0} = \frac{1}{\left(1+\dfrac{x}{np}\right)^{np+x+\frac{1}{2}}\left(1-\dfrac{x}{nq}\right)^{nq-x+\frac{1}{2}}}$$

Hence,

$$\log_e\left(\frac{y_x}{y_0}\right) = -(np+x+\tfrac{1}{2})\log_e\left(1+\frac{x}{np}\right) - (nq-x+\tfrac{1}{2})\log_e\left(1-\frac{x}{nq}\right)$$

$$= -\left(np+x+\tfrac{1}{2}\right)\left(\frac{x}{np} - \frac{x^2}{2n^2p^2} + \frac{x^3}{3n^3p^3} + \ldots\right)$$

$$-\left(nq-x+\tfrac{1}{2}\right)\left(-\frac{x}{nq} - \frac{x^2}{2n^2q^2} - \frac{x^3}{3n^3q^3} - \ldots\right)$$

After a little rearrangement this becomes—

$$\log_e\left(\frac{y_x}{y_0}\right) = -\frac{x^2}{2npq} + \frac{x^2(p^2+q^2)}{4n^2p^2q^2} - \frac{q-p}{2npq}x + \frac{q^2-p^2}{6n^2p^2q^2}x^3$$

$$+ \text{ terms of order } \frac{1}{n^3} \text{ and higher}$$

Since $q+p=1$, we have, neglecting the terms of order $\dfrac{1}{n^3}$ and higher, which are small compared with the others when n is large—

$$\log_e\left(\frac{y_x}{y_0}\right) = -\frac{x^2}{2npq} + \frac{x^2(p^2+q^2)}{4n^2p^2q^2} + \frac{q-p}{2npq}\left(-x + \frac{x^3}{3npq}\right) \qquad . \text{ (8.13)}$$

Put, as before, $npq = \sigma^2$, where σ is the standard deviation of the binomial. If n be large, the second term is small compared with the first.

Further, since we need not consider values of $\dfrac{x}{\sigma}$ much greater than 3, if $\dfrac{q-p}{\sqrt{npq}}$ be small, we can neglect the whole of the third term. On these assumptions we have—

$$\log_e \frac{y_x}{y_0} = -\frac{x^2}{2\sigma^2}$$

or

$$y_x = y_0 e^{-\frac{x^2}{2\sigma^2}} \qquad . \qquad . \qquad . \qquad . \text{ (8.14)}$$

as before.

The expression $\dfrac{q-p}{\sqrt{npq}}$ is merely $\sqrt{\beta_1}$, and so we have in effect simply assumed β_1 small; however much p and q differ we can always make $\sqrt{\beta_1}$ as small as we please by increasing n sufficiently.

8.17 Hence, whether or not p is equal to q, the binomial distribution tends to the form of the continuous curve ((8.9) and (8.14)) when n becomes large, at least for the material part of the range. As a matter of fact, the correspondence between the binomial and the curve is surprisingly close even for comparatively low values of n, provided that p and q are fairly near equality. The student may care to draw the curve with the aid of the tables given at the end of this book (see below, **8.26**) and compare it with some of the simpler binomials drawn to the same scale.

8.18 The curve

$$y = y_0 e^{\frac{-x^2}{2\sigma^2}}$$

is called the *normal curve*. A population classified according to a continuous variate whose ideal frequency-distribution is a normal curve is called a normal population.

The applications of the normal curve are by no means limited to distributions of the binomial type. Before we refer to its many practical and theoretical applications, however, we shall give a short account of its main properties.

Properties of the normal curve

8.19 The normal curve is obviously symmetrical about the point $x=0$, for its equation is independent of the sign of x. At this point the ordinate has its maximum value. The mean, the median and the mode coincide, and the curve is, in fact, that drawn in fig. 4.5, page 81, and taken as the ideal form of the symmetrical curve.

8.20 The curve is specified completely by defining the mean (the origin of x), the standard deviation σ and the value y_0.

In actual practice, as, for example, when we are trying to fit a normal curve to given data, we are not given y_0 itself, but have to calculate it from the fact that the area of the curve must be equal, on the chosen scale, to the total number of observations. For this reason we wish to find the area under the curve

$$y = y_0 e^{-\frac{x^2}{2\sigma^2}}$$

8.21   From **4.14** it will be seen that the area of a histogram, that is to say, the total number of observations which it represents, is given by

$$\text{Area} = \sum_{r=1}^{r=n} (f_r) \times h$$

where h is the width of the interval, f_r is the frequency in the rth interval and there are n intervals.

As the histogram tends towards the continuous curve the width of the intervals becomes smaller and the number of terms in the summation becomes larger. For the normal curve, which extends to infinity on either side of the mean, the limit to which the sum tends as the intervals become indefinitely small and the number of terms indefinitely large is written

$$\int_{-\infty}^{\infty} y_0 e^{-\frac{x^2}{2\sigma^2}} dx$$

the sign $\int$ being a conventional form of the summation sign S and dx representing the infinitesimally small value of h.

This is the notation of the integral calculus, and the quantity $\int_{-a}^{b} F(x)dx$ is said to be the integral of $F(x)$ with respect to x between the limits $-a$ and $+b$. In this book we shall not use the methods of the integral calculus, and accordingly it will be necessary for us to state certain results without proof. It will be sufficient if the student bears in mind that the process of integration is one of proceeding to the limit in cases of straightforward summation with which he is already familiar.

8.22   The area of the curve

$$y = y_0 e^{-\frac{x^2}{2\sigma^2}}$$

is then

$$\int_{-\infty}^{\infty} y_0 e^{-\frac{x^2}{2\sigma^2}} dx$$

and this is equal to

$$y_0 \sigma \times \sqrt{2\pi} = 2 \cdot 506627 y_0 \sigma$$

Hence the curve

$$y = \frac{1}{\sigma\sqrt{2\pi}} e^{-\frac{x^2}{2\sigma^2}}$$

has unit area, and for this reason the equation of the normal curve is usually written in the standard form

$$y = \frac{1}{\sigma\sqrt{2\pi}} e^{-\frac{x^2}{2\sigma^2}} \qquad . \qquad . \qquad . \qquad . \quad (8.15)$$

From this the form corresponding to a distribution of any given frequency is immediately written down. In fact, if the frequency is N, the corresponding normal curve is

$$y = \frac{N}{\sigma\sqrt{2\pi}} e^{-\frac{x^2}{2\sigma^2}} \qquad . \qquad . \qquad . \qquad . \quad (8.16)$$

Constants of the normal curve

8.23 The mean of the curve is, as we have seen, located at the origin. If we wish to write the curve with reference to some other point as origin, we can do so in the form

$$y = \frac{1}{\sigma\sqrt{2\pi}} e^{-\frac{1}{2\sigma^2}(x-m)^2} \qquad . \qquad . \qquad . \qquad . \quad (8.17)$$

where m is the excess of the mean over the value chosen as origin.

The standard deviation of the curve is σ, and the variance is accordingly σ^2.

The higher moments are calculated by the processes of the integral calculus. Since the nth moment about the mean is given by

$$\mu_n = \Sigma(fx^n)$$

we have, proceeding to the limit, that the nth moment of the normal curve is

$$\mu_n = \frac{1}{\sigma\sqrt{2\pi}} \int_{-\infty}^{\infty} x^n e^{-\frac{x^2}{2\sigma^2}} dx$$

If n is odd this vanishes, as it must for any symmetrical curve. If n is even we have—

$$\mu_n = \frac{n!}{2^{\frac{1}{2}n}(\frac{1}{2}n)!} \sigma^n \qquad . \qquad . \qquad . \qquad . \quad (8.18)$$

and hence,

$$\mu_4 = \frac{4.3.2}{2.2.2} \sigma^4 = 3\sigma^4 \qquad . \qquad . \qquad . \qquad . \quad (8.19)$$

8.24 From these results it follows that—

$$\left. \begin{array}{l} \beta_1 = \gamma_1 = 0 \\ \beta_2 = 3, \quad \gamma_2 = 0 \end{array} \right\} \qquad . \qquad . \qquad . \qquad . \quad (8.20)$$

i.e. the normal curve has zero kurtosis. This is, in fact, the origin of the choice of the apparently arbitrary value 3 in the definitions of platy- and lepto-kurtosis (**7.14**).

We may also state without proof the important result that all cumulants of the normal curve of orders higher than the second vanish identically.

8.25 The mean deviation of the normal curve is—

$$\sigma\sqrt{\frac{2}{\pi}}=0\cdot79788\ .\ .\ .\ \sigma$$

This is the origin of the rule given in **6.22**, that the mean deviation is approximately $\frac{4}{5}$ of the standard deviation. The result is true of the normal curve, and very approximately true of curves which do not differ markedly from the normal form. The rules that a range of 6 times the standard deviation includes the great majority of the observations (**6.13**) and that the quartile deviation is about $\frac{2}{3}$ of the standard deviation (**6.25**) were also suggested by the properties of the normal curve (see below, **8.28** and **8.29**).

Ordinates of the normal curve

8.26 The normal curve is so important that tables have been prepared to give (1) the ordinate of the curve corresponding to any given value of x, i.e. the values of $\dfrac{1}{\sqrt{2\pi}}e^{-\frac{x^2}{2}}$, and (2) the areas of the curve to the right and the left of any given ordinate, i.e. the values of $\dfrac{1}{\sqrt{2\pi}}\displaystyle\int_{x}^{\infty}e^{-\frac{x^2}{2}}dx$ and $\dfrac{1}{\sqrt{2\pi}}\displaystyle\int_{-\infty}^{x}e^{-\frac{x^2}{2}}dx$. Table 1 of the Appendix gives the values of the ordinate for values of x proceeding by steps of one-tenth of the standard deviation. The values are, of course, the same for positive as for negative values of x. More extended tables will be found in *Tables for Statisticians and Biometricians, Part I.*

The ordinate of any normal curve corresponding to a specified value of the variate is easily obtained from the table, as may be seen from the following example—

Example 8.3.—To find the ordinate of the normal curve given by—

$$y=\frac{10,000}{4\sqrt{2\pi}}e^{-\frac{x^2}{32}}$$

corresponding to the variate value $x=7$.
Here

$$N=10,000,\qquad \sigma=4$$

Altering the value of σ is equivalent to altering the scale of x. The ordinate in this curve corresponding to $x=7$ will be the same as the ordinate of the curve of unit s.d. corresponding to $x=\frac{7}{4}=1\cdot75$.
From Appendix Table 1, when

$$x=1\cdot8\qquad y=0\cdot07895$$
$$x=1\cdot7\qquad y=0\cdot09405$$

Hence, by simple interpolation, when

$$x = 1\cdot75 \qquad y = 0\cdot08650$$

The ordinate is $10,000/4$ times this, i.e. is equal to 216.   This is accurate to the nearest unit.

Area of the normal curve—the probability integral

8.27   A table of the areas of the normal curve cut off by ordinates at specified values of x is given in Table 2 of the Appendix.   As in the case of the table of ordinates, this table is applicable to all normal curves, whatever the value of their standard deviation, the areas cut off on

$$y = \frac{1}{\sqrt{2\pi}} e^{-\frac{x^2}{2}} \text{ by ordinates at } x \text{ being the same as those cut off on } y = \frac{1}{\sigma\sqrt{2\pi}} e^{-\frac{x^2}{2\sigma^2}}$$

by ordinates at $\frac{x}{\sigma}$.   More extended tables will again be found in *Tables for Statisticians and Biometricians, Part I.*

The area of the normal curve to the left of the ordinate at x or, it may be, between the ordinates at 0 and x—conventions differ—is sometimes termed the *probability integral* or the *error function*.   These names arise from the use of the function in the theory of sampling and the theory of errors respectively.

Example 8.4.—Find the frequency represented by the smaller area of the curve $y = \dfrac{10,000}{4\sqrt{2\pi}} e^{-\frac{x^2}{32}}$ cut off by the ordinate at $x = 7$.

Here

$$\sigma = 4, \qquad \frac{x}{\sigma} = 1\cdot75$$

For $\dfrac{x}{\sigma} = 1\cdot75 = 1\cdot5 + 0\cdot25$ the table gives the value $0\cdot9599$.   Hence the smaller fraction equals $1 - 0\cdot9599 = 0\cdot0401$ and multiplying this by $10,000$, we have the frequency represented, i.e. 401.

Example 8.5.—A hundred coins are thrown a number of times.   How often approximately in 10,000 throws may (1) exactly 65 heads, (2) 65 heads or more, be expected ?

The number of heads is given by the terms in

$$10,000(\tfrac{1}{2} + \tfrac{1}{2})^{100}$$

The standard deviation is $\sqrt{0\cdot5 \times 0\cdot5 \times 100} = 5$, $\dfrac{N}{\sigma} = 2,000$, and the exponent is large enough for us to be able to take the distribution as normal.

The mean number of heads is 50, and $65-50=3\sigma$. The frequency of a deviation of 3σ is given at once by Appendix Table 1 as $2,000 \times 0\cdot00443 = 8\cdot86$, or nearly 9 throws in 10,000. A throw of 65 heads will therefore be expected about 9 times.

The frequency of throws of 65 heads *or more* is given by Appendix Table 2, but a little caution must now be used, owing to the discontinuity of the distribution. A throw of 65 heads is equivalent to a range of $64\cdot5\text{--}65\cdot5$ on the continuous scale of the normal curve, the division between 64 and 65 coming at $64\cdot5$. $64\cdot5-50=+2\cdot9\sigma$, and a deviation of $+2\cdot9\sigma$ or more will only occur, as given by the table, 187 times in 100,000 throws, or, say, 19 times in 10,000.

8.28 From the table of areas we can find approximately the position of the quartiles. In fact, we require the value of $\dfrac{x}{\sigma}$ which will give us $0\cdot75$ as the greater fraction of the area. From the table we see that this value must lie between $0\cdot67$ and $0\cdot68$. Simple interpolation gives

$$\left\{0\cdot67+0\cdot01\frac{14}{31}\right\}=0\cdot675$$

a more exact result is

$$\text{Quartile deviation}=0\cdot67448975\sigma . \qquad . \qquad . \ (8.21)$$

This is the origin of the rough rule that the semi-interquartile range is usually about $\frac{2}{3}$ of the standard deviation.

8.29 We also observe from the table that an ordinate 3σ from the mean cuts off an area $0\cdot99865$ of the whole. The smaller fraction left is therefore $0\cdot00135$ of the whole. Since the curve is symmetrical, it follows that a range of 3σ on each side of the mean will cut off all but twice this, i.e. all but $0\cdot00270$ of the whole. This again is the origin of the rule that such a range includes the great majority of the observations.

The normal distribution as an error distribution

8.30 We have deduced the normal distribution as a limiting form of the binomial distribution when n, the exponent, is large. This however, is only one of the ways in which the normal curve occurs in statistical literature, and Gauss was led to it by a totally different line of reasoning, viz. by inquiring what law of distribution errors of observation should obey in order to make the arithmetic mean of a set of measurements the most likely value of the " true " magnitude.

8.31 Suppose we take a population of measurements of some magnitude, and consider the population of deviations from the true value. Let us further suppose that any deviation is the result of the operation of an indefinitely large number of small causes, each producing a small perturbation. Let us assume that the small perturbations are all equal, and that positive and negative perturbations are equally likely.

Then it may be shown that the distribution of errors x about the true value (taken as zero) is given by the law—

$$y = \frac{1}{\sigma\sqrt{2\pi}} e^{-\frac{x^2}{2\sigma^2}}$$

For, if δ is the amount of the perturbation, and positive and negative perturbations are equally likely, the expected frequency of m positive errors and $n-m$ negative errors in N observations is the term $(\frac{1}{2})^m(\frac{1}{2})^{n-m}$ in $N(\frac{1}{2}+\frac{1}{2})^n$, and the actual error is $m\delta-(n-m)\delta=(2m-n)\delta$. Similarly, the frequency of the actual error $\{2(m+1)-n\}\delta$ is given by the term in $(\frac{1}{2})^{m+1}(\frac{1}{2})^{n-m-1}$; and so on. Proceeding to the limit, as n becomes large, we get the stated result precisely as for the limiting process of **8.15**.

8.32 In the theory of errors it is more customary to write—

$$h^2 = \frac{1}{2\sigma^2}$$

so that the distribution becomes—

$$y = \frac{h}{\sqrt{\pi}} e^{-h^2x^2} \qquad . \qquad . \qquad . \qquad . \qquad (8.22)$$

h is called the " precision " (cf. **6.17**). As h increases, the normal curve becomes narrower and hence h measures in a sense the closeness of the bulk of observations to the true value.

The occurrence of normal distributions in nature

8.33 It was found at an early date that error distributions followed the normal law more or less closely, though it must be admitted not with any great exactitude. The fact that many populations, particularly biometrical populations such as those classified according to height and weight, lie distributed round the mean in a humped curve which is not unlike the normal curve, gave rise in the first half of the nineteenth century to keen interest. Although the term " normal " had not then been applied, there appears to have been a feeling that the curve was the ideal to which most distributions should in some degree attain, and that an explanation was demanded if they did not. The normal curve was, in fact, to the early statisticians what the circle was to the Ptolemaic astronomers.

8.34 Workers during the latter half of the nineteenth century were more careful not to let their theories outrun their facts, and as the data accumulated it became evident that the normal distribution was no more usual than any other type. In fact, rather the reverse, so that the occurrence of a normal distribution was to be regarded as something abnormal. " The reader may well ask," said Karl Pearson, " is it not possible to find material which obeys within probable limits the normal law ? I reply, yes, but this law is not a universal law of nature. We must hunt for cases."

The belief in the validity of the normal law in the theory of errors died harder. " As M. Lippmann once said to me," says Poincaré, in his *Calcul des Probabilités*, "everybody believes in the law of errors, the experimenters because they think it is a mathematical theorem, the mathematicians because they think it is an experimental fact."

8.35 One must, however, be careful not to go too far in seeking to avoid an over-emphasis on the practical occurrence of the normal curve. A certain number of distributions, more particularly those relating to measurements on plants and animals, are approximately of the normal form. As an example, we may take the distribution of Table 4.7, which we show in fig. 8.3 fitted with a normal curve.

Place of the normal curve in theory

8.36 Strangely enough, the realisation that the normal distribution did not correspond to any widespread natural effect did not diminish its importance in statistical theory. On the contrary, the normal distribution has increased in importance in recent years. It is instructive to consider why this is so.

In the first place, the normal curve and the normal integral have numerous mathematical properties which make them attractive and comparatively easy to manipulate. We have, for instance, already seen that the moments and cumulants of the normal curve are expressible in simple forms.

Now the normal form is reasonably close to many distributions of the humped type. If, therefore, we are ignorant of the exact nature of a humped distribution, or know the form but find it mathematically intractable, we may assume as a first approximation that the distribution is normal and see where this assumption leads us. It is not infrequently found that a population represented in this way is sufficiently accurately specified for the purposes of the inquiry.

8.37 Secondly, we shall find, when we come to consider sampling distributions, that many of the populations which occur are of the normal form, either exactly or to a satisfactory degree of approximation.

8.38 Thirdly, the theory of the normal curve has been applied to the graduation of curves which are not normal.

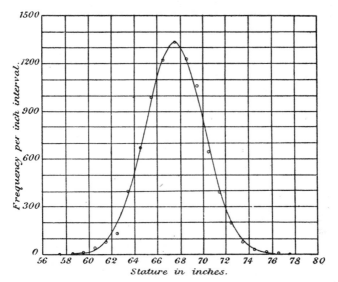

Fig. 8.3.—The distribution of stature for adult males in the British Isles (fig. 4.6, page 83), fitted with a normal curve
To avoid confusing the figure, the frequency-polygon has not been drawn in, the tops of the ordinates being shown by small circles.

It is possible to develop a technique for expressing a given distribution in the form of an infinite series whose terms depend on the quantity $e^{-\frac{x^2}{2}}$ and certain dependent functions.

8.39 Fourthly, distributions which are not normal can sometimes be brought to a form approximating to the normal by a transformation of the variate.   A population which is skew with respect to a variate x, for instance, might be normal when we take $\sqrt{x}$ as the variate.   We gave an example of this kind of effect in Exercise 4.6, page 100, where we saw that a population of men classified according to their weight was skew, whereas a population classified according to height (which we may take to be roughly proportional to the cube root of the weight) is nearly normal.

The Poisson distribution
8.40 We have found that the limit to the binomial would be a normal curve even if p and q were unequal, provided that n were increased sufficiently to make $(q-p)$ small compared with $\sqrt{npq}$.   We now propose to find the limit to the same series if one of the chances, say q, becomes indefinitely

small and n is increased sufficiently to keep nq finite, but not necessarily large—practical values are in fact usually small.

Let us suppose that q is very small and that qn is equal to the finite number m.

In the binomial $(p+q)^n$, the term

$$\frac{n!}{r!\,(n-r)!}q^r p^{n-r}$$

$$=\frac{n!}{r!\,(n-r)!}\left(\frac{m}{n}\right)^r\left(1-\frac{m}{n}\right)^{n-r}$$

$$=\frac{m^r}{r!}\left(1-\frac{m}{n}\right)^n\times\frac{n!}{(n-r)!\,n^r\left(1-\frac{m}{n}\right)^r}\qquad .\qquad .\ (8\ 23)$$

Now the limit of $\left(1-\dfrac{m}{n}\right)^n$ as n becomes large $=e^{-m}$.

Applying Stirling's approximation (**8.16**) when n is large, the term

$$\frac{n!}{(n-r)!\,n^r\left(1-\dfrac{m}{n}\right)^r}\qquad .\qquad .\qquad .\ (8.24)$$

$$=\frac{\sqrt{2\pi n}\,e^{-n}n^n}{\sqrt{2\pi(n-r)}\,e^{-n+r}(n-r)^{n-r}n^r\left(1-\dfrac{m}{n}\right)^r}$$

$$=\frac{e^{-r}}{\left(1-\dfrac{r}{n}\right)^n}\cdot\frac{\left(1-\dfrac{r}{n}\right)^{r-\frac{1}{2}}}{\left(1-\dfrac{m}{n}\right)^r}$$

Now the limit of $\left(1-\dfrac{r}{n}\right)^n=e^{-r}$, as we need not consider terms in which r exceeds quantities of the order $\sqrt{nq}$, and the limits of $\left(1-\dfrac{r}{n}\right)^{r-\frac{1}{2}}$, $\left(1-\dfrac{m}{n}\right)^r$ are both unity. Hence the limit of (8.24) is unity, and the limit of (8.23) is

$$\frac{m^r e^{-m}}{r!}$$

8.41 Hence the successive terms in the binomial are

$$e^{-m},\qquad e^{-m}m,\qquad e^{-m}\frac{m^2}{2!},\qquad e^{-m}\frac{m^3}{3!},\qquad \text{etc.}$$

and the limit of $(q+p)^n$ is

$$e^{-m}\left(1+m+\frac{m^2}{2!}+\frac{m^3}{3!}+\ \cdots\ \right)\qquad .\qquad .\qquad .\ (8.25)$$

This expression is called Poisson's distribution, or Poisson's exponential limit. It was first published by Poisson in 1837, but has subsequently been rediscovered by numerous writers.

Constants of the Poisson distribution

8.42 Taking an origin located at the first term of the distribution, we have—

$$\mu_1' = e^{-m}\left[0 + m + \left(\frac{m^2}{2!} \times 2\right) + \left(\frac{m^3}{3!} \times 3\right) + \cdots\right]$$

$$= me^{-m}\left(1 + \frac{m}{1!} + \frac{m^2}{2!} + \cdots\right)$$

$$= me^{-m}e^{m}$$

$$= m$$

$$\mu_2' = e^{-m}\left[0 + m + \left(\frac{m^2}{2!} \times 2^2\right) + \left(\frac{m^3}{3!} \times 3^2\right) + \cdots\right]$$

$$= e^{-m}\left[m + \left(\frac{m^2}{1!} \times 2\right) + \left(\frac{m^3}{2!} \times 3\right) + \cdots\right]$$

$$= me^{-m}\left(1 + \frac{m}{1!}(1+1) + \frac{m^2}{2!}(2+1) + \cdots\right)$$

$$= me^{-m}\left(1 + \frac{m}{1!} + \frac{m^2}{2!} + \cdots + m + \frac{m^2}{1!} + \cdots\right)$$

$$= me^{-m}(e^m + me^m)$$

$$= m(m+1)$$

It may also be shown that—

$$\mu_3' = m(m^2 + 3m + 1) = m\{(m+1)^2 + m\}$$
$$\mu_4' = m(m^3 + 6m^2 + 7m + 1)$$

From these results we have immediately—

$$\text{Mean} = m \qquad \cdot \qquad \cdot \qquad \cdot \qquad \cdot \qquad (8.26)$$
$$\mu_2 = m(m+1) - m^2$$
$$= m$$
$$\sigma = \sqrt{m} \qquad \cdot \qquad \cdot \qquad \cdot \qquad \cdot \qquad (8.27)$$

Hence,

$$\sigma^2 = m = \text{mean}$$

8.43 The third and fourth moments about the mean will be found to be—

$$\mu_3 = m \qquad \cdot \qquad \cdot \qquad \cdot \qquad \cdot \qquad (8.28)$$
$$\mu_4 = 3m^2 + m \qquad \cdot \qquad \cdot \qquad \cdot \qquad (8.29)$$

so that

$$\beta_1 = \frac{\mu_3^2}{\mu_2^3} = \frac{m^2}{m^3} = \frac{1}{m} \qquad \cdot \quad \cdot \quad \cdot \quad \cdot \quad (8.30)$$

$$\beta_2 = \frac{\mu_4}{\mu_2^2} = \frac{3m^2 + m}{m^2} = 3 + \frac{1}{m} \qquad \cdot \quad \cdot \quad \cdot \quad (8.31)$$

These results should be compared with the expressions

$$\beta_1 = \frac{(p-q)^2}{npq}$$

$$\beta_2 = 3 + \frac{1 - 6pq}{pqn}$$

for the binomial. They are, as might be expected, the limits of those expressions when $q = \dfrac{m}{n}$ and n is large.

8.44 We may state without proof that *all* the cumulants of the Poisson distribution are equal to m.

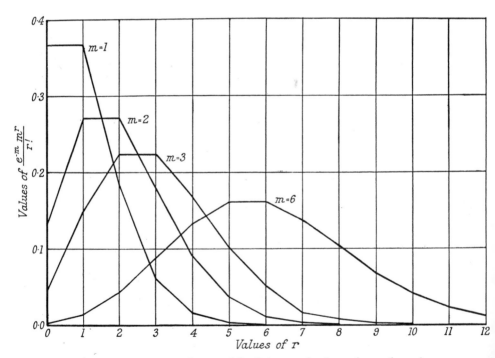

Fig. 8.4.—Frequency-polygons of the Poisson series for various values of m

8.45 Tables of the limit $e^{-m}\dfrac{m^r}{r\,!}$ for various values of m and r have been published by several authorities. One such set will be found in *Tables for Statisticians and Biometricians, Part I.*

The form of the frequency-polygon of the distribution (which, like the binomial and unlike the normal, is discontinuous) can be judged from fig. 8.4, in which the polygons for various values of m are drawn. It will be seen that for low values of m the polygon is very skew, but that for larger values it tends towards a symmetrical form.

8.46 The condition that p or q shall be small, np or nq remaining finite, implies that in practice we should expect to find a Poisson distribution in cases where the chance of any individual being a " success " was small. Such a case might arise, for example, in considering the deaths from a rare disease in a population, the chance of any individual dying from it being small.

8.47 Attention to the fact that comparatively rare events are not haphazard was first directed by Quetelet and von Bortkiewicz. The latter's data of the number of men killed by the kick of a horse in certain Prussian army corps in twenty years (1875–94) have become classical.

The frequency-distribution of the number of deaths in 10 corps per army corps per annum over twenty years was—

Deaths	Frequency
0	109
1	65
2	22
3	3
4	1

The mean of this distribution is $0 \cdot 61$ and there are 200 cases. Taking $m = 0 \cdot 61$, we find the following values for various numbers of deaths per annum—

Deaths	Frequency assigned by Poisson's Limit
0	108·7
1	66·3
2	20·2
3	4·1
4	0·7 (4 and over)

If we calculate σ^2 for the actual distribution, we find—

$$\sigma = 0 \cdot 78, \qquad \sigma^2 = 0 \cdot 6079$$

Hence, σ^2 is nearly equal to the mean, which is in accordance with theory. The agreement is, in fact, very much closer than is usual. Many distributions are now available for the frequency of individuals who have met with 0, 1, 2, . . . accidents, e.g. in factories, during a given period of time, and more often than not such distributions give a value of the variance exceeding the mean. This state of affairs can be accounted for on the assumption that the individuals at risk have varying degrees of " accident-proneness," and the assumption has been corroborated by finding that those individuals who have the largest number of accidents in one period are, on the whole, those who have most accidents during a succeeding period.

A more modern example of the occurrence of the distribution is given in the following data relating to the incidence of flying bombs (V1) in an area in south London. An area of 144 square kilometers was selected for which the mean density of bombs appeared constant. To test the hypothesis that the bombs fell in clusters the area was divided into 576 squares of $\frac{1}{4}$ kilometer each and a count made of the numbers of squares containing 0, 1, 2, etc. bombs, of which there were 537 altogether. A comparison with the frequencies given by a Poisson distribution is as follows (data from R. D. Clarke, 1948, *Jour. Inst. Act.*, **72**, No. 335)—

Number of flying bombs per square	Actual number of squares	Theoretical number given by the Poisson distribution
0	229	226·74
1	211	211·39
2	93	98·54
3	35	30·62
4	7	7·14
5 and over	1	1·57
Total	576	576·00

The agreement is extraordinarily close and there appears no evidence that the bombs " clustered " otherwise than by chance.

It is an interesting reflection that although the cavalry of 1875 developed into the flying bomb of 1945 the laws of probability seem to have endured over this span of 70 years.

Another example of the Poisson distribution is given in Exercise 8.17 at the end of this chapter. The early instances of the distribution were nearly all demographic, and for some time it remained more of a curiosity than a useful tool. In 1907, however, " Student " drew attention to a class of hæmacytometer counts to which the distribution seemed appropriate, and since that time it has found several important biological applications. It also appears in problems of controlling road and telephone traffic.

Pearson curves

8.48 The process of obtaining the normal curve as a limit of the binomial suggested to Karl Pearson an investigation into a series of analogous curves which may be regarded as limits to skew binomials or to distributions from a finite population, e.g. by drawing r balls at a time from a bag which contains a finite number N of black and white balls in given proportions. One such curve was of the form

$$y = y_0 \left(1 + \frac{x}{\alpha} \right)^{\gamma\alpha} e^{-\gamma x}$$

This set of curves, divided into twelve types, which were later regarded from rather a different standpoint, can be made to fit a large number of the distributions occurring in practice.

In the curve given above, γ, α and the origin can all be obtained from the first three moments. For the other curves of Pearson's system, except some degenerate types, the first four moments are necessary to specify the constants of the curve completely. The distributions considered hitherto have required in addition to the area (number of observations), either the mean only (Poisson) or the mean and standard deviation (normal curve) to determine their constants; but the principle of fitting for the more general curves remains the same. The actual moments of the curves are equated to the moments expressed in terms of the constants, such as γ and α, which are to be found. For full details of these curves, the method of determining the type to choose and the method of fitting, the student is referred to Elderton's *Frequency Curves and Correlation* and Kendall and Stuart's *Advanced Theory of Statistics*, vol. 1.

SUMMARY

1. If the chance of the success of an event is p, and of its failure q, then, provided that the chance remains constant throughout the trials, the expected frequencies of 0, 1, 2, . . . successes in N sets of n trials are the 1st, 2nd, etc. terms in the binomial

$$N(q+p)^n$$

2. The mean of the binomial is pn and its standard deviation is $\sqrt{npq}$.

3. For the binomial—

$$\beta_1 = \frac{(q-p)^2}{npq}, \qquad \beta_2 = 3 + \frac{1-6pq}{pqn}$$

4. If neither p nor q is small, the binomial tends for large values of n to the form

$$y = y_0 e^{-\frac{x^2}{2\sigma^2}}$$

5. This curve, which may also be written

$$y = \frac{N}{\sigma\sqrt{2\pi}} e^{-\frac{x^2}{2\sigma^2}}$$

is called the normal curve.

6. The standard deviation of the normal curve is σ. Its third moment is zero, and the fourth moment is $3\sigma^4$. Hence

$$\beta_1 = 0, \qquad \beta_2 = 3$$

All cumulants higher than the second are zero.

7. In the theory of errors the normal population is usually written—

$$y = \frac{h}{\sqrt{\pi}} e^{-h^2 x^2}$$

$h = \frac{1}{\sigma\sqrt{2}}$ being called the precision.

8. The mean deviation of the normal curve is

$$\sigma\sqrt{\frac{2}{\pi}} = 0 \cdot 79788 \ldots \sigma$$

and the quartile deviation (semi-interquartile range) is $0 \cdot 67448975 \ldots \sigma$

9. A range 3σ on each side of the mean of the normal curve contains $0 \cdot 9973$ of the distribution.

10. If p or q is small and one of pn, qn is finite and equal to m, the binomial distribution tends to the limit

$$e^{-m}\left(1 + m + \frac{m^2}{2!} + \ldots + \frac{m^r}{r!} + \ldots \right)$$

This is called the Poisson distribution.

11. The mean of the Poisson distribution is m, and σ^2 also equals m.

12. For the Poisson distribution—

$$\beta_1 = \frac{1}{m}, \qquad \beta_2 = 3 + \frac{1}{m}$$

and all the cumulants are equal to m.

EXERCISES

8.1 A perfect cubic die is thrown a large number of times in sets of 8. The occurrence of a 5 or a 6 is called a success. In what proportion of the sets would you expect 3 successes ?

8.2 The following data, due to W. F. R. Weldon, show the results of throwing 12 dice 4,096 times, a throw of 4, 5 or 6 being called a success—

Successes	Frequency	Successes	Frequency
0	—	7	847
1	7	8	536
2	60	9	257
3	198	10	71
4	430	11	11
5	731	12	—
6	948	Total	4,096

Find the expected frequencies, and compare the actual mean and standard deviation with those of the expected distribution.

8.3   In the previous example find the equation of the normal curve which has the same mean, standard deviation and total frequency as the observed distribution.

Find the frequencies to be expected if the distribution were represented exactly by the ordinates of this curve and compare them with the actual frequencies.

8.4   Assuming that half the population are consumers of chocolate, so that the chance of an individual being a consumer is $\frac{1}{2}$, and assuming that 100 investigators each take ten individuals to see whether they are consumers, how many investigators would you expect to report that three people or less were consumers ?

8.5   An irregular six-faced die is thrown, and the expectation that in 10 throws it will give five even numbers is twice the expectation that it will give four even numbers. How many times in 10,000 sets of 10 throws would you expect it to give no even numbers ?

8.6   If two normal populations have the same total frequency but the σ of one is k times that of the other, show that the maximum frequency of the first is $\dfrac{1}{k}$ that of the other.

8.7   Find graphically or otherwise the point of inflection of the normal curve, and show that it occurs at a distance σ from the mean ordinate.

8.8   Show that if np be a whole number, the mean of the binomial coincides with the greatest term.

8.9   Show that if two symmetrical binomial distributions of degree n (and of the same number of observations) are so superposed that the rth term of the one coincides with the $(r+1)$th term of the other, the distribution formed by adding superposed terms is a symmetrical binomial of degree $(n+1)$.

[Note.—It follows that if two normal distributions of the same area and standard deviation are superposed so that the difference between the means is small compared with the standard deviation, the compound curve is very nearly normal.]

8.10   Calculate the ordinates of the binomial $1,024 \ (0 \cdot 5 + 0 \cdot 5)^{10}$, and compare them with those of the normal curve.

8.11   If skulls are classified as *dolichocephalic* when the length-breadth index is under 75, *mesocephalic* when the same index lies between 75 and 80, and *brachycephalic* when the index is over 80, find approximately (assuming that the distribution is normal) the mean and standard deviation of a series in which 58 per cent are stated to be dolichocephalic, 38 per cent mesocephalic and 4 per cent brachycephalic.

8.12   Find the deciles of the normal curve.

8.13   Write down the normal population which has the same mean and (uncorrected) standard deviation as that of the last column of Table 4.7, page 82, and find the mean deviation and quartile deviation. Compare the results with the corresponding quantities for the actual distribution.

8.14   Proceed similarly for the skew population of Table 4.8, page 84.

8.15   In Exercise 8.4, if 1,000 investigators each choose 100 individuals, how many would you expect to report that more than 60 persons are consumers?

8.16   Taking the population of screws of Table 4.3, page 72, find the normal population which has the same standard deviation and a mean of 1 inch. Compare the frequencies given by this population with the actual frequencies.

8.17   The following data (Lucy Whitaker, *Biometrika*, 1914, **10**, 36) give the number of deaths of women over 85 published in *The Times* during 1910–12—

Number of deaths per day	Frequency
0	364
1	376
2	218
3	89
4	33
5	13
6	2
7	1

Find the frequencies of the Poisson distribution which has the same mean as this distribution, and compare your results with the actual frequencies. For the purpose of this example, simple interpolation in the tables given in *Tables for Statisticians and Biometricians* is sufficient.

8.18   In the data of the previous exercise calculate the first four cumulants.

CHAPTER NINE

CORRELATION AND REGRESSION

Bivariate populations

9.1 In Chapters 4 to 8 we considered the members of a population classified according to the values of a single variable ; and we saw how they could be grouped into a frequency-distribution whose character-istics could be described by certain constants. We have now to proceed to the case of two variables, in which each member of the population will exhibit two values, one for each of the variables under consideration.

A population of this kind is called a *bivariate* population. One of our main topics will be the way in which the two variables are related in the population.

9.2 If the corresponding values of the two variables are noted for each member, the methods of classification employed in the previous chapters may be applied to both variables. We can thus group our data into a table of double entry, or contingency table (Chapter 3), showing the frequencies of pairs of values lying within given class-intervals. Six such tables are given below as illustrations for the following variables : Table 9.1, two measurements on a shell ; Table 9.2, ages of husbands and their wives in marriages taking place in England and Wales in 1933 ; Table 9.3, statures of fathers and their sons ; Table 9.4, age and yield of milk in cows ; Table 9.5, the rate of discount and ratio of reserves to deposits in American banks; Table 9.6, the birth rate per thousand and the total numbers of births in the registration districts of England in 1941.

Arrays and correlation tables

9.3 Each row in such a table gives the frequency-distribution of the first variable for the members of the population in which the second variable lies within the limits stated on the left of the row. Similarly for the columns. As " columns " and " rows " are distinguished only by the accidental circumstances of the one set running vertically and the other horizontally, and the difference has no statistical significance, the word *array* has been suggested as a convenient term to denote either a row or a column.

If the values of X in one array are associated with values of Y in an interval centred at Y_n, then Y_n is called the *type* of the array.

TABLE 9.1—Correlation between (1) antero-posterior and (2) dorso-ventral diameter in lower valve of Pecten opercularis

(Condensed from a Table given by C. B. Davenport, *Proc. Amer. Ac.*, 1903, **39**, 149)

(Measurements in millimetres)

(2) Dorso-ventral diameter, mm.	(1) Antero-posterior diameter, mm.														Total
	37-39	40-42	43-45	46-48	49-51	52-54	55-57	58-60	61-63	64-66	67-69	70-72	73-75	76-78	
37-39	4	—	—	—	—	—	—	—	—	—	—	—	—	—	4
40-42	1	12	6	—	—	—	—	—	—	—	—	—	—	—	19
43-45	—	1	35	12	—	—	—	—	—	—	—	—	—	—	48
46-48	—	—	1	35	22	1	—	—	—	—	—	—	—	—	59
49-51	—	—	—	2	22	17	3	—	—	—	—	—	—	—	44
52-54	—	—	—	—	—	29	68	8	—	—	—	—	—	—	105
55-57	—	—	—	—	—	—	32	90	25	—	—	—	—	—	147
58-60	—	—	—	—	—	—	—	14	59	7	—	—	—	—	80
61-63	—	—	—	—	—	—	—	—	4	13	3	1	—	—	21
64-66	—	—	—	—	—	—	—	—	—	—	5	1	—	—	6
67-69	—	—	—	—	—	—	—	—	—	—	—	1	—	1	2
70-72	—	—	—	—	—	—	—	—	—	—	—	—	—	2	2
Total	5	13	42	49	44	47	103	112	88	20	8	3	—	3	537

9.4 A grouped frequency-distribution of the type of Tables 9.1 to 9.6 may then be termed a bivariate frequency-distribution ; but if we are particularly interested in the relationship between the two variates it is sometimes called a *correlation table*. The difference between a correlation table and a contingency table lies in the fact that the latter term may be, and usually is, applied to tables classified according to unmeasured quantities or imperfectly defined intervals.

9.5 We need add very little to what was said in Chapter 4 about the choice and magnitude of class-intervals and the classification of data. When the intervals have been fixed, the table is readily compiled from the raw material by taking a large sheet of paper ruled with arrays properly

TABLE 9.2—Correlation between ages of (1) husband and (2) wife in marriages in
England and Wales in 1933

Figures in hundreds—certain marriages in which no age was specified are omitted.

(Data from Registrar-General's Statistical Review of England and Wales for 1933, Tables, Part II, Civil)

(2) Age of wife (Years)	(1) Age of husband (Years)													Total
	15–	20–	25–	30–	35–	40–	45–	50–	55–	60–	65–	70–	75–	
15–	33	189	56	8	2	—	—	—	—	—	—	—	—	288
20–	18	682	585	106	19	5	2	1	—	—	—	—	—	1,418
25–	1	140	511	179	40	14	6	3	1	1	—	—	—	896
30–	—	11	75	101	42	20	10	5	2	1	1	—	—	268
35–	—	2	10	24	28	19	13	8	5	2	1	—	—	112
40–	—	—	1	5	9	14	12	10	6	4	2	1	—	64
45–	—	—	—	1	3	5	9	9	7	4	3	1	—	42
50–	—	—	—	—	—	1	3	7	6	5	3	1	—	26
55–	—	—	—	—	—	—	1	3	5	4	3	1	—	17
60–	—	—	—	—	—	—	—	1	1	4	3	2	—	11
65–	—	—	—	—	—	—	—	—	1	1	3	2	1	8
70–	—	—	—	—	—	—	—	—	—	1	1	1	3
Total	52	1,024	1,238	424	143	78	56	47	34	26	20	9	2	3,153

headed in the same way as the final table and entering a small mark in the compartment corresponding to the variate values exhibited by each individual. If facility of checking be of great importance, each pair of recorded values may be entered on a separate card and these dealt into little packs on a board ruled in squares, or into a divided tray ; each pack can then be run through to see that no card has been mis-sorted. The difficulty as to the intermediate observations—values of the variables corresponding to divisions between class-intervals—will be met in the same way as before if the value of one variable alone be intermediate, the unit of frequency being divided between two adjacent compartments. If both values of the pair be intermediates, the observation must be divided between *four* adjacent compartments, and thus quarters as well as halves

TABLE 9.3—Correlation between (1) stature of father and (2) stature of son : 1 or 2 sons only of each father

Measurements in inches

(From Karl Pearson and Alice Lee, *Biometrika*, 1903, **2**, 415)

(2) Stature of son	(1) Stature of father																	Totals
	58·5–59·5	59·5–60·5	60·5–61·5	61·5–62·5	62·5–63·5	63·5–64·5	64·5–65·5	65·5–66·5	66·5–67·5	67·5–68·5	68·5–69·5	69·5–70·5	70·5–71·5	71·5–72·5	72·5–73·5	73·5–74·5	74·5–75·5	
59·5–60·5	—	—	—	—	·5	·5	1	—	—	—	—	—	—	—	—	—	—	2
60·5–61·5	—	·25	—	—	·5	—	—	—	—	—	—	—	—	—	—	—	—	1·5
61·5–62·5	—	·5	·25	2·25	·5	·5	—	—	—	—	—	—	—	—	—	—	—	3·5
62·5–63·5	1	1·5	1	3·75	2·25	2	1	—	1	—	—	—	—	—	—	—	—	20·5
63·5–64·5	2	1	1·5	4·75	3	4·25	4	·25	·5	1·25	—	—	·25	—	—	—	—	38·5
64·5–65·5	—	·25	2	2·25	5·25	9·5	8	5	2·75	5·5	1·5	·25	1·25	—	—	—	—	61·5
65·5–66·5	—	—	1·5	2	7·5	13·75	13·5	9·25	7·5	16	3·5	·75	2·5	—	—	—	—	89·5
66·5–67·5	—	—	1	2	5·25	10	19·75	16·75	17·5	19·5	5·25	2·5	3·25	·5	1	—	—	148
67·5–68·5	—	—	·75	—	3·5	9·5	12·75	26·5	25·75	23·5	12·5	2	8·5	3·5	2·25	—	—	173·5
68·5–69·5	—	—	—	—	3·25	5	10·25	24·25	31·5	24	23·5	13·75	10	6·25	2·25	—	—	149·5
69·5–70·5	—	—	—	—	2	3·25	10	18·75	16	19·5	29	13·25	14·5	9·5	3·5	1·5	—	128
70·5–71·5	—	—	—	—	·5	2·5	5·75	18·25	11·75	19	22·5	21·5	10·75	8	5	1	1	108
71·5–72·5	—	—	—	—	·5	1	5	10·75	10·75	10·75	14·75	19·5	10	8·5	2·75	·5	1	63
72·5–73·5	—	—	—	—	—	·25	3	8·75	7	7·75	10·75	20·75	7·5	6·25	3·25	·5	1	42
73·5–74·5	—	—	—	—	—	—	1·5	2·5	3	7·5	11·25	11·25	6·5	3·25	3·25	·5	·5	29
74·5–75·5	—	—	—	—	—	—	·75	1·5	2·5	—	6·5	6	2·5	1	1·75	—	2	8·5
75·5–76·5	—	—	—	—	—	—	—	—	—	—	—	2·5	·5	·75	1	—	—	4
76·5–77·5	—	—	—	—	—	—	—	—	—	—	—	1	—	·25	1·5	—	—	4
77·5–78·5	—	—	—	—	—	—	—	—	—	—	—	1	—	·25	·75	—	—	3
78·5–79·5	—	—	—	—	—	—	—	—	—	—	—	—	—	—	·25	—	—	·5
Totals	3	3·5	8	17	33·5	61·5	95·5	142	137·5	154	141·5	116	78	49	28·5	4	5·5	1,078

may occur in the table, as for example, in Table 9.3. In this case the statures of fathers and sons were measured to the nearest quarter-inch and subsequently grouped by 1-inch intervals : a pair in which the recorded stature of the father is $60 \cdot 5$ in. and that of the son $62 \cdot 5$ in. is accordingly entered as $0 \cdot 25$ to each of the four compartments under the columns $59 \cdot 5$–$60 \cdot 5$, $60 \cdot 5$–$61 \cdot 5$, and the rows $61 \cdot 5$–$62 \cdot 5$, $62 \cdot 5$–$63 \cdot 5$.

Frequency-surface and stereogram

9.6 The distribution of frequency for two variables may be represented by a surface in three dimensions in the same way as the frequency-distribution for a single variable may be represented by a curve in two. We may imagine the surface to be obtained by erecting at the centre of every compartment of the correlation table a vertical of length proportionate to the frequency in that compartment, and joining up the tops of the verticals. If the compartments were made smaller and smaller while the class-frequencies remained finite, the irregular figure so obtained would approximate more and more closely towards a continuous curved surface —a *frequency-surface*—corresponding to the frequency-curves for single variables of Chapter 4. The volume of the frequency-solid over any area drawn on its base gives the frequency of pairs of values falling within that area, just as the area of the frequency-curve over an interval of the base line gives the frequency of observations within that interval.

9.7 Similarly, a figure analogous to the frequency-polygon or the histogram may be constructed by drawing the frequency-distributions for all arrays of the one variable, to the same scale, on sheets of cardboard, cutting-out and erecting the cards vertically on a base-board at equal distances apart, or by marking out a base-board in squares corresponding to the compartments of the correlation table, and erecting on each square a rod of wood of height proportionate to the frequency. Such solid representations of frequency-distributions for two variables are sometimes termed *stereograms*.

9.8 It is impossible, however, to group the majority of frequency-surfaces, in the same way as the frequency-curves, under a few simple types : the forms are too varied. The simplest ideal type is one in which every section of the surface is a symmetrical curve—the first type of Chapter 4, fig. 4.5, page 81. Like the symmetrical distribution for the single variable, this is a very rare form of distribution in economic statistics, but approximate illustrations may be drawn from anthropometry. Fig. 9.1 shows the ideal form of the surface, somewhat truncated, and fig. 9.3 the distribution of Table 9.3, which approximates to the same type— the difference in steepness is, of course, merely a matter of scale. The maximum frequency occurs in the centre of the whole distribution, and the surface is symmetrical round the vertical through the maximum, equal frequencies occurring at equal distances from the mode on opposite sides.

TABLE 9.4—Correlation between (1) age in years and (2) yield of milk per week in 4,912 Ayrshire cows

(Data from J. F. Tocher, "An Investigation of the Milk Yield of Dairy Cows," *Biometrika*, 1928, 20B, 106)

(2) Yield of milk per week (gallons) central value of interval	(1) Age in years																Totals
	3	4	5	6	7	8	9	10	11	12	13	14	15	16	17	18	
8									1								1
9		2	2		1												5
10	3	5	1	1	3												13
11	2	10	8	7	1	4			2								33
12	2	30	17	9	5	2	1	2	1	1				1			71
13	2	71	29	18	9	9	4	1	4	1	3	1					151
14	9	76	57	38	23	24	4	6	4	2	1		1				236
15	11	115	79	43	34	23	7	8	9	5	4				1		339
16	11	149	119	74	59	34	11	16	12	7	5	2					499
17	15	148	131	94	58	49	23	15	17	6	5	1	1		1		552
18	16	146	132	83	73	51	32	22	11	6	2	1					585
19	11	117	112	113	87	51	39	33	13	10	3	3	1		1	1	586
20	10	97	107	79	69	49	35	30	9	10	4	3	1		1		496
21	8	63	93	88	70	32	25	29	10	7	1	2	2				448
22	3	42	63	49	45	27	31	18	12	3	1	2	1	1			284
23	5	19	33	38	38	19	14	17	3	7	1		1				214
24	1	20	23	34	27	20	17	9	3	2	1		1				153
25	2	10	15	22	17	15	13	10	2	4							112
26	3	7	13	7	4	5	8	4	2	3							58
27		2	7	9	5	2	2	2	3								35
28			2	1	4	1	4	1	2								13
29			2	2	4	2	1				1						15
30			2	1			3		1								4
31				2			2										5
32																	2
33																	1
34									1								1
Totals	112	1,129	1,047	812	636	419	276	223	122	75	32	15	7	2	4	1	4,912

TABLE 9.5—Correlation between (1) call discount rates and (2) percentage of reserves on deposits in New York Associated Banks (Weekly Returns)

(From "Statistical Studies in the New York Money Market," by J. P. Norton. Publications of the Department of the Social Sciences, Yale University; The Macmillan Co., 1902. Note that, after the column headed 8 per cent, blank columns have been omitted to save space.

(2) Percentage ratio of reserves to deposits	(1) Call discount rates																					Totals
	1	1·5	2	2·5	3	3·5	4	4·5	5	5·5	6	6·5	7	7·5	8	9	10	12	15	20	25	
21									1													2
22							1															1
23									1													1
24						1	2	1								1					1	9
25					2	6	2	6	4	4	2	1	2		3		2		1			42
26			10	9	14	12	13	12	16	6	11	4	7		6	1	2	1	1	1	2	85
27		1	30	23	20	11	15	17	19	9	11	3	4		1	2	2		1			124
28		5	48	17	16	3	7	3	7	1	9	2	3				1				1	115
29	3	9	12	10	8	4	6	3	1		2		2									109
30	1	12	6	2	4	2	4	1	2													53
31	8	14	10	8	5	1	2	1	1													36
32	15	8	4	1				1														53
33	15	11	1				2															32
34	2	5	1																			14
35	8	2	1																			14
36	7	1	1																			10
37	8	2	1																			9
38	9	8																				11
39	19	3																				21
40	7	2																				15
41	7																					10
42	8																					10
43	1																					1
44	1																					1
45	2																					2
Totals	121	93	125	70	69	40	52	45	52	20	35	10	18	—	10	4	7	1	3	1	4	780

TABLE 9.6—Correlation between (1) Birth rate per thousand and (2) Number of births in the registration districts of England in 1941

(Five large towns with more than 6,000 births and a few exceptional districts with less than ten inhabitants have been excluded.) The ranges of birth-rate are from 6·0 to 6·9 inclusive and so on and hence presumably really run from 5·95 to 6·95, etc. Similarly the class limits for births are 0-199 etc. and the mid points 99·5 etc. Note the exclusion of certain empty rows and columns to save space

(Data compiled from Registrar-General's Statistical Review of England and Wales for 1941)

(2) Number of births	(1) Birth-rate per thousand																						Totals
	6–	7–	8–	9–	10–	11–	12–	13–	14–	15–	16–	17–	18–	19–	20–	21–	22–	23–	24–	26–	28–	29–	
0–	3	4	9	22	57	72	75	99	65	59	39	27	25	10	1	3	4	1	2	1	1	1	580
200–	—	1	—	2	7	34	42	48	66	67	44	36	18	9	5	4	1	—	2	—	1	—	387
400–	—	—	—	4	3	6	15	22	15	24	20	7	9	6	3	—	3	—	—	—	—	—	137
600–	—	—	—	1	1	2	4	6	12	5	16	5	4	3	1	1	—	—	—	—	—	—	61
800–	—	—	—	—	—	—	3	2	5	2	3	3	4	2	—	1	1	1	—	—	—	—	27
1,000–	—	—	—	—	—	1	2	4	5	6	5	4	3	—	2	—	—	—	—	—	—	—	32
1,200–	—	—	—	—	—	2	1	4	2	6	3	1	1	—	—	—	—	—	—	—	—	—	20
1,400–	—	—	—	—	—	1	1	4	3	1	1	1	1	—	—	—	—	—	—	—	—	—	13
1,600–	—	—	—	—	—	—	1	1	1	1	1	1	1	—	—	—	—	—	—	—	—	—	7
1,800–	—	—	—	—	—	—	1	1	2	3	1	1	—	1	—	—	—	—	—	—	—	—	10
2,000–	—	—	—	—	—	—	—	—	—	1	1	—	1	—	—	—	—	—	—	—	—	—	4
2,200–	—	—	—	—	—	—	—	1	—	1	1	—	—	—	—	—	—	—	—	—	—	—	3
2,400–	—	—	—	—	—	—	—	—	2	—	2	—	—	—	—	—	—	—	—	—	—	—	4
2,600–	—	—	—	—	—	—	—	1	—	—	1	—	—	—	—	—	—	—	—	—	—	—	2
2,800–	—	—	—	—	—	—	—	1	—	—	1	1	—	—	—	—	—	—	—	—	—	—	3
3,000–	—	—	—	—	—	—	—	—	—	—	—	—	—	—	—	—	—	—	—	—	—	—	0
3,200–	—	—	—	—	—	—	—	—	—	—	1	—	—	—	—	—	—	—	—	—	—	—	1
3,400–	—	—	—	—	—	—	1	—	—	—	—	—	—	—	—	—	—	—	—	—	—	—	1
3,600–	—	—	—	—	—	—	—	1	—	—	—	—	—	—	—	—	—	—	—	—	—	—	1
3,800–	—	—	—	—	—	—	—	—	—	—	1	—	—	—	—	—	—	—	—	—	—	—	1
4,000–	—	—	—	—	—	—	—	—	—	—	1	—	—	—	—	—	—	—	—	—	—	—	1
4,200–	—	—	—	—	—	—	—	—	—	—	—	1	—	—	—	—	—	—	—	—	—	—	1
4,400–	—	—	—	—	—	—	—	—	—	—	1	—	—	—	—	—	—	—	—	—	—	—	1
5,200–	—	—	—	—	—	—	—	—	1	—	—	—	—	—	—	—	—	—	—	—	—	—	1
Totals	3	5	9	29	69	118	145	194	180	174	139	94	67	32	12	9	9	1	4	2	2	1	1,298

TABLE 9.7—Showing the monthly index-numbers of prices of (1) animal feeding-stuffs and (2) home-grown oats in England and Wales for 1931-1935
The index-numbers are based on prices in corresponding months of 1911-1913
(Data from Agricultural Market Report for England and Wales)

Month	Index of feeding-stuffs price	Index of oats price	Month	Index of feeding-stuffs price	Index of oats price
1931 Jan.	78	84	1933 July	85	75
Feb.	77	82	Aug.	83	79
Mar.	85	82	Sept.	80	78
Apr.	88	85	Oct.	78	78
May	87	89	Nov.	80	76
June	82	90	Dec.	83	75
July	81	88			
Aug.	77	92	1934 Jan.	82	80
Sept.	76	83	Feb.	83	91
Oct.	83	89	Mar.	85	87
Nov.	97	98	Apr.	83	84
Dec.	93	99	May	82	81
			June	85	83
1932 Jan.	95	102	July	88	83
Feb.	97	102	Aug.	101	92
Mar.	102	105	Sept.	102	98
Apr.	99	105	Oct.	98	94
May	97	107	Nov.	96	94
June	94	107	Dec.	98	95
July	94	101			
Aug.	97	106	1935 Jan.	98	100
Sept.	92	96	Feb.	92	99
Oct.	89	90	Mar.	92	96
Nov.	90	85	Apr.	90	98
Dec.	90	81	May	88	97
			June	86	98
1933 Jan.	92	84	July	83	99
Feb.	91	85	Aug.	80	92
Mar.	90	84	Sept.	81	90
Apr.	86	81	Oct.	86	89
May	85	76	Nov.	83	87
June	85	77	Dec.	82	83

The next simplest type of surface corresponds to the second type of frequency-curve—the moderately asymmetrical. Most, if not all, of the distributions of arrays are asymmetrical and like the distributions of fig. 4.7 ; the surface is consequently asymmetrical, and the maximum does not lie in the centre of the distribution. This form is fairly common, and illustrations might be drawn from a variety of sources—economics, meteorology, anthropometry, etc. The data of Table 9.4 will serve as an example. The total distributions and the distributions of the majority of the arrays are asymmetrical, the rows being markedly so. The maximum frequency lies towards the upper end of the table in the compartment under the row headed " 16 " and column headed " 4 ". The frequency falls off very rapidly towards the lower ages, and slowly in the direction of old age.

Apart from these two forms, it seems impossible to delimit empirically any simple types. Tables 9.5 and 9.6 are given simply as illustrations of

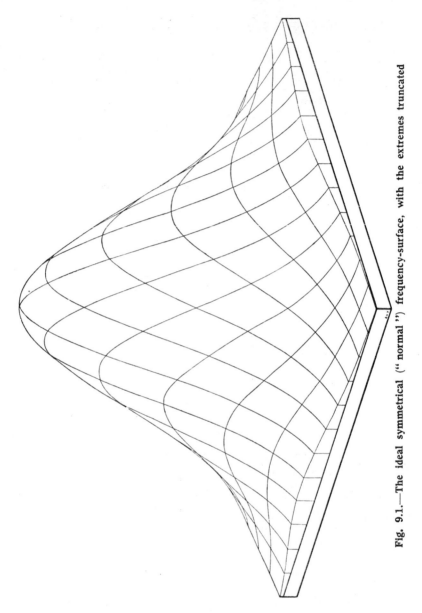

Fig. 9.1.—The ideal symmetrical (" normal ") frequency-surface, with the extremes truncated

two very divergent forms. Fig. 9.2 gives a graphical representation of the former by the method corresponding to the histogram of Chapter 4, the frequency in each compartment being represented by a square pillar. The distribution of frequency is very characteristic, and quite different from that of any of the Tables 9.1 to 9.4.

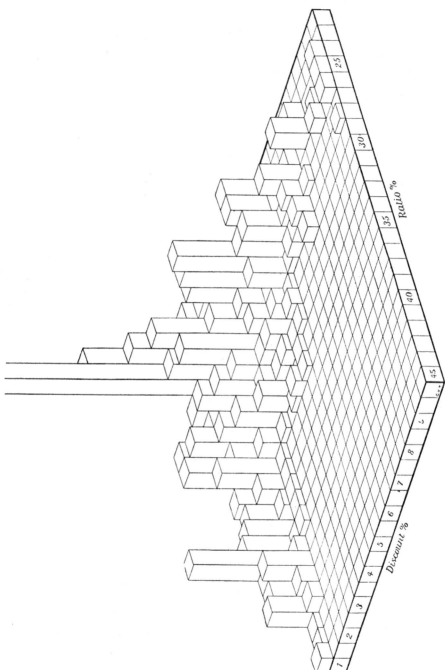

Fig. 9.2.—Frequency-surface for the rate of discount and ratio of reserves to deposits in American banks (data of Table 9.5)

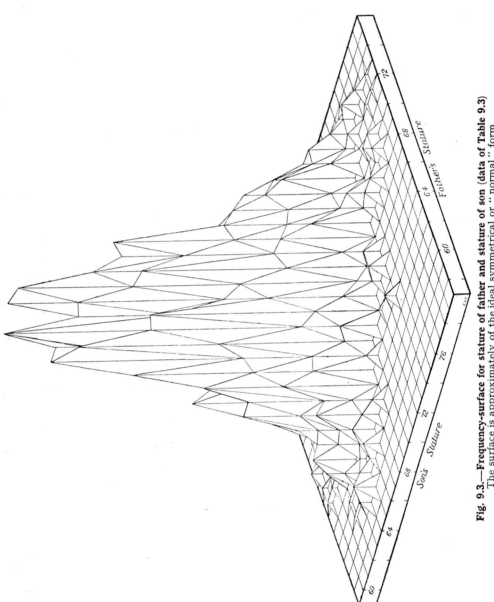

Fig. 9.3.—Frequency-surface for stature of father and stature of son (data of Table 9.3)
The surface is approximately of the ideal symmetrical or " normal " form

The scatter diagram

9.9 There is another method of representing bivariate data graphically which is particularly useful for ungrouped data. Take, for instance, the data of Table 9.7, giving the index-numbers of prices of animal feeding-stuffs and home-grown oats for each month of the years 1931-35. There are only 60 pairs of values, and the data cannot be grouped into a frequency-distribution with class-intervals of reasonable size without

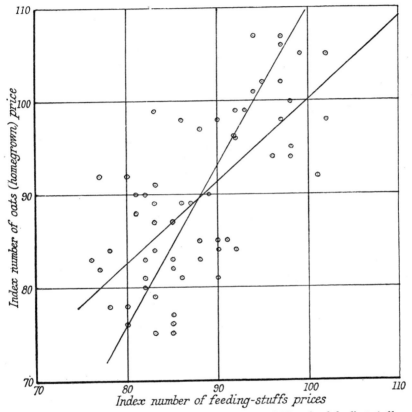

Fig. 9.4.—Scatter diagram of index-numbers of prices of (1) animal feeding-stuffs and (2) home-grown oats (Table 9.7)

For the meaning of the straight lines, see Example 9.1, page 223

giving rise to irregular frequencies. We may, however, proceed as follows—

On squared paper take two axes at right angles, one axis corresponding to the variable X and the other to the variable Y (see fig. 9.4). To each member of the population there will correspond a pair of values X, Y, which in turn will correspond to a point whose abscissa on the diagram is X and whose ordinate is Y. Thus the population, when represented in this way, will give a swarm of points on the diagram, and we can interpret the ways in which these points cluster or scatter as properties of the relationship between the two variables. Fig. 9.4 shows the data of Table 9.7 plotted in this way. It will be observed that the points tend to distribute themselves so that high and low values of X correspond to high and low values of Y respectively.

Such a figure is called a *scatter diagram.*

9.10 We can also represent a grouped bivariate frequency table on a scatter diagram, though less satisfactorily and with some labour. For this purpose axes are taken as before and abscissæ and ordinates drawn to correspond to the divisions of the frequency table. The diagram will then be divided into compartments corresponding to the compartments of the table. In each compartment we place a number of dots equal to the frequency in the corresponding compartment of the table. We have, as a rule, no guide as to the disposition of these dots within their respective cells, and hence it is usual to place them in some symmetrical arrangement so that they are, as nearly as may be, spread uniformly through the cells.

The difficulty of inserting the dots when the frequencies are large will be obvious, and, in fact, such a scatter diagram rarely tells us more than we can see from an inspection of the table itself. In contrast to this, the scatter diagram of the data of Table 9.7 gives a much better picture of the dependence of the two variates than can be obtained by mere inspection of the ungrouped data of the table.

9.11 It is clear that a correlation table may be treated by the methods discussed in Chapter 3, which are applicable to all contingency tables, however formed. But the coefficient of contingency merely tells us whether two variables are related, and if so, how closely. The methods we shall now discuss go much further than this. The numerical character of the variates and the arrangement of the correlation table in class-intervals of equal widths enable us to approach the problem of investigating the relationship between the variates with additional precision.

9.12 If the two variates in a contingency table are independent, the distributions in parallel arrays are similar (**3.18**) ; hence their averages and dispersions, i.e. their means and standard deviations, must be the same. In general they will not be the same, and we are thus led to inquire into the relation between the values of the means and standard deviations in different arrays and the departure of the distribution from complete independence.

9.13 The mean is the most important constant, in general, and for the present we shall concentrate our attention upon it. Although the values in arrays are scattered about their respective means, it is in most cases profitable to inquire how the means of arrays are related ; this will throw a good deal of light on the important question whether high values of one variate show any tendency to be associated, on the average, with high values of the other variate.

If possible, we also wish to know how great a divergence of one variate from its mean is associated with a given divergence of the other, and to obtain some idea of how closely the relation is usually fulfilled.

Lines of regression

9.14 Let us then consider the means of arrays. Let OX, OY be two axes at right angles representing the scales of the two variates. As in the case of the scatter diagram we can plot the positions of the means ; for example, if the mean of a row whose variate value is centred at y_1 is m_1, we can plot the point whose abscissa is m_1 and whose ordinate is y_1. There will thus be one point corresponding to each row and one to each column. In practice, to distinguish the two, the means of rows are denoted by small circles and the means of columns by small crosses. Fig. 9.8 shows such a diagram drawn for the data of Table 9.3.

The means of rows and the means of columns will, in general, lie more or less closely round smooth curves. For example, in fig. 9.8 they lie, very approximately, on straight lines, RR and CC in the figure. Such curves are said to be *curves of regression*, and their equations with reference to the axes OX and OY are called *regression equations*. If the lines of regression are straight, the regression is said to be *linear*. In the contrary case it is said to be *curvilinear*.

9.15 The term " regression " is not a particularly happy one from the etymological point of view, but it is so firmly embedded in statistical literature that we make no attempt to replace it by an expression which would more suitably express its essential properties. It was introduced by Galton in connection with the inheritance of stature. Galton found that the sons of fathers who deviate x inches from the mean height of all fathers themselves deviate from the mean height of all sons by less than x inches, i.e. there is what Galton called a " regression to mediocrity." In general the idea ordinarily attached to the word " regression " does not touch upon this connotation, and it should be regarded merely as a convenient term.

9.16 If two variates are independent, their regression lines are straight and at right angles, the means of rows lying on a line parallel to the axis OY and the means of columns on a line parallel to the axis OX, for the distributions in parallel arrays are similar (see fig. 9.5). In any case drawn from actual data, of course, the means might not lie exactly on straight lines, owing to fluctuations of sampling.

9.17 The cases with which the experimentalist, e.g. the chemist or physicist, has to deal, where the observations are all crowded closely round a single line, lie at the opposite extreme from independence. The entries fall into a few compartments only of each array, and the means of rows and of columns lie approximately on one and the same curve, like the line RR of fig. 9.6.

9.18 The ordinary cases of statistics are intermediate between these two extremes, the lines of means being neither perpendicular as in fig. 9.5, nor coincident as in fig. 9.6. One problem of the statistician is to find expressions which will suffice to describe the regression lines, either exactly or to a satisfactory degree of approximation.

In general this is a difficult problem, and the theory of curvilinear regression is as yet incomplete. We can, however, make considerable progress by confining ourselves to the cases in which the regression is linear. Cases of this kind are more frequent than might be supposed, and in other cases the means of arrays lie so irregularly, owing to the paucity of the observations, that the real nature of the regression curve is not indicated and a straight line will give as good an approximation as a more elaborate curve.

9.19 Consider the simplest case in which the means of rows lie exactly on a straight line RR (fig. 9.7). Let M_2 be the mean value of Y, and let RR cut M_2x, the horizontal through M_2, in M. Then it may be shown that the vertical through M must cut OX in M_1, the mean of X. For, let the slope of RR to the vertical, i.e. the tangent of the angle M_1MR or ratio of kl to lM, be b_1, and let deviations from My, Mx be denoted by x and y.

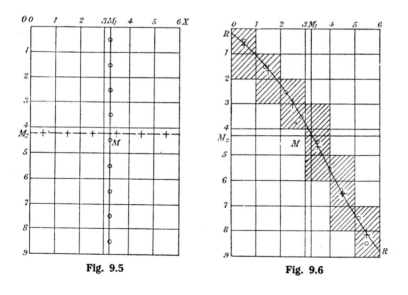

Fig. 9.5   Fig. 9.6

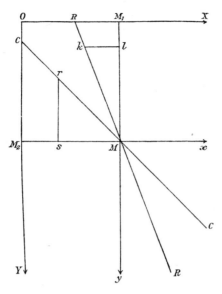

Fig. 9.7

Then for any one row of type y in which the number of observations is n, $\Sigma(x)=nb_1y$, and therefore for the whole table, since $\Sigma(ny)=0$, $\Sigma(x)=b_1\Sigma(ny)=0$. M_1 must therefore be the mean of X, and M may accordingly be termed the mean of the whole distribution.

Knowing that RR passes through the mean of the distribution, we can determine it completely if we know the value of b_1.

For any one row we have

$$\Sigma(xy)=y\Sigma(x)=nb_1y^2$$

Therefore for the whole table

$$\Sigma(xy)=b_1\Sigma(y^2)n=Nb_1\sigma_y^2$$

Let us write

$$p=\frac{1}{N}\Sigma(xy) \quad . \qquad . \qquad . \qquad . \qquad . \quad (9.1)$$

Then

$$b_1=\frac{p}{\sigma_y^2} \qquad . \qquad . \qquad . \qquad . \qquad . \quad (9.2)$$

Similarly, if CC be the line on which lie the means of columns and b_2 is the slope to the horizontal,

$$b_2=\frac{p}{\sigma_x^2} \qquad . \qquad . \qquad . \qquad . \qquad . \quad (9.3)$$

Now let us define

$$r = \frac{p}{\sigma_x \sigma_y} = \frac{\Sigma(xy)}{\sqrt{\Sigma(x^2)\Sigma(y^2)}} \qquad . \qquad . \qquad . \quad (9.4)$$

Then

$$b_1 = r\frac{\sigma_x}{\sigma_y} \text{ and } b_2 = r\frac{\sigma_y}{\sigma_x} \qquad . \qquad . \qquad . \quad (9.5)$$

and the equations of RR and CC, referred to the centre of the distribution, are

$$x = r\frac{\sigma_x}{\sigma_y}y \text{ and } y = r\frac{\sigma_y}{\sigma_x}x \qquad . \qquad . \qquad . \quad (9.6)$$

and, referred to the origin 0,

$$X - M_1 = \frac{r\sigma_x}{\sigma_y}(Y - M_2), \qquad Y - M_2 = \frac{r\sigma_y}{\sigma_x}(X - M_1) \qquad (9.7)$$

9.20   Let us now proceed to the case when the means of arrays are not situated on a straight line.   This we shall treat by finding the next best thing—straight lines which are the closest fit to the means.

The expression " closest fit," as applied to the fitting of curves to points, is one which we deal with at length in Chapter 15, and it is only necessary to say at this stage that the straight line RR of closest fit to the means of rows, i.e.

$$x = a_1 + b_1 y$$

will be determined by evaluating a_1 and b_1 so as to make the expression

$$E = \Sigma\{x - (a_1 + b_1 y)\}^2$$

(that is, the sum of the squares of the horizontal distances of the points representing the observations from RR) a minimum.   Here x and y, as before, denote deviations from the respective means of X and Y, and the summation is taken over all values of x and y.

We have, expanding E,

$$E = \Sigma(a_1^2) - 2\Sigma\{a_1(x - b_1 y)\} + \Sigma(x - b_1 y)^2$$

The second term on the right vanishes, since $\Sigma(x) = \Sigma(y) = 0$ and hence

$$E = \Sigma(a_1^2) + \Sigma(x - b_1 y)^2$$

Now a_1 and b_1 can be chosen independently, and hence E is a minimum only if $\Sigma(a_1^2) = 0$, i.e.

$$a_1 = 0 \qquad . \qquad . \qquad . \qquad . \qquad . \quad (9.8)$$

Thus the line of closest fit goes through the mean of the distribution.

Hence,

$$E = \Sigma(x - b_1 y)^2$$
$$= \Sigma(x^2) - 2b_1 \Sigma(xy) + b_1{}^2 \Sigma(y^2)$$
$$= \Sigma(y^2) \left\{ b_1{}^2 - 2b_1 \frac{\Sigma(xy)}{\Sigma(y^2)} + \frac{\Sigma(x^2)}{\Sigma(y^2)} \right\}$$
$$= \Sigma(y^2) \left[\left\{ b_1 - \frac{\Sigma(xy)}{\Sigma(y^2)} \right\}^2 + \frac{\Sigma(x^2)}{\Sigma(y^2)} - \left\{ \frac{\Sigma(xy)}{\Sigma(y^2)} \right\}^2 \right]. \qquad (9.9)$$

This is a minimum when the first term (a square) is zero, i.e. when

$$b_1 = \frac{\Sigma(xy)}{\Sigma(y^2)} \qquad \qquad \qquad (9.10)$$

which is the same as equation (9.2).

We may show similarly that the line of closest fit CC, given by

$$y = a_2 + b_2 x$$

has

$$a_2 = 0, \qquad b_2 = \frac{\Sigma(xy)}{\Sigma(x^2)},$$

which is the same as equation (9.3).

If we regard the equation

$$x = a_1 + b_1 y$$

as one for estimating x from y, we may take $x - a_1 - b_1 y$ as the error of estimation, and E will then be the sum of the squares of such errors. The condition that E is a minimum is then equivalent to the condition that the sum of squares of errors of estimation shall be a minimum. This is one form of the so-called " Principle of Least Squares " (see Chapter 15).

9.21 Equations (9.6) and (9.7) are thus of general application. If the regression is exactly linear they give the lines of regression. If the regression departs from linearity, either owing to sampling effects or owing to real divergences, they give the " best " straight regression lines which the data admit. We may regard the equations as either (a) equations for estimating an individual x from its associated y (or y from its associated x) in such a way that the sum of squares of errors of estimation is a minimum ; or (b) equations for estimating the *mean* of the x's associated with a particular y (or the mean of y's associated with a particular x) in such a way that the sum of the squares of errors of estimation is a minimum, each mean being counted proportionately to the number of observations on which it is based.

Coefficient of correlation

9.22 The coefficient r defined in equation (9.4) is of very great importance. It is called the *coefficient of correlation.*

r cannot exceed $+1$ or be less than -1.

For, from equation (9.9) we see that the value of E is

$$\Sigma(x-b_1 y)^2 = \Sigma(x^2) - \frac{\{\Sigma(xy)\}^2}{\Sigma(y^2)} = \Sigma(x^2)\{1-r^2\} \qquad . \qquad . \quad (9.11)$$

But E is the sum of a number of squares and cannot be negative. Hence,

$$1-r^2 \geqslant 0$$

which proves the result.

If $r=+1$, the regression equations are identical, as may be seen from equations (9.6), and hence the lines RR and CC coincide. In this case it follows from (9.11) that for all pairs of values of the variates

$$x-b_1 y=0$$

i.e. all values lie on a single straight line. Thus to one value of x there

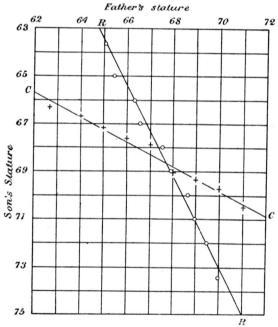

Fig. 9.8.—Correlation between stature of father and stature of son (Table 9.3)
Means of rows shown by circles and means of columns by crosses : $r=+0\cdot51$

corresponds one, and only one, value of y. This is the case we mentioned in **9.17**, and since high values of x correspond to high values of y, the variables may be said to be perfectly positively correlated.

Similarly, if $r=-1$, the pairs of values all lie on a single straight line as before, but high values of one will be associated with low values of the

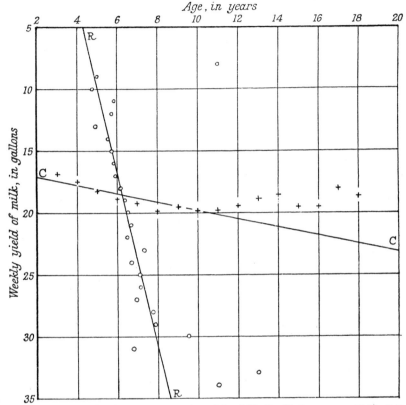

Fig. 9.9.—Correlation between age and weekly yield of milk from cows (Table 9.4)
Means of rows shown by circles and means of columns by crosses : $r=+0\cdot22$

other. In this case we can say that the variates are perfectly negatively correlated.

Finally, if the variates are independent, r is zero, for b_1 and b_2 are zero, and the lines of regression are parallel to OX and OY. It does *not* follow, however, that if r is zero the variates are independent ; the fact that r is zero implies only that the means of arrays lie *scattered around* two straight lines which do not exhibit any definite trend away from the horizontal or the vertical as the case may be. Two variates for which r is zero may, however, be spoken of as *uncorrelated*. Table 9.6 will serve as a case where the variates are almost uncorrelated but by no means independent,

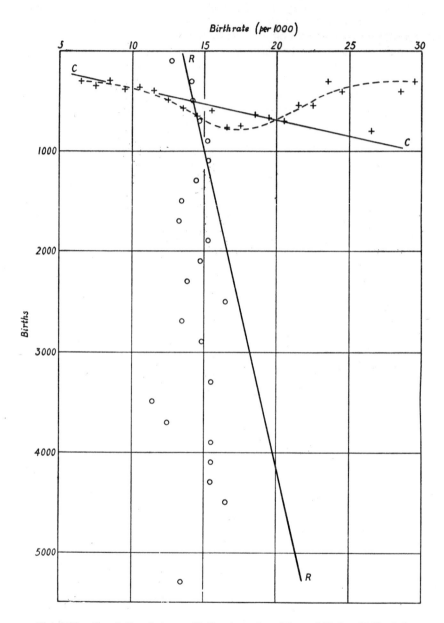

Fig. 9.10.—Correlation between birth-rate and number of births (Table 9.6)
Means of rows shown by circles and means of columns by crosses : $r = +0 \cdot 17$

r being small $(0 \cdot 17)$ (see fig. 9.10), but the coefficient of contingency C (for the grouping of Exercise 9.3) $0 \cdot 30$.　Figs. 9.8 and 9.9 are drawn from the data of Tables 9.3 and 9.4, for which r has the values $+0 \cdot 51$ and $+0 \cdot 22$ respectively.　The student should study such tables and diagrams closely, and endeavour to accustom himself to estimating the value of r from the general appearance of the table.

It does *not* follow that if x and y are functionally related their correlation is unity, unless the relationship is linear.　Cf Exercise 10.9.

Coefficients of regression

9.23　The two quantities

$$b_1 = \frac{r\sigma_x}{\sigma_y}, \qquad b_2 = \frac{r\sigma_y}{\sigma_x}$$

are called *coefficients of regression*, b_1 being the regression of x on y, or deviation in x corresponding on the average to a unit change in y, and b_2 being similarly the regression of y on x.

The coefficient of correlation is always a pure number, but the coefficients of regression are only pure numbers if the variates are the same in kind ; for they depend on the ratio $\dfrac{\sigma_x}{\sigma_y}$, and consequently on the units in which x and y are measured.

Since r is not greater than unity, one of the coefficients of regression is less than unity ; but the other may be greater than unity, if $\dfrac{\sigma_x}{\sigma_y}$ or $\dfrac{\sigma_y}{\sigma_x}$ be large.

9.24　The two standard deviations,

$$s_x = \sigma_x \sqrt{1 - r^2}, \qquad s_y = \sigma_y \sqrt{1 - r^2}$$

are of considerable importance.　It follows from (9.11) that s_x is the standard deviation of $(x - b_1 y)$, and similarly s_y is the standard deviation of $(y - b_2 x)$.　Hence we may regard s_x and s_y as the standard errors (root-mean-square errors) made in estimating x from y and y from x by the respective regression equations

$$x = b_1 y, \qquad y = b_2 x.$$

s_x may also be regarded as a kind of average standard deviation of a row about RR, and s_y as an average standard deviation of a column about CC. In an ideal case, where the regression is truly linear and the standard deviations of all parallel arrays are equal, a case to which the distribution of Table 9.3 is a rough approximation,[1] s_x is the standard deviation of the x-array and s_y the standard deviation of the y-array.　Hence s_x and s_y are sometimes termed the " standard deviations of arrays."

---

[1] Tables in which the standard deviations of arrays are equal are sometimes said to be " homoscedastic " ; in the contrary case " heteroscedastic."

Calculation of the coefficient of correlation

9.25   We now proceed to the arithmetical work involved in calculating the correlation coefficient.

For this purpose we use the formula (9.4), i.e.

$$r = \frac{\Sigma(xy)}{N \sigma_x \sigma_y} = \frac{\Sigma(xy)}{\sqrt{\Sigma(x^2)\Sigma(y^2)}}$$

The calculation of $\Sigma(x^2)$, or σ_x, and of $\Sigma(y^2)$, or σ_y, proceeds exactly as in Chapter 6.   The only expression of a novel type is the quantity $\frac{1}{N}\Sigma(xy)$, which we may call the first product-moment or the *covariance* of the distribution.[1]   As in the case of univariate distributions, the form of the arithmetic is slightly different according as the observations are grouped or ungrouped.

9.26   Our work is greatly simplified by the use of devices similar to those employed in calculating the means and other moments of univariate distributions.

(*a*) We take working means for the two variates, obtained by inspection, and transfer our moments to those about the means after the bulk of the arithmetic has been performed.   For the first product-moment we have, in fact, if ξ, η are the deviations from the working means and $\bar{\xi}$, $\bar{\eta}$ the deviations of the true means from the working means—

$$\xi = x + \bar{\xi}, \qquad \eta = y + \bar{\eta}$$

Hence,

$$\xi\eta = xy + \bar{\xi}y + x\bar{\eta} + \bar{\xi}\bar{\eta}$$

Summing for all members of the population, since $\Sigma(\bar{\xi}y) = \bar{\xi}\Sigma(y) = 0$ and similarly $\Sigma(x\bar{\eta}) = 0$, x and y being deviations from the true means,

$$\Sigma(\xi\eta) = \Sigma(xy) + N\bar{\xi}\bar{\eta}$$

Hence,

$$\Sigma(xy) = \Sigma(\xi\eta) - N\bar{\xi}\bar{\eta} \qquad . \qquad . \qquad . \qquad . \quad (9.12)$$

This gives us the product-moment about the true means in terms of the product-moment about the working means and the deviations of the true means from the working means.

---

[1] In generalisation of the definition of moments of a univariate distribution in Chapter 7 we may define the product-moments of a bivariate population as

$$\mu_{rs} = \frac{1}{N}\Sigma(fx^r y^s)$$

where f is the frequency and the variates are measured from their means.   This gives us

$$\mu_{11} = \frac{1}{N}\Sigma(fxy)$$

the quantity we have called p in equation (9.1).

(b) As a check on the rather heavy arithmetic which is frequently involved, it is advisable to use a method similar to that of **6.11**. We have

$$\Sigma(\xi+1)(\eta+1)=\Sigma(\xi\eta)+\Sigma(\xi)+\Sigma(\eta)+N \quad . \quad . \quad . \quad (9.13)$$

If, therefore, we calculate $\Sigma(\xi+1)(\eta+1)$ as well as $\Sigma(\xi\eta)$, we shall have in the above equation a check on the accuracy of our work.

(c) We take the class-intervals as units and transfer to other units afterwards as desired.

Example 9.1, Table 9.8.—Let us investigate the correlation and regressions of the variates of Table 9.7, the data of which are ungrouped. The variates are (1) the price index-number of animal feeding-stuffs, X, and (2) the price index-number of home-grown oats, Y. The values of the variates themselves are shown in columns 2 and 3 of Table 9.8. We take a working mean at $X=90$ and $Y=90$, and the deviations from these values are shown in columns 4 and 5. The remaining columns 6 to 13 give the squares and product of the deviations together with the various auxiliary quantities used for checking purposes. Finally, the various sums are shown at the bottom of the table.

In practice it is as well to show the negative values which may occur in columns 4, 5, 6, 7, 12 and 13 (particularly the last two) in a separate column, so as to facilitate addition and avoid mistakes. We have refrained from this course for convenience of printing.

As check on the arithmetic we have—

$$-118=\Sigma(\xi)=\Sigma(\xi+1)-N=-58-60$$
$$2,924=\Sigma(\xi+1)^2=\Sigma(\xi^2)+2\Sigma(\xi)+N=3,100-236+60$$

etc., and

$$2,493=\Sigma(\xi+1)(\eta+1)=\Sigma(\xi\eta)+\Sigma(\xi)+\Sigma(\eta)+N$$
$$=2,565-118-14+60$$
$$=2,493$$

We have, then, about the working means—

$$\bar{\xi}=-\frac{118}{60}=-1\cdot9667$$

$$\bar{\eta}=-\frac{14}{60}=-0\cdot2333$$

$$\sigma_x^2=\frac{3,100}{60}-\bar{\xi}^2=47\cdot7989, \qquad \sigma_x=6\cdot914$$

$$\sigma_y^2=\frac{4,814}{60}-\bar{\eta}^2=80\cdot1789, \qquad \sigma_y=8\cdot954$$

$$p=\frac{\Sigma(xy)}{N}=\frac{\Sigma(\xi\eta)}{N}-\bar{\xi}\bar{\eta}=42\cdot75-0\cdot4589=42\cdot2911$$

$$r=\frac{p}{\sigma_x\sigma_y}=\frac{42\cdot2911}{61\cdot9080}=+0\cdot68$$

TABLE 9.8—Correlation between monthly index-numbers of prices of (1) animal feeding-stuffs and (2) home-grown oats in years 1931-35

1 Month	2 X	3 Y	4 ξ	5 η	6 $\xi+1$	7 $\eta+1$	8 ξ^2	9 $(\xi+1)^2$	10 η^2	11 $(\eta+1)^2$	12 $\xi\eta$	13 $(\xi+1)(\eta+1)$
1931 Jan.	78	84	−12	−6	−11	−5	144	121	36	25	72	55
Feb.	77	82	−13	−8	−12	−7	169	144	64	49	104	84
Mar.	85	82	−5	−8	−4	−7	25	16	64	49	40	28
Apr.	88	85	−2	−5	−1	−4	4	1	25	16	10	4
May	87	89	−3	−1	−2	—	9	4	1	—	3	—
June	82	90	−8	—	−7	1	64	49	—	1	—	−7
July	81	88	−9	−2	−8	−1	81	64	4	1	18	8
Aug.	77	92	−13	2	−12	3	169	144	4	9	−26	−36
Sept.	76	83	−14	−7	−13	−6	196	169	49	36	98	78
Oct.	83	89	−7	−1	−6	—	49	36	1	—	7	—
Nov.	97	98	7	8	8	9	49	64	64	81	56	72
Dec.	93	99	3	9	4	10	9	16	81	100	27	40
1932 Jan.	95	102	5	12	6	13	25	36	144	169	60	78
Feb.	97	102	7	12	8	13	49	64	64	169	84	104
Mar.	102	105	12	15	13	16	144	169	225	256	180	208
Apr.	99	105	9	15	10	16	81	100	225	256	135	160
May	97	107	7	17	8	18	49	64	289	324	119	144
June	94	107	4	17	5	18	16	25	289	324	68	90
July	94	101	4	11	5	12	16	25	121	144	44	60
Aug.	97	106	7	16	8	17	49	64	256	289	112	136
Sept.	92	96	2	6	3	7	4	9	36	49	12	21
Oct.	89	90	−1	—	—	1	1	—	—	1	—	—
Nov.	90	85	—	−5	1	−4	—	1	25	16	—	−4
Dec.	90	81	—	−9	1	−8	—	1	81	64	—	−8
1933 Jan.	92	84	2	−6	3	−5	4	9	36	25	−12	−15
Feb.	91	85	1	−5	2	−4	1	4	25	16	−5	−8
Mar.	90	84	—	−6	1	−5	—	1	36	25	—	−5
Apr.	86	81	−4	−9	−3	−8	16	9	81	64	36	24
May	85	76	−5	−14	−4	−13	25	16	196	169	70	52
June	85	77	−5	−13	−4	−12	25	16	169	144	65	48
July	85	75	−5	−15	−4	−14	25	16	225	196	75	56
Aug.	83	79	−7	−11	−6	−10	49	36	121	100	77	60
Sept.	80	78	−10	−12	−9	−11	100	81	144	121	120	99
Oct.	78	78	−12	−12	−11	−11	144	121	144	121	144	121
Nov.	80	76	−10	−14	−9	−13	100	81	196	169	140	117
Dec.	83	75	−7	−15	−6	−14	49	36	225	196	105	84
1934 Jan.	82	80	−8	−10	−7	−9	64	49	100	81	80	63
Feb.	83	91	−7	1	−6	2	49	36	1	4	−7	−12
Mar.	85	87	−5	−3	−4	−2	25	16	9	4	15	8
Apr.	83	84	−7	−6	−6	−5	49	36	36	25	42	30
May	82	81	−8	−9	−7	−8	64	49	81	64	72	56
June	85	83	−5	−7	−4	−6	25	16	49	36	35	24
July	88	83	−2	−7	−1	−6	4	1	49	36	14	6
Aug.	101	92	11	2	12	3	121	144	4	9	22	36
Sept.	102	98	12	8	13	9	144	169	64	81	96	117
Oct.	98	94	8	4	9	5	64	81	16	25	32	45
Nov.	96	94	6	4	7	5	36	49	16	25	24	35
Dec.	98	95	8	5	9	6	64	81	25	36	40	54
1935 Jan.	98	100	8	10	9	11	64	81	100	121	80	99
Feb.	92	99	2	9	3	10	4	9	81	100	18	30
Mar.	92	96	2	6	3	7	4	9	36	49	12	21
Apr.	90	98	—	8	1	9	—	1	64	81	—	9
May	88	97	−2	7	−1	8	4	1	49	64	−14	−8
June	86	98	−4	8	−3	9	16	9	64	81	−32	−27
July	83	99	−7	9	−6	10	49	36	81	100	−63	−60
Aug.	80	92	−10	2	−9	3	100	81	4	9	−20	−27
Sept.	81	90	−9	—	−8	1	81	64	—	1	—	−8
Oct.	86	89	−4	−1	−3	—	16	9	1	—	4	—
Nov.	83	87	−7	−3	−6	−2	49	36	9	4	21	12
Dec.	82	83	−8	−7	−7	−6	64	49	49	36	56	42
Total	—	—	−118	−14	−58	46	3,100	2,924	4,814	4,846	2,565	2,493

Further, working the regressions in the way best to avoid errors in rounding off,

$$b_1 = \frac{p}{\sigma_y{}^2} = 0 \cdot 527$$

$$b^2 = \frac{p}{\sigma_x{}^2} = 0 \cdot 885$$

Thus the correlation coefficient is $0 \cdot 68$, and the regression equations, referred to the means, are—

$$\overset{\cdot}{x} = 0 \cdot 527y$$

$$y = 0 \cdot 885x$$

If we prefer to express these equations with origin at $X = 0$, $Y = 0$, we have—

$$X - (90 - 1 \cdot 97) = X - 88 \cdot 03 = 0 \cdot 527(Y - 89 \cdot 77)$$

$$Y - (90 - 0 \cdot 23) = Y - 89 \cdot 77 = 0 \cdot 885(X - 88 \cdot 03)$$

which reduce to

$$X = 0 \cdot 527Y + 40 \cdot 72 \qquad . \qquad . \qquad . \qquad . \qquad (a)$$

$$Y = 0 \cdot 885X + 11 \cdot 86 \qquad . \qquad . \qquad . \qquad . \qquad (b)$$

The lines of regression are drawn on the scatter diagram of fig. 9.4.

The standard errors made in using these equations to estimate the index-number of oats from animal feeding-stuffs, and *vice versa*, are—

$$\sigma_x\sqrt{1 - r^2} = 5 \cdot 07$$

$$\sigma_y\sqrt{1 - r^2} = 6 \cdot 57$$

Equation (a) tells us that a rise of one point in the price index-number of oats is accompanied *on the average* by a rise of $0 \cdot 527$ point in the price index-number of feeding stuffs. Similarly, equation (b) tells us that a rise of one point in the index for feeding-stuffs is accompanied *on the average* by a rise of $0 \cdot 885$ point in the price of oats.

It is important to note that the regression equations do not tell us whether a variation in one variate is *caused* by a variation in the other ; all we know is that the two vary together, and so far as the regression equations show, either the feeding-stuffs price may exert an influence on the oats price, or *vice versa*, or their common variation may be due to some other cause affecting both. This is only one instance of a difficulty which pervades the theory of correlation and regression, namely, that of *interpreting* results in terms of causal factors.

TABLE 9.9.—Correlation between (1) length of mother-frond, (2) length of daughter-frond, in Lemna minor

(The frequencies are the figures printed in ordinary type. The numbers in heavy type are the deviation-products ($\xi\eta$))

(Unpublished data; G. U. Yule)

(1) Length of mother-frond (mm. of camera drawing enlarged 24:1).

(2) Length of daughter-frond	60–66	66–72	72–78	78–84	84–90	90–96	96–102	102–108	108–114	114–120	120–126	126–132	132–138	138–144	144–150	150–156	156–162	162–168	Total
60–66		2 **42**																	2
66–72			1 **24**	1 **3**	2 **18**														3
72–78			1 **25**	3 **20**	1 **15**	5													9·5
78–84		4 **24**	2 **5**	3 **16**	6 **12**	8 **6·5**	2												26·5
84–90	2 **21**		3 **20**	5 **4·5**	12 **9**	8 **4·5**	3 **6**	5 **0**											27·5
90–96		1 **12**	15 **3·5**	12 **5**	9 **6·5**	4 **4·5**	8 **3**	4 **0**											33·5
96–102	1 **14**		10	8 **8**	6 **4·5**	7 **2**	4 **2**	0 **0**	1 **3**										24·5
102–108			1 **0**	4 **8**	3 **7·5**	7 **0**	3·5 **0**	9 **0**	3 **0**										39
108–114					4 **8**	5 **0**	5·5 **5·5**	6 **6**	4 **0**	2 **2**	1								22·5
114–120					8 **1**	2 **5**	1 **4·5**	5·5 **0**	2 **3**	2 **3**	6 **7**								22
120–126					2 **6**	5 **4**	3 **3**	2 **0**	3 **3**	3 **6**	7 **9**	2 **12**							23
126–132					2 **9**	4 **1**	3 **8**	3 **0**	1 **4**	8	2 **12**	2 **16**	3 **20**						15
132–138						6 **1**		1 **0**		2	2 **15**	16		2 **30**					8
138–144						8 **1**		0 **1**	6	10 **2**	15		1 **30**	1 **36**					6
144–150						10		0	1	12		1 **28**						1 **63**	1
150–156													1 **30**						—
156–162																			—
162–168															1 **60**				1
Total	3	7	10·5	34·5	36·5	38·5	25·5	41·5	22	15	16	6	5	3	1	—	—	1	266

Example 9.2, Table 9.9.—We now consider an example based on grouped data. In this we have omitted the auxiliary quantities necessary for checking in order to save space.

(Unpublished data ; measurements by G. U. Yule.) The two variables are (1) X, the length of a mother-frond of duckweed (*Lemna minor*) ; (2) Y, the length of the daughter-frond. The mother-frond was measured when the daughter-frond separated from it, and the daughter-frond when its first daughter-frond separated. Measures were taken from camera drawings made with the Zeiss-Abbe camera under a low power, the actual magnification being 24 : 1. The units of length in the tabulated measurements are millimetres on the drawings.

The arbitrary origin for both X and Y was taken at 105 mm. The following are the values found for the constants of the single distributions—

$$\bar{\xi} = -1 \cdot 058 \text{ intervals} = -6 \cdot 3 \text{mm.} \qquad M_1 = 98 \cdot 7 \text{ mm. on drawing}$$
$$= 4 \cdot 11 \text{ mm. actual}$$

$$\sigma_x = 2 \cdot 828 \text{ intervals} = 17 \cdot 0 \text{ mm. on drawing} = 0 \cdot 707 \text{ mm. actual}$$

$$\bar{\eta} = -0 \cdot 203 \text{ interval} = -1 \cdot 2 \text{ mm.} \qquad M_2 = 103 \cdot 8 \text{ mm. on drawing}$$
$$= 4 \cdot 32 \text{ mm. actual}$$

$$\sigma_y = 3 \cdot 084 \text{ intervals} = 18 \cdot 5 \text{ mm. on drawing} = 0 \cdot 771 \text{ mm. actual}$$

To calculate $\Sigma(\xi\eta)$ the value of $\xi\eta$ is first written in every compartment of the table against the corresponding frequency, treating the class-interval as unit. In Table 9.9 frequencies are shown in ordinary type and the values of $\xi\eta$ in heavy type. In making these entries the sign of the product may be neglected, but it must be remembered that this sign will be positive in the upper left-hand and lower right-hand quadrants, and negative in the two others. The frequencies are then collected, according to the magnitude and sign of $\xi\eta$, in columns 2 and 3 of Table 9.10. When columns 2 and 3 are completed they should be checked to see that no frequency has been dropped, which may readily be done by adding together the total of the two columns and the frequency in the 8th row and 8th column of Table 9.9 (the row and column for which $\xi\eta = 0$), care being taken not to count twice the frequency in the compartment common to the two. This grand total must clearly be equal to N, the total number of observations, which in this case is 266. The numbers in column 4 are given by deducting the entries in column 3 from those in column 2. The totals so obtained are multiplied by $\xi\eta$ (column 1) and the products entered in column 5 or 6 according to sign. The algebraic sum of these totals gives

$$\Sigma(\xi\eta) = +1519 \cdot 5$$

TABLE 9.10

1 $\xi\eta$	2 Frequencies + Quadrants	3 Frequencies − Quadrants	4 Total	5 Products +	6 Products −
1	—	8·5	− 8·5	—	8·5
2	17	13·5	+ 3·5	7	—
3	10·5	9	+ 1·5	4·5	—
4	13·5	6·5	+ 7	28	—
5	2	0·5	+ 1·5	7·5	—
6	13·5	5	+ 8·5	51	—
8	13	1	+12	96	—
9	9	4	+ 5	45	—
10	6·5	1	+ 5·5	55	—
12	17·5	—	+17·5	210	—
14	1	—	+ 1	14	—
15	6	—	+ 6	90	—
16	7	—	+ 7	112	—
18	2	—	+ 2	36	—
20	8	—	+ 8	160	—
21	2	—	+ 2	42	—
24	6	—	+ 6	144	—
25	1	—	+ 1	25	—
28	1	—	+ 1	28	—
30	3	—	+ 3	90	—
36	1	—	+ 1	36	—
40	1	—	+ 1	40	—
42	2	—	+ 2	84	—
60	1	—	+ 1	60	—
63	1	—	+ 1	63	—
Totals	145·5 49 71·5 266	49	—	+ 1,528 − 8·5 1,519·5	− 8·5

Hence, dividing by 266,

$$\frac{1}{N}\Sigma(\xi\eta)=5\cdot712$$

$$p=5\cdot712-\bar{\xi}\bar{\eta}=5\cdot712-0\cdot215$$
$$=5\cdot497$$

Hence.

$$r=\frac{p}{\sigma_x\sigma_y}=\frac{5\cdot497}{2\cdot828\times3\cdot084}=+0\cdot63$$

The regression of daughter-frond on mother-frond is 0·69 (a value which will not be affected by altering the units of measurement for both mother- and daughter-fronds, as such an alteration will affect both standard deviations equally). Hence, the regression equation giving the average actual length (in millimetres) of daughter-fronds for mother-fronds of the actual length X is

$$Y = 1 \cdot 48 + 0 \cdot 69X$$

We leave it to the student to work out the second regression equation giving the average length of mother-fronds for daughter-fronds of length Y, and to check the whole work by a diagram showing the lines of regression and the means of arrays for the central portion of the table.

Example 9.3, Table 9.2.—The following device is frequently useful, and saves a considerable amount of labour in calculating the product term $\Sigma(xy)$.

We have—

$$\Sigma(x-y)^2 = \Sigma(x^2) - 2\Sigma(xy) + \Sigma(y^2) . \qquad . \qquad . \qquad \text{(i)}$$

and

$$\Sigma(x+y)^2 = \Sigma(x^2) + 2\Sigma(xy) + \Sigma(y^2) \qquad . \qquad . \qquad \text{(ii)}$$

Hence, knowing $\Sigma(x^2)$ and $\Sigma(y^2)$, we can find $\Sigma(xy)$ if we know either $\Sigma(x-y)^2$ or $\Sigma(x+y)^2$. These quantities are often easier to calculate than $\Sigma(xy)$ itself.

Consider the data of Table 9.2. In the usual way, taking a working mean centred in the intervals $X = 25-$ years, $Y = 25-$ years, we have, in units of five years—

$$\bar{\xi} = +0 \cdot 2924 \qquad \bar{\eta} = -0 \cdot 2353$$
$$\Sigma(\xi^2) = 9{,}708 \qquad \Sigma(\eta^2) = 7{,}090$$
$$\sigma_x = 1 \cdot 730 \qquad \sigma_y = \cdot 481$$

Now the value of $\xi - \eta$ is constant down diagonals which run from the top left hand to the bottom right hand of the table. In fact, for the principal diagonal, running from $X = 15-, Y = 15-$ through $X = 20-,$ $Y = 20-$, etc., $\xi - \eta = 0$. For the diagonal above this, running from $X = 20-, Y = 15-$ through $X = 25-, Y = 20-$, etc., $\xi - \eta = 1$, and so on. Let us then find the diagonal totals. We find—

$\xi - \eta$	Frequency in diagonal
-3	4
-2	34
-1	280
0	1,398
1	1,051
2	263
3	73
4	31
5	12
6	5
7	2
	3,153

The total is the total frequency, which gives a check on the work.

The value of $\Sigma(\xi-\eta)^2$ for the whole table is then obtained from the above table by squaring the values in the left-hand column, multiplying by the corresponding frequency in the right-hand column and adding. We get

$$\Sigma(\xi-\eta)^2 = (9\times4)+(4\times34)+(1\times280)+ \ldots +(49\times2)$$
$$= 4,286$$

Hence, from (i),

$$4,286 = 9,708+7,090-2\Sigma(\xi\eta)$$
$$\therefore \quad \Sigma(\xi\eta) = 6,256$$
$$p = \frac{6,256}{3,153} - \overline{\xi\eta} = +2\cdot0529$$

whence

$$r = \frac{p}{\sigma_x\sigma_y} = +\frac{2\cdot0529}{1\cdot730\times1\cdot481} = 0\cdot80$$

The regression equations may now be obtained in the usual manner.

In the above work we chose equation (i) in preference to equation (ii) because the frequencies are seen by inspection to run mainly from the top left hand to the bottom right hand of the table. Had they run from the top right hand to the bottom left hand we should probably have found it better to use equation (ii).

9.27　The student should be careful to remember the following points in working—

(1) To give $\Sigma(\xi\eta)$ and $(\overline{\xi\eta})$ their correct signs in finding the true mean deviation product p.

(2) To express σ_x and σ_y in terms of the class-interval as a unit, in the value of $r=p/\sigma_x\sigma_y$, for these are the units in terms of which p has been calculated.

(3) To use the proper units for the standard deviations (not class-intervals in general) in calculating the coefficients of regression : in forming the regression equation in terms of the absolute values of the variables, for example, as above, the work will be wrong unless means and standard deviations are expressed in the same units.

Fluctuations of sampling

9.28　Further, it must always be remembered that correlation coefficients, like other statistical measures, are subject to fluctuations of sampling. We shall consider this point at some length in later chapters (18 and 21), since the correlation coefficient has certain individual features which make it of special interest from the sampling point of view. We may, however, at this stage stress that if the number of observations is small, no significance can be attached to small, or even moderately large, values of r as indicating a real correlation in the population from which the observations are drawn. For example, if $N=36$, a value of $r=\pm0\cdot5$ may be a chance result, though a very infrequent one, in sampling from an uncorrelated population. If $N=100$, $r=\pm0\cdot3$ may similarly be a mere fluctuation of sampling, though again a very infrequent one. The student should therefore be careful in interpreting his coefficients.

Corrections for grouping

9.29 In this connection we may mention the question whether, in calculating the correlation coefficient from grouped data, any correction is to be made analogous to the Sheppard correction for grouping which we have considered in the case of univariate data. In the examples considered in the foregoing we have not made such corrections.

It appears that, when the distribution is reasonably symmetrical and obeys conditions similar to those enunciated in **6.12**, page 133, we may, with advantage, correct the standard deviations σ_x, σ_y, by applying to each the formula

$$\sigma^2(\text{corrected}) = \sigma^2 - \frac{h^2}{12}$$

where h is the width of the interval. The product term $\Sigma(xy)$ needs no such correction.

We pointed out in **6.12**, however, that sampling fluctuations usually obliterate any correction for grouping unless the size of the sample is large. It may, as before, be suggested that unless $N=1,000$ or more, it is hardly worth while making the correction. For example, in Tables 9.1–9.6, Tables 9.1 and 9.5 have a frequency less than 1,000 and the corrections are not to be applied—in any case they would not be applied to Tables 9.5 and 9.6, which violate the conditions as to " tapering off."

9.30 Finally, it should be borne in mind that any coefficient, e.g. the coefficient of correlation or the coefficient of contingency, gives only a part of the information afforded by the original data or the correlation table. The correlation table itself, or the original data if no correlation table has been compiled, should always be given, unless considerations of space or of expense absolutely preclude the adoption of such a course.

SUMMARY

1. A population every member of which bears one of the values of each of two variates is said to be bivariate. If the members are grouped according to class-intervals of the two variables, we have a bivariate frequency-distribution.

2. The bivariate frequency-distribution may be represented by a frequency-surface or by a stereogram. Ungrouped data (and, less conveniently, grouped data) can be represented on a scatter diagram.

3. The means of arrays of a bivariate frequency-distribution may be represented as points by reference to a pair of rectangular axes along which are measured values of the variables. The means of rows and those of columns will in general lie respectively about two smooth curves, called lines of regression. The equations of these curves are called regression equations.[1]

4. The regression equations may be regarded as expressions for estimating from a given value of one variate the average corresponding value of the other.

5. The coefficient of correlation (product-moment correlation coefficient) between two variables X and Y is given by—

$$r = \frac{\Sigma(xy)}{\sqrt{\Sigma(x^2)\Sigma(y^2)}}$$

$$= \frac{p}{\sigma_x \sigma_y}$$

where x, y are the values of the variables measured from their respective means, and $p = \dfrac{\Sigma(xy)}{N}$.

6. The correlation coefficient r cannot be less than -1 or greater than $+1$. If $r = \pm 1$ the variables are perfectly correlated, the points corresponding to pairs of values x, y all lying on a straight line. If $r = -1$ the variables are perfectly negatively correlated, low values of one corresponding to high values of the other. If $r = +1$ the variables are perfectly positively correlated, high values of one corresponding to high values of the other.

7. The linear regression equation of X on Y (referred to axes through their respective means) is

$$x = b_1 y$$

where

$$b_1 = \frac{r\sigma_x}{\sigma_y} = \frac{p}{\sigma_y^2}$$

and that of Y on X is

$$y = b_2 x$$

where

$$b_2 = \frac{r\sigma_y}{\sigma_x} = \frac{p}{\sigma_x^2}$$

b_1 and b_2 being called coefficients of regression, or simply regressions.

---

[1] Curvilinear regression lines, like straight regression lines, may also be defined for ungrouped data by an extension of the principle of making sums of squares of errors of estimate a minimum.

8. The straight lines of regression are such that the sums of squares of errors of estimate, $\Sigma(x-b_1 y)^2$ and $\Sigma(y-b_2 x)^2$, are a minimum. If the quotients of these sums by N are denoted by $s_x{}^2, s_y{}^2$,

$$s_x{}^2 = \sigma_x{}^2(1-r^2)$$

$$s_y{}^2 = \sigma_y{}^2(1-r^2)$$

EXERCISES

9.1   Find the correlation coefficient and the equations of regression for the following values of X and Y—

X	Y
1	2
2	5
3	3
4	8
5	7

[As a matter of practice it is never worth calculating a correlation coefficient for so few observations : the figures are given solely as a short example on which the student can test his knowledge of the work.]

9.2   (Data from W. Little : Labour Commission Report, Vol. 5, Part 1, 1894, and Official Returns.)
    The figures in the table on p. 234 show (1) the estimated average earnings of agricultural labourers, X, (2) the percentage of population in receipt of poor law relief, Y, (3) the ratio of the number of paupers receiving outdoor relief to the number receiving relief in workhouses, Z, for certain districts in England and Wales in 1893.
    Find the correlations between X and Y, Y and Z, and Z and X.   Draw scatter diagrams to illustrate the various joint distributions.

9.3   Verify the data in the table heading p. 235 for the under-mentioned tables of this chapter.   Calculate the means of rows and columns and draw a diagram showing the lines of regression for the data of Table 9.1 (Sheppard's correction used only in Table 9.4.)
    In calculating the coefficient of contingency (coefficient of mean square contingency) use the following groupings, so as to avoid small scattered frequencies at the extremities of the tables and also excessive arithmetic—
    Table 9.1.   Group together (1) two top rows, (2) three bottom rows, (3) two first columns, (4) four last columns, leaving centre of table as it stands.

Table for Exercise 9.2

Union	Estimated average earnings of agricultural labourers Shillings and pence per week		Percentage of population in receipt of Poor Law relief	Ratio of number of paupers receiving outdoor relief to the number receiving relief in workhouses
	s.	d.		
1. Glendale . . .	20	9	2·40	6·40
2. Wigton . . .	20	3	2·29	4·04
3. Garstang . . .	19	8	1·39	7·90
4. Belper . . .	18	6	1·92	3·31
5. Nantwich . . .	17	8	2·98	7·85
6. Atcham . . .	17	6	1·17	0·45
7. Driffield . . .	17	1	3·79	10·00
8. Uttoxeter . . .	17	0	3·01	4·43
9. Wetherby . . .	17	0	2·39	4·78
10. Easingwold . .	16	11	2·78	4·73
11. Southwell . .	16	6	3·09	6·66
12. Hollingbourn . .	16	4	2·78	1·22
13. Melton Mowbray .	16	3	2·61	4·27
14. Truro . . .	16	3	4·33	7·50
15. Godstone . . .	16	0	3·02	4·44
16. Louth . . .	16	0	4·20	8·34
17. Brixworth . .	15	9	1·29	0·69
18. Crediton . .	15	8	5·16	9·89
19. Holbeach . .	15	6	4·75	4·00
20. Maldon . . .	15	6	4·64	6·02
21. Monmouth. .	15	4	4·26	8·27
22. St. Neots . . .	15	3	1·66	1·58
23. Swaffham . .	15	0	5·37	16·04
24. Thakeham . .	15	0	3·38	1·96
25. Thame . . .	15	0	5·84	9·28
26. Thingoe . . .	15	0	4·63	8·72
27. Basingstoke . .	15	0	3·93	2·97
28. Cirencester . .	15	0	4·54	5·38
29. North Witchford .	14	10	3·42	3·24
30. Pewsey . . .	14	9	5·88	7·61
31. Bromyard . .	14	9	4·36	5·87
32. Wantage . . .	14	9	3·85	5·50
33. Stratford-on-Avon .	14	7	3·92	3·58
34. Dorchester. .	14	6	4·48	6·93
35. Woburn . . .	14	6	5·67	6·02
36. Buntingford . .	14	4	4·91	4·92
37. Pershore . . .	13	6	4·34	4·64
38. Langport . . .	12	6	5·19	10·56

Table 9.3.   Regroup by 2-inch intervals, 58·5–60·5, etc., for father, 59·5–61·5, etc., for son.   If a 3-inch grouping be used (58·5–61·5, etc., for both father and son), the coefficient of mean square contingency is 0·465.

Table 9.4.   For columns, group those headed 3 and 4, 5 and 6, 7 and 8, 9 and 10, 11 and over ; for rows, group those headed 8–11, 12–13, 14–15, 16–17, 18–19, 20–21, 22–23, 24–25, 26–27, 28 and over.

Table for Exercise 9.3

	9.1	9.3	9.4	9.6
Mean of X . . .	55·3 mm.	67·70 in	6·22 yrs	14·54 per thou.
,, ,, Y . . .	53·1 ,,	68·66 ,,	18·61 gal	379·47 births
Standard deviation of X .	6·86 ,,	2·72 ,,	2·21 yrs	2·87 per thou.
,, ,, Y .	5·77 ,,	2·75 ,,	3·37 gal	505·24 births
Coefficient of correlation .	+0·97	+0·51	+0·22	+0·17
Coefficient of contingency (for the grouping stated below)	0·90	0·51	0·26	0·30

Table 11.6. For columns, take singly those for 0–, 200–, group 400– and 600– and group 800– and over. Rows, group those headed 6–11, 12 and 13, 14 and 15, 16–18, 19 and over.

9.4 (Data from Statistical Review of England and Wales for 1933, Tables, Part 1, p. 3, and part 2, p. 6.) The following show mean annual birth and death rates in England and Wales for quinquennia since 1876. Find the correlation between birth and death rates.

Period	Mean annual Live birth rate per 1,000 of population	Mean annual death rate per 1,000 of population
1876–80	35·3	20·8
1881–85	33·5	19·4
1886–90	31·4	18·9
1891–95	30·5	18·7
1896–1900	29·3	17·7
1901–1905	28·2	16·0
1906–1910	26·3	14·7
1911–15	23·6	14·3
1916–20	20·1	14·4
1921–25	19·9	12·2
1926–30	16·7	12·1

9.5 The following figures (S. Rowson, *Journ. Roy. Sta. Soc.*, vol. 99, 1936), give the relationship between the density of population and seating capacity of cinemas in various districts of Great Britain.

Find the correlation between density of population and proportion of cinemas with (1) seating capacity 500 or less, (2) seating capacity 2,000 or more.

District	Density of population per square mile	Percentage of cinemas	
		(1) Seating 500 or less	(2) Seating 2,000 or more
Scotland . . .	163	13·4	4·3
North Wales . . .	165	42·5	0·0
West of England . . .	380	38·2	2·1
Eastern Counties . . .	431	38·8	1·3
South Wales . . .	440	22·4	1·2
North of England . .	487	16·0	1·2
Yorkshire and district . .	594	15·5	3·1
Midlands	710	20·2	1·6
Home Counties (excl. London)	794	28·2	3·0
Lancashire . . .	2,157	13·5	3·6

9.6 Show that the coefficient of correlation is the geometric mean of the coefficients of regression; verify from the data of Examples 9.1, 9.2 and 9.3 that the arithmetic mean of the coefficients of regression is greater than the coefficient of correlation.

9.7 The tangent of the difference of angles A and B is given by—

$$\tan (A - B) = \frac{\tan A - \tan B}{1 + \tan A \tan B}$$

Deduce that the smaller angle between regression lines is θ, given by—

$$\tan \theta = \frac{1 - r^2}{r} \frac{\sigma_x \sigma_y}{\sigma_x^2 + \sigma_y^2}$$

and interpret this result when $r = 0$ and $r = \pm 1$.

CHAPTER TEN

NORMAL CORRELATION

The bivariate normal surface

10.1 Our study of the normal curve in Chapter 8 may be extended to yield a corresponding expression for the frequency-distribution of pairs of values of two variates. This bivariate normal distribution, known also as "*the bivariate normal surface*," "*the normal correlation surface*" or simply "*the normal surface*," occupies a central position in the theory of bivariate frequency-distributions, and bears to them a relation similar to that borne by the normal curve to the frequency-distributions of a single variate.

The normal surface is of great historical importance, as the earlier work on correlation is, almost without exception, based on the assumption of such a distribution ; though when it was recognised that the properties of the correlation coefficient could be deduced, as in Chapter 9, without reference to the form of the distribution of frequency, a knowledge of this special type of frequency-surface ceased to be so essential. But the generalised normal law is of importance in the theory of sampling : it serves to describe very approximately certain actual distributions (e.g. of measurements on man) ; and if it can be assumed to hold good, some of the expressions in the theory or correlation, notably the standard deviations of arrays (and, if more than two variables are involved, the partial correlation coefficients), can be assigned more simple and definite meanings than in the general case. The student should, therefore, be familiar with the more fundamental properties of the distribution.

10.2 Consider first the case in which the two variables are completely independent. Let the distributions of frequency for the two variables x_1 and x_2 singly be given by

$$\left. \begin{array}{l} y_1 = y_1' \exp(-x_1{}^2/2\sigma_1{}^2) \\ y_2 = y_2' \exp(-x_2{}^2/2\sigma_2{}^2) \end{array} \right\} \qquad . \qquad . \qquad . \quad (10.1)$$

Then, assuming independence, the frequency-distributions of pairs of values must, by the rule of independence, be given by

$$y_{12} = y'_{12} \exp\left\{ -\tfrac{1}{2}\left(\frac{x_1{}^2}{\sigma_1{}^2} + \frac{x_2{}^2}{\sigma_2{}^2} \right) \right\} . \qquad . \qquad . \quad (10.2)$$

where

$$y'_{12} = \frac{y_1' y_2'}{N} = \frac{N}{2\pi\sigma_1\sigma_2} \qquad \cdot \qquad \cdot \qquad \cdot \qquad (10.3)$$

Equation (10.2) gives a normal correlation surface for one special case, the correlation coefficient being zero. If we put $x_2 = a$ constant, we see that every section of the surface by a vertical plane parallel to the x_1-axis, i.e. the distribution of any array of x_1's, is a normal distribution, with the same mean and standard deviation as the total distribution of x_1's ; and a similar statement holds for the arrays of x_2's ; these properties must hold good, of course, as the two variables are assumed independent (cf. **3.18**). The contour lines of the surface, that is to say, lines drawn on the surface at a constant height, are a series of similar ellipses with major and minor axes parallel to the axes of x_1 and x_2 and proportional to σ_1 and σ_2, the equations to the contour lines being of the general form

$$\frac{x_1^2}{\sigma_1^2} + \frac{x_2^2}{\sigma_2^2} = c^2 \qquad \cdot \qquad \cdot \qquad \cdot \qquad (10.4)$$

Pairs of values of x_1 and x_2 related by an equation of this form are, therefore, equally frequent.

10.3 Now suppose we have two correlated variates x_1 and x_2, and let the regression of x_1 on x_2 be b_{12} and that of x_2 on x_1 be b_{21}. Let r_{12} be the coefficient of correlation between x_1 and x_2.

Consider the new variates defined by the equations

$$x_{1.2} = x_1 - b_{12}x_2$$
$$x_{2.1} = x_2 - b_{21}x_1$$

This is a notation which we shall later extend considerably.

Then x_1 and $x_{2.1}$ are uncorrelated, as are x_2 and $x_{1.2}$. ·

For

$$\Sigma(x_1 x_{2.1}) = \Sigma\{x_1(x_2 - b_{21}x_1)\}$$
$$= \Sigma(x_1 x_2) - b_{21}\Sigma(x_1)^2$$
$$\frac{1}{N}\Sigma(x_1 x_{2.1}) = r_{12}\sigma_{x_1}\sigma_{x_2} - \frac{r_{12}\sigma_{x_2}}{\sigma_{x_1}}\sigma_{x_1}^2$$
$$= 0$$

and similarly for $\Sigma(x_2 x_{1.2})$.

Writing σ_1, σ_2 for the standard deviations of x_1, x_2, we see that the standard deviation $\sigma_{1.2}$ of $x_{1.2}$ is given by

$$\sigma^2{}_{1.2}=\frac{1}{N}\Sigma(x^2_{1.2})=\frac{1}{N}\Sigma(x_1-b_{12}x_2)^2$$

$$=\{\sigma_1^2-2b_{12}r_{12}\sigma_1\sigma_2+b_{12}^2\sigma_2^2\}$$

$$=\{\sigma_1^2-2r_{12}^2\sigma_1^2+r_{12}^2\sigma_1^2\}$$

$$=\sigma_1^2(1-r_{12}^2)$$

and similarly $\sigma_{2.1}$ the standard deviation of $x_{2.1}$ is given by

$$\sigma_{2.1}^2=\sigma_2^2(1-r_{12}^2)$$

We obtained these results in a slightly different form in **9.22** and **9.24**.

10.4 Suppose further that x_1 and $x_{2.1}$ are not only uncorrelated, but independent, and that each is normally distributed.

In accordance with equation (10.2), we must have for the frequency-distribution of pairs of deviations of x_1 and $x_{2.1}$

$$y_{12}=y'_{12}\exp\left\{-\tfrac{1}{2}\left(\frac{x_1^2}{\sigma_1^2}+\frac{x_{2.1}^2}{\sigma_{2.1}^2}\right)\right\} \qquad . \qquad . \qquad (10.5)$$

But

$$\frac{x_1^2}{\sigma_1^2}+\frac{x_{2.1}^2}{\sigma_{2.1}^2}=\frac{x_1^2}{\sigma_1^2(1-r_{12}^2)}+\frac{x_2^2}{\sigma_2^2(1-r_{12}^2)}-2r_{12}\frac{x_1x_2}{\sigma_1\sigma_2(1-r_{12}^2)}$$

$$=\frac{x_1^2}{\sigma_{1.2}^2}+\frac{x_2^2}{\sigma_{2.1}^2}-2r_{12}\frac{x_1x_2}{\sigma_{1.2}\sigma_{2.1}}$$

Evidently we should also have arrived at precisely the same expression if we had taken the distribution of frequency for x_2 and $x_{1.2}$, and reduced the exponent

$$\frac{x_2^2}{\sigma_2^2}+\frac{x_{1.2}^2}{\sigma_{1.2}^2}$$

We have, therefore, the general expression for the normal correlation surface for two variables—

$$y_{12}=y'_{12}\exp\left\{-\tfrac{1}{2}\left(\frac{x_1^2}{\sigma_{1.2}^2}+\frac{x_2^2}{\sigma_{2.1}^2}-2r_{12}\frac{x_1x_2}{\sigma_{1.2}\sigma_{2.1}}\right)\right\} \qquad . \qquad . \qquad (10.6)$$

Further, since x_1 and $x_{2.1}$, x_2 and $x_{1.2}$, are independent, we must have :

$$y'_{12}=\frac{N}{2\pi\sigma_1\sigma_{2.1}}=\frac{N}{2\pi\sigma_2\sigma_{1.2}}=\frac{N}{2\pi\sigma_1\sigma_2(1-r_{12}^2)^{\frac{1}{2}}} \qquad . \qquad . \qquad (10.7)$$

Expressing $\sigma_{1.2}$ and $\sigma_{2.1}$ in terms of σ_1, σ_2 and r_{12}, we have the alternative form

$$y_{12}=\frac{N}{2\pi\sigma_1\sigma_2\sqrt{1-r_{12}^2}}\exp\left\{-\frac{1}{2(1-r_{12}^2)}\left(\frac{x_1^2}{\sigma_1^2}-\frac{2r_{12}x_1x_2}{\sigma_1\sigma_2}+\frac{x_2^2}{\sigma_2^2}\right)\right\} \qquad . \qquad (10.8)$$

Properties 'of the normal surface

10.5 For any given value h_2 of x_2 the distribution of the array of x_1's is given by

$$y_{12} = y'_{12} \exp\left\{ -\tfrac{1}{2}\left(\frac{x_1^2}{\sigma_{1.2}^2} + \frac{h_2^2}{\sigma_{2.1}^2} - 2r_{12}\frac{x_1 h_2}{\sigma_{1.2}\sigma_{2.1}} \right) \right\}$$

$$= y'_{12} \exp\left(-\frac{h_2^2}{2\sigma^2} \right)\exp\left\{ -\frac{\left(x_1 - r_{12}\dfrac{\sigma_1}{\sigma_2}h_2\right)^2}{2\sigma_{1.2}^2} \right\}$$

This is a normal distribution of standard deviation $\sigma_{1.2}$, with a mean deviating by $r_{12}\dfrac{\sigma_1}{\sigma_2}h_2$ from the mean of the whole distribution of x_1's.

Hence, since h_2 may be any value, we have the important results—

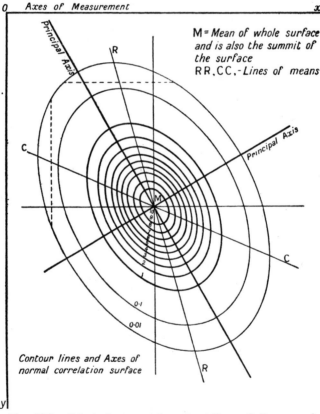

O   *Axes of Measurement*   *x*

M = *Mean of whole surface and is also the summit of the surface*
RR.CC,- *Lines of means*

Principal Axis

R

C

Principal Axis

M

C

R

0·1

0·01

Contour lines and Axes of normal correlation surface

y

Fig. 10.1.—Principal axes and contour lines of the normal correlation surface

(1) that the standard deviations of all arrays of x_1 are the same, and equal to $\sigma_{1.2}$;

(2) that the regression of x_1 on x_2 is strictly linear.

Similarly, it follows that the s.d.'s of all arrays of x_2 are equal to $\sigma_{2.1}$, and that the regression of x_2 on x_1 is linear.

10.6 The contour lines are, as in the case of independence, a series of concentric and similar ellipses ; the major and minor axes are, however, no longer parallel to the axes of x_1 and x_2, but make a certain angle with them.   Fig. 10.1 illustrates the calculated form of the contour lines for one case, RR and CC being the lines of regression.   As each line of regression cuts every array of x_1 or of x_2 in its mean, and as the distribution of every array is symmetrical about its mean, RR must bisect every horizontal chord and CC every vertical chord, as illustrated by the two chords shown by dotted lines ; it also follows that RR cuts all the ellipses in the points of contact of the horizontal tangents to the ellipses, and CC in the points of contact of the vertical tangents.   The surface or solid itself, somewhat truncated, is shown in fig. 9.1, page 208.

10.7 Since, as we see from fig. 10.1, a normal surface for two correlated variables may be regarded merely as a certain surface for which r is zero turned round through some angle, and since for every angle through which it is turned the distributions of all x_1 arrays and x_2 arrays are normal, it follows that every section of a normal surface by a vertical plane is a normal curve, i.e. the distributions of arrays taken at any angle across the surface are normal.

10.8 It also follows that, since the total distributions of x_1 and x_2 must be normal for every angle through which the surface is turned, the distributions of totals given by slices or arrays taken at any angle across a normal surface must be normal distributions.   But these would give the distributions of functions like $ax_1 \pm bx_2$, and consequently (1) the distribution of any linear function of two normally distributed variables x_1 and x_2 must also be normal ; (2) the correlation between any two linear functions of two normally distributed variables must be normal correlation.

Result (1) is very important, and may easily be extended to cover the case of n variables $x_1 \ldots x_n$.   Suppose, in fact, we have n such variables each of which is normally distributed, and a linear function $ax_1 + bx_2 + \ldots + hx_n$.   Since $ax_1 + bx_2$ is normally distributed, $(ax_1 + bx_2) + cx_3$ is normally distributed, and hence so is $(ax_1 bx_2 + cx_3) + dx_4$, and so on.   Thus the function $ax_1 + \ldots + hx_n$ is normally distributed.

Hence, the sum of n normal variates is distributed normally ; and in particular the mean of n normal variates is distributed normally.   More particularly still, the means of samples of n from a normal population are normally distributed.

10.9 Returning to the normal surface, it is interesting to inquire what is the angle θ through which the surface has been turned from the position for which the correlation was zero. The major and minor axes of the ellipses are sometimes termed the *principal axes*. If ξ_1, ξ_2 be the co-ordinates referred to the principal axes (the ξ_1-axis being the x_1-axis in its new position), we have for the relation between ξ_1, ξ_2, x_1, x_2, the angle θ being taken as positive for a rotation of the x_1-axis which will make it, if continued through 90°, coincide in direction and sense with the x_2-axis,

$$\left.\begin{array}{l} \xi_1 = x_1 \cos \theta + x_2 \sin \theta \\ \xi_2 = x_2 \cos \theta - x_1 \sin \theta \end{array}\right\} \qquad . \qquad . \qquad . \ (10.9)$$

But, since ξ_1, ξ_2 are uncorrelated, $\Sigma(\xi_1 \xi_2) = 0$. Hence, multiplying together equations (10.9) and summing,

$$0 = (\sigma_2{}^2 - \sigma_1{}^2) \sin 2\theta + 2r_{12}\sigma_1\sigma_2 \cos 2\theta$$

$$\tan 2\theta = \frac{2r_{12}\sigma_1\sigma_2}{\sigma_1{}^2 - \sigma_2{}^2} \qquad . \qquad . \qquad . \ (10.10)$$

It should be noticed that if we *define* the principal axes of any distribution for two variables as being a pair of axes at right angles for which the variables ξ_1, ξ_2 are uncorrelated, equation (10.10) gives the angle that they make with the axes of measurement whether the distribution be normal or not.

10.10 The two standard deviations, say S_1 and S_2, about the principal axes are of some interest, for evidently from **10.2** the major and minor axes of the contour ellipses are proportional to these two standard deviations. They may be most readily determined as follows. Squaring the two transformation equations (10.9), summing and adding, we have—

$$S_1{}^2 + S_2{}^2 = \sigma_1{}^2 + \sigma_2{}^2 \quad . \qquad . \qquad . \ (10.11)$$

Referring the surface to the axes of measurement, we have for the central ordinate, by equation (10.7),

$$y'_{12} = \frac{N}{2\pi\sigma_1\sigma_2(1 - r_{12}^2)^{\frac{1}{2}}}$$

Referring it to the principal axes, by equation (10.3),

$$y'_{12} = \frac{N}{2\pi S_1 S_2}$$

But these two values of the central ordinate must be equal, therefore

$$S_1 S_2 = \sigma_1\sigma_2(1 - r_{12}^2)^{\frac{1}{2}} \qquad . \qquad . \qquad . \ (10.12)$$

(10.11) and (10.12) are a pair of simultaneous equations from which S_1 and S_2 may be very simply obtained in any arithmetical case. Care must, however, be taken to give the correct signs to the square root in solving.

S_1+S_2 is necessarily positive, and S_1-S_2 also if r is positive, the major axes of the ellipses lying along ξ_1 ; but if r be negative, S_1-S_2 is also negative. It should be noted that, while we have deduced (10.12) from a simple consideration depending on the normality of the distribution, it is really of general application (like equation (10.11)), and may be obtained at somewhat greater length from the equations for transforming co-ordinates.

10.11   As an example of the application of the foregoing theory to a practical case, we proceed to consider the distribution of Table 9.3, page 202, showing the correlation between stature of father and son, and to test, as far as we can by elementary methods, whether a normal surface will fit the data.

10.12   The first important property of the normal distribution is the linearity of regression.   This was well illustrated for these data in fig. 9.8 (page 218).   Subject to some investigation as to the deviations from strict linearity which may occur as the result of sampling fluctuations, we may conclude that the regression is appreciably linear.   We shall consider a test of linearity in later chapters (see Chapter 21).

10.13   The second important property is the constancy of the standard deviation for all parallel arrays.
   The standard deviations of the ten columns from that headed $62\cdot5\text{--}63\cdot5$ onwards are—

2·56	2·60
2·11	2·26
2·55	2·26
2·24	2·45
2·23	2·33

the mean being 2·36.   The standard deviations again only fluctuate irregularly round their mean value.   The mean of the first five is 2·34, of the second five 2·38, a difference of only 0·04 ; of the first group, two are greater and three are less than the mean, and the same is true of the second group.   There does not seem to be any indication of a general tendency for the standard deviation to increase or decrease as we pass from one end of the table to the other.   We are not yet in a position to test how far the differences from the average standard deviation might have arisen in sampling from a record in which the distribution was strictly normal, but, as a fact, a rough test suggests that they might have done so.

10.14   Next we note that the distributions of all arrays of a normal surface should themselves be normal.   Owing, however, to the small numbers of observations in any array, the distributions of arrays are very irregular, and their normality cannot be tested in any very satisfactory way ; we can only say that they do not exhibit any marked or regular asymmetry.   But we can test the allied property of a normal correlation table, viz. that the totals of arrays must give a normal distribution even if the arrays be taken diagonally across the surface, and not parallel to either axis of measurement. From an ordinary correlation table we cannot find the totals of such diagonal arrays exactly, but the totals of arrays at an angle of 45° will be given with sufficient accuracy for our present purpose by the totals of lines of diagonally adjacent compartments. Referring again to Table 9.3, and forming the totals of such diagonals (running up from left to right), we find, starting at the top left-hand corner of the table, the following distribution—

0·25	78·75
2	81·25
3·25	66·5
6·25	59·25
8	42·25
9·75	30·75
17	29·25
34·5	19
42	10·75
46·25	7
60·5	4·25
67·5	3·5
85·75	1·75
87·25	1
78	0·25
94·25	

Total 1078

The mean of this distribution is at 0·359 of an interval above the centre of the interval with frequency 78 ; its standard deviation is 4·757 intervals, or, remembering that the interval is $1/\sqrt{2}$ of an inch, 3·364 inches. (This value may be checked directly from the constants for the table given in Exercise 9.3, page 235, for we have, from the first of the transformation equations (12.9),

$$\sigma_\xi{}^2 = \sigma_1{}^2 \cos^2 \theta + \sigma_2{}^2 \sin^2 \theta + 2r_{12}\sigma_1\sigma_2 \sin \theta \cos \theta$$

and inserting $\sigma_1 = 2·72$, $\sigma_2 = 2·75$, $r_{12} = 0·51$, $\sin \theta = \cos \theta = 1/\sqrt{2}$, find $\sigma_\xi = 3·361$.) Drawing a diagram and fitting a normal curve, we have fig. 10.2 ; the distribution is rather irregular but the fit is fair ; certainly there is no marked asymmetry, and, so far as the graphical test goes, the distribution may be regarded as appreciably normal. One of the greatest divergences of the actual distribution from the normal curve occurs in the almost central interval with frequency 78 ; the difference between the observed and calculated frequencies is here 12 units, but nevertheless it

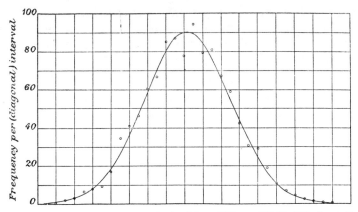

Fig. 10.2.—Distribution of frequency obtained by addition of Table 9.3 along diagonals running up from left to right, fitted with a normal curve

may well have occurred as a fluctuation of sampling. In fact, anticipating our discussion of the use of the standard error (standard deviation of simple sampling) in testing the significance of sampling fluctuations (**17.4**), we may note that the standard error in this case is $\sqrt{npq}$, where n is the number of observations and p and q the chances of an individual falling or not falling within the given interval. p may be taken as $90/1078$, and therefore the standard error is

$$\sqrt{1078 \cdot \frac{90}{1078} \cdot \frac{988}{1078}} = 9 \cdot 1$$

The observed deviation, 12, is not much greater than this and may therefore have occurred as a sampling fluctuation. We have used here the exact expression for the standard error, but since p is small we might have used the approximation $\sqrt{pn} = \sqrt{90} = 9 \cdot 5$. This last is useful as giving a test which can be applied on sight.

10.15 So far, we have seen (1) that the regression is approximately linear; (2) that, in the arrays which we have tested, the standard deviations are approximately constant, or at least that their differences are only small, irregular and fluctuating; (3) that the distribution of totals for one set of diagonal arrays is approximately normal. These results suggest, though they cannot completely prove, that the whole distribution of frequency may be regarded as approximately normal, within the limits of fluctuations of sampling. We may therefore apply a more searching test, viz. the form of the contour lines and the closeness of their fit to the contour ellipses of the normal surface. It may, however, be seen that no very close fit can be expected. Since the frequencies in the compartments of the table are small, the standard error of any frequency is given approximately by its square root (**17.15**), and this implies a standard error of about 5 units at the centre of the table, 3 units for a frequency of 9, or 2 units for a frequency of 4 ; fluctuations of these magnitudes are quite possible and might cause wide divergences in the corresponding contour lines.

10.16 Using the suffix 1 to denote the constants relating to the distribution of stature for fathers, and 2 the same constants for the sons,

$$N = 1078 \qquad M_1 = 67 \cdot 70 \qquad M_2 = 68 \cdot 66$$
$$\sigma_1 = 2 \cdot 72 \qquad \sigma_2 = 2 \cdot 75 \qquad r_{12} = 0 \cdot 51$$

Hence we have from equation (10.7),

$$y'_{12} = 26 \cdot 7$$

and the complete expression for the fitted normal surface is

$$y = 26 \cdot 7 \, \exp\left\{ -\tfrac{1}{2}\left(\frac{x_1^2}{5 \cdot 47} + \frac{x_2^2}{5 \cdot 60} - \frac{x_1 x_2}{5 \cdot 43} \right) \right\}$$

The equation to any contour ellipse will be given by equating the index of e to a constant, but it is very much easier to draw the ellipses if we refer them to their principal axes. To do this we must first determine θ, S_1 and S_2. From (10.10),

$$\tan 2\theta = -46 \cdot 49$$

whence $2\theta = 91° \, 14'$, $\theta = 45° \, 37'$, the principal axes standing very nearly at an angle of 45° with the axes of measurement, owing to the two standard deviations being very nearly equal. They should be set off on the diagram, not with a protractor, but by taking $\tan \theta$ from the tables (1.022) and calculating points on each axis on either side of the mean.

To obtain S_1 and S_2 we have, from (10.11) and (10.12),

$$S_1{}^2 + S_2{}^2 = 14 \cdot 961$$
$$2S_1 S_2 = 1 \cdot 868$$

Adding and subtracting these equations from each other and taking the square root,

$$S_1 + S_2 = 5 \cdot 275$$
$$S_1 - S_2 = 1 \cdot 447$$

whence $S_1 = 3 \cdot 36$, $S_2 = 1 \cdot 91$; owing to the principal axes standing nearly at 45° the first value is sensibly the same as that found for σ_ξ in **10.14.** The equations to the contour ellipses, referred to the principal axes, may therefore be written in the form—

$$\frac{\xi_1^2}{(3 \cdot 36)^2} + \frac{\xi_2^2}{(1 \cdot 91)^2} = c^2$$

the major and minor semi-axes being $3 \cdot 36 \times c$ and $1 \cdot 91 \times c$ respectively. To find c for any assigned value of the frequency y we have—

$$y_{12} = y'_{12} e^{-\frac{1}{2}c^2}$$

$$c^2 = \frac{2(\log y'_{12} - \log y_{12})}{\log e}$$

Supposing that we desire to draw the three contour ellipses for $y=5$, 10 and 20, we find $c=1 \cdot 83$, $1 \cdot 40$ and $0 \cdot 76$, or the following values for the major and minor axes of the ellipses : semi-major axes, $6 \cdot 15$, $4 \cdot 70$, $2 \cdot 55$; semi-minor axes, $3 \cdot 50$, $2 \cdot 67$, $1 \cdot 45$. The ellipses drawn with these axes are shown in fig. 10.3, very much reduced, of course, from the original

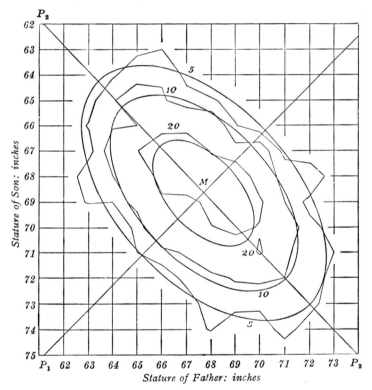

Fig. 10.3.—Contour lines for the frequencies 5, 10 and 20 of the distribution of Table 11.3, and corresponding contour ellipses of the fitted normal surface
P_1P_1, P_2P_2, principal axes ; M, mean.

drawing, one of the squares shown representing a square inch on the original. The actual contour lines for the same frequencies are shown by the irregular polygons superposed on the ellipses, the points on these polygons having been obtained by simple graphical interpolation between the frequencies in each row and each column—diagonal interpolation between the frequencies in a row and the frequencies in a column not being used. It will be seen that the fit of the two lower contours, is on the whole, fair, especially considering the high standard errors. In the case of the central contour, $y=20$, the fit looks very poor to the eye, but if the ellipse be compared carefully with the table, the figures suggest that here again we have only to deal with the effects of fluctuations of sampling. For father's stature$=66$ in., son's stature$=70$ in., there is a frequency of $18\cdot75$, and an increase in this much less than the standard error would bring the actual contour outside the ellipse. Again, for father's stature$=68$ in. son's statute$=71$ in., there is a frequency of 19, and an increase of a single unit would give a point on the actual contour below the ellipse. Taking the results as a whole, the fit must be considered quite as good as we could expect with such small frequencies.

Isotropic character of the normal surface

10.17 The normal distribution of frequency for two variables is an isotropic distribution, to which all the theorems of **3.16** apply. For if we isolate the four compartments of the correlation table common to the rows and columns centring round values of the variables x_1, x_2, x_1', x_2', we have for the ratio of the cross-products (frequency of $x_1 x_2$ multiplied by frequency of $x_1' x_2'$, divided by frequency of $x_1 x_2'$ multiplied by frequency of $x_1' x_2$),

$$\exp \frac{r_{12}}{\sigma_{1.2}\sigma_{2.1}}(x_1'-x_1)(x_2'-x_2)$$

Assuming that $x_1'-x_1$ has been taken of the same sign as $x_2'-x_2$, the exponent is of the same sign as r_{12}. Hence, the association for this group of four frequencies is also of the same sign as r_{12}, the ratio of the cross-products being unity, or the association zero, if r_{12} is zero. In a normal distribution, the association is therefore of the same sign—the sign of r_{12}—for every tetrad of frequencies in the compartments common to two rows and two columns ; that is to say, the distribution is isotropic. It follows that every grouping of a normal distribution is isotropic whether the class-intervals are equal or unequal, large or small and the sign of the association for a normal distribution grouped down to 2×2-fold form must always be the same whatever the axes of division chosen.

10.18 These theorems are of importance in the applications of the theory of normal correlation to the treatment of qualitative characters which are subjected to a manifold classification. The contingency tables for such characters are sometimes regarded as groupings of a normal distribution of frequency, and the coefficient of correlation is determined on this hypothesis by a special procedure (see below, **11.29**, page 268).

Before applying this procedure it is well, therefore, to see whether the distribution of frequency may be regarded as approximately isotropic, or reducible to isotropic form by some alteration in the order of rows and columns (**3.16** and **3.17**). If only reducible to isotropic form by some rearrangement, this rearrangement should be effected before grouping the table to 2×2-fold form for the calculation of the correlation coefficient by the process referred to. If the table is not reducible to isotropic form by any rearrangement, the process of calculating the coefficient of correlation on the assumption of normality is to be avoided. Clearly, even if the table be isotropic it need not be normal, but at least the test for isotropy affords a rapid and simple means for excluding certain distributions which are not even remotely normal. Table 3.2, page 50, might possibly be regarded as a grouping of normally distributed frequency if rearranged as suggested in **3.15**—it would be worth the investigator's while to proceed further and compare the actual distribution with a fitted normal distribution—but Table 3.4 could not be regarded as normal, and could not be rearranged so as to give a grouping of normally distributed frequency.

10.19 If the frequencies in a contingency table be not large, and also if the contingency or correlation be small, the influence of casual irregularities due to fluctuations of sampling may render it difficult to say whether the distribution may be regarded as essentially isotropic or not. In such cases some further condensation of the table by grouping together adjacent rows and columns, of some process of " smoothing " by averaging the frequencies in adjacent compartments, may be of service. The correlation table for stature in father and son (Table 9·3), for instance, is obviously not strictly isotropic as it stands : we have seen, however, that it appears to be normal, within the limits of fluctuations of sampling, and it should consequently be isotropic within such limits. We can apply a rough test by regrouping the table in a much coarser form, say with four rows and four columns : the table below exhibits such a grouping,

TABLE 10.1—(Condensed from Table 9.3, p. 202)

Son's stature (inches)	Father's stature (inches)				Total
	Under 65·5	65·5-67·5	67·5-69·5	69·5 and over	
Under 66·5	97·5	74·25	34·75	10·5	217
66·5-68·5	76·5	108	85	52	321·5
68·5-70·5	33·25	64·75	95	84·5	277·5
70·5 and over	14·75	32·5	80·75	134	262
Total	222	279·5	295·5	281	1,078

the limits of rows and of columns having been so fixed as to include not less than 200 observations in each array.

Taking the ratio of the frequency in column 1 to the sum of the frequencies in columns 1 and 2 for each successive row, and so on for the other pairs of columns, we find the following series of ratios—

TABLE 10.2—Ratio of frequency in column m to frequency in column m plus frequency in column (m+1) of Table 10.1

| Row | Columns | | |
	1 and 2	2 and 3	3 and 4
1	0·568	0·681	0·768
2	0·415	0·560	0·620
3	0·339	0·405	0·529
4	0·312	0·287	0·376

These ratios decrease continuously as we pass from the top to the bottom of the table, and the distribution, as condensed, is therefore isotropic. The student should form one or two other condensations of the original table to 3- ×3- or 4- ×4-fold form : he will probably find them either isotropic or diverging so slightly from isotropy that an alteration of the frequencies, well within the margin of possible fluctuations of sampling, will render the distribution isotropic.

Relationship between contingency and normal correlation

10.20   It was shown by Karl Pearson that if a normal bivariate population is divided into sections so as to form a contingency table, the coefficient of mean square contingency, C, tends to the value r in magnitude as the intervals become finer and finer, though of course it is always positive in sign.   It was, in fact, the relation

$$r = \pm \sqrt{\frac{\phi^2}{1 + \phi^2}}$$

where ϕ^2 is the mean-square contingency, which led Pearson to identify C with the expression on the right.

The values of C and r for the distributions of some of the tables of Chapter 9 were compared in Exercise 9.3, page 235.

SUMMARY

1. The equation of the normal surface is

$$y_{12} = \frac{N}{2\pi\sigma_1\sigma_2\sqrt{1-r_{12}^2}} \exp\left\{-\frac{1}{2(1-r_{12}^2)}\left(\frac{x_1^2}{\sigma_1^2} - \frac{2r_{12}x_1x_2}{\sigma_1\sigma_2} + \frac{x_2^2}{\sigma_2^2}\right)\right\}$$

where σ_1 is the s.d. of x_1, σ_2 that of x_2, and r_{12} the correlation between x_1 and x_2.

This may also be written

$$y_{12} = \frac{N\sqrt{1-r^2}}{2\pi\sigma_{1.2}\sigma_{2.1}} \exp\left\{-\frac{1}{2}\left(\frac{x_1^2}{\sigma_{1.2}^2} - \frac{2r_{12}x_1x_2}{\sigma_{1.2}\sigma_{2.1}} + \frac{x_2^2}{\sigma_{2.1}^2}\right)\right\}$$

where

$$\sigma_{1.2}^2 = \sigma_1^2(1-r_{12}^3), \qquad \sigma_{2.1}^2 = \sigma_2^2(1-r_{12}^2)$$

2. For two variates normally correlated the standard deviations of parallel arrays are equal and the regressions are linear.

3. Any section of the normal surface by a vertical plane is a normal curve, and a section by a horizontal plane is an ellipse. The ellipses given by horizontal sections are similar and similarly situated.

4. The bivariate normal distribution is isotropic.

5. A linear function of variates, each of which is normally distributed, is also normally distributed.

EXERCISES

10.1   Deduce equation (10.12) from the equations for transformation of co-ordinates without assuming the normal distribution.

10.2   Hence show that if the pairs of observed values of x_1 and x_2 are represented by points on a plane, and a straight line drawn through the mean, the sum of the squares of the distances of the points from this line is a minimum if the line is the major principal axis.

10.3   The coefficient of correlation with reference to the principal axes being zero, and with reference to other axes *something*, there must be some pair of axes at right angles for which the correlation is a maximum, i.e. is numerically greatest without regard to sign. Show that these axes make an angle of 45° with the principal axes, and that the maximum value of the correlation is

$$\pm\frac{S_1{}^2 - S_2{}^2}{S_1{}^2 + S_2{}^2}$$

10.4 (Sheppard, *Phil. Trans. Roy. Soc.* A, 1898, **192**, 101.)   A fourfold table is formed from a normal correlation table, taking the points of division between A and α, B and β, at the medians, so that $(A)=(\alpha)=(B)=(\beta)=N/2$.   Show that

$$r=\cos\left(1-\frac{2(AB)}{N}\right)\pi$$

10.5   Show that the points of inflection of the sections of the normal surface by vertical planes through the mean of the distribution lie on an ellipse ; and show how this ellipse may be used to give the standard deviations of such sections.

10.6   Hence find the minimum and maximum standard deviations which can be taken by such sections, and show that any specified value of the s.d. between the minimum and maximum will be given by two, and only two, sections.

10.7   Assuming that the heights of fathers and sons are distributed in the bivariate normal form with a correlation which is positive but not unity and with the same means and variances, show that fathers of more than average height tend to have sons whose height, though above average, is less than that of their respective fathers.   Show also that sons of more than average height tend to have fathers whose height is less than that of their respective sons.   Explain why these two results are not inconsistent.

10.8   Find the conditions that the surface

$$z=k \exp \ (ax^2+2hxy+by^2)$$

can represent a normal correlation surface whose variates are x and y. Assuming these conditions satisfied, express σ_1, σ_2 and r_{12} in terms of a, h and b.

10.9   Corresponding to x-values, $-n$, $-(n-1)$ . . . $-1, 0, 1, \ldots (n-1)$, n, the y-values are the cubes of the x-values.   Show that the covariance **(9.25)** of x and y is given by

$$\mu_{11}=\frac{2n^5}{5} + \text{lower powers of } n.$$

Hence show that for large n the correlation is approximately $\sqrt{0\cdot84}=0\cdot916$ and thus is not unity although the variates are functionally related.

10.10   In a bivariate normal population the standard deviation of any x-array is k times that of the x-variate as a whole.   Show that the correlation is $\sqrt{(1-k^2)}$.

CHAPTER ELEVEN

FURTHER THEORY OF CORRELATION

Methods of estimating the product-moment correlation coefficient

11.1 The only strict method of calculating the correlation coefficient is that described in Chapter 10, from the formula

$$r = \frac{\Sigma(xy)}{\sqrt{\Sigma(x^2)\Sigma(y^2)}}$$

Where possible this formula should be employed. It sometimes happens, however, owing to incomplete data, that we are constrained to use some method of approximation. Furthermore, the large amount of arithmetical labour involved in applying the ordinary formula may sometimes be avoided by approximations which are sufficiently accurate for the purpose in view. We therefore proceed to give a few methods of this kind. They are not recommended for general use as they will, as a rule, lead to different results in different hands.

11.2 (1) The means of rows and columns are plotted on a diagram, and lines fitted to the points by eye, say by shifting about a stretched black thread until it seems to run as near as may be to all the points. If b_1, b_2 be the slopes of these two lines to the vertical and the horizontal respectively,

$$r = \sqrt{b_1 b_2}$$

Hence the value of r may be estimated from any such diagram as fig. 9.8 or 9.9, in the absence of the original table. Further, if a correlation table be not grouped by equal intervals, it may be difficult to calculate the product sum, but it may still be possible to plot approximately a diagram of the two lines of regression, and so determine roughly the value of r. Similarly, if only the means of two rows and two columns, or of one row and one column in addition to the means of the two variables, are known, it will still be possible to estimate the slopes of RR and CC, and hence the correlation coefficient.

(2) The means of one set of arrays only, say the rows, are calculated, and also the two standard deviations σ_x and σ_y. The means are then plotted on a diagram, using the standard deviation of each variable as the unit of measurement, and a line fitted by eye. The slope of this line to the vertical is r. If the standard deviations be not used as the units of measure-

ment in plotting, the slope of the line to the vertical is $r\sigma_x/\sigma_y$, and hence r will be obtained by dividing the slope by the ratio of the standard deviations.

This method, or some variation of it, is often useful as a makeshift when the data are too incomplete to permit of the proper calculation of the correlation, only one line of regression and the ratio of the dispersions of the two variables being required : the ratio of the quartile deviations, or other simple measures of dispersion, will serve quite well for rough purposes in lieu of the ratio of standard deviations. As a special case, we may note that if the two dispersions are approximately the same, the slope of RR to the vertical is r.

Plotting the medians of arrays on a diagram with the quartile deviations as units, and measuring the slope of the line, was the method of determining the correlation coefficient used by Galton, to whom the introduction of such a coefficient is due.

(3) If s_1 be the standard deviation of errors of estimate like $x - b_1 y$, we have, from **9.24**,

$$s_x{}^2 = \sigma_x{}^2(1 - r^2)$$

and hence,

$$r = \sqrt{1 - \frac{s_x{}^2}{\sigma_x{}^2}}$$

But if the dispersions of arrays do not differ largely, and the regression is nearly linear, the value of s_x may be estimated from the average of the standard deviations of a few rows, and r determined—or rather estimated —accordingly. Thus in Table 9.3 the standard deviations of the ten columns headed 62·5–63·5, 63·5–64·5, etc., are—

2·56	2·26
2·11	2·26
2·55	2·45
2·24	2·33
2·23	—
2·60	Mean 2·359

The standard deviation of the stature of all sons is 2·75 : hence approximately

$$r = \sqrt{1 - \left(\frac{2 \cdot 359}{2 \cdot 75}\right)^2}$$
$$= 0 \cdot 514$$

This is the same as the value found by the product-sum method to the second decimal place. It would be better to take an average by counting the square of each standard deviation once for each observation in the column (or " weighting " it with the number of observations in the column), but in the present case this would only lead to a very slightly different result, viz. $s=2\cdot362$, $r=0\cdot512$.

Non-linear regression

11.3 We referred in Chapter 9 to the fact that the treatment of cases when the regression is non-linear is somewhat difficult. We may, by the methods of Chapter 15, and otherwise, fit curves of any order to the means of arrays, just as we have fitted straight lines to them ; but the handling of these regression curves and their interpretation is far more complicated.

11.4 It is therefore desirable, wherever possible, to deal with variates which result in linear regression. Now it sometimes happens that if a relation between X and Y be suggested, we may, either by theory or by previous experience, throw that relation into the form

$$Y=A+B\phi(X)$$

where A and B are the only unknown constants to be determined. If a correlation table be then drawn up between Y and $\phi(X)$ instead of Y and X, the regression will be approximately linear. Thus in Table 9.5, page 205, if X be the rate of discount and Y the percentage of reserves on deposits, a diagram of the curves of regression suggests that the relation between X and Y is approximately of the form

$$X(Y-B)=A$$

A and B being constants ; that is,

$$XY=A+BX$$

Or, if we make XY a new variable, say Z,

$$Z=A+BX$$

Hence, if we draw up a new correlation table between X and Z the regression will probably be much more closely linear.

If the relation between the variables be of the form

$$Y=AB^X$$

we have

$$\log Y=\log A+X\log B$$

and hence the relation between $\log Y$ and X is linear. Similarly, if the relation be of the form

$$X^nY=A$$

we have

$$\log Y=\log A-n\log X$$

and so the relation between $\log Y$ and $\log X$ is linear. By means of such artifices for obtaining correlation tables in which the regression is linear, it may be possible to do a good deal in difficult cases whilst using elementary methods only.

The correlation ratios

11.5 In view of the importance of linearity of regression it is desirable to have some criterion which will enable a judgment to be formed whether a regression is, within the limits permitted by sampling fluctuations, linear in any given case. We now proceed to discuss a coefficient designed for this purpose.

Consider a bivariate frequency table, and let s_{px} be the standard deviation of the pth array of X's. Let n_p be the number of observations in this array.

Let

$$\sigma^2{}_{ax} = \frac{1}{N}\Sigma(n_p s^2{}_{px}) \qquad . \qquad . \qquad . \qquad . \quad (11.1)$$

Then $\sigma^2{}_{ax}$ is the weighted mean of the variances of arrays, obtained as suggested in the last sentence of **11.2** (3). Now, let

$$\sigma^2{}_{ax} = \sigma^2{}_x(1 - \eta^2{}_{xy}) \qquad . \qquad . \qquad . \qquad . \quad (11.2)$$

or

$$\eta^2{}_{xy} = 1 - \frac{\sigma^2{}_{ax}}{\sigma^2{}_x} \qquad . \qquad . \qquad . \qquad . \quad (11.3)$$

Then η_{xy} is called the *correlation ratio* of X on Y. Similarly, η_{yx}, defined by

$$\eta^2{}_{yx} = 1 - \frac{\sigma^2{}_{ay}}{\sigma^2{}_y}$$

is called the *correlation ratio* of Y on X.

11.6 The correlation ratios may be put in another form, which is much more convenient for purposes of calculation.

In fact, if M_x is the mean of all the X's and m_{px} the mean of an array, we have, as in equation (6.6),

$$N\sigma^2{}_x = \Sigma(n_p\{s^2{}_{px} + (M_x - m_{px})^2\})$$

or, using σ_{mx} to denote the standard deviation of m_{px}, obtained by " weighting " each m_{px} according to n_p, the number of observations in the array in which it occurs,

$$\sigma^2{}_x = \sigma^2{}_{ax} + \sigma^2{}_{mx} \qquad . \qquad . \qquad . \quad (11.4)$$

Hence, substituting in (11.3),

$$\eta_{xy} = \frac{\sigma_{mx}}{\sigma_x} \qquad . \qquad . \qquad . \qquad . \quad (11.5)$$

The correlation ratio of X on Y is therefore determined when we have found the standard deviation of X and the standard deviation of the means of its arrays.

11.7 In **9.22** we saw that

$$\sigma_x^2(1-r^2)=\frac{1}{N}\Sigma(x-b_1y)^2 \quad . \qquad . \qquad . \qquad (11.6)$$

where $x-b_1y=0$ is the line of regression of x on y, x and y being the values of X and Y measured from the mean of the distribution.

Now, for any array for which y is constant,

$$\frac{1}{N}\Sigma(x-b_1y)^2=\frac{1}{N}\Sigma\{(x-m_{px})+(m_{px}-b_1y)\}^2$$

$$=\frac{n_p}{N}s_{px}^2+\frac{n_p}{N}(m_{px}-b_1y)^2$$

the product term vanishing since $\Sigma(x-m_{px})=0$. Hence, summing for all arrays of y,

$$\sigma_x^2(1-r^2)=\sigma_{ax}^2+\Sigma\frac{n_p}{N}\left\{(m_{px}-b_1y)^2\right\}$$

But

$$\sigma_x^2(1-\eta_{xy}^2)=\sigma_{ax}^2$$

Hence,

$$\sigma_x^2(\eta_{xy}^2-r^2)=\Sigma\left\{\frac{n_p}{N}(m_{px}-b_1y)^2\right\} \qquad . \qquad . \qquad . \qquad (11.7)$$

From this we see that η_{xy} cannot be less than r in absolute value.

If $\eta_{xy}^2=r^2$, then

$$\Sigma\{n_p(m_{px}-b_1y)^2\}=0$$

i.e.

$$m_{px}-b_1y=0$$

for all arrays. This means that the mean m_{px} must be on the line of regression for all arrays, i.e. that the regression is linear.

11.8 The divergence of η^2 from r^2 therefore measures the departure of the regression from linearity. It should, however, be noted that sampling fluctuations may cause $\eta^2 - r^2$ to deviate from zero even when the regression is truly linear. We give later a method of testing the significance of observed fluctuations of this kind.

Calculation of the correlation ratio

11.9 The table on page 259 illustrates the form of the arithmetic for the calculation of the correlation ratio of son's stature on father's stature (Table 9.3). In the first column is given the type of the array (stature of father) ; in the second, the mean stature of sons for that array ; in the third, the difference of the mean of the array from the mean stature of all sons. In the fourth column these differences are squared, and in the sixth they are multiplied by the frequency of the array, two decimal places only having been retained as sufficient for the present purpose. The sum-total of the last column divided by the number of observations (1078) gives $\sigma^2_{my} = 2 \cdot 058$, or $\sigma_{my} = 1 \cdot 43$. As the standard deviation of the sons' stature is $2 \cdot 75$ in., $\eta_{yx} = 0 \cdot 52$. Before taking the differences for the third column of such a table, it is as well to check the means of the arrays by recalculating from them the mean of the whole distribution, i.e. multiplying each array-mean by its frequency, summing and dividing by the number of observations. The form of the arithmetic may be varied, if desired, by working from zero as origin, instead of taking differences from the true mean. The square of the mean must then be subtracted from $\Sigma(fm^2_y)/N$ to give σ^2_{my}.

11.10 If the second correlation ratio for this table be worked out in the same way, the value will be found to be the same to the second place of decimals : the two correlation ratios for this table are, therefore, very nearly identical, and only slightly greater than the correlation coefficient ($0 \cdot 51$). Both regressions, as follows from the last section, are very nearly linear, a result confirmed by the diagram of the regression lines (fig. 9.8, page 218). On the other hand, it is evident from fig. 9.10, page 220, that we should expect the two correlation ratios for Table 9.6 to differ considerably from each other and from the correlation coefficient.

The student should notice that the correlation ratio only affords a satisfactory test when the number of observations is sufficiently large for a grouped correlation table to be formed. In the case of a short series of observations such as that given in Table 9.7, page 207, the method is inapplicable.

Rank correlation coefficients

11.11 In calculating the coefficient of correlation from the product-moment it is necessary that the data should be definitely measured. If they are not so measured we cannot, in general, determine the coefficient,

Example 11.1.—Calculation of the correlation ratio

Sons's stature on father's stature

(Data of Table 9.3, page 202)

1 Type of array (Father's stature)	2 Mean of array (Son's stature)	3 Difference from mean of all sons (68·66)	4 Square of difference	5 Frequency	6 Frequency × (difference)^2
59	64·67	−3·99	15·9201	3	47·76
60	65·64	−3·02	9·1204	3·5	31·92
61	66·34	−2·32	5·3824	8	43·06
62	65·56	−3·10	9·6100	17	163·37
63	66·68	−1·98	3·9204	33·5	131·33
64	66·74	−1·92	3·6864	61·5	226·71
65	67·19	−1·47	2·1609	95·5	206·37
66	67·61	−1·05	1·1025	142	156·56
67	67·95	−0·71	0·5041	137·5	69·31
68	69·07	+0·41	0·1681	154	25·89
69	69·39	+0·73	0·5329	141·5	75·41
70	69·74	+1·08	1·1664	116	135·30
71	70·50	+1·84	3·3856	78	264·08
72	70·87	+2·21	4·8841	49	239·32
73	72·00	+3·34	11·1556	28·5	317·93
74	71·50	+2·84	8·0656	4	32·26
75	71·73	+3·07	9·4249	5·5	51·84
Total	....	....	....	1,078	2,218·42

$$\sigma^2_{my} = 2218\cdot42 / 1078 = 2\cdot058 \qquad \sigma_{my} = 1\cdot43$$
$$\eta_{yx} = 1\cdot43 / 2\cdot75 = 0\cdot52$$

though we may sometimes approximate to it by one of the methods of 11.2.

But there may be more serious obstacles than imperfect grouping in the way of finding the correlation between two variates. In the examples we have considered up to the present the qualities we have discussed have been easily measurable, involving such familiar concepts as height, weight, age and so forth. In certain types of inquiry we may have to deal with qualities which are not expressible as numbers of units of an objective kind.

11.12 Consider, for instance, the relation between mathematical and musical ability in a class of students. "Ability," whether of a general or a specific kind, is a variate in the sense that it varies from one individual to another ; and it may be a numerical variate if we can decide on some unequivocal way of measuring it. A very common mode of attempting to do so is by allotting marks to each student. But such methods are open to many objections, not the least of which is that different examiners would give different marks to the same person. A correlation between the marks obtained for mathematics and music would, therefore, be likely to depend to some extent on the examiner, and would not reflect accurately the relationship between the two qualities.

11.13 Difficulties of this type disappear to some extent if we arrange the students *in order* of their ability, but do not attempt to assess it numerically. There will still be some divergence of opinion between different examiners, perhaps, but it will not as a rule be so serious. We then allot to each student a number which indicates his position in the arrangement according to ability, the first being number 1, the second number 2, and so on. The students are then said to be *ranked*, and the number of a particular individual is his *rank* (cf. **6.33**).

11.14 A procedure of this kind is useful in the treatment not only of data which can be ordered but not exactly measured, but of measurable data also. For instance, we can easily rank a number of men according to height without actually measuring them. It is also comparatively easy to rank a number of shades of a colour, or a number of countries according to their importance in the export market, where precise numerical measurement would be very troublesome.

In the extreme case we may have situations in which individuals can be ordered but not measured. Suppose, for example, we have a pack of cards in which a particular suit, say hearts, is in the correct order ace, two, . . . king. We then shuffle the pack and examine the order of the heart cards with the intention of discussing whether the shuffling process was a good one. The relationship between the orders before and after shuffling is evidently a possible basis of comparison ; but there is not even a *theoretically* measurable variate corresponding to " order " in this case.

11.15 If we have a set of individuals ranked according to two different qualities it is natural to inquire whether the ranks can be made to give us some measure of the degree of relation between the two qualities.

Suppose we have n individuals, whose ranks according to quality A are $X_1, X_2, X_3, \ldots X_n$, and according to quality B are $Y_1, Y_2, Y_3, \ldots Y_n$, where the X's and Y's are merely permutations of the first n natural numbers. Let $d_k = X_k - Y_k$.

The values of d form a convenient measure of the closeness of the correspondence between A and B. If all the d's are zero the correspondence is perfect, for an individual whose rank is X_k for A will also be X_k for B. We cannot, however, take the sum of the d's as a measure of correspondence, because that sum is zero ; for the sum of the differences of the X's and Y's is the difference of the sums of the X's and the Y's, each of which is the sum of the first n natural numbers.

A possible measure which suggests itself is the sum of the absolute values of the d's, i.e. $\Sigma|d|$. This measure and its mean $\frac{1}{n}\Sigma|d|$ have, in fact, been used, but like the mean deviation (**6.18**) they have certain analytical disadvantages.

11.16 A more convenient coefficient is obtained as follows—

The values of X range from 1 to n. Their sum is $\dfrac{n(n+1)}{2}$, and their mean is accordingly $\dfrac{n+1}{2}$. This value is also the mean of the Y's.

Let us denote by x_k the value of $X_k - \dfrac{n+1}{2}$, i.e. the divergence of X_k from the mean. Similarly for y_k, which we define as $Y_k - \dfrac{n+1}{2}$.

Write

$$\rho = \frac{\Sigma(xy)}{\sqrt{\Sigma(x^2)\Sigma(y^2)}} \qquad . \qquad . \qquad . \qquad . \quad (11.8)$$

This is the product-moment coefficient of correlation between X and Y. We shall call ρ Spearman's *rank correlation coefficient*. It may be expressed very simply in terms of n and the d's.

For, as we saw in **6.15**, $\Sigma(x^2) = \Sigma(y^2) = \dfrac{1}{12}(n^3 - n)$

Now,

$$\Sigma(d^2) = \Sigma(X_k - Y_k)^2 = \Sigma(x-y)^2$$
$$= \Sigma(x^2) + \Sigma(y^2) - 2\Sigma(xy)$$

Hence,

$$\Sigma(xy) = \tfrac{1}{2}\left\{ \frac{n^3 - n}{6} - \Sigma(d^2) \right\}$$

and substituting in (11.8)—

$$\rho = 1 - \frac{6\Sigma(d^2)}{n^3 - n} \qquad . \qquad . \qquad . \qquad . \quad (11.9)$$

Example 11.2.—The rankings of ten students in mathematics and music are as follows—

Mathematics : 1, 2, 3, 4, 5, 6, 7, 8, 9, 10

Music : 6, 5, 1, 4, 2, 7, 8, 10, 3, 9

What is the coefficient of rank correlation ?

The differences d are (mathematical rank minus musical rank)

$-5, -3, +2, 0, +3, -1, -1, -2, +6, +1$

These add to zero, as they should.

The squares of d are

25, 9, 4, 0, 9, 1, 1, 4, 36, 1

which add up to 90.

Hence, from (11.9),

$$\rho = 1 - \frac{540}{990} = +0 \cdot 45$$

11.17 The rank correlation coefficient varies from $+1$ to -1. If the rank correlation is perfect, all the d's are zero. If, on the other hand, the ranks are such that the first, second, third in one order correspond to the nth, $(n-1)$th, $(n-2)$th, . . . in the other, $\rho=-1$. The proof is slightly different according to whether n is even or odd. If it is odd, say $=2m+1$, the d's are

$$2m, \quad 2m-2, \ . \ . \ . \quad 2, \quad 0, \quad -2, \ . \ . \ . \quad -(2m-2), \quad -2m$$

and

$$\Sigma(d^2) = 2\{(2m)^2 + (2m-2)^2 + \ . \ . \ . \ +2^2\}$$
$$= \frac{8m(m+1)(2m+1)}{6}$$

Hence,

$$\rho = 1 - \frac{8m(m+1)(2m+1)}{(2m+1)\{(2m+1)^2-1\}} = -1$$

If n is even, say $=2m$,

$$\Sigma(d^2) = 2\{(2m-1)^2 + \ . \ . \ . \ +1^2\}$$
$$= \frac{2m}{3}(4m^2-1)$$

and

$$\rho = -1 \text{ as before.}[1]$$

11.18 A second rank correlation coefficient which has certain advantages over Spearman's may be obtained as follows: Consider again the data of Example 11.2, and consider the order of each possible pair in the two rankings. If any pair is in the same order in both we allot it the score $+1$, if in the opposite order the score -1. For instance, of the pairs 65, 61, 64, 62, 67 the first four are in the reverse order in the second ranking as compared with the first and each scores -1; the fifth, 67, is in the same order and hence scores $+1$; and so on. There are $^{10}C_2 = 45$ possible pairs. The maximum score, if both rankings are the same, is 45. The minimum score, if one is the inverse of the other, is -45. In our present example the total score will be found to be 15. We then define a rank correlation coefficient τ as

$$\tau = \frac{\text{Score}}{\text{Maximum possible score}}$$
$$= \frac{15}{45} = 0 \cdot 33$$

---

[1]The property of varying between $+1$ and -1 does not belong to a similar coefficient proposed by Spearman, and known as his " foot-rule," viz. $R = 1 - \frac{3\Sigma(|d|)}{n^2-1}$.

It may be shown in the above manner that R varies from $-0 \cdot 5$ to $+1$, and for this reason alone R seems an undesirable coefficient.

11.19 Generally, if S is the score in a ranking of n we have

$$\tau = \frac{S}{\frac{1}{2}n(n-1)} . \qquad . \qquad . \qquad . \qquad (11.10)$$

τ may also be regarded, in a sense, as a product-moment correlation. Suppose that for any two ranks i, j, we allot the value $+1$ if $i > j$ and -1 if $i < j$. Call this value a_{ij}, so that

$$a_{ij} = \begin{matrix} 1 & i > j \\ -1 & i < j \end{matrix} \Bigg\}$$

Similarly let b_{ij} represent a corresponding quantity in the second ranking. We then have

$$\tau = \frac{\Sigma(a_{ij} \, b_{ij})}{\sqrt{\Sigma(a^2_{ij}) \, \Sigma(b^2_{ij})}} \qquad . \qquad . \qquad . \qquad (11.11)$$

for $\Sigma(a^2_{ij})$ is merely the number of possible pairs $\frac{1}{2}n(n-1)$ and the numerator is the score S as defined above.

Example 11.3.—A set of 15 recruits are given a preliminary test to admit them to a course of training and, after the completion of training, a proficiency test. Their ranks are—

Candidate . .	A	B	C	D	E	F	G	H	I	J	K	L	M	N	O
Rank (prelim.)	7	4	1	3	14	13	10	12	5	9	8	2	11	15	6
Rank (profic.) .	4	6	3	7	15	11	14	12	1	13	5	2	9	10	8

Does this suggest that the preliminary test was a good predictor of the results in the proficiency test ?

To calculate τ it is convenient to rearrange one ranking so as to be in the natural order $1, \ldots n$. If we do so for the ranking in the preliminary score we have, for the ranking in the proficiency score—

$$3 \quad 2 \quad 7 \quad 6 \quad 1 \quad 8 \quad 4 \quad 5 \quad 13 \quad 14 \quad 9 \quad 12 \quad 11 \quad 15 \quad 10 \ldots (a)$$

The score obtained by considering the first member 3, in conjunction with the others is $12-2=10$, for there must be 12 members greater than 3 and 2 less than it. Similarly the score (apart from that involving the 3 which has already been counted) involving the 2 is found to be 11. That involving the 7 is 4. The total score (the reader should check this result) is then

$$10+11+4+5+10+5+8+7-2-3+4-1+0-1=57$$

Thus, since the maximum possible score is 105 we have

$$\tau = \frac{57}{105} = +0 \cdot 54$$

indicating a moderate, but not a very high, correlation between the rankings in the two tests.

When one ranking is in the natural order a slightly simpler method of calculating τ may be used. In the ranking (a) we count the number of members greater than 3 lying to the right of 3 (giving 12), then the number greater than 2 lying to the right of 2 (again 12) and so on. If R is the total score so obtained

$$\tau = \frac{2R}{\frac{1}{2}n(n-1)} - 1, \qquad . \qquad . \qquad . \qquad . \qquad (11.12)$$

a relation which the reader can easily prove for himself.

11.20 It is useful to remember that for large n the following relation usually holds approximately except for values of ρ or τ near to unity—

$$\rho = \frac{3\tau}{2} \qquad . \qquad . \qquad . \qquad . \qquad . \qquad (11.13)$$

For instance, in the data of Example 11.2 we found $\rho = 0 \cdot 45$ and $\tau = 0 \cdot 33$.

11.21 It is rather more troublesome to calculate τ than to calculate ρ, but τ has advantages for more advanced work.

(a) Where sampling effects are in question the significance of τ may be tested by known methods but little is known about ρ except in one special case (cf. **19.31–19.34**).

(b) τ may be extended to partial rank correlations.

(c) If an extra member is added to the ranking (as, for instance, if one has been accidentally omitted or further information arrives late) it is easier to recalculate τ than ρ. In fact, in making a new determination of ρ, it may be necessary to re-rank many of the members and hence to recalculate the values of d; whereas for τ we need only consider the additional scores attaching to the new member added.

Tied ranks

11.22 In some classes of ranking work, as for instance in arranging students in order of merit, it is impossible to distinguish between a number of adjacent individuals. In such a case it is customary to average the ranks and to assign the same rank to each even though it may be fractional.

For example, in a ranking of 10, we may be able to assign one individual to the rank 1, but be unable to decide which of the next two members shall be second and which third. They are therefore " tied " and each is given the rank $\frac{1}{2}(2+3)=2\frac{1}{2}$. The next member is then ranked 4, and so on. If we had to tie the next three members we should allot to each the rank $\frac{1}{3}(4+5+6)=5$. The general procedure will now be clear.

11.23 When ranks are tied we have a choice in the calculation of ρ and τ. Let us in the first place determine the effect on the sum of squares of the ranks of tying t individuals occupying the ranks $k+1$, $k+2$, . . . $k+t$. The sum of squares of untied ranks is—

$$(k+1)^2+(k+2)^2+ \ . \ . \ . \ (k+t)^2=tk^2+kt(t+1)+\tfrac{1}{6}t(t+1)(2t+1)$$

The sum of squares of the tied ranks is—

$$t\{k+\tfrac{1}{2}(t+1)\}^2=tk^2+kt(t+1)+\tfrac{1}{4}t(t+1)^2$$

The difference is then—

$$\tfrac{1}{6}t(t+1)(2t+1)-\tfrac{1}{4}t(t+1)^2=\tfrac{1}{12}(t^3-t)$$

Consequently, if we tie t ranks the sum of squares is lowered by $\tfrac{1}{12}(t^3-t)$. The mean value of the ranks is the same, $\frac{1}{2}(n+1)$ and hence the variance of the tied ranking is lowered by $\tfrac{1}{12n}(t^3-t)$. Moreover, the effect of tying different sets is evidently additive, so that if we have a ranking with ties of t_1, t_2, . . . t_l and

$$T_X= \sum_{j=1}^{l} \tfrac{1}{12}(t_j^3-t_j)$$

the variance of the ranking is—

$$\frac{1}{n}\Sigma(x^2)=\tfrac{1}{12}(n^2-1)-\frac{1}{n}T_X \qquad . \qquad . \qquad . \quad (11.14)$$

Similarly it will be found that

$$\frac{1}{n}\Sigma(xy)=\tfrac{1}{12}(n^2-1)-\frac{1}{2n}\Sigma(d^2)-\frac{1}{2n}T_X-\frac{1}{2n}T_Y. \qquad . \quad (11.15)$$

where T_Y is the quantity corresponding to T_X for the second ranking.

Hence, if we continue to regard ρ as the product-moment correlation of the rankings we have—

$$\rho=\frac{\frac{1}{6}(n^3-n)-(T_X+T_Y)-\Sigma(d^2)}{\{\frac{1}{6}(n^3-n)-2T_X\}^{\frac{1}{2}}\{\frac{1}{6}(n^3-n)-2T_Y\}^{\frac{1}{2}}} \qquad . \qquad . \quad (11.16)$$

as compared with the simple formula (11.9) to which it reduces if $T_X=T_Y=0$.

11.24 The reader will sometimes find other formulae in use. For instance, (11.9) is sometimes used as it stands for tied ranks. This is certainly wrong. An alternative is to convert $\Sigma(xy)$ for ties as in (11.15) but not to correct the variances, which leads to the formula

$$\rho = 1 - \frac{6\{\Sigma(d^2) + T_X + T_Y\}}{n^3 - n} \qquad . \qquad . \qquad . \quad (11.17)$$

to which (11.16) reduces if we put $T_X = T_Y = 0$ in the denominator only.

11.25 From some points of view (11.17) may be justifiable. Suppose we have two judges who rank a number of candidates identically, though there are ties present. In such a case (11.16) is the form to use, for we are measuring the agreement between them and the correlation should be unity. Both judges may be wrong, but that is not the point. We are measuring their agreement, not their accuracy.

But if we have one observer ranking a number of objects *which really have an objective order* (11.17) may be preferable. The observer may tie certain ranks because of an inability to distinguish between the individuals concerned. In using (11.17) we take this into account in ascertaining the covariance of (11.15) : but in deciding to make allowance in the variance we are refusing, so to speak, to give him credit for clustering his values because he ought not to do so, there being a really objective order. The effect of using (11.17) instead of (11.16), of course, is to give a lower value to ρ, which appears to conform to the common-sense requirements of the position wherein we are measuring the observer's ability to rank individuals in their real order.

11.26 In the calculation of τ we allot to any tied pair the score 0, this being the intermediate point between the scores of $+1$ or -1 which would result if one were greater than the other. The effect of this is to lower the maximum possible score for X by

$$U_X = \tfrac{1}{2}\Sigma\{t(t-1)\} \qquad . \qquad . \qquad . \quad (11.18)$$

the summation taking place over the ties as for T_X. Corresponding to (11.16) we shall then have

$$\tau = \frac{S}{\{\tfrac{1}{2}n(n-1) - U_X\}^{\frac{1}{2}}\{\tfrac{1}{2}n(n-1) - U_Y\}^{\frac{1}{2}}} \qquad . \qquad . \quad (11.19)$$

and corresponding to (11.17)

$$\tau = \frac{S}{\tfrac{1}{2}n(n-1)} \qquad . \qquad . \qquad . \quad (11.20)$$

In both these formulae the score S is, of course, affected by ties.

Example 11.4.—Two foremen rank ten employees according to suitability for promotion as follows—

Employee	A	B	C	D	E	F	G	H	I	J
Foreman 1	$1\frac{1}{2}$	$1\frac{1}{2}$	3	4	6	6	6	8	$9\frac{1}{2}$	$9\frac{1}{2}$
Foreman 2	1	2	4	4	4	6	7	8	9	10

In the first ranking there are three sets of ties and we have—

$$T_X = \tfrac{1}{12}\{(2^3-2)+(3^3-3)+(2^3-2)\}$$
$$=3$$

Similarly

$$T_Y = \tfrac{1}{12}(3^3-3)$$
$$= 2$$

The differences d are

$$\tfrac{1}{2}, -\tfrac{1}{2}, \ -1, \ 0, \ 2, \ 0, \ -1, \ 0, \ \tfrac{1}{2}, \ -\tfrac{1}{2}$$

and hence

$$\Sigma(d^2)=7$$

Hence from (11.16)

$$\rho = \frac{165-3-2-7}{\sqrt{(159\times161)}}$$
$$=0.956$$

The scores S contributing to τ, taking the first employee A with the others, then B with C . . . J and so on, will be found to be

$$8+8+5+5+3+3+3+2+0=37$$

We also have

$$U_X = \tfrac{1}{2}\{2+3.2+2\}$$
$$=5$$
$$U_Y=3$$

Hence, from (11.19)

$$\tau = \frac{37}{\sqrt{(40\times42)}}$$
$$=0.903$$

Either coefficient indicates a high degree of agreement between the judges.

Relationship between rank correlation and product-moment correlation

11.27 The rank correlation coefficients as we have introduced them are merely measures like the coefficients of association, contingency and product-moment correlation, of the correspondence between two quantities. Like those coefficients, they are affected by sampling fluctuations.

They are, however, more easily calculated than most coefficients, and for this reason some writers have advocated their use as a substitute for the product-moment coefficient between the actual measurements, and for estimating the product-moment coefficient from a normal population. We proceed to examine this practice briefly.

Grade correlation

11.28 We referred at the end of Chapter 6 to such quantities as quartiles, deciles and percentiles, which are values of the variate dividing the total frequency into certain specified proportions. For instance, the seventh decile is the variate value such that seven-tenths of the distribution lie below it, i.e. exhibit values of the variate less than the decile.

Generally, we may regard the *grade* of an individual as the proportion of individuals which lie below him (cf. **6.31**). If the population is continuous, the range of grades will also be continuous.

11.29 To each individual in a bivariate population there will be attached two grade numbers, one for each variate, and if the population is correlated the grades will also be correlated. In fact, it has been shown that if the population is normal, ρ_g, the grade correlation, and r, the ordinary correlation (both calculated by the product-moment method), are related by the equation

$$r = 2 \sin\left(\frac{\pi \rho_g}{6}\right) \qquad . \qquad . \qquad . \qquad . \quad (11.21)$$

11.30 Ranks and grades are connected by a simple relation. In fact, if an individual is of rank k, there are $k-1$ individuals below him (assuming that the ranking proceeds from the lowest variate value). If we admit, conventionally, that one-half of the individual is to be regarded as lying to the left of the line of division which he makes, and one-half to the right, his grade, g_k, is given by

$$g_k = (k-1) + \tfrac{1}{2} = k - \tfrac{1}{2} \qquad . \qquad . \qquad . \quad (11.22)$$

It follows that the correlation between ranks is the same as the correlation between grades. But in a population which is finite and discontinuous (and ranking is in practice applied to comparatively small populations of twenty or thirty individuals) *it does not follow that*

$$r = 2 \sin\left(\frac{\pi \rho}{6}\right) \qquad . \qquad . \qquad . \qquad . \quad (11.23)$$

Equation (11.21) was obtained by considering grades in a continuous population, and equation (11.23) is at best an approximation, depending on assumptions which are often of doubtful legitimacy. This is a fact which has not always been appreciated. We may, perhaps, clarify the point by considering the data of Example 11.2.

Example 11.5.—In Example 11.2 we found—

$$\rho = +0.45$$

If we apply (11.23) we find—

$$r = 2 \sin 13.5°$$

$$= +0.47$$

Let us consider what this means.

The value r purports to be a correlation coefficient such as would have been obtained by the product-moment method if the two variates had been measurable in the ordinary way. Let us, for the sake of argument, agree that mathematical and musical abilities are capable of measurement.

Now there are only ten members in this population, and it cannot be regarded with any degree of accuracy as a continuous normal population. The use of (11.23) in finding the correlation *in the population of ten* is therefore of doubtful validity, to say the least.

But it is possible to look at this from rather a different point of view, and to regard the ten students as a sample from a practically infinite population which *is* continuous and normal. The value r is then taken to be an estimate of the correlation coefficient in this population.

The legitimacy of this procedure will depend on the extent to which the grade correlation in the sample can be taken to represent the grade correlation in the population. It will, we think, be sufficiently evident from the smallness of the sample that the two are likely to diverge considerably owing to sampling fluctuations.

Furthermore, in the comparatively small samples to which (11.23) is applied—the labour of calculating the rank correlation coefficient for large samples is very tedious—it is difficult to obtain any satisfactory evidence from the data themselves that the population can properly be regarded as normal ; and even if the distribution of each of the variates, taken singly, can be rendered normal by some appropriate transformation of the variate which squeezes or stretches the scale of measurement, it does not necessarily follow that the correlation distribution can in this way be rendered normal.

As a matter of interest we may record that, corresponding to (11.16) for ρ we have also the relation

$$r = \sin \frac{\pi\tau}{2} \qquad . \qquad . \qquad . \qquad . \qquad . \quad (11.24)$$

The use of this equation is, of course, subject to the same objections as lie against (11.23).

Use of (11.23) and (11.24) should therefore be made with the utmost reserve. It would probably be better to avoid them altogether and rely on the rank correlation coefficient.

11.31 The relationship between the product-moment coefficient and the rank correlation coefficients might profitably be subjected to further investigation, particularly for small numbers of individuals. As we have just seen, with the present state of our knowledge, the use of the rank coefficient is not to be recommended as a brief method of estimating the product-moment coefficient. It is, however, of service as a quick method of gauging relations between variates which are not normally distributed and in any case it is useful where the variates can be ranked but not measured for either practical or theoretical reasons.*

Tetrachoric r

11.32 To complete our account of methods which have been devised as alternatives to the use of the product-moment correlation coefficient in cases where, for some reason, that coefficient cannot be computed, we may refer to a process specially adapted to the 2×2 contingency table.

Consider such a table in the schematic form—

	A	Not-A	Total
B . .	a	b	$a+b$
Not-B .	c	d	$c+d$
Total	$a+c$	$b+d$	N

Let us assume that our attributes A and B are, in theory, based on measurable quantities ; and let us suppose further that the population would be normally distributed with respect to those quantities as variates. Then we may regard the above table as the result obtained by dividing a bivariate normal population into four sections, a division of the X-variate at some point, say h, and a division of the Y-variate at some point k. If we picture the population as a solid figure, as in fig. 9.1, page 208, the frequencies a, b, c and d will be the volumes into which the population is divided by planes perpendicular to the X and Y axes through the points $X=h$ and $Y=k$, respectively.

The problem then arises, given a, b, c and d, what are the values of h and k (in terms of the standard deviations of X and Y), and what is the value of r?

---

* For some further developments of this subject see Kendall's *Rank Correlation Methods*, Third edition 1962

11.33 A discussion of this problem, which involves some difficult mathematics, is outside the scope of this book. The student may be referred to Kendall and Stuart's *Advanced Theory of Statistics*, vol. 2, for an account of the method and to *Tables for Statisticians and Biometricians*, Parts I and II, for tables which are almost indispensable in working out *r* for any given case.

A value of *r* obtained in this way is said to be *tetrachoric*.

The coefficient has often been used to obtain a value of the correlation (so-called) for a contingency table, using some reduction to the four-fold form by amalgamating adjacent arrays, or possibly making more than one such reduction and averaging the results. As such tables are very often far from normal, it is always desirable to test the normality by using more than one reduction. In any case the reader should be informed precisely as to the reduction used.

The product-moment correlation coefficient for a 2×2 table

11.34 The correlation coefficient is in general only calculated for a table with a considerable number of rows and columns, such as those given in Chapter 9. In some cases, however, a theoretical value is obtainable for the coefficient, which holds good even for the limiting case when there are only two values possible for each variable (e.g. 0 and 1) and consequently two rows and two columns (cf. Exercises 11.5 and 11.6). It is therefore of some interest to obtain an expression for the coefficient in this case in terms of the class-frequencies.

Using the notation of Chapters 1-3 the table may be written in the form—

Values of second variable	Values of first variable X_1 X'_1		Total
X_2	(AB)	(αB)	(B)
X'_2	$(A\beta)$	$(\alpha\beta)$	(β)
Total	(A)	(α)	N

Taking the centre of the table as arbitrary origin and the class-interval, as usual, as the unit, the co-ordinates of the mean are—

$$\bar{\xi} = \frac{1}{2N}\{(\alpha) - (A)\} \qquad \bar{\eta} = \frac{1}{2N}\{(\beta) - (B)\}$$

The standard deviations σ_1, σ_2 are given by

$$\sigma_1{}^2 = 0 \cdot 25 - \bar{\xi}^2 = (A)(\alpha)/N^2$$
$$\sigma_2{}^2 = 0 \cdot 25 - \bar{\eta}^2 = (B)(\beta)/N^2$$

Finally,

$$\Sigma(xy) = \tfrac{1}{4}\{(AB)+(\alpha\beta)-(A\beta)-(\alpha B)\}-N\bar{\xi}\bar{\eta}$$

Writing

$$(AB)-(A)(B)/N=\delta$$

(as in Chapter 2) and replacing $\bar{\xi}$, $\bar{\eta}$ by their values, this reduces to

$$\Sigma(xy)=\delta$$

Whence

$$r=\frac{N\delta}{\sqrt{(A)(\alpha)(B)(\beta)}} \quad . \quad . \quad . \quad . \quad (11.25)$$

We may also put this in the form

$$r^2=\frac{\chi^2}{N} \quad . \quad . \quad . \quad . \quad (11.26)$$

where χ^2 is the square contingency as defined in **3.8**.

This value of r can be used as a coefficient of association, but, unlike the association coefficient of Chapter 2, which is unity if either $(AB)=(A)$ or $(AB)=(B)$, r only becomes unity if $(AB)=(A)=(B)$. This is the only case in which both frequencies (αB) and $(A\beta)$ can vanish so that (AB) and $(\alpha\beta)$ correspond to the frequencies of two points, $X_1\,Y_1$, $X_2\,Y_2$ on a line. Obviously this alone renders the numerical values of the two coefficients quite incomparable with each other. But further, while the association coefficient is the same for all tables derived from one another by multiplying rows or columns by arbitrary coefficients, the correlation coefficient (11.25) is greatest when $(A)=(\alpha)$ and $(B)=(\beta)$, i.e. when the table is symmetrical, and its value is lowered when the symmetrical table is rendered asymmetrical by increasing or reducing the number of A's or B's. For moderate degrees of association, the association coefficient gives much the larger values. The two coefficients possess, in fact, essentially different properties, and are *different* measures of association in the same sense that the geometric and arithmetic means are different forms of average, or the semi-interquartile range and the standard deviation different measures of dispersion.

11.35 The student should realise that the product-sum correlation and the tetrachoric correlation are also two entirely different measures with quite different properties. The one is in no sense an approximation to the other, and the two may often differ largely.

Intraclass correlation

11.36 We have previously considered correlations between two definite defined variates, such as age and yield of milk in cows, or stature of father and stature of son ; but there occurs, mainly in biological studies, a rather different kind of correlation which we will now proceed to discuss.

Suppose we are examining the relationship between the heights of brothers, and consider a pair of brothers. Our two variates will be (1) the height of the first brother, and (2) the height of the second brother. The question is, which are we to regard as the first brother and which as the second? It is not difficult to lay down rules which would enable us to make a distinction—for instance, we might take the elder brother first, or the taller brother first. But if we did this and drew up a correlation table for all such pairs, we should not be answering the question as to the relation between brothers in general, for we should only get a correlation between the height of taller brothers and that of shorter brothers, or the height of elder brothers and the height of younger brothers.

11.37 The relationship of brotherhood is in fact symmetrical; if A is the brother of B, then B is the brother of A. When we are considering only the relationship in height implied by relationship of blood, there is no relevant character to enable us to single out one brother as the first.

We accordingly treat the problem by taking each pair of brothers in two ways: (1) with the height of A as the first variate and that of B as the second, and (2) with the height of B as the first variate and that of A as the second. Similarly, if there are k brothers in the family, we enter in the correlation table the results of taking pairs in all possible ways, which number $k(k-1)$. For example, if we have a family containing three brothers with heights 5 ft. 9 in., 5 ft. 10 in. and 5 ft. 11 in., they may be regarded as giving six pairs of variate values—

5 ft. 9 in. with 5 ft. 10 in.	5 ft. 10 in. with 5 ft. 9 in.
5 ft. 9 in. with 5 ft. 11 in.	5 ft. 11 in. with 5 ft. 9 in.
5 ft. 10 in. with 5 ft. 11 in.	5 ft. 11 in. with 5 ft. 10 in.

11.38 Generally, if we have n families, each with k members, there will be $nk(k-1)$ pairs, and hence the same number of entries in the table.

Such a table is called an *intraclass correlation table*, and the correlation between the two variates is called *intraclass correlation*.

Tables in which all the families have the same number are of particular importance, and we will consider them first. It is, however, permissible to apply the term intraclass correlation to the symmetrical table derived from families which have different numbers of members. This case we shall consider in **11.42**.

11.39 The intraclass correlation table has certain peculiarities, and is not of such a general type as the ordinary table which we have considered hitherto (and which, for the purposes of distinction, is sometimes called an *interclass* table).

Let the variate values in the first family be

$$x_{11} \; x_{12} \; \cdots \; x_{1k}$$

those in the second family being

$$x_{21} \ x_{22} \ . \ . \ . \ x_{2k}$$

and so on, those in the nth family being

$$x_{n1} \ x_{n2} \ . \ . \ . \ x_{nk}$$

Consider the mean of the X-variate.

In the table the value x_{11} will be associated as an X-variate with each of the $(k-1)$ values $x_{12} \ldots x_{1k}$. Hence it appears $(k-1)$ times. Similarly, every other value appears $(k-1)$ times. Hence the sum of the marginal row, corresponding to the X-variate, is $(k-1)\Sigma(x)$, the summation extending over all values. But there are $nk(k-1)$ members in the table. Hence,

$$\bar{X} = \frac{1}{nk(k-1)}(k-1)\Sigma(x)$$

$$= \frac{1}{nk}\Sigma(x) \qquad . \qquad . \qquad . \qquad . \qquad . \quad (11.27)$$

Similarly,

$$\bar{Y} = \frac{1}{nk}\Sigma(x) \qquad . \qquad . \qquad . \qquad . \qquad . \quad (11.28)$$

i.e. the means of the variates are the same. This must evidently be the case, for the table is symmetrical.

For the variance of X we have—

$$\sigma_x{}^2 = \frac{1}{nk(k-1)}\{\text{Sum of } (x - \bar{X})^2\}$$

and since each $x - \bar{X}$ occurs $(k-1)$ times,

$$\sigma_x{}^2 = \frac{1}{nk}\Sigma(x - \bar{X})^2 \qquad . \qquad . \qquad . \qquad . \quad (11.29)$$

the summation, as before, extending over all the values of x.

Similarly,

$$\sigma_y{}^2 = \frac{1}{nk}\Sigma(x - \bar{Y})^2$$

$$= \frac{1}{nk}\Sigma(x - \bar{X})^2$$

$$= \sigma_x{}^2$$

We therefore write

$$\sigma = \sigma_x = \sigma_y$$

11.40   For the correlation coefficient r we have

$$\sigma^2 r = \frac{1}{nk(k-1)} \Sigma'(x_{ij}-\bar{X})(x_{im}-\bar{X}) \ . \qquad . \qquad . \quad (11.30)$$

where the summation Σ' extends over all the possible pairs.

We can put this formula into a much simpler form.

Consider the terms in (11.30) for which the first term is $(x_{11}-\bar{X})$. They will be the $(k-1)$ terms of the following series—

$$(x_{11}-\bar{X})(x_{12}-\bar{X})+(x_{11}-\bar{X})(x_{13}-\bar{X})+ \ . \ . \ . \ +(x_{11}-\bar{X})(x_{1k}-\bar{X})$$

$$=(x_{11}-\bar{X})\{(x_{12}+x_{13}+ \ . \ . \ . \ +x_{1k})-(k-1)\bar{X}\}$$

Now write

$$\bar{X}_1 = \frac{1}{k}(x_{11}+x_{12}+ \ . \ . \ . \ +x_{1k}) \ . \qquad . \qquad . \quad (11.31)$$

i.e. $\bar{X}_1$ is the mean of the members of the first family.   Then our expression becomes

$$(x_{11}-\bar{X})\{k\bar{X}_1-x_{11}-(k-1)\bar{X}\}$$

$$=(x_{11}-\bar{X})\{k(\bar{X}_1-\bar{X})+\bar{X}-x_{11}\}$$

$$=k(\bar{X}_1-\bar{X})(x_{11}-\bar{X})-(x_{11}-\bar{X})^2$$

The sum Σ' of (11.30) will contain nk such terms.

Hence,

$$nk(k-1)\sigma^2 r = k\Sigma(\bar{X}_1-\bar{X})(x_{11}-\bar{X})-\Sigma(x_{11}-\bar{X})^2 \ . \qquad . \quad (11.32)$$

the summation extending over all the nk members.

Now,

$$k\Sigma(\bar{X}_1-\bar{X})(x_{11}-\bar{X})$$

$$=\text{sum of } n \text{ terms like } k \times k(\bar{X}_1-\bar{X})(\bar{X}_1-\bar{X})$$

$$=k^2\Sigma''(\bar{X}_1-\bar{X})^2$$

Σ'' extending over the n families ; and

$$\Sigma(x_{11}-\bar{X})^2=nk\sigma^2$$

Hence, from (11.32),

$$nk(k-1)\sigma^2 r=k^2\Sigma''(\bar{X}_1-\bar{X})^2-\sigma^2 nk$$

Now $\frac{1}{n}\Sigma''(\bar{X}_1-\bar{X})^2$ is the variance of the means of families about the mean of the whole.   Calling this σ_m^2, we have

$$nk(k-1)\sigma^2 r=k^2 n\sigma_m^2-\sigma^2 nk$$

$$\{1+r(k-1)\}\sigma^2=k\sigma_m^2 \qquad . \qquad . \qquad . \quad (11.33)$$

This result gives us the intraclass correlation in terms of the variance of the distribution (according to either variate) and the variance of the means of families.

Example 11.6.—In five families of 3 the heights of brothers are : 5′ 9″, 5′ 10″, 5′ 11″ ; 5′ 10″, 5′ 11″, 6′ 0″ ; 5′ 11″, 6′ 0″, 6′ 1″ ; 6′ 0″, 6′ 1″, 6′ 2″ ; 6′ 1″, 6′ 2″, 6′ 3″.   Find the intraclass coefficient of correlation. Here the mean of the whole $=6'$.

$$\sigma^2 = \frac{1}{5\times 3}\{9+4+1+4+1+1+1+1+4+1+4+9\}$$

$$= \frac{40}{15} = \frac{8}{3}$$

$$\sigma_m{}^2 = \frac{1}{5}\{4+1+0+1+4\} = 2$$

Hence, from (11.33),

$$\{1+2r\}\frac{8}{3} = 3\times 2$$

$$1+2r = 2\cdot 25$$

$$r = +0\cdot 625$$

11.41 We may notice two rather unusual results which follow from equation (11.33).

In the first place, since $\sigma_m{}^2$ is not negative,

$$1+r(k-1) \geqslant 0$$

and hence,

$$r \geqslant -\frac{1}{k-1}$$

Thus, whereas the interclass correlation coefficient can vary from -1 to $+1$, the intraclass coefficient cannot be less than $-\frac{1}{k-1}$. For example, in families of threes the intraclass coefficient cannot be less than $-\frac{1}{2}$.

Secondly, let us consider the correlation within a single family, i.e. when $n=1$.

In this case, $\sigma_m{}^2 = 0$, and hence

$$r = -\frac{1}{k-1}$$

For $k=2, 3, 4, \ldots$ this gives the successive values of $r= -1, -\frac{1}{2}, -\frac{1}{3}, \ldots$ It is clear that the first value is correct, for the two values x_1 and x_2 determine only two points (x_1x_2) and (x_2x_1), and the slope of the line joining them is negative.

The student should notice that a corresponding negative association will arise between the first and second members of the pair if all possible pairs are chosen from a population in which the variates can assume only two values, say 0 and 1, or in which only A's and not-A's are distinguished. We use this result later in **17.36.**

11.42. Reverting now to the more general case, suppose we have n families whose members number $k_1, k_2, \ldots k_n$.

The ith family contributes $k_i(k_i-1)$ pairs to the intraclass table, and hence the total number of pairs is $\Sigma\{k_i(k_i-1)\}=N$, say, the summation extending over the n families.

Let the variate values be

$$x_{11}\ x_{12}\ \cdot\ \cdot\ \cdot\ x_{1k1}$$
$$x_{21}\ x_{22}\ \cdot\ \cdot\ \cdot\ x_{2k2}$$
$$\cdot\qquad\cdot\qquad\cdot\qquad\cdot$$
$$x_{n1}\ x_{n2}\ \cdot\ \cdot\ \cdot\ x_{nk_n}$$

As in **11.41,** we see that in the intraclass table each member of the first family appears (k_1-1) times, each of the second (k_2-1) times, and so on. Hence,

$$\bar{X}=\bar{Y}=\frac{1}{N}\Sigma\{(k_i-1)\Sigma'(x_{ij})\}\qquad\cdot\qquad\cdot\qquad\cdot\quad(11.34)$$

the summation Σ' being carried over all members of the ith family and Σ over all families.

Similarly,

$$\sigma_X{}^2=\sigma_Y{}^2=\frac{1}{N}\Sigma''\{(k_i-1)\Sigma(x_{ij}-\bar{X})^2\}\qquad\cdot\qquad\cdot\quad(11.35)$$

and

$$\sigma^2 r=\frac{1}{N}\Sigma''\{(x_{ij}-\bar{X})(x_{im}-\bar{X})\}$$

the summation extending over all possible pairs.
and this, as in **11.40,** reduces to

$$N\sigma^2 r=\Sigma\{k_i{}^2(\bar{X}_i-\bar{X})^2\}-\Sigma\Sigma'(x_{ij}-\bar{X})^2\qquad\cdot\qquad\cdot\quad(11.36)$$

These formulæ are considerably more complex than those of **11.40,** but reduce to those forms if k_i is constant for all families.

SUMMARY

1. In cases where the data are incomplete, or in order to avoid lengthy calculation, it is possible to use various methods of approximating to the product-moment coefficient of correlation, provided that the regression is approximately linear.

2. Cases in which the regression is non-linear can sometimes be reduced to the linear case by a suitable transformation of the variates.

3. The correlation ratio of X on Y is given by

$$\eta_{xy}^2 = 1 - \frac{\sigma_{ax}^2}{\sigma_x^2}$$

$$= \frac{\sigma_{mx}^2}{\sigma_x^2}$$

where σ_x^2 is the variance of X, σ_{ax}^2 is the weighted average of the variances of arrays and σ_{mx}^2 the variance of the means of X-arrays, weighted according to the number of individuals in the arrays.

4. $\eta_{xy}^2 - r^2$ cannot be negative, and if it is zero the regression of X on Y is linear.

5. Spearman's rank correlation coefficient is given by

$$\rho = \frac{\Sigma(xy)}{\sqrt{\Sigma(x^2)\Sigma(y^2)}}$$

where x and y are the deviations of the ranks X and Y from the mean $\frac{n+1}{2}$.

6. If

$$d_k = (X_k - Y_k)$$

$$\rho = 1 - \frac{6\Sigma(d^2)}{n^3 - n}$$

7. The rank correlation coefficient τ is given by

$$\tau = \frac{S}{\frac{1}{2}n(n-1)}$$

$$= \frac{2R}{\frac{1}{2}n(n-1)} - 1$$

where S is the sum of scores obtained by allocating $+1$ if pairs of ranks are in the same order in the two rankings and -1 in the contrary case; and R is the sum of scores for positive scores only.

8. The coefficient of intraclass correlation is given by

$$\{1 + r(k-1)\}\sigma^2 = k\sigma_m^2$$

where σ is the standard deviation of X and Y, and σ_m is the standard deviation of the means of families, there being n families each of k members.

EXERCISES

11.1 Find to 3 places of decimals the correlation ratio of X on Y and of Y on X for the distribution of cows of Table 9.4, page 204 ($r = +0\cdot219$). Hence, show that

$$\eta_{xy}^2 - r^2 = 0\cdot011$$
$$\eta_{yx}^2 - r^2 = 0\cdot023$$

11.2 Find the correlation ratios of the distribution of marriages of Table 9.2.

11.3 In a test of ability to distinguish shades of colour, 15 discs of various shades, whose true orders are 1, 2, . . . 15, are arranged by a subject in the order 7, 4, 2, 3, 1, 10, 6, 8, 9, 5, 11, 15, 14, 12, 13. Find the rank correlation coefficients ρ and τ between the real and the observed ranks.

11.4 Ten competitors in a beauty contest are ranked by three judges in the orders

1, 6, 5, 10, 3, 2, 4, 9, 7, 8
3, 5, 8, 4, 7, 10, 2, 1, 6, 9
6, 4, 9, 8, 1, 2, 3, 10, 5, 7

Use rank correlation coefficients to discuss which pair of judges has the nearest approach to common tastes in beauty.

11.5 (Cf. Pearson, " On a Generalised Theory of Alternative Inheritance," *Phil. Trans.*, A, 1904, **203**, 53.) If we consider the correlation between number of recessive couplets in parent and in offspring, in a Mendelian population breeding at random (such as would ultimately result from an initial cross between a pure dominant and a pure recessive), the correlation is found to be $1/3$ for a total number of couplets n. If $n=1$, the only possible numbers of recessive couplets are 0 and 1, and the correlation table between parent and offspring reduces to the form

Offspring	Parent 0	1	Total
0	5	1	6
1	1	1	2
Total	6	2	8

Verify the correlation, and work out the association coefficient Q.

11.6 (Cf. the above, and also Snow, *Proc. Roy. Soc.*, B, 1910, **83**, 42.) For a similar population the correlation between brothers, assuming a practically infinite size of family, is $5/12$. The table is

Second brother	First brother 0	1	Total
0	41	7	48
1	7	9	16
Total	48	16	64

Verify the correlation, and work out the association coefficient Q.

11.7 Establish equation (11.26).

11.8 Show by drawing a graph that the values of x and $2\sin\dfrac{\pi x}{6}$ are never very different for the range $-1 \leqslant x \leqslant 1$ and that the greatest difference is about $0\cdot018$ (Cf. equation (11.23)).

11.9 Referring to the notation of **11.34**, show that we have the following expressions for the regressions in a fourfold table—

$$r\frac{\sigma_1}{\sigma_2} = \frac{N\delta}{(B)(\beta)} = \frac{(AB)}{(B)} - \frac{(A\beta)}{(\beta)}$$

$$r\frac{\sigma_2}{\sigma_1} = \frac{N\delta}{(A)(\alpha)} = \frac{(AB)}{(A)} - \frac{(\alpha B)}{(\alpha)}$$

Verify on the tables of Exercises 11.5 and 11.6.

11.10 In four pea-pods, each containing eight peas, the weights of the peas are, in hundredths of a gramme : 43, 46, 48, 42, 50, 45, 45 and 49 ; 33, 34, 37, 39, 32, 35, 37 and 41 ; 56, 52, 50, 51, 54, 52, 49 and 52 ; 36, 37, 38, 40, 40, 41, 44 and 44. Find the coefficient of intraclass correlation.

11.11 (Data from O.H. Latter, *Biometrika*, 1905, **4**, 363.)
The following table shows the length of cuckoos' eggs fostered by various birds—

Foster parent	Length of egg (units ½ millimetre)											Totals
	40	41	42	43	44	45	46	47	48	49	50	
Robin . . .	1	1	8	3	9	13	20	6	11	2	2	76
Wren . . .	7	5	14	8	9	6	3	2	—	—	—	54
Hedge-sparrow .	—	—	2	5	14	13	13	3	5	—	3	58
Totals . .	8	6	24	16	32	32	36	11	16	2	5	188

Find the coefficient of intraclass correlation, and state how many entries there would be in the intraclass correlation table.

11.12 If t consecutive ranks are replaced by a single tie, show that, for both ρ and τ, the resulting coefficients are the means of the $t\,!$ coefficients obtained by permuting the t original ranks in all possible ways. Show that this remains true if there are several sets of tied ranks in either ranking.

CHAPTER TWELVE

PARTIAL CORRELATION

Mutiple correlation

12.1 In Chapters 9 to 11 we developed the theory of the correlation between a single pair of variables. But in the case of statistics of attributes we found it necessary to proceed from the theory of simple association for a single pair of attributes to the theory of association for several attributes, in order to be able to deal with the complex causation characteristic of statistics ; and similarly the student will find it impossible to advance very far in the discussion of many problems in correlation without some knowledge of the theory of *multiple correlation,* or correlation between several variables.

For example, in considering the relationship between the number of children per family, level of income and age at marriage, it might be found that the number of children was negatively correlated with income and also with age at marriage ; and the question might arise how far the first correlation was affected by the fact that people with higher incomes tend to marry later. The question could not at the present stage be answered by working out the correlation coefficient between the last pair of variables, for we have as yet no guide as to how far a correlation between the variables 1 and 2 can be accounted for by correlations between 1 and 3 and 2 and 3.

Again, a marked positive correlation might be observed between, say, the bulk of a crop and the rainfall during a certain period, and practically no correlation between the crop and the accumulated temperature during the same period ; and the question might arise whether the last result might not be due merely to a negative correlation between rain and accumulated temperature, the crop being favourably affected by an increase of accumulated temperature *if other things were equal,* but failing as a rule to obtain this benefit owing to the concomitant deficiency of rain. In the problem of inheritance in a population, the corresponding problem is of great importance, as already indicated in Chapter 2. It is essential . for the discussion of possible hypotheses to know whether an observed correlation between, say, grandson and grandparent can or cannot be accounted for solely by observed correlations between grandson and parent, parent and grandparent.

Partial regressions and correlation coefficients

12.2 Problems of this type, in which it is necessary to consider simultaneously the relations between at least three variables, and possibly more, may be treated by a simple and natural extension of the method used in the case of two variables. The latter case was discussed by forming linear equations between the two variables, assigning such values to the constants as to make the sum of the squares of the errors of estimate as low as possible : the more complicated case may be discussed by forming linear equations between any one of the n variables involved, taking each in turn, and the $n-1$ others, again assigning such values to the constants as to make the sum of the squares of the errors of estimate a minimum. If the variables are $X_1, X_2, X_3, \ldots X_n$, the equation will be of the form

$$X_1 = a + b_2 X_2 + b_3 X_3 + \ldots + b_n X_n$$

If in such a *generalised regression equation* we find a sensible positive value for any one coefficient such as b_2, we know that there must be a positive correlation between X_1 and X_2 that cannot be accounted for by mere correlations of X_1 and X_2 with X_3, X_4 or X_n, for the effects of changes in these variables are allowed for in the remaining terms on the right. The magnitude of b_2 gives, in fact, the mean change in X_1 associated with a unit change in X_2 when all the remaining variables are kept constant.

The correlation between X_1 and X_2 indicated by b_2 may be termed a *partial correlation*, as corresponding with the *partial association* of Chapter 2, and it is required to deduce from the values of the coefficients b, which may be termed *partial regressions, partial coefficients of correlation* giving the correlation between X_1 and X_2 or other pair of variables *when the remaining variables $X_3 \ldots X_n$ are kept constant*, or when changes in these variables are corrected or allowed for, so far as this may be done with a linear equation. For examples of such generalised regression equations the student may turn to the illustrations worked out later in this chapter.

12.3 With this explanatory introduction, we may now proceed to the algebraic theory of such generalised regression equations and of multiple correlation in general. It will first, however, be as well to revert briefly to the case of two variables. In Chapter 9, to obtain the greatest possible simplicity of treatment, the value of the coefficient $r = p / \sigma_1 \sigma_2$ was deduced on the special assumption that the means of all arrays were strictly collinear, and the meaning of the coefficient in the more general case was subsequently investigated. Such a process is not conveniently applicable when a number of variables are to be taken into account, and the problem has to be faced directly : i.e. *required, to determine the coefficients and constant term, if any, in a regression equation, so as to make the sum of the squares of the errors of estimate a minimum.*

12.4 To solve this problem we proceed as in **9.20**.

Let us measure the variates $X_1 \ldots X_n$ from their respective means, denoting the quantities so obtained by $x_1 \ldots x_n$.

Then the regression equation of, say, x_1 on $x_2 \ldots x_n$ may be written in the form

$$x_1 = a_1 + b_2 x_2 + b_3 x_3 + \ldots + b_n x_n$$

We have to find $a_1, b_2, \ldots b_n$ such that

$$E_1 = \Sigma(x_1 - a_1 - b_2 x_2 - \ldots - b_n x_n)^2$$

is a minimum, the summation taking place over all sets of values of $x_1 \ldots x_n$.

Now,

$$E_1 = \Sigma(a_1{}^2) + \Sigma(x_1 - b_2 x_2 - \ldots - b_n x_n)^2$$

the product term

$$2\Sigma\{a_1(x_1 - b_2 x_2 - \ldots - b_n x_n)\}$$

vanishing, since x_1, etc. are measured from the mean.

Hence we have, for the minimum value of E_1,

$$a_1 = 0$$

Now, if b_2 is chosen so that E_1 is a minimum, the value of E_1, when $(b_2 + \delta)$ is substituted for b_2, is increased no matter how small δ may be ; i.e.

$$\Sigma\{x_1 - (b_2 + \delta)x_2 - \ldots - b_n x_n\}^2 \geqslant \Sigma(x_1 - b_2 x_2 - \ldots - b_n x_n)^2$$

Expanding the left-hand side, and neglecting δ^2, which can be made as small as we please compared with δ,

$$\Sigma(x_1 - b_2 x_2 - \ldots - b_n x_n)^2 - 2\Sigma\{x_2(x_1 - b_2 x_2 - \ldots - b_n x_n)\}\delta$$
$$\geqslant \Sigma(x_1 - b_2 x_2 - \ldots - b_n x_n)^2$$

or

$$\Sigma\{x_2(x_1 - b_2 x_2 - \ldots - b_n x_n)\}\delta \leqslant 0$$

Now this is to be true for all small values of δ, positive or negative. If $\Sigma\{x_2(x_1 - b_2 x_2 - \ldots - b_n x_n)\}$ were not zero, this would be impossible, for if it were positive, say, we could take δ positive and the inequality would not be satisfied.

Hence,

$$\Sigma\{x_2(x_1 - b_2 x_2 - \ldots - b_n x_n)\} = 0$$

Similarly, considering b_3 instead of b_2, we have

$$\Sigma\{x_3(x_1 - b_2 x_2 - \ldots - b_n x_n)\} = 0$$

and so on, there being $(n-1)$ equations. These are sufficient to determine the $(n-1)$ quantities $b_2 \ldots b_n$, and hence our problem is solved.

Notation

12.5 At this point we introduce a flexible notation which will enable us to consider any regression equation.

We write—

$$x_1 = b_{12.34\,\ldots\,n} x_2 + b_{13.24\,\ldots\,n} x_3 + \cdots + b_{1n.23\,\ldots\,(n-1)} x_n \qquad (12.1)$$

The quantities b are *partial regression coefficients*. The first subscript attached to the b is the subscript of the letter on the left (the dependent variable). The second subscript is that of the x to which it is attached. These are called *primary subscripts*.

After the primary subscripts, and separated from them by a point, are placed the subscripts of the remaining variables on the right. These are called *secondary subscripts*.

Equation (12.1) is the regression equation of x_1. Similarly, in accordance with the rules we have just laid down, we have—

$$x_2 = b_{21.34\,\ldots\,n} x_1 + b_{23.14\,\ldots\,n} x_3 + \cdots + b_{2n.13\,\ldots\,(n-1)} x_n$$

and so on.

It should be noted that the order in which the secondary subscripts are written is immaterial; but this is not true of the primary subscripts; e.g. $b_{12.3\,\ldots\,n}$ and $b_{21.3\,\ldots\,n}$ denote quite distinct coefficients, x_1 being the dependent variable in the first case and x_2 in the second.

A coefficient with p secondary subscripts may be termed a *regression of the pth order*. The regressions b_{12}, b_{21}, b_{13}, b_{31}, etc., obtained by considering two variables alone, may be regarded as of order zero, and may be termed *total*, as distinct from *partial*, regressions.

12.6 If the regressions $b_{12.34\,\ldots\,n}$, $b_{13.24\,\ldots\,n}$, etc., be assigned the " best " values, as determined by the method of least squares, the difference between the actual value of x_1 and the value assigned by the right-hand side of the regression equation (12.1), that is, the error of estimate, will be denoted by $x_{1.23\,\ldots\,n}$; i.e. as a definition we have—

$$x_{1.23\,\ldots\,n} = x_1 - b_{12.34\,\ldots\,n} x_2 - b_{13.24\,\ldots\,n} x_3 - \cdots - b_{1n.23\,\ldots\,(n-1)} x_n \quad (12.2)$$

where x_1, x_2, ... x_n are assigned any one set of observed values. Such an error (or *residual*, as it is sometimes called), denoted by a symbol with p secondary suffixes, will be termed a *deviation* of the pth order.

Finally, we will define a generalised standard deviation $\sigma_{1.23\,\ldots\,n}$ by the equation

$$N\sigma_{1.23\,\ldots\,n}^2 = \Sigma(x_{1.23\,\ldots\,n}^2) \qquad\qquad\qquad (12.3)$$

N being, as usual, the number of observations. A standard deviation denoted by a symbol with p secondary suffixes will be termed a standard deviation of the pth order, the standard deviations σ_1, σ_2, etc., being regarded as of order zero, the standard deviations $\sigma_{1.2}$, $\sigma_{2.1}$, etc., of the first order, and so on.

12.7 In the case of two variables, the correlation coefficient r_{12} may be regarded as defined by the equation

$$r_{12} = (b_{12}b_{21})^{\frac{1}{2}}$$

We shall generalise this equation in the form

$$r_{12.34\ldots n} = (b_{12.34\ldots n}b_{21.34\ldots n})^{\frac{1}{2}} \qquad . \qquad . \qquad . \quad (12.4)$$

This is at present a pure definition of a new symbol, and it remains to be shown that $r_{12.34\ldots n}$ may really be regarded as, and possesses all the properties of, a correlation coefficient ; the name may, however, be applied to it, pending the proof. A correlation coefficient with p secondary subscripts will be termed a *correlation of order* p. Evidently, in the case of a correlation coefficient, the order in which both primary and secondary subscripts is written is indifferent, for the right-hand side of equation (12.4) is unaltered by writing 2 for 1 and 1 for 2. The correlations r_{12}, r_{13}, etc., may be regarded as of order zero, and spoken of as *total*, as distinct from *partial*, correlations.

The normal equations

12.8 All the quantities we have just defined are expressible in terms of the total and partial regression coefficients, and particular importance therefore attaches to the equations which give those coefficients. The equations of **12.4** may be written

$$\Sigma(x_2 x_{1.23\ldots n}) = 0 \qquad . \qquad . \qquad . \qquad . \quad (12.5)$$

etc., there being $(n-1)$ equations for each regression equation.

These equations are called the *normal equations*.

12.9 If the student will follow the process by which (12.5) was obtained, he will see that when the condition is expressed that $b_{12.34\ldots n}$ shall possess the " least-square " value, x_2 enters into the product-sum with $x_{1.23\ldots n}$; when the same condition is expressed for $b_{13.24\ldots n}$, x_3 enters into the product-sum, and so on. Taking each regression in turn, in fact, every x the suffix of which is included in the secondary suffixes of $x_{1.23\ldots n}$ enters into the product-sum. The normal equations of the form (12.5) are therefore equivalent to the theorem—

The product-sum of any deviation of order zero with any deviation of higher order is zero, provided the subscript of the former occur among the secondary subscripts of the latter.

12.10   But it follows from this that

$$\Sigma(x_{1.34\ldots n}x_{2.34\ldots n})=\Sigma\{x_{1.34\ldots n}(x_2-b_{23.4\ldots n}x_3-\cdots-b_{2n.34\ldots(n-1)}x_n)\}$$

$$=\Sigma(x_{1.34\ldots n}x_2)$$

Similarly,

$$\Sigma(x_{1.34\ldots n}x_{2.34\ldots n})=\Sigma(x_1 x_{2.34\ldots n})$$

Similarly again,

$$\Sigma(x_{1.34\ldots n}x_{2.34\ldots(n-1)})=\Sigma(x_{1.34\ldots n}x_2)$$

and so on.   Therefore, quite generally,

$$
\left.
\begin{aligned}
\Sigma(x_{1.34\ldots n}x_{2.34\ldots n}) &=\Sigma(x_{1.34\cdots(n-1)}x_{2.34\ldots n}) \\
&= \quad\cdot\qquad\cdot\qquad\cdot \\
&=\Sigma(x_1 x_{2.31\ldots n}) \\
&=\Sigma(x_{1\,34\ldots n}x_{2\,34\ldots(n-1)}) \\
&= \quad\cdot\qquad\cdot\qquad\cdot \\
&=\Sigma(x_{1.34\ldots n}x_2)
\end{aligned}
\right\}
\qquad . \qquad . \qquad . \quad (12.6)
$$

Comparing all the equal product-sums that may be obtained in this way, we see that *the product-sum of any two deviations in which all the secondary subscripts of the first occur among the secondary subscripts of the second is unaltered by omitting any or all of the secondary subscripts of the first, and, conversely, the product-sum of any deviation of order* p *with a deviation of order* p+q, *the* p *subscripts being the same in each case, is unaltered by adding to the secondary subscripts of the former any or all of the* q *additional subscripts of the latter.*

It follows therefore from (12.5) that *any product-sum is zero if all the subscripts of the one deviation occur among the secondary subscripts of the other.*   As the simplest case, we may note that x_1 is uncorrelated with $x_{2.1}$, and x_2 uncorrelated with $x_{1.2}$.

The theorems of this and of the preceding paragraph are of fundamental importance, and should be carefully remembered.

12.11   We can now show that the quantities r defined by (12.4) are really coefficients of correlation.   In fact we have, from the results of **12.9** and **12.10,**

$$
\begin{aligned}
0 &=\Sigma(x_{2.34\ldots n}x_{1.234\cdots n}) \\
&=\Sigma\{x_{2.34\ldots n}(x_1-b_{12.34\ldots n}x_2-\text{terms in }x_3\text{ to }x_n)\} \\
&=\Sigma(x_1 x_{2.34\ldots n})-b_{12.34\ldots n}\Sigma(x_2 x_{2.31\ldots n}) \\
&=\Sigma(x_{1.34\ldots n}x_{2.34\ldots n})-b_{12.34\ldots n}\Sigma(x^2_{2.34\ldots n})
\end{aligned}
$$

That is,

$$b_{12.34\ldots n}=\frac{\Sigma(x_{1.34\ldots n}x_{2.31\ldots n})}{\Sigma(x^2_{2.34\ldots n})} \qquad . \qquad . \qquad . \quad (12.7)$$

But this is the value that would have been obtained by taking a regression equation of the form

$$x_{1.34\ldots n}=b_{12.34\ldots n}x_{2.34\ldots n}$$

and determining $b_{12.34\ldots n}$ by the method of least squares, i.e. $b_{12.34\ldots n}$ is the regression of $x_{1.34\ldots n}$ on $x_{2.34\ldots n}$. It follows at once from (12.4) that $r_{12.34\ldots n}$ is the correlation between $x_{1.34\ldots n}$ and $x_{2.34\ldots n}$, and from (12.7) that we may write

$$b_{12.34\ldots n} = r_{12.34\ldots n} \frac{\sigma_{1.34\ldots n}}{\sigma_{2.34\ldots n}} \qquad . \qquad . \qquad . \quad (12.8)$$

an equation identical with the familiar relation $b_{12} = r_{12}\sigma_1/\sigma_2$, with the secondary suffixes $34\ldots n$ added throughout.

To illustrate the meaning of the equation by the simplest case, if we had three variables only, x_1, x_2 and x_3, the value of $b_{12.3}$ or $r_{12.3}$ could be determined (1) by finding the correlations r_{13} and r_{23} and the corresponding regressions b_{13} and b_{23}; (2) working out the residuals $x_1 - b_{13}x_3$ and $x_2 - b_{23}x_3$ for all associated deviations; (3) working out the correlation between the residuals associated with the same values of x_3. The method would not, however, be a practical one, as the arithmetic would be extremely lengthy, much more lengthy than the method given below for expressing a correlation of order p in terms of correlations of order $p-1$.

Expression of standard deviation in terms of standard deviations and coefficients of lower orders

12.12 *Any standard deviation of order* p *may be expressed in terms of a standard deviation of order* p−1 *and a correlation of order* p−1. *For,*

$$\Sigma(x_{1.23\ldots n})^2 = \Sigma(x_{1.23\ldots (n-1)}x_{1.23\ldots n})$$
$$= \Sigma(x_{1.23\ldots (n-1)})(x_1 - b_{1n.23\ldots (n-1)}x_n - \text{terms in } x_2 \text{ to } x_{n-1})$$
$$= \Sigma(x_{1.23\ldots (n-1)}^2) - b_{1n.23\ldots (n-1)}\Sigma(x_{1.23\ldots (n-1)}x_{n.23\ldots (n-1)})$$

or, dividing through by the number of observations—

$$\sigma_{1.23\ldots n}^2 = \sigma_{1.23\ldots (n-1)}^2(1 - b_{1n.23\ldots (n-1)}b_{n1.23\ldots (n-1)})$$
$$= \sigma_{1.23\ldots (n-1)}^2(1 - r_{1n.23\ldots (n-1)}^2) \qquad . \qquad . \qquad . \quad (12.9)$$

This is again the relation of the familiar form

$$\sigma_{1.n}^2 = \sigma_1^2(1 - r_{1n}^2)$$

with the secondary suffices $23\ldots(n-1)$ added throughout. It is clear from (12.9) that $r_{1n.23\ldots(1-n)}$, like any correlation of order zero, cannot be numerically greater than unity. It also follows at once that if we have been estimating x_1 from x_2, x_3, $\ldots x_{n-1}$, x_n will not increase the accuracy of estimate unless $r_{12.23\ldots(n-1)}$ (not r_{1n}) differ from zero. This condition is somewhat interesting, as it leads to rather unexpected results. For example, if $r_{12} = +0\cdot8$, $r_{13} = +0\cdot4$, $r_{23} = +0\cdot5$, it will not be possible to estimate x_1 with any greater accuracy from x_2 and x_3 than from x_2 alone, for the value of $r_{13.2}$ is zero (see below, **12.15**).

12.13 It should be noted that, in equation (12.9), any other subscript can be eliminated in the same way as subscript n from the suffix of $\sigma_{1.23\ldots n}$, so that a standard deviation of order p can be expressed in p ways in terms of standard deviations of the next lower order. This is useful as affording an independent check on arithmetic. Further, $\sigma_{1.23\ldots(n-1)}$ can be expressed in the same way in terms of $\sigma_{1.23\ldots(n-2)}$, and so on, so that we must have

$$\sigma_{1.23\ldots n}^2=\sigma_1^2(1-r_{12}^2)(1-r_{13.2}^2)(1-r_{14.23}^2)\cdots(1-r_{1n.23\ldots(n-1)}^2) \quad (12.10)$$

This is an extremely convenient expression for arithmetical use; the arithmetic can again be subjected to an absolute check by eliminating the subscripts in a different, say the inverse, order. Apart from the algebraic proof, it is obvious that the values must be identical; for if we are estimating one variable from n others, it is clearly indifferent in what order the latter are taken into account.

$\sigma_{1.23\ldots n}$ can also be expressed in terms of σ_1 and the total correlation coefficients. We have

$$\Sigma(x_{1.23\ldots n})^2=\Sigma\{x_1(x_{1.23\ldots n})\}=N\sigma_{1.23\ldots n}^2$$

Hence, expanding $x_{1.23\ldots n}$,

$$\sigma_1^2-b_{12.3\ldots n}r_{12}\sigma_1\sigma_2-b_{13.2\ldots n}r_{13}\sigma_1\sigma_3-\cdots=\sigma_{1.23\ldots n}^2$$

The $(n-1)$ normal equations involving $x_{1.23\ldots n}$ are

$$\Sigma(x_2 x_{1.23\ldots n})=0,\ \text{etc.}$$

i.e. expanding,

$$r_{21}\sigma_1\sigma_2-b_{12.3\ldots n}\sigma_2^2-b_{13.2\ldots n}r_{23}\sigma_2\sigma_3\cdots=0$$

$$r_{31}\sigma_1\sigma_3-b_{12.3\ldots n}r_{32}\sigma_3\sigma_2-b_{13.2\ldots n}\sigma_3^2\cdots=0,\ \text{etc.}$$

Regarding the n equations so obtained as equations in the quantities b, we have, on elimination, the determinant

$$\begin{vmatrix} \sigma_1^2-\sigma_{1.23\ldots n}^2 & r_{12}\sigma_1\sigma_2 & r_{13}\sigma_1\sigma_3 & \cdots & r_{1n}\sigma_1\sigma_n \\ r_{21}\sigma_2\sigma_1 & \sigma_2^2 & r_{23}\sigma_2\sigma_3 & \cdots & r_{2n}\sigma_2\sigma_n \\ \cdot\ \cdot & \cdot\ \cdot & \cdot\ \cdot & & \cdot\ \cdot \\ r_{n1}\sigma_n\sigma_1 & r_{n2}\sigma_n\sigma_2 & r_{n3}\sigma_n\sigma_3 & \cdots & \sigma_n^2 \end{vmatrix}=0$$

Dividing the sth row by σ_s and the tth column by σ_t, this gives—

$$\begin{vmatrix} 1-\dfrac{\sigma_{1.23\ldots n}^2}{\sigma_1^2} & r_{12} & r_{13} & \cdots & r_{1n} \\ r_{21} & 1 & r_{23} & \cdots & r_{2n} \\ \cdot\ \cdot & \cdot\ \cdot & \cdot\ \cdot & & \cdot\ \cdot \\ r_{n1} & r_{n2} & r_{n3} & \cdots & 1 \end{vmatrix}=0$$

Write ω for the determinant

$$\begin{vmatrix} 1 & r_{12} & \ldots & r_{1n} \\ r_{21} & 1 & \ldots & r_{2n} \\ \cdot & \cdot & \cdot & \cdot \\ r_{n1} & r_{n2} & \ldots & 1 \end{vmatrix}$$

and let ω_{11} be the minor of the term in the first row and column. Then

$$\omega - \frac{\sigma^2_{1.23\ldots n}}{\sigma^2_1}\omega_{11} = 0$$

$$\frac{\sigma^2_{1.23\ldots n}}{\sigma^2_1} = \frac{\omega}{\omega_{11}} \qquad . \qquad . \qquad . \quad (12.11)$$

Similarly,

$$\frac{\sigma^2_{2.13\ldots n}}{\sigma^2_2} = \frac{\omega}{\omega_{22}}$$

and so on.

These results exhibit $\sigma^2_{1.23\ldots n}$, etc., in a symmetrical form.

Expression of regression coefficients in terms of coefficients of lower orders
12.14 Any regression of order p may be expressed in terms of regressions of order $p-1$. For we have—

$$\Sigma(x_{1.34\ldots n}x_{2.34\ldots n}) = \Sigma(x_{1.34\ldots(n-1)}x_{2.34\ldots n})$$
$$= \Sigma(x_{1.34\ldots(n-1)})(x_2 - b_{2n.34\ldots(n-1)}x_n - \text{terms in } x_3 \text{ to } x_{n-1})$$
$$= \Sigma(x_{1.34\ldots(n-1)}x_{2.34\ldots(n-1)}) - b_{2n.34\ldots(n-1)}\Sigma(x_{1.34\ldots(n-1)}x_{n.34\ldots(n-1)})$$

Replacing $b_{2n.34\ldots(n-1)}$ by $b_{n2.34\ldots(n-1)}\sigma^2_{2.34\ldots(n-1)}/\sigma^2_{n.34\ldots(n-1)}$

we have—

$$b_{12.34\ldots n}\sigma^2_{2.34\ldots n} = b_{12.34\ldots(n-1)}\sigma^2_{2.34\ldots(n-1)} - b_{1n.34\ldots(n-1)}b_{n2.34\ldots(n-1)}\sigma^2_{2.34\ldots(n-1)}$$

or, from (12.9),

$$b_{12.34\ldots n} = \frac{b_{12.34\ldots(n-1)} - b_{1n.34\ldots(n-1)}b_{n2.34\ldots(n-1)}}{1 - b_{2n.34\ldots(n-1)}b_{n2.34\ldots(n-1)}} \qquad (12.12)$$

The student should note that this is an expression of the form

$$b_{12.n} = \frac{b_{12} - b_{1n}b_{n2}}{1 - b_{2n}b_{n2}}$$

with the subscripts $34 \ldots (n-1)$ added throughout. The coefficient $b_{12.34\ldots n}$ may therefore be regarded as determined from a regression equation of the form

$$x_{1.34\ldots(n-1)} = b_{12.34\ldots n}x_{2.34\ldots(n-1)} + b_{1n.23\ldots(n-1)}x_{n.34\ldots(n-1)}$$

i.e. it is the partial regression of $x_{1.34\ldots(n-1)}$ on $x_{2.34\ldots(n-1)}$, $x_{n.34\ldots(n-1)}$ being given. As any other secondary suffix might have been eliminated in lieu of n, we might also regard it as the partial regression of $x_{1.45\ldots n}$ on $x_{2.45\ldots n}$, $x_{3.45\ldots n}$ being given, and so on.

Expression of correlation coefficient in terms of coefficients of lower orders

12.15 From equation (12.12) we may readily obtain a corresponding equation for correlations. For (12.12) may be written—

$$b_{12.34 \ldots n} = \frac{r_{12.34 \ldots (n-1)} - r_{1n.34} \ldots (n-1) r_{2n.34} \ldots (n-1)}{1 - r_{2n.34}^2 \ldots (n-1)} \cdot \frac{\sigma_{1.34} \ldots (n-1)}{\sigma_{2.34} \ldots (n-1)}$$

Hence, writing down the corresponding expression for $b_{21.34 \ldots n}$ and taking the square root—

$$r_{12.34 \ldots n} = \frac{r_{12.34 \ldots (n-1)} - r_{1n.34} \ldots (n-1) r_{2n.34} \ldots (n-1)}{(1 - r_{1n.34}^2 \ldots (n-1))^{\frac{1}{2}}(1 - r_{2n.34}^2 \ldots (n-1))^{\frac{1}{2}}} \qquad (12.13)$$

This is, similarly, the expression for three variables—

$$r_{12.n} = \frac{r_{12} - r_{1n} r_{2n}}{(1 - r_{1n}^2)^{\frac{1}{2}}(1 - r_{2n}^2)^{\frac{1}{2}}}$$

with the secondary subscripts added throughout, and $r_{12.34 \ldots n}$ can be assigned interpretations corresponding to those of $b_{12.34 \ldots n}$ above. Evidently equation (12.13) permits of an absolute check on the arithmetic in the calculation of all partial coefficients of an order higher than the first, for any one of the secondary suffixes of $r_{12.34 \ldots n}$ can be eliminated so as to obtain another equation of the same form as (12.13), and the value obtained for $r_{12.34 \ldots n}$ by inserting the values of the coefficients of lower order in the expression on the right must be the same in each case.

Practical procedure

12.16 The equations now obtained provide all that is necessary for the arithmetical solution of problems in multiple correlation. The best mode of procedure on the whole, having calculated all the correlations and standard deviations of order zero, is (1) to calculate the correlations of higher order by successive applications of equation (12.13) ; (2) to calculate any required standard deviations by equation (12.10) ; (3) to calculate any required regressions by equation (12.8) ; the use of equation (12.12) for calculating the regressions of successive orders directly from one another is comparatively clumsy. We will give two illustrations, the first for three and the second for four variables. The introduction of more variables does not involve any difference in the form of the arithmetic, but rapidly increases the amount.

Example 12.1.—In Exercise 9.2, page 234, we gave some data of (1) the average earnings of agricultural labourers, (2) the percentage of the population in receipt of poor law relief, (3) the ratios of the numbers in receipt of outdoor relief to those relieved in the workhouse, for 38 rural districts. Required to work out the partial correlations, regressions, etc., for these three variables.

Using as our notation X_1=average earnings, X_2=percentage of population in receipt of relief, X_3=out-relief ratio, the first constants determined are—

$$M_1=15\cdot9 \text{ shillings} \qquad \sigma_1=1\cdot71 \text{ shillings} \qquad r_{12}=-0\cdot66$$
$$M_2=3\cdot67 \text{ per cent} \qquad \sigma_2=1\cdot29 \text{ per cent} \qquad r_{13}=-0\cdot13$$
$$M_3=5\cdot79 \qquad\qquad \sigma_3=3\cdot09 \qquad\qquad\quad r_{23}=+0\cdot60$$

To obtain the partial correlations, equation (12.13) is used direct in its simplest form—

$$r_{12.3}=\frac{r_{12}-r_{13}r_{23}}{(1-r_{13}^2)^{\frac{1}{2}}(1-r_{23}^2)^{\frac{1}{2}}}$$

The work is best done systematically and the results collected in tabular form, especially if logarithms are used, as many of the logarithms occur repeatedly. First, it will be noted that the logarithms of $(1-r^2)^{\frac{1}{2}}$ occur in all the denominators ; these had, accordingly, better be worked out at once and tabulated (col. 2 of the table below). In column 3 the product term of the numerator of each partial coefficient is entered, i.e.

1	2	3	4	5	6	7	8	9
						Correlation of first order		
	$\log\sqrt{1-r^2}$	Product term	Numerator	log num.	log denom.	log	Value	$\log\sqrt{1-r^2}$
$r_{12}=-0\cdot66$	$\bar{1}\cdot87580$	$-0\cdot0780$	$-0\cdot5820$	$\bar{1}\cdot76492$	$\bar{1}\cdot89938$	$\bar{1}\cdot86554$	$r_{12.3}-0\cdot73$	$\bar{1}\cdot83216$
$r_{13}=-0\cdot13$	$\bar{1}\cdot99629$	$-0\cdot3960$	$+0\cdot2660$	$\bar{1}\cdot42488$	$\bar{1}\cdot77889$	$\bar{1}\cdot64599$	$r_{13.2}+0\cdot44$	$\bar{1}\cdot95267$
$r_{23}=+0\cdot60$	$\bar{1}\cdot90309$	$+0\cdot0858$	$+0\cdot5142$	$\bar{1}\cdot71113$	$\bar{1}\cdot87209$	$\bar{1}\cdot83904$	$r_{23.1}+0\cdot69$	$\bar{1}\cdot85946$

the product of the two other coefficients on the remaining lines in column 1 ; subtracting this from the coefficient on the same line in column 1, we have the numerator (col. 4) and can enter its logarithm. The logarithm of the denominator (col. 6) is obtained at once by adding the two logarithms of $(1-r^2)^{\frac{1}{2}}$ on the remaining lines of the table, and subtracting the logarithms of the denominators from those of the numerators, we have the logarithms of the correlations of the first order. It is also as well to calculate at once, for reference in the calculation of standard deviations of the second order, the values of $\log\sqrt{1-r^2}$ for the first-order coefficients (col. 9).

Having obtained the correlations, we can now proceed to the regressions. If we wish to find all the regression equations, we shall have six regressions to calculate from equations of the form

$$b_{12.3}=r_{12.3}\sigma_{1.3}/\sigma_{2.3}$$

These will involve all the six standard deviations of the first order $\sigma_{1.2}$, $\sigma_{1.3}$, $\sigma_{2.1}$, $\sigma_{2.3}$, etc. The standard deviations of the first order are not in themselves of much interest, but the standard deviations of the second order are important, as being the standard errors or root-mean-square errors of estimate made in using the regression equations of the second order. We may save needless arithmetic, therefore, by replacing the standard deviations of the first order by those of the second, omitting the former entirely, and transforming the above equation for $b_{12.3}$ to the form

$$b_{12.3} = r_{12.3}\sigma_{1.23}/\sigma_{2.13}$$

This transformation is a useful one and should be noted by the student. The values of each σ may be calculated twice independently by the formulæ of the form

$$\sigma_{1.23} = \sigma_1(1 - r_{12}^2)^{\frac{1}{2}}(1 - r_{13.2}^2)^{\frac{1}{2}}$$
$$= \sigma_1(1 - r_{13}^2)^{\frac{1}{2}}(1 - r_{12.3}^2)^{\frac{1}{2}}$$

so as to check the arithmetic; the work is rapidly done if the values of $\log \sqrt{1 - r^2}$ have been tabulated. The values found are—

$$\log \sigma_{1.23} = 0 \cdot 06146 \qquad \sigma_{1.23} = 1 \cdot 15$$
$$\log \sigma_{2.13} = \bar{1} \cdot 84584 \qquad \sigma_{2.13} = 0 \cdot 70$$
$$\log \sigma_{3.12} = 0 \cdot 34571 \qquad \sigma_{3.12} = 2 \cdot 22$$

From these and the logarithms of the r's we have—

$$\log b_{12.3} = 0 \cdot 08116, \quad b_{12.3} = -1 \cdot 21 \quad \bigg| \quad \log b_{13.2} = \bar{1} \cdot 36174 \quad b_{13.2} = +0 \cdot 23$$
$$\log b_{21.3} = \bar{1} \cdot 64993, \quad b_{21.3} = -0 \cdot 45 \quad \bigg| \quad \log b_{23.1} = \bar{1} \cdot 33917 \quad b_{23.1} = +0 \cdot 22$$
$$\log b_{31.2} = \bar{1} \cdot 93024, \quad b_{31.2} = +0 \cdot 85 \quad \bigg| \quad \log b_{32.1} = 0.33891 \quad b_{32.1} = +2 \cdot 18$$

That is, the regression equations are—

(1) $x_1 = -1 \cdot 21x_2 + 0 \cdot 23x_3$
(2) $x_2 = -0 \cdot 45x_1 + 0 \cdot 22x_3$
(3) $x_3 = +0 \cdot 85x_1 + 2 \cdot 18x_2$

or, transferring the origins to zero—

(1) *Earnings* $\quad X_1 = +19 \cdot 0 - 1 \cdot 21X_2 + 0 \cdot 23X_3$
(2) *Pauperism* $\quad X_2 = +9 \cdot 55 - 0 \cdot 45X_1 + 0 \cdot 22X_3$
(3) *Out-relief ratio* $X_3 = -15 \cdot 7 + 0 \cdot 85X_1 + 2 \cdot 18X_2$

The units are throughout one shilling for the earnings X_1, 1 per cent for the pauperism X_2 and 1 for the out-relief ratio X_3.

Now let us examine the light thrown by these results on the relationship between the variables.

The first and second regression equations are those of most practical importance. The argument was once advanced that the giving of out-relief tended to lower earnings, and the total coefficient ($r_{13} = -0 \cdot 13$) between earnings (X_1) and out-relief (X_3), though very small, does not seem inconsistent with such a hypothesis. The partial correlation coefficient ($r_{13.2} = +0 \cdot 44$) and the regression equation (1), however, indicate that in unions with a *given* percentage of the population in receipt of relief (X_2) the earnings were highest where the proportion of out-relief was highest ; and this is, in so far, against the hypothesis of a tendency to lower wages. It remained possible, of course, that out-relief might adversely affect the *possibility of earning*, e.g. by limiting the employment of the old.

As regards pauperism, the argument might be advanced that the observed correlation ($r_{23} = +0\cdot60$) between pauperism and out-relief was in part due to the negative correlation ($r_{13} = -0\cdot13$) between earnings and out-relief. Such a hypothesis would have little to support it in view of the smallness and doubtful significance of r_{13}, and is definitely contradicted by the positive partial correlation $r_{23.1} = +0\cdot69$ and the second regression equation. The third regression equation shows that the proportion of out-relief was on the whole highest where earnings were highest and pauperism greatest. It should be noticed, however, that a negative ratio is clearly impossible, and consequently the relation cannot be strictly linear ; but the third equation gives *possible* (positive) average ratios for all the combinations of pauperism and earnings that actually occur.

Example 12.2 (*Four variables*).—As an illustration of the form of the work in the case of four variables, we will take a portion of the data from another investigation into the causation of pauperism.

The variables are the ratios of the values in 1891 to the values in 1881 (taken as 100) of—

1. The percentage of the population in receipt of relief,
2. The ratio of the numbers given outdoor relief to the numbers relieved in the workhouse,
3. The percentage of the population over 65 years of age,
4. The population itself,

in the metropolitan group of 32 unions, and the fundamental constants (means, standard deviations and correlations) are as follows—

TABLE 12.1

1 Means		2 Standard deviations		3 Correlation coefficient		4 $\log \sqrt{1-r^2}$
1	104·7	1	29·2	12	+0·52	$\bar{1}\cdot93154$
2	90·6	2	41·7	13	+0·41	$\bar{1}\cdot96003$
3	107·7	3	5·5	14	−0·14	$\bar{1}\cdot99570$
4	111·3	4	23·8	23	+0·49	$\bar{1}\cdot94038$
—	—	—	—	24	+0·23	$\bar{1}\cdot98820$
—	—	—	—	34	+0·25	$\bar{1}\cdot98598$

It is seen that the average changes are not great ; the percentages of the population in receipt of relief increased on an average by 4·7 per cent, the out-relief ratio dropped by 9·4 per cent and the percentage of the old increased by 7·7 per cent, while the population of the unions rose on the average by 11·3 per cent. At the same time the standard deviations of the first, second and fourth variables are very large. As a matter of fact, while in one union the pauperism decreased by nearly 50 per cent and in others by 20 per cent, in some there were increases of 60, 80 and

TABLE 12.2

	1	2	3	4		5
	Correlation coefficient (zero order)	Product term of numerator	Numerator	Correlation coefficient (first order)		$\log \sqrt{1-r^2}$
12	$+0\cdot52$	$+0\cdot2009$	$+0\cdot3191$	$12\cdot3$	$+0\cdot4013$	$\bar{1}\cdot96187$
13	$+0\cdot41$	$+0\cdot2548$	$+0\cdot1552$	$13\cdot2$	$+0\cdot2084$	$\bar{1}\cdot99035$
23	$+0\cdot49$	$+0\cdot2132$	$+0\cdot2768$	$23\cdot1$	$+0\cdot3553$	$\bar{1}\cdot97070$
12	$+0\cdot52$	$-0\cdot0322$	$+0\cdot5522$	$12\cdot4$	$+0\cdot5731$	$\bar{1}\cdot91355$
14	$-0\cdot14$	$+0\cdot1196$	$-0\cdot2596$	$14\cdot2$	$-0\cdot3123$	$\bar{1}\cdot97772$
24	$+0\cdot23$	$-0\cdot0728$	$+0\cdot3028$	$24\cdot1$	$+0\cdot3580$	$\bar{1}\cdot97022$
13	$+0\cdot41$	$-0\cdot0350$	$+0\cdot4450$	$13\cdot4$	$+0\cdot4642$	$\bar{1}\cdot94731$
14	$-0\cdot14$	$+0\cdot1025$	$-0\cdot2425$	$14\cdot3$	$-0\cdot2746$	$\bar{1}\cdot98297$
34	$+0\cdot25$	$-0\cdot0574$	$+0\cdot3074$	$34\cdot1$	$+0\cdot3404$	$\bar{1}\cdot97326$
23	$+0\cdot49$	$+0\cdot0575$	$+0\cdot4325$	$23\cdot4$	$+0\cdot4590$	$\bar{1}\cdot94863$
24	$+0\cdot23$	$+0\cdot1225$	$+0\cdot1075$	$24\cdot3$	$+0\cdot1274$	$\bar{1}\cdot99645$
34	$+0\cdot25$	$+0\cdot1127$	$+0\cdot1373$	$34\cdot2$	$+0\cdot1618$	$\bar{1}\cdot99424$

90 per cent ; similarly, in the case of the out-relief, in several unions the ratio was decreased by 40 to 60 per cent, a consistent anti-out-relief policy having been enforced ; in others the ratio was doubled, and more than doubled. As regards population, the more central districts showed decreases ranging up to 20 and 25 per cent, the circumferential districts increases of 45 to 80 per cent. The correlations of order zero are not large, the changes in the rate of pauperism exhibiting the highest correlation with changes in the out-relief ratio, slightly less with changes in the proportion of old and very little with changes in population.

The correlations of the second order are obtained in two steps. In the first place, the six coefficients of order zero are grouped in four sets of three, corresponding to the four sets of three variables formed by omitting each one of the four variables in turn (Table 12.2, col. 1). Each of these sets of three coefficients is then treated in the same manner as in the last example, and so the correlations of the first order (Table 12.2, col. 4) are obtained. The first-order coefficients are then regrouped in sets of three, with the same secondary suffix (Table 12.3, col. 1), and these are treated precisely in the same way as the coefficients of order zero. In this way, it will be seen, the value of each coefficient of the second order is arrived at in two ways independently, and so the arithmetic is checked : $r_{12.34}$ occurs in the first and fourth lines, for instance, $r_{13.24}$ in the second and seventh, and so on. Of course slight differences may occur in the last digit if a sufficient number of digits is not retained, and for this reason the intermediate work should be carried to a greater degree of accuracy than is necessary in the final result ; thus four places of decimals were retained throughout in the intermediate work of this example, and three in the final result. If he carries out an independent calculation, the student may differ slightly from the logarithms given in this and the following work, if more or fewer figures are retained.

TABLE 12.3

1		2	3	4		5
Correlation coefficient (first order)		Product term of numerator	Numerator	Correlation coefficient (second order)		$\log \sqrt{1-r^2}$
12·4	+0·5731	+0·2131	+0·3600	12·34	+0·457	$\bar{1}$·94901
13·4	+0·4642	+0·2631	+0·2011	13·24	+0·276	$\bar{1}$·98277
23·4	+0·4590	+0·2660	+0·1930	23·14	+0·266	$\bar{1}$·98408
12·3	+0·4013	−0·0350	+0·4363	12·34	+0·457	—
14·3	−0·2746	+0·0511	−0·3257	14·23	−0·359	$\bar{1}$·97013
24·3	+0·1274	−0·1102	+0·2376	24·13	+0·270	$\bar{1}$·98359
13·2	+0·2084	−0·0505	+0·2589	13·24	+0·276	—
14·2	−0·3123	+0·0337	−0·3460	14·23	−0·359	—
34·2	+0·1618	−0·0651	+0·2269	34·12	+0·244	$\bar{1}$·98664
23·1	+0·3553	+0·1219	+0·2334	23·14	+0·266	—
24·1	+0·3580	+0·1209	+0·2371	24·13	+0·270	—
34·1	+0·3404	+0·1272	+0·2132	34·12	+0·244	—

Having obtained the correlations, the regressions can be calculated from the third-order standard deviations by equations of the form (as in the last example),

$$b_{12.34} = r_{12.34} \frac{\sigma_{1.234}}{\sigma_{2.134}}$$

so the standard deviations of lower orders need not be evaluated. Using equations of the form

$$\sigma_{1.234} = \sigma_1 (1 - r_{12}^2)^{\frac{1}{2}} (1 - r_{13.2}^2)^{\frac{1}{2}} (1 - r_{14.23}^2)^{\frac{1}{2}}$$
$$= \sigma_1 (1 - r_{14}^2)^{\frac{1}{2}} (1 - r_{13.4}^2)^{\frac{1}{2}} (1 - r_{12.34}^2)^{\frac{1}{2}}$$

we find :

$$\log \sigma_{1.234} = 1·35740 \qquad \sigma_{1.234} = 22·8$$
$$\log \sigma_{2.134} = 1·50597 \qquad \sigma_{2.134} = 32·1$$
$$\log \sigma_{3.124} = 0·65773 \qquad \sigma_{3.124} = 4·55$$
$$\log \sigma_{4.123} = 1·32914 \qquad \sigma_{4.123} = 21·3$$

All the twelve regressions of the second order can be readily calculated, given these standard deviations and the correlations, but we may confine ourselves to the equation giving the changes in pauperism (X_1) in terms of other variables as the most important.   It will be found to be

$$x_1 = 0 \cdot 325 x_2 + 1 \cdot 383 x_3 - 0 \cdot 383 x_4$$

or, transferring the origins and expressing the equation in terms of percentage ratios,

$$X_1 = -31 \cdot 1 + 0 \cdot 325 X_2 + 1 \cdot 383 X_3 - 0 \cdot 383 X_4$$

or, again, in terms of percentage changes (ratio — 100)—
Percentage change in pauperism

$$\begin{aligned}
&= +1 \cdot 4 \text{ per cent} \\
&\quad +0 \cdot 325 \text{ times the change in out-relief ratio} \\
&\quad +1 \cdot 383 \quad \text{,,} \quad \text{,,} \quad \text{,,} \quad \text{proportion of old} \\
&\quad -0 \cdot 383 \quad \text{,,} \quad \text{,,} \quad \text{,,} \quad \text{population}
\end{aligned}$$

These results render the interpretation of the total coefficients, which might be equally consistent with several hypotheses, more clear and definite. The questions would arise, for instance, whether the correlation of changes in pauperism with changes in out-relief might not be due to correlation of the latter with the other factors introduced, and whether the negative correlation with changes in population might not be due solely to the correlation of the latter with changes in the proportion of old.   As a matter of fact, the partial correlations of changes in pauperism with changes in out-relief and in proportion of old are slightly less than the total correlations, but the partial correlation with changes in population is numerically greater, the figures being—

$$\begin{array}{ll}
r_{12} = +0 \cdot 52 & r_{12.34} = +0 \cdot 46 \\
r_{13} = +0 \cdot 41 & r_{13.24} = +0 \cdot 28 \\
r_{14} = -0 \cdot 14 & r_{14.23} = -0 \cdot 36
\end{array}$$

So far, then, as we have taken the factors of the case into account, there appears to have been a true correlation between changes in pauperism and changes in out-relief, proportion of old and population—the latter serving, of course, as some index to changes in general prosperity.   The relative influences of the three factors are indicated by the regression equation above.

In this and the previous example we have had to consider only three or four independent variables.   For five or more the number of partial correlations and regressions increases rapidly (see Exercise 12.6) and it becomes impracticable to compute them all without great labour.   In such circumstances, where we are primarily interested in the regression of one variate on the others it may well be easier to solve direct the normal equations given at the end of 12.4, either by progressive elimination of

variables in the usual manner for simultaneous linear equations or by
evaluating determinants systematically. See the comments on this point
in **13.27–13.29**.

Aids to calculation

12.17 To facilitate the computation of partial correlation and regression
coefficients, various tables of such quantities as

$$1-r^2, \quad \sqrt{1-r^2}, \quad \frac{1}{\sqrt{(1-r_{13}^2)(1-r_{12}^2)}}$$

have been prepared. See, for instance, T. L. Kelley's *Statistical Tables*.

The generalised scatter diagram

12.18 The scatter diagram in two dimensions may be generalised to
three dimensions, and may also be used as a mental construct for higher
dimensions, though no actual model can of course be made.

Consider the case of three variates. The values of X_1, X_2 and X_3
associated with any given individual may be regarded as determining a
point in space whose co-ordinates are X_1, X_2 and X_3. The totality of
individuals will therefore give us a swarm of points in three-dimensional
space, which will lie distributed in certain ways about planes of regression.
The closeness with which the points lie to the regression planes is a
measure of the adequacy of the representation by regression equations.
In figure 12.1 we give a diagrammatic representation of the data of
Example 12.1 with the regression plane of X_1 on the other two variables.

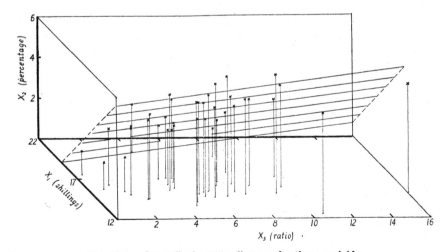

Fig. 12.1.—Generalised scatter diagram for three variables
Data of Example 12.1. X_1=average earnings, X_2=percentage of population in
receipt of relief, X_3=out-relief ratio.

Coefficient of multiple correlation

12.19 Consider the regression equation for x_1,

$$x_1 = b_{12.3 \ldots n} x_2 + b_{13.2 \ldots n} x_3 + \ldots + b_{1n.2 \ldots (n-1)} x_n$$

Let us write the right-hand side of this equation as $e_{1.23 \ldots n}$, so that in virtue of (12.2),

$$e_{1.23 \ldots n} = x_1 - x_{1.23 \ldots n} \qquad . \qquad . \qquad . \quad (12.14)$$

Now consider the correlation between x_1 and $e_{1.23 \ldots n}$. We have in virtue of the theorem of **12.10**—

$$\begin{aligned}
\Sigma(x_1 e_{1.23 \ldots n}) &= \Sigma\{x_1(x_1 - x_{1.23 \ldots n})\} \\
&= \Sigma(x_1{}^2) - \Sigma\{x_1(x_{1.23 \ldots n})\} \\
&= \Sigma(x_1{}^2) - \Sigma(x_{1.23 \ldots n})^2 \\
&= N(\sigma_1^2 - \sigma_{1.23 \ldots n}^2)
\end{aligned}$$

Also,

$$\begin{aligned}
\Sigma(e_{1.23 \ldots n})^2 &= \Sigma(x_1 - x_{1.23 \ldots n})^2 \\
&= N(\sigma_1^2 - \sigma_{1.23 \ldots n}^2)
\end{aligned}$$

Hence, the correlation between x_1 and $e_{1.23 \ldots n}$

$$= \frac{\sigma_1^2 - \sigma_{1.23 \ldots n}^2}{\sigma_1 \sqrt{\sigma_1^2 - \sigma_{1.23 \ldots n}^2}}$$

$$= \frac{\sqrt{\sigma_1^2 - \sigma_{1.23 \ldots n}^2}}{\sigma_1}$$

We shall call this quantity $R_{1(23 \ldots n)}$. We have immediately—

$$\sigma_{1.23 \ldots n}^2 = \sigma_1^2(1 - R_{1(23 \ldots n)}^2) \qquad . \qquad . \qquad (12.15)$$

$R_{1(2 \ldots n)}$ is called the *multiple correlation coefficient* between x_1 and $x_2 \ldots x_n$. We have, similarly, multiple correlations between x_1 and fewer variables. $R_{1(2 \ldots n)}$ is called an $(n-1)$-fold multiple correlation coefficient. $R_{1(2 \ldots \overline{n-1})}$ would be an $(n-2)$-fold coefficient, and so on.

12.20 The value of R may be calculated either directly from equation (12.15), or by substituting in that equation the value of $\sigma_{1.23 \ldots n}^2$ obtained in (12.10), which gives—

$$1 - R_{1(23 \ldots n)}^2 = (1 - r_{12}^2)(1 - r_{13.2}^2)(1 - r_{14.23}^2) \ldots (1 - r_{1.n23 \ldots (n-1)}^2) \quad (12.16)$$

Properties of the multiple correlation coefficient

12.21 $R_{1(23 \ldots n)}$, being the correlation between x_1 and $e_{1.23 \ldots n}$, measures how closely x_1 can be represented by the regression equation. If $R = 1$, x_1 can be perfectly represented by such an equation, i.e. is a linear function of $x_2 \ldots x_n$. In this case $\sigma_{1.23 \ldots n}^2 = 0$, i.e. all the residuals are zero.

It may, in fact, be shown that $R_{1(23\ldots n)}$ is greater than the correlation between x_1 and any linear function of $x_2\ldots x_n$ other than that expressed in the regression equation, i.e. $e_{1.23\ldots n}$. Putting this another way, the regression coefficients in $e_{1.23\ldots n}$ may be determined by the condition that the correlation between x_1 and $e_{1.23\ldots n}$ is a maximum.

R is necessarily positive or zero

12.22 This is true, since the product term $\Sigma(x_1 e_{1.23\ldots n})$ is positive, being equal to $N(\sigma_1^2 - \sigma_{1.23\ldots n}^2)$, and we see from (12.10) that $\sigma_1^2 \geqslant \sigma_{1.23\ldots n}^2$.

Further, from (12.16),

$$1 - R_{1(23\ldots n)}^2 \leqslant 1 - r_{12}^2$$

i.e. R is not numerically less than r_{12}. Similarly, it is not numerically less than any other total or partial correlation coefficient which can appear in (12.16). Hence, $R_{1(2\ldots n)}$ *is not numerically less than any possible constituent coefficient of correlation.*

It follows from this that if $R_{1(2\ldots n)} = 0$, all the correlation coefficients involving x_1 are zero, i.e. the variate x_1 is *completely uncorrelated with the other variates.*

12.23 Further, even if all the variables X_1, X_2, $\ldots X_n$ were strictly uncorrelated in the original population as a whole, we should expect r_{12}, $r_{13.2}$, $r_{14.23}$, etc. to exhibit values (whether positive or negative) differing from zero in a limited sample. Hence, R will not tend, on an average of such samples, to be zero, but will fluctuate round some mean value. This mean value will be the greater the smaller the number of observations in the sample, and also the greater the number of variables. When only a small number of observations is available it is, accordingly, little use to deal with a large number of variables. As a limiting case, it is evident that if we deal with n variables and possess only n observations, all the partial correlations of the highest possible order will be unity. We shall deal with the question of the significance of an observed value of R in Chapter 22.

Example 12.3.—In Example 12.1 we found—

$$r_{12} = -0\cdot 66$$
$$r_{13.2} = +0\cdot 44$$

Hence, from (12.16),

$$1 - R_{1(23)}^2 = \{1 - (0\cdot 66)^2\}\{1 - (0\cdot 44)^2\}$$
$$= 0\cdot 455$$

whence

$$R_{1(23)} = 0\cdot 74$$

Similarly, it will be found that

$$R_{2(13)} = 0 \cdot 84$$

and

$$R_{3(12)} = 0 \cdot 70$$

The student may verify by inspection that these values are greater than the corresponding constituent values.

Expression of regressions and correlations in terms of coefficients of higher orders

12.24 It is obvious that as equations (12.12) and (12.13) enable us to express regressions and correlations of higher orders in terms of those of lower orders, we must similarly be able to express the coefficients of lower in terms of those of higher orders. Such expressions are sometimes useful for theoretical work. Using the same method of expansion as in previous cases, we have—

$$0 = \Sigma(x_{1.23 \ldots n} x_{2.34 \ldots (n-1)})$$
$$= \Sigma(x_1 x_{2.34 \ldots (n-1)}) - b_{12.34 \ldots n} \Sigma(x_2 x_{2.34 \ldots (n-1)})$$
$$- b_{1n.23 \ldots (n-1)} \Sigma(x_n x_{2.34 \ldots (n-1)})$$

That is,

$$b_{12.34 \ldots (n-1)} = b_{12.34 \ldots n} + b_{1n.23 \ldots (n-1)} b_{n2.34 \ldots (n-1)}$$

In this equation the coefficient on the left and the last on the right are of order $n-3$, the other two of order $n-2$. We therefore wish to eliminate the last coefficient on the right. Interchanging the suffixes 1 for n and n for 1, we have—

$$b_{n2.34 \ldots (n-1)} = b_{n2.13 \ldots (n-1)} + b_{n1.23 \ldots (n-1)} b_{12.34 \ldots (n-1)}$$

Substituting this value for $b_{n2.34 \ldots (n-1)}$ in the first equation, we have—

$$b_{12.34 \ldots (n-1)} = \frac{b_{12.34 \ldots n} + b_{1n.23 \cdots (n-1)} b_{n2.13 \ldots (n-1)}}{1 - b_{1n.23 \ldots (n-1)} b_{n1.23 \ldots (n-1)}} \qquad (12.17)$$

This is the required equation for the regressions ; it is the equation

$$b_{12} = \frac{b_{12.n} + b_{1n.2} b_{n2.1}}{1 - b_{1n.2} b_{n1.2}}$$

with secondary suffixes 34 . . . $(n-1)$ added throughout. The corresponding equation for the correlations is obtained at once by writing down equation (12.17) for $b_{21.34\ldots(n-1)}$ and taking the square root of the product ; this gives—

$$r_{12.34\ldots(n-1)} = \frac{r_{12.34\ldots n} + r_{1n.23\ldots(n-1)} r_{2n.13\ldots(n-1)}}{(1 - r_{1n.23\ldots(n-1)}^2)^{\frac{1}{2}}(1 - r_{2n.13\ldots(n-1)}^2)^{\frac{1}{2}}} \qquad (12.18)$$

which is similarly the equation

$$r_{12} = \frac{r_{12.n} + r_{1n.2} r_{2n.1}}{(1 - r_{1n.2}^2)^{\frac{1}{2}}(1 - r_{2n.1}^2)^{\frac{1}{2}}}$$

with the secondary suffixes 34 ... $(n-1)$ added throughout.

Conditions of consistence among correlation coefficients

12.25 Equations (12.13) and (12.18) imply that certain limiting inequalities must hold between the correlation coefficients in the expression on the right in each case in order that real values (values between ± 1) may be obtained for the correlation coefficient on the left. These inequalities correspond precisely with those " conditions of consistence " between class-frequencies with which we dealt in Chapter 1, but we propose to treat them only briefly here. Writing (12.13) in its simplest form for $r_{12.3}$, we must have $r_{12.3}^2 \leqslant 1$ or

$$\frac{(r_{12} - r_{13} r_{23})^2}{(1 - r_{13}^2)(1 - r_{23}^2)} \leqslant 1$$

that is,

$$r_{12}^2 + r_{13}^2 + r_{23}^2 - 2r_{12} r_{13} r_{23} \leqslant 1 \qquad . \qquad . \qquad . \qquad (12.19)$$

if the three r's are consistent with one another. If we take r_{12}, r_{13} as known, this gives as limits for r_{23},

$$r_{12} r_{13} \pm \sqrt{1 - r_{12}^2 - r_{13}^2 + r_{12}^2 r_{13}^2}$$

Similarly, writing (12.18) in its simplest form for r_{12} in terms of $r_{12.3}$, $r_{13.2}$ and $r_{23.1}$, we must have—

$$r_{12.3}^2 + r_{13.2}^2 + r_{23.1}^2 + 2r_{12.3} r_{13.2} r_{23.1} \leqslant 1 \qquad . \qquad . \qquad (12.20)$$

and therefore, if $r_{12.3}$ and $r_{13.2}$ are given, $r_{23.1}$ must lie between the limits

$$-r_{12.3} r_{13.2} \pm \sqrt{1 - r_{12.3}^2 - r_{13.2}^2 + r_{12.3}^2 r_{13.2}^2}$$

The following table gives the limits of the third coefficient, in a few special cases, for the three coefficients of zero order and of the first order respectively—

Value of		Limits of	
r_{12} or $r_{12.3}$	r_{13} or $r_{13.2}$	r_{23}	$r_{23.1}$
0	0	± 1	± 1
± 1	± 1	$+1$	-1
± 1	∓ 1	-1	$+1$
$\pm \sqrt{0\cdot 5}$	$\pm \sqrt{0\cdot 5}$	$0, +1$	$0, -1$
$\pm \sqrt{0\cdot 5}$	$\mp \sqrt{0\cdot 5}$	$0, -1$	$0, +1$

The student should notice that the set of three coefficients of order zero and value unity are only consistent if either one only, or all three, are positive, i.e. $+1, +1, +1$, or $-1, -1, +1$; but not $-1, -1, -1$. On the other hand, the set of three coefficients of the first order and value unity are only consistent if one only, or all three, are negative : the only consistent sets are $+1, +1, -1$ and $-1, -1, -1$. The values of the two given r's need to be very high if even the sign of the third can be inferred ; if the two are equal, they must be at least equal to $\sqrt{0\cdot 5}$ or $0\cdot 707\ldots$ Finally, it may be noted that no two values for the known coefficients ever permit an inference of the value zero for the third ; the fact that 1 and 2, 1 and 3 are uncorrelated, pair and pair, permits no inference of any kind as to the correlation between 2 and 3, which may lie anywhere between $+1$ and -1.

Fallacies in the interpretation of correlation coefficients

12.26 We do not think it necessary to add to this chapter a detailed discussion of the nature of fallacies on which the theory of multiple correlation throws much light. The general nature of such fallacies is the same as for the case of attributes, and was discussed fully in Chapter 2. It suffices to point out the principal sources of fallacy which are suggested at once by the form of the partial correlation

$$r_{12.3} = \frac{r_{12} - r_{13} r_{23}}{\sqrt{(1 - r_{13}^2)(1 - r_{23}^2)}} \qquad . \qquad . \qquad . \qquad (a)$$

and from the form of the corresponding expression for r_{12} in terms of the partial coefficients—

$$r_{12} = \frac{r_{12.3} + r_{13.2} r_{23.1}}{\sqrt{(1 - r_{13.2}^2)(1 - r_{23.1}^2)}} \qquad . \qquad . \qquad (b)$$

From the form of the numerator of (a) it is evident (1) that even if r_{12} be zero, $r_{12.3}$ will not be zero unless either r_{13} or r_{23}, or both, are zero. If r_{13} and r_{23} are of the same sign, the partial correlation will be negative ; if of opposite sign, positive. Thus the quantity of a crop might appear to be unaffected, say, by the amount of rainfall during some period preceding harvest : this might be due merely to a correlation between rain and low temperature, the partial correlation between crop and rainfall being positive and important. We may thus easily misinterpret a coefficient of correlation which is zero. (2) $r_{12.3}$ may be, indeed often is, of opposite sign to r_{12}, and this may lead to still more serious errors of interpretation.

From the form of the numerator of (b), on the other hand, we see that, conversely, r_{12} will not be zero even though $r_{12.3}$ is zero, unless either $r_{13.2}$ or $r_{23.1}$ is zero. This corresponds to the theorem of **2.26,** and indicates a source of fallacies similar to those there discussed.

12.27 We have seen that $r_{12.3}$ is the correlation between $x_{1.3}$ and $x_{2.3}$, and that we might determine the value of this partial correlation by drawing up the actual correlation table for the two residuals in question. Suppose, however, that instead of drawing up a single table we drew up a series of tables for values of $x_{1.3}$ and $x_{2.3}$ associated with values of x_3 lying within successive class-intervals of its range. In general, the value of $r_{12.3}$ would not be the same (or approximately the same) for all such tables, but would exhibit some systematic change as the value of x_3 increased. Hence $r_{12.3}$ should be regarded, in general, as of the nature of an average correlation : the cases in which it measures the correlation between $x_{1.3}$ and $x_{2.3}$ for *every* value of x_3 (cf. below **12.31**) are probably exceptional. The process for determining partial associations (cf. Chapter 2) is, it will be remembered, thorough and complete, as we always obtain the actual tables exhibiting the association between, say, A and B in the population of C's and the population of γ's : that two such associations may differ materially is illustrated by Example 2.9, page 34. It might sometimes serve as a useful check on partial correlation work to reclassify the observations by the fundamental methods of Chapter 2.

Multivariate normal correlation

12.28 The theorems and results of Chapter 10 in regard to normal correlation can be extended to the case of n variates, which we have studied in this chapter.

In fact, suppose we have n variates x_1, x_2 x_3, . . . x_n, measured from their respective means, with standard deviations σ_1, σ_2, σ_3, . . . σ_n. Let us first consider the simple case in which they are normally distributed and each is completely independent of the others.

Then, if $y_1 \ldots _n$ denote the frequency of the combination of deviations $x_1, x_2, \ldots x_n$, we have—

$$y_{12} \ldots _n = y'_{12} \ldots _n e^{-\frac{1}{2}\phi(x_1, x_2, \ldots x_n)}$$

where

$$\phi(x_1, x_2, \ldots x_n) = \frac{x_1^2}{\sigma_1^2} + \frac{x_2^2}{\sigma_2^2} + \frac{x_3^2}{\sigma_3^2} + \ldots + \frac{x_n^2}{\sigma_n^2}$$

(12.21)

Now consider the variates $x_1, x_{2.1}, x_{3.12}, \ldots x_{n.12 \ldots (n-1)}$. Whether $x_1, x_2, \ldots x_n$ are correlated or not, these variates are uncorrelated, in virtue of **12.10**. Let us further suppose they are independent and normally distributed. Then their distribution is given by

$$y_{12 \ldots n} = y'_{12 \ldots n} e^{-\frac{1}{2}\phi(x_1, x_{2.1} \ldots x_{n.12 \ldots (n-1)})} \quad . \quad (12.22)$$

where

$$\phi(x_1, x_{2.1}, \ldots x_{n.12 \ldots (n-1)}) = \frac{x_1^2}{\sigma_1^2} + \frac{x_{2.1}^2}{\sigma_{2.1}^2} + \ldots + \frac{x_{n.12 \ldots (n-1)}^2}{\sigma_{n.12 \ldots (n-1)}^2} \quad . \quad (12.23)$$

and

$$y'_{12 \ldots n} = \frac{N}{(2\pi)^{\frac{n}{2}} \sigma_1 \sigma_{2.1} \ldots \sigma_{n.12 \ldots (n-1)}} \quad . \quad . \quad (12.24)$$

The expression (12.23) may be put in a more convenient form. It may be shown, but we omit the proof, that

$$
\begin{aligned}
\phi = &\frac{x_1^2}{\sigma_{1.23 \ldots n}^2} + \frac{x_2^2}{\sigma_{2\,13 \ldots n}^2} + \ldots + \frac{x_n^2}{\sigma_{n.12 \ldots (n-1)}^2} \\
&- 2r_{12\,3 \ldots n} \frac{x_1 x_2}{\sigma_{1.23 \ldots n}\sigma_{2\,13 \ldots n}} - \ldots \\
&- 2r_{(n-1)n.12 \ldots (n-2)} \frac{x_{n-1} x_n}{\sigma_{n-1.1 \ldots (n-2)n}\sigma_{n.1 \ldots (n-1)}} \quad . \quad (12.25)
\end{aligned}
$$

which exhibits the form as symmetrical in $x_1 \ldots x_n$.
Now we showed in **12.13** that

$$\sigma_{1.23 \ldots n}^2 = \frac{\omega}{\omega_{11}} \sigma_1^2$$

etc.

In precisely the same way it may be shown that

$$\sigma_{1.23 \ldots n} \sigma_{2.13 \ldots n} / r_{12.3 \ldots n} = -\frac{\omega}{\omega_{12}} \sigma_1 \sigma_2$$

ω_{12} being the minor in ω of the term in the first row and the second column.
If we substitute these and analogous values in (12.22), we get—

$$y_{12 \ldots n} = \frac{N}{(2\pi)^{\frac{n}{2}} \sigma_1 \sigma_2 \ldots \sigma_n \sqrt{\omega}} e^{-\frac{1}{2}\phi}$$

where

$$\phi = \frac{1}{\omega}\left\{ \omega_{11} \frac{x_1^2}{\sigma_1^2} + \omega_{22}\frac{x_2^2}{\sigma_2^2} + \ldots + 2\omega_{12}\frac{x_1 x_2}{\sigma_1 \sigma_2} + \ldots + 2\omega_{n.n-1}\frac{x_n x_{n-1}}{\sigma_n \sigma_{n-1}} \right\} \quad (12.26)$$

This is a form which is very frequently quoted.

12.29 From these formulæ several important results follow immediately.

In the first place, for any fixed values $h_2 \ldots h_n$ of $x_2 \ldots x_n$, the exponent (12.25) becomes—

$$\frac{x_1^2}{\sigma_{1.23\ldots n}^2} - 2r_{12.34\ldots n}\frac{x_1 h_2}{\sigma_{1.23\ldots n}\sigma_{2.13\ldots n}} - \ldots - \frac{2r_{1n.2\ldots(n-1)}x_1 h_n}{\sigma_{1.23\ldots n}\sigma_{n.1\ldots(n-1)}} + \text{constant terms}$$

$$= \left\{\frac{x_1}{\sigma_{1.23\ldots n}} - \frac{r_{12.3\ldots n}h_2}{\sigma_{2.13\ldots n}} - \ldots - \frac{r_{1n.2\ldots(n-1)}h_n}{\sigma_{n.1\ldots(n-:)}}\right\}^2 + \text{constant terms.}$$

Hence x_1 is distributed normally about the mean, m_1, given by

$$\frac{m_1}{\sigma_{1.23\ldots n}} = \frac{r_{12.3\ldots n}}{\sigma_{2.13\ldots n}}h_2 + \ldots + \frac{r_{1n.2\ldots(n-1)}}{\sigma_{n.1\ldots(n-1)}}h_n \quad . \quad (12.27)$$

Hence every array of every order is normally distributed.

It follows in a similar way that any linear function of the x's is distributed normally.

In particular, all deviations of any order and with any number of suffixes are normally distributed.

12.30 Secondly, as will be seen from (12.27), the regression of x_1 on the other variables is linear. It follows that the regression of any variate on any or all of the others is linear. In (12.27), for instance, the expressions $\dfrac{r_{12.3\ldots n}\sigma_{1.23\ldots n}}{\sigma_{2.13\ldots n}}$, etc., are the partial regressions $b_{12.3\ldots n}$, etc.

12.31 If, in equation (12.23) any fixed values be assigned to $x_{3.12}$ and all the following deviations, the correlation between x_1 and x_2, on expanding $x_{2.1}$, is, as we have seen, normal correlation. Similarly, if any fixed values be assigned to x_1, to $x_{4.123}$, and all the following deviations, on reducing $x_{3.12}$ to the second order we shall find that the correlation between $x_{2.1}$ and $x_{3.1}$ is normal correlation, the correlation coefficient being $r_{23.1}$, and so on. That is to say, using k to denote any group of secondary suffixes, (1) *the correlation between any two deviations $x_{m.k}$ and $x_{n.k}$ is normal correlation*; (2) *the correlation between the said deviation is $r_{mn.k}$ whatever the particular fixed values assigned to the remaining deviations.* The latter conclusion, it will be seen, renders the meaning of partial correlation coefficients much more definite in the case of normal correlation than in the general case. In the general case $r_{mn.k}$ represents merely the average correlation, so to speak, between $x_{m.k}$ and $x_{n.k}$: in the normal case $r_{mn.k}$ is constant for all the sub-groups corresponding to particular assigned values of the other variables. Thus in the case of three variables which are normally correlated, if we assign any given value to x_3, the correlation between the associated values of x_1 and x_2 is $r_{12.3}$: in the general case $r_{12.3}$, if actually worked out for the various sub-groups corresponding, say, to increasing values of x_3, would probably exhibit some continuous change, increasing or decreasing as the case might be.

12.32 It will be noticed that all the preceding work in this chapter assumes the correlations to have been determined by the product-sum formula. The method has also been applied to correlations obtained in other ways, e.g. from four-fold or contingency tables. In spite of the favourable results of an experimental test (Newbold, *Biometrika,* 1925, **17**, 251) this procedure remains of doubtful value.

12.33 It has been shown, however, that for the rank correlation coefficient τ a meaning can be assigned to partial coefficients calculated by a formula analogous to (12.13) for three variables, e.g., for three rankings 1, 2, 3, we have—

$$\tau_{12.3} = \frac{\tau_{12} - \tau_{13}\,\tau_{23}}{\{(1 - \tau_{13}^2)(1 - \tau_{23}^2)\}^{\frac{1}{2}}} \qquad . \qquad . \qquad . \quad (12.28)$$

expressing the relationship between rankings 1 and 2 if the influence of ranking 3 is eliminated. No similar results are known for Spearman's ρ.

SUMMARY

1. The regression equation of x_1 on $x_2, x_3 \ldots x_n$ is written—

$$x_1 = b_{12.34 \ldots n} x_2 + b_{13.24 \ldots n} x_3 + \cdots + b_{1n.23 \ldots (n-1)} x_n$$

The deviation $x_{1.23 \ldots n}$ is defined as

$$x_1 - b_{12.34 \ldots n} x_2 - b_{13.24 \ldots n} x_3 - \cdots - b_{1n.23 \cdots (n-1)} x_n$$

and $\sigma_{1.23 \ldots n}$ is the standard deviation of $x_{1.23 \ldots n}$.

2. The equations giving the regression coefficients are—

$$\Sigma(x_2 x_{1.23 \ldots n}) = 0$$
$$\Sigma(x_3 x_{1.23 \ldots n}) = 0$$
$$\cdot \qquad \cdot \qquad \cdot \qquad \cdot$$
$$\Sigma(x_n x_{1.23 \ldots n}) = 0$$

and similar equations with $x_{2.13 \ldots n}$, etc.

3. The product-sum of any two deviations is unaltered by omitting any or all of the secondary subscripts of the first, if, and only if, all the secondary subscripts of the first occur among the secondary subscripts of the second; conversely, the product-sum of any deviation of order p with a deviation of order $p+q$, the p subscripts being the same in each case, is unaltered by adding to the secondary subscripts of the former any or all of the q additional subscripts of the latter.

4.
$$b_{12.34 \ldots n} = r_{12.34 \ldots n} \frac{\sigma_{1.34 \ldots n}}{\sigma_{2.34 \ldots n}}$$

5. Any standard deviation of order p can be expressed in terms of a standard deviation of order $p-1$ and a correlation of order $p-1$. In fact,

$$\sigma^2_{1.23\ldots n}=\sigma^2_{1.23\ldots (n-1)}(1-r^2_{1n.23\ldots (n-1)})$$

6.
$$\sigma^2_{p.23\ldots n}=\frac{\omega\sigma_p{}^2}{\omega_{pp}}$$

where ω is the determinant

$$\begin{vmatrix} 1 & r_{12} & r_{13} & \cdots & r_{1n} \\ r_{21} & 1 & r_{23} & \cdots & r_{2n} \\ & \cdot & \cdot & \cdot & \\ r_{n1} & r_{n2} & r_{n3} & \cdots & 1 \end{vmatrix}$$

and ω_{pp} is the minor of the element in the pth row and the pth column.

7. Any regression of order p may be expressed in terms of regressions of order $p-1$. In fact,

$$b_{12.34\ldots n}=\frac{b_{12.34\ldots (n-1)}-b_{1n.34\ldots (n-1)}b_{n2.34\ldots (n-1)}}{1-b_{2n.34\ldots (n-1)}b_{n2.34\ldots (n-1)}}$$

8. Similarly, for correlations—

$$r_{12.34\ldots n}=\frac{r_{12.34\ldots (n-1)}-r_{1n.34\ldots n-1)}r_{2n.34\ldots (n-1)}}{(1-r^2_{1n.34\ldots (n-1)})^{\frac{1}{2}}(1-r^2_{2n.34\ldots (n-1)})^{\frac{1}{2}}}$$

9. The coefficient of multiple correlation $R_{1(23\ldots n)}$ is given by

$$\sigma^2_{1.23\ldots n}=\sigma^2_1(1-R^2_{1(23\ldots n)})$$

or

$$\frac{\omega}{\omega_{11}}=1-R^2_{1(23\ldots n)}$$

Also,

$$1-R^2_{1(23\ldots n)}=(1-r^2_{12})(1-r^2_{13.2})(1-r^2_{14.23})\ldots(1-r^2_{1n.23\ldots (n-1)})$$

10. R is necessarily not less than zero. If it is zero, the variate to which it refers is completely uncorrelated with the other variates. If $R=1$, there is a linear relation between the variates.

11. The multivariate normal surface may be written—

$$y_{12\ldots n}=\frac{N}{(2\pi)^{\frac{n}{2}}\sigma_1\sigma_2\ldots\sigma_n\sqrt{\omega}}e^{-\frac{1}{2}\phi}$$

where

$$\phi=\frac{1}{\omega}\left\{\omega_{11}\frac{x_1{}^2}{\sigma_1{}^2}+\omega_{22}\frac{x_2{}^2}{\sigma_2{}^2}+\cdots+2\omega_{12}\frac{x_1x_2}{\sigma_1\sigma_2}+\cdots+2\omega_{n.n-1}\frac{x_nx_{n-1}}{\sigma_n\sigma_{n-1}}\right\}$$

EXERCISES

12.1 (Hooker, *J. R. Stat. Soc.* 1907, **65**, 1). The following means, standard deviations and correlations are found for

X_1=Seed-hay crops in cwts. per acre,
X_2=Spring rainfall in inches,
X_3=Accumulated temperature above 42° F. in spring,

in a certain district of England during twenty years.

$$M_1 = 28\cdot02 \qquad \sigma_1 = 4.42 \qquad r_{12} = +0\cdot80$$
$$M_2 = 4\cdot91 \qquad \sigma_2 = 1\cdot10 \qquad r_{13} = -0\cdot40$$
$$M_3 = 594 \qquad \sigma_3 = 85 \qquad r_{23} = -0\cdot56$$

Find the partial correlations and the regression equation for hay-crop on spring rainfall and accumulated temperature.

12.2 In Exercise 12.1, find the multiple correlation coefficient of each variate on the other two.

12.3 (The following figures must be taken as an illustration only : the data on which they were based do not refer to uniform times or areas.)

X_1=Deaths of infants under 1 year per 1,000 births in same year (infantile mortality).
X_2=Number per thousand of married women occupied for gain.
X_3=Death-rate of persons over 5 years of age per 10,000.
X_3=Number per thousand of population living two or more to a room (overcrowding).

Taking the figures below for thirty urban areas in England and Wales, find the partial correlations and the regression equation for infantile mortality on the other factors.

$$M_1 = 164 \qquad \sigma_1 = 20\cdot0 \qquad r_{12} = +0\cdot49 \qquad r_{23} = +0\cdot15$$
$$M_2 = 158 \qquad \sigma_2 = 74\cdot9 \qquad r_{13} = +0\cdot78 \qquad r_{24} = -0\cdot37$$
$$M_3 = 143 \qquad \sigma_3 = 22\cdot4 \qquad r_{14} = +0\cdot20 \qquad r_{34} = +0\cdot23$$
$$M_4 = 205 \qquad \sigma_4 = 130\cdot0$$

12.4 In Exercise 12.3, find the multiple correlation coefficient of X_1 on X_2 and X_3; and of X_1 on the other three variates.

12.5 (Data from W. F. Ogburn, " Factors in the Variation of Crime among Cities," *Jour. Amer. Stat. Assoc.*, 1935, **30**, 12).
For certain large cities in the U.S.A.—

X_1=Crime rate, being the number of known offences per thousand of population.
X_2=Percentage of male inhabitants.
X_3=Percentage of total inhabitants who are foreign-born males.

X_4=Number of children under 5 years of age per thousand married women between 15 and 44 years of age.

X_5=Church membership, being number of church members 13 years of age and over per 100 of total population 13 years of age and over.

$M_1=19\cdot9$	$\sigma_1=7\cdot9$	$r_{12}=+0\cdot44$	$r_{24}=-0\cdot19$
$M_2=49\cdot2$	$\sigma_2=1\cdot3$	$r_{13}=-0\cdot34$	$r_{25}=-0\cdot35$
$M_3=10\cdot2$	$\sigma_3=4\cdot6$	$r_{14}=-0\cdot31$	$r_{34}=+0\cdot44$
$M_4=481\cdot4$	$\sigma_4=74\cdot4$	$r_{15}=-0\cdot14$	$r_{35}=+0\cdot33$
$M_5=41\cdot6$	$\sigma_5=10\cdot8$	$r_{23}=+0\cdot25$	$r_{45}=+0\cdot85$

Find the regression equation of X_1 on the other four variables.   Find also $R_{1(2345)}$.

Find, further, $r_{15.3}$, $r_{15.4}$ and $r_{15.34}$.   Discuss the influence of church membership on crime for these data.

12.6   Show that for n variates there are $^nC_2$ total correlation coefficients, $(n-2)^nC_2$ correlation coefficients of order 1, $^{n-2}C_2{}^nC_2$ correlation coefficients of order 2, and $^{n-2}C_s{}^nC_2$ of order s.   Hence show that there are $n(n-1)2^{n-3}$ correlation coefficients and $n(n-1)2^{n-2}$ regression coefficients.

12.7   Find the number of multiple correlation coefficients of order s and the total number of such coefficients for n variables.

12.8   If all the correlations of order zero are equal, say $=r$, what are the values of the partial correlations of successive orders ?

Under the same conditions, what is the limiting value of r if all the equal correlations are negative and n variables have been observed ?

12.9   Write down from inspection the values of the partial correlations for the three variables

$$X_1,\ X_2,\ \text{and}\ X_3=aX_1+bX_2$$

12.10   If the relation

$$ax_1+bx_2+cx_3=0$$

holds for all sets of values of x_1, x_2 and x_3, what must the partial correlations be ?

CHAPTER THIRTEEN

CORRELATION AND REGRESSION

SOME PRACTICAL PROBLEMS

13.1 The student should be careful to note that the coefficient of correlation, like an average or a measure of dispersion, only exhibits in a summary form one aspect of the facts on which it is based. Some very real difficulties arise both in the selection of variables for which the coefficient is to be computed and in the interpretation of the results when obtained. In the present chapter we shall consider some of these practical problems and indicate how they mould from the outset the scope and nature of an inquiry based on correlations and regressions.

The modifiable unit

13.2 Table 13.1 shows, for each of the 48 agricultural counties of England in 1936, the yields per acre of wheat and potatoes. The order of arrangement is the one given in the official *Agricultural Statistics*.

It is a natural and meaningful question to ask whether there is any correlation between these yields, so that, for example, we may know whether an area of high wheat-yield is also one of high potato-yield.

Taking the values of Table 13.1 as they stand we find a correlation of +0·2189, a value which the student can verify for himself as an exercise. But we observe that these yields per acre are given for 48 geographical areas the boundaries of which are quite arbitrary so far as crop yields are concerned. What would happen if we took other geographical areas? Should we get the same correlation or not?

We can explore this question to some extent by combining the areas as given. Suppose we group the counties in pairs and determine for each of the 24 resulting pairs the simple arithmetic mean yields as exemplified in the figures following Table 13.1 on the next page.

Since most of the areas are contiguous this is the kind of result we might get if larger areas ·than counties were recorded. The yields per acre so calculated are not necessarily those of the grouped pairs because the total yields may be greater in one member of the pair than in the other ; but the process will serve for the purposes of illustration.

There are now 24 members and the correlation between the yields will be found to be +0·2963 against +0·2189 for the original 48. If we repeat the process and group our 24 pairs (in order as they stand) we find for the resulting 12 members a correlation of +0·5757. In practice we should not compute a correlation for a smaller number of values but if we pursue the condensing process to the bitter end and group our 12 values into 6, we find a correlation of $+0\cdot7649$; and finally, by grouping the six into three, we have a correlation of $+0\cdot9902$.

TABLE 13.1.—Yields of wheat and potatoes in 48 counties in England in 1936

County	Wheat (cwts. per acre)	Potatoes (tons per acre)	County	Wheat (cwts. per acre)	Potatoes (tons per acre)
Bedford	16·0	5·3	Northampton	14·3	4·9
Huntingdon	16·0	6·6	Peterborough	14·4	5·6
Cambridge	16·4	6·1	Buckingham	15·2	6·4
Ely	20·5	5·5	Oxford	14·1	6·9
Suffolk, West	18·2	6·9	Warwick	15·4	5·6
Suffolk, East	16·3	6·1	Shropshire	16·5	6·1
Essex	17·7	6·4	Worcester	14·2	5·7
Hertford	15·3	6·3	Gloucester	13·2	5·0
Middlesex	16·5	7·8	Wiltshire	13·8	6·5
Norfolk	16·9	8·3	Hereford	14·4	6·2
Lincoln (Holland)	21·8	5·7	Somerset	13·4	5·2
,, (Kesteven)	15·5	6·2	Dorset	11·2	6·6
,, (Lindsey)	15·8	6·0	Devon	14·4	5·8
Yorkshire (East Riding)	16·1	6·1	Cornwall	15·4	6·3
Kent	18·5	6·6	Northumberland	18·5	6·3
Surrey	12·7	4·8	Durham	16·4	5·8
Sussex (East)	15·7	4·9	Yorkshire (N.R.)	17·0	5·9
Sussex (West)	14·3	5·1	,, (W.R)	16·9	6·5
Berkshire	13·8	5·5	Cumberland	17·5	5·8
Hampshire	12·8	6·7	Westmorland	15·8	5·7
Isle of Wight	12·0	6·5	Lancashire	19·2	7·2
Nottingham	15·6	5·2	Cheshire	17·7	6·5
Leicester	15·8	5·2	Derby	15·2	5·4
Rutland	16·6	7·1	Stafford	17·1	6·3

	Wheat (cwts.)	Potatoes (tons)
Bedfordshire and Huntingdonshire	16·0	5·95
Cambridgeshire and Ely	18·45	5·80
Suffolk West and Suffolk East	17·25	6·5

13.3 We have thus found correlations ranging from $0\cdot2189$ to $0\cdot9902$. Nor is this all. We may well expect that if our 48 counties were divided into smaller areas the resulting correlation would be smaller than $0\cdot2189$. On the face of it we seem to be able to produce any value of the correlation from 0 to 1 merely by choosing an appropriate size of the unit of area for which we measure the yields. Is there then, any " real " correlation between wheat and potato-yields or are our results illusory ?

13.4 This example serves to bring out an important distinction between two different types of data to which correlation analysis may be applied.

The difficulty does not arise when we are considering the relationship, say, between heights of fathers and sons. The ultimate unit in this case is the individual father or son whose height is a unique non-modifiable numerical measurement. We cannot divide a single pair of father-and-son into smaller units ; nor can we amalgamate two pairs to give measurements of the same type as that of the single pair. The same is true of the data of Table 9.1 (correlation between measurements on shells), of Table 9.2 (correlation between ages of husband and wife), and of Table 9.4 (correlation between age and weekly milk-yield of cows) — the shell, the married couple and the cow are *non-modifiable units.*

13.5 On the other hand, our geographical areas chosen for the calculation of crop yields are *modifiable units*, and necessarily so. Since it is impossible (or at any rate agriculturally impracticable) to grow wheat and potatoes on the same piece of ground simultaneously we must, to give our investigation any meaning, consider an area containing both wheat and potatoes ; and this area is modifiable at choice. A similar effect arises whenever we try to measure concomitant variation extending over continuous regions of space or time. For example, a regional death-rate must necessarily relate to a modifiable geographical area ; and rainfall, regional prices, production of goods or services are quantities of the same type. In the case where observations are taken over time, examples are imports and exports, cost of living, and stock-exchange prices. Suppose, for instance, that we are interested in a possible relationship over time between the marriage-rate and the wholesale price index, the suggestion being that in prosperous times, when the price index is relatively high, more people can afford to marry. Are we to correlate figures compiled on a monthly basis, a quarterly basis, an annual basis or a triennial basis ? The unit of time is essentially modifiable.

13.6 From the example we have given as to crop-yields it will be clear that the magnitude of a correlation will, in general, depend on the unit chosen if that unit is modifiable. Our correlations will accordingly measure the relationship between the variates *for the specified units chosen for the work.* They have no absolute validity independently of those units, but are relative to them. They measure, as it were, not only the variation of the quantities under consideration, but the properties of the unit-mesh which we have imposed on the system in order to measure it.

13.7 The student should not now go to the other extreme and claim that, since a large range of values of correlation coefficients may be obtained according to the choice of a modifiable unit, a particular value has no significance and that any inquiry based on correlations in the modifiable case is useless. It is of some significance to know that the correlation between wheat- and potato-yields in the 48 counties of England in 1936 was $0 \cdot 2189$. A comparison of a series of such values over a period of years might well throw light on changes in farm practice or soil fertility ; the correlation and the corresponding regression indicates how far we may expect to predict the potato crop from a knowledge of the earlier-harvested wheat crop—in this particular case, not very far. But we must emphasise the necessity, in this type of work, of not losing sight of the fact that our results depend on our units.   The point assumes particular importance when we are trying to disentangle causal factors. It is a fact that wheat- and potato-yields in the 48 counties of England were correlated in 1936 ; but it is a geographical as well as an agricultural fact.   We cannot infer without additional inquiry that soil which produces good crops of wheat tends to produce good crops of potatoes.

The attenuation effect

13.8   There is a distinct type of grouping-effect in correlation analysis which leads to a very similar increase in correlations with increasing size of geographical area.   Suppose we are interested in the relationship between income and size of family in a certain country.   Ignoring minor difficulties as to what constitutes a family in some cases, we have a non-modifiable unit.   If time, patience and money were available in sufficient quantity we might be able to ascertain the income and family-size for each unit in the country ; but in practice (unless we performed an *ad hoc* sampling inquiry) we should probably have regard to totals and averages available for regions and districts.   We might, for instance, attempt to estimate the mean number per family for census districts and estimate the mean income from fiscal or local taxation data.   Effectively we should then be grouping the non-modifiable units into larger units which are themselves, within limits, modifiable.

13.9   Suppose we have two variables x, y each of which can be regarded as the sum of a systematic and a random element

$$\left.\begin{array}{l} x = \xi + e \\ y = \eta + f \end{array}\right\} \qquad . \qquad . \qquad . \qquad . \qquad (13.1)$$

We may, for example, imagine that there is some causal factor affecting ξ and η simultaneously and hence resulting in a correlation between x and y ; but that other components e and f are unrelated to ξ and η and to each other.

Without loss of generality we may suppose that ξ and e are measured about their means, in which case x will also be measured about its mean. We then have

$$\Sigma(x^2) = \Sigma(\xi^2) + 2\Sigma(\xi e) + \Sigma(e^2)$$

and since ξ and e are uncorrelated we have, on dividing by the number of the population

$$\text{var } x = \text{var } \xi + \text{var } e \qquad . \qquad . \qquad . \qquad (13.2)$$

where we write var x for the variance of x.   Equation (13.2) is a particular case of a theorem which we shall consider in more detail in the next chapter (14.2).

Similarly we shall have

$$\text{var } y = \text{var } \eta + \text{var } f \qquad . \qquad . \qquad . \qquad (13.3)$$

and, writing cov (x, y) for the covariance of x and y

$$\text{cov } (x, y) = \text{cov } (\xi, \eta) \qquad . \qquad . \qquad . \qquad (13.4)$$

Let us now denote the correlation between x and y by r and that between ξ and η by r'. We then have

$$r = \frac{\text{cov } (x, y)}{\{\text{var } x \text{ var } y\}^{\frac{1}{2}}}$$

$$= \frac{\text{cov } (\xi, \eta)}{\{(\text{var } \xi + \text{var } e)(\text{var } \eta + \text{var } f)\}^{\frac{1}{2}}}$$

$$= \frac{\text{cov } (\xi, \eta)}{\{\text{var } \xi \text{ var } \eta\}^{\frac{1}{2}}} \cdot \frac{1}{\left\{\left(1 + \dfrac{\text{var } e}{\text{var } \xi}\right)\left(1 + \dfrac{\text{var } f}{\text{var } \eta}\right)\right\}^{\frac{1}{2}}}$$

$$= \frac{r'}{\left\{\left(1 + \dfrac{\text{var } e}{\text{var } \xi}\right)\left(1 + \dfrac{\text{var } f}{\text{var } \eta}\right)\right\}^{\frac{1}{2}}} \qquad . \qquad . \qquad . \qquad (13.5)$$

Now a variance is essentially non-negative and hence each part of the denominator on the right hand side of (13.5) is greater than unity. Consequently r is less than r'; that is to say, a correlation calculated from the observed values is reduced, or we may say *attenuated* by the effect of the factors expressed by e and f.

13.10 Now suppose that we group units, bearing x and y values, either geographically or in time. In virtue of a sampling effect which we shall study later (Chapter 17) the proportionate variance var e/var ξ will be reduced. For the present we assume this; but the reader will probably accept it as probable from the consideration that systematic effects represented by ξ and η will be cumulative, whereas random effects represented by e and f tend to cancel out—the larger the number of units we group, the less, relatively speaking, will their total be affected by erratic fluctuations.

It follows that the denominator in (13.5) will also be reduced as we increase the size of the grouping; and consequently, if r' is constant r will continually increase as we group more and more individuals.

13.11 This is the kind of effect we frequently find. It is not necessarily due to the system which we have just discussed, though that system provides a possible explanation. There may be other effects such as " patchiness " in the total area under consideration, which would lead to r' itself changing with increased grouping and might either enhance or counteract the effect of grouping on random components. What explanation we seek in individual cases depends on the individual circumstances. We can only leave the reader with the warning to watch very carefully the possibility of grouping effects, particularly in economic investigations.

Example 13.1—(Gehlke and Biehl, *J. Am. Stat. Ass. Supp*, 1934, **29**, 169)

A study was made of the relationship between male juvenile delinquency, expressed as absolute numbers, and the median monthly rental in Cleveland, Ohio. The 252 census tracts were grouped successively into 200, 175, 150, 125, 100, 50 and 25 areas, consisting so far as possible of the same size and comprising contiguous territory.

The correlation coefficients, including that for the original 252 tracts, ran $-0 \cdot 502$, $-0 \cdot 569$, $-0 \cdot 580$, $-0 \cdot 606$, $-0 \cdot 662$, $-0 \cdot 667$, $-0 \cdot 685$, $-0 \cdot 763$. The characteristic increase of correlation with size of area is clear. The corresponding correlations between *rates* of male juvenile delinquency and median monthly rentals were $-0 \cdot 516$, $-0 \cdot 504$, $-0 \cdot 480$, $-0 \cdot 475$, $-0 \cdot 563$, $-0 \cdot 524$, $-0 \cdot 579$, $-0 \cdot 621$. Here the increase is not uniform but it begins to appear as the grouping becomes more condensed.

TABLE 13.2.—Numbers of wireless receiving licences issued during the year in the U.K. and numbers of notified mental defectives in England and Wales

(Date from Statistical Abstract for the United Kingdom. Cmd. 5903, 1939)

Year	Number of wireless receiving licences issued (thousands)	Number of notified mental defectives per 10,000 of estimated population
1924	1,350	8
1925	1,960	8
1926	2,270	9
1927	2,483	10
1928	2,730	11
1929	3,091	11
1930	3,647	12
1931	4,620	16
1932	5,497	18
1933	6,260	19
1934	7,012	20
1935	7,618	21
1936	8,131	22
1937	8,593	23

Note : The year for the purposes of the wireless licence records is the fiscal year April/March ; for the mental defective records the census date is January 1st.

Nonsense correlations

13.12 In Table 13.2 we show the number of wireless receiving licences taken out from 1924 to 1937 in the United Kingdom and the number of notified mental defectives per 10,000 in England and Wales for the same period. A glance at these figures shows that they are very highly correlated. The correlation coefficient is, in fact, 0·998.

Now, facetiousness apart, it cannot be contended that listening to the radio conduces to notifiable mental defect or vice-versa. The correlation appears to be nonsensical. Before dismissing it as such, however, we must concede that the possibility of causal connection cannot be entirely excluded. For instance, it might be argued that the period in question was one of great technical progress in many scientific fields; that one effect of this movement was the development of broadcasting and the general spread of the practice of listening evinced by the increased number of licences taken out; that another effect was the greater interest in psychological ailments and increased facilities for treatment, resulting in either more discoveries of mental defect or greater readiness to submit cases to medical notice. Whether this is the right explanation is doubtful, but it is a possible rational explanation of what at first sight seems absurd.

13.13 The more reasonable explanation is that the strength of the correlation is an accident; and our point will have been made if the reader understands what sort of an accident it is. When we consider sampling in Chapter 16 *et seq.* we shall discuss the nature of sampling distributions and shall point out that occasionally, by sheer chance, an improbable event may arise. In sampling from a bivariate normal population, for instance, as we have pointed out above (**9.28**) a high correlation may appear even when the parent is uncorrelated, albeit rather rarely. This, however, arises in sampling where members are chosen independently. In the case of our nonsense-correlation we have taken a sequence of values moving through time, each very dependent on the one before. Our present effect, accordingly, is not a sampling fluctuation as ordinarily understood.

13.14 It may, none the less, be regarded as accidental. Suppose we have two series in time, each of which is moving fairly steadily upwards or downwards (i.e. increasing or decreasing more or less uniformly from one year to the next). Clearly such series will appear as highly correlated, positively or negatively, if we happen to choose for consideration periods of time in which the movement of each series is in the same direction. But the reasons for the movements may be quite unrelated or at least so remote that we cannot claim any "real" connection between the two series. Increased numbers of radio licences are due to the invention of radio communication and the steady movement towards the saturation of a latent demand. This is probably quite unrelated to the development in notifications of mental defectives. It may well be that in a future period the numbers of licences may decline with a declining population while the numbers of notified defectives increase.

13.15 It is possible to have nonsense-correlations in space as well as in time, though good examples are hard to find. As we move from north to south across Europe, for example, the proportion of Roman Catholics in the population probably increases—there are few in Scotland and a great many in Sicily. At the same time we should probably find a decrease in the average height. If, therefore, we were to correlate height and proportion of Catholics (we have not tried the experiment) we should probably find quite a substantial negative correlation ; but if so it would be obvious nonsense in our present usage of the word.

Variate-differences

13.16 Figure 13.1 shows, for the period 1838-1914, the movements of (a) the infantile mortality (deaths of infants under one year of age per 1,000 births in the same year) and (b) the general mortality (deaths at all ages per 1,000 living) in England and Wales. A very cursory inspection of the diagram shows that the two varied together—when the infantile mortality rose from one year to the next the general mortality did the same, with only seven or eight exceptions to the rule during the whole period under review. The correlation between the annual values of the two may be expected to be positive, because the infantile death-rate forms part of the general death-rate ; but it would not be very high as the general mortality fell more or less steadily from 1875 onwards whereas the infantile mortality rose to a peak in 1898. During a long period of time the correlation may nearly vanish, for the two mortalities are affected by largely different causes. In this sense, a high correlation for a short period might be "nonsense" (though this is stretching our usage rather far) if it was interpreted as implying a strong causal nexus in the long run.

13.17 To exhibit the closeness of the relation between infantile and general mortality *for such causes as show marked changes from one year to the next* it will be best to proceed by correlating the annual *changes*, and not the annual values. The work would be arranged in the following form (only sufficient years being given to exhibit the principle of the process), and the correlation worked out between the figures of columns 3 and 5—

1 Year	2 Infantile mortality per 1,000 births	3 Increase or decrease from year before	4 General mortality per 1,000 living	5 Increase or decrease from year before
1838	159	—	22·4	—
1839	151	−8	21·8	−0·6
1840	154	+3	22·9	+1·1
1841	145	−9	21·6	−1·3
1842	152	+7	21·7	+0·1
1843	150	−2	21·2	−0·5

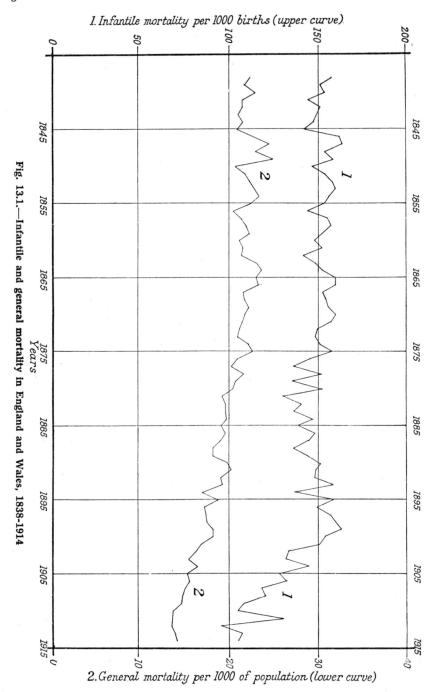

Fig. 13.1.—Infantile and general mortality in England and Wales, 1838-1914

For the period to which the diagram refers, viz. 1838–1914, the following constants were found by this method—

Infantile mortality, mean annual change   − 0·71
,,   ,,   , standard deviation   10·76
General mortality, mean annual change   − 0·11
,,   ,,   , standard deviation   1·13
Coefficient of correlation   + 0·69

This is a much higher correlation than would arise from the mere fact that the deaths of infants form part of the general mortality, and consequently there must be a high correlation between the annual changes in the mortality of those who are over and under 1 year of age, respectively.

13.18 The procedure of the foregoing section has been called the " variate-difference correlation method." By taking first differences instead of the variate values themselves, the slower changes of the two variates with time are to some extent eliminated, and we are able to study the effect of short-term variations. To eliminate the secular changes more completely it may be desirable to proceed to second differences, i.e. to work out the successive differences of the differences in column 3 and column 5 before correlating. It may even be desirable to proceed to third, fourth or higher differences before correlating. The method should, however, be used with caution in such cases, particularly with short series. Correlation coefficients obtained from higher differences are not always reliable, and their interpretation becomes a matter of considerable difficulty. We return to the subject later in Chapters 26 and 27 on time-series, where will also be found a method more adapted to the case of time-series in which wave-like oscillations appear to be imposed on the general trend.

13.19 When an inquiry involving correlation or regression analysis is undertaken the variables to be considered are sometimes determined at the outset by the nature of the questions which are to be answered. If, for example, we are asked to investigate the relationship between the annual suicide rate and the annual number of bankruptcies in a particular country our variables are specified and all that remains is to obtain the data and to work on them. There may, indeed, be practical difficulties in obtaining the data for the right years or the right areas but this is not a matter in which theoretical considerations can help us.

13.20 More usually, the type of inquiry we are asked to undertake is less definitely specified. We may wish to investigate the relationship between a number of quantities or factors which are not directly measureable, e.g. the relation between weather and the prevalence of epidemic disease. There is no single measurement corresponding to " weather " and we have to select a number of variables to represent it such as temperature, rainfall, or cloudiness. Each of these, in general, may be modifiable or non-modifiable and we have an additional element of choice in the precise form of the variate which we select.

13.21 In the extreme case we may not even know which factors will emerge from our analysis as important. Suppose we are interested in the factors which encourage or prevent tuberculosis and attempt to throw some light on the subject by considering variations in the incidence of the disease in different areas. What factors are we to select as " independent " ? It is easy to write down a long list of possible factors—income, overcrowding, rainfall, sunshine, height above sea-level and so forth. Assuming for the moment that we can measure all these factors, how far do we have to take them into account, and can we do so without rendering the analysis quite unwieldy ?

There is no simple answer to these questions. In the remainder of the chapter we shall give a short account of some of the resources at the investigator's disposal in particular cases.

A practical example

13.22 Some of the questions which arise are illustrated in an investigation by Hooker (*J. R. Stat. Soc.* 1907, **65**, 1) into the relationship between the yield of certain crops (cereals, roots and hay) and the weather.

The material question here was how far crop-yields *in the same area* vary with the weather. Geographical variation was therefore not in point, and Hooker considered the series of values over a period of years for a single area. Climatic, soil, and farm-practice conditions vary so much over the United Kingdom that any attempt to take geographical variation into account would have complicated the analysis enormously. By choosing one area we eliminate some of the variables and can concentrate on climatic factors. Our gain in simplicity may, of course, be offset by loss of generality—we cannot assume that our results will hold good for other areas where different conditions exist. We must also be careful to ascertain that, even in the area under consideration, our series of years is not so long that there are material changes which would obscure climatic effects, such as exhaustion of soil fertility or a switch from arable to grass farming.

13.23 There then arises the problem of selecting the appropriate area. The desiderata are (1) that it should be reasonably homogeneous from the meteorological standpoint and (2) it should be large enough to present a representative variety of soil. Hooker chose a group of eastern counties, consisting of Lincoln, Huntingdon, Cambridge, Norfolk, Suffolk, Essex, Bedford and Hertford, as fulfilling these conditions. The group included the county with the largest acreage of each of the ten crops investigated with the single exception of permanent grass.

13.24 Produce statistics for the more important crops of England and Wales have been issued by the Ministry of Agriculture since 1885. The figures are based on estimates of yield furnished by local official estimators all over the country. Estimates are published for separate counties and for groups of counties (divisions), but not for smaller units of area, though the crop estimators usually submit returns for parishes.

The data in this case are thus provided by the official publications. Their nature limits the inquiry in space (since we must choose areas based on counties) and in time (since figures are not available prior to 1885). We must also assume that the estimates are reasonably accurate. The field of choice in most economic inquiries is limited by such factors as these.

13.25 Having decided on our crop-figures we have to consider the weather factors. The produce of a crop is dependent on the weather of a long preceding period, and it is naturally desired to find the influence of the weather at successive stages during this period, and to determine, for each crop, which period of the year is of most critical importance as regards weather. It must be remembered, however, that the times of both sowing and harvest are themselves very largely dependent on the weather, and consequently, on an average of many years, the limits of the critical period will not be very well defined. If, therefore, we correlate the produce of the crop (X) with the characteristics of the weather (Y) during successive intervals of the year, it will be as well not to make these intervals too short. It was accordingly decided to take successive groups of 8 weeks, overlapping each other by 4 weeks, i.e. weeks 1–8, 5–12, etc. Correlation coefficients were thus obtained at 4-week intervals, but based on 8 weeks' weather.

13.26 Finally, we have to decide what measurable characteristics of the weather are to be taken into account. Prior knowledge suggests that the two most important are rainfall and temperature. The two provide quite enough labour for a first investigation.

(a) The rainfall for a particular county is to some extent a modifiable unit, for no measurements are taken of the total precipitation on a given area. Hooker took records of weekly rainfall from eight stations within the total area under consideration and used the average of these figures as the first characteristic of the weather.

(b) Temperatures were taken from the records of the same stations. The average temperatures, however, do not give quite the sort of information that is required : at temperatures below a certain limit (about 42° Fahr.) there is very little growth, and the growth increases in rapidity as the temperature rises above this point (within limits). It was therefore decided to utilise the figures for " accumulated temperatures above 42° Fahr.," i.e. the total number of day-degrees above 42° during each of the 8-weekly periods, as the second characteristic of the weather ; these " accumulated temperatures," moreover, show much larger variations than mean temperatures.

Reference should be made to Hooker's paper for a more detailed account of the inquiry and its results.

Economy in the number of variables

13.27 In the agricultural case we have just considered there was a large body of prior knowledge available to assist in determining the field of inquiry and the variables which were likely to give significant and meaningful results. This is not always the case. In discussing the geographical variation of mortality our prior knowledge would suggest considering as independent variates such factors as age-distribution, proportion of males and density of population. We could, however, without difficulty extend the list of possible factors almost indefinitely, e.g. by including hours of sunshine, wage levels, adequacy of medical attention and standards of nutrition. In an investigation into the variation of crime among American cities Ogburn (*J. Am. Stat. Ass.* 1935, **30**, 12) listed no fewer than 26 factors including birth-rate, proportion of negroes and proportion of foreign-born immigrants, as well as the more obvious ones such as efficacy of the police system and proportion of males.

13.28 With adequate data and sufficient patience, of course, we can work out the regression of our variable on all these others. But the practical difficulties, including those of computation, are prohibitive ; and sometimes there are theoretical difficulties into the bargain. The reader who consults some earlier inquiries in which arithmetical enthusiasm was not tempered by common sense will find that there are more variables than observations and that the resulting high correlations may mean next to nothing. In any case, ten variables are about as many as can be conveniently managed, and even that number throws a severe strain on the computer.

13.29 It is therefore necessary at an early stage to economise in the number of variables—

(*a*) As in the agricultural example we may limit the scope of the inquiry. This is what the physicist does in the laboratory by holding other factors as constant as experimental conditions will allow. By taking a particular factor as constant (within reasonable limits) we may ignore its effect on the regression equation. Subject to practical limitations we exclude in this way those factors which are expected to have the least effect. We can always bring them into account later one by one if necessary.

(*b*) Certain of the variables may be grouped and expressed, at least approximately, in terms of one of them or of some other summarising coefficient. In considering the relationship between employment and retail prices, for instance, we need not bring into account as a separate variate every retail commodity entering into the household budget. An index of retail prices would probably be quite sufficient. Again, in a mortality inquiry we might suppose that ability to pay for medical attention and standards of nutrition were sufficiently closely linked to wage-levels to justify us in using wage-levels to represent capacity to pay the doctor's bills and to buy enough food.

(c) As we have already mentioned, we may proceed by selecting two or three of the most promising variables to see whether the regression line containing them satisfactorily accounts for the data (as judged, for example, by the magnitude of the multiple correlation coefficient.)   If it does not we may add further variates until a good fit is obtained.

13.30   To conclude this chapter we may refer to some approaches to the problem of statistical relationship which have been developed for particular purposes but are capable of more general application.

A regression equation expresses the " best " linear relationship between a dependent variable and a set of given independent variables, " best " in this connection being somewhat arbitrarily defined by minimising a certain sum of squares.   Let us look at this geometrically.   Given a set of points in n dimensions where n is the total number of variables, dependent and independent together, we find as the regression of one on the others that plane which lies closest to the points ; " closest " being defined so as to minimise the sum of squares of distances from the points to the place *in the direction parallel to the axis of the dependent variate*.   The student can picture this situation easily enough in the two- and three-dimensional case ; and further dimensions, though impossible to imagine spatially, add nothing new to the principles.

13.31   Now our cluster of points, though specified by means of n variables and hence in an n dimensional space, may in fact lie, at least approximately, in a space of fewer dimensions.   For instance the cluster of points of Figure 12.1 (lying in three dimensions) might perhaps lie on a plane or even on a line.   We may, therefore, be able to find new variables, expressible as linear functions of the old, which represent the data equally well but require fewer independent variables.

The approach is one aspect of the subject known as *factor analysis*.   It seeks to isolate, from a complex of variables, a small number of factors which will account for most of the variation. We cannot give here any indication of the various techniques which have been developed, mainly in psychology, to carry out the analysis, for most of them involve advanced mathematics as well as some complicated theoretical problems.   The reader who wishes to pursue the subject may refer to *Factor Analysis* by Holzinger and Harman or to Kendall's *A Course in Multivariate Analysis*, 1961.

13.32   A somewhat different line of inquiry known as *confluence analysis* has been followed by Scandinavian writers, mainly by Ragnar Frisch. This involves heavy calculations and in effect, depends on working out all the possible regressions in order to see how far the appearance of a new variate disturbs the previous coefficients.   For some account of the method see Frisch's *Confluence Analysis*, 1934 (Oslo) and Reiersol, *Econometrica*, 1941, **2**, 1.

SUMMARY

1. Units may be modifiable or non-modifiable. For modifiable units the values of correlations depend on the size of the units and must be interpreted accordingly.

2. When units are grouped and correlations calculated from some summary features of the group, such as averages, there may be a tendency for the correlations to increase with the size of the grouping. Conversely as the grouping becomes finer the coefficients may be attenuated.

3. Correlations for series which are developing in time may be misleadingly high if the series accidentally happen to move togethei.

4. To elucidate short-term variation in time-series it may be preferable to correlate changes from one period to the next rather than the actual values of the series. This conception is the origin of the variate-difference method which must, however, be used with great caution.

5. In a general inquiry involving correlation or regression analysis efforts are necessary to economise in the number of independent variables.

EXERCISES

13.1   Examine how far Tables 9.5 and 9.6 are based on modifiable units.

13.2   The following table shows, for the United Kingdom, the population and the infantile mortality for certain years—

Year	Population (000)	Deaths of infants per 1,000 births approx. at census date
1871	31,485	144
1881	34,885	134
1891	37,733	141
1901	41,459	140
1911	45,222	108
1921	47,123	81
1931	47,289	67

Show that the values are correlated.   How far would you regard this as a nonsense-correlation ?

(Data from the Statistical Abstract for the U.K.Cmd. 5908, 1939.   The figures for 1931 exclude the territory now forming Eire but this may be ignored for the purpose of the example.)

13.3   The following table shows the number of steam ships registered as belonging to the United Kingdom and the receipts from horse-drawn vehicle-licenses in Great Britain for certain years—

Year	Number of steam vessels	Receipts from licences on horse-drawn vehicles
1924	10,690	140,719
1925	10,526	118,847
1926	10,262	98,459
1927	10,032	80,302
1928	9,959	64,675
1929	9,855	51,199
1930	9,729	40,878
1931	9,529	32,303
1932	9,248	25,700
1933	8,900	21,288
1934	8,622	17,661
1935	8,306	14,481
1936	8,032	11,579
1937	7,702	9,177

Bearing in mind the development of diesel-propelled ships and of the motor car, consider how far the correlation between these figures may be regarded as nonsense.

CHAPTER FOURTEEN

MISCELLANEOUS THEOREMS INVOLVING
THE CORRELATION COEFFICIENT

Algebraical convenience of the correlation coefficient

14.1 It has already been pointed out that a statistical measure, if it is to be widely useful, should lend itself readily to algebraical treatment. The arithmetic mean and the standard deviation derive their importance largely from the fact that they fulfil this requirement better than any other averages or measures of dispersion ; and the following illustrations, while giving a number of results that are of value in one branch or another of statistical work, suffice to show that the correlation coefficient can be treated with the same facility. This might indeed be expected, seeing that the coefficient is derived, like the mean and standard deviation, by a straightforward process of summation.

The standard deviation of the sum or difference of variables

14.2 Let X_1, X_2 be two variables, and Z stand for their sum or difference.

Let z, x_1, x_2 denote deviations of the several variables from their arithmetic means. Then, if

$$Z = X_1 \pm X_2$$

evidently

$$z = x_1 \pm x_2$$

Squaring both sides of the equation and summing,

$$\Sigma(z^2) = \Sigma(x_1{}^2) + \Sigma(x_2{}^2) \pm 2\Sigma(x_1 x_2)$$

That is, if r be the correlation between x_1 and x_2, and σ, σ_1, σ_2 the respective standard deviations,

$$\sigma^2 = \sigma_1{}^2 + \sigma_2{}^2 \pm 2r\sigma_1\sigma_2 \quad . \qquad . \qquad . \qquad . \quad (14.1)$$

If x_1 and x_2 are uncorrelated, we have the important special case

$$\sigma^2 = \sigma_1{}^2 + \sigma_2{}^2 \qquad . \qquad . \qquad . \qquad . \quad (14.2)$$

The student should notice that in this case the standard deviation of the sum of corresponding values of the two variables is the same as the standard deviation of their difference. If we write var X for the variance of X and cov (X, Y) for the covariance of X and Y we may express (14.1) as

$$\text{var } (X \pm Y) = \text{var } X + \text{var } Y \pm 2 \text{ cov } (X, Y) \qquad (14.3)$$

and (14.2) as

$$\text{var } (X \pm Y) = \text{var } X + \text{var } Y \qquad . \qquad . \qquad . \qquad (14.4)$$

The same process will evidently give the standard deviation of a linear function of any number of variables. For the sum of a series of variables $X_1, X_2, \ldots X_N$, we must have—

$$\sigma^2 = \sigma_1{}^2 + \sigma_2{}^2 + \ldots + \sigma_N{}^2 + 2r_{12}\sigma_1\sigma_2 + 2r_{13}\sigma_1\sigma_3$$
$$+ \ldots + 2r_{23}\sigma_2\sigma_3 + \ldots$$

r_{12} being the correlation between X_1 and X_2, r_{23} the correlation between X_2 and X_3, and so on.

Influence of errors of observation on the standard deviation

14.3 The results of **14.2** may be applied to the theory of errors of observation. Let us suppose that, if *any* value of X be observed a large number of times, the arithmetic mean of the observations is approximately the true value, the arithmetic mean error being zero. Then, the arithmetic mean error being zero for all values of X, the error, say, δ, is uncorrelated with X. In this case, if x_1 be an observed deviation from the arithmetic mean, and x the true deviation, we have from the preceding—

$$\text{var } x_1 = \text{var } x + \text{var } \delta \qquad . \qquad . \qquad . \qquad (14.5)$$

The effect of errors of observation is, consequently, to increase the standard deviation above its true value. The student should notice that the assumption made does not imply the *complete independence* of X and δ : he is quite at liberty to suppose that errors fluctuate more, for example, with large than with small values of X, as might very probably happen. In that case the contingency coefficient between X and δ would not be zero, although the correlation coefficient might still vanish as supposed.

14.4 If certain observations be repeated so that we have in every case two measures x_1 and x_2 of the same deviation x, it is possible to obtain the true standard deviation σ_x if the further assumption is legitimate that the errors δ_1 and δ_2 are uncorrelated with each other. On this assumption

$$\Sigma(x_1 x_2) = \Sigma(x + \delta_1)(x + \delta_2)$$
$$= \Sigma(x^2)$$

and accordingly

$$\text{var } x = \sigma_x{}^2 = \frac{\Sigma(x_1 x_2)}{N} \qquad . \qquad . \qquad : \qquad . \qquad (14.6)$$

(This formula is part of Spearman's formula for the correction of the correlation coefficient ; cf. **14.6**.)

Influence of errors of observation on the correlation coefficient

14.5 Let x_1, y_1 be the observed deviations from the arithmetic means, x, y the true deviations, and δ, ϵ the errors of observation. Of the four quantities x, y, δ, ϵ we will suppose x and y alone to be correlated. On this assumption

$$\Sigma(x_1 y_1) = \Sigma(xy) \qquad . \qquad . \qquad . \qquad . \qquad . \quad (14.7)$$

It follows at once that

$$\frac{r_{xy}}{r_{x_1 y_1}} = \frac{\sigma_{x_1}\sigma_{y_1}}{\sigma_x \sigma_y}$$

and consequently the observed correlation is less than the true correlation. This difference, it should be noticed, no mere increase in the number of observations can in any way lessen.

Spearman's theorems

14.6 If, however, the observations of both x and y be repeated, as assumed in **14.4**, so that we have two measures x_1 and x_2, y_1 and y_2 of every value of x and y, the true value of the correlation can be obtained by the use of equations (14.6) and (14.7), on assumptions similar to those made above. For we have—

$$r_{xy}^2 = \frac{\Sigma(x_1 y_1)\Sigma(x_2 y_2)}{\Sigma(x_1 x_2)\Sigma(y_1 y_2)} = \frac{\Sigma(x_1 y_2)\Sigma(x_2 y_1)}{\Sigma(x_1 x_2)\Sigma(y_1 y_2)}$$

$$= \frac{r_{x_1 y_1} r_{x_2 y_2}}{r_{x_1 x_2} r_{y_1 y_2}} = \frac{r_{x_1 y_2} r_{x_2 y_1}}{r_{x_1 x_2} r_{y_1 y_2}} \qquad . \qquad . \qquad . \quad (14.8)$$

Or, if we use all the four possible correlations between observed values of x and observed values of y,

$$r_{xy}^4 = \frac{r_{x_1 y_1} r_{x_2 y_2} r_{x_1 y_2} r_{x_2 y_1}}{(r_{x_1 x_2} r_{y_1 y_2})^2} \qquad . \qquad . \qquad . \quad (14.9)$$

Equation (14.9) is the original form in which Spearman gave his correction formula. It will be seen to imply the assumption that, of the six quantities $x, y, \delta_1, \delta_2, \epsilon_1, \epsilon_2$, only x and y are correlated. The correction given by the second part of equation (14.8), also suggested by Spearman, seems, on the whole, to be safer, for it eliminates the assumption that the errors in x and in y, in the same series of observations, are uncorrelated. An insufficient though partial test of the correctness of the assumptions may be made by correlating $x_1 - x_2$ with $y_1 - y_2$: this correlation should vanish. Evidently, however, it may vanish from symmetry without thereby implying that all the correlations of the errors are zero.

Mean and standard deviation of an index

14.7 The means and standard deviations of non-linear functions of two or more variables can in general only be expressed in terms of the means and standard deviations of the original variables to a first approximation, on the assumption that deviations are small compared with the mean values of the variables. Thus, let it be required *to find the mean and standard deviation of a ratio or index* $Z = X_1/X_2$, in terms of the constants for X_1 and X_2. Let I be the mean of Z, M_1 and M_2 the means of X_1 and X_2. Then,

$$I = \frac{1}{N}\Sigma\left(\frac{X_1}{X_2}\right) = \frac{1}{N}\frac{M_1}{M_2}\Sigma\left(1 + \frac{x_1}{M_1}\right)\left(1 + \frac{x_2}{M_2}\right)^{-1}$$

Expand the second bracket by the binomial theorem, assuming that x_2/M_2 is so small that powers higher than the second can be neglected. Then, to this approximation,

$$I = \frac{1}{N}\frac{M_1}{M_2}\left[N - \frac{1}{M_1 M_2}\Sigma(x_1 x_2) + \frac{1}{M_2{}^2}\Sigma(x_2{}^2)\right]$$

That is, if r be the correlation between x_1 and x_2, and if $v_1 = \sigma_1/M_1$, $v_2 = \sigma_2/M_2$,

$$I = \frac{M_1}{M_2}(1 - rv_1v_2 + v_2{}^2) \qquad . \qquad . \qquad . \qquad . \qquad (14.10)$$

If s be the standard deviation of Z, we have—

$$s^2 + I^2 = \frac{1}{N}\Sigma\left(\frac{X_1}{X_2}\right)^2$$

$$= \frac{1}{N}\frac{M_1{}^2}{M_2{}^2}\Sigma\left(1 + \frac{x_1}{M_1}\right)^2\left(1 + \frac{x_2}{M_2}\right)^{-2}$$

Expanding the second bracket again by the binomial theorem, and neglecting terms of all orders above the second—

$$s_2 + I^2 = \frac{1}{N}\frac{M_1{}^2}{M_2{}^2}\Sigma\left(1 + \frac{x_1}{M_1}\right)^2\left(1 - 2\frac{x_2}{M_2} + 3\frac{x_2{}^2}{M_2{}^2}\right)$$

$$= \frac{M_1{}^2}{M_2{}^2}(1 + v_1{}^2 - 4rv_1v_2 + 3v_2{}^2)$$

or from (14.10)—

$$s^2 = \frac{M_1{}^2}{M_2{}^2}(v_1{}^2 - 2rv_1v_2 + v_2{}^2) \qquad . \qquad . \qquad . \qquad (14.11)$$

which we may also write as

$$\mathrm{var}\,(X_1/X_2) = \frac{M_1{}^2}{M_2{}^2}\left\{\frac{\mathrm{var}\,X_1}{M_1{}^2} - \frac{2\,\mathrm{cov}\,(X_1,\,X_2)}{M_1 M_2} + \frac{\mathrm{var}\,X_2}{M_2{}^2}\right\} \qquad . \qquad . \qquad (14.12)$$

Correlation between indices

14.8 The following problem affords a further illustration of the use of the same method. *Required to find approximately the correlation between two ratios* $Z_1 = X_1/X_3$, $Z_2 = X_2/X_3$, X_1, X_2 *and* X_3 *being uncorrelated.*

Let the means of the two ratios or indices be I_1, I_2, and the standard deviations s_1, s_2; these are given approximately by (14.10) and (14.11) of the last section. The required correlation ρ will be given by—

$$N\rho s_1 s_2 = \Sigma\left(\frac{X_1}{X_3} - I_1\right)\left(\frac{X_2}{X_3} - I_2\right)$$

$$= \Sigma\left(\frac{X_1 X_2}{X_3^2}\right) - NI_1 I_2$$

$$= \frac{M_1 M_2}{M_3^2}\Sigma\left(1 + \frac{x_1}{M_1}\right)\left(1 + \frac{x_2}{M_2}\right)\left(1 + \frac{x_3}{M_3}\right)^{-2} - NI_1 I_2$$

Neglecting terms of higher order than the second as before and remembering that all correlations are zero, we have—

$$\rho s_1 s_2 = \frac{M_1 M_2}{M_3^2}(1 + 3v_3^2) - I_1 I_2$$

$$= \frac{M_1 M_2}{M_3^2}v_3^2$$

where, in the last step, a term of the order v_3^4 has again been neglected. Substituting from (14.11) for s_1 and s_2, we have finally—

$$\rho = \frac{v_3^2}{\sqrt{(v_1^2 + v_3^2)(v_2^2 + v_3^2)}} \qquad . \qquad . \qquad . \quad (14.13)$$

This value of ρ is obviously positive, being equal to $0 \cdot 5$ if $v_1 = v_2 = v_3$; and hence even if X_1 and X_2 are independent, the indices formed by taking their ratios to a common denominator X_3 will be correlated. The value of ρ was termed by Karl Pearson the " spurious correlation." Thus, if measurements be taken, say, on three bones of the human skeleton, and the measurements grouped in threes absolutely at random, there will, nevertheless, be a positive correlation, probably approaching $0 \cdot 5$, between the indices formed by the ratios of two of the measurements to the third. To give another illustration, if two individuals both observe the same series of magnitudes quite independently, there may be little, if any, correlation between their absolute errors. But if the errors be expressed as percentages of the magnitude observed, there may be considerable correlation. It does not follow of necessity that the correlations between indices or ratios are misleading. If the indices are uncorrelated, there will be a similar " spurious " correlation between the absolute measurements $Z_1 X_3 = X_1$ and $Z_2 X_3 = X_2$, and the answer to the question whether the correlation between indices or that between absolute measures is misleading depends on the further question whether the indices or the absolute measures are the quantities directly determined by the causes under investigation.

The case considered, where X_1, X_2, X_3 are uncorrelated, is only a special one ; for the general discussion see K. Pearson, *Proc. Roy. Soc.* 1897, **60**, 489. For an interesting study of actual illustrations see J. W. Brown and others, *J. Roy. Stat. Soc.*, 1914, **77**, 317.

Correlation due to heterogeneity of material

14.9 The following theorem offers some analogy with the theorem of **2.26** for attributes : *If X and Y are uncorrelated in each of two records, they will nevertheless exhibit some correlation when the two records are mingled, unless the mean value of X in the second record is identical with that in the first record, or the mean value of Y in the second record is identical with that in the first record, or both.*

This follows almost at once, for if M_1, M_2 are the mean values of X in the two records, K_1, K_2 the mean values of Y, N_1, N_2 the numbers of observations, and M, K the means when the two records are mingled, the product-sum of deviations about M, K is—

$$N_1(M_1-M)(K_1-K)+N_2(M_2-M)(K_2-K)$$

Evidently the first term can only be zero if $M=M_1$ or $K=K_1$. but the first condition gives—

$$\frac{N_1M_1+N_2M_2}{N_1+N_2}=M_1$$

that is,

$$M_1=M_2$$

Similarly, the second condition gives $K_1=K_2$. Both the first and second terms can, therefore, only vanish if $M_1=M_2$ or $K_1=K_2$. Correlation may accordingly be created by the mingling of two records in which X and Y vary round different means.

Reduction of correlation due to mingling of uncorrelated with correlated pairs

14.10 Suppose that n_1 observations of x and y give a correlation coefficient—

$$r_1=\frac{\Sigma(xy)}{n_1\sigma_x\sigma_y}$$

Now, let n_2 pairs be added to the material, the means and standard deviations of x and y being the same as in the first series of observations, but the correlation zero. The value of $\Sigma(xy)$ will then be unaltered, and we shall have—

$$r_2 = \frac{\Sigma(xy)}{(n_1 + n_2)\sigma_x\sigma_y}$$

Whence

$$\frac{r_2}{r_1} = \frac{n_1}{n_1 + n_2} \qquad . \qquad . \qquad . \qquad . \qquad (14.14)$$

Suppose, for example, that a number of bones of the human skeleton have been disinterred during some excavations, and a correlation r_2 is observed between pairs of bones presumed to come from the same skeleton, this correlation being rather lower than might have been expected, and subject to some uncertainty owing to doubts as to the allocation of certain bones. If r_1 is the value that would be expected from other records, the difference might be accounted for on the hypothesis that, in a proportion $(r_1 - r_2)/r_1$ of all the pairs, the bones do not really belong to the same skeleton, and have been virtually paired at random.

The weighted mean

14.11 The arithmetic mean M of a series of values of a variable X was defined as the quotient of the sum of those values by their number N, or

$$M = \Sigma(X)/N$$

If, on the other hand, we multiply each individual observed value of X by some numerical coefficient or *weight* W, the quotient of the sum of such products by the sum of the weights is defined as a *weighted mean* of X, and may be denoted by M'; so that

$$M' = \Sigma(WX)/\Sigma(W)$$

The distinction between " weighted " and " unweighted " means is, it should be noted, very often formal rather than essential, for the " weights " may be regarded as actual, estimated or virtual frequencies. The weighted mean then becomes simply an arithmetic mean, in which some new quantity is regarded as the unit. Thus, if we are given the means M_1, M_2, M_3. . . . M_r of r series of observations, but do not know the number of observations in every series, we may form a general average by taking the arithmetic mean of all the means, viz. $\Sigma(M)/r$, treating the series as the unit. But if we know the number of observations in every series it will be better to form the *weighted mean* $\Sigma(NM)/\Sigma(N)$, weighting each mean in proportion to the number of observations in the series on which it is based. The second form of average would be quite correctly spoken of as a weighted mean of the means of the several series : at the same time, it is simply the arithmetic mean of all the series pooled together, i.e. the arithmetic mean obtained by treating the observation and not the series as the unit.

14.12   To give an arithmetical illustration, if a commodity is sold at different prices in different markets, it will be better to form an average price, not by taking the arithmetic mean of the several market prices, treating the market as the unit, but by weighting each price in proportion to the quantity sold at that price, if known, i.e. treating the unit of quantity as the unit of frequency.   Thus, if wheat has been sold in market A at an average price of 29s. 1d. per quarter, in market B at an average price of 27s. 7d. and in market C at an average price of 28s. 4d., we may, if no statement is made as to the quantities sold at these prices (as very often happens in the case of statements as to market prices), take the arithmetic mean (28s. 4d.) as the general average.   But if we know that 23,930 qrs. were sold at A, only 26 qrs. at B and 3,933 qrs. at C, it will be better to take the *weighted mean*

$$\frac{(29\text{s. }1\text{d.} \times 23,930) + (27\text{s. }7\text{d.} \times 26) + (28\text{s. }4\text{d.} \times 3,933)}{27,889} = 29\text{s.}$$

to the nearest penny.   This is appreciably higher than the arithmetic mean price, which is lowered by the undue importance attached to the small markets B and C.

14.13   In the case of index-numbers for exhibiting the changes in average prices from year to year, it may make a sensible difference whether we take the simple arithmetic mean of the index-numbers for different commodities in any one year as representing the price-level in that year, or *weight* the index-numbers for the several commodities according to their importance from some point of view.   If, for example, our standpoint be that of some average consumer, we may take as the *weight* for each commodity the sum which he spends on that commodity in an average year, so that the frequency of each commodity is taken as the number of shillings or pounds spent thereon instead of simply as unity.   We revert to this topic in Chapter 25.

14.14   Rates or ratios like the birth-, death- or marriage-rates of a country may be regarded as weighted means.   For, treating the rate for simplicity as a fraction, and not as a rate per 1,000 of the population,

$$\text{Birth-rate of whole country} = \frac{\text{Total births}}{\text{Total population}}$$

$$= \frac{\Sigma(\text{Birth-rate in each district} \times \text{population in that district})}{\Sigma(\text{Population of each district})}$$

i.e. the rate for the whole country is the mean of the rates in the different districts, weighting each in proportion to its population.   We use the weighted and unweighted means of such rates as illustrations in **14.16** below.

14.15 It is evident that any weighted mean will in general differ from the unweighted mean of the same quantities, and it is required to find an expression for this difference. If r be the correlation between weights and variables, σ_w and σ_x the standard deviations and $\bar{w}$ the mean weight, we have at once

$$\Sigma(WX)=N(M\bar{w}+r\sigma_w\sigma_x)$$

whence

$$M'=M+r\sigma_x\frac{\sigma_w}{\bar{w}} \qquad . \qquad . \qquad . \qquad . \quad (14.15)$$

That is to say, if the weights and variables are positively correlated, the weighted mean is the greater ; if negatively, the less. In some cases r is very small, and then weighting makes little difference, but in others the difference is large and important, r having a sensible value and $\sigma_x\sigma_w/\bar{w}$ a large value.

14.16 The difference between weighted and unweighted means of death-rates, birth-rates or other rates on the population in different districts is, for instance, nearly always of importance. For instance, in 1941, the birth-rates per 1,000 civilian population in Lancashire were—

> County Boroughs .... 16·1
> Urban Districts   .... 14·7
> Rural Districts   .... 14·4

The mean value of these three is 15·07 whereas the birthrate for Lancashire as a whole was 15·5, a reflection of the well-known fact that the more populous areas have the higher birth-rate. The death-rates, excluding civilian war-deaths, were—

> County Boroughs .... 15·6
> Urban Districts   .... 13·2
> Rural Districts   .... 11·0

with a mean of 13·27, against a (weighted) mean for the whole county of 14·5. There appears to be a positive correlation between death-rate and size of population as well as between birth rate and population, though no doubt for different reasons. Urban aggregations have a larger proportion of the young than rural areas, and hence a higher birth-rate, but on the other hand living conditions are more unfavourable to life and this factor outbalances the effect of the more favourable age-composition on the death-rate.

Age-composition may exert a similar effect on marriage rates. For

instance, persons married per 1,000 in the regions of England and Wales
in 1941 were as follows—

South East	....	....	21·6
North I	....	....	19·5
North II	....	....	19·0
North III	....	....	19·9
North IV	....	....	19·9
Midland I	....	....	20·0
Midland II	....	....	19·2
East	....	....	19·0
South-west	....	....	17·2
Wales I	....	....	20·1
Wales II	....	....	16·3

The mean of these figures is 19·25 whereas the marriage rate for the
whole country was 20·1. The explanation is that the more populous
areas contain a greater proportion of younger people and hence have a
higher marriage-rate.

14.17 The principle of weighting finds one very important application
in the treatment of such rates as death-rates, which are largely affected
by the age and sex composition of the population. Neglecting, for
simplicity, the question of sex, suppose the numbers of deaths are noted
in a certain district for, say, the age-groups $0-$, $10-$, $20-$, etc., in which
the fractions of the whole population are p_1, p_2, etc., where $\Sigma(p)=1$.
Let the death-rates for the corresponding age-groups be d_1, d_2, etc. Then
the ordinary or *crude* death-rate for the district is

$$D=\Sigma(dp) \quad . \quad . \quad . \quad . \quad . \text{(14.16)}$$

For some other district taken as a basis of comparison, perhaps the
country as a whole, the death-rates and fractions of the population in the
several age-groups may be δ_1, δ_2, δ_3, . . ., π_1, π_2, π_3, . . ., and the crude
death-rate

$$\Delta=\Sigma(\delta\pi) \quad . \quad . \quad . \quad . \text{(14.17)}$$

Now, D and Δ differ either because the d's and δ's differ or because
the p's and π's differ, or both. It may happen that really both districts
are about equally healthy, and the death-rates approximately the same
for all age-classes, but, owing to a difference of *weighting*, the first average
may be markedly higher than the second, or *vice versa*. If the first
district be a rural district and the second urban, for instance, there will be
a larger proportion of the old in the former, and it may possibly have a
higher crude death-rate than the second, in spite of lower death-rates in
every class. The comparison of crude death-rates is therefore liable to
lead to erroneous conclusions. The difficulty may be got over by averaging
the age-class death-rates in the district not with the weights p_1, p_2, p_3, . . .,

given by its own population, but with the weights π_1, π_2, π_3, . . . given by the population of the standard district. The *standardised death-rate* for the district will then be

$$D' = \Sigma(d\pi) \quad . \quad . \quad . \quad . \quad (14.18)$$

and D' and Δ will be comparable as regards age-distribution. There is obviously no difficulty in taking sex into account as well as age if necessary. The death-rates must be noted for each sex separately in every age-class and averaged with a system of weights based on the standard population. The method is also of importance for comparing death-rates in different classes of the population, e.g. those engaged in given occupations, as well as in different districts, and is used for both these purposes in the publications of the Registrar-General for England and Wales.

14.18 Difficulty may arise in practical cases from the fact that the death-rates d_1, d_2, d_3, . . . are not known for the districts or classes which it is desired to compare with the standard population, but only the crude rates D and the fractional populations of the age-classes p_1, p_2 p_3, . . . The difficulty may be partially obviated (cf. **2.30** and Example 2.10, pp. 38–40) by forming what is termed an *index* death-rate Δ' for the class or district, Δ' being given by

$$\Delta' = \Sigma(\delta p) \quad . \quad . \quad . \quad . \quad (14.19)$$

i.e. the rates of the standard population averaged with the weights of the district population. It is the crude death-rate that there would be in the district if the rate in every age-class were the same as in the standard population. An approximate standardised death-rate for the district or class is then given by

$$D'' = D \times \frac{\Delta}{\Delta'} \quad . \quad . \quad . \quad . \quad (14.20)$$

D'' is not necessarily, nor generally, the same as D'. It can only be the same if

$$\frac{\Sigma(d\pi)}{\Sigma(dp)} = \frac{\Sigma(\delta\pi)}{\Sigma(\delta p)}$$

This will hold good if, e.g., the death-rates in the standard population and the district stand to one another in the same ratio in all age-classes, i.e. $\delta_1/d_1 = \delta_2/d_2 = \delta_3/d_3 \doteqdot$ etc. This method of standardisation was used in the Annual Summaries of the Registrar-General for England and Wales.

14.19 Both methods of standardisation—that of **14.17** and that of **14.18**—are of great importance. They are obviously applicable to other rates besides death-rates, e.g. birth-rates. Further, they may readily be extended into quite different fields. Thus it has been suggested that standardised *average heights* or standardised *average weights* of the children in different schools might be obtained on the basis of a standard school population of given age and sex composition, or indeed of given composition as regard hair- and eye-colour as well.

14.20   In 14.11-14.16 we have dealt only with the theory of the weighted arithmetic mean, but it should be noted that any form of average can be weighted.   Thus a weighted median can be formed by finding the value of the variable such that the sum of the weights of lesser values is equal to the sum of the weights of greater values.   A weighted mode could be formed by finding the value of the variable for which the sum of the weights was greatest, allowing for the smoothing of casual fluctuations. Similarly, a weighted geometric mean could be calculated by weighting the logarithms of every value of the variable before taking the arithmetic mean, i.e.

$$\log\, G_w = \frac{\Sigma(W \log X)}{\Sigma(W)}$$

SUMMARY

1. The standard deviation of the sum of variables X_1, X_2, $\ldots$ X_N is given by

$$\sigma^2 = \sigma_1{}^2 + \sigma_2{}^2 + \ldots + \sigma_N{}^2 + 2r_{12}\sigma_1\sigma_2 + 2r_{13}\sigma_1\sigma_3 + \ldots + 2r_{23}\sigma_2\sigma_3 + \ldots$$

which may also be written

$$\text{var}\,\{\Sigma(X)\} = \Sigma(\text{var}\,X) + \Sigma\{\text{cov}(X_i, X_j)\},\, i \neq j$$

2. In particular, the variance of the sum of N uncorrelated variates is the sum of their variances.

3. If X_1, X_2 and X_3 are uncorrelated, the indices $\dfrac{X_1}{X_3}$, $\dfrac{X_2}{X_3}$ will nevertheless be correlated in general.

4. If X and Y are uncorrelated in each of two separate records, they will be correlated in the sum of the two records, unless either the means of X or the means of Y, or both, are the same in the two records.

5. If correlated and uncorrelated material is mingled, the correlation in the total is lower than that in the correlated portion.

6. An arithmetic mean is weighted when, in the calculation of $\dfrac{1}{N}\Sigma(X)$, each value of the variate is multiplied by a weight W.

7. The weighted arithmetic mean is greater or less than the unweighted mean according as the weights and variables are positively or negatively correlated.

EXERCISES

14.1 (Data from the Decennial Supplements to the Annual Reports of the Registrar-General for England and Wales.) The following particulars are found for 36 small registration districts in which the number of births in a decade ranged between 1,500 and 2,500—

Decade	Proportion of male births per 1,000 of all births	
	Mean	Standard deviation
1881–1890 . .	508·1	12·80
1891–1900 . .	508·4	10·37
Both decades .	508·25	11·65

It is believed, however, that a great part of the observed standard deviation is due to mere " fluctuations of sampling " of no real significance.

Given that the correlation between the proportions of male births in a district in the two decades is $+0\cdot36$, estimate (1) the true standard deviation freed from such fluctuations of sampling ; (2) the standard deviation of fluctuations of sampling, i.e. of the errors produced by such fluctuations in the observed proportions of male births.

14.2 The coefficients of variation for breadth, height and length of certain skulls are $3\cdot89$, $3\cdot50$ and $3\cdot24$ per cent respectively. Find the " spurious correlation " between the breadth/length and height/length indices, absolute measures being combined at random so that they are uncorrelated.

14.3 (Data from Boas, communicated to Pearson ; cf. Fawcett and Pearson, *Proc. Roy. Soc.*, **62**, p. 413) From short series of measurements on American Indians, the mean coefficient of correlation found between father and son, and father and daughter, for cephalic index, is $0\cdot14$; between mother and son, and mother and daughter, $0\cdot33$. Assuming these coefficients should be the same if it were not for the looseness of family relations, find the proportion of children not due to the reputed father.

14.4 Find the correlation between X_1+X_2 and X_2+X_3, X_1, X_2 and X_3 being uncorrelated.

14.5 Find the correlation between X_1 and aX_1+bX_2, X_1 and X_2 being uncorrelated.

14.6 (Referring to **13.17**.) Use the answer to Exercise 14.5 to estimate, very roughly, the correlation that would be found between annual movements in infantile and general mortality if the mortality of those under and over 1 year of age were uncorrelated. Note that—

General mortality per 1,000 of population $\Big\}$ =Infantile mortality per 1,000 births $\times$

$\dfrac{\text{Births}}{\text{Population}}$ +Deaths over one year per 1,000 of population

and treat the ratio of births to population as if it were constant at a rough average value, say $0\cdot032$. The standard deviation of annual movements in infantile mortality is (*loc. cit.*) $10\cdot76$, and that of annual movements in mortality other than infantile may be taken as sensibly the same as that of general mortality, or, say, $1\cdot13$ units.

14.7 If the relation

$$ax_1+bx_2+cx_3=0$$

holds for all values of x_1, x_2 and x_3 (which are, in our usual notation, deviations from the respective arithmetic means), find the correlations between x_1, x_2 and x_3 in terms of their standard deviations and the values of a, b and c.

14.8 What is the effect on a weighted mean of errors in the weights of the quantities weighted, such errors being uncorrelated with one another, with the weights or with the variables: (1) if the arithmetic mean values of the errors are zero, (2) if the arithmetic mean values of the errors are not zero?

14.9 The following are the variances of the rainfall (1) for January to March, (2) for April to December, (3) for the whole year, at Greenwich in the eighty years 1841-1920, the unit being a millimetre—

January-March	.	.	.	$\sigma_1{}^2=$ 1,521
April-December.	.	.	.	$\sigma_2{}^2=$ 8,968
Whole year	.	.	.	$\sigma^2=$10,754

Find the correlation between the rainfall in January-March and April-December.

14.10 If of three variables A, B, C, the variance of the sum of A and B is the sum of the variances of A and B and the variance of the sum of B and C is the sum of the variances of B and C; show that the variance of the sum of A and C is not necessarily the sum of the variances of A and C. What must be the correlation between $A+B$ and $B+C$ for this to be true?

CHAPTER FIFTEEN

SIMPLE CURVE FITTING

The problem

15.1   In this chapter we turn aside somewhat from the line of development of previous chapters in order to study a subject of considerable theoretical and practical importance—the representation of relationship between two variables by simple algebraic expressions.   Our work on correlation has already led us to fit regression lines and planes to the means of arrays. We now attack a rather more general problem.   An illustration will make clear the type of inquiry involved.

TABLE 15.1.—**Estimated distance and velocities of recession of 10 extra-galactic nebulae**

(Edwin Hubble and Milton L. Humason, " The Velocity-distance Relation among Extra-galactic Nebulae," *Contributions from Mount Wilson Observatory*, Carnegie Institute of Washington, No. 427 ; *Astrophysical Journal*, 1931, **74**, 43).

Constellation in which the nebula is situated	Mean velocity (kilometres per second)	Distance (millions of parsecs)
Isolated Nebula II .	630	1·20
Virgo . .	890	1·82
Isolated Nebula I .	2,350	3·31
Pegasus . .	3,810	7·24
Pisces . .	4,630	6·92
Cancer . .	4,820	9·12
Perseus . .	5,230	10·97
Coma . .	7,500	14·45
Ursa Major .	11,800	22·91
Leo . . .	19,600	36·31

Table 15.1 shows the estimated distance and velocities of recession of certain nebulæ in the outlying parts of the visible universe.

A little inspection of the table will show that there appears to be some relation between distance and velocity—the greater the one, the greater the other, with only one exception.   A diagram makes the relation clearer still.   In fig. 15.1 we have taken the two variables velocity and distance as rectangular co-ordinates y and x, and have marked for each nebula a point whose co-ordinates are the distance and velocity of that nebula. The ten points so obtained evidently lie very approximately on a straight line or, to express the same fact algebraically, the ten values of the variables are closely represented by an equation of the form

$$y = a_0 + a_1 x \qquad . \qquad . \qquad . \qquad . \qquad (15.1)$$

where we use small letters to denote current co-ordinates.

15.2 No straight line, however, passes exactly through all the points, although a great many lines may be drawn which nearly do so. The question then arises, is there a straight line which fits the points better than all others, and if so, which is it ? Or, in other language, what values of a_0 and a_1 in equation (15.1) must we take to get the best representation of the linear relationship between the two variables ? And, as a further question, can we devise a measure of the closeness of the fit of the various lines which can be drawn ?

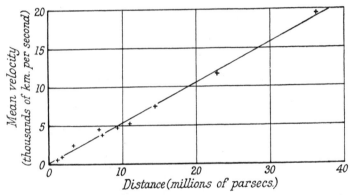

Fig. 15.1.—Relationship between distance and velocity of recession in certain extragalactic nebulae. (Table 15.1)

15.3 In the foregoing illustration it is clear from the data or from the diagram that a linear relationship between the variables gives a very close picture of the truth. In other cases the points of the diagram will lie more or less on a curve, and no straight line will give a satisfactory representation. We should then wish to investigate whether the dependence of y on x may be suitably represented by the more general equation

$$y = a_0 + a_1 x + a_2 x^2 + \dots + a_p x^p \qquad . \qquad . \qquad . \qquad (15.2)$$

which, in the diagram, corresponds to a curve of the type known as parabolic. The number p indicates the *degree* of the parabola, and we speak of quadratic, cubic, quartic parabolas, meaning curves of type (15.2) with $p = 2, 3, 4$, respectively.

15.4 Our general problem may, then be stated as follows : Given n pairs of values of two variables, X_1Y_1, X_2Y_2, ... X_nY_n, to express the values of one of them as nearly as may be in terms of the other by an equation of the form (15.2) ; and to measure the closeness of the approximation of the values of y given by the equation to the actual values. In geometrical language, given n points in a plane, to fit to them a curve of the parabolic type (15.2) and to measure the closeness of fit.

15.5 The representation of data in this way may serve several purposes. In the first place, it may present the relationship between the two variables in a useful summary form. Secondly, it may be used to interpolate, i.e. to estimate the values of one variable which would correspond to specified values of the other. In fig. 15.1, for example, the straight line which has been drawn in, and whose equation is obtained below, tells us what we might expect to be the velocity of a nebula whose distance is, say, 20 million parsecs, on the assumption that the linear relation holds good for nebulæ in general.

15.6 Again, the representation may also be very suggestive to the theorist. The linear form of the relationship between the variables of Table 15.1 involves more than a convenient summary of the facts, and has inspired a great deal of research into the nature of the physical universe. In such cases, the derived equation is regarded as the expression of a law of nature, and the deviations of the observed values from those given by it are interpreted as fluctuations arising from experimental error or secondary perturbations. This standpoint is common in physics, in which data often lie very closely about a smooth curve.

The method of least squares

15.7 Let us suppose that we have n pairs of values X_1Y_1, ... X_nY_n, and that we wish to represent them by an equation of the type (15.2). Our problem is, having fixed the value of p, to determine the constants a_0, a_1, ... a_p in terms of the observed values X, Y, so as to get the best possible fit.

The expression " best possible fit " may be defined in more than one way, and consequently there is no unique method of determining the constants. Several methods have been proposed, and our choice between them is determined mainly by convenience. One way, which is suggested by the geometrical representation, is to choose the curve of equation (15.2) so that the sum of the distances (taken as positive) of the points from it is a minimum, the sum of the distances being regarded as a measure of goodness of fit, and the " best " fit being given by the curve of specified degree for which that sum is least. But this method, whatever its theoretical attractions, suffers from the disadvantage that it is difficult to apply in practice except for the straight line.

An alternative method, which is in almost universal use at the present time, is that known as the *Method of Least Squares*, and we proceed to discuss it at length. We have already used it to find regression lines (**9.20** and **12.4**).

15.8 If we substitute for the value x_r in equation (15.2) we get a quantity y_r, given by

$$y_r = a_0 + a_1 X_r + a_2 X_r^2 + \ldots + a_p X_r^p \qquad . \qquad (15.3)$$

This is not in general the same as Y_r, and we therefore define the residual ξ_r as

$$\xi_r = Y_r - y_r = Y_r - a_0 - a_1 X_r - \ldots - a_p X_r^p \qquad . \qquad (15.4)$$

There will be n residuals, one for each pair X, Y, and they are all zero if, and only if, the curve is a perfect fit. We then take the sum of the squares of residuals—

$$U = \Sigma(\xi_r^2) = \Sigma(Y_r - a_0 - a_1 X_r - \ldots - a_p X_r^p)^2 \qquad . \qquad (15.5)$$

If U is zero, each residual must be zero, and the data are represented perfectly by the equation. Except in this case, U is positive. The further the points lie from the curve of equation (15.2), the greater U will be. U therefore provides one measure of the closeness of fit. From this standpoint, the best fit will be that for which U is least.

The Method of Least Squares adopts this criterion, and states that *the constants a shall be determined so that U is a minimum.*

15.9 The reason for taking the sum of *squares* of residuals, rather than the sum of residuals simply, is akin to that which led us to prefer the standard deviation to the mean deviation as a measure of dispersion (Chap. 6), namely, that the former is more convenient in theory and leads to equations which are easier to handle in practice.

15.10 It was formerly the custom, and is so still in works on the theory of observations, to derive the method of least squares from certain theoretical considerations, the assumed normality of the distribution of errors of observations being one such. It is, however, more than doubtful whether the conditions for the theoretical validity of the method are realised in statistical practice, and the student would do well to regard the method as recommended chiefly by its comparative simplicity and by the fact that it has stood the test of experience.

15.11 Consider now the quantity U, given by equation (15.5). a_0, a_1, ... a_p are to be chosen so that this is a minimum, say U_0. Let us imagine this done.

If, now, we substitute in equation (15.5) $a_0+\epsilon_0$ for a_0, $a_1+\epsilon_1$ for a_1, $a_2+\epsilon_2$ for a_2, and so on, we shall get a quantity U_1 given by

$$U_1=\Sigma\{Y-(a_0+\epsilon_0)-(a_1+\epsilon_1)X-\ \ldots\ -(a_p+\epsilon_p)X^p\}^2$$

and U_1 is greater than U_0 for all values of $\epsilon_0,\ \epsilon_1,\ \ldots\ \epsilon_p$.

Now,

$$
\begin{aligned}
U_1&=\{\Sigma(Y-a_0-a_1X-\ \ldots\ -a_pX^p)-(\epsilon_0+\epsilon_1X+\ \ldots\ +\epsilon_pX^p)\}^2\\
&=\Sigma(Y-a_0-a_1X-\ \ldots\ -a_pX^p)^2\\
&\quad-2\Sigma(Y-a_0-a_1X-\ \ldots\ -a_pX^p)(\epsilon_0+\epsilon_1X+\ \ldots\ +\epsilon_pX^p)\\
&\quad+\Sigma(\epsilon_0+\epsilon_1X+\ \ldots\ +\epsilon_pX^p)^2
\end{aligned}
$$

The first of these terms is equal to U_0. Hence, if $U_1 \geqslant U_0$, we must have

$$
\begin{aligned}
&-2\Sigma(Y-a_0-a_1X-\ \ldots\ -a_pX^p)(\epsilon_0+\epsilon_1X+\ \ldots\ +\epsilon_pX^p)\\
&+\Sigma(\epsilon_0+\epsilon_1X+\ \ldots\ +\epsilon_pX^p)^2\geqslant 0\ \ .\qquad .\qquad .\qquad .\qquad .\quad (15.6)
\end{aligned}
$$

This is to be true for all values of $\epsilon_0\ \ldots\ \epsilon_p$. Let us then take these quantities to be very small. The second term in equation (15.6), depending as it does on the squares of the ϵ's, will be small compared with the first, and may be neglected. (15.6) will then be true only if the first term vanishes, for otherwise the ϵ's could be so chosen in sign as to make the first term negative.

Hence,

$$\Sigma(Y-a_0-a_1X-\ \ldots\ -a_pX^p)(\epsilon_0+\epsilon_1X+\ \ldots\ +\epsilon_pX^p)=0\ \ .\quad (15.7)$$

This is true for *all* small values of the ϵ's. Hence the coefficients of $\epsilon_0,\ \epsilon_1,\ \ldots\ \epsilon_p$ all vanish, i.e. we have—

$$
\left.
\begin{aligned}
&\Sigma(Y)\ \ -a_0n\ \ \ -a_1\Sigma(X)\ \ \ -\ \ldots\ -a_p\Sigma(X^p)\ \ \ \ =0\\
&\Sigma(YX)\ -a_0\Sigma(X)\ -a_1\Sigma(X^2)\ \ -\ \ldots\ -a_p\Sigma(X^{p+1})\ =0\\
&\Sigma(YX^2)-a_0\Sigma(X^2)-a_1\Sigma(X^3)\ \ -\ \ldots\ -a_p\Sigma(X^{p+2})\ =0\\
&\qquad\qquad\ \ .\qquad\quad .\qquad\quad .\qquad .\qquad .\qquad .\\
&\Sigma(YX^p)-a_0\Sigma(X^p)-a_1\Sigma(X^{p+1})-\ \ldots\ -a_p\Sigma(X^{2p})\qquad =0
\end{aligned}
\right\}\quad (15.8)
$$

The equations (15.8) give us $p+1$ equations in the $(p+1)$ unknowns $a_0\ \ldots\ a_p$. Hence they may be solved so as to give the a's in terms of the calculable quantities $\Sigma(X)$, $\Sigma(X^2)$, $\ldots$ $\Sigma(X^{2p})$, $\Sigma(Y)$, $\Sigma(YX)$, $\ldots$ $\Sigma(YX^p)$.

15.12 It will be seen that the solution of these equations depends on the evaluation of the various summed quantities. A first step is therefore to calculate these sums, and this is done by a process very similar to that used in finding the moments of a distribution.

We can, in fact, express the equations in terms of moments. Dividing each equation by n, and remembering that $\mu_r'=\frac{1}{n}\Sigma(X^r)$, we have—

$$
\begin{aligned}
\frac{1}{n}\Sigma(Y) \quad -a_0 \quad -a_1\mu_1' \quad -a_2\mu_2' \quad -\ldots a_p\mu_p' \quad &=0 \\
\frac{1}{n}\Sigma(YX) -a_0\mu_1'-a_1\mu_2' \quad -a_2\mu_3' \quad -\ldots -a_p\mu_p'+1 &=0 \\
\cdot \quad \cdot \quad \cdot \quad \cdot \quad \cdot \quad \cdot \quad \cdot \quad \cdot \quad \cdot& \\
\frac{1}{n}\Sigma(YX^p)-a_0\mu_p'-a_1\mu'_{p+1}-a_2\mu'_{p+2}-\ldots -a_p\mu'_{2p} &=0
\end{aligned}
\right\} \quad (15.9)
$$

Equations for fitting a straight line

15.13 In the simplest case, that of a straight line, we have $p=1$, and the equations (15.9) become—

$$
\left.\begin{aligned}
\frac{1}{n}\Sigma(Y) \quad &=a_0+a_1\mu_1' \\
\frac{1}{n}\Sigma(YX)&=a_0\mu_1'+a_1\mu_2'
\end{aligned}\right\} \qquad . \qquad . \qquad . \quad (15.10)
$$

In particular, if X and Y are measured about their means and hence are denoted by x, y, we have—

$$\mu_1=0$$
$$\Sigma(y)=0$$

and hence, from (15.10),

$$a_0=0$$

$$a_1=\frac{1}{n\mu_2}\Sigma(yx)$$

so that the fitted line is

$$y=x\frac{1}{n\mu_2}\Sigma(yx) \qquad . \qquad . \qquad . \qquad . \quad (15.11)$$

i.e. passes through the mean of X and Y. This is, in fact, the first regression equation of (9.6) (p. 216) in another form.

15.14 In equation (15.2) it is customary to call x the " independent " variable and y the " dependent " variable. In any given case it is, as a rule, possible to regard either of the variables under consideration as the independent variable, and the other as the dependent variable. We shall then get two expressions, one giving variable A in terms of variable B, the other giving B in terms of A ; and there will be two curves of closest fit, just as there are two regression lines in the theory of correlation.

These two curves are not, in general, the same, and the result sounds a little paradoxical until we examine how the two curves are derived. We have, in fact, two definitions of closest fit, one minimising residuals of the type $(A - a_0 - a_1 B - \ldots)^2$, the other minimising residuals of the type $(B - a_0' - a_1' A - \ldots)^2$. On *a priori* grounds there is nothing to choose between the two.

15.15 Which of the two forms we choose will depend in practice on a variety of circumstances. Sometimes one variable is clearly marked out as the independent variable. For example, in considering the way in which a population varies with time, it is almost inevitable to regard the former as dependent on the latter, and not *vice versa*. In other cases the choice is dictated by the purpose in view. For instance, in expressing the relationship between current and resistance in an electric circuit, an investigator would probably take as the independent variable that factor over which he had direct control. Frequently, however, there is no guide of this kind, and it may be necessary to ascertain both curves. See **15.27** below.

Calculation

15.16 The calculations necessary to fit a curve by the method of least squares fall into two stages. First of all, the sums of squares which appear in equation (15.8) must be found, or, what amounts to the same thing, the moments. To fit a curve of degree p it is necessary to find $2p$ sums of the type $\Sigma(X^k)$ and $p+1$ sums of the type $\Sigma(YX^k)$ (including $\Sigma(Y)$). The work is best carried out systematically after the manner of Chapter 7, and several devices considerably shorten the arithmetical labour.

(*a*) By a suitable choice of origin and unit we can often reduce the given values of X and Y to smaller numbers—a great help in calculating the higher powers and sums. For instance, if the values of Y were 625, 650, 675, 700, we could take an origin at $y=625$, and a scale of one unit $=25$, and our new values would then be 0, 1, 2, 3.

(*b*) If the values of the independent variable proceed by equal steps, and particularly if there is an odd number of them, the labour of calculation is enormously reduced. We shall consider this important case in some detail below (**15.22**).

When the various sums have been ascertained, the second stage, that of the solution of the equations (15.8), may be carried through. For a curve of degree p there are $p+1$ of these equations. They are linear in the unknowns a, and their solution offers only arithmetical difficulty.

15.17 Before proceeding to consider some examples, we may remark on one point of theoretical interest. It is always possible to fit a curve of degree p exactly to $p+1$ points; for instance, a straight line can be drawn to pass exactly through two points, a cubic parabola through four points, and so on. Thus, if we have n points we can always find a curve of degree $n-1$ which is an exact fit. But in practice n is rarely less than ten, and a fitted curve of degree as high as this would have no practical value and very little theoretical interest. It is only exceptionally that use is found for fitted curves of degree higher than the fourth.

We will now consider some examples.

Example 15.1.—Let us fit a straight line to the data of Table 15.1. To illustrate the method we will deal with both cases, taking first distance and then velocity as the independent variable.

Denoting, then, distance by x and velocity by y, we wish to fit a curve of the form

$$y = a_0 + a_1 x$$

For this we require $\Sigma(X)$, $\Sigma(X^2)$, $\Sigma(Y)$ and $\Sigma(YX)$. For the alternative case we shall also require $\Sigma(Y^2)$.

The arithmetic is shown in Table 15.2. In successive columns we write, for each nebula, Y, X, X^2, YX and Y^2. Totals are shown at the foot of the columns.

TABLE 15.2.—Practical work for fitting a straight line to the data of Table 15.1

Constellation	Mean velocity (000 km. per second) Y	Distance (millions of parsecs) X	X^2	YX	Y^2
Isolated Nebula II	0·63	1·20	1·4400	0·7560	0·3969
Virgo . .	0·89	1·82	3·3124	1·6198	0·7921
Isolated Nebula I	2·35	3·31	10·9561	7·7785	5·5225
Pegasus. .	3·81	7·24	52·4176	27·5844	14·5161
Pisces . .	4·63	6·92	47·8864	32·0396	21·4369
Cancer . .	4·82	9·12	83·1744	43·9584	23·2324
Perseus . .	5·23	10·97	120·3409	57·3731	27·3529
Coma . .	7·50	14·45	208·8025	108·3750	56·2500
Ursa Major .	11·80	22·91	524·8681	270·3380	139·2400
Leo . .	19·60	36·31	1318·4161	711·6760	384·1600
Total .	61·26	114·25	2371·6145	1261·4988	672·8998

Equations (15.8) then become

$$\Sigma(Y) - a_0 n - a_1 \Sigma(X) = 0$$
$$\Sigma(YX) - a_0 \Sigma(X) - a_1 \Sigma(X^2) = 0$$

or

$$61 \cdot 26 - 10a_0 - 114 \cdot 25a_1 = 0$$
$$1261 \cdot 4988 - 114 \cdot 25a_0 - 2371 \cdot 6145a_1 = 0$$

Multiplying the first of these by 114·25 and the second by 10, and subtracting, we get

$$5616 \cdot 033 - 10{,}663 \cdot 0825a_1 = 0$$
$$a_1 = 0 \cdot 527 \text{ (more accurately, } 0 \cdot 526{,}680{,}066)$$

and hence,

$$a_0 = 0 \cdot 109 \text{ (more accurately, } 0 \cdot 108,680,240)$$

So that

$$y = 0 \cdot 109 + 0 \cdot 527x \qquad . \qquad . \qquad . \qquad (a)$$

This line is shown in fig. 15.1.

If we wish to express distance in terms of velocity, we have, interchanging X and Y in equations (15.8)—

$$x = a_0' + a_1'y$$
$$\Sigma(X) - a_0'n - a_1'\Sigma(Y) = 0$$
$$\Sigma(XY) - a_0'\Sigma(Y) - a_1'\Sigma(Y^2) = 0$$

or

$$114 \cdot 25 - 10a_0' - 61 \cdot 26a_1' = 0$$
$$1261 \cdot 4988 - 61 \cdot 26a_0' - 672 \cdot 8998a_1' = 0$$

whence

$$a_0' = -0 \cdot 135$$
$$a_1' = 1 \cdot 89$$

and

$$x = -0 \cdot 135 + 1 \cdot 89y \qquad . \qquad . \qquad . \qquad (b)$$

Equations (a) and (b) are nearly identical, for dividing (a) by $0 \cdot 527$ and rearranging, we have—

$$x = -0 \cdot 207 + 1 \cdot 90y$$

This is exceptional, and results from the closeness with which the points lie to a straight line. The correlation between X and Y is, in fact, $0 \cdot 997$.

Reduction of data to linear form

15.18 *Example* 15.2.—It sometimes happens that we may reduce data to a linear form by some simple transformation. Table 15.3, for example, shows the number of fronds of a duckweed plant on fourteen successive days. The number of fronds (N) clearly does not increase uniformly with time (x), and the curve of growth is not linear, as may be seen by graphing N against x. There are theoretical reasons for inquiring whether the law of growth may be represented by an equation of the form

$$N = ae^{bx}$$

A population which conformed to this equation would have the property that its rate of increase at any moment was proportional to the size of the population at that moment—its "birth-rate," so to speak, would be a constant.

Taking logarithms, we have—

$$\log_e N = \log_e a + bx$$

and if we now write $y=\log_e N$, we have—

$$y=\log_e a+bx$$

which is linear in x and y.

We should, of course, have a relation of the same form, with different values of the constants a and b, if we took logarithms to base 10, which is usually the more convenient procedure.

We therefore try the effect of fitting a straight line to x (the time) and $\log_{10} N$ (log number of fronds). From fig. 15.2 it will be seen that the fit is a close one.

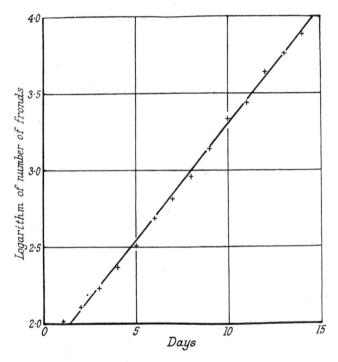

Fig. 15.2.—Straight line fitted to data of Table 15.3.   (Growth of duckweed)

The preliminary work is shown in Table 15.3.   We find first Y, corresponding to $\log_{10} N$, then $\Sigma(X)$, $\Sigma(Y)$, $\Sigma(X^2)$, $\Sigma(YX)$.   For this particular example we do not require $\Sigma(Y^2)$.   In view of the simple character of the values of X there is little saving in taking other origins or units for X and Y, although, if we were fitting a curve of higher order, it might be an advantage to take a different origin for X.

TABLE 15.3.—Growth of duckweed

(V. H. Blackman, *Nature*, 6th June, 1936, quoting data of Ashby and Oxley.)

Number of fronds N	$\log_{10} N$ Y	Days X	X^2	YX
100	2·0000000	1	1	2·0000000
127	2·1038037	2	4	4·2076074
171	2·2329961	3	9	6·6989883
233	2·3673559	4	16	9·4694236
323	2·5092025	5	25	12·5460125
452	2·6551384	6	36	15·9308304
654	2·8155777	7	49	19·7090439
918	2·9628427	8	64	23·7027416
1,406	3·1479853	9	81	28·3318677
2,150	3·3324385	10	100	33·3243850
2,800	3·4471580	11	121	37·9187380
4,140	3·6170003	12	144	43·4040036
5,760	3·7604225	13	169	48·8854925
8,250	3·9164539	14	196	54·8303546
Total . .	40·8683755	105	1015	340·9594891

Equations (15.8) then become—

$$\Sigma(Y) - na_0 - a_1\Sigma(X) = 0$$
$$\Sigma(YX) - a_0\Sigma(X) - a_1\Sigma(X^2) = 0$$

or

$$40 \cdot 8683755 - 14a_0 - 105a_1 = 0$$
$$340 \cdot 9594891 - 105a_0 - 1015a_1 = 0$$

whence

$$a_0 = 1 \cdot 785$$
$$a_1 = 0 \cdot 1514$$

and

$$y = 1 \cdot 785 + 0 \cdot 1514x \qquad . \qquad . \qquad . \qquad (a)$$

Raising this to power 10, and remembering that $10^y = N$, we have—

$$N = 10^{1 \cdot 785} \times 10^{0 \cdot 1514x} \qquad . \qquad . \qquad . \qquad (b)$$

which we may also write, expressing the powers of 10 as actual numbers—

$$N = 60 \cdot 95 \times (1 \cdot 417)^x$$

15.19 *Example* 15.3.—The process of taking logarithms may be applied to both variables. In Table 15.4 are given the costs per unit of electricity sold (η) and the number of units sold per head of the population served by the undertaking (ξ) for 27 electricity undertakings. The data were taken from the Returns of the Electricity Commission for 1933-34, which cover about six hundred undertakings, by selecting every twenty-fifth. They are, therefore, only a comparatively small sample, but they reflect fairly accurately the general relationship between ξ and η for the whole number of undertakings.

This relationship is illustrated by fig. 15.3, on which ξ is graphed against η. It will be seen that, broadly, the larger the number of units sold per head, the lower the cost per unit.

The points of fig. 15.3 lie, in fact, about a curve which suggests a relation of the form—

$$\eta = a\xi^{-b}$$

As ξ becomes larger, η becomes smaller, and as ξ tends to zero, η tends to infinity. Let us try to fit a curve of this kind to the data.

We have—

$$\log \eta = \log a - b \log \xi$$

and, putting

$$y = \log \eta, \qquad x = \log \xi$$

$$y = \log a - bx$$

which is linear. We therefore proceed to fit a straight line to log η and log ξ.

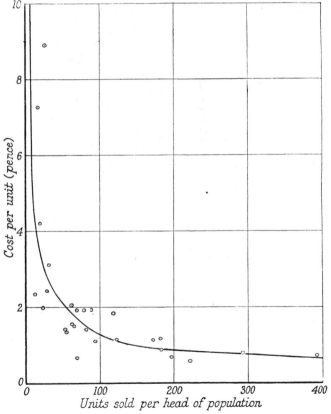

Fig. 15.3.—Curve fitted to data of Table 15.4

The preliminary work is shown in Table 15.4. Equations (15.8) become, in the usual way,

$$5 \cdot 2493 - 27a_0 - 50 \cdot 1311a_1 = 0$$
$$7 \cdot 3008 - 50 \cdot 1311a_0 - 97 \cdot 1450a_1 = 0$$

whence

and

$$a_0 = 1 \cdot 31 \qquad a_1 = -0 \cdot 601$$

$$y = 1 \cdot 31 - 0 \cdot 601x \qquad . \qquad . \qquad . \qquad (a)$$

From which

$$\eta = 10^{1 \cdot 31} \xi^{-0 \cdot 601} \qquad . \qquad . \qquad . \qquad (b)$$

or

$$\eta = 20 \cdot 42 \xi^{-0 \cdot 601}$$

Fig. 15.4 shows the values of y plotted against those of x. The straight line we have found cannot be described as a good fit, but so far as the eye can judge it is as good as any simple curve is likely to be. It expresses the general relation between x and y; but, naturally, local circumstances cause individual values to deviate appreciably from this relation. Statistical data which are not produced under laboratory conditions are very often of this nature. The fitted curve expresses a general trend, but individual cases may lie well away from it in a number of instances.

Fitting of more general curves

15.20 *Example* 15.4—We must now consider the fitting of curves of order higher than the first.

Table 15.5 on p. 356 shows the percentage loss of weight (Y) for certain temperatures (X) in experiments on the oven-drying of soils. Since X is here the controllable factor, it is natural to take it as the independent variable, and we shall express Y in terms of X.

The data are shown graphically in fig. 15.5. We shall find successively the straight line, quadratic parabola and cubic parabola of closest fit. We shall therefore require sums of powers of X up to $\Sigma(X^6)$ and sums of products up to $\Sigma(YX^3)$. We also require, for later work, $\Sigma(Y^2)$.

The preliminary work is shown in Table 15.5. We might, perhaps, have abbreviated the arithmetic slightly by taking an origin of x at $X = 100$ and of y at $Y = 3$, but the saving would not have been large. Data of this kind frequently give rise to large figures in the higher sums, and a machine is a great help in the calculation. For instance, with a machine the sums $\Sigma(YX)$, etc., can be found by continuous addition, without the necessity for writing each individual contribution in the relative column.

For the straight line of closest fit, equations (15.8) become—

$$82 \cdot 97 - 16a_0 - 2642a_1 = 0$$
$$14{,}736 \cdot 19 - 2642a_0 - 474{,}050a_1 = 0$$

whence

$$a_0 = 0 \cdot 660 \quad \text{and} \quad a_1 = 0 \cdot 02741$$
(more accurately, $0 \cdot 659{,}759{,}789$ and $0 \cdot 027{,}408{,}722$)

TABLE 15.4.—Reduction of non-linear relation to linear form
Relationship between Working Costs per Unit and Number of Units Sold in 27 Electricity Undertakings.

(Data from Return of Engineering and Financial Statistics, 1933-34—Electricity Commission.)

Name of undertaking	Working costs per unit sold (pence) η	Units sold (excluding bulk supplies) per head of population ξ	$\log \eta = Y$	$\log \xi = X$	YX	X^2
Aberdare	1·53	63·1	0·18469	1·8000	0·3324	3·2400
Barry U.D.C.	2·36	12·1	0·37291	1·0828	0·4038	1·1725
Bredbury and Romiley	0·70	394·2	−0·15490	2·5957	−0·4021	6·7377
Chesterfield	0·56	220·5	−0·25181	2·3434	−0·5901	5·4915
Earby	1·41	52·4	0·14922	1·7193	0·2566	2·9560
Grange	1·88	119·4	0·27416	2·0770	0·5694	4·3139
Holmfirth	1·17	181·6	0·06819	2·2591	0·1541	5·1035
Lincoln	0·78	293·8	−0·10791	2·4681	−0·2663	6·0915
Mexborough	1·13	170·4	0·05308	2·2315	0·1185	4·9796
Nuneaton	0·86	184·1	−0·06550	2·2651	−0·1484	5·1307
Redcar	1·91	68·0	0·28103	1·8325	0·5150	3·3581
Slaithwaite	1·40	80·7	0·14613	1·9069	0·2787	3·6363
Tanfield	2·41	29·0	0·38202	1·4624	0·5587	2·1386
West Lancs R.D.C.	·1·37	53·4	0·13672	1·7275	0·2362	2·9843
Dumfries Corp.	1·10	93·0	0·04139	1·9685	0·0815	3·8750
Tobermory	4·21	19·9	0·62428	1·2989	0·8109	1·6871
Aberayron	8·9	25·6	0·94939	1·4082	1·3369	1·9830
Brixham Gas and Electric Co.	3·13	30·4	0·49554	1·4829	0·7348	2·1990
Chudleigh Co.	7·28	16·7	0·86213	1·2227	1·0541	1·4950
Foots Cray Co.	1·92	77·8	0·28330	1·8910	0·5357	3·5759
Lewes Co.	1·14	120·1	0·05690	2·0795	0·1183	4·3243
Newcastle Electric Light Co.	0·64	68·8	−0·19382	1·8376	−0·3562	3·3768
Ramsgate Co.	1·57	60·5	0·19590	1·7818	0·3490	3·1748
Steyning Co.	1·06	93·9	0·02531	1·9727	0·0499	3·8915
West Devon Co.	1·98	22·1	0·29667	1·3444	0·3988	1·8074
Coatbridge and Airdrie Co.	0·68	196·2	−0·16749	2·2927	−0·3840	5·2565
Skelmorlie Co.	2·05	60·1	0·31175	1·7789	0·5546	3·1645
Total	—	—	5·24928	50·1311	7·3008	97·1450

and the straight line is—

$$y = 0·660 + 0·02741x \qquad (a)$$

For the quadratic parabola, equations (15.8) are—

$$\Sigma(Y) \quad -na_0 \quad -a_1\Sigma(X) \quad -a_2\Sigma(X^2) = 0$$
$$\Sigma(YX) \quad -a_0\Sigma(X) -a_1\Sigma(X^2) \quad -a_2\Sigma(X^3) = 0$$
$$\Sigma(YX^2) \quad -a_0\Sigma(X^2) -a_1\Sigma(X^3) -a_2\Sigma(X^4) = 0$$

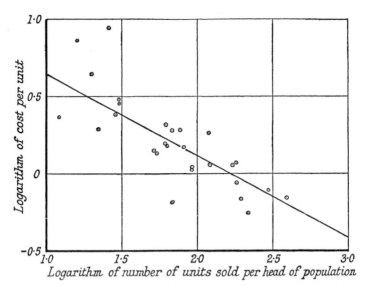

Fig. 15.4.—Straight line fitted to logarithms of data of Table 15.4

These become, on substitution,

$$82 \cdot 97 - 16a_0 - 2642a_1 - 474{,}050a_2 = 0$$
$$14{,}736 \cdot 19 - 2642a_0 - 474{,}050a_1 - 91{,}244{,}582a_2 = 0$$
$$2{,}819{,}909 \cdot 45 - 474{,}050a_0 - 91{,}244{,}582a_1 - 18{,}553{,}164{,}842a_2 = 0$$

giving

$$a_0 = 3 \cdot 551, \qquad a_1 = -0 \cdot 009291, \qquad a_2 = 0 \cdot 00010695$$

(more accurately, $3 \cdot 550{,}990{,}2$, $-0 \cdot 009{,}291{,}235{,}7$, and $0 \cdot 000{,}106{,}954{,}12$) and the parabola is—

$$y = 3 \cdot 551 - 0 \cdot 009291x + 0 \cdot 00010695x^2 \qquad (b)$$

For the cubic parabola, equations (15.8) are—

$$\Sigma(Y) \quad -na_0 \quad -a_1\Sigma(X) \quad -a_2\Sigma(X^2) \quad -a_3\Sigma(X^3) = 0$$
$$\Sigma(YX) \quad -a_0\Sigma(X) \quad -a_1\Sigma(X^2) \quad -a_2\Sigma(X^3) \quad -a_3\Sigma(X^4) = 0$$
$$\Sigma(YX^2) \quad -a_0\Sigma(X^2) \quad -a_1\Sigma(X^3) \quad -a_2\Sigma(X^4) \quad -a_3\Sigma(X^5) = 0$$
$$\Sigma(YX^3) \quad -a_0\Sigma(X^3) \quad -a_1\Sigma(X^4) \quad -a_2\Sigma(X^5) \quad -a_3\Sigma(X^6) = 0$$

which become—

$$82 \cdot 97 - 16a_0 - 2642a_1 - 474{,}050a_2 - 91{,}244{,}582a_3 = 0$$
$$14{,}736 \cdot 19 - 2642a_0 - 474{,}050a_1 - 91{,}244{,}582a_2 - 18{,}553{,}164{,}842a_3 = 0$$
$$2{,}819{,}909 \cdot 45 - 474{,}050a_0 - 91{,}244{,}582a_1 - 18{,}553{,}164{,}842a_2 - 3{,}930{,}294{,}225{,}302a_3 = 0$$
$$571{,}902{,}362 \cdot 11 - 91{,}244{,}582a_0 - 18{,}553{,}164{,}842a_1 - 3{,}930{,}294{,}225{,}302a_2 - 858{,}077{,}668{,}755{,}250a_3 = 0$$

It is not really necessary to write out the large numbers of the later equations as fully as we have done, and a certain amount of approximation is allowable. The student should, however, be careful not to introduce it too soon, as neglected quantities may become of cumulative importance in the solution of the equations.

By straightforward but rather strenuous arithmetic we find—

$$a_0 = 7 \cdot 783, \qquad a_1 = -0 \cdot 08940$$
$$a_2 = 0 \cdot 0005875, \qquad a_3 = -0 \cdot 0000009189$$

(more accurately,

$$a_0 = 7 \cdot 782,526,861, \qquad a_1 = -0 \cdot 089,402,395,60$$
$$a_2 = 0 \cdot 000,587,479,234,2, \qquad a_3 = -0 \cdot 000,000,918,891,069,8)$$

The smallness of the coefficients a_2 and a_3 does not mean that they are of minor importance, since in the equation for y they are multiplied by terms in x^2 and x^3, which may be large.

The cubic parabola is, then,

$$y = 7 \cdot 783 - 0 \cdot 08940x + 0 \cdot 0005875x^2 - 0 \cdot 0000009189x^3$$

which we may also write as—

$$y = 7 \cdot 783 - 8 \cdot 940\frac{x}{100} - 5 \cdot 875\left(\frac{x}{100}\right)^2 - 0 \cdot 9189\left(\frac{x}{100}\right)^3 \qquad . \quad (c)$$

Fig. 15.5 shows the data graphically, with the straight line and cubic parabola of closest fit.

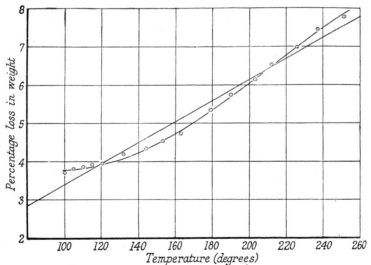

Fig. 15.5.—Straight line and cubic parabola of closest fit to the data of Table 15.5.

TABLE 15.5.—Curve-fitting to express the relationship between temperature and percentage loss in weight of certain soil samples
(Data from J. R. H. Coutts, " ' Single Value ' Soil Properties : V. On the Changes Produced in a Soil by Oven-drying," *Journal Agricultural Science*, 1930, **20,** 541.)

Percentage loss in weight Y	Temperature (degrees) X	Y²	X²	X³	X⁴	X⁵	X⁶	YX	YX²	YX³
3·71	100	13·7641	10,000	1,000,000	100,000,000	10,000,000,000	1,000,000,000,000	371·00	37,100·00	3,710,000·00
3·81	105	14·5161	11,025	1,157,625	121,550,625	12,762,815,625	1,340,095,640,625	400·05	42,005·25	4,410,551·25
3·86	110	14·8996	12,100	1,331,000	146,410,000	16,105,100,000	1,771,561,000,000	424·60	46,706·00	5,137,760·00
3·93	115	15·4449	13,225	1,520,875	174,900,625	20,113,571,875	2,313,060,765,625	451·95	51,974·25	5,977,038·75
3·96	121	15·6816	14,641	1,771,561	214,358,881	25,937,424,601	3,138,428,376,721	479·16	57,978·36	7,015,381·56
4·20	132	17·6400	17,424	2,299,968	303,595,776	40,074,642,432	5,289,852,801,024	554·40	73,180·80	9,659,865·60
4·34	144	18·8356	20,736	2,985,984	429,981,696	61,917,364,224	8,916,100,448,256	624·96	89,994·24	12,959,170·56
4·51	153	20·3401	23,409	3,581,577	547,981,281	83,841,135,993	12,827,693,806,929	690·03	105,574·59	16,152,912·27
4·73	163	22·3729	26,569	4,330,747	705,911,761	115,063,617,043	18,755,369,578,009	770·99	125,671·37	20,484,433·31
5·35	179	28·6225	32,041	5,735,339	1,026,625,681	183,765,996,899	32,894,113,444,921	957·65	171,419·35	30,684,063·65
5·74	191	32·9476	36,481	6,967,871	1,330,863,361	254,194,901,951	48,551,226,272,641	1,096·34	209,400·94	39,995,579·54
6·14	203	37·6996	41,209	8,365,427	1,698,181,681	344,730,881,243	69,980,368,892,329	1,246·42	253,023·26	51,363,721·78
6·51	212	42·3801	44,944	9,528,128	2,019,963,136	428,232,184,832	90,785,223,184,384	1,380·12	292,385·44	62,028,113·28
6·98	226	48·7204	51,076	11,543,176	2,608,757,776	589,579,257,376	133,244,912,279,976	1,577·48	356,510·48	80,571,368·48
7·44	237	55·3536	56,169	13,312,053	3,154,956,561	747,724,704,957	177,210,755,074,809	1,763·28	417,897·36	99,041,674·32
7·76	251	60·2176	63,001	15,813,251	3,969,126,001	996,250,626,251	250,058,907,189,001	1,947·76	488,887·76	122,710,827·76
82·97	2,642	459·4363	474,050	91,244,582	18,553,164,842	3,930,294,225,302	858,077,668,755,250	14,736·19	2,819,909·45	571,902,362·11

15.21 Although a graph will usually suggest whether a straight line or quadratic parabola is likely to give a satisfactory fit, it will not as a rule be much guide in deciding whether further terms will repay the labour of calculation. This can be judged, at least roughly, by calculating the terms given by the polynomial (to as high a degree as it has been carried) for the observed values of x, and then observing the run of the residuals. If the signs run more or less at random it will hardly be worth while to calculate another term ; but if a series of positive residuals is followed by a series of negative residuals, these by another series of positive residuals, etc., it will probably be worth while to proceed further. Moreover, the coefficients for a parabola of order k are no guide to those of order $k+1$. For instance, in Example 15.4, the values of a_0 for the straight line, square parabola and cubic parabola are $0\cdot660, 3\cdot551, 7\cdot783$; and those of a_1 are $0\cdot02741, -0\cdot009291, -0\cdot08940$. From this information we could not guess even the sign of these coefficients in the parabola of order 4, and if we wished to fit such a curve five equations of the type (15.8) would have to be solved *ab initio*.

The student, therefore, should not fall into the error of thinking that parabolas of successive orders will resemble each other in their lower terms, or that the fitting of a curve of order $k+1$ is merely a question of adding an extra term to a curve of order k. It would be a great convenience if this were so, and, in fact, methods have been devised whereby one variate can be expressed in terms of certain polynomials of the other in such a way that this advantage is secured. The theory of these so-called " orthogonal " polynomials is, however, outside the scope of the present work.

The case when the independent variable proceeds by equal steps

15.22 When the independent variable x proceeds by steps of equal amount h, the arithmetical solution of equations (15.8) can be greatly simplified, particularly if the number of values is odd. In such a case we take h as the unit of x and an origin at the middle term. The values of x will then be $-k, -(k-1), -(k-2), \ldots -2, -1, 0, 1, 2, \ldots (k-2), (k-1), k$, and owing to the symmetry of this series the sums of odd powers of x will vanish, i.e. $\Sigma(X), \Sigma(X^3), \Sigma(X^5)$, etc. are all zero. Equations (15.8) then become, taking p as odd,

$$
\begin{aligned}
\Sigma(Y) &\quad -na_0 &\quad -a_2\Sigma(X^2) &\quad -a_4\Sigma(X^4) \ldots =0\\
\Sigma(YX) &\quad -a_1\Sigma(X^2) &\quad -a_3\Sigma(X^4) \ldots &\quad =0\\
&\quad . &\quad . &\quad .\\
&\quad . &\quad . &\quad .\\
\Sigma(YX^{p-1}) -a_0\Sigma(X^{p-1}) &\quad -a_2\Sigma(X^{p+1}) \ldots &\quad &\quad =0\\
\Sigma(YX^p) &\quad -a_1\Sigma(X^{p+1}) &\quad -a_3\Sigma(X^{p+3}) \ldots &\quad =0
\end{aligned}
\tag{15.12}
$$

and not only is the number of terms reduced, but the equations split into two sets, one in a_0, a_2, a_4, etc., and the other in a_1, a_3, a_5, etc. Moreover, the sums of even powers of X are twice the sums of powers of the first k natural numbers, which may be easily found, either from tables or from known formulæ.

Example 15.5.—Table 15.6 shows the population of England and Wales in certain census years from 1811 onwards. Taking the time as the independent variable, we choose as the unit of X the period of ten years, and the origin at the mid-point of the range, 1871. The preliminary work for the fitting of curves up to the cubic form is shown in the table.

For the cubic parabola, equations (15.8) are, then,

$$
\begin{array}{llll}
314 \cdot 09 - 13a_0 & -182a_2 & =0 \\
474 \cdot 77 & -182a_1 & -4550a_3 & =0 \\
4520 \cdot 45 - 182a_0 & -4550a_2 & =0 \\
11{,}632 \cdot 97 & -4550a_1 & -134{,}342a_3 & =0
\end{array}
$$

whence

$$
\begin{array}{ll}
a_0 = 23 \cdot 299 & a_1 = \;\; 2 \cdot 895 \\
a_2 = \;\; 0 \cdot 06153 & a_3 = -0 \cdot 01147
\end{array}
$$

The parabola is, therefore,

$$y = 23 \cdot 299 + 2 \cdot 895x + 0 \cdot 06153x^2 - 0 \cdot 01147x^3 \tag{a}$$

Fig. 15.6 shows the data graphically, together with this cubic.

Incidentally, this example illustrates one point of some importance. Over the years 1811 to 1931 the cubic gives a fair fit, and might be used to estimate the population at intermediate years. But for extrapolation it is of very little value. We could not estimate the population for 1961 with any confidence by putting $x=9$ in the cubic; still less that for later years. Unless there are good reasons for supposing that the fitted curve is an accurate representation of a theoretical relationship, it is dangerous to assume that a fitted parabola can be used outside the range for which it was ascertained.

It would be instructive for the student to fit merely a segment of some actual series and note how rapidly the curve calculated from the segment diverged from the observations outside its limits. It has been shown that even within the limits of the fitted observations the fit tends to be worst as the limits are approached. The higher powers of x become of greater and greater effect the more we diverge from the centre of the fitted segment and tend, so to speak, to " wag the tail " of the curve.

15.23 If the number of values of x is even, we have a choice of two methods of procedure. We can take h as unit and the origin at one of the two middle values; or we can take $\frac{1}{2}h$ as unit and origin midway between the two central values. In the first case, the sums of odd powers will no longer vanish, but they will nevertheless be easily calculable,

TABLE 15.6.—Curve-fitting to growth of population in England and Wales
(Data from Registrar-General's Statistical Review of England and Wales, 1933, Tables, Part II.)

Year	Popu-lation (mil'ns) Y	X	X^2	X^3	X^4	X^6	YX	YX^2	YX^3
1811	10·16	−6	36	−216	1,296	46,656	−60·96	365·76	− 2,194·56
1821	12·00	−5	25	−125	625	15,625	−60·00	300·00	− 1,500·00
1831	13·90	−4	16	− 64	256	4,096	−55·60	222·40	− 889·60
1841	15·91	−3	9	− 27	81	729	−47·73	143·19	− 429·57
1851	17·93	−2	4	− 8	16	64	−35·86	71·72	− 143·44
1861	20·07	−1	1	− 1	1	1	−20·07	20·07	− 20·07
1871	22·71	0	0	0	—	—	—	—	—
1881	25·97	1	1	1	1	1	25·97	25·97	25·97
1891	29·00	2	4	8	16	64	58·00	116·00	232·00
1901	32·53	3	9	27	81	729	97·59	292·77	878·31
1911	36·07	4	16	64	256	4,096	144·28	577·12	2,308·48
1921	37·89	5	25	125	625	15,625	189·45	947·25	4,736·25
1931	39·95	6	36	216	1,296	46,656	239·70	1,438·20	8,629·20
Total	314·09	0	182	0	4,550	134,342	474·77	4,520·45	11,632·97

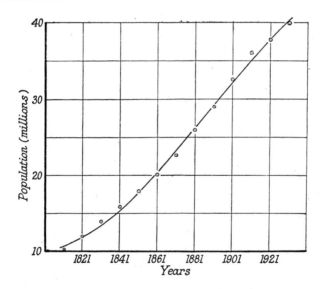

Fig. 15.6.—Cubic parabola fitted to the data of Table 15.6

since all terms except a single outlying member in the summation will cancel out in pairs. In the second case the sums of odd powers will vanish, but the other sums will no longer be twice those of the first k natural numbers, but of the first k odd numbers. In either case the solution of the equations (15.8) is not difficult.

Calculation of the sum of squares of residuals

15.24   The eye is not a reliable guide to the closeness with which a given curve lies to data, and it is desirable to have some more accurate measure of the closeness of fit.   For this purpose we require to be able to find the sum of the squares of residuals U.   We know by our method of ascertaining the curve that this will be less than the corresponding quantity for any other curve of the same degree, and our interest is centred on how close this is to the ideal value zero.

To calculate the sum of squares of residuals it is not necessary to calculate each separate residual.   In fact, for the parabola of order p we have—

$$U = \Sigma(Y - a_0 - a_1 X - a_2 X^2 - \ldots - a_p X^p)^2$$
$$= \Sigma\{Y(Y - a_0 - a_1 X - \ldots - a_p X^p)\}$$

for the terms of the type $\Sigma\{a_k X^k(Y - a_0 - a_1 X - \ldots - a_p X^p)\}$ vanish in virtue of equations (15.8).   Hence,

$$U = \Sigma(Y^2) - a_0\Sigma(Y) - a_1\Sigma(YX) - \ldots - a_p\Sigma(YX^p) \qquad . \quad (15.13)$$

The constants a and the sums which appear in this expression have already been found, with the exception of $\Sigma(Y^2)$ in some cases.   With this additional quantity we can find U.

Example 15.6.—Let us find U for the data of Example 15.4 for the straight line and the two parabolas.

For the line
$$U = \Sigma(Y^2) - a_0\Sigma(Y) - a_1\Sigma(YX)$$

Here
$$\Sigma(Y) = 82 \cdot 97, \qquad \Sigma(YX) = 14{,}736 \cdot 19$$
$$\Sigma(Y^2) = 459 \cdot 4363, \qquad a_0 = 0 \cdot 659{,}759{,}789$$
$$a_1 = 0 \cdot 027{,}408{,}722$$

Hence,
$$U = 459{,}4363 - 54 \cdot 74027 - 403 \cdot 90014$$
$$= 0 \cdot 7959$$

For the quadratic parabola—
$$U = \Sigma(Y^2) - a_0\Sigma(Y) - a_1\Sigma(YX) - a_2\Sigma(YX^2)$$

and here
$$a_1 = \quad 3 \cdot 550{,}990{,}2$$
$$a_1 = -0 \cdot 009{,}291{,}235{,}7$$
$$a_2 = \quad 0 \cdot 000{,}106{,}954{,}12$$

whence
$$U = 0 \cdot 1271$$

Similarly, for the cubic
$$U = 0 \cdot 0485$$

The value of U therefore decreases from $0\cdot7959$ for the straight line to $0\cdot0485$ for the cubic. This is what we should expect, for the addition of extra terms means that we have additional constants at our disposal in the task of minimising U.

To obtain U with any accuracy by the foregoing method it is necessary to ascertain the a's to a considerable number of decimal places.

Measurement of the closeness of fit

15.25 The value of U enables us to make some sort of comparison between the fits of different curves to the same data ; but it is not, in itself, a satisfactory measure of fit, since it does not permit of the comparison of the fits of curves to different data. The measure U/n, which is the variance of errors of estimation, suggests itself, but this, like U, is not absolute, being dependent on the units in which we are working. For a satisfactory measure some form of ratio would have to be taken.

Such a ratio arises in a natural way if we consider the correlation between the actual values of Y and those " predicted " by the polynomial.

Let us, without loss of generality, suppose that the values are measured from their mean, and let y_r be the value given by the polynomial and Y_r be the actual value. Then, as in **15.24**,

$$\Sigma(y^2)=\Sigma(Yy) \qquad . \qquad . \qquad . \qquad (15.14)$$

$$U=\Sigma\{Y(Y-y)\}$$
$$=\Sigma(Y^2)-\Sigma(Yy) \qquad . \qquad . \qquad (15.15)$$

Writing σ_r, σ_y for the standard deviations of Y and y, and R for the correlation between them, we get, from (15.14),

$$\sigma_y{}^2=R\sigma_r\sigma_y$$

or

$$\sigma_y=R\sigma_r \qquad . \qquad . \qquad . \qquad (15.16)$$

and from (15.15),

$$\frac{U}{n}=\sigma_r{}^2-R\sigma_r\sigma_y$$

or

$$R\frac{\sigma_y}{\sigma_r}=1-\frac{U}{n\sigma_r{}^2} \qquad . \qquad . \qquad . \qquad (15.17)$$

Hence, substituting for σ_y from (15.16),

$$R^2=1-\frac{U}{n\sigma_r{}^2} \qquad . \qquad . \qquad . \qquad (15.18)$$

which gives the correlation in terms of the ratio of U/n and the variance $\sigma_r{}^2$.

R is, in fact, analogous to the multiple correlation coefficient and the correlation ratio, and the equation (15.18) should be compared with equation (11.3), page 256, and equation (12.15), page 298.

Example 15.7.—In Example 15.1 we have, using the data of Table 15.2 and the constants found—

$$\sigma_r{}^2 = 67 \cdot 28998 - (6 \cdot 126)^2$$
$$= 29 \cdot 762,104$$
$$U = 1 \cdot 835,777,255$$
$$R^2 = 1 - \frac{1 \cdot 835,777,255}{297 \cdot 62104} = 0 \cdot 993,831,830$$
$$R = 0 \cdot 99691$$

For the soil data of Examples 15.4 and 15.6 we find—

For the straight line $R = 0 \cdot 98627$
For the cubic $R = 0 \cdot 99917$

Thus, judged by the value of R, the straight line of Example 15.1 is a better fit than that of Example 15.4, but a worse fit than the cubic of the latter.

15.26 As a general comment on the scope of the methods of curve-fitting described in this chapter, we may remark that although polynomials can always be fitted to data, the student should not assume that even the polynomial of closest fit will necessarily be a *satisfactory* fit. It may exhibit peculiarities of behaviour which are entirely absent from the data themselves. He may well ask, when confronted by a given set of data, how he is to know whether they may be satisfactorily represented by a polynomial. The answer is that he must fit one and see. Some further remarks on this point are given later in **24.12**, where similar questions arise in connection with interpolation and graduation.

15.27 The reader must be mindful of the fact that in the type of curve-fitting discussed above there is an essential difference between the roles of the independent and the dependent variables, which accounts for there being two curves according to which variable is regarded as independent. If y is the dependent and x the independent variable the minimisation of the sum of squares of residuals in the manner of **15.8** is equivalent to supposing that if there is a " true " law under which y is equal to a polynomial in x, the " errors " observed are in the dependent variable y, not in x. *Per contra*, if we suppose that the errors are in x, we must minimise the sum of squares of residuals in x, which makes the latter the dependent variable.

15.28 Suppose, however, that x and y are known to be related by a linear equation but that *both* variables are subject to error. What is then the appropriate method of finding the best estimate of the unknown relation ? If the errors are small, as seems to be the case in Example 15.1, an approximation is given by the methods we have used because the two lines of closest fit are nearly identical. But where the errors may be large, and in any case as a theoretical problem where both variates are subject to error, we may require to find a *unique* relation most probably (in some sense) representing the truth. This sort of problem may very well arise, for example, in physics where it is assumed that there exists a definite functional relationship between two quantities (the pressure and the reciprocal of the volume of a gas or the length and temperature of a metal rod) both of which are subject to errors of measurement.

15.29 This type of problem is extraordinarily difficult to solve and we have no space to discuss it here at any length. A single illustration of the complications which arise will have to suffice.

A plausible procedure to determine a unique straight line fitting a set of points on a scatter diagram is to minimise the sum of squares of perpendiculars from the points on to the line. This is equivalent to finding the principal axis (**10.9**) which, in a sense, may be regarded as " closest " to the points. But unfortunately this line will vary according to the scale of measurement of the variates—if we double the scale of one and hence enlarge the scatter diagram by the factor 2 in one direction, the new line has a different equation from the old and the difference is not merely that the transformed variate is in the new scale. Geometrically, we may say that right-angles are not preserved in a diagram if it is stretched in one direction, so that perpendiculars from points to lines do not remain perpendiculars under such a transformation. The procedure we are considering, therefore, whatever its merits as providing empirically a line of closest fit, is open to the theoretical objection that the answer it gives depends on the scale of measurement, which in many problems is repugnant to commonsense requirements. We do not, for example, expect the linear law connecting the length of a rod with its temperature to depend on whether we are measuring the latter in Centigrade, Fahrenheit or absolute units. The procedure is reasonably plausible if both variables are of the same kind, e.g. both temperatures, so that a change of scale affects both to the same extent. The difficulties become intensified if the underlying law is not linear.*

SUMMARY

1. A parabola of the form $y=a_0+a_1x+a_2x^2+ \ldots +a_px^p$ may be fitted to data by choosing the constants a so that the sum of squares of residuals $U=\Sigma(Y-a_0-a_1X-a_2X^2- \ldots -a_pX^p)^2$ is a minimum.

2. This method leads to the equations

$$\Sigma(Y) \quad -na_0 \quad -a_1\Sigma(X) \quad -a_2\Sigma(X^2) \quad - \ldots \quad -a_p\Sigma(X^p) \quad =0$$
$$\Sigma(YX) \quad -a_0\Sigma(X) \quad -a_1\Sigma(X^2) \quad -a_2\Sigma(X^3) \quad - \ldots \quad -a_p\Sigma(X^{p+1}) =0$$
$$\Sigma(YX^p) \quad -a_0\Sigma(X^p) \quad -a_1\Sigma(X^{p+1}) \quad -a_2\Sigma(X^{p+2}) - \ldots \quad -a_p\Sigma(X^{2p}) \quad =0$$

* For a useful review of the problem see D.V. Lindley, *Supp. J. Roy. Statist. Soc.*, 1947, **9**, 218.

3. Non-linear data may sometimes be reduced to the linear form by a simple transformation of one or both the variables.

4. The sum of squares of residuals may be found from the formula

$$U = \Sigma(Y^2) - a_0\Sigma(Y) - a_1\Sigma(YX) - \ldots - a_p\Sigma(YX^p)$$

5. One measure of the goodness of fit of the parabola to the data is given by R, the correlation between actual and " predicted " values of the variate. R is given by

$$R^2 = 1 - \frac{U}{n\sigma_Y^2}$$

where Y is the dependent variable.

EXERCISES

15.1 Fit a straight line and parabolas of the second and third orders to the following data, taking X to be the independent variable—

X	Y
0	1
1	1·8
2	1·3
3	2·5
4	6·3

and find the sum of squares of residuals in the three cases.

15.2 (Data quoted by P. L. Fegiz, " Le variazioni stagionali della natalità," *Metron*, vol. 5, 1925, No. 4, p. 127.) The following figures show the relation between duration of marriage and average number of children per marriage in Norway in 1920—

Duration of marriage (years)	Average number of children
0– 1	0·48
5– 6	2·09
10–11	3·26
15–16	4·33
20–21	5·14
25–26	5·63
30–31	5·77

By the method of least squares find equations of the first, second and third orders expressing the number of children in terms of the duration of marriage. Compare the values given by these expressions for a duration of 17-18 years with the true value 4·67.

15.3 The pressure of a gas and its volume are known to be related by an equation of the form $pv^\gamma =$ constant.

In a certain experiment the following volumes of a quantity of the gas were observed for the pressures specified. Find the value of γ by fitting a straight line to the logarithms of p and v, taking p to be the independent variable.

p (kg. per square cm.) .	0·5	1·0	1·5	2·0	2·5	3·0
v (litres) . . .	1·62	1·00	0·75	0·62	0·52	0·46

15.4 The following are the gross output and the gross output per £100 of labour employed, for a selected number of farms—

Gross output (units)	Gross output per £100 labour (units)
63	40
223	155
755	188
165	78
1,535	315
3,193	290
2,238	259
1,228	231
2,695	255

Fit a quadratic parabola to these data, taking gross output as the independent variable.

CHAPTER SIXTEEN

PRELIMINARY NOTIONS ON SAMPLING

The problem

16.1 In practical problems the statistician is often confronted with the necessity of discussing a population of which he cannot examine every member. For example, an inquirer into the heights of the population of Great Britain cannot afford the time or expense required to measure the height of each individual ; nor can a farmer who wants to know what proportion of his potato crop is diseased examine every single potato.

In such cases the best an investigator can do is to examine a limited number of individuals and hope that they will tell him, with reasonable trustworthiness, as much as he wants to know about the population from which they come. We are thus led naturally to the question : what can be said about a population when we can examine only a limited number of its members ? This question is the origin of the *Theory of Sampling.*

16.2 A sample from a population is a selected number of individuals each of which is a member of the population. As a very special case the sample may consist of the entire population.

It is a matter of common belief, founded on experience and intuition, that a sample will tell us something about the parent population. The corn merchant, whose livelihood depends on his ability to ascertain the quality of the grain which he handles, is content to assess it by thrusting a conical trowel into the middle of a sack and scrutinising the sample he gets. He believes that the sample will be representative of the whole, and experience justifies him. He buys and sells on the basis of judgment from samples. It is also a matter of common belief that the larger a sample becomes the more likely it is to reflect accurately the conditions in the parent population.

To these and similar beliefs the theory of sampling gives a logical basis and a system of quantitative measurement. In this chapter we give a general survey of the fundamental ideas and the technique of sampling. In later chapters we shall develop these ideas and discuss their applications in various fields.

Types of population

16.3 Before we consider sampling itself, however, it is desirable to look a little closer into the various types of population which we shall have to investigate.

By a *finite population* we shall mean a population which contains a finite number of members. Such, for instance, is the population of inhabitants of Great Britain and the population of books in the British Museum.

Similarly, by an *infinite* population we shall mean a population containing an infinite number of members. Such, for instance, is the population of pressures at various points in the atmosphere, or the population of possible sizes of the wheat crop, for, although there are limits to the size, the actual tonnage can take any numerical value within those limits.

In many cases the number of members in a population is so large as to be practically infinite. Moreover, a theoretical discussion of an infinite population is frequently easier than a discussion of a finite population, and a large class of problems may be treated by assuming that the parent population is infinite, without introducing any sensible error.

It may be worth remarking that in a few cases we may be ignorant whether or not the population under discussion is infinite. The population of stars is an example.

Existent and hypothetical population

16.4 By the logical extension of the idea of a population of concrete objects, which we shall call an *existent population*, we are able to construct the idea of a *hypothetical population*.

Consider the throws of a die. Each throw will be regarded as an individual. There is an infinite number of throws which can be made with the die, provided that it does not wear out. Let us then define as our population of discussion all the *possible* throws of the die.

In doing so we are clearly making some new step ; for our population is to be conceived as having no existence in reality but only in imagination. We can give actuality to some members of the population by throwing the die, but we can never produce them all. Even if the die were locked away in a safe and never thrown at all there would still be a population of possible throws.

Such a population is called a *hypothetical* population. We may define it formally as the aggregate of all the conceivable ways in which a specified event can happen. Other examples of hypothetical populations are the population of all values which the bank rate can have in ten years' time, and the population of the possible ways in which three balls can be arranged on a billiard table.

16.5 A hypothetical population may, in fact, be imagined around any observed event. We have only to picture all the circumstances before the event happens ; the population is then all the possible ways in which it could happen. Which of the ways it *will* happen does not affect the population. We know that "from the chaos of predestination and the night of our forebeing " some one individual will emerge to assume the mantle of reality ; but which one that will be is another and more difficult question.

16.6 The student of metaphysics would perhaps criticise the thoughts expressed briefly in the previous two sections, but we have no space to go further into the philosophical implications of the idea of hypothetical populations. The problems which arise in this connection have, however, far more than an abstract interest. They lie at the root of a great many practical statistical problems, and most students, however utilitarian their outlook, will find that a clear perception of the issues involved may save a lot of thought and labour at a subsequent stage.

Population of populations

16.7 Just as a population may contain a number of sub-populations, so any given population may be a member of some more widely defined population. For example, the population of inhabitants of Great Britain is a member of the population of populations, each of which consists of the inhabitants of some European country.

Similarly, any existent population may be regarded as one member of a hypothetical population of populations. For instance, the normal population of men whose heights have a mean of 65 inches and standard deviation 3 inches is a member of the hypothetical population of all populations which are normally distributed with respect to height.

16.8 We shall sometimes have to discuss aggregates which it is difficult to regard as composed of individual members at all—for example, we may wish to sample a reservoir of water to test for pollution. In theory, perhaps, we could in such a case regard the reservoir as a population composed of molecules each of which was an individual, but in practice, as we shall see, this is not usually a convenient method of approach. Such populations may frequently be treated as composed of arbitrary units, e.g. the reservoir may be regarded as composed of so many pints of fluid. Similarly, a 280-lb. sack of flour may be regarded as composed of 4,480 ounces, and we can, if we like, regard it as weighed out into one-ounce packets.

16.9 We can now turn to discuss the aims which usually underlie a sampling inquiry.

Briefly, the fundamental object of sampling is to give the maximum information about the parent population with the minimum effort. We must, therefore, consider the type of information we require and the methods by which it is to be obtained.

16.10 In sampling a population we usually have in mind one or more of its variates. For instance, when we sample the population of Great Britain, we are not so much interested in the individuals as human beings as in one of their qualities, such as height or weight, or perhaps the correlation between height and weight. Our object will then be to get, from the sample, an idea of the frequency-distribution in the parent population according to the chosen variates.

The ideal for the purpose would be to express this distribution in some mathematical form such as a Pearson curve (**8.48**). It may be, however, that the parent population will not admit of this representation, or that the sample is not large enough for us to venture on it with any confidence.

In such cases we attempt to find estimates of certain constants of the parent population. Very often this is all we need. We can, for example, form a very fair idea of the height distribution of the population of Great Britain if we know the mean and the standard deviation. If we can go further, and find the third and fourth moments, our idea will be better still.

Theory of estimation

16.11 Hence, a large part of the theory of sampling is devoted to finding from the sample estimates of certain constants of the parent population. Such constants include the measures of position and of dispersion together with the moments and measures of skewness; and, in multivariate populations, the various total and partial correlations.

In general, there are more ways than one of estimating a constant from the data of the sample. Some of these ways will be better than others. The *Theory of Estimation* treats of these and cognate matters. It seeks to investigate the conditions which an estimate should obey, what are the best estimates to employ in given circumstances, and how good other estimates are in comparison.

Precision of estimates

16.12 It will be obvious that knowledge derived from a sample is not of the categorical kind customary in mathematics. If we have 1,000 balls in a bag and draw 999 of them which turn out to be black, it is always *possible* that the remaining one is of some other colour. It is, however, so improbable, that in most practical cases we should be justified in concluding that the balls were all black.

If we did draw such a conclusion, and acted upon it, we should be basing our action, not upon certainty, but on probability. One does this kind of thing, of course, in nearly all everyday actions almost without noticing it. Some events, such as the death of a man before reaching the age of 150, have such a high degree of probability that we never regard them as other than certain; other events, such as the possibility of rain to-morrow, are so uncertain that we should hesitate to make an important decision contingent upon them.

16.13 The second aim of the theory of sampling is, therefore, to determine as objectively as possible what degree of confidence we can put in our estimates when they are obtained. This we do in terms of probability as far as we can; if this proves impossible, we sometimes have to rely on intuitive impressions or the results of previous experience, which are not expressible in quantitative terms.

Put in another way, we may say that our object is to determine the *precision* of an estimate. We attempt to do this by assigning limits to the probable divergence between the estimate based on the sample and the true value of the estimated quantity in the population.

16.14 The accuracy of the estimate will depend on (*a*) the way in which the estimate is made from the data of the sample, and (*b*) the way in which the sample was obtained. Consideration of the first leads us again to the theory of estimation. The second leads us to study the *technique of sampling* and the *design of statistical inquiries*.

Tests of significance

16.15 If the sample is small we cannot, as a rule, assign to the estimates we obtain sufficiently narrow limits to locate the population value with any serviceable accuracy. For example, a correlation of $+0\cdot5$ in a sample of twelve might arise, rather infrequently, from a normal population in which the true correlation was as high as $+0\cdot9$ or as low as zero. For such samples our questions are accordingly framed in more qualitative terms : we do not ask, " What is the value of the correlation in the population ? " but, " Is the observed value *significant* of the existence of any correlation at all in the population, whatever its value ? " In other words, we wish to know whether the observed value could have arisen from a population in which the true correlation is zero. If our conclusion is that it could not, we may say that the sample value is significant of correlation, although we cannot say with much confidence what that correlation is.

Much of the investigation arising out of small samples is thus of a rather special character, and deals with *tests of significance*. The methods developed for the purpose of conducting such tests can be, and not infrequently are, applied also to large samples, either alone or supplementary to the direct approach of forming more or less precise estimates of the various quantities which specify the parent population.

Types of sampling

16.16 The process of forming a sample consists of choosing a predetermined number of individuals from the parent population. The choice may be exercised in three ways—

(*a*) By selecting the individuals at random (the meaning of " random " is discussed below).

(*b*) By selecting the individuals according to some purposive principle.

(*c*) By a mixture of (*a*) and (*b*).

Thus, in taking a sample of the inhabitants of Great Britain to study their income we might, according to method (*a*), select the individuals at random from census returns ; or according to (*b*) we might, knowing roughly the average incomes in various age-groups, purposely select from each group an individual whose income was somewhere near the average in that group ; or (c) we might decide to take ten individuals from each group and select those ten by method (a).

16.17 Sampling of type (a) is called *random sampling*. That of type (b) is called *purposive sampling*. That of type (c) is sometimes referred to as *mixed sampling*. If the population is divided into " strata " by purposive methods and then a portion of the sample is taken from each " stratum," the sampling is said to be *stratified*.

The application of each of these types may be affected by what is known as *bias*. This is the name given to perturbations which influence the nature of the choice and make it something other than what the experimenter intends it to be. Bias may be due to imperfect instruments, the personal qualities of the observer, defective technique, or other causes. Like experimental error, it is difficult to eliminate entirely, but usually may be reduced to relatively small dimensions by taking proper care.

By an obvious extension of the nomenclature, we talk of a sample obtained by random sampling as a random sample, that obtained by purposive sampling as a purposive sample, and so on.

Random sampling
16.18 The reader no doubt already has some intuitive ideas about randomness of choice. We may give a formal definition of random sampling by saying that the selection of an individual from a population is random when each member of the population has the same chance of being chosen. Similarly, a sample of n individuals is random when it is chosen in such a way that, when the choice is made, all possible samples of n have an equal chance of being selected.

16.19 The first question arising out of this definition which we have to consider is : How are we to obtain a random sample ?

This question is more difficult than it appears at first sight. It might be thought that any purely haphazard method of selection would give a random sample. For example, if we wished to obtain a random sample of local tradesmen, one way which suggests itself is to take a Trades Directory, open it " at random " and take the first name on which the eye alights, repeating the process until the sample is of the required size. Or again, if we wished to obtain a random sample of wheat growing in a field, it might be thought that a satisfactory method would be to throw a hoop in the air " at random " and select all the plants over which it fell.

16.20 That such methods are apt to be deceptive may be seen from the two examples we have just given. In the first, if we consulted a Trades Directory which had already been used, we should probably find that it opened at some pages more readily than at others ; we should therefore tend to get the more popular tradesmen. Moreover, our eye might tend to be caught by long names or peculiar names. In either case some tradesmen would have a greater chance of being chosen than others, and the sample would not be random.

TABLE 16.1.—Height measurements of wheat. Frequencies of plants chosen by eye in ranks 1-8

F. Yates, " Some Examples of Biased Sampling," *Annals of Eugenics*, 1935, **6**, 202.

Date	Observation	Ascending order of magnitude rank								Total	Expectation in each class
		1	2	3	4	5	6	7	8		
May 31	Shoot height	9	7	11	8	11	18	21	31	116	14·5
June 28	Ear height	9	19	27	23	15	10	5	4	112	14

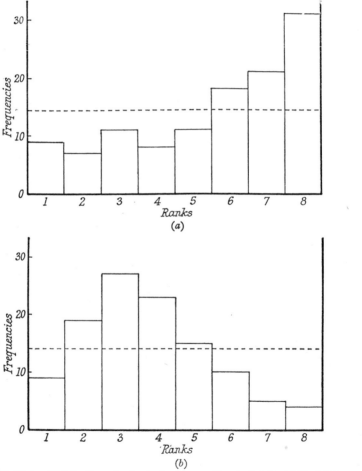

Fig. 16.1.—Distribution of wheat plants according to height (Table 16.1)
(*a*) Distribution of shoot heights (31st May) in ranks 1-8
(*b*) Distribution of ear heights (28th June) in ranks 1-8

Again, in the second example, our hoop might tend to be caught by the taller ears of wheat, or we might tend unconsciously to throw it towards parts of the field where the wheat looked to be about the average height. These and other factors would destroy the random character of the sampling.

Human bias

16.21 Experience has, in fact, shown that the human being is an extremely poor instrument for the conduct of a random selection. Wherever there is any scope for personal choice or judgment on the part of the observer, bias is almost certain to creep in. Nor is this a quality which can be removed by conscious effort or training. Nearly every human being has, as part of his psychological make-up, a tendency away from true randomness in his choices.

We may illustrate the unreliability of free choice on the part of even a trained observer by taking an example of height measurements in samples of wheat plants. In the course of certain work at the Rothamsted Experimental Station, sets of eight wheat plants were selected for measurement. Six of these shoots were chosen by purely random methods. The other two were chosen " at random " by eye. If, in any set, the eight shoots were ranged in order of magnitude, the two chosen by eye could have any places from one to eight; and if they, in common with the other six, were really random, they should have occupied these places with equal frequency in a reasonably large number of sets. Table 16.1 shows the resulting frequencies in the ranks one to eight for 116 sets taken on 31st May (before the ears of wheat had formed) and 112 sets taken on 28th June (after the ears had formed).

Fig. 16.1 shows the same results graphically, the dotted line giving the frequencies to be expected if the choice was really random.

The divergence of the actual from the expected results is very striking, and clearly cannot be attributed to fluctuations of sampling. It will be seen that on 31st May, before the ears had formed, the observer was strongly biased towards the taller shoots ; whereas in June, after the ears had formed, he was biased strongly towards a central position and avoided short and tall plants.

16.22 Sight is not the only sense which may bias a sampling method. In certain experiments counters of the same shape but of different colours were put into a bag and chosen one at a time, the counter chosen being put back and the bag thoroughly shaken before the next trial. On the face of it this appears to be a purely random method of drawing the counters. Nevertheless, there emerged a persistent bias against counters of one particular colour. After careful investigation the only explanation seemed to be that these particular counters were slightly more greasy than the others, owing to peculiarities of the pigment, and hence slipped through the sampler's fingers.

The student may perform similar experiments for himself. One of the simplest is to ask a friend to recite " at random " one hundred digits, including zero, and then count the number of odd ones. If the numbers are really random, the number of even ones and odd ones should be about equal, but there will frequently be found a bias one way or the other.

16.23 Enough has been said to show that if we are to evolve a satisfactory method of random sampling we must eliminate all personal choice. The method of selection must, therefore, follow some code of procedure which leaves nothing to the observer's idiosyncrasies.

It may sound a little paradoxical to obtain true randomness·by following rules of procedure. We are reminded of Bertrand's question : " How can we talk of the laws of chance, which is the negation of all law ? " The ensuing sections will, it is hoped, remove any doubts on this head.

Technique of random sampling

16.24 The methods adopted in any given case to ensure as far as possible that the sampling is random depend to some extent on the size and nature of the population. Certain modes of procedure which are convenient for small populations are not so for large populations. We shall also see that sampling from a hypothetical population has a special significance and special difficulties of its own.

16.25 The criterion that every individual should have an equal chance of being chosen may be put in a somewhat different form. If the method of selection is independent of the properties of the sampled population which it is desired to investigate, there will, so far as those properties are concerned, be no reason why one individual should be chosen rather than another. Hence all values of the properties which occur in the population will have an equal chance of being chosen. If, therefore, we can produce a mode of procedure which bears no relation to the properties of the parent population which we are discussing, we may expect that it will give a random sample, so far as those properties are concerned.

16.26 We may now consider a few examples of the kind of procedure to which this rule leads.

Suppose we wish to take a sample of the inhabitants of a street. They are already arranged in houses, and for the sake of simplicity we will take our problem to be that of selecting a number of houses, whose occupants will comprise our sample.

Let us take as our rule of procedure the selection of every tenth house, starting at some arbitrary point. Unless there are peculiar circumstances, it is presumable that the properties we are investigating, which may, for instance, be income or size of family, are not grouped periodically along the street. The method of selection is then independent of the properties of the population and the sampling will be random.

If, however, the street were divided into blocks by cross-streets at every tenth house, so that every house in our sample was a corner house, and therefore, possibly, a shop, it is easy to see that the sample is no longer random. Shops occur, in fact, along that street with period ten, and since our method of selection has also that period, the method and the qualities under investigation are no longer independent.

16.27. We might then fall back on a different method. If we take a pack of plain cards, as similar as we can get them, we can make one card correspond to one of the houses by writing on it the number of the house in the street. The pack would then be a kind of miniature of the population for sampling purposes. We can draw a sample of houses by drawing a sample of cards, and if we shuffle the pack well we have every reason to hope that a random sample will result, for it is hard to imagine any way in which the method of shuffling and drawing could be dependent on the properties of the population. It is not impossible to make it so, however. For instance, if the ink with which we wrote the numbers on the cards was slightly adhesive, the larger numbers would not be so easy to draw out as the small ones, and we should tend to get houses at one end of the street. If such houses were of the poorer class, our sample for the purpose of investigating income would not be random.

Lottery sampling

16.28 The method we have just described, of constructing a miniature population which is easily handled, is one of the most reliable methods of drawing a random sample. It is the method usually adopted in drawing the winning numbers in sweepstakes and lotteries. In such cases the population is the aggregate of persons owning tickets in the lottery. To every member of this population there corresponds a number, the totality of which numbers, written on pieces of paper, comprises the miniature population. In practice, these pieces are placed in similar containers, usually small metal cylinders, and thrown into a large rotating drum, in which they are thoroughly mixed or " randomised."

16.29 The practical difficulties of constructing the miniature population and of shuffling it are, however, severe if the parent population is at all large. The method is, of course, inapplicable on theoretical grounds if the population is not finite. To save the trouble of work with tickets it is often possible to use numerical methods.

Suppose we require a set of points on the celestial sphere, as for example if stars were uniformly distributed and we wanted a sample of stars. We will take a point to be defined on the celestial sphere by latitude and longitude (though this is not the way in which astronomers usually express it), and will ignore difficulties arising from the existence of double stars or unresolved objects. What we want, then, is a set of random pairs of latitudes and longitudes. As a crude method we might take an atlas of the world and choose the figure set out in the index for places arranged alphabetically. But it is easy to see that this method is unsound ; for there will be more names associated with the more populous districts, and hence the values given in the index will tend to cluster round certain points and avoid others—there will be none in the middle of seas or at the poles, so that the pole star has no chance of being selected.

Let us then take a set of statistical tables and open it haphazardly. We shall be confronted with a page of figures, and if we take, say, the tenth figure in each row we shall probably get a set of digits which are random. Suppose the first ten digits obtained in this way were 7, 0, 4, 7, 9, 6, 8, 2, 9, 1. We might then take our star to be defined by latitude 70° 47·9′ and longitude 68° 29·1 . Another page will give us another star, and so on.

Random sampling numbers

16.30 The difficulty in applying the method we have just described lies in ensuring that the numbers we obtain are really random. Many tables of figures, such as logarithm tables, may fail to give random digits because there is a relation between the figures in successive rows. To obviate this difficulty certain Tables of Random Sampling Numbers have been constructed.

One such set, due to L. H. C. Tippett, consists of 41,600 digits taken from census reports and combined by fours to give 10,400 four-figure numbers. We give here the first forty sets as an illustration of their general appearance—

2952	6641	3992	9792	7979	5911	3170	5624
4167	9524	1545	1396	7203	5356	1300	2693
2370	7483	3408	2762	3563	1089	6913	7691
0560	5246	1112	6107	6008	8126	4233	8776
2754	9143	1405	9025	7002	6111	8816	6446

The reader may wonder how it was ensured that these digits are random. They were chosen haphazard, but the real guarantee of their randomness lies in practical tests. We may say at once that Tippett's numbers have been subjected to numerous investigations which make their randomness for many practical cases highly probable. A further set of numbers (100,000 in all) was constructed by Kendall and Babington Smith using a randomising machine. These also were carefully tested after construction. The use of random sampling numbers will be apparent from the following examples—

Example 16.1.—To take a random sample of 10 from the population of 8585 men of Table 4.7, page 82.

Here we have 8585 individuals. We will number them from 1 to 8585. The problem of selecting ten men at random is then that of finding ten numbers at random between 1 and 8585. We therefore take a page of random sampling numbers and select the first ten on the page which are not greater than 8585. Thus, if our page were the one on which appear the

numbers we have quoted above, our individuals would be those corresponding to the numbers, reading across.

2952, 6641, 3992, 7979, 5911, 3170, 5624, 4167, 1545, 1396

If we imagine the numbering to be done in order of height, starting with
the shortest and ending with the tallest, we see that the first individual falls
in the group 66—", the second in the group 69—", and so on. The height-
ranges in which the ten individuals fall are, in fact, in inches—

66—, 69—, 67—, 71—, 68--, 66—, 68—, 67—, 65--, 65—

Let us take their heights as being given by the centre points of these ranges,
and find their mean. We have—

$$M - \tfrac{7}{16} = \tfrac{1}{10}(66 + 69 + \ldots + 65)$$
$$= 67 \cdot 2$$

Hence the mean is $67 \cdot 6$ inches, as against the true value of $67 \cdot 46$ inches in
the whole population.

Example 16.2.—To take a sample of $\dot{5}$ from the distribution of screw
lengths of Table 4.3, page 72.

Here we have 206 individuals. It would clearly be a waste to use only
numbers from 0001 to 0206 for the screws and to neglect the rest, and we
are able to bring nearly all numbers into play by the following device.
We note that 206 goes 48 times into 10,000, with a certain remainder. In
fact, $206 \times 48 = 9{,}888$. We therefore attach 48 numbers to each screw.
Taking them in order, beginning at the shortest, we let the first screw
correspond to the numbers 0001 to 0048, the second to 0049 to 0096, the
third to 0097 to 0144, and so on, the 206th screw corresponding to the
numbers 9841 to 9888. Numbers above 9888 we leave out of account.
Referring to the table, we see that there is one screw in the first category
(5 to 6 thousandths short of an inch), four in the second (4 to 5 thousandths
short of an inch), and so on. The numbers corresponding to screws in the
different categories will then be 0001-0048, 0049-0240, 0241-0768, and
so on ; or, in tabular form.

We now take five random sampling numbers from the tables. For
instance, we might take the five in the first column of **16.30**, i.e. 2952,
4167, 2370, 0560, 2754. The screws corresponding to these numbers will
be $1 \cdot 5$, $0 \cdot 5$, $1 \cdot 5$, $3 \cdot 5$ and $1 \cdot 5$ thousandths short of the inch respectively.

If we had obtained two numbers, say 0001 and 0002 in the first category,
we should have been faced with the necessity for a decision on how the
sampling was to be regarded, for there is only one screw in this category.
If we suppose that a sampled screw is abstracted from the population, it can
only be drawn once ; and hence we should have had to ignore all numbers
in the category 0001 to 0048 subsequent to that which first occurs. If, on
the other hand, the screw is replaced, we can draw it as often as we like.

Difference in length from 1 inch (thousandths)	Numbers corresponding	Difference in length from 1 inch (thousandths)	Numbers corresponding
−6 to −5	0001—0048	+1 to +2	5857—7488
−5 to −4	0049—0240	+2 to +3	7489—8688
−4 to −3	0241—0768	+3 to +4	8689—9456
−3 to −2	0769—1824	+4 to +5	9457—9840
−2 to −1	1825—3024	+5 to +6	9841—9888
−1 to 0	3025—4320		
˚0 to +1	4321−5856		

Example 16.3.—In Example 2.5, page 25, we had the following data giving the association between inoculation against cholera and exemption from attack in 818 subjects—

	Not attacked	Attacked	Total
Inoculated .	276 (0001–3312)	3 (3313–3348)	279
Not inoculated .	473 (3349–9024)	66 (9025–9816)	539
Total .	749	69	818

Let us take a sample of 10 from this population.

We observe that 818 goes into 10,000 twelve times, with a certain remainder. In fact, $10,000 = 12 \times 818 + 184$. We can therefore attach 12 random sampling numbers to each member of the population. To the 276 inoculated-not-attacked individuals we attach the numbers 0001 to 3312 (12×276). To the 3 inoculated-attacked individuals we attach the numbers 3313 to 3348 (a range of 36, equal to 3×12). Similarly for the remaining individuals. The random sampling numbers corresponding to the individuals in the four compartments of the table are shown in brackets above.

We then take ten random sampling numbers from the tables, say the first ten, reading across, from the numbers given in **16.30**. If we had come across a number greater than 9816 we should have ignored it. The first number, 2952, gives us an individual falling in the inoculated-not-attacked class ; the second, 6641, gives us a member of the not-inoculated-not-attacked class; and so on. The 10 numbers give the following results—

	Not attacked	Attacked	Total
Inoculated .	2	0	2
Not inoculated .	6	2	8
Total .	8	2	10

Example 16.4.—Strictly speaking, random sampling numbers are applicable only to sampling from a finite population, for we cannot attach a different number to each member of an infinite aggregate. But, by the following device, we can apply the tables to draw samples from a continuous (and therefore infinite) population which is specified by a mathematical equation in such a way as to give us the proportion of the total frequency in given *ranges* of the variate.

In fact, let us draw a sample from a normal population with unit standard deviation and unit total frequency.

Let us take ranges of 0·1 on each side of the central ordinate. Table 2 of the Appendix will then give us the proportion of the frequency lying in these ranges. As in Example 16.1, we divide up the numbers from 0000 to 9999 in proportion to these frequencies, and this is, in fact, a particularly simple matter. All we have to do, for the positive values of the variate, is to take the figures in the table, which have four figures. For example, for the first interval 0·0 to 0·1, there will correspond the numbers 5000 to 5398; to the interval 0·1 to 0·2, the numbers 5399 to 5793; to the interval 0·2 to 0·3, the numbers 5794 to 6179; and so on. For the negative values of the variate we have, similarly, for 0·0 to −0·1, the numbers 4601 to 4999; for −0·1 to −0·2, the numbers 4206 to 4600; for −0·2 to −0·3, the numbers 3820 to 4205; and so on, there being as many numbers in any negative range as in the corresponding positive range. Occasionally doubt may arise in assigning a number to a given interval owing to the difficulty of rounding up a figure ending in 5. In practice it is not likely to make any difference which interval we choose; if it threatens to do so, we can take the doubtful number to refer alternately to the two possible intervals.

Having assigned numbers to the ranges, we select from the random sampling numbers tables in the ordinary way. For instance, a number 5500 will correspond to a member in the range 0·1 to 0·2. If we wish to ascertain the mean of a sample, or some similar function of the variate values, we take the variate value of any individual to be the centre of the interval in which it falls. This is an approximation, but the narrowness of the intervals justifies it in most practical cases.

Sampling from infinite populations

16.31 The methods we have just been discussing are appropriate only to those cases in which the population is finite, so that it was possible to associate with each individual one or more random sampling numbers ; or to populations which, though infinite, can be treated by the method of Example 16.4 owing to their complete specification according to the variate under discussion. The required conditions are met with in much of the material treated in practice, particularly in demographic and economic work ; but in other work the population may be either infinite or so large as to be infinite for all practical purposes, and a different technique must therefore be used.

Consider, for example, the problem of drawing a random sample from a sack of flour. We clearly cannot number all the particles in the sack, nor could we extract any given particles and examine them. We might, perhaps, reduce this case to that of a finite population by weighing out the flour into small, say one-ounce, packets and then sampling the packets. This is a kind of mixed sampling. But it is also possible to handle the problem by a special technique, as follows.

First of all, we mix the flour thoroughly. We then divide it into two halves and select one half. (It does not matter which, but for convenience we may imagine two heaps, one on the right and one on the left, and select left and right alternately.) We then divide the half we have chosen into two further halves, and again select one. The process is continued until the sample has reached a manageable size. We may reasonably suppose that it is random, especially if the flour is well mixed at each stage before being divided into two.

A similar technique may be used for many " continuous " substances, such as milk, grain, cement, etc.

Sampling from hypothetical populations

16.32 The technique for drawing random samples brings out a fundamental difference between existent and hypothetical populations. Taking a simple but typical case, let us draw a sample from the population of throws of a die.

The methods we have previously used are quite obviously inapplicable here. We cannot construct a card population, because we do not know the nature of the parent population. Nor can we put all the possible throws in a heap, and select from it by continued subdivision. In fact, there is only one thing we can do, and that is to throw the die, and take our results as a sample.

What reason have we to suppose that this is a *random* sample ? The answer lies partly in theory and partly in technique. In the first place, we must adapt our method of throwing so that the sampling conditions, so far as we can see, remain constant throughout the experiment. This is a matter of technique, and our methods can, in fact, be tested. But since our population does not exist for us to examine separately, the only knowledge about it being derived from the sample itself, it will be clear on a little reflection how difficult it is to say that every other possibility in the population had an equal chance of occurring. We return to this point in **16.35** and **16.36** below. Basically our assumption is that our throws behave *as if* they were being chosen at random from an existent population. The justification for this is our general knowledge of the behaviour of dice.

The importance of random sampling

16.33 We have already remarked on the importance of being able to gauge the error of an estimate made from a sample. The practical use of the theory of random sampling lies largely in the fact that it allows us to measure objectively, in terms of probability, errors of estimation or the significance of a result obtained from a random sample. The purposive methods to which we refer below do not do this, or at least have not yet been made to do so. The present trend among statisticians is, therefore, on the whole, in favour of the use of random sampling methods except in certain special cases.

16.34 At this point we may bring forward two important considerations.

In the first place, it must not be forgotten that random sampling *may* produce the most unrandom-looking results. For instance, we usually regard a hand of cards at bridge as a random sample from the population of 52 which comprise the pack ; but it is not unknown for a hand of 13 spades to be dealt. The fact that the sample looks purposive, therefore, *proves* nothing. But it does provide a basis for strong presumptions. How strong those presumptions may be the student may judge for himself by imagining what he would think of a card party at which he got 13 spades twice in succession.

Secondly, we can never be absolutely certain that a method of sampling is random. There are doubts on *a priori* grounds because for any given method there are always *conceivable* sources of bias, and we can never rule out entirely the possibility that some of these sources are present. The utmost we can do is to make their presence extremely unlikely by taking great care with the experiment.

16.35 We can, however, apply tests to judge the randomness of a sampling method. If we draw a single sample from a known population, the result will tell us nothing about the method adopted; but if we take a large number of samples they should, if the sampling is random, be distributed in a certain way, and for some populations we can calculate mathematically what that way ought to be. If, therefore, we apply our sampling method to such a parent population and find the results widely divergent from expectation, we have every reason to suspect our sampling technique. *Per contra*, if the results and expectation are in accord, there is good ground for reliance on the sampling.

16.36 Tests of this kind presuppose that we know the form of the parent population. In sampling from a hypothetical population we do not know this, and are forced to estimate it from the sample. Clearly, we cannot use this estimate to criticise the method by which the sample was obtained without some closer inquiry.

Similar problems may arise for existent populations when we do not know the nature of the parent population but have to estimate some or all of its characteristics from the data of the sample. In such cases it is extremely difficult to be completely satisfied that the sampling is random. Frequently the best we can do is to use a method which has been found satisfactory for other populations and hope, in the absence of any indication to the contrary, that it will also be satisfactory for the present population.

Purposive sampling

16.37 We have already pointed out the dangers of introducing bias if the observer gives rein to his inclinations in choosing a sample, and have stressed the fact that in general there does not exist a method of assessing the degree of accuracy of an estimate made from a purposive sample. In spite of these handicaps, however, there are cases where purposive selection is a useful method. In this book we shall not consider it in any great detail, because the reliance placed upon it depends largely on the circumstances of the case, remains to a great extent a matter of personal opinion, and is not capable of being discussed by elementary methods. Nevertheless, our brief survey would be incomplete without some reference to it.

16.38 Let us first of all consider the case of an observer who wishes to take a sample of two or three turnips from a cart-load. A *random* sample might give us several very large or very small turnips, though it is unlikely to do so. But if we allow the observer to run his eye over the whole load and then choose, he is most likely to take what he regards as average turnips—i.e. average in size, weight, shape, and whatever other quality may be in his mind.

It may be claimed, with some plausibility, that this purposive method is more likely to give us a sample which is *typical* or *representative* of the population than a random method. The random sample may vary widely from the average, whereas the purposive sample does not. This gives the latter an advantage as a rule ; but it may be pointed out—

(*a*) That as the sample becomes larger the random sample becomes more and more representative of the parent, whereas, owing to bias, the purposive sample in general does not.

(*b*) That in many cases the object of the sample is to give us information about the whole of the population ; the purposive sample might tell us more about the mean weight of the turnips, but would probably give a worse idea of the variance of the weights because the observer has deliberately chosen values near the mean.

16.39 If we had to choose between pure random sampling and purposive sampling, our choice would probably be determined by balancing the uncertainties of the former, which are mainly due to fluctuations of chance, and the uncertainties of the latter, which are mainly due to bias. In practice, however, it is often possible to combine the two methods in *stratified sampling* and gain some of the advantages of each while minimising their disadvantages.

The essentials of this process lie in dividing the parent population into strata and taking a random sample from each stratum. For instance, if we are taking a sample of earned incomes, we might first group individuals into classes "earning up to £500 per annum," "earning from £500 to £1,000 per annum," and so on, and then choose a random sample from each class. Or, if we wanted a sample of farms in Great Britain, we might first classify them roughly as "devoted mainly to arable crops," "devoted mainly to milk production," "devoted mainly to vegetable growing," etc., and again take a random sample from each group.

16.40 Finally, we may also sample a population by first of all arranging its individuals in groups. This amounts to taking a different sampling unit. For instance, in sampling the population of Great Britain we might, as a matter of convenience, take streets or local government districts instead of individual human beings as our unit. We have already had an instance of this type when we suggested as one way of sampling a sack of flour that it might be weighed out first into one-ounce packets. The process is obviously more convenient when this grouping has been done for us, e.g., in census returns.

16.41 Each branch of science and industry presents its own sampling problems, and it would be difficult to expand the foregoing discussion so as to include the detailed requirements of the worker in every sphere. We shall revert to the general subject of sampling in Chapter 23, and conclude this chapter with an example of the way in which all the methods we have described may be pressed into service in order to give a sample which is as representative as practical limitations will allow.

It is the practice in England for manufacturers of sugar from sugar beet to pay the growers according to the sugar content of their product. The beet, which is not unlike a parsnip, is delivered to the factory in lots of at least several tons with a certain amount of waste material, such as earth, adhering to it. The problem is, then, (a) to find the net weight of the beet when cleaned and ready for the slicing process, which is the first stage in the extraction of the sugar, and (b) to ascertain the sugar content. The method of procedure is as follows—

The gross weight of the load of beet usually is first obtained by weighing the lorry which contains it when full, and when empty. From the middle of the load of beet is then abstracted about 28 pounds, which is carefully weighed, and then cleaned and weighed again. The difference in the weights gives the " tare," that is to say, the proportion of waste matter, and a proportional amount is deducted from the whole load to give the net weight of beet. This process is equivalent to taking a random sample and assuming that the value of the " tare " in the sample is the value in the whole population.

The sample of washed beet is then laid out on a table and arranged with the roots in order of size. From this sample a smaller sample is taken by choosing a beet every so often. This is a process of pure purposive selection.

The reduced sample is still inconveniently large, so it is reduced by taking a slice from each beet. It is known that the sugar in the root is not distributed homogeneously (although it is roughly symmetrical about the axis of the root), so trained men are employed to slice one section with a rasp, the section being that which would be obtained by cutting the root from the thick end to the tapered end into two symmetrical halves and then repeating the process one or more times. This selection again is purposive in so far as the shape of the section is based on knowledge of the distribution of the sugar, but random in so far as it is a matter of chance what is the longitude of the particular slice chosen.

When each beet has been treated in this way there is given a heap of pulp which may be analysed. The heap is, however, as a rule still too large. It is therefore well mixed and divided into four heaps. Two heaps are thrown away, one is reduced to 26 grammes and analysed by the factory and one, similarly reduced, is analysed by the grower's representative. This last method of selection is a random method adapted for a population which cannot readily be enumerated.

The final sample therefore appears as the result of four successive sampling methods, two of which are random, one purposive, and one a mixture of purposive and random.

SUMMARY

1. Sampling may be random, purposive or mixed.

2. Random sampling owes its importance to the fact that we can assess the results obtained from it in terms of probability.

3. The presence of an element of choice on the part of the observer introduces the danger of bias, and should not be permitted where it can be avoided.

4. Random samples may conveniently be drawn by the use of card populations or of random sampling numbers.

5. The sampling technique adopted in any given case will depend largely on the circumstances of that case and the resources of the observer. At the present time the reliability of estimates made from samples is partly a matter of individual opinion founded on intuitive ideas, unless the sampling methods are random.

EXERCISES

16.1 Draw a random sample of 20 from the population of men of the last column of Exercise 4.6 (inhabitants of the United Kingdom classified according to weight). Find the mean of the sample and compare it with the mean of the population.

16.2 Deal yourself a hand of 13 cards from an ordinary pack of 52 playing cards and count the number of court cards. Use your result to estimate the number of court cards in the whole pack.

Repeat the experiment ten times, taking a new deal each time, and compare the mean of your results with the true value, 12.

16.3 Suggest a method for obtaining a random sample of words from the English language by the use of random sampling numbers and a dictionary.

16.4 Draw a sample of 30 from the population of the last column of Table 4.7, and find the standard deviation. Compare your result with the standard deviation of the population.

16.5 Suggest a possible source of bias in the following—

(a) A barrel of apples is sampled by taking a handful from the top.

(b) A mixture of sand and sawdust is sampled by scooping up a quantity from the bottom.

(c) A set of digits is taken by opening a Telephone Directory at random and choosing the telephone numbers in the order in which they appear on the page.

(d) Readers of a newspaper are sampled by printing in it an invitation to them to send up their observations on some topical event.

(e) Investigators into the size of families in a town conduct a house-to-house inquiry (1) in the morning, (2) in the afternoon, ignoring those houses at which there is no reply.

16.6 Draw 100 samples of 10 from a normal population by means of random sampling numbers, and form the frequency-distribution of their means.

16.7 In the data obtained in Exercise 16.6, form the frequency-distribution of the root-mean-square deviations of the samples about the mean of the parent population.

16.8 Draw 100 samples of 10 from the Poisson population of **8.47**, page 194, and form the frequency-distribution of their means.

16.9 Draw 500 samples of 4 from the population of Australian marriages of Table 4.8, page 84, and form the frequency-distribution of their range.

16.10 Draw a sample of 50 from the population of Table 9.4, page 204 (4912 dairy cows), and find the correlation in the sample between age in years and yield of milk per week. Compare your result with the correlation in the population.

CHAPTER SEVENTEEN

THE SAMPLING OF ATTRIBUTES

LARGE SAMPLES

The problem

17.1 In dealing with the theory of sampling we shall find it convenient to preserve the formal distinction between attributes and variables which we drew earlier in this book. The theory of the sampling of attributes is in many respects simpler than that of variables, and in this chapter we shall confine ourselves to it. We shall begin by considering a type of sampling which we shall call *simple*, involving certain limitations on the generality of the problem, and shall then proceed to examine the removal of these limitations in order to deal with the general case.

17.2 The sampling of attributes may be regarded as the drawing of samples from a population containing A's and not-A's. The number of A's in each sample, or the proportion of A's, will form part of the data provided by the samples.

We shall find it convenient to adopt the nomenclature of 8.3 and to speak of the drawing of an individual on sampling as an " event." The appearance of the attribute A may be called a " success " and the non-appearance a " failure." Thus, in sampling a human population for the proportions of the two sexes, we might say of a sample of 100, 45 of which were male, that the sample consisted of 100 events, 45 of which were successes and 55 failures. (It might, of course, be more convenient—and would certainly be more courteous—to reverse the names and call the occurrence of a female a " success " and of a male a " failure.")

Simple sampling

17.3 By *simple* sampling we mean random sampling in which each event has the same chance p of success, and in which the chances of success of different events are independent, whether previous trials have been made or not. These conditions hold good, for instance, in the throwing of a die or the tossing of a coin ; the chance of getting heads with a coin is not affected by what was obtained on the previous trials, and remains constant no matter how many trials are made, provided, of course, that the coin does not begin to wear or is not falsely manipulated by the experimenter.

Simple sampling is a particular form of random sampling, as we have defined it in the previous chapter. Suppose, for example, we take a sample of two from a population consisting of 6 men and 4 women under random sampling conditions, i.e. so that at each of the two events which constitute the sample every member of the population has an equal chance of being chosen. If, at the first trial, we draw a man, the chance of doing so being $\frac{6}{10}$, there will be 5 men and 4 women left in the population, and the chance of obtaining a man on the second trial will be $\frac{5}{9}$. This is not the same as the chance on the first trial, and hence the sampling is not simple, though it is random.

Mean and standard deviation in simple sampling of attributes

17.4 Suppose now that we take N samples with n events in each. The chance of success of each event is p and of its failure $q=1-p$. As in **8.6,** the frequencies of samples with 0, 1, 2, . . . successes are the terms in the series $N(q+p)^n$, i.e.

$$N\left\{q^n+nq^{n-1}p+\frac{n(n-1)}{2}q^{n-2}p^2+ \ldots +nqp^{n-1}+p^n\right\}$$

As in **8.9,** this distribution has mean M given by

$$M=np$$

and standard deviation (**8.10**)

$$\sigma=\sqrt{npq} \qquad . \qquad . \qquad . \qquad . \qquad (17.1)$$

17.5 In lieu of recording the number of successes in each sample we might have recorded the proportion of successes, that is, $\frac{1}{n}$th of the number in each sample. As this would amount to dividing all figures of the record by n, the mean proportion of successes must be p, and the standard deviation of the proportion of successes is given by

$$s=\sqrt{\frac{pq}{n}} \qquad . \qquad . \qquad . \qquad . \qquad (17.2)$$

Equations (17.1) and (17.2) are of fundamental importance.

Example 17.1.—The following results, due to Weldon, are of interest. Weldon threw 12 dice 4,096 times, a throw of 4, 5 or 6 being called a success. We have, then, 4,096 samples of 12 from the population consisting of all possible throws of the dice.

If the dice are all true, the chance of success is $\frac{1}{2}$. Hence, the theoretical mean $M=6$; theoretical value of the standard deviation $\sigma=\sqrt{0\cdot5\times0\cdot5\times12}$ $=1\cdot732$.

The following was the frequency-distribution observed—

Successes	Frequency	Successes	Frequency
0	—	7	847
1	7	8	536
2	60	9	257
3	198	10	71
4	430	11	11
5	731	12	—
6	948		
		Total	4,096

Mean $M=6\cdot139$, standard deviation $\sigma=1\cdot712$. The proportion of successes is $6\cdot139/12=0\cdot512$ instead of $0\cdot5$.

Example 17.2.—(G. U. Yule.) The following may be taken as an illustration based on a smaller number of observations : Three dice were thrown 648 times, and the numbers of 5's or 6's noted at each throw. $p=1/3$, $q=2/3$; theoretical mean 1 ; standard deviation $0\cdot816$.

Frequency-distribution observed—

Successes	Frequency
0	179
1	298
2	141
3	30
Total	648

$M=1\cdot034$, $\sigma=0\cdot823$. Actual proportion of successes $0\cdot345$.

17.6 The value pn is sometimes called the " expected " value of the number of successes in the sample. It is not only the mean value of all samples, but is the most probable value and is also representative, i.e. it bears the same ratio p to the number in the sample as the number of individuals with attribute A in the population bears to the total number in the population. The divergences of the number of successes from the expected value in any given random sample give rise to what we have hitherto called fluctuations of random sampling. They are to be regarded as deviations due to the nature of the sampling process, and not indicative of any real properties of the population itself.

17.7 Equations (17.1) and (17.2) enable us to deal with the question which has arisen several times in earlier chapters of this book, namely, when can we say that observed deviations from the expected values in a sample of attributes are due to some real effect and are not merely attributable to sampling fluctuations ?

The binomial distribution, to which samples classified according to the frequencies of an attribute give rise, is a single-humped type which approximates very closely to the normal for large values of n, the number in the sample. It follows that the great majority of its members lie within a range $\pm 3\sigma$ on each side of the mean, i.e. of $\pm 3\sqrt{npq}$ on each side of the value np. If the distribution is exactly normal, $0\cdot 9973$ of the curve lies within this range (**8.29**). We can therefore say that if a particular sample gives a value of p outside this range, the deviation from the expected value is most unlikely to have arisen from fluctuations of simple sampling. If n is large, the chances are about 3 in a thousand that it arose in that way.

It must be emphasised that the free use of the 3σ rule is justified only if n is large.

Example 17.3.—In the experiments of Example 17.1, 25,145 throws of a 4, 5 or 6 were made out of 49,152 throws altogether. The chance of throwing one of these numbers is $\frac{1}{2}$, and hence the expected value is 24,576. The observed number was thus 569 in excess of this. Can the deviation from the expected value be due to fluctuations of simple sampling?

The standard deviation of simple sampling is

$$\sigma = \sqrt{npq} = \sqrt{\tfrac{1}{2} \times \tfrac{1}{2} \times 49152}$$
$$= 110\cdot 9$$

The deviation observed is $5\cdot 13$ times this quantity, and it is therefore most improbable that it arose as a sampling fluctuation. We must therefore seek some other explanation of the deviation, and it seems reasonable to suspect that the dice were slightly biased.

The problem might, of course, have been attacked equally well from the standpoint of *proportion* instead of the actual numbers of successes. This proportion is $0\cdot 5116$ instead of the expected $0\cdot 5000$, the difference in excess being $0\cdot 0116$. The standard deviation of the proportion is

$$s = \sqrt{\frac{1}{2} \times \frac{1}{2} \times \frac{1}{49152}} = 0\cdot 00226$$

and the difference observed is $5\cdot 13$ times this, which is the same ratio as before, as of course it must be.

Example 17.4.—(Data from the *Second Report of the Evolution Committee of the Royal Society*, 1905, p. 72.)

Certain crosses of the pea, *Pisum sativum*, gave 5,321 yellow and 1,804 green seeds. The expectation is 25 per cent of green seeds on a Mendelian hypothesis. Can the divergences from the expected values have arisen from fluctuations of simple sampling only?

The numerical difference from the expected result is 23. The standard deviation of simple sampling is

$$\sigma = \sqrt{0\cdot 25 \times 0\cdot 75 \times 7125} = 36\cdot 6$$

The divergence from theory is only about $0\cdot 6$ of this, and hence may very well have arisen from fluctuations of simple sampling.

Standard error

17.8 We shall very frequently have to use the standard deviation of sampling, and it is convenient to have a shorter name for this quantity. We shall call it the *standard error*. The use of the word error is justified in this connection by the fact that we usually regard the expected value as the true value, and divergences from it as errors of estimation due to sampling effects ; but the student should not attach too much significance to the particular term " error."

In most of our work the term " standard error " will be applied to the standard deviation of *simple* sampling ; but it has a rather wider meaning, embracing this one, which we shall discuss in considering the sampling of variables (**18.22**, cf. also **17.31**).

We may, then, summarise the foregoing in the statement that frequencies differing from the expected frequency by more than 3 times the standard error are almost certainly not due to fluctuations of sampling. They point to some departure of the sampling from simplicity, which may in turn point either to some flaw in the sampling technique or to causal effects in the population itself.

Probable error

17.9 Instead of the standard error, some authorities have used a quantity called the *probable error*, which is $0 \cdot 67449$ times the standard error. This practice arose from the fact that in the normal curve the quartiles are distant $0 \cdot 67449\sigma$ from the mean, so that the probability that a deviation is in excess of the probable error is $\frac{1}{2}$, and is equal to the probability of a deviation being less than the probable error. The rule that the observed deviation should not be greater than 3 times the standard error is then approximately equivalent to a rule that it should not exceed $4 \cdot 5$ times the probable error.

The use of the probable error is declining, and we recommend the student to eschew it.

17.10 In Examples **17.1** to **17.4** we dealt with cases where p, the probability of success, was known *a priori*. In many cases it is not known, and further consideration is necessary before we can apply equations (17.1) and (17.2) to such cases.

To fix the ideas, let us suppose that we have a simple sample of 1,000 individuals from the inhabitants of Great Britain, and find that 36 per cent of them have blue eyes and the remainder have eyes of some other colour. What can we infer about the proportion of blue-eyed individuals in the whole population ?

In this instance we do not know the proportion p of blue-eyed individuals in the population. We do know that the standard error is $\sqrt{1000pq}$. Now, whatever p and q are, pq cannot exceed $\frac{1}{4}$, and hence the standard error cannot exceed $\frac{1}{2}\sqrt{1000}$, or 16. Hence, whatever p is, a simple sample should give a number of successes within 3 times this, or 48, of the expected frequency pn. This is $4 \cdot 8$ per cent of the sample, and we thus may say that the proportion of blue-eyed people in the whole population is $36 \pm 4 \cdot 8$ per cent, i.e. that it lies between $31 \cdot 2$ and $40 \cdot 8$ per cent.

17.11 We may, however, make a rather better estimate. We have seen that the standard error is small compared with the expected value, and hence with the observed value. If, therefore, in calculating the standard error we take the observed values of p and q *in the sample* instead of the unknown true values of p and q, we shall not involve ourselves in very great error.

Thus, taking p to be $0 \cdot 36$, $q = 0 \cdot 64$,

$$\sigma = \sqrt{npq} = \sqrt{0 \cdot 36 \times 0 \cdot 64 \times 1000}$$

$$= 15 \cdot 18$$

Hence, $3\sigma = 45 \cdot 5$ approximately, and the limits are now $36 \pm 4 \cdot 6$ or $31 \cdot 4$ and $40 \cdot 6$—slightly narrower than those previously obtained.

17.12 In this example we have taken the proportion of successes in the sample to be an estimate of the proportion of successes in the population, and have set limits to the range within which the true proportion probably lies. There are other reasons, of an advanced theoretical character which we shall not specify, for taking p in the sample as an estimate of p in the population, but the student will probably concede that it is the most reasonable thing to do in the circumstances. We must, however, look a little more closely into the assumption that this estimate may be used in calculating the standard error.

17.13 The assumption is a justifiable one if n is large and neither p nor q is small. For in such a case, the standard error of the proportion p is $\sqrt{\dfrac{pq}{n}}$, and this is small compared with p unless p itself is small.

If, then, the standard error of p is small, the value of p estimated from the sample must be close to the real value, and we shall not introduce any serious error by taking the estimated value in evaluating the formula $\sqrt{\dfrac{pq}{n}}$.

17.14 Precisely how large n must be for this approximation to be valid it is not easy to say. Samples of 1,000 are almost certainly large enough, and we may often apply the foregoing procedure with considerable confidence to much smaller samples, say of 100. For samples below that figure it is as well to examine carefully the circumstances of any given case and to proceed with caution.

We shall have more to say on this matter when we consider the sampling of variables (**18.17** and **18.18**).

For the remainder of this chapter we shall assume that our samples are "large," that is to say, that the approximations involved in our assumptions as to the estimate of p are valid.

Example 17.5.—A sample of 900 days is taken from meteorological records of a certain district, and 100 of them are found to be foggy. What are the probable limits to the percentage of foggy days in the district ?

Anticipating somewhat our discussion of simple sampling, we will assume that the conditions of this problem give a simple sample.

Hence,

$$p=\tfrac{1}{9}, \qquad q=\tfrac{8}{9}$$

Standard error of the proportion of foggy days

$$=\sqrt{\frac{pq}{n}}=\sqrt{\frac{1}{9}\times\frac{8}{9}\times\frac{1}{900}}$$

$$=0\cdot0105$$

$$=1\cdot05 \text{ per cent.}$$

Hence, taking $\tfrac{1}{9}$ to be the estimate of the number of foggy days, we have that the limits are $11\cdot11$ per cent $\pm3\cdot15$ per cent, i.e. 8 per cent and $14\cdot25$ per cent approximately.

Example 17.6.—A biased penny is tossed 100 times and comes down heads 70 times. What are the probable limits to the probability of getting a head in a single trial ?

We require to know the limits of p. If we assume that 100 is a large sample, we have—

$$\sqrt{\frac{pq}{n}}=\sqrt{\frac{1}{100}\times\frac{7}{10}\times\frac{3}{10}}=0\cdot0458$$

The limits are therefore $0\cdot70\pm(3\times0\cdot0458)$

$$=0\cdot70\pm0\cdot1374$$

$$=0\cdot56 \text{ and } 0\cdot84 \text{ approximately}$$

If we feel any doubt as to the validity of using estimates of p and q from a sample of 100 in calculating the standard error, we may proceed as follows—

The standard error of p cannot exceed $\sqrt{\frac{1}{100}\times\frac{1}{2}\times\frac{1}{2}}$, i.e. $0\cdot05$. Hence the value of p lies almost certainly within the limits $0\cdot70 \pm 0\cdot15$, i.e. $0\cdot55$ and $0\cdot85$.

$$\text{If } p=0\cdot55, \qquad \sqrt{\frac{pq}{n}}=0\cdot04975$$

$$\text{If } p=0\cdot85, \qquad \sqrt{\frac{pq}{n}}=0\cdot03571$$

For intermediate values of p, $\sqrt{\dfrac{pq}{n}}$ lies between these limits. Hence the maximum value of the standard error is $0\cdot04975$, and p lies between the limits $0\cdot70 \pm 0\cdot14925$, i.e.

$$0\cdot55075 \text{ and } 0\cdot84925$$

It will be seen that these limits are nearly equal to those obtained on the assumption that $p=q=\frac{1}{2}$, and are not very different from those we got by assuming $p=0\cdot70$. There would, however, be an appreciable difference if p had been small, say $0\cdot10$.

17.15 If one of the two proportions p and q becomes very small, equation (17.1) may be put into an approximate form that is very useful. Suppose p to be the proportion that becomes very small, so that we may neglect p^2 compared with p ; then

$$pq=p-p^2=p \text{ approximately}$$

and consequently we have approximately—

$$\sigma=\sqrt{np}=\sqrt{M} \qquad . \qquad . \qquad . \qquad . \qquad (17.3)$$

That is to say, *if the proportion of successes be small, the standard deviation of the number of successes is the square root of the mean number of successes.* Hence we can find the standard error even though p be unknown provided only we know that it is small.

This is, in fact, the case when the binomial becomes the Poisson series (8.40). For such distributions the rule that a range of 6σ includes the great majority of the observations remains valid, as may be seen from the diagram on page 192, but the limits assigned to the standard error of the mean M may be too wide on the left of the mean. For example, if $M=1$, $\sigma=1$, and a range of 3 units to the left of the mean carries us to a value of -2, whereas there can be no part of the frequency with negative values of the variate.

17.16 It will be noticed that the standard error depends only on the value of p and the size of the sample, and that therefore the range within which p probably lies is independent of the size of the population. This appears a little paradoxical, because one might expect that a sample which was, say, 20 per cent of the population would enable closer limits to be set than one which was 10 per cent of the population. The ordinary man nearly always believes that a sample of only 1/1000 of the population necessarily gives much less trustworthy results than a sample of say, 1/10, without regard to its actual size, but the belief is quite unjustified.

The explanation is to be found in the nature of simple sampling itself. We shall see overleaf that the conditions under which simple sampling arises in practice are such that either the population is actually or practically infinite, or each member drawn for a sample is put back in the population before the next is drawn. In either case the population is inexhaustible, and no sample is any nearer to including all its members than another sample. It is, therefore, not surprising to find that the size of the population does not appear in the formula for the standard error.

17.17 A further notable fact is that the standard error of p varies inversely as the square root of n, and not inversely as n itself. Thus, as n becomes larger the standard error becomes smaller, which is what we should expect, but the standard error decreases proportionately to the square root of n. For instance, if a sample of 100 gives us a standard error of 10 per cent, it will take a sample of 400 to halve that error, and a sample 100 times as large, i.e. 10,000, to reduce the error to one-tenth or one per cent.

Precision

17.18 The standard error may fairly be taken to measure the unreliability of an estimate of p ; the greater the standard error, the greater the fluctuations of the observed proportion, although the true proportion is the same throughout. The reciprocal of the standard error $(1/s)$, on the other hand—or some convenient multiple of the reciprocal—may be regarded as a measure of *reliability*, or, as it is sometimes termed, *precision*, and consequently *the reliability or precision of an observed proportion varies as the square root of the number of observations on which it is based.*

The limitations of simple sampling

17.19 In order to realise the limitations on the use of the formulæ of equations (17.1) and (17.2), it is necessary to consider what are the conditions which will give rise to simple sampling in practice. Supposing, for example, that we observe among groups of 1,000 persons, at different times or in different localities, the various percentages of individuals possessing certain characteristics—dark hair, or blindness, or insanity, and so forth. Under what conditions should we expect the observed percentages to obey the law of sampling that we have found, and show a standard deviation given by equation (17.2) ?

17.20 In the first place, the condition that p, the probability of drawing an individual with attribute A on random sampling, remains constant, and in particular is the same for all samples, means that the proportion of individuals with attribute A in the population must remain constant at the drawing of each sample. Consequently, if formula (17.2) is to hold good in our practical case of sampling there must not be a difference in any essential respect—i.e. in any character that can affect the proportion observed—between the localities from which the samples are drawn, nor, if the samples have been made at different epochs, must any essential change have taken place during the period over which the observations are spread. Where the causation of the character observed is more or less unknown, it may, of course, be difficult or impossible to say what differences or changes are to be regarded as essential, but where we have more knowledge the condition laid down enables us to exclude certain cases at once from the possible applications of formula (17.1) or (17.2). Thus it is obvious that the theory of simple sampling cannot apply to the variations of the death-rate in localities with populations of different age and sex composition, or to death-rates in a mixture of healthy and unhealthy districts, or to death-rates in successive years during a period of continuously improving sanitation. In all such cases variations due to definite causes are superposed on the fluctuations of sampling.

17.21 Secondly, the proportion of individuals with attribute A must remain constant for the drawing of each individual member of the sample. This is again a very marked limitation. To revert to the case of death-rates, formulæ (17.1) and (17.2) would not apply to the numbers of persons dying in a series of samples of 1,000 persons, even if these samples were all of the same age and sex composition, and living under the same sanitary conditions, unless, further, each sample only contained persons of one sex and one age. For if each sample included persons of both sexes and different ages, the condition would be broken, the chance of death during a given period not being the same for the two sexes, or for the young and the old. The groups would not be homogeneous in the sense required by the conditions from which our formulæ have been deduced.

17.22 We pointed out in **17.3** that sampling from a finite population is not simple owing to the fact that the abstraction of an individual alters the chance of success at the next trial. In practice there are three important cases in which the condition for the constancy of p is satisfied :

(*a*) If the individuals are replaced at each drawing before the next drawing is made ; for in this case the constitution of the population is the same at each trial, and hence the chance of success must also be the same.

(*b*) If the population is infinite ; for in this case the withdrawal of a finite number of members does not affect the proportion of individuals in the population possessing the attribute in question.

(*c*) If the population is very large, p may be taken to be constant without sensible error, provided that the sample is not also large. This is a very important case, and justifies the application of the theory of simple sampling to many practical data.

Suppose, for instance, we are sampling the population of the United Kingdom for sex ratio, and decide to take a sample of 1,000. Suppose again, for the purposes of illustration, that the whole population consists of 23 million women and 22 million men. The chance of getting a man at the first trial will then be $\dfrac{22,000,000}{45,000,000}$. If we succeed in getting a man, the chance of doing so at the second trial will be $\dfrac{21,999,999}{44,999,999}$. Even if we draw 999 men the chance of success at the thousandth trial would be

$\dfrac{21,999,001}{44,999,001}$. All these chances, to a close approximation, are equal, and we can assume them to be so without fear of appreciable error. The case would, of course, have stood differently if our sample had numbered several millions.

17.23 A third condition for simple sampling was explicitly stated in our definition in **17.3**. The individual events must be completely independent of one another, like the throws of a die, or sensibly so, like the drawing of balls from a bag containing a number of balls which is large compared with the number drawn. Reverting to the illustration of a death-rate, our formulæ would not apply even if the sample populations were composed of persons of one age and one sex, if we were dealing, for example, with deaths from an infectious or contagious disease. For if one person in a certain sample has contracted the disease in question, he has increased the possibility of others doing so, and hence of dying from the disease. The same thing holds good for certain classes of deaths from accident, e.g. railway accidents due to derailment, and explosions in mines : if such an accident is fatal to one person it is probably fatal to others also, and consequently the annual returns show large and more or less erratic variations.

17.24 It is evident that these conditions very much limit the field of practical cases of an economic or sociological character to which formulæ (17.1) and (17.2) can apply without considerable modification. The formulæ appear, however, to hold to a high degree of approximation in certain biological cases, notably in the proportions of offspring of different types obtained on crossing hybrids, and, with some limitations, to the proportions of the two sexes at birth. It is possible, accordingly, that in these cases all the necessary conditions are fulfilled, but this is not a necessary inference from the mere applicability of the formulæ. In the case of the sex ratio at birth it seems doubtful whether the rule applies to the frequency of the sexes in individual families of given numbers, but it does apply fairly closely to the sex ratios of births in different localities, and still more closely to the ratios in one locality during successive periods. That is to say, if we note the number of males in a series of groups of n births each, the standard deviation of that number is approximately $\sqrt{npq}$, where p is the chance of a male birth ; or, otherwise, $\sqrt{pq/n}$ is the standard deviation of the proportion of male births.

Applications of simple sampling
17.25 We have already shown in examples how the theory of simple sampling can be used to gauge the precision of an estimate of the proportion of individuals in a population which possess an attribute A, and to set limits outside which that proportion probably does not lie. We now turn to further applications of the theory in the checking and control of the interpretation of statistical results.

17.26 *Case* 1.—Given the expected frequency in a sample and the observed frequency of successes, it is desired to know whether the deviation of the second from the first can have arisen from fluctuations of simple sampling.

This is a case which we have discussed in Examples 17.3 and 17.4. From the expected frequency we can calculate the standard error, and if the deviation is more than 3 times this quantity it almost certainly did not arise from fluctuations of random sampling.

17.27 One caution is necessary here. If the deviation is less than 3 times the standard error, it does not follow that the expected frequency divided by the number in the sample is really the proportion of individuals possessing the attribute A in the population. In other words, if the expected value is derived from some hypothesis, such as the Mendelian hypothesis in the case of Example 17.4, the fact that the deviation lies within the limits of 3 times the standard error does not prove the hypothesis correct. It only indicates that experiment and hypothesis are not in disagreement. Furthermore, if the deviation lay without those limits, the hypothesis would not necessarily be disproved, for the fault might lie with the randomness of the sampling.

17.28 *Case* 2.—Two samples from distinct materials or different populations give proportions of A's p_1 and p_2, the numbers of observations in the samples being n_1 and n_2 respectively. (*a*) Can the difference between the two proportions have arisen merely as a fluctuation of simple sampling, the two populations being really similar as regards the proportion of A's therein ? (*b*) If the difference indicated were a real one, might it vanish, owing to fluctuations of sampling, in other samples taken in precisely the same way ? This case corresponds to the testing of an association which is indicated by a comparison of the proportion of A's amongst B's and β's.

(*a*) We have no theoretical expectation in this case as to the proportion of A's in the population from which either sample has been taken.

Let us find, however, whether the observed difference between p_1 and p_2 may not have arisen solely as a fluctuation of simple sampling, the proportion of A's being really the same in both cases, and given, let us say, by the (weighted) mean proportion in our two samples together, i.e. by

$$p_0 = \frac{n_1 p_1 + n_2 p_2}{n_1 + n_2}$$

(the best guide that we have).

Let ϵ_1, ϵ_2 be the standard errors in the two samples, then

$$\epsilon_1{}^2 = p_0 q_0 / n_1, \qquad \epsilon_2{}^2 = p_0 q_0 / n_2$$

If the samples are simple samples in the sense of the previous work, then the mean difference between p_1 and p_2 will be zero, and the standard error of the difference ϵ_{12}, the samples being independent, will be given by

$$\epsilon_{12}^2 = p_0 q_0 \left(\frac{1}{n_1} + \frac{1}{n_2}\right) \qquad . \qquad . \qquad . \qquad (17.4)$$

If the observed difference is less than some three times ϵ_{12}, it may have arisen as a fluctuation of simple sampling only.

(b) If, on the other hand, the proportions of A's are not the same in the material from which the two samples are drawn, but p_1 and p_2 are the true values of the proportions, the standard errors of sampling in the two cases are

$$\epsilon_1{}^2 = p_1 q_1 / n_1, \qquad \epsilon_2{}^2 = p_2 q_2 / n_2$$

and consequently

$$\epsilon_{12}^2 = \frac{p_1 q_1}{n_1} + \frac{p_2 q_2}{n_2} \qquad . \qquad . \qquad . \qquad (17.5)$$

If the difference between p_1 and p_2 does not exceed some three times this value of ϵ_{12}, it may be obliterated by an error of simple sampling on taking fresh samples in the same way from the same material.

The student will note that in arriving at these results we have assumed that the unknown values p_0, p_1, p_2 are given to a sufficient degree of approximation by estimates from the samples. This, as we have seen, is justified if n be large.

Example 17.7.—(Data from J. Gray, " Memoir on the Pigmentation Survey of Scotland," *Jour. of the Royal Anthropological Institute*, 1907, 37). The following are extracted from the tables relating to hair-colour of girls at Edinburgh and Glasgow—

	Of medium hair-colour	Total observed	Per cent medium
Edinburgh . .	4,008	9,743	41·1
Glasgow . .	17,529	39,764	44·1

Can the difference observed in the percentage of girls of medium hair-colour have arisen solely through fluctuations of sampling ?

In the two towns together the percentage of girls with medium hair-colour is 43·5 per cent. If this were the true percentage, the standard error of sampling for the difference between percentages observed in samples of the above sizes would be—

$$\epsilon_{12} = (43 \cdot 5 \times 56 \cdot 5)^{\frac{1}{2}} \times \left(\frac{1}{9743} + \frac{1}{39,764}\right)^{\frac{1}{2}}$$

$$= 0 \cdot 56 \text{ per cent.}$$

The actual difference is $3 \cdot 0$ per cent, or over 5 times this, and could not have arisen through the chances of simple sampling.

If we assume that the difference is a real one and calculate the standard error by equation (17.5), we arrive at the same value, viz, $0 \cdot 56$ per cent. With such large samples the difference could not, accordingly, be obliterated by the fluctuations of simple sampling alone.

17.29 *Case 3.*—Two samples are drawn from distinct material or different populations, as in the last case, giving proportions of A's p_1 and p_2, but in lieu of comparing the proportion p_1 with p_2 it is compared with the proportion of A's in the two samples together, viz. p_0, where, as before,

$$p_0 = \frac{n_1 p_1 + n_2 p_2}{n_1 + n_2}$$

Required to find whether the difference between p_1 and p_0 can have arisen as a fluctuation of simple sampling, p_0 being the true proportion of A's in both samples.

This case corresponds to the testing of an association which is indicated by a comparison of the proportion of A's amongst the B's with the proportion of A's in the population. The general treatment is similar to that of Case 2, but the work is complicated owing to the fact that errors in p_1 and p_0 are not independent.

If ϵ_{01} be the standard error of the difference between p_1 and p_0, we have at once—

$$\epsilon_{01}^2 = \epsilon_0{}^2 + \epsilon_1{}^2 - 2r_{01}\epsilon_0\epsilon_1$$

$$= p_0 q_0 \left\{ \frac{1}{n_1 + n_2} + \frac{1}{n_1} - 2r_{01} \frac{1}{\sqrt{n_1}\sqrt{n_1 + n_2}} \right\}$$

r_{01} being the correlation between errors of simple sampling in p_1 and p_0. But from the above equation relating p_0 to p_1 and p_2, writing it in terms of deviations in p_0, p_1 and p_2, multiplying by the deviation in p_1 and summing, we have, since errors in p_1 and p_2 are uncorrelated—

$$r_{01} = \frac{n_1}{n_1 + n_2} \cdot \frac{\epsilon_1}{\epsilon_0} = \sqrt{\frac{n_1}{n_1 + n_2}}$$

Therefore finally—

$$\epsilon_{01}^2 = \frac{p_0 q_0}{n_1 + n_2} \cdot \frac{n_2}{n_1} \qquad . \quad . \quad . \quad (17.6)$$

Unless the difference between p_0 and p_1 exceed, say, some three times this value of ϵ_{01}, it may have arisen solely by the chances of simple sampling.

It will be observed that if n_1 be very small compared with n_2, ϵ_{01} approaches, as it should, the standard error for a sample of n_1 observations.

We omit, in this case, the allied problem whether, if the difference between p_1 and p_0 indicated by the samples were real, it might e wiped out in other samples of the same size by fluctuations of simple s mpling alone. The solution is a little complex, as we no longer have $\epsilon_0{}^2 = p_0 q_0 / (n_1 + n_2)$.

Example 17.8.—Taking now the figures of Example 17.7, suppose that we had compared the proportion of girls of medium hair-colour in Edinburgh with the proportion in Glasgow and Edinburgh together. The former is $41 \cdot 1$ per cent, the latter $43 \cdot 5$ per cent, difference $2 \cdot 4$ per cent. The standard error of the difference between the percentages observed in the sub-sample of 9,743 observations and the entire sample of 49,507 observations is, therefore,

$$\epsilon_{01} = (43 \cdot 5 \times 56 \cdot 5)^{\frac{1}{2}} \left(\frac{39,764}{49,507 \times 9743} \right)^{\frac{1}{2}} = 0 \cdot 45 \text{ per cent.}$$

The actual difference is over five times this (the ratio must, of course, be the same as in Example 17.7), and could not have occurred as a mere error of sampling.

Effect of removing the limitations of simple sampling

17.30   Let us now consider the effect on the standard error of the removal of the conditions of simple sampling which we discussed in **17.19** to **17.24**.

The breakdown of the condition we discussed in **17.20**, namely, that the proportion of A's in the population should remain constant for all samples, might occur if we took a number of samples from a changing population or from different strata of a population which was not homogeneous.

We may represent such circumstances in a case of artificial chance by supposing that for the first f_1 throws of n dice the chance of success for each die is p_1, for the next f_2 throws p_2, for the next f_3 throws p_3, and so on, the chance of success varying from time to time, just as the chance of death, even for individuals of the same age and sex, varies from district to district. Suppose, now, that the records of all these throws are pooled together. The mean number of successes per throw of the n dice is given by

$$M = \frac{n}{N}(f_1 p_1 + f_2 p_2 + f_3 p_3 + \ldots) = n p_0$$

where $N = \Sigma(f)$ is the whole number of throws, and p_0 is the mean value $\Sigma(fp)/N$ of the varying chance p. To find the standard deviation of the number of successes at each throw, consider that the first set of throws contributes to the sum of the squares of deviations an amount

$$f_1[n p_1 q_1 + n^2 (p_1 - p_0)^2]$$

$n p_1 q_1$ being the square of the standard deviation for these throws, and $n(p_1 - p_0)$ the difference between the mean number of successes for the first set and the mean for all the sets together. Hence the standard deviation σ of the whole distribution is given by the sum of all quantities like the above, or

$$N\sigma^2 = n\Sigma(fpq)+n^2\Sigma\{f(p-p_0)^2\}$$

Let σ_p be the standard deviation of p, then the last sum is $Nn^2\sigma_p^2$, and substituting $1-p$ for q, we have—

$$\sigma^2 = np_0-np_0^2-n\sigma_p^2+n^2\sigma_p^2$$
$$= np_0q_0+n(n-1)\sigma_p^2 . \qquad . \qquad . \qquad . \qquad (17.7)$$

This is the formula corresponding to equation (17.1); if we deal with the standard deviation of the *proportion* of successes, instead of that of the absolute number, we have, dividing through by n^2, the formula corresponding to equation (17.2), viz.—

$$s^2 = \frac{p_0q_0}{n} + \frac{n-1}{n}\sigma_p^2 . \qquad . \qquad . \qquad . \qquad (17.8)$$

17.31 If n be large and s_0 be the standard error calculated from the mean proportion of successes p_0, equation (17.8) is sensibly of the form

$$s^2 = s_0^2+\sigma_p^2$$

We have thus analysed s^2 into two parts, s_0^2 the portion due to deviations from the mean p_0, and σ_p^2 the portion due to variations of the p's about their mean. The former we may regard as the contribution to s^2 due to chance fluctuations; the latter as the contribution due to real variation of the proportions among the different strata of the population.

In conformity with later work we shall continue to call s (or σ if we are dealing with frequencies) the standard error, although the sampling is no longer simple. The deviation s is still, in fact, the standard deviation of the various sample values of p about the mean value. The term s_0 (or $\sqrt{np_0q_0}$), on the other hand, is what the standard error would have been if the sampling had been simple, and from the above equation we accordingly see that the effect of the breakdown of the first condition for simple sampling is to increase the standard error.

We may illustrate the effect of variations in p on the data of Table **17.1**, showing the percentages of the electorate voting in municipal elections in England, in various groups according to size of electorate. (The figures in the original returns for percentages are given to the first place of decimals, so the intervals are centred at $20\cdot45$, $27\cdot45$, etc.)

At the foot of the table we show the actual variances s^2 and the theoretical variances based on the formula pq/n. For instance, in the size group 0—5,000 we have $p = 0\cdot5621$ and take n as the mid-point of the range, namely 2,500. The variance (in terms of percentages, not proportions) is then $(0\cdot5621 \times 0\cdot4379 \times 100^2)/2,500 = 0\cdot98$.

Now it is clear from these data that the theoretical variances are only a very small proportion of the actual variances. In short we cannot assume, even in electorates of about the same size, that the numbers voting are distributed in the binomial form. There is, so to speak, no "proneness to vote" common to all electors and represented by the proportion p. There are (as we know for elections) substantial variations between electorates, represented by the variances $s^2 - s_0^2$.

The effect of these results on "straw votes" for the forecasting of elections is evident. We cannot measure the standard error of proportions in samples of persons indicating their voting intentions by the simple-sampling formulæ.

TABLE 17.1.—Percentages of electorate voting in municipal elections in England in 1945
County boroughs and boroughs with more than 100,000 voters omitted. "Electorate" includes only those persons entitled to vote on this occasion, i.e., persons in non-contested areas are excluded.
Data from Registrar-General's Review of England and Wales for 1946, Tables Part II Civil.

Percentage of electorate voting	Size of electorate					
	0 to 5,000	5,001 to 10,000	10,001 to 15,000	15,001 to 20,000	20,001 to 50,000	50,001 to 100,000
20–	—	1	2	—	1	1
25–	3	6	2	2	5	3
30–	10	17	12	9	16	5
35–	20	18	13	14	20	9
40–	40	44	31	10	31	10
45–	39	44	32	9	33	3
50–	82	39	26	14	25	1
55–	77	54	21	9	17	—
60–	72	31	12	6	6	—
65–	42	12	6	5	2	—
70–	32	5	3	—	—	—
75–	12	1	2	—	—	—
80–	3	—	—	—	—	—
85–	1	1	—	—	—	—
90–	—	—	—	1	—	—
Totals	433	272	162	79	156	32
Means	56·21	50·51	48·81	47·83	45·56	39·79
Variances s^2. . .	120·12	113·45	111·43	140·36	82·80	85·91
Theoretical variances s_0^2	0·98	0·33	0·20	0·14	0·07	0·03
$\sqrt{(s^2 - s_0^2)}$ . . .	10·9	10·6	10·5	11·9	9·1	9·3

The figures of this case also bring out clearly one important consequence of (17.8), viz. that if we make n large, s becomes sensibly equal to σ_p, while if we make n small, s becomes more nearly equal to $p_0 q_0/n$. Hence, if we want to know the significant standard deviation of the proportion p —the measure of its fluctuation owing to definite causes—n should be made as large as possible ; if, on the other hand, we want to obtain good illustrations of the theory of simple sampling, n should be made small. If n be very large, the actual standard error may evidently become almost indefinitely large compared with the standard deviation of *simple* sampling.

Thus during the twenty years 1855–74 the death-rate in England and Wales fluctuated round a mean value of $22 \cdot 2$ per thousand with a standard deviation (s) of $0 \cdot 86$. Taking the mean population as roughly 21 millions, the standard deviation of simple sampling (s_0) is approximately

$$\sqrt{\frac{22 \times 978}{21 \times 10^6}} = 0 \cdot 032 \text{ per thousand}$$

This is only about one twenty-seventh of the actual value.

17.32 Now consider the effect of altering the second condition of simple sampling dealt with in **17.21**, viz. the circumstances that regulate the appearance of the character observed shall be the same for every individual or every sub-class in each of the populations from which samples are drawn. Suppose that in a group of n dice thrown the chances for m_1 dice are p_1, q_1 ; for m_2 dice, p_2, q_2, and so on, the chances varying for different dice, but being constant throughout the experiment. The case differs from the last, as in that the chances were the same for every die at any one throw, but varied from one throw to another ; now they are constant from throw to throw, but differ from one die to another as they would in any ordinary set of badly made dice. Required to find the effect of these differing chances.

For the mean number of successes we evidently have—

$$M = m_1 p_1 + m_2 p_2 + m_3 p_3 + \cdots$$

$$= n p_0$$

p_0 being the mean chance $\Sigma(mp)/n$. To find the standard deviation of the number of successes at each throw, it should be noted that this may be regarded as made up of the number of successes in the m_1 dice for which the chances are p_1, q_1, together with the number of successes amongst the m_2 dice for which the chances are p_2, q_2, and so on ; and these numbers of successes are all independent. Hence,

$$\sigma^2 = m_1 p_1 q_1 + m_2 p_2 q_2 + m_3 p_3 q_3 + \cdots$$

$$= \Sigma(mpq)$$

Substituting $1 - p$ for q, as before, and using σ_p to denote the standard deviation of p,

$$\sigma^2 = n p_0 q_0 - n \sigma_p{}^2 \qquad . \qquad . \qquad . \qquad . \quad (17.9)$$

or if s be, as before, the standard error of the *proportion* of successes,

$$s^2 = \frac{p_0 q_0}{n} - \frac{\sigma_p{}^2}{n} \qquad . \qquad . \qquad . \quad (17.10)$$

Hence, in this case the standard error s is less than the standard error of simple sampling.

17.33 The extent to which the standard error is affected may conceivably be considerable. To take a limiting case, if p be zero for half the events and unity for the remainder, $p_0 = q_0 = \frac{1}{2}$, and $\sigma_p = \frac{1}{2}$, so that s is zero. To take another illustration, still somewhat extreme, if the values of p are uniformly distributed over the whole range between 0 and 1, $p_0 = q_0 = \frac{1}{2}$ as before, but $\sigma_p{}^2 = 1/12 = 0 \cdot 0833$ (**6.15**, p. 136). Hence, $s^2 = 0 \cdot 1667/n$, $s = 0 \cdot 408/\sqrt{n}$, instead of $0 \cdot 5/\sqrt{n}$, the value of s if the chances are $\frac{1}{2}$ in every case. In most practical cases, however, the effect will be much less. Thus the standard deviation of simple sampling for a death-rate of, say, 14 per thousand in a population of uniform age and one sex is $(14 \times 986)^{\frac{1}{2}}/\sqrt{n} = 118/\sqrt{n}$. In a population of the age composition of that of England and Wales, however, the death-rate is not, of course, uniform, but varies from a high value in infancy (say 64 per thousand), through very low values (2 to 3 per thousand) in childhood to continuously increasing values in old age ; the standard deviation of the rate within such a population is roughly about 24 per thousand. But the effect of this variation on the standard deviation of simple sampling is quite small, for, as calculated from equation (17.10),

$$s^2 = \frac{1}{n}(14 \times 986 - 576)$$

$$s = 115/\sqrt{n}$$

as compared with $118/\sqrt{n}$.

17.34 We have, finally, to pass to the condition referred to in **17.23**, and to discuss the effect of a certain amount of dependence between the several " events " in each sample. We shall suppose, however, that the two other conditions are fulfilled, the chances p and q being the same for every event at every trial, and constant throughout the experiment. The standard deviation for each event is $(pq)^{\frac{1}{2}}$ as before, but the events are no longer independent ; instead, therefore, of the simple expression

$$\sigma^2 = npq$$

we must have (cf. **14.2**, p. 327)

$$\sigma^2 = npq + 2pq(r_{12} + r_{13} + \ldots + r_{23} + \ldots)$$

where r_{12}, r_{13}, etc. are the correlations between the results of the first and second, first and third events, and so on—correlations for variables (number of successes) which can only take the values 0 and 1, but may nevertheless be treated as ordinary variables. There are $n(n-1)/2$ correlation coefficients, and if, therefore, r is the arithmetic mean of the correlations, we may write—

$$\sigma^2 = npq[1 + r(n-1)] \qquad . \qquad . \qquad . \qquad . \quad (17.11)$$

The standard deviation of simple sampling will therefore be increased or diminished according as the average correlation between the results of the single events is positive or negative, and the effect may be considerable, as σ may be reduced to zero or increased to $n(pq)^{\frac{1}{2}}$. For the standard deviation of the proportion of successes in each sample we have the equation

$$s^2 = \frac{pq}{n}[1+r(n-1)] \qquad . \qquad . \qquad . \qquad . \quad (17.12)$$

17.35 It should be noted that, as the means and standard deviations for our variables are all identical, r is the correlation coefficient for a table formed by taking all possible pairs of results in the n events of each sample.

It should also be noted that the case when r is positive covers the departure from the rules of simple sampling discussed in **17.30-17.31**; for if we draw successive samples from different records, this introduces the positive correlation at once, even although the results of the events *at each trial* are quite independent of one another.   Similarly, the case discussed in **17.32-17.33** is covered by the case when r is negative ; for if the chances are not the same for every event at each trial, and the chance of success for some one event is above the average, the mean chance of success for the remainder must be below it.   The present case is, however, best kept distinct from the other two, since a positive or negative correlation may arise for reasons quite different from those discussed in **17.30-17.33**.

17.36 As a simple illustration, consider the important case of sampling from a limited population, e.g. of drawing n balls in succession from the whole number w in a bag containing pw white balls and qw black balls. On repeating such drawings a large number of times, we are evidently equally likely to get a white ball or a black ball for the first, second or nth ball of the sample ; the correlation table formed from all possible pairs of every sample will therefore tend in the long run to give just the same form of distribution as the correlation table formed from all possible pairs of the w balls in the bag.   But from **11.41**, page 276, we know that the correlation coefficient for this table is $-1/(w-1)$, whence

$$\sigma^2 = npq\left(1-\frac{n-1}{w-1}\right)$$

$$= npq\frac{w-n}{w-1}$$

If $n=1$, we have the obviously correct result that $\sigma=(pq)^{\frac{1}{2}}$, as in drawing from unlimited material ; if, on the other hand, $n=w$, σ becomes zero as it should, and the formula is thus checked for simple cases.   For drawing 2 balls out of 4, σ becomes $0\cdot816$ $(npq)^{\frac{1}{2}}$; for drawing 5 balls out of 10, $0\cdot745(npq)^{\frac{1}{2}}$; in the case of drawing half the balls out of a very large number, it approximates to $(0\cdot5npq)^{\frac{1}{2}}$, or $0\cdot707(npq)^{\frac{1}{2}}$.

17.37 In the case of contagious or infectious diseases, or of certain forms of accident that are apt, if fatal at all, to result in wholesale deaths, r is positive, and if n be large (as it usually is in such cases), a very small value of r may easily lead to a very great increase in the observed standard deviation. It is difficult to give a really good example from actual statistics, as the conditions are hardly ever constant from one year to another, but the following will serve to illustrate the point. During the twenty years 1887–1906 there were 2,107 deaths from explosions of fire-damp or coal-dust in the coal-mines of the United Kingdom, or an average of 105 deaths per annum. From **17.15** it follows that this should be the square of the standard deviation of simple sampling, or the standard deviation itself approximately 10·3. But the square of the actual standard deviation (the standard error) is 7,178, or its value 84·7, the numbers of deaths ranging between 14 (in 1903) and 317 (in 1894). This large standard deviation, to judge from the figures, is partly, though not wholly, due to a general tendency to decrease in the numbers of deaths from explosions in spite of a large increase in the number of persons employed ; but even if we ignore this, the magnitude of the standard deviation can be accounted for by a very small value of the correlation r, expressive of the fact that if an explosion is sufficiently serious to be fatal to one individual, it will probably be fatal to others also. For if σ_0 denote the standard deviation of simple sampling, σ the standard deviation of sampling given by equation (17.11), we have—

$$r = \frac{\sigma^2 - \sigma_0{}^2}{(n-1)\sigma_0{}^2}$$

Whence, from the above data, taking the numbers of persons employed underground at a rough average of 560,000,

$$r = \frac{7,073}{560,000 \times 105} = +0\cdot00012$$

17.38 Summarising the preceding paragraphs, **17.30-17.37**, we see that if the chances p and q differ for the various populations, districts, years, materials, or whatever they may be from which the samples are drawn, the standard deviation observed (the standard error) will be greater than the standard deviation of simple sampling, as calculated from the average values of the chances; if the average chances are the same for each population from which a sample is drawn, but vary from individual to individual or from one sub-class to another within the population, the standard deviation observed (the standard error) will be less than the standard deviation of simple sampling as calculated from the mean values of the chances ; finally, if p and q are constant, but the events are no longer independent, the observed standard deviation (the standard error) will be greater or less than the simplest theoretical value according as the correlation between the results of the single events is positive or negative. These conclusions further emphasise the need for caution in the use of standard errors. If we find that the standard deviation in some case of sampling exceeds the standard deviation of simple sampling, two interpretations are possible : *either* that p and q are different in the various populations from which samples have been drawn (i.e. that the variations are more or less significant), *or* that the results of the events are positively correlated *inter se*. If the actual standard deviation fall short of the standard deviation of simple sampling two interpretations are again possible : *either* that the chances p and q vary for different individuals or sub-classes in each population, while approximately constant from one population to another, *or* that the results of the events are negatively correlated *inter se*. Even if the actual standard deviation approaches closely to the standard deviation of simple sampling, it is only a conjectural and not a necessary inference that all the conditions of " simple sampling " are fulfilled. Possibly, for example, there may be a positive correlation r between the results of the different events, masked by a variation of the chances p and q in sub-classes of each population.

An alternative approach

17.39 The results of this chapter have been studied from a rather different point of view by a continental school of statisticians, among whose names those of Lexis and Charlier are prominent.

Lexis considers a number of samples of n individuals in which the proportions of successes observed are $p_1, p_2, \ldots p_N$, and sets himself to investigate the nature of the population from which they were drawn— whether it is homogeneous and the samples may be regarded as obtained by simple sampling, whether it varies in time or place so that the samples are not simple, and so on. He takes p to be the mean of the observed values $p_1 \ldots p_N$, and writes—

$$r = 0 \cdot 67449 \sqrt{\frac{pq}{n}}$$

He then defines

$$R = 0 \cdot 67449 \sqrt{\frac{\Sigma (p_k - p)^2}{N - 1}}$$

where the summation extends over all values of $p_1 \ldots p_N$, and writes

$$Q = \frac{R}{r}$$

17.40 Now, if the sampling is simple we may, in large samples, take the mean p to be an estimate of the true value, and r to be an estimate of the probable error of simple sampling of p. Also, we may take the quantity R to be an estimate of the probable error of p (see **21.7**).

Hence, for large samples, R is approximately equal to r, and $Q=1$. This case, which is what we have called simple sampling, Lexis calls " normal dispersion."

17.41 On the other hand, if the population is not constant while the samples are drawn, or if they come from different parts of a patchy population, we get the case discussed in **17.30**. R is no longer an estimate of the probable error of a constant p, but may be split into two parts, one due to the sampling fluctuations of the observed values of p round the mean value, the other due to the variations of the true values round that mean. R will therefore be greater than r, as may be seen from equation (17.8), and $Q>1$. This case Lexis calls " supernormal dispersion."

17.42 Similarly, in the case discussed in **17.32** we get R less than r, and hence $Q<1$. This case Lexis calls " subnormal dispersion," and speaks of the data which give rise to it as " constrained " (*gebundene*).

The quantity Q is analogous to a quantity χ^2, which we shall consider at some length in Chapter 20 in discussing the significance of the deviations of observed frequencies from theoretical expectation.

SUMMARY

1. Under simple sampling conditions, the proportion of successes in a sample may be taken as an estimate of the proportion of successes in the parent population.

2. If p is the proportion of successes in the population, the standard error of simple sampling of the *number* of successes is given by

$$\sigma = \sqrt{npq}$$

and of the *proportion* of successes by

$$s = \sqrt{\frac{pq}{n}}$$

3. The probability that an observed number of successes deviates from the expected number by more than three times the standard error is very small. This fact enables us to set limits to the range within which the observed frequency lies when we know the theoretical frequency.

4. For large samples, the observed frequency of successes may be used to calculate the standard error, and this fact enables us to set limits to the range within which the theoretical frequency lies when we know the observed frequency.

5. For several samples, if the chance of success varies from sample to sample but remains constant within a sample, the standard error of the *number* of successes is given by

$$\sigma^2 = np_0q_0 + n(n-1)\sigma_p{}^2$$

and of the *proportion* of successes by

$$s^2 = \frac{p_0q_0}{n} + \frac{n-1}{n}\sigma_p{}^2$$

where p_0 is the mean of the varying chance of success, σ_p is the standard deviation of p, and n is the number of individuals in each sample.

If n is large and s_0 is the standard deviation calculated from the mean p_0, this last equation is approximately

$$s^2 = s_0{}^2 + \sigma_p{}^2$$

6. If the chance of success varies between the individuals of a sample but does not vary as between the different samples,

$$\sigma^2 = n p_v q_0 - n \sigma_p{}^2$$

$$s^2 = \frac{p_0 q_0}{n} - \frac{\sigma_p{}^2}{n}$$

7. If the chance of success remains constant for each member of each sample, but the events are not independent,

$$\sigma^2 = npq\{1 + r(n-1)\}$$

$$s^2 = \frac{pq}{n}\{1 + r(n-1)\}$$

where r is the mean of the correlations between the results of the events.

EXERCISES

17.1 Compare the actual with the theoretical mean and standard deviation for the following record of 6,500 throws of 12 dice, 4, 5 or 6 being reckoned as a " success "—

Successes	Frequency	Successes	Frequency
0	1	7	1,351
1	14	8	844
2	103	9	391
3	302	10	117
4	711	11	21
5	1,231	12	3
6	1,411		
		Total	6,500

17.2 (Quetelet, " Lettres . . . sur la théorie des probabilités.")

Balls were drawn from a bag containing equal numbers of black and white balls, each ball being returned before drawing another.   The records were then grouped by counting the number of black balls in consecutive 2's, 3's, 4's, 5's, etc.   The following are the distributions so derived for grouping by 5's, 6's, and 7's. Compare actual with theoretical means and standard deviations.

Successes	(a) Grouping by fives	(b) Grouping by sixes	(c) Grouping by sevens
0	30	17	9
1	125	65	34
2	277	166	104
3	224	192	151
4	136	166	148
5	27	69	95
6	—	8	40
7	—	—	4
Total	819	683	585

17.3 The proportion of successes in the data of Exercise 17.1 is 0·5097. Find the standard deviation of the proportion with the given number of throws, and state whether you would regard the excess of successes as probably significant of bias in the dice.

17.4 In the 4,096 drawings on which Exercise 17.2 is based 2,030 balls were black and 2,066 white. Is this divergence probably significant of bias ?

17.5 (Data from Report I, Evolution Committee of the Royal Society, page 17.) In breeding certain stocks, 408 hairy and 126 glabrous plants were obtained. If the expectation is one-fourth glabrous, is the divergence significant, or might it have occurred as a fluctuation of sampling ?

17.6 400 eggs are taken at random from a large consignment, and 50 are found to be bad. Estimate the percentage of bad eggs in the consignment and assign limits within which the percentage probably lies.

17.7 In a certain association table (data from Exercise 2.5) the following frequencies were obtained—

$$(AB) = 309, \quad (A\beta) = 214, \quad (\alpha B) = 132, \quad (\alpha\beta) = 119$$

Can the association of the table have arisen as a fluctuation of simple sampling, the true association being zero ?.

17.8 The sex ratio at birth is sometimes given by the ratio of male to female births, instead of the proportion of male to total births. If Z is the ratio, i.e. $Z = p/q$, show that the standard error of Z is approximately $(1+Z)\sqrt{\dfrac{Z}{n}}$, n being large, so that deviations are small compared with the mean.

17.9 In a random sample of 500 persons from town A, 200 are found to be consumers of cheese. In a sample of 400 from town B, 200 are also found to be consumers of cheese. Discuss the question whether the data reveal a significant difference between A and B so far as the proportion of cheese-consumers is concerned.

17.10   In a newspaper article of 1,600 words in English 36 per cent of the words are found to be of Anglo-Saxon origin. Assuming that simple sampling conditions hold, estimate the proportion of Anglo-Saxon words in the writer's vocabulary and assign limits to that proportion.

Suggest possible causes which might break down the three conditions for simple sampling.

17.11   If a series of random samples of different sizes is taken from the same material, show that the standard deviation of the observed proportions of successes in such sets is s, where

$$s^2 = \frac{pq}{H}$$

and H is the harmonic mean of the numbers in the samples.

17.12   Apply the result of the previous exercise to the following data (A. D. Darbishire, *Biometrika*, vol. 3, page 30), giving percentages to the nearest unit of albinos obtained in 121 litters from hybrids of Japanese waltzing mice by albinos, crossed *inter se*—

Percentage	Frequency	Percentage	Frequency
0	40	40	3
14	4	43	2
17	9	50	16
20	9	57	1
22	1	60	3
25	10	67	4
29	3	80	1
33	13	100	2

Calculate the actual standard deviation and compare it with the result given by the formula of the previous exercise. The expected proportion of albinos is 25 per cent, and the sizes of the litters are given in Example 5.5, page 121

17.13   In a case of mice-breeding (see reference above) the harmonic mean number in a litter was $4 \cdot 735$, and the expected proportion of albinos 50 per cent. Find the standard deviation of simple sampling for the proportion of albinos in a litter, and state whether the actual standard deviation ($21 \cdot 63$ per cent) probably indicates any *real* variation, or not.

17.14   If for one half of n events the chance of success is p and the chance of failure q, whilst for the other half the chance of success is q and the chance of failure p, what is the standard deviation of the number of successes, the events being all independent?

17.15 Corresponding to the case of equation (17.8) show that if the values of p are small so that the binomial tends to the Poisson limit with parameter M, the variance of the numbers of successes observed is given by

$$s^2 = \overline{M} + \sigma_M^2$$

where $\overline{M}$ is the mean value of M and σ_M is the standard deviation.

17.16 Similarly, corresponding to equation (17.10), show that

$$s^2 = \overline{M}$$

so that the usual equation for the standard error holds notwithstanding departures from simple sampling of the type here considered. (cf. equation (17.3)).

17.17 The following are the deaths from smallpox during the twenty years 1882–1901 in England and Wales—

1882	1,317	1892	431
83	957	93	1,457
84	2,234	94	820
85	2,827	95	223
86	275	96	541
87	506	97	25
88	1,026	98	253
89	23	99	174
90	16	1900	85
91	49	1901	356

The death-rate from smallpox being very small, the rule of **17.15** may be applied to estimate the standard deviation of simple sampling. Assuming that the excess of the actual standard deviation over this can be entirely accounted for by a correlation between the results of exposure to risk of the individuals composing the population, estimate r. The mean population during the period may be taken in round numbers as 29 millions.

CHAPTER EIGHTEEN

THE SAMPLING OF VARIABLES

LARGE SAMPLES

Sampling of variables

18.1 We are now able to proceed from the sampling of attributes to the sampling of variables. Whereas in the last chapter we were interested in the question whether a member of a sample did or did not exhibit a particular attribute, we now have to study individuals which may take any of the values of a variable. It will no longer be possible, therefore, for us to classify each member of a sample under one of two heads, success or failure ; in general the values of the variate given by different trials will be spread over a range, which may be unlimited, limited by practical considerations, as in the case of height in human beings, or limited by theoretical considerations, as in the case of the correlation coefficient, which cannot lie outside the range $+1$ to -1.

18.2 To give concreteness to our discussions we shall occasionally find it useful to consider the sampling of variables as a kind of ticket sampling. We may picture our population as made up of tickets, each bearing a recorded value of some variable X. Sampling may then be imagined to consist of the drawing of tickets and the noting of the values of X which they bear. In the great majority of cases with which we shall deal, X may have any value over a continuous range, and the ticket population is to be conceived as being actually or practically infinite.

18.3 As in the case of attributes, our principal objects in studying these samples will be (*a*) to compare observation with expectation and to see how far deviations of one from the other can be attributed to fluctuations of sampling ; (*b*) to estimate from samples some characteristic of the parent population, such as the mean of a variate ; and (*c*) to gauge the reliability of our estimates.

In order to grasp satisfactorily the ideas and assumptions upon which work of this kind is based, it is necessary to develop some theoretical considerations which have already been touched upon in the last chapter. This we now proceed to do.

Sampling distributions

18.4 If we take a number of samples from a population and calculate some function,[1] such as the mean or the standard deviation, of each sample, we shall in general get a series of different values, one for each sample. If the number of samples is at all large, these values may be grouped in a frequency distribution ; and as the number of samples becomes larger, this distribution will approach the " ideal " form of a continuous curve. Such a distribution is called a *sampling distribution*.

18.5 As an illustration, consider the population of 8,585 men, classified according to height, of Table 4.7, page 82. In Chapter 16 we showed how to draw a random sample of 10 individuals from this population, and for one sample we calculated the mean. The following table shows the 100 values of the sample mean obtained by taking 100 such samples arranged in the form of a frequency table—

TABLE 18.1.—Frequency distribution of means of samples of 10 from the population of the last column of Table 4.7 page 82

Value of mean in sample (inches) less $\frac{7}{16}$ inch	Number of samples with specified values of the mean
64·4–	1
64·8–	—
65·2–	1
65·6–	11
66·0–	12
66·4–	16
66·8–	22
67·2–	18
67·6–	14
68·0–	4
68·4–	1
Total	100

This distribution is not very regular, owing to the smallness of the total frequency.

18.6 As a second illustration we take some data obtained with random sampling numbers from a bivariate normal population with correlation +0·9. 500 samples of 10 were taken and the correlation coefficient of each sample worked out. The frequency distribution of the 500 values was as follows (data adapted from P. R. Rider, " Distribution of Correlation Coefficient in Small Samples," *Biometrika*, vol. 24, 1932, page 382)—

---

[1] Quantities such as means, standard deviations, moments, correlation coefficients and so forth will be referred to generically as " parameters." It is the modern practice to reserve this word for a population value and to denote the corresponding sample value by the word "Statistic." Thus a sample-mean is a statistic which forms the estimate of a population-mean, the parameter.

TABLE 18.2.—Frequency distribution of correlation coefficients in samples of 10 from a normal population

Value of r in sample	Frequency
$-0 \cdot 1 - 0 \cdot 0$	2
$0 \cdot 0 - 0 \cdot 1$	0
$0 \cdot 1 - 0 \cdot 2$	0
$0 \cdot 2 - 0 \cdot 3$	2
$0 \cdot 3 - 0 \cdot 4$	4
$0 \cdot 4 - 0 \cdot 5$	7
$0 \cdot 5 - 0 \cdot 6$	30
$0 \cdot 6 - 0 \cdot 7$	44
$0 \cdot 7 - 0 \cdot 8$	102
$0 \cdot 8 - 0 \cdot 9$	178
$0 \cdot 9 - 1 \cdot 0$	131
Total	500

Here the distribution is more regular, the number of samples being five times as large. In general we expect that as the number of samples increases, the distribution will tend more and more to a continuous curve.

Use of the sampling distribution

18.7 Let us suppose that we are given the sampling distribution of a statistic, and that the frequency (y) may be represented in terms of the variate (x) by a continuous curve,

$$y = f(x)$$

The frequency with which a given value x_0 of the statistic occurs in a large number of samples will be represented by the ordinate of the curve at the point whose abscissa is x_0. We have had an example of this in the normal curve.

The number of samples which give a value of x greater than x_0 will be represented by the area to the right of the ordinate at x_0; the number giving a value less than x_0 will be represented by the remaining area to the left.

Hence, the chance that any sample chosen at random from all possible samples will give a value of x greater than x_0 is given by the area to the right of the ordinate at x_0 divided by the total area of the curve, which represents the total number of samples; and the chance that the sample will give a value of x less than x_0 is given by the area to the left of the ordinate of x_0 divided by the total area.

Similarly, the chance that a sample would give a value of x lying between, say, x_1 and x_2 is the area lying between the ordinates at the points x_1 and x_2 divided by the total area.

18.8   In 8.21 we referred to the fact that areas could be expressed in the notation of the integral calculus.   In fact, we may write the area of the curve between x_1 and x_2 as

$$\int_{x_1}^{x_2} f(x) dx$$

and hence we may express P, the probability that a sample will give a value between x_1 and x_2, as

$$P = \int_{x_1}^{x_2} f(x) dx \Big/ \int_{-\infty}^{\infty} f(x) dx$$

where we assume the extreme limits to be $\pm \infty$ as in the normal curve. In particular, the probability that the sample will give a value of x greater than x_0 is given by

$$P = \frac{\int_{x_0}^{\infty} f(x) dx}{\int_{-\infty}^{\infty} f(x) dx}$$

As a rule, we can choose our units so that the area of the curve is unity. This simplifies the above expressions; for the denominator, being equal to unity, may be omitted.

18.9   Now let us suppose that, knowing the form of the sampling distribution and hence being able to calculate P for any given x_0, we take a sample and find that it gives a very low value of P.   We are then faced with three possibilities: either a very improbable event has occurred; or the assumptions on which we obtained the sampling distribution were incorrect; or there is something wrong with our sampling technique. Which of these explanations we adopt is to some extent a matter of choice, but if we have tested our sampling, or on other grounds have no reason to suspect it, we shall, as a rule, be led to query the hypotheses on which the sampling distribution was obtained.

   This, in effect, is what we did in the previous chapter.   It so happens that in the simple sampling of attributes we know that the exact form of the sampling distribution is $N(q+p)^n$, where p is the chance of success. Without examining this distribution too closely we can say that only a very small part of it lies outside the range $\pm 3\sigma$.   Hence, if we find a sample giving a value outside the range $\pm 3\sqrt{npq}$, we suspect the hypothesis on which the distribution was based; and this, unless we prefer to suppose that our sampling was not in fact simple, leads us to suspect the value of p, which completely determines the sampling distribution.

18.10   In the previous chapter we regarded the probability of a sample giving a value differing by more than 3σ from the mean value as so remote that in every case we should be justified in looking for some definite cause of the discrepancy. This is only a conventional range, based upon the empirical fact that in most single-humped populations it includes nearly all the members ; but it is a convenient one to take and we shall use it again below. For certain purposes, however, we might be prepared to use a narrower range which, though not giving such a small probability that a sample lay outside it, yet indicated considerable improbability in the divergence of observation from expectation, and enabled us to criticise the validity of our hypotheses with some degree of assurance. We give one or two examples below.

18.11 In practice nearly all the sampling distributions we have to consider are based on simple sampling. It is therefore convenient to speak briefly of a " sampling distribution," meaning thereby a sampling distribution obtained under simple (and random) conditions.

Example 18.1.—The sampling distribution of a statistic is a normal population with mean 9 units and standard deviation 2 units. What is the probability that a sample will give a value of the statistic greater than 12 units ?

Here the value 12 is three units, i.e. $1 \cdot 5\sigma$, to the right of the mean. The required probability is therefore the area of the normal curve to the right of an ordinate $1 \cdot 5\sigma$ to the right of the mean, divided by the total area of the curve.

This ratio can be obtained at once from Table 2 of the Appendix. We see, in fact, that the greater fraction of the area of the curve corresponding to $\frac{x}{\sigma} = 1 \cdot 5$ is $0 \cdot 9332$. The smaller fraction is therefore $0 \cdot 0668$, which gives us the required probability.

Example 18.2.—If the sampling distribution of a statistic is normal, with zero mean and standard deviation σ, what is the value of the statistic such that the chances are 99 to 1 against a sample giving a value in excess of that value ?

We have to find x such that the area of the curve to the right of the ordinate at x is $0 \cdot 01$. or the area to the left $0 \cdot 99$.

From Appendix Table 2—

$$\text{If } \frac{x}{\sigma} = 2 \cdot 32, \text{ greater fraction of area} = 0 \cdot 9898$$

$$\text{and if } \frac{x}{\sigma} = 2 \cdot 33 \quad ,, \qquad ,, \qquad ,, \qquad = 0 \cdot 9901$$

Hence, to the nearest second place of decimals the required value is $2 \cdot 33\sigma$.

Example 18.3.—It very frequently happens in sampling inquiries that we are interested in the probability that a sample value exceeds a given value x_0 *in absolute value,* i.e. that it is greater than x_0 or less than

$-x_0$. We can ascertain this probability without much trouble from the ordinary table of areas of the normal curve if the distribution is normal. Consider, for instance, the data of Example 18.1. Here we found the probability that a sample would give a value greater than $1 \cdot 5\sigma$. If we want the probability that it would give a value greater than $1 \cdot 5\sigma$ in absolute value, we have—

$$P = \text{Area to right of ordinate at } 1 \cdot 5\sigma$$
$$+ \text{Area to left of ordinate at } -1 \cdot 5\sigma$$

Since the curve is symmetrical, the two areas in question are equal, and

$$P = 2(1 - 0 \cdot 9332)$$
$$= 0 \cdot 1336$$

18.12 To apply the results of **18.7** to **18.11** in practice for the purpose of discussing the population from which the samples came, we require to know two things : (a) What is the relation between the sampling distribution and the parent distribution, and (b) what is the form, at least approximately, of the sampling distribution of a given statistic from a given population ?

18.13 If the sampling is to be of much use in enabling us to estimate the value of a parameter in the parent, we should expect most of our estimates to be somewhere near the mark, and only comparatively few to be very far from the true value of the quantity estimated ; and further, we expect that, in general, the further the estimates are from the truth the fewer there will be of them.

To put this more formally, we expect that the sampling distribution will have a peak somewhere close to the value of the parameter which corresponds to the true value in the parent. If it does not, the distribution is probably biased and our samples are likely to be misleading.

The first *desideratum* in our sampling is, therefore, that it shall not lead to a biased distribution. We have seen in Chapter 16 the difficulties of eliminating bias in the sampling process itself. Where, therefore, the more practical considerations alluded to in that chapter impose no limitation, we must use unbiased sampling ; and this means that our sampling must be random. In this connection it must be remembered that we cannot judge from the samples themselves whether the sampling is random or not, though we may suspect it. Separate tests, or the use of some accredited method, are to be recommended where practicable.

18.14 Knowledge of the form of the sampling distribution of a statistic, even of an approximate kind, is by no means easy to secure. We saw that in the case of the simple sampling of attributes it was possible to deduce the sampling distribution in an exact form. We are not always in this fortunate position here—in fact, rarely so. The principal difficulties are—

(a) The form of the parent population frequently is unknown.

(b) Even if the form of the parent is known, certain of its constants may be unknown ; for instance, we may know that a population is normal but be ignorant of its mean and standard deviation.

(c) If the parent is completely known, the form of the sampling distribution can be deduced theoretically in certain circumstances, and in particular if the sampling is simple ; but in practice the mathematical problems which arise usually are very complex, and even if they are tractable may be of no use owing to the enormous arithmetical labour involved in expressing a solution in serviceable form.

18.15 If the samples are small these difficulties are formidable, even for simple sampling. With large samples, however, we are able to make certain legitimate approximations and assumptions which greatly simplify the problem. For the rest of this chapter and in the next we shall be concerned solely with large samples.

Simple sampling of variables

18.16 We shall also be thinking mainly in terms of simple sampling (**17.3**). It is unnecessary to recapitulate here the discussion of simple sampling which we gave in the previous chapter. The assumptions which we considered in **17.19** to **17.24** apply *mutatis mutandis* to the simple sampling of variables.

(a) We assume that we are drawing from precisely the same record during the whole of the sampling ; if we picture our parent population as a card population, the chance of drawing a card with any given value X is the same for each sample.

(b) We assume not only that we are drawing from the same record throughout, but that *each of our cards* at each drawing may be regarded quite strictly as drawn from the same record (or from identically similar records) : e.g. if our card record is contained in a series of bundles, we must not make it a practice to take the first card from bundle number 1, the second card from bundle number 2, and so on, or else the chance of drawing a card with a given value of X, or a value within assigned limits, may not be the same for each individual card at each drawing.

(c) We assume that the drawing of each card is entirely independent of that of every other, so that the value of X recorded on card 1, at each drawing, is uncorrelated with the value of X recorded on card 2, 3, 4, and so on. It is for this reason that we spoke of the record, in **18.2**, as containing a practically infinite number of cards, for otherwise the successive drawings at each sampling would not be independent : if the bag contains ten tickets only, bearing the numbers 1 to 10, and we draw the card bearing 1, the average of the following cards drawn will be higher than the mean of all cards drawn ; if, on the other hand, we draw the 10, the average of the following cards will be lower than the mean of all cards— i.e. there will be a negative correlation between the number on the card taken at any one drawing and the card taken at any other drawing.   Without making the number of cards in the bag indefinitely large, we can, as already pointed out for the case of attributes, eliminate this correlation by replacing each card before drawing the next.

Approximations in the theory of large samples

18.17   We can now consider the approximations which are possible in the theory of large samples.

In the first place, since we have supposed bias to be eliminated, the sample values of a statistic will be grouped about the true value, and if the samples are large, will differ by comparatively small quantities from that value.   Hence, we may take a sample value as an estimate of the true value.   That is to say, if we have a large sample (which may consist of a number of samples run together), we may calculate the parameter from it precisely as we should proceed if we were calculating the parameter for the population as a whole, and take that value as our estimate.   Thus, the mean of the sample may be taken as an estimate of the mean of the population.

18.18   This rule is not quite so obvious as it appears.   Suppose, for example, that we are estimating the standard deviation of a population. In accordance with the previous paragraph we should take the standard deviation of the sample.   But in calculating this quantity we should have to use deviations, not from the true mean, but from the mean in the sample, which may differ from the true mean and to that extent affect the value of the estimate.   We shall, in fact, see later that if $x_1, x_2 \ldots x_n$ are the values in the sample and $\bar{x}$ their mean, there are reasons for preferring the estimate $s^2 = \dfrac{1}{n-1}\Sigma(x-\bar{x})^2$ to the estimate $s^2 = \dfrac{1}{n}\Sigma(x-\bar{x})^2$ for the variance.   If n is large, however, the difference is unimportant ; we can ignore it until we come to deal with small samples.

18.19   Secondly, as in the case of attributes, we can use these estimates in calculating the constants of the sampling distribution, since they differ only by small quantities from the real values.   We saw, for instance, that we were justified in taking the value of p in a large sample in calculating the standard deviation $\sqrt{npq}$ of the sampling distribution. We shall find that the standard deviation of the sampling distribution of the mean of samples from a normal population involves the standard deviation of the parent ; and in this case we can evaluate that quantity by using the standard deviation of the sample in place of the unknown standard deviation of the parent.

18.20 Finally, it is a very remarkable fact that the sampling distributions of many statistics, obtained under simple sampling conditions, tend for large samples to a single-humped form either exactly or very closely normal. The evidence for this statement is partly theoretical, partly experimental. It may be shown that, for simple samples from a normal population, the sampling distributions of most statistics are exactly normal for large samples—some, in fact, are normal for small samples. Following up this work, a number of experiments has been carried out on populations which are not normal ; and it appears that the parent can deviate quite markedly from the normal form without affecting the normality of the sampling distribution to any great extent provided, as before, that the samples are large.

In most of our work we shall not require to assume that the sampling distribution is normal. It will be sufficient to assume that a range of 3σ on each side of the mean includes the major portion of the distribution, and we can confidently take this to be so unless the parent exhibits very marked skewness.

18.21 It will now be apparent that the difficulties we specified in **18.14** have to a great extent been met. Provided that we know the parent distribution to be not unduly skew, we need not know its exact form ; and the sampling distribution can be represented satisfactorily, if not exactly specified, by a mean and standard deviation which may be estimated from the data of the sample.

Standard error

18.22 As in the last chapter, we shall refer to the standard deviation of the sampling distribution as the standard error. In most cases we shall be dealing with simple sampling distributions, but it is convenient to use the term in this wider sense, although the word " error " is not altogether appropriate in some instances. In general, as we have seen, we are justified in taking a range of ± 3 times the standard error as determining limits outside which the value of the parameter given by a sample probably does not lie. We can therefore use the standard error, as we have already used it for attributes, to gauge the precision of an estimate or to permit a judgment being made of the divergence between expected and observed values.

In the remainder of this chapter, and in the next, we shall therefore be concerned mainly in finding expressions for the standard errors of the various parameters which we have to estimate. Their use we shall illustrate in examples as we go along. In certain cases we shall also consider the effect of a breakdown in the conditions of simple sampling.

Standard of error of a quantile, quartile and median

18.23 Let us first of all consider the case of quantiles, which is intimately related to that of attributes.

Consider the distribution of a variate X in an indefinitely large sample. (This is not necessarily the same as the distribution in the parent, owing to the possible presence of bias ; but if bias is excluded, and the sampling is simple, it is the same as the parent form.)

Let X_p be a value of X such that pN values of X in this distribution lie above it and qN below it. Thus, if the sampling is unbiased, $p=\frac{1}{10}$ would give us the upper decile in the indefinitely large sample, $p=\frac{1}{2}$ the median, and so on.

A sample of n will contain various values of X. Let the proportion of values above X_p be $p+\delta$; and let ϵ be the adjustment to be made in X_p so that the proportion of values of X above $X_p+\epsilon$ is p. The values δ and ϵ may be regarded as sampling fluctuations.

Considering now the sample of n, we have that

$$\text{the proportion of values above } X_p \quad = p+\delta$$

$$\text{,, \quad\quad ,, \quad\quad ,, } \quad X_p+\epsilon = p$$

Hence,

$$\delta = \text{proportion of values between } X_p \text{ and } X_p+\epsilon$$

Now if n be large, the proportion of values between X_p and $X_p+\epsilon$ in the sample will, to a close approximation, be the proportion of values between those quantities in the distribution of an indefinitely large sample. Consider then this distribution and let the standard deviation of X in it be σ. If we take the distribution as drawn to scale with unit standard deviation and unit area, the proportion of values between X_p and $X_p+\epsilon$ is the area of the curve between ordinates at the points $\dfrac{X_p}{\sigma}$ and $\dfrac{X_p+\epsilon}{\sigma}$.

Now if n be large, ϵ will be small, for the value of a parameter in the sample of n will lie close to the value in the indefinitely large sample.

Hence the area between $\dfrac{X_p}{\sigma}$ and $\dfrac{X_p+\epsilon}{\sigma}$ is approximately rectangular, and if we call the $\dfrac{X_p}{\sigma}$ ordinate y_p, the area will be $y_p \times \dfrac{\epsilon}{\sigma}$.

Hence,

$$\delta = y_p \times \frac{\epsilon}{\sigma}$$

or

$$\epsilon = \frac{\sigma}{y_p}\delta$$

Now δ is the deviation of the observed proportion from the value p; and from our study of attributes we know that the observed proportion $p + \delta$ will centre round the mean p with standard deviation $\sqrt{\dfrac{pq}{n}}$.

Hence δ centres round zero mean with standard deviation $\sqrt{\dfrac{pq}{n}}$. Since ϵ bears a constant ratio $\dfrac{\sigma}{y_p}$ to δ, it follows that ϵ will be distributed about zero mean with standard deviation

$$\sqrt{\operatorname{var}(x_p)} = \sigma_{xp} = \frac{\sigma}{y_p}\sqrt{\frac{pq}{n}} \qquad . \qquad . \qquad . \qquad (18.1)$$

18.24 If the distribution in an indefinitely large sample be normal we can take the values of y_p from the tables of the ordinate of the norma curve (Appendix Table 1). From tables carried to further places o decimals we have, for the various values of p which correspond to th decides,

	Value of y_p
Median	0·3989423
Deciles 4 and 6 . . .	0·3863425
„ 3 and 7 . . .	0·3476926
„ 2 and 8 . . .	0·2799619
„ 1 and 9 . . .	0·1754983
Quartiles	0·3177766

Inserting these values of y_p in equation (18.1), we have the following values for the standard errors of the median, deciles, etc.—

	Standard error is $\sigma/\sqrt{n}$ multiplied by
Median	1·25331
Deciles 4 and 6 . . .	1·26804
„ 3 and 7 . . .	1·31800
„ 2 and 8 . . .	1·42877
„ 1 and 9 . . .	1·70942
Quartiles	1·36263

It will be seen that the influence of fluctuations of sampling on the several quantiles increases as we depart from the median : the standard error of the quartiles is nearly one-tenth greater than that of the median, and the standard error of the first or ninth decile more than one-third greater.

18.25 Consider further the influence of the form of the frequency-distribution on the standard error of the median, as this is an important form of average. For a distribution with a given number of observations and a given standard deviation the standard error varies inversely as y_p. Hence for a distribution in which y_p is small, for example a U-shaped distribution, the standard error of the median will be relatively high, and it will, in so far, be an undesirable form of average to employ. On the other hand, in the case of a distribution which has a high peak in the centre, so as to exhibit a value of y_p large compared with the standard deviation, the standard error of the median will be relatively low. We can create such a " peaked " distribution by superposing a normal curve with a small standard deviation on a normal curve with the same mean and a relatively large standard deviation. To give some idea of the reduction in the standard error of the median that may be effected by a moderate change in the form of the distribution, let us find for what ratio of the standard deviations of two such curves, having the same area, the standard error of the median reduces to $\sigma/\sqrt{n}$, where σ is of course the standard deviation of the compound distribution.

Let σ_1, σ_2 be the standard deviations of the two distributions, and let there be $n/2$ observations in each. Then

$$\sigma = \sqrt{\frac{\sigma_1{}^2 + \sigma_2{}^2}{2}} \qquad . \qquad . \qquad (18.2)$$

On the other hand, the value of y_p is

$$\left\{ \frac{1}{2\sqrt{2\pi}\sigma_1} + \frac{1}{2\sqrt{2\pi}\sigma_2} \right\} \sqrt{\frac{\sigma_1{}^2 + \sigma_2{}^2}{2}} \qquad . \qquad . \qquad (18.3)$$

Hence, the standard error of the median is

$$\sqrt{\frac{2\pi}{n} \frac{\sigma_1\sigma_2}{\sigma_1 + \sigma_2}} \qquad . \qquad . \qquad . \qquad (18.4)$$

(18.4) is equal to $\sigma/\sqrt{n}$ if

$$\frac{(\sigma_1 + \sigma_2)\sqrt{\sigma_1{}^2 + \sigma_2{}^2}}{2\sqrt{\pi\sigma_1\sigma_2}} = 1$$

and writing $\sigma_2/\sigma_1 = \rho$, that is if

$$\frac{(1+\rho)\sqrt{1+\rho^2}}{2\sqrt{\pi\rho}} = 1$$

or

$$\rho^4 + 2\rho^3 + (2 - 4\pi)\rho^2 + 2\rho + 1 = 0$$

This equation may be reduced to a quadratic and solved by taking $\rho + \dfrac{1}{\rho}$ as a new variable. The roots found give $\rho = 2 \cdot 2360 \ldots$ or $0 \cdot 4472 \ldots$, the one root being merely the reciprocal of the other. The standard error of the median will therefore be $\sigma/\sqrt{n}$, in such a compound distribution, if the standard deviation of the one normal curve is, in round numbers, about $2\frac{1}{4}$ times that of the other. If the ratio be greater, the standard error of the median will be less than $\sigma/\sqrt{n}$. The distribution for which the standard error of the median is exactly equal to $\sigma/\sqrt{n}$ is shown in fig. 18.1 ; it will be seen that it is by no means a very striking form of distribution ; at a hasty glance it might almost be taken as normal. In the case of distributions of a form more or less similar to that shown, it is evident that we cannot at all safely estimate by eye alone the relative standard error of the median as compared with $\sigma/\sqrt{n}$.

18.26 In the case of a grouped frequency-distribution in which the number of observations is large enough to give a fairly smooth distribution, we can use a alternative form which does not involve a knowledge of the standard deviation of the distribution in a very large sample. In fact, in such a case the sample itself is large enough to give us a satisfactory approximation to the distribution in an indefinitely large sample. Let f_p be the frequency per class-interval at the given percentile—simple interpolation will give us the value with quite sufficient accuracy for practical purposes, and if the figures run irregularly they may be smoothed. Let σ be the value of the standard deviation expressed in class-intervals, and let n be the number of observations as before. Then, since y_p is the ordinate of the frequency-distribution when drawn with unit standard deviation and unit area, we must have

$$y_p = \frac{\sigma}{n} f_p$$

But this gives at once for the standard error *expressed in terms of the class-interval as unit*

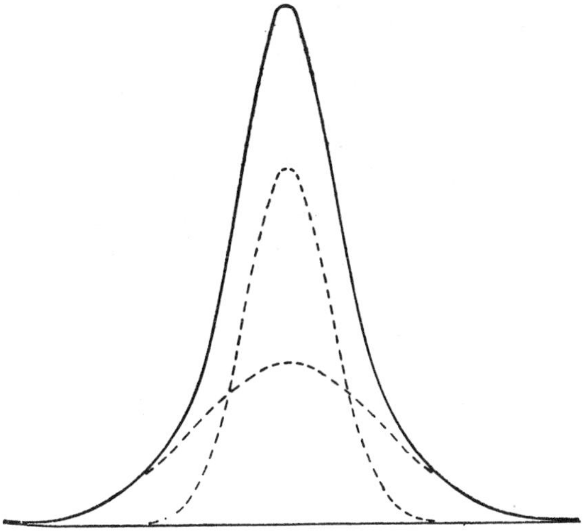

Fig. 18.1

$$\sigma_{x_p} = \frac{\sqrt{npq}}{f_p} \qquad \cdot \qquad \cdot \qquad \cdot \qquad \cdot \qquad \cdot \quad (18.5)$$

Example 18.4.—Consider the data of Table 4.7, page 82, giving the distribution of 8,585 men according to height. Let us take these data to be a sample from the population of men in the United Kingdom at that time. The number of observations is 8,585, and the standard deviation 2·57 in., the distribution being approximately normal : $\sigma/\sqrt{n}=0\cdot027737$, and, multiplying by the factor $1\cdot253\ldots$ given in the table in **18.24**, this gives $0\cdot0348$ as the standard error of the median, on the assumption of normality of the distribution.

Using the direct method of equation (18.5), we find the median to be $67\cdot47$ **(5.20)**, which is very nearly at the centre of the interval with a frequency 1,329. Taking this as being, with sufficient accuracy for our present purpose, the frequency per interval at the median, the standard error is

$$\tfrac{1}{2}\frac{\sqrt{8585}}{1329} = 0\cdot0349$$

As we should expect, the value is practically the same as that obtained from the value of the standard deviation on the assumption of normality.

Three times the standard error is $0\cdot1047$, and we accordingly conclude that the median in the population lies within about $0\cdot1$ inch of $67\cdot47$, the sample value, provided that the sampling is simple.

Example 18.5.—Let us find the standard error of the first and ninth deciles as another illustration. On the assumption that the distribution is normal, these standard errors are the same, and equal to $0\cdot027737 \times 1\cdot70942=0\cdot0474$. Using the direct method, we find by simple interpolation the approximate frequencies per interval at the first and ninth deciles respectively to be 590 and 570, giving standard errors of $0\cdot0471$ and $0\cdot0488$, mean $0\cdot0479$, slightly in excess of that found on the assumption that the frequency is given by the normal curve. The student should notice that the class-interval is, in this case, identical with the unit of measurement, and consequently the answer given by equation (18.5) does not require to be multiplied by the magnitude of the interval.

Correlation between errors of quantiles

18.27　In finding the standard error of the difference between two quantiles in the same distribution, the student must be careful to note that the errors in two such quantiles are not independent. Consider the two quantiles for which the values of p and q are $p_1\ q_1$, $p_2\ q_2$, respectively, the first named being the lower of the two quantiles. These two quantiles divide the whole area of the frequency curve into three parts, the areas of which are proportional to q_1, $1-q_1-p_2$, and p_2. Further, since the errors in the first quantile are directly proportional to the errors in q_1, and the errors in the second quantile are directly proportional but of opposite sign to the errors in p_2, the correlation between errors in the two quantiles will be the same as the correlation between errors in q_1 and p_2, but of opposite sign. But if there be a deficiency of observations below the lower quantile, producing an error δ_1 in q_1, the missing observations will tend to be spread over the two other sections of the curve in proportion to their respective areas,[1] and will therefore tend to produce an error

$$\delta_2 = -\frac{p_2}{p_1}\delta_1$$

in p_2. If, then, r be the correlation between errors in q_1 and p_2, ϵ_1 and ϵ, the respective standard errors, we have—

$$r\frac{\epsilon_2}{\epsilon_1} = -\frac{p_2}{p_1}$$

Or, inserting the values of the standard errors,

$$r = -\sqrt{\frac{p_2 q_1}{q_2 p_1}}$$

The correlation between the quantiles is the same in magnitude but opposite in sign ; it is obviously positive, and consequently

$$\left.\begin{array}{r}\text{Correlation between errors}\\ \text{in two quantiles}\end{array}\right\} = +\sqrt{\frac{p_2 q_1}{q_2 p_1}} \qquad (18.6)$$

If the two quantiles approach very close together, q_1 and q_2 p_1, and p_2 become sensibly equal to one another, and the correlation becomes unity, as we should expect. An alternative derivation is suggested in **19.3**.

Standard error of semi-interquartile range

18.28 Let us apply the above value of the correlation between quantiles to find the standard error of the semi-interquartile range for the normal curve. Inserting $q_1 = p_2 = \frac{1}{4}$, $q_2 = p_1 = \frac{3}{4}$, we find $r = \frac{1}{3}$. Hence the standard error of the interquartile range is, applying the ordinary formula for the standard deviation of a difference, $2/\sqrt{3}$ times the standard error of either quartile, or the standard error of the *semi*-interquartile range $1/\sqrt{3}$ times the standard error of a quartile. Taking the value of the standard error of a quartile from the table in **18.24**, we have, finally,

$$\left.\begin{array}{r}\text{Standard error of the semi-}\\ \text{interquartile range in a}\\ \text{normal distribution}\end{array}\right\} = 0\cdot 78672\frac{\sigma}{\sqrt{n}} \qquad . \quad (18.7)$$

Of course the standard deviation of the interquartile, or semi-interquartile, range can readily be worked out in any particular case, using equation (18.5) and the value of the correlation given above ; it is best to work out such standard errors from first principles, applying the usual formula for the standard deviation of the difference of two correlated variables **(14.2)**.

---

[1] This statement is, perhaps, not obviously true, and the assumption which it represents is not a necessary condition for the validity of equation (18.6). The alternative approach of **19.3** avoids using it.

18.29 If there is any failure of the conditions of simple sampling, the formulæ of the preceding sections cease, of course, to hold good. We need not, however, enter again into a discussion of the effect of removing the several restrictions, for the effect on the standard error of p was considered in detail in Chapter 17, and the standard error of any quantile is directly proportional to the standard error of p.

Standard error of the arithmetic mean

18.30 Let us now determine the standard error of the arithmetic mean.

Suppose we note separately at each drawing the value recorded on the first, second, third ... and nth card of our sample. The standard deviation of the values on each separate card will tend in the long run to be the same, and indentical with the standard deviation σ of x in an indefinitely large sample, drawn under the same conditions. Further, the value recorded on each card is (as we assume) uncorrelated with that on every other. The standard deviation of the sum of the values recorded on the n cards is therefore $\sqrt{n}\sigma$, and the standard deviation of the mean of the sample is consequently 1 /nth of this ; or,

$$\sigma_m = \frac{\sigma}{\sqrt{n}} \qquad . \qquad . \qquad . \qquad (18.8)$$

This is a most important and frequently cited formula, and the student should note that it has been obtained without any reference to the size of the sample or to the form of the frequency-distribution. It is therefore of perfectly general application, if σ be known. We can verify it against our formula for the standard deviation of sampling in the case of attributes. The standard deviation of the number of successes in a sample of m observations is $\sqrt{mpq}$: the standard deviation of the total number of successes in n samples of m observations each is therefore $\sqrt{nmpq}$: dividing by n we have the standard deviation of the mean number of successes in the n samples, viz. $\sqrt{mpq}$ /$\sqrt{n}$, agreeing with equation (18.8).

Example 18.6.—In the height distribution considered in Examples 18.4 and 18.5 we found that σ /$\sqrt{n}$=0·0277 approximately. This is then the standard error of the mean of the distribution.

If we regard the data as a simple sample from the population of men in the United Kingdom, we may take the mean, i.e. 67·46 inches, as an estimate of the mean in the population. Three times the standard error is very small, 0·083 inch, and we can therefore locate the mean in the population with considerable accuracy.

The standard error in this case, however, gives a misleading idea as to the accuracy attained in determining the average stature in the United Kingdom ; the sample was not chosen under conditions which gave every individual an equal chance of being chosen.

Comparison of the standard errors of the median and the mean

18.31 For a normal curve the standard error of the mean is to the standard error of the median approximately as 100 to 125 (cf. **18.24**), and in general the standard errors of the two stand in a somewhat similar ratio for a distribution not differing largely from the normal form. For the distribution of statures used as an illustration in Example 18.4, the standard error of the median was found to be 0·0349 : the standard error of the mean is only 0·0277. The distribution being very approximately normal, the ratio of the two standard errors, viz. 1·26, assumes almost exactly the theoretical magnitude.

As such cases as these seem on the whole to be more common and typical, we stated in **5.23** that the mean is *in general* less affected than the median by errors of sampling. At the same time we also indicated the exceptional cases in which the median might be the more stable—cases in which the mean might, for example, be affected considerably by small groups of widely outlying observations, or in which the frequency-distribution assumed a form resembling fig. 18.1, but even more exaggerated as regards the height of the central " peak " and the relative length of the " tails." Such distributions are not uncommon in some economic statistics, and they might be expected to characterise some forms of experimental error. If, in these cases, the greater stability of the median is sufficiently marked to outweigh its disadvantages in other respects, the median may be the better form of average to use. Fig. 18.1 represents a distribution in which the standard errors of the mean and of the median are the same. Further, in some experimental cases it is conceivable that the median may be less affected by definite experimental errors, the average of which does not tend to be zero, than is the mean—this is, of course, a point quite distinct from that of errors of sampling.

Means of two samples

18.32 When we have two samples from some record which exhibit different means, a very common question which we wish to ask is : Can the difference be accounted for by sampling fluctuations, i.e. can the two samples have come from the same population ?

If the two samples are independent and come from the same population under simple conditions, evidently ϵ_{12}, the standard error of the difference of their means, is given by

$$\epsilon_{12}^2 = \sigma^2\left(\frac{1}{n_1} + \frac{1}{n_2}\right) \qquad . \qquad . \qquad . \qquad . \qquad (18.9)$$

If an observed difference exceed three times the value of ϵ_{12} given by this formula, it can hardly be ascribed to fluctuations of sampling. If, in a practical case, the value of σ is not known *a priori*, we must substitute an observed value, and it would seem natural to take as this value the standard deviation in the two samples thrown together. If, however, the standard deviations of the two samples themselves differ more than can be accounted for on the basis of fluctuations of sampling alone (see below, **19.14**), we evidently cannot assume that both samples have been drawn from the same record : the one sample must have been drawn from a record or a population exhibiting a greater standard deviation than the other. If two samples be drawn quite independently from different populations, indefinitely large samples from which exhibit the standard deviations σ_1 and σ_2, the standard error of the difference of their means will be given by

$$\epsilon_{12}^2 = \frac{\sigma_1^2}{n_1} + \frac{\sigma_2^2}{n_2} \qquad . \qquad . \qquad . \qquad . \quad (18.10)$$

This is, indeed, the formula usually employed for testing the significance of the difference between two means in any case ; seeing that the standard error of the mean depends on the standard deviation only, and not on the mean, of the distribution, we can inquire whether the two populations from which samples have been drawn differ in mean *apart from any difference in dispersion.*

18.33   If two quite independent samples be drawn from the same population, but instead of comparing the mean of the one with the mean of the other we compare the mean m_1 of the first with the mean m_0 of both samples together, the use of (18.9) or (18.10) is not justified, for errors in the mean of the one sample are correlated with errors in the mean of the two together.   Following precisely the lines of the similar problem in **17.29**, we find that this correlation is $\sqrt{n_1/(n_1+n_2)}$, and hence

$$\epsilon_{01}^2 = \sigma^2 \frac{n_2}{n_1(n_1+n_2)} \qquad . \qquad . \qquad . \qquad . \quad (18.11)$$

Effect on standard error of mean of breakdown of conditions for simple sampling

18.34   Let us consider briefly the effect on the standard error of the mean if the conditions of simple sampling as laid down in **18.16** cease to apply.

If we do not draw from the same record all the time, but first draw a series of samples from one record, then another series from another record with a somewhat different mean and standard deviation, and so on, or if we draw the successive samples from essentially different parts of the same record, the standard error will be greatly increased.

For suppose we draw k_1 samples from the first record, for which the standard deviation (in an indefinitely large sample) is σ_1, and the mean differs by d_1 from the mean of all the records together (as ascertained by large samples in numbers proportionate to those now taken), k_2 samples from the second record, for which the standard deviation is σ_2, and the mean differs by d_2 from the mean of all the records together, and so on. Then for the samples drawn from the first record the standard error of the mean will be $\sigma_1/\sqrt{n}$, but the distribution will centre round a value differing by d_1 from the mean for all the records together ; and so on for the samples drawn from the other records. Hence, if σ_m be the standard error of the mean in all the records taken together, N the total number of samples,

$$N\sigma_m{}^2 = \Sigma\left(\frac{k\sigma^2}{n}\right) + \Sigma(kd^2)$$

But the standard deviation σ_0 for all the records together is given by

$$N\sigma_0{}^2 = \Sigma(k\sigma^2) + \Sigma(kd^2)$$

Hence, writing $\Sigma(kd^2) = Ns_m{}^2$,

$$\sigma_m{}^2 = \frac{\sigma_0{}^2}{n} + \frac{n-1}{n}s_m{}^2 \qquad . \qquad . \qquad . \quad (18.12)$$

This equation corresponds precisely to equation (17.8), page 401. The standard error of the mean, if our samples are drawn from different records or from essentially different parts of the entire record may be increased indefinitely as compared with the value it would have in the case of simple sampling. If, for example, we take the statures of samples of n men in a number of different districts of England, and the standard deviation of all the statures observed is σ_0, the standard deviation of the means for the different districts will not be $\sigma_0/\sqrt{n}$, but will have some greater value, dependent on the real variation in mean stature from district to district.

18.35 If we are drawing from the same record throughout, but always draw the first card from one part of that record, the second card from another part, and so on, and these parts differ more or less, the standard error of the mean will be decreased. For if, in large samples drawn from the subsidiary parts of the record from which the several cards are taken, the standard deviations are σ_1, σ_2, . . . σ_n, and the means differ by d_1, d_2, . . . d_n from the mean for a large sample from the entire record, we have—

$$\sigma_0{}^2 = \frac{1}{n}\Sigma(\sigma^2) + \frac{1}{n}\Sigma(d^2)$$

Hence,

$$\sigma_m{}^2 = \frac{1}{n^2}\Sigma(\sigma^2)$$

$$= \frac{\sigma_0{}^2}{n} - \frac{s_m{}^2}{n} \qquad . \qquad . \qquad . \qquad . \quad (18.13)$$

The last equation again corresponds precisely with that given for the same departure from the rules of simple sampling in the case of attributes (equation (17.10), page 403). If, to vary our previous illustration, we had measured the statures of men in each of n different districts, and then proceeded to form a set of samples by taking one man from each district for the first sample, one man from each district for the second sample, and so on, the standard deviation of the means of the samples so formed would be appreciably less than the standard error of simple sampling $\sigma_0/\sqrt{n}$. As a limiting case, it is evident that if the men in each district were all of precisely the same stature, the means of all the samples so compounded would be identical; in such a case, in fact, $\sigma_0=s_m$, and consequently $\sigma_m=0$. To give another illustration, if the cards from which we were drawing samples had been arranged in order of the magnitude of X recorded on each, we would get a much more stable sample by drawing one card from each successive nth part of the record than by taking the sample according to our previous rules—e.g. shaking them up in a bag and taking out cards blindfold, or using some equivalent process.

The result is perhaps of some practical interest. It shows that, if we are actually taking samples from a large area, different districts of which exhibit markedly different means for the variable under consideration, and are limited to a sample of n observations, if we break up the whole area into n sub-districts, each as homogeneous as possible, and take a contribution to the sample from each, we will obtain a *more stable* mean by this orderly procedure than will be given, for the same number of observations, by any process of selecting the districts from which samples shall be taken by chance. There may, however, be a greater risk of biased error. These conclusions seem in accord with common sense. We consider this subject further in Chapter 23.

18.36 Finally, suppose that, while our conditions (*a*) and (*b*) of **18.16** hold good, the magnitude of the variable recorded on one card drawn is no longer independent of the magnitude recorded on another card, e.g. that if the first card drawn at any sampling bears a high value, the next and following cards of the same sample are likely to bear high values also. In these circumstances, if r_{12} denote the correlation between the values on the first and second cards, and so on,

$$s_m{}^2 = \frac{\sigma^2}{n} + 2\frac{\sigma^2}{n^2}(r_{12}+r_{13}+ \ldots +r_{23}+ \ldots)$$

There are $n(n-1)/2$ correlations; and if, therefore, r is the arithmetic mean of them all, we may write—

$$\sigma_m{}^2 = \frac{\sigma^2}{n}[1+r(n-1)] \qquad . \qquad . \qquad . \quad (18.14)$$

As the means and standard deviations of $x_1, x_2, \ldots x_n$ are all identical,

r may more simply be regarded as the correlation coefficient for a table formed by taking all possible pairs of the n values in every sample. If this correlation be positive, the standard error of the mean will be increased, and for a given value of r the increase will be the greater, the greater the size of the samples. If r be negative, on the other hand, the standard error will be diminished. Equation (18.14) corresponds precisely to equation (17.12), page 405.

As was pointed out in **17.35**, the case when r is positive covers the case discussed in **18.34** ; for if we draw successive samples from different records, such a positive correlation is at once introduced, although the drawings of the several cards *at each* sampling are quite independent of one another. Similarly, the case discussed in **18.35** is covered by the case of negative correlation, for if each card is always drawn from a separate and distinct part of the record, the correlation between any two x's will on the average be negative ; if some one card be always drawn from a part of the record containing low values of the variable, the others must on an average be drawn from parts containing relatively high values. It is as well, however, to keep the three cases distinct, since a positive or negative correlation may arise for reasons quite different from those considered in **18.34** and **18.35**.

SUMMARY

1. A knowledge of the sampling distribution of a statistic enables us to ascertain the probability that a given sample will exhibit a value of the statistic between specified limits.

2. The sampling distribution of many statistics tends to the normal form, or at least a single-humped form, for large values of n, the number in the sample, if the sampling is simple.

3. This fact enables us to take a range of ± 3 times the standard error as providing limits within which a sample value of the statistic will probably lie ; with the further assumption of normality of the sampling distribution we can determine the probability that a sample value will lie within any specified limits.

4. In a large sample the values of statistics in the sample may be taken to be estimates of the values in the population, if the sample is simple. Further, these values may be used instead of the values in the population in calculating the standard errors of the statistics.

5. The standard error of the median of a normal distribution is given by

$$\text{s.e.} = 1 \cdot 25331 \frac{\sigma}{\sqrt{n}}$$

where σ is the standard deviation in an indefinitely large sample and n is the number in the sample.

6. With the same notation the standard error of the arithmetic mean is

$$\text{s.e.} = \frac{\sigma}{\sqrt{n}}$$

whatever the form of the distribution.

7. If a series of samples of n is drawn from different populations or from different parts of a non-homogeneous population,

$$\sigma_m{}^2 = \frac{\sigma_0{}^2}{n} + \frac{n-1}{n} s_m{}^2$$

where σ_m is the standard error of the mean, σ_0 is the standard deviation in all the samples taken together, and s_m is the standard deviation of means of indefinitely large samples about the mean of all samples.

8. If samples are drawn so that each member comes from a different section of a non-homogeneous population,

$$\sigma_m{}^2 = \frac{\sigma_0{}^2}{n} - \frac{s_m{}^2}{n}$$

where σ_m, σ_0 and s_m are defined as before.

9. If there is a correlation between the results of the drawing of successive individuals,

$$\sigma_m{}^2 = \frac{\sigma^2}{n}[1 + r(n-1)]$$

where σ_m is the standard error of the mean, σ the standard deviation in an indefinitely large sample, and r is the mean correlation between results of pairs of individuals.

EXERCISES

18.1 If the sampling distribution of a statistic is normal, find the probability that a sample value will differ from the central value by more than twice the probable error.

18.2 In the height distribution of the United Kingdom given in Table 4.7, page 82, assumed to be normal, with mean $67 \cdot 46$ inches and standard deviation $2 \cdot 57$ inches, find the probability that an individual chosen in the same way as the members of the distribution will be between 5 and 6 feet in height.

18.3 For the data of the last column of Exercise 4.6, page 100, find the standard error of the median ($154 \cdot 7$ lbs.) and the standard errors of the two quartiles ($142 \cdot 5$ lbs. and $168 \cdot 4$ lbs.)

18.4 For the same distribution find the standard error of the semi-interquartile range.

18.5 The standard deviation of the same distribution is 21·3 lbs. Find the standard error of the mean and compare it with the standard error of the median (Exercise 18.3).

18.6 Taking the values of the median and the quartiles of the marriage distribution of Table 4.8, page 84, from Example 7.8, page 100, find their standard errors.

18.7 In the same distribution the mean is 29·4 years and the standard deviation 8 years, approximately. Find the standard error of the mean and compare it with that of the median.

18.8 For the same distribution find the standard error of the quartiles, assuming it to be normal with mean 29·4 years and standard deviation 8 years, and compare your results with those obtained in Exercise 18.6.

18.9 Find the standard error of the 27th percentile of the normal distribution.

18.10 (Imaginary data.) A random sample of 1,000 men from the North of England shows their mean wage to be £2 7s. per week, with a standard deviation of £1 8s. A sample of 1,500 men from the South of England gives a mean wage of £2 9s. per week, with a standard deviation of £2. Discuss the suggestion that the mean rate of wages varies as between the two regions.

18.11 Two populations have the same mean but the standard deviation of one is twice that of the other. Show that in samples of 500 from each drawn under simple random conditions the difference of the means will in all probability not exceed 0·3σ, where σ is the smaller standard deviation ; and assuming the distribution of the difference of means to be normal, find the probability that it exceeds half that amount.

18.12 A random sample of 1,000 farms in a certain year gives an average yield of wheat of 2,000 lbs. per acre, with a standard deviation of 192 lbs. A random sample of 1,000 farms in the following year gives an average yield of 2,100 lbs. per acre, with a standard deviation of 224 lbs. Show that these data are inconsistent with the hypothesis that the average yields in the country as a whole were the same in the two years.

Would you modify this conclusion if the farms in the second sample were the same as those in the first ?

18.13 Find the mean and median of the U-shaped distribution of Table 4.14, page 96, and compare their standard errors. (For the purpose of this exercise the median frequency may be found by simple interpolation, but this gives a value on the high side.)

18.14 The mean of a certain normal distribution is equal to the standard error of the mean of samples of 100 from that distribution. Find the probability that the mean of a sample of 25 from the distribution will be negative.

18.15 If it costs a shilling to draw one member of a sample, how much would it cost, in sampling from a population with mean 100 and standard deviation 10, to take sufficient members to ensure that the mean of the sample in all probability would be within 0·01 per cent of the true value ? Find the extra cost necessary to double the precision.

18.16 Consider the data of Table 4.7, page 82, giving the distribution of men by height in each of the four countries which then formed part of the United Kingdom. The means and standard deviations of the four distributions are given in Exercise 5.1, page 122 and Exercise 6.1, page 148.

What is the standard error of the mean of a sample which consists of 400 men, 100 chosen at random from each of the four countries ?

CHAPTER NINETEEN

THE SAMPLING OF VARIABLES

LARGE SAMPLES, CONTINUED

The problem

19.1 We have just considered the standard errors of the most important measures of location, the median and the mean, and of certain measures of dispersion, the quantiles and the semi-interquartile range. We now proceed to discuss the standard errors of other important parameters, including the standard deviation, moments and correlation coefficients. All that we have said in regard to sampling distributions generally in **18.1** to **18.22** applies equally well to this chapter ; and we shall throughout the following sections be thinking of simple sampling unless we state explicitly to the contrary.

Standard errors of moments[1]

19.2 The data from which we calculate the moments are arranged into a certain number of groups. Suppose there are m such groups, and that the expected frequencies falling into them are y_1, y_2, . . . y_m, where $y_1 + y_2 + \ . \ . \ . \ + y_m = \Sigma(y) = n$, n being the number in the sample. The expected frequencies are, as shown below, proportional to the frequencies in the various groups of the parent population.

Let us in the first place recapitulate some of our earlier work by finding the standard error of one of the frequencies, say y_s, due to fluctuations of sampling.

The probability that an individual chosen from the population falls into the sth group is $\dfrac{y_s}{n}$. The probability that it does not is $1 - \dfrac{y_s}{n}$. For n individuals the distribution of frequencies is given by the binomial

$$n\left\{\left(1 - \frac{y_s}{n}\right) + \frac{y_s}{n}\right\}^n$$

with an expected value y_s and a standard deviation

$$\sigma_{y_s} = \sqrt{n\frac{y_s}{n}\left(1 - \frac{y_s}{n}\right)}$$

---

[1] The student whose main interest lies in the practical application of the results of this chapter may prefer to omit paragraphs **19.2** to **19.8**.

Now, if the sample is large, we can take the observed frequency in the sth group in calculating the standard error of the frequency of that group. Taking this observed frequency as our estimate of y_s, its standard error, σ_{y_s}, is given by

$$\text{var } (y_s) = \sigma^2_{y_s} = y_s\left(1 - \frac{y_s}{n}\right). \qquad . \qquad . \qquad . \quad (19.1)$$

This in another form, is our familiar result for the sampling of attributes.

19.3   We may now find the correlation between errors in y_s and errors in another group-frequency, say y_t.   It is evident that such a correlation will exist, for if y_s falls below its expected value, some other frequencies must be increased.

Consider the variance of $y_s + y_t$.   We have, from (14.3), page 327,

$$\text{var } (y_s+y_t) = \text{var } y_s + \text{var } y_t + 2 \text{ cov } (y_s, y_t) \qquad . \qquad . \quad (19.2)$$

Substituting for the variances from (19.1) with the similar expression

$$\text{var } (y_s+y_t) = (y_s+y_t)\left(1 - \frac{y_s+y_t}{n}\right)$$

we find, after a little rearrangement

$$2 \text{ cov } (y_s, y_t) = (y_s+y_t)\left(1 - \frac{y_s+y_t}{n}\right) - y_s\left(1 - \frac{y_s}{n}\right) - y_t\left(1 - \frac{y_t}{n}\right)$$

whence

$$\text{cov } (y_s, y_t) = -\frac{y_s y_t}{n} \qquad . \qquad . \qquad . \qquad . \quad (19.3)$$

This is a more general case of the correlation between quantiles which we considered in **18.27**.   For the correlation between y_s and y_t we have, on dividing (19.3) by the standard deviations—

$$r_{y_s y_t} = -\frac{1}{n}\left\{\frac{\dfrac{y_s}{1-\dfrac{y_s}{n}} \cdot \dfrac{y_t}{1-\dfrac{y_t}{n}}}{}\right\}^{\frac{1}{2}}$$

19.4   By definition the qth moment about an arbitrary point is μ'_q where

$$n\mu'_q = \Sigma(x_s^q\, y_s)$$

x being the variate measured from the arbitrary point.   We write a deviation in a quantity μ'_q or y_s as $\delta\mu'_q$ or δv_s as the case may be.   (The symbol δ is not to be regarded as a number multiplying μ'_r or y_s but as part of the single quantity $\delta\mu'_q$ or δy_s.)

Squaring both sides,

$$n^2(\delta\mu'_q)^2 = (x_1{}^q\delta y_1 + x_2{}^q\delta y_2 + \dots + x_n{}^q\delta y_n)^2$$
$$= \Sigma\{x_s{}^{2q}(\delta y_s)^2\} + 2\Sigma'(x_s{}^q x_t{}^q \delta y_s \delta y_t)$$

where Σ' denotes summation over all values of s and t except those for which $s = t$.

This equation holds for any one sample, and we have to sum it for all samples. Carrying out this summation first (in which s and t are fixed), and substituting from equations (19.1) and (19.3) on the right-hand side, we have—

$$n^2 \operatorname{var} \mu_q' = n^2\sigma_{\mu_q}^{2'} = \Sigma\left\{x_s^{2q}y_s\left(1-\frac{y_s}{n}\right)\right\} - 2\Sigma'\left(\frac{x_s^q x_t^q y_s y_t}{n}\right)$$

$$= \Sigma(x_s^{2q}y_s) - \frac{1}{n}\Sigma(x_s^q y_s)\Sigma(x_t^q y_t)$$

$$= n\mu_{2q}' - n\mu_q'^2$$

Hence,

$$\sqrt{\operatorname{var} \mu_q'} = \sigma_{\mu_q}' = \sqrt{\frac{\mu_{2q}' - \mu_q'^2}{n}} \qquad . \qquad . \qquad . \qquad . \qquad (19.4)$$

Example 19.1.—Let us find the standard error of the first moment, or mean h.

We have, from (19.4)—

$$\sigma_{\mu_1} = \sqrt{\frac{\mu_2' - \mu_1'^2}{n}}$$

$$= \sqrt{\frac{\mu_2' - h^2}{n}}$$

Now $\mu_2' - h^2$ is the second moment μ_2 about the mean, i.e. is σ^2. Hence,

$$\sigma_{\mu_1}' = \sigma_h = \sqrt{\frac{\sigma^2}{n}} = \frac{\sigma}{\sqrt{n}}$$

which is the result we have already found in **18.30**.

Correlation between errors in the qth and rth moments, both about the same fixed point

19.5 As in **19.4** we have—

$$n\delta\mu_q' = \Sigma(x_s^q \delta y_s)$$
$$n\delta\mu_r' = \Sigma(x_s^r \delta y_s)$$

Multiplying,

$$n^2\delta\mu_q'\delta\mu_r' = \Sigma(x_s^{q+r}\delta y_s^2) + \Sigma'\{(x_s^q x_t^r + x_s^r x_t^q)(\delta y_s \delta y_t)\}$$

and summing for all samples,

$$n^2 \operatorname{cov}(\mu_q', \mu_r') = \Sigma(x_s^{q+r} \operatorname{var} y_s) + \Sigma'[(x_s^q x_t^r + x_s^r x_t^q)\{\operatorname{cov}(y_s, y_t)\}]$$

On substitution for var y_s and cov (y_s, y_t) from (19.1) and (19.3), the right-hand side reduces to $n\mu'_{q+r} - n\mu'_q\mu'_r$, and hence,

$$\text{cov}(\mu'_q, \mu'_r) = \frac{\mu'_{q+r} - \mu'_q\mu'_r}{n} \qquad . \qquad . \qquad . \quad (19.5)$$

Standard error of the moments about the mean

19.6 In **19.4** and **19.5** we have considered moments about a fixed point. In practice we have to deal more usually with moments about the mean *of the sample*. Since this mean is itself subject to sampling fluctuations, the standard errors of moments about the mean will not in general be the same as those about a fixed point

If h is the mean we have, by definition,

$$n\mu_q = \Sigma\{(x_s - h)^q y_s\}$$
$$= \Sigma(x_s^q y_s) - qh\Sigma(x_s^{q-1}y_s) + T$$

where T is written generally for an expression involving h^2 and higher powers of h.

Now let h vary to $h + \delta h$, y_s vary to $y_s + \delta y_s$, and μ_q vary to $\mu_q + \delta\mu_q$. We have—-

$$n(\mu_q + \delta\mu_q) = \Sigma\{x_s^q(y_s + \delta y_s)\} - q(h + \delta h)\Sigma\{x_s^{q-1}(y_s + \delta y_s)\} + T$$

Subtracting the equation for $n\mu_q$,

$$n\delta\mu_q = \Sigma(x_s^q\delta y_s) - q\delta h\Sigma(x_s^{q-1}y_s) - q\Sigma(x_s^{q-1}\delta h\delta y_s) + U$$
$$= n\delta\mu'_q - nq\mu'_{q-1}\delta h - nq\delta h\delta\mu'_{q-1} + U$$

where U will involve h and higher powers. We may neglect the term in $\delta h\delta\mu'_{q-1}$ as being small compared with the remaining terms. Squaring and summing for all samples,

$$\text{var } \mu_q = \text{var } \mu'_q + q^2\mu'^2_{q-1} \text{ var } h - 2q\mu'_{q-1} \text{ cov}(h, \mu'_q) + U$$

Substituting for var μ'_q etc. from (19.4) and (19.5),

$$\text{var } \mu_q = \frac{\mu'_{2q} - \mu'^2_q \quad q^2\mu'_2\mu'^2_{q-1} - 2q\mu'_{q-1}\mu_{q-1}}{n} + U$$

Now put $h = 0$. U vanishes and the moments become moments about the mean and may therefore be written without dashes. Hence,

$$\sqrt{\text{var } \mu_q} = \sigma_{\mu_q} = \sqrt{\frac{\mu_{2q} - \mu_q^2 + q^2\mu_2\mu_{q-1}^2 - 2q\mu_{q-1}\mu_{q+:}}{n}} \qquad . \quad (19.6)$$

Correlation between two moments both measured about the mean

19.7 In a similar way it may be shown that

$$\text{cov}(\mu_q, \mu_r) = \frac{\mu_{q+r} - \mu_q\mu_r + qr\mu_2\mu_{q-1}\mu_{r-1} - r\mu_{q+1}\mu_{r-1} - q\mu_{q-1}\mu_{r+1}}{n} \qquad (19.7)$$

We omit the algebra for the sake of brevity.

Correlation between errors in a moment about a fixed point and in a moment about the mean

19.8 Let us first of all find the correlation between deviations in a group-frequency y_t and the moment μ_q' about a fixed point. We have:

$$n\mu_q' = \Sigma(x_s{}^q y_s)$$

Hence,

$$n\delta\mu_q'\delta y_t = \delta y_t\Sigma(x_s{}^q\delta y_s)$$
$$= x_t{}^q(\delta y_t)^2 + \Sigma'(x_s{}^q\delta y_s\delta y_t)$$

the summation Σ' being taken over all values of s except $s=t$.

Hence, summing for all samples,

$$n \operatorname{cov}(\mu_q', y_t) = x_t{}^q y_t\left(1 - \frac{y_t}{n}\right) - \Sigma'\left(\frac{x_s{}^q y_s y_t}{n}\right)$$

$$= y_t\left\{x_t{}^q - \Sigma\left(\frac{x_s{}^q y_s}{n}\right)\right\}$$

$$= y_t\{x_t{}^q - \mu_q'\}$$

Hence,

$$\operatorname{cov}(\mu_q', y_t) = \frac{y_t}{n}(x_t{}^q - \mu_q') \qquad . \qquad . \qquad . \qquad . \quad (19.8)$$

Similarly, for the product-sum of deviations in y_t and the moment μ_q about the mean, we have—

$$\operatorname{cov}(\mu_q, y_t) = \frac{y_t}{n}(x_t{}^q - \mu_q') - \frac{qy_t}{n}(x_t - h)\mu'_{-1}$$

$$+ \text{terms in } h \text{ and higher powers}$$

Putting $h=0$, the right-hand side reduces to

$$\frac{y_t}{n}(x_t{}^q - \mu_q - qx_t\mu_{q-1}) \qquad . \qquad . \qquad . \quad (19.9)$$

For the product-sum of errors in μ_q' and μ_r,

$$n\delta\mu_q' = \Sigma(x_s{}^q\delta y_s)$$
$$\delta\mu_r = \delta\mu_r' - r\delta h\mu'_{r-1} + U$$

where U, as before, denotes an expression involving h and higher powers. Hence,

$$n\delta\mu_q'\delta\mu_r = \Sigma(x_s{}^q\delta y_s\delta\mu_r') - \Sigma(x_s{}^q\delta y_s r\delta h\mu'_{r-1}) + U$$

Summing for all deviations,

$$\operatorname{cov}(\mu_q', \mu_r) = \Sigma\{x_s{}^q \operatorname{cov}(y_s, \mu_r')\} - \Sigma\{x_s{}^q r\mu'_{r-1} \operatorname{cov}(h, y_s)\} + U$$

and substituting from (19.8) and (19.9) the right-hand side becomes

$$\frac{\mu'_{q+r} - \mu_q'\mu_r'}{n} - \frac{r\mu'_{q+1}\mu'_{r-1}}{n} + U$$

Put $h=0$. Then,

$$\text{cov}\,(\mu_q', \mu_r) = \frac{\mu_{q+r} - \mu_q\mu_r - r\mu_{q+1}\mu_{r-1}}{n} \qquad . \qquad . \quad (19.10)$$

Use of Sheppard's corrections in evaluating standard errors.

19.9 Theoretically, Sheppard's corrections for grouping are not to be used in evaluating the moments which enter into the general equations for standard errors obtained in the previous sections. For, as the corrected values differ from the uncorrected values only by constants depending on the width of the interval, the sampling deviations of corrected and uncorrected moments are equal, and hence so are their standard errors. But the standard errors of uncorrected moments are given by the equations we have obtained in the foregoing section, and hence those equations are applicable to corrected moments provided that the uncorrected values are used in them.

In practice, however, it seems to make very little difference which moments we use, unless the sample is very large indeed. But as the uncorrected values have to be obtained before the corrected values can be calculated, and are therefore usually available, it is as well to use the uncorrected values wherever possible.

Standard error of the variance

19.10 Armed with the general results of the foregoing sections, we can discuss the standard errors of a large class of parameters.

From equation (19.6), putting $q=2$, we have, since $\mu_1=0$,

$$\sqrt{\text{var}\,\mu_2} = \sigma_{\mu_2} = \sqrt{\frac{\mu_4 - \mu_2{}^2}{n}} \qquad . \qquad . \quad (19.11)$$

which gives the standard error of the variance μ_2.

If the parent population is normal,

$$\mu_2 = \sigma^2, \qquad \mu_4 = 3\sigma^4 \quad (8.23)$$

and hence,

$$\sigma_{\mu_2} = \sqrt{\frac{3\sigma^4 - \sigma^4}{n}} = \sigma^2\sqrt{\frac{2}{n}}$$

$$= \mu_2\sqrt{\frac{2}{n}} \qquad . \qquad . \qquad . \qquad . \quad (19.12)$$

Standard error of the standard deviation

19.11 If μ_2 is the variance, we have—

$$\mu_2 = \sigma^2$$

Hence,

$$\mu_2 + \delta\mu_2 = (\sigma + \delta\sigma)^2$$
$$= \sigma^2 + 2\sigma\delta\sigma + (\delta\sigma)^2$$

Neglecting $\delta\sigma^2$ in comparison with $\delta\sigma$,

$$\delta\mu_2 = 2\sigma\delta\sigma$$

Squaring and summing for all samples,

$$\text{var } \mu_2 = \sigma^2_{\mu_2} = 4\sigma^2 \text{ var } \sigma$$

Hence,

$$\sqrt{\text{var } \sigma} = \sigma_\sigma = \frac{1}{2\sigma}\sigma_{\mu_2} = \sqrt{\frac{\mu_4 - \mu_2^2}{4\mu_2 n}} \qquad . \qquad . \qquad . \quad (19.13)$$

If the parent distribution is normal this reduces to

$$\sqrt{\text{var } \sigma} = \sigma_\sigma = \frac{\sigma}{\sqrt{2n}} \qquad . \qquad . \qquad . \qquad . \quad (19.14)$$

19.12   The form of equation (19.14) has been widely used for the standard error of σ without due regard to the nature of the parent population, and the student should guard against this mistake.

We have, in fact, from (19.13)—

$$\sigma_\sigma = \frac{\sqrt{\mu_2}}{\sqrt{2n}}\sqrt{\frac{1}{2}\left(\frac{\mu_4}{\mu_2^2} - 1\right)}$$

$$= \frac{\sigma}{\sqrt{2n}}\left(1 + \frac{\beta_2 - 3}{2}\right)^{\frac{1}{2}}$$

How far σ_σ can be taken to be the value (19.14) therefore depends on how close the factor $\left(1 + \frac{\beta_2 - 3}{2}\right)^{\frac{1}{2}}$ is to unity, i.e. depends on the kurtosis of the parent distribution.

The following table shows the value of this factor for various values of β_2—

β_2	$\left(1 + \frac{\beta_2 - 3}{2}\right)^{\frac{1}{2}}$
2	0·7071
3	1·0000
4	1·2247
5	1·4142
6	1·5811
7	1·7321
8	1·8708
9	2·0000

It thus appears that if the population is leptokurtic the real standard error is greater than that given by the assumption of normality, and may be twice as great or even more. If the population is platykurtic the real standard error is less than the " normal " value.

If $\dfrac{\beta_2-3}{2}$ is small, the factor $\left(1+\dfrac{\beta_2-3}{2}\right)^{\frac{1}{2}}$ is approximately $1+\dfrac{\beta_2-3}{4}$.

This differs from unity by more than 5 per cent if β_2 is less than $2\cdot8$ or more than $3\cdot2$. Hence, values of β_2 lying outside the range $2\cdot8$ to $3\cdot2$ (and they are more common than not in practice) will give an error of more than 5 per cent if the population is assumed to be normal.

Example 19.2.—For the height distribution of Table 4.7, page 82, we have found that $\sigma=2\cdot57$ inches, $n=8585$. The population may be taken to be normal, for β_2 from the sample is $3\cdot149$ (Example 7.9, page 164) and hence the standard error of $\sigma=\dfrac{2\cdot57}{\sqrt{2\times8585}}=0\cdot02$ approximately.

Hence, we may say that the s.d. in the population almost certainly lies in the range $2\cdot57\pm0\cdot06$, assuming that the sampling is simple.

Example 19.3.—The distribution of Australian marriages of Table 4.8, page 84, has uncorrected moments μ_2 and μ_4, in class-intervals, as follows—

$$\mu_2 = 7\cdot0570$$
$$\mu_4 = 408\cdot7382 \qquad \text{(Example 7.2, page 157.)}$$

Hence,

$$\sigma = \sqrt{\overline{\mu_2}} = 2\cdot6565$$

The standard error of $\sigma = \sqrt{\dfrac{\mu_4-\mu_2{}^2}{4\mu_2 n}}$

$$= \sqrt{\dfrac{408\cdot7382-(7\cdot0570)^2}{4\times7\cdot0570\times301,785}}$$

$$= 0\cdot00649 \text{ class-intervals}$$

As we should expect from such a large sample, the standard error is very small, and we conclude that the standard deviation of the parent lies in the range $2\cdot6565\pm0\cdot0195$.

It may be pointed out that if we take these data as a sample of Australian marriages in general, we may be violating the conditions of simple sampling, for the distribution most likely changes from year to year.

Example 19.4.—In the previous example we worked throughout with uncorrected values. The corrected moments (Example 7.4, page 159) are—

$$\mu_2 = 6\cdot9736$$
$$\mu_4 = 405\cdot2389$$

We then have, for the corrected value of σ,

$$\sigma = \sqrt{6 \cdot 9736}$$
$$= 2 \cdot 641$$

But the standard error of σ is $0 \cdot 00649$ as in the previous example, for we must use the uncorrected values in calculating it.

As a matter of fact, if we had used the corrected values we should have found the value $0 \cdot 00654$—a practically negligible difference even for a sample of this size.

Finally, let us compare this value with that given by the assumption of normality. We have—

$$\sigma_\sigma = \frac{\sigma}{\sqrt{2n}} = \frac{2 \cdot 6565}{\sqrt{603{,}570}}$$

$$= 0 \cdot 00342 \text{ class-intervals}$$

i.e. only about half the true value. This is in accordance with the result of Example 7.6, for β_2 is over 8.

Comparative effects of sampling fluctuations and corrections for grouping

19.13 Writing temporarily $\sigma_1{}^2$ for the uncorrected value of the variance and $\sigma_2{}^2$ for the corrected value, we have—

$$\sigma_2{}^2 = \sigma_1{}^2 - \frac{h^2}{12}$$

or

$$\frac{\sigma_2{}^2}{\sigma_1{}^2} = 1 - \frac{1}{12}\frac{h^2}{\sigma_1{}^2}$$

If the class-interval is chosen so as to make the number of intervals d

then $6\sigma_1$ would be about dh and $\dfrac{h}{\sigma_1}$ about $\dfrac{6}{d}$. Hence

$$\frac{\sigma_2{}^2}{\sigma_1{}^2} = 1 - \frac{3}{d^2}$$

or, since $\dfrac{3}{d^2}$ is small

$$\frac{\sigma_2}{\sigma_1} = 1 - \frac{3}{2d^2}$$

For instance, if d is 20, the corrected value is about $0 \cdot 375$ per cent less than the uncorrected value.

Now, for a normal population,

$$\sigma_\sigma = \frac{\sigma}{\sqrt{2n}}$$

and if n is, say, 1,000, the standard error is $\dfrac{\sigma}{44\cdot72}=0\cdot0224\sigma=2\cdot24$ per cent of σ. Thus Sheppard's correction amounts to no more than about one-sixth of the standard error, and to make it gives an almost misleading idea of precision in most practical cases.

It was for this reason that we recommended (**6.12** and **9.29**) that the Sheppard corrections should not be applied if the total frequency is less than 1,000. On the other hand, in Examples 19.3 and 19.4 the correction is large compared with the standard error and can reasonably be made, owing to the largeness of the sample.

Comparison of standard deviations of two samples

19.14 As in **18.32**, where we considered the comparison of the means of two samples, if the samples are independent and come from the same population the standard error of the difference of their standard deviations is given by

$$\epsilon_{12}^2 = \frac{\mu_4-\mu_2{}^2}{4\mu_2}\left\{\frac{1}{n_1}+\frac{1}{n_2}\right\} \qquad . \qquad . \qquad . \quad (19.15)$$

where n_1, n_2 are the numbers in the samples, or, if the population be normal,

$$\epsilon_{12}^2 = \frac{\sigma^2}{2}\left\{\frac{1}{n_1}+\frac{1}{n_2}\right\} \qquad . \qquad . \qquad . \quad (19.16)$$

If the two samples are drawn from different populations with constants μ_2, μ_4 and ν_2, ν_4, the standard error of the difference of the standard deviations is given by

$$\epsilon_{12}^2 = \frac{\mu_4-\mu_2{}^2}{4\mu_2 n_1}+\frac{\nu_4-\nu_2{}^2}{4\nu_2 n_2} \qquad . \qquad . \qquad . \quad (19.17)$$

or

$$\epsilon_{12}^2 = \frac{\sigma_1{}^2}{2n_1}+\frac{\sigma_2{}^2}{2n_2} \qquad . \qquad . \qquad . \quad (19.18)$$

if the population be normal.

Again, if the standard deviation of one sample is compared with the standard deviation of the two samples when pooled, the standard error of the difference is, if the distribution be normal,

$$\epsilon_{01}^2 = \frac{\sigma^2}{2}\,\frac{n_2}{n_1(n_1+n_2)} \qquad . \qquad . \qquad . \quad (19.19)$$

These results can be used to test the significance of differences between standard deviations precisely as the equations of **18.32** and **18.33** were used to test the significance of differences between means.

Standard error of third and fourth moments about the mean

19.15 From equation (19.6), putting $q = 3$,

$$\sigma_{\mu_3.} = \sqrt{\frac{\mu_6 - \mu_3{}^2 - 6\mu_4\mu_2 + 9\mu_2{}^3}{n}} \qquad . \qquad . \quad (19.20)$$

If the distribution is normal,

$$\mu_6 = 15\sigma^6, \qquad \mu_4 = 3\sigma^4, \qquad \mu_3 = 0, \qquad \mu_2 = \sigma^2$$

Hence,

$$\sigma_{\mu_3} = \frac{\sigma^3}{\sqrt{n}}\sqrt{15 - 18 + 9} = \sigma^3\sqrt{\frac{6}{n}} \qquad . \qquad . \quad (19.21)$$

Similarly, from equation (19.6), putting $q = 4$,

$$\sigma_{\mu_4} = \sqrt{\frac{\mu_8 - \mu_4{}^2 - 8\mu_5\mu_3 + 16\mu_2\mu_3{}^2}{n}} \qquad . \quad (19.22)$$

If the distribution is normal, $\mu_8 = 105\sigma^8$, $\mu_5 = 0$.
Hence,

$$\sigma_{\mu_4} = \frac{\sigma^4}{\sqrt{n}}\sqrt{105 - 9}$$

$$= \sigma^4\sqrt{\frac{96}{n}} \qquad . \qquad . \quad (19.23)$$

Example 19.5.—For the height distribution of Table 4.7 we have (Example 7.1, page 153)—

$$\mu_2 \text{ (uncorrected)} = 6\cdot6168$$
$$\mu_3 \text{ (uncorrected)} = -0\cdot2078$$
$$\mu_4 \text{ (uncorrected)} = 137\cdot6892$$

and from Example 7.3, page 159—

$$\mu_2 \text{ (corrected)} = 6\cdot5335$$
$$\mu_3 \text{ (corrected)} = -0\cdot2078$$
$$\mu_4 \text{ (corrected)} = 134\cdot4100$$

We did not calculate higher moments, and hence cannot use equations (19.20) and (19.22) with these data. The distribution is, however, approximately normal. Hence, from (19.21),

$$\sigma_{\mu_3} = \sigma^3\sqrt{\frac{6}{8585}} = 0\cdot45 \text{ approximately}$$

The value of μ_3 cannot therefore be judged significantly different from zero, which is what we should expect, for we have assumed the population to be normal.

From (19.23) we have—

$$\sigma_{\mu_4} = \sigma^4\sqrt{\frac{96}{8585}}$$

$$= 4\cdot63 \text{ approximately}$$

These are calculated from the uncorrected value of σ. We may infer that μ_4 (corrected) lies within the range $134\cdot41\pm13\cdot89$. The Sheppard correction is only $3\cdot28$, and is submerged in the possible sampling deviation, even for a sample of 8585. What we have said in **19.13** applies, in fact, *a fortiori* to the higher moments.

19.16 It will be evident that the standard errors of moments of high order are very large ; for the moments increase rapidly, and the standard error of the moment of order q depends on the moment of order $2q$. For example, in the normal distribution, for $q=6$, $\mu_{2q}=10{,}395\sigma^{12}$ and σ_{μ_6} will be of the order $\dfrac{100\sigma^6}{\sqrt{n}}$, whereas $\mu_6=15\sigma^6$. Unless, therefore, n is at least 400, the range $3\sigma_{\mu_6}$ will be greater than the value of μ_6, and hence we cannot locate the value of μ_6 in the population with any exactness. Our approximations, in fact, break down if the deviations are large.

The large sampling errors of moments of high orders prevent the use of moments higher than the fourth in most practical problems.

Correlation between errors in mean and standard deviation

19.17 From equation (19.10), putting $q=1$, $r=2$, and remembering that $\mu_1=0$, we have—

$$\frac{\mathfrak{z}}{\sqrt{n}}\sigma_{\mu_2}r_{h\mu_2} = \frac{\mu_3}{n}$$

Hence, if $\mu_3=0$, errors in the mean and variance, and hence in the mean and s.d., are uncorrelated. In particular, we have the important result that errors in the mean and s.d. in a normal population are uncorrelated. In actual fact they are independent, even for small samples, but we shall have to state this result without proof.

Standard error of the coefficient of variation

19.18 The coefficient of variation V is defined as

$$V = \frac{100\sigma}{h}$$

$$= \frac{100\sqrt{\mu_2}}{h}$$

Hence,

$$V+\delta V = \frac{100\sqrt{\mu_2+\delta\mu_2}}{h+\delta h}$$

$$= \frac{100\sqrt{\mu_2}}{h}\left(1+\frac{\delta\mu_2}{\mu_2}\right)^{\frac{1}{2}}\left(1+\frac{\delta h}{h}\right)^{-1}$$

$$= V\left\{1+\frac{\delta\mu_2}{2\mu_2}\right\}\left\{1-\frac{\delta h}{h}\right\}$$

Neglecting quantities small compared with $\delta\mu_2$ and δh, this becomes

$$V\left\{1+\frac{\delta\mu_2}{2\mu_2}-\frac{\delta h}{h}\right\}$$

Hence,

$$\frac{\delta V}{V} = \frac{\delta\mu_2}{2\mu_2}-\frac{\delta h}{h}$$

$$\frac{(\delta V)^2}{V^2} = \frac{(\delta\mu_2)^2}{4\mu_2^2}+\frac{(\delta h)^2}{h^2}-\frac{1}{\mu_2 h}\delta\mu_2\delta h$$

Summing for all samples we have—

$$\frac{\sigma_V^2}{V^2} = \frac{\text{var }\mu_2}{4\mu_2^2}+\frac{\text{var }h}{h^2}-\frac{\text{cov }(\mu_2,\,h)}{\mu_2 h}$$

If the distribution is normal—

$$\sigma_{\mu_2}^2 = \frac{2\sigma^4}{n}, \qquad \sigma_h^2 = \frac{\sigma^2}{n}$$

and cov $(\mu_2,\,h) = 0$ (**19.17**).
    Hence,

$$\frac{\sigma_V^2}{V^2} = \frac{1}{2n}+\frac{\sigma^2}{h^2 n}$$

$$= \frac{1}{2n}\left\{1+\frac{2V^2}{10^4}\right\}$$

Hence,

$$\sigma_V = \frac{V}{\sqrt{2n}}\sqrt{1+\frac{2V^2}{10^4}} \qquad . \qquad . \qquad . \quad (19.24)$$

In many practical cases the second term differs little from unity and $\frac{V}{\sqrt{2n}}$ will give a sufficiently precise result.

Standard error of β_1 and β_2

19.19 The standard errors of β_1 and β_2 can be deduced in a similar manner.

In fact,

$$\beta_1 = \frac{\mu_3{}^2}{\mu_2{}^3}$$

$$\beta_1 + \delta\beta_1 = \frac{(\mu_3 + \delta\mu_3)^2}{(\mu_2 + \delta\mu_2)^3}$$

which, after some reduction, gives

$$\delta\beta_1 = \frac{2\mu_3\delta\mu_3}{\mu_2{}^3} - \frac{3\mu_3{}^2}{\mu_2{}^4}\delta\mu_2$$

Squaring and summing for all samples—

$$\sigma_{\beta_1}^2 = \frac{4\mu_3{}^2}{\mu_2{}^6}\,\text{var}\,\mu_3 + \frac{9\mu_3{}^4}{\mu_2{}^8}\,\text{var}\,\mu_2 - \frac{12\mu_3{}^3}{\mu_2{}^7}\,\text{cov}\,(\mu_3, \mu_2)$$

$$n\sigma_{\beta_1}^2 = \frac{4\mu_3{}^2}{\mu_2{}^6}\,(\mu_6 - \mu_3{}^2 - 6\mu_4\mu_2 - 9\mu_2{}^3)$$

$$+ \frac{9\mu_3{}^4}{\mu_2{}^8}(\mu_4 - \mu_2{}^2) - \frac{12\mu_3{}^3}{\mu_2{}^7}(\mu_5 - 4\mu_2\mu_3)$$

In terms of β_1, β_2, β_3 and β_4 (see page 159, footnote, for definition of the higher β's),

$$\text{var}\,\beta_1 = \frac{\beta_1}{n}\{4\beta_4 - 24\beta_2 + 36 + 9\beta_1\beta_2 - 12\beta_3 + 35\beta_1\} \qquad . \ (19.25)$$

Similarly,

$$\text{var}\,\beta_2 = \frac{1}{n}\{\beta_6 - 4\beta_2\beta_4 + 4\beta_2{}^3 - \beta_2{}^2 + 16\beta_2\beta_1 - 8\beta_3 + 16\beta_1\} \qquad . \ (19.26)$$

The labour of evaluating these quantities may be obviated by the use of tables given in *Tables for Statisticians and Biometricians, Part I*.

19.20 There is here one important point to be noted. In equation (19.24), if $V=0$, $\sigma_V=0$. Similarly, in equation (19.25), if $\beta_1=0$, $\sigma_{\beta_1}=0$. It might be thought from this that if in a large sample we find in the one case that $V=0$ (and hence that $\sigma=0$), or in the other case that the distribution is symmetrical, then $V=0$ or $\beta_1=0$ in the population. This is not necessarily true.

V will vanish only if all members of the sample give the same value of the variate. If the sample is large, it will be evident that if there is any variation in the parent it must be small; but it is not impossible that members should exist showing deviations from the observed value. The explanation is to be found in the terms which we have neglected in our approximations. These, though in general small compared with the terms retained, may be important if the terms retained themselves vanish. Futhermore, our assumption that the sample value is the same as the parent value may be unjustified if both are very small compared with their difference. Equations such as (19.24) and (19.25) must, there-fore, be treated carefully in the neighbourhood of values which cause them to vanish.

19.21 From the foregoing work the student will have no difficulty in accepting the statement that it is possible to calculate the standard error of any quantity which is expressible as a function of the moments. Such a standard error would, however, be applicable only to a value which had actually been calculated from the moments, and not arrived at by some other means. We shall not pursue the subject further in this book, but we may point out that the standard errors of certain quantities, such as an approximation to the Pearson measure of skewness (**7.12**), have been tabulated in *Tables for Statisticians and Biometricians* for different values of β_1 and β_2. The same tables also contain some results of interest in connection with the sampling distributions of range.

We now turn to the parameters of multivariate universes, the correla-tion coefficients, regression coefficients, and some of the measures of association.

Standard error of the correlation coefficient

19.22 For samples from a normal population the standard error of the correlation coefficient is given by

$$\sigma_r = \frac{1-r^2}{\sqrt{n}} \qquad . \qquad . \qquad . \qquad . \quad (19.27)$$

A proof of this result would take us beyond the scope of the present work. It has to be used with reserve for values of the correlation near to unity, since the distribution in such a case is markedly skew unless the sample is very large, say, at least 500. When there is any doubt it is better to use an alternative test given in **21.33**.

The formula applies also to partial correlations.

19.23 Formula (19.27) is sometimes used to estimate the precision of correlation coefficients obtained by the use of the product-moment formula without reference to the nature of the population. This practice is hardly to be commended, although sometimes there is nothing better to do. It is, however, possible to generalise the procedure of sections **19.2** to **19.8** to the bivariate case, and it may be shown that

$$\frac{\sigma_r^2}{r^2} = \frac{1}{n}\left\{\frac{\mu_{22}}{\mu_{11}^2} + \frac{1}{4}\frac{\mu_{40}}{\mu_{20}^2} + \frac{1}{4}\frac{\mu_{04}}{\mu_{2}^2} + \frac{1}{2}\frac{\mu_{22}}{\mu_{20}\mu_{02}} - \frac{\mu_{31}}{\mu_{11}\mu_{20}} - \frac{\mu_{13}}{\mu_{11}\mu_{02}}\right\} \qquad (19.28)$$

(For the definition of the bivariate moments, see footnote, page 222).

In addition, if the regression is linear, denoting the β_2's of the two variates considered separately by β_2, β_2',

$$\sigma_r{}^2 = \frac{(1-r^2)^2}{n}\left\{1-\frac{r^2}{4(1-r^2)}(\beta_2-3+\beta_2'-3\right\} \qquad . \quad (19.29)$$

which reduces to (19.27) if the kurtosis is zero.

If the distribution is not normal and r is not small, the difference between the values given by (19.27) and (19.29) may be considerable ; but it may be noticed that the value given by (19.27) is less than that given by (19.29) if the distribution is platykurtic for both variates, and greater if the distribution is leptokurtic for both variates.

19.24 In particular, it may be shown that for a 2×2 table in which the frequencies are (AB), $(A\beta)$, (αB) and $(\alpha\beta)$, the standard error of the correlation coefficient calculated by the product-moment method on the assumption that the frequencies are concentrated at points is given by

$$\sigma_r{}^2 = \frac{1}{n}\left\{1-r^2+(r+\tfrac{1}{2}r^3)\frac{[(A)-(\alpha)][(B)-(\beta)]}{\sqrt{(A)(\alpha)(B)(\beta)}}\right.$$
$$\left.-\tfrac{3}{4}r^2\left[\frac{[(A)-(\alpha)]^2}{(A)(\alpha)}+\frac{[(B)-(\beta)]^2}{(B)(\beta)}\right]\right\} \qquad (19.30)$$

19.25 The standard error of tetrachoric r, as calculated in the manner of **11.32**, is given by very complicated expressions which we do not reproduce. The coefficient is very sensitive to departures of the parent from normality, and no satisfactory test of significance seems to be known.

Example 19.6.—In the data of Table 9.3, page 202, we found that the correlation between the stature of the father and the stature of the son was $0 \cdot 51$. Regarding these data as a sample of 1078 from the population of fathers and sons, we have—

$$\text{Standard error of } r = \frac{1-r^2}{\sqrt{n}} = \frac{1-(0\cdot51)^2}{\sqrt{1078}}$$
$$= 0\cdot023 \text{ approximately}$$

Hence, if the sampling was simple, the correlation in the population most probably lies within $0 \cdot 44$ and $0 \cdot 58$. It is thus undoubtedly real.

Example 19.7.—In considering data from 14,416 cows, J. F. Tocher found a negative correlation of $0 \cdot 0796$ between yield of milk per week and percentage of butter fat. Is this significant, i.e., could it have arisen from an uncorrelated population by sampling fluctuations ?

If $r=0$,

$$\sigma_r = \frac{1}{\sqrt{n}} = \frac{1}{\sqrt{14,416}}$$
$$= 0\cdot008$$

The correlation observed is ten times this, and small though it is, could not have arisen from sampling fluctuations.

In this example we may reiterate the caution to be observed in inferring from the sample anything about the population (cows in Scotland) as a whole. The records were, in fact, taken by the Scottish Milk Records Association from constituent associations at various years between 1908 and 1923. The conditions of simple sampling may, therefore, have been violated both in regard to time and in regard to place.

Standard error of the coefficient of regression

19.26 The standard error of the coefficient of regression from a normal population is given by

$$\sigma_{b_{12}} = \frac{\sigma_1 \sqrt{1-r_{12}^2}}{\sigma_2 \sqrt{n}} = \frac{\sigma_{1.2}}{\sigma_2 \sqrt{n}} \qquad . \qquad . \qquad . \quad (19.31)$$

This again applies to a regression coefficient of any order, total or partial, i.e., in terms of our general notation, k denoting any collection of secondary subscripts other than 1 or 2,

$$\left. \begin{array}{l} \text{Standard error of } b_{12.k} \\ \text{for a normal distribution} \end{array} \right\} = \frac{\sigma_{1.2k}}{\sigma_{2.k} \sqrt{n}}$$

The correlation ratio and coefficient of multiple correlation

19.27 It has been shown that the sampling distributions of the correlation ratio and the multiple correlation coefficient from normal populations do *not* tend to the normal form for large samples, although they do give single-humped distributions. The use of a standard error in such cases must be made with great caution, and it is probably better to apply one of the tests of significance which we shall consider later in connection with the theory of small samples. The formula usually given for the standard error of the correlation ratio is an approximate one—

$$\sigma_\eta = \frac{1-\eta^2}{\sqrt{n}} \qquad . \qquad . \qquad . \qquad . \quad (19.32)$$

19.28 Somewhat similar remarks apply to the coefficient $\zeta = \eta^2 - r^2$ which, as we saw in **11.8**, may be used to test the linearity of regression. The use of a standard error for ζ in an attempt to gauge the significance of a departure from linearity has been subjected to very damaging criticism.

Example 19.8.—Consider the data of Example 12.2, page 293 (relation between pauperism, age of population and number of population). We found—

$$x_1 = 0 \cdot 325 x_2 + 1 \cdot 383 x_3 - 0 \cdot 383 x_4$$

Taking this to be given by a random sample from a normal population, is the value $0 \cdot 325$ significant ?

We have—

$$\sigma_{b_{12.34}} = \frac{\sigma_{1.234}}{\sigma_{2.34}\sqrt{n}} = \frac{\sigma_{1.234}\sqrt{1-r_{21.34}^2}}{\sigma_{2.134}\sqrt{n}}$$

$$= \frac{22\cdot8\sqrt{1-0\cdot457^2}}{32\cdot1\sqrt{32}}$$

$$= 0\cdot11$$

The coefficient $b_{12.34}$ is therefore significant.

In this example the number in the sample is not as large as one might wish and the standard error is probably underestimated; but if any doubt exists it is possible to make more definite tests by the methods of Chapter 21.

Standard error of coefficient of association

19.29 We may refer briefly to the quantities treated in Chapters 2 and 3, in considering the association of attributes.

The coefficient of association, Q, defined in **2.15**, has a standard error given by

$$\sigma_Q = \frac{1-Q^2}{2}\sqrt{\frac{1}{(AB)}+\frac{1}{(A\beta)}+\frac{1}{(\alpha B)}+\frac{1}{(\alpha\beta)}} \qquad . \qquad . \quad (19.33)$$

This quantity is not infinite, as might at first sight appear, if one of the cell frequencies vanishes, because in that case $1-Q^2$ also vanishes; in fact, in such an event $\sigma_Q=0$.

Standard error of the coefficient of mean-square contingency

19.30 The determination of the standard error of the coefficient of mean-square contingency is a matter of considerable mathematical complexity, and even when approximations are employed, leads to expressions which are tedious to calculate in practice. For a detailed discussion we must refer the student to the original memoirs (K. Pearson, *Biometrika*, 1913, **9**, 22 and T. Kondo, *Biometrika*, 1929, **21**, 376).

Spearman's rank correlation coefficient

19.31 Unlike most of the parameters we have been considering, the distribution of Spearman's rank correlation coefficient is discontinuous, and to that extent resembles the binomial. Very little is known about the distribution except in the important case when the correlation in the population is zero. The other cases are sometimes treated by assuming a normal continuous distribution in the parent and working from ranks to grades and thence to the product-moment coefficient of correlation by the equations (11.21) and (11.23) of **11.29**; but this procedure is not to be recommended.

The case when the correlation in the population is zero, i.e., when all possible permutations of the ranks occur with equal frequency, has to some extent been investigated. It was shown by " Student " in 1907 that the standard deviation of Spearman's rank correlation coefficient is given by the simple equation

$$\sigma_\rho = \frac{1}{\sqrt{n-1}} \qquad . \qquad . \qquad . \qquad . \qquad (19.34)$$

This cannot be taken to be a standard error in the ordinary way, because the distribution is not normal for small samples. It has also been shown that the distribution tends to normality as n increases, but for low values of n the normal distribution gives an unsatisfactory approximation. For values of n greater than 8 the significance of an observed ρ can be tested in the t-distribution (see below, **21.25**) by entering the tables with $t = \rho\sqrt{(n-2)}/\sqrt{(1-\rho^2)}$ and $\nu = n-2$.

The rank correlation coefficient τ

19.32 For the coefficient τ more information is available. Kendall (*Advanced Theory of Statistics, Vol.* 1, chapter 16) has given the actual distribution up to and including $n=10$ in the case where all possible rankings occur equally frequently, and has shown that the distribution tends to normality more rapidly than that of ρ. For values greater than $n=10$ the distribution can be assumed to be normal with a standard error given by

$$\sigma_\tau = \sqrt{\frac{2(2n+5)}{9n(n-1)}} \qquad . \qquad . \qquad . \qquad (19.35)$$

19.33 Tests of ρ or τ based on the results given in the two preceding sections take as the hypothesis that there is no correlation in the population. For instance, suppose a value of τ in a ranking of 15 was found to be 0·6. For the standard error we find, from (19.35), a value of 0·19. The observed value exceeds thrice this amount and is significant. Our argument is as follows—

If there were no correlation in the population from which this ranking is supposed to have been drawn as a sample, the order of appearance of one variate is just as likely as any other order. Consequently, in continued sampling we should, in the long run, obtain all possible rankings of one variate with any particular ranking of the other. The population of values of τ so generated has a standard deviation given by (19.35). Our observed value is very improbable in relation to this distribution, and hence we suspect the hypothesis that the variates are independent.

19.34 But we have said nothing about the case when the variates are not independent in the population and the foregoing results cannot be used to test the difference of two rank correlation coefficients. Nothing appears to be known on this point in relation to ρ, but some light has been thrown on it in regard to τ. In fact it may be shown—

(a) That the observed value of τ is a good estimate of the value in the parent population;

(b) That the standard error of τ is *not greater than* $\sqrt{\dfrac{2}{n}(1-\tau^2)}$

This limit is in some cases nearly reached so that no lower limit appears possible. The test based on it may be rather insensitive but it seems unlikely that any improvement can be effected unless some further assumption is made about the nature of the parent population. (For the further theory of this subject see Kendall's *Rank Correlation Methods*, 1948, Griffin).

SUMMARY

1. The following are the standard errors of the parameters named, the parent population being assumed normal--

Variance	$\sigma^2\sqrt{\dfrac{2}{n}}$
Standard deviation	$\dfrac{\sigma}{\sqrt{2n}}$
Coefficient of variation	$\dfrac{V}{\sqrt{2n}}\sqrt{1+\dfrac{2V^2}{10^4}}$
Correlation coefficient	$\dfrac{1-r^2}{\sqrt{n}}$
Regression coefficient	$\dfrac{\sigma_1\sqrt{1-r^2}}{\sigma_2\sqrt{n}}$ or $\dfrac{\sigma_{1.2}}{\sigma_2\sqrt{n}}$

2. The standard error of the qth moment measured about the mean is given by

$$\sigma_{\mu_q} = \sqrt{\frac{\mu_{2q}-\mu_q^2+q^2\mu_2\mu_{q-1}^2-2q\mu_{q-1}\mu_{q+1}}{n}}$$

3. The correlation between errors in the qth and rth moments, both measured about the mean, is given by

$$\mathrm{cov}\,(\mu_r,\mu_q) = \frac{\mu_{q+r}-\mu_q\mu_r+qr\mu_2\mu_{q-1}\mu_{r-1}-r\mu_{q+1}\mu_{r-1}-q\mu_{q-1}\mu_{r+1}}{n}$$

4. From the results of (2) and (3), and similar results for moments about a fixed point, it is possible to calculate the standard error of any function of the moments.

5. In the normal population, errors in the mean and standard deviation are uncorrelated.

6. In calculating the standard errors of moments the uncorrected values should be used.

7. It is unsafe to use the formulæ for standard errors appropriate to the normal population in cases where the population is suspected to differ from the normal form ; in particular, the formula for the standard error of the standard deviation, $\dfrac{\sigma}{\sqrt{2n}}$, should not be used for parent populations which are markedly lepto- or platy-kurtic.

8. Tests are given for the significance of the rank correlation coefficient ρ and τ when no parental correlation exists. When there is parent correlation an upper limit to the standard error of τ is given by

$$\sqrt{\frac{2}{n}(1-\tau^2)}$$

EXERCISES

19.1   In the weight distribution of Exercise 4.6, page 100, last column, find the standard error of the standard deviation. Compare it with the value obtained on the assumption that the parent distribution is normal.

19.2   In the same data, compare the ratio of the s.e. of the s.d. to the s.d. with the ratio of the s.e. of the semi-interquartile range to the semi-interquartile range.

19.3   Show that for a normal population the standard error of the s.d. is less than the standard error of the semi-interquartile range.

19.4   In a sample of 1,000 the mean is found to be $17 \cdot 5$ and the standard deviation $2 \cdot 5$.   In another sample of 800 the mean is 18 and the standard deviation $2 \cdot 7$.   Assuming that the samples are independent, discuss whether the two samples can have come from populations which have the same standard deviation.

19.5   Find the correlation between errors in the mean and standard deviation for the height distribution of 8585 men of Table 4.7, page 82, and do the same for the marriage distribution of Table 4.8, page 84.

19.6   Find the standard errors of the first four cumulants as calculated from the moments.

19.7   Samples of 10,000 are taken from a normal population.   For what even moments does the standard error of the moment lie within 10 per cent of the value of that moment ?

19.8 For samples of (*a*) 100, (*b*) 1,000, draw a graph showing how the standard error of the correlation coefficient from a normal population varies with *r*.

19.9 (Data quoted by M. F. Hoadley, " Note on the Association of Relative Laterality of Hand and Eye from the Cambridge Anthropometric Data," *Biometrika*, 1928, **20B**, 401.)

Three experiments were conducted to determine the relationship between laterality of hand and laterality of eye. The correlations between (1) difference of strength of grip and (2) difference in visual acuity were—

$$-0\cdot02410 \qquad \text{(3234 subjects)}$$
$$-0\cdot00738 \qquad \text{(4003 subjects)}$$
$$+0\cdot02962 \qquad \text{(1447 subjects)}$$

Find the standard errors of the three correlation coefficients, and hence show that it cannot be concluded that there is any significant correlation between laterality of hand and laterality of eye.

19.10 Find the standard errors of the partial correlation coefficients of Example 12.1, page 290. Hence state whether any one is not significantly different from zero, and if so, which. For the purpose of this exercise normality may be assumed, although in all probability the actual data do not emanate from a normal population.

THE χ^2 DISTRIBUTION

20.1   In Chapters 17 to 19 we have seen that a knowledge of the sampling distribution of a statistic gives us a means of judging from samples the relationship between fact and theory. For instance, in Example 17.3, page 389, we were able to infer from a knowledge of the binomial distribution that the dice which provided the data were probably biased; and in Example 18.6, page 428, we could apply a knowledge of the distribution of the mean of samples from a normal population to reject the hypothesis that the mean in the population was less than 67 inches.

In the present chapter we shall discuss a particular sampling distribution of profound importance in statistical theory, and shall note its applications to the testing of accordance between fact and hypothesis in a wide range of cases.

Cells

20.2   In what follows we shall consider only data giving the frequencies of individuals falling within various categories. Statistical data, as will have been evident from the examples already given in this book, are very often of this type.

Such data, whether relating to attributes or to continuous variates or to a mixture of both, will in practice be arranged in compartments. For example, in the association table on page 20 there are four compartments, corresponding to the four ultimate classes. In the table of frequencies within various height ranges (Table 4.7, page 82), each range determines a compartment, and the data consists of 8585 individuals distributed in 21 groups.

It is convenient to have a name for these compartments. We shall call them *cells*. The frequency falling in a cell will be referred to as the *cell frequency*.

One and the same table may contain frequencies of more than one order, and frequencies of different orders must be kept distinct. Thus an association table has four cells with frequencies of the second order and two sets of two (the border frequencies) of the first order. A $p \times q$ contingency table has pq cells of the second order (to condense our terminology) and a set of p and a set of q of the first order. Each such set must be considered by itself. The tests of this chapter are applicable

to any homogeneous set, but not to a " mixed " set comprising cells of
different orders.

20.3 We shall denote the number of cells in the presentation of a set
of data by n, and the cell frequency occurring in the rth cell by $\tilde{m}_r$. Thus,
in the table of page 82 we have, numbering the cells downwards—

$$\tilde{m}_1 = 2$$
$$\tilde{m}_2 = 4$$
$$\tilde{m}_3 = 14$$
$$\cdot \quad \cdot \quad \cdot \quad \cdot$$
$$\tilde{m}_{21} = 2$$

20.4 In the class of cases we shall consider, we wish to compare the
actual values $\tilde{m}$ with the cell frequencies which would exist if a particular
hypothesis H were exactly verified. These latter values we shall denote
by the letter m, so that the theoretical frequency in the rth cell is m_r.

The cell frequencies m, are sometimes referred to as the " expected "
values on the hypotheses H. This is rather a special use of the word
" expected," in the sense we have already given, namely, that the m_r's
assume the values which they would take if the hypothesis were exactly
verified for the particular set of data.

We shall write—

$$x_r = \tilde{m}_r - m_r \qquad . \qquad . \qquad . \qquad . \qquad (20.1)$$

so that the x_r's are the excesses of the actual over the expected frequencies.

Clearly the quantities x embody all the information in the data about
the discrepancies between theory and fact. If the x's are all zero, fact
and theory are in perfect agreement. If the x's are large, the agreement
is poor.

Example 20.1.—As a simple example let us consider the 2×2 contingency table of Example 2.5, page 25. Numbering the cells from left
to right we have—

$$\tilde{m}_1 = 276, \qquad \tilde{m}_2 = 3$$
$$\tilde{m}_3 = 473, \qquad \tilde{m}_4 = 66$$

Now let our hypothesis H be that inoculation and exemption from attack
are independent. If this be so, the expected frequencies are—

$$m_1 = 255 \cdot 5, \qquad m_2 = 23 \cdot 5$$
$$m_3 = 493 \cdot 5, \qquad m_4 = 45 \cdot 5$$

and hence we have —

$$x_1 = \tilde{m}_1 - m_1 = 20 \cdot 5, \qquad x_2 = -20 \cdot 5$$
$$x_3 = -20 \cdot 5, \qquad x_4 = 20 \cdot 5$$

The x's are, in fact, in this particular case, the numbers we referred to in
Chapter 2 as δ-numbers. We have already considered them as reflecting
the divergence of fact from theory.

Constraints

20.5 In the example we have just considered, one important effect is to be noted, viz. that when we have calculated one independent frequency, say m_1, the other three follow arithmetically from the fact that the two frequencies in any row or column must add up to the border frequency in that row or column.

In fact, we have—

$$\left. \begin{aligned} x_1 + x_2 &= 0 \\ x_1 + x_3 &= 0 \\ x_2 + x_4 &= 0 \end{aligned} \right\} \qquad . \qquad . \qquad . \qquad . \qquad (20.2)$$

We need not add $x_3 + x_4 = 0$, since this is given by the last two equations in conjunction with the first. There are only three independent equations.

Thus, whatever our hypothesis H may be, the conditions of the problem impose limitations, expressed by the equations (20.2), on the way in which the m's and the x's may be chosen. If one m or one x is fixed by H, the other three are determinate in accordance with the conditions of the data themselves.

Similarly, suppose we wished to examine the height data of page 82 in the light of the hypothesis that the parent distribution, of which this is a sample, is normal with given mean and standard deviation. With the aid of the table of the probability integral we can determine the cell frequencies on this hypothesis ; but again the problem imposes a limitation on the way in which the theoretical cell frequencies are assigned, namely, that they must add up to the total number 8585 of the sample. When 20 frequencies are fixed, the other is determined by mere arithmetic.

20.6 In general, when the conditions of the problem impose limitations of this kind on the number of cell frequencies which may be fixed by H we say, borrowing an expression from Statics, that they impose *constraints*. In the example of the 2×2 contingency table there were three independent constraints, expressed by the equations (20.2). In the case of the height distribution there is one constraint expressed by the fact that the sum of the cell frequencies must be 8585.

Linear constraints

20.7 Constraints which involve linear equations in the cell frequencies (i.e. equations containing no squares or higher powers of the frequencies) are called *linear constraints*. The two instances above are of this type. Linear constraints are of paramount importance, and we shall shortly confine our attention to them alone.

Degrees of freedom

20.8 We denote the number of independent constraints in a set of data by κ. We then define the number ν by the simple equation

$$\nu = n - \kappa$$

and call ν the number of *degrees of freedom* of the aggregate of cells. It is the number of cell frequencies which can be assigned at will, the remaining κ following from the conditions to which the data are subject.

Thus, for the 2×2 table $\kappa = 3$ and $\nu = 1$, for, as we have seen, the fixing of one cell frequency fixes them all. For the height distribution $\kappa = 1$, $\nu = 20$.

Example 20.2.—Let us find the number of degrees of freedom of a $p \times q$ contingency table.

The constraints of such a table are similar to those of the 2×2 table. Thus the sum of the cell frequencies in each row is determined as being the border frequency in that row, and similarly for the columns. Hence each of the p columns and q rows imposes a constraint. From the total $p + q$ constraints we must, however, subtract one, for they are not algebraically independent; there is one relation between them, expressed by the fact that the sum of the border column equals the sum of the border row, namely, the total frequency N.

Hence there are $p + q - 1$ independent linear constraints. Hence,

$$\begin{aligned}
\nu &= n - \kappa \\
&= pq - (p + q - 1) \\
&= (p - 1)(q - 1)
\end{aligned}$$

We might have got this result more directly by considering that the cell frequencies in the first $p - 1$ columns and $q - 1$ rows are determinable at will, the rest following automatically from the border frequencies. Hence the number of degrees of freedom, being the number of cells which can be so filled, is $(p - 1)(q - 1)$ as before.

20.9 Now let us consider a set of data arranged in n cells, the total frequency being N.

The theoretical frequency in the rth cell is m_r. This means that the chance of an individual falling into this cell is $\dfrac{m_r}{N}$, and the chance of its not doing so is $\left(1 - \dfrac{m_r}{N}\right)$. We may regard the actual frequencies $\tilde{m}$ as having been arrived at by distributing the N individuals among the n cells in such a way that the chance of an individual falling into the rth cell is $\dfrac{m_r}{N}$. Hence the probability that of the N individuals, $\tilde{m}_r$ fall into the rth cell and the remainder elsewhere is the term involving

$$\left(\frac{m_r}{N}\right)^{\tilde{m}_r}\left(1 - \frac{m_r}{N}\right)^{N - \tilde{m}_r}$$

in the binomial

$$\left\{\frac{m_r}{N} + \left(1 - \frac{m_r}{N}\right)\right\}^{N}$$

Thus, this binomial will give us the relative frequencies of the various values which $\tilde{m}_r$ can take in different samples, of which the actual data form one.

If N is fairly large and $\dfrac{m_r}{N}$ is not small, this distribution is approximately normal with mean m_r. That is to say, $\tilde{m}_r$ is distributed normally about a mean m_r, or x_r is distributed normally about zero mean.

Definition of χ^2

20.10 We now define the quantity χ^2 by the equation

$$\chi^2 = \Sigma\left(\frac{x_r^2}{m_r}\right) = \Sigma\left\{\frac{(\tilde{m}_r - m_r)^2}{m_r}\right\} \qquad . \qquad . \quad (20.3)$$

the summation being taken over the n cells.

The student can verify for himself that this definition is consistent with that given in equation (3.4), page 52, for the particular case of divergence from independence in a contingency table.

We can write χ^2 in a slightly different form. For

$$\chi^2 = \Sigma\left\{\frac{(\tilde{m}_r - m_r)^2}{m_r}\right\} = \Sigma\left(\frac{\tilde{m}_r^2}{m_r}\right) - 2\Sigma\left(\frac{\tilde{m}_r m_r}{m_r}\right) + \Sigma\left(\frac{m_r^2}{m_r}\right)$$

$$= \Sigma\left(\frac{\tilde{m}_r^2}{m_r}\right) - 2\Sigma(\tilde{m}_r) + \Sigma(m_r)$$

$$= \Sigma\left(\frac{\tilde{m}_r^2}{m_r}\right) - N \qquad . \qquad . \qquad . \quad (20.4)$$

This corresponds to equation (3.7), page 53.

20.11 If $\chi^2 = 0$ all the x's are zero, and hence the actual cell frequencies coincide with the expected cell frequencies. On the other hand, if some or all of the x's are large, χ^2 will be large.

It will thus be evident that χ^2 affords a measure of the correspondence between fact and theory. It must not be forgotten, however, that it ignores the signs of the x's and hence takes no cognisance of certain information which those signs may convey. We shall take up this point again later.

20.12 If the use of χ^2 is to be satisfactory, we must be able to distinguish significant values from those which may have arisen by sampling fluctuations. This leads us to inquire what is the probability of getting a particular value of χ^2 from a set of $\tilde{m}_r$'s chosen at random, and this in turn leads to the question : What is the sampling distribution of χ^2 ?

We shall not give a proof here of the important answer to this question, but shall content ourselves with quoting it and indicating briefly the method by which it is obtained.

We have already seen that the sum of n normally distributed variates is itself normally distributed (**10.8**). The sum of the *squares* of n normal variates is not so distributed, however. In fact, the sum of the squares of n normal variates, drawn from a population with unit standard deviation and zero mean is distributed in a form given by the equation

$$y = y_0 e^{-\frac{\Sigma^2}{2}} \Sigma^{n-1} \qquad . \qquad . \qquad . \qquad . \quad (20.5)$$

where Σ^2 is the sum in question.

Now it has already been shown that under the conditions assumed the x's are each distributed normally about zero mean, and it may be shown further that χ^2 may be regarded as the sum of the squares of ν variates each distributed normally with unit s.d. and about a zero mean. Hence the distribution of χ^2 is given by

$$y = y_0 e^{-\frac{\chi^2}{2}} \chi^{\nu-1} \qquad . \qquad . \qquad . \qquad . \quad (20.6)*$$

20.13 It follows, as in **18.8**, that if we take a random set of $\tilde{m}$'s and calculate χ^2 from them, the probability of getting a value of χ^2 as great as, or greater than, this observed value χ_0^2, is the area of the curve (20.6) to the right of the ordinate at χ_0 divided by the total area of the curve ; or, in the language of the integral calculus,

$$P = \frac{\int_{\chi_0}^{\infty} y_0 e^{-\frac{\chi^2}{2}} \chi^{\nu-1} d\chi}{\int_0^{\infty} y_0 e^{-\frac{\chi^2}{2}} \chi^{\nu-1} d\chi} \qquad . \qquad . \qquad . \quad (20.7)\dagger$$

The curve, as we shall see later, extends from 0 to $+\infty$, which accounts for the limits of the integral in the denominator of the above expression.

---

* Since the variate in this expression is χ, the distribution should, perhaps, be known as the χ-distribution, not the χ^2-distribution. The latter name is, however, in universal use, and the tables of the integral of equation (20.7) are usually prepared with argument χ^2.

† The actual values of P are, expanding this integral,

$$P = \sqrt{\frac{2}{\pi}} \int_{\chi}^{\infty} e^{-\frac{1}{2}\chi^2} d\chi + \sqrt{\frac{2}{\pi}} e^{-\frac{1}{2}\chi^2} \left(\frac{\chi}{1} + \frac{\chi^3}{1.3} + \frac{\chi^5}{1.3.5} + \cdots + \frac{\chi^{\nu-2}}{1.3.5 \ldots (\nu-2)} \right)$$

if ν is odd

$$= e^{-\frac{1}{2}\chi^2} \left(1 + \frac{\chi^2}{2} + \frac{\chi^4}{2.4} + \frac{\chi^6}{2.4.6} + \cdots + \frac{\chi^{\nu-2}}{2.4.6 \ldots (\nu-2)} \right)$$

if ν is even

The first term of the first series may be obtained from the probability integral. Values of P for given χ^2 and ν are provided in *Tables for Statisticians and Biometricians*, a new edition of which, in course of preparation, gives more detailed tables than have hitherto been available.

Tabulation of P for the χ^2 distribution

20.14 The rather formidable result of equation (20.7) need occasion no alarm to the student who is unacquainted with the notation and methods of the integral calculus. The function P has been tabulated for certain ranges of ν and χ^2 in the same way as the probability for the normal curve, and the tables are in most cases sufficient for the practical application of the results of the present chapter. More convenient is the table given in Appendix Table 3, which shows the values of χ^2 for given values of ν and P.

20.15 It is desirable to point out that other writers have used different letters to denote the number of degrees of freedom. Karl Pearson, in the tables to which we have just referred, used the number n', which is one more than our ν. R. A. Fisher writes n instead of our ν, so that we have—

$$\nu = n' - 1 \text{ (Pearson)} = n \text{ (Fisher)}$$

We have thought it desirable to introduce the symbol ν in order to avoid confusion with the use of n' and n as numbers in a sample or in a population.

The χ^2 test of significance when the theoretical cell frequencies are known *a priori*

20.16 Armed with Appendix Table 3, we can now proceed as follows—

Having decided on the hypothesis to be tested, we calculate from it the theoretical frequencies m_r. (For the present we assume that this can be done without reference to the observed frequencies $\tilde{m}_r$. The contrary case will be considered later.)

From the m_r's and the $\tilde{m}_r$'s we calculate χ^2 according to (20.3) or (20.4). We also ascertain ν.

Then, from the table we determine whereabouts this value of χ^2 lies in relation to P.

The value P gives us the probability that on random sampling we should get a value of χ^2 as great as, or greater than, the value actually obtained.

Now, if P is small, our data give us an improbable value of χ^2. Thus we have the alternative conclusions that either (a) an improbable event has occurred, or (b) that the divergence of fact from theory is significant of some real effect and cannot be attributed to fluctuations of sampling. The smaller P is, the more we incline to the latter alternative ; if we do decide to adopt it, the inferences we draw will depend on the nature of the problem. Sometimes it will lead us to reject our hypothesis. Sometimes it will lead us to suspect our sampling technique.

The following examples will illustrate the type of reasoning involved in applying the χ^2 test.

Example 20.3.—In some experiments on dice-throwing W. F. R. Weldon rolled 12 dice 26,306 times, observing at each throw the number of dice recording a 5 or a 6.

If the dice are unbiased, the chance of getting a 5 or a 6 with one die is $\frac{1}{3}$. Hence the chances with 12 dice of getting 12 5's or 6's, 11 5's or 6's, etc., are the successive terms in the binomial $(\frac{1}{3}+\frac{2}{3})^{12}$. Hence the theoretical frequencies in 26,306 throws are the terms in 26,306 $(\frac{1}{3}+\frac{2}{3})^{12}$. These are our m_r's.

The following table shows the actual $(\tilde{m}_r)$ and the theoretical (m_r) frequencies, together with the values of $\dfrac{(\tilde{m}_r-m_r)^2}{m_r}$.

TABLE 20.1—12 dice thrown 26,306 times, a throw of 5 or 6 reckoned a success

Number of successes	Observed frequency $(\tilde{m})$	Theoretical frequency (m)	$\tilde{m}-m$ (x)	$\dfrac{(\tilde{m}-m)^2}{m}$
0	185	203	− 18	1·596
1	1,149	1,217	− 68	3·800
2	3,265	3,345	− 80	1·913
3	5,475	5,576	−101	1·829
4	6,114	6,273	−159	4·030
5	5,194	5,018	+176	6·173
6	3,067	2,927	+140	6·696
7	1,331	1,254	+ 77	4·728
8	403	392	+ 11	0·309
9	105	87	+ 18	3·724
10 and over	18	14	+ 4	1·143
Totals	26,306	26,306	0	35·941

Hence $\chi^2=35\cdot941$, and $\nu=$one less than the number of cells$=10$.

From the *Tables for Statisticians and Biometricians* we have, when $\nu=10$ $(n'=11)$,

$$P = 0\cdot000857 \quad \text{for} \quad \chi^2 = 30$$
$$P = 0\cdot000017 \quad \text{for} \quad \chi^2 = 40$$

Evidently when $\chi^2=35\cdot941$, P will be extremely small. If we want to evaluate it exactly we can proceed by the methods given in the Tables. In fact $P=0\cdot000086$.

Alternatively, from Appendix Table 3 we see that when $\chi^2=23\cdot209$ and $\nu=10$, the value of P is $0\cdot01$. Thus P for $\chi^2=35\cdot941$ must be much less than this value.

We may therefore say that the correspondence between theory and fact is very poor. The extreme improbability of the observed event enables us to say with some confidence that the divergence between the two is significant, and hence that either our sampling technique or our hypothesis is at fault. Now in this experiment Weldon took particular care with the dice-throwing, and we may regard it as unlikely that there was anything seriously wrong with the randomness of the sampling. We are therefore led to doubt our hypothesis that the dice were unbiased.

Briefly, then, the χ^2 test suggests that the dice were biased.

Example 20.4.—The following table shows the result of inoculation against cholera on a certain tea estate—

TABLE 20.2

	Not-attacked	Attacked	Total
Inoculated . . $\cdot\{$	431 (427·7)	5 (8·3)	436
Not-inoculated . $\cdot\{$	291 (294·3)	9 (5·7)	300
Total .	722	14	736

We shall explain the figures in brackets presently. The question on which we want to throw light is : Is there any significant association between inoculation and attack ?

To answer this, let us take for our hypothesis H the supposition that they are independent. If this is so, the expected frequencies, calculated in the manner of Chapter 2, are those given in brackets. These we take to be the m_r's, the $\tilde{m}_r$'s being the actual frequencies. We then have—

$$\chi^2 = (3\cdot3)^2\left\{\frac{1}{427\cdot7}+\frac{1}{8\cdot3}+\frac{1}{294\cdot3}+\frac{1}{5\cdot7}\right\} = 3\cdot27$$

and

$$\nu = 1$$

From Appendix Table 3 for $\chi^2=2\cdot706$, $P=0\cdot10$ and for $\chi^2=3\cdot841$, $P=0\cdot05$. For our observed value of $3\cdot27$, P lies between $0\cdot05$ and $0\cdot10$.

Thus if H is true, our data give a result which would be obtained between 5 and 10 times in a hundred trials. This is infrequent, but not very infrequent. Moreover, the theoretical frequencies in the " attacked " column are not very large. We should therefore be unjustified in rejecting H on this evidence, but we can say that the data lend some colour to the supposition that H is not correct.

To sum up, the χ^2 test shows that the data incline us, though not strongly, to the belief that inoculation and attack are associated.

Example 20.5.—(Imaginary data.) An investigator into chocolate consumption divided the United Kingdom into eight areas and took a random sample from each, the individuals so obtained being classified as consumers or non-consumers of chocolate. His results were as follows—

TABLE 20.3

Area number	1	2	3	4	5	6	7	8	Total
Consumers . .	56 (55)	87 (81)	142 (152)	71 (69)	88 (90)	72 (72)	100 (95)	142 (144)	758
Non-consumers .	17 (18)	20 (26)	58 (48)	20 (22)	31 (29)	23 (23)	•25 (30)	48 (46)	242
Total	73	107	200	91	119	95	125	190	1,000

Do these results suggest that the consumption of chocolate varies from place to place ?

Let us take as our hypothesis H the supposition that it does not, i.e. that the two attributes in the above table are independent. The theoretical frequencies m_r are then those shown in brackets, and we have—

$$\chi^2 = \frac{1^2}{55} + \frac{6^2}{81} + 14 \text{ similar terms}$$

$$= 6 \cdot 28$$

The table has two rows and eight columns, and hence $\nu = (2-1)(8-1) = 7$. From Appendix Table 3 we have for $\nu = 7$, $\chi^2 = 6 \cdot 346$, $P = 0 \cdot 50$; or alternatively, from the *Tables for Statisticians and Biometricians* for $\nu = 7$ $(n' = 8)$,

$$\text{if } \chi^2 = 6, \qquad P = 0 \cdot 539750$$
$$\text{if } \chi^2 = 7, \qquad P = 0 \cdot 428880$$

Hence, for $\chi^2 = 6 \cdot 28$, $P = 0 \cdot 51$ approximately.

Thus there is no cause to suspect our hypothesis, and the data do not suggest that the proportion of consumers of chocolate varies from place to place, at least so far as this test is concerned.

Properties of the χ^2 distribution
20.17 The curves

$$y = y_0 e^{-\frac{\chi^2}{2}} \chi^{\nu-1}$$

and the probability function P derived from them, have several interesting properties which are worth noticing. As χ^2 is essentially positive, we consider only positive values of the variate.

(*a*) In the first place, it will be seen that when $\nu = 1$ the curve is the normal curve with unit standard deviation, for positive values of the variate. Thus the test for $\nu = 1$ may be reduced to testing the significance of deviations of a normally distributed variate.

(b) When $\nu > 1$ the curve is of the single-humped type. It is tangential to the x-axis at the origin ($\chi^2=0$), rises to a maximum where $\chi^2=\nu-1$ and then falls more slowly to zero as χ^2 increases indefinitely. It is thus skew to the right.

(c) As ν increases, the curve becomes more and more symmetrical. In fact, when ν is large, $\sqrt{2\chi^2}$ is distributed approximately normally about a mean $\sqrt{2\nu-1}$ with unit standard deviation. This result, due to R. A. Fisher, enables us to dispense with tables of P for large values of ν, say $\nu > 30$, and to use the normal integral instead. In practice large values of ν are rather infrequent.

Example 20.6.—To find P when $\chi^2=64$ and $\nu=41$.

We know that $\sqrt{2\chi^2}$ is distributed normally about mean $\sqrt{82-1}=9$ with unit standard deviation. When $\chi^2=64$, $\sqrt{2\chi^2}=11\cdot314$, which therefore has a deviation $2\cdot314$ to the right of the mean. Hence we have to find the area of the probability curve to the right of the ordinate which is $2\cdot314$ units to the right of the mean. From Appendix Table 2 this is seen to be $0\cdot0103$ approximately.

Conditions for the application of the χ^2 test

20.18 We may conveniently bring together at this point the various precautions which should be observed in applying the χ^2 distribution to a test of significance.

(a) In the first place, N must be reasonably large. Otherwise the x's are not normally distributed.

This is a condition which is almost always fulfilled in practice. It is difficult to say exactly what constitutes largeness, but as an arbitrary figure we may say that N should be at least 50, however few the cells.

(b) No theoretical cell frequency should be small. Here again it is hard to say what constitutes smallness, but 5 should be regarded as the very minimum, and 10 is better.

In practice, data not infrequently contain cell frequencies below these limits. As a rule the difficulty may be met by amalgamating such cells into a single cell. Thus, in Example 20.3 above, the theoretical numbers of throws with 10, 11 and 12 successes are (to the nearest integer) 13, 1 and 0. Instead of putting each into a separate cell we have run them together into one cell " 10 and over."

(c) The constraints must be linear. The reason for this condition has not emerged explicitly in the foregoing because we omitted the stage in the proof of the χ^2 distribution at which it occurs.

20.19 To these three conditions we may add the following remarks, which should also be borne in mind when the χ^2 test is being used.

(a) The χ^2 test tells us the probability of getting, on a random sample, a value of χ^2 equal to or higher than the actual value. If this probability is small we are justified in suspecting a significant divergence between theory and experiment.

We cannot proceed, however, in the reverse direction and say that if P is not small our hypothesis is proved correct. All that we can say is that the test reveals no grounds for supposing the hypothesis incorrect; or alternatively, that so far as the χ^2 test is concerned, data and hypothesis are in agreement.

(b) Nor do only small values of P lead us to suspect our hypothesis or our sampling technique. A value of P very near to unity may also do so.

This rather surprising result arises in this way: a large value of P normally corresponds to a small value of χ^2, that is to say a very close agreement between theory and fact. Now such agreements are rare—almost as rare as great divergences.

We are just as unlikely to get very good correspondence between fact and theory as we are to get very bad correspondence and, for precisely the same reasons, we must suspect our sampling technique if we do. In short, very close correspondence is *too good to be true*.

The student who feels some hesitation about this statement may like to reassure himself with the following example. An investigator says that he threw a die 600 times and got exactly 100 of each number from 1 to 6. This is the theoretical expectation, $\chi^2=0$ and $P=1$, but should we believe him? We might, if we knew him very well, but we should probably regard him as somewhat lucky, which is only another way of saying that he has brought off a very improbable event.

20.20　At this point we can resume a topic which we laid on one side in **20.11**, namely the signs of the x's, which are ignored by χ^2.

It may happen that χ^2 has quite a moderate value and P is not small when all the positive x's are on one side of the mode of the theoretical distribution and all the negative x's on the other. There will thus be a consistent " shift " of the $\tilde{m}$'s one way or the other from the m's. This may give us a value of the mean quite outside the limits of sampling. Again, if the x's are all negative in the cells farthest removed from the mean, the standard deviation may show an almost impossible divergence from expectation.

Thus, although the χ^2 test may reveal no cause to suspect the hypothesis, a closer examination of the x's may.

Example 20.7.—Consider the following dice data (Table 20.4) (Weldon, see Example 19.1.)

Now, in this example, all the x's are negative up to 5 successes, positive from 6 to 10 successes, and negative again for 11 to 12 successes. This is almost one of the cases we referred to earlier in this section.

We have, in fact, already found (Example 17.3, page 389) that the mean deviates from the expected value by $5 \cdot 13$ times the standard error.

TABLE 20.4.—12 dice thrown 4.096 times, a throw of 4, 5 or 6 points reckoned a success

Number of successes	Observed frequency ($\tilde{m}$)	Expected frequency (m) $4096(\frac{1}{2}+\frac{1}{2})^{12}$	$\tilde{m}-m$ (x)	$\dfrac{(\tilde{m}-m)^2}{m}$
0	0	1	-1	1·0000
1	7	12	-5	2·0833
2	60	66	-6	0·5455
3	198	220	-22	2·2000
4	430	495	-65	8·5354
5	731	792	-61	4·6982
6	948	924	24	0·6234
7	847	792	55	3·8194
8	536	495	41	3·3960
9	257	220	37	6·2227
10	71	66	5	0·3788
11	$\left.\begin{matrix}11\\0\end{matrix}\right\}11$	$\left.\begin{matrix}12\\1\end{matrix}\right\}13$	$\left.\begin{matrix}-1\\-1\end{matrix}\right\}-2$	0·3077
12				
Totals	4096	4096	0	$33\cdot8104=\chi^2$

From the tables we find—

ν	n'	χ^2	P
12	13	30	0·002792
12	13	40	0·000072

Hence, by simple interpolation for $\chi^2=33\cdot8104$, $P=0\cdot0018$.

As a matter of fact, simple interpolation is of very little value for small values of P (cf. **24.12**), and this value is wide of the mark, the true value being $0\cdot00072$. Appendix Table 3 shows us that P is less than $0\cdot01$.

From the extended tables of the normal integral in *Tables for Statisticians and Biometricians, Part I*, we have—

Greater fraction of the area of a normal
curve for a deviation 5·13 . . . 0·9999998551
Area in the tail of the curve . . . 0·0000001449
Area in both tails . . . . 0·0000002898

so that the probability of getting such a deviation (+ or −) on random sampling is only about 3 in 10,000,000.

Comparing this with the value of P, we see that the data are really more divergent from theory than the χ^2 test would lead us to suppose.

20.21 Hence, if the signs of the x's show any marked peculiarities, it is as well to apply as many supplementary tests as are available, and not to rely on the χ^2 test alone. Such tests would include those for the significance of the mean and standard deviation, which we have already discussed.

Levels of significance

20.22 In the examples we have given above, our judgment whether P was small enough to justify us in suspecting a significant difference between fact and theory has been more or less intuitive. Most people would agree, in Example 20.3, that a probability of only 0·0001 is so small that the evidence is very much in favour of the supposition that the dice were biased. But we shall not always get such a decisive result. Suppose we had obtained $P=0·1$, so that the odds against the event are nine to one. Is this value small enough to lead us to suspect the dice ? If it is not, would $P=0·01$ be small enough ? Where, if anywhere, can we draw the line ?

The odds against the observed event which influence a decision one way or the other depend to some extent on the caution of the investigator. Some people (not necessarily statisticians) would regard odds of ten to one as sufficient. Others would be more conservative and reserve judgment until the odds were much greater. It is a matter of personal taste.

20.23 There are, however, two values of P which are widely used to provide a rough line of demarcation between acceptance and rejection of the significance of observed deviations. These values are $P=0·05$ and $P=0·01$, and are said to define 5 per cent and 1 per cent *levels of significance*. The value $P=0·001$, i.e. the 0·1 per cent level, is also used. A value of P less than 0·05 will be said to fall *below* the 5 per cent level of significance, and so on. The values of the 5 per cent and the 1 per cent levels, among others, are tabulated in Appendix Table 3.

Example 20.8.—Let us consider the data of Exercise 2.11. In experiments on the Spahlinger anti-tuberculosis vaccine the following results were obtained. (As before, the figures in brackets are the independence values.)

	Died or seriously affected	Unaffected or not seriously affected	Total
Inoculated . . .	6 (8·87)	13 (10·13)	19
Not inoculated or inoculated with control media	8 (5·13)	3 (5·87)	11
Total	14	16	30

Here,
$$\chi^2 = 4·75 \quad \text{and} \quad \nu = 1$$
From Appendix Table 3 we have when $\nu=1$ for $P=0·05$, $\chi^2=3·841$, and we have for $P=0·01$, $\chi^2= 6·635$, so that P lies between the 5 per cent level of significance and the 1 per cent level.

If, therefore, we take the 5 per cent level as appropriate to this case, the results are significant ; but if we are more conservative and take the 1 per cent level, the results are not significant. In this particular case the position is complicated by the relative smallness of the theoretical cell frequencies.

The additive property of χ^2

20.24 It sometimes happens, by the repetition of experiments or otherwise, that we have a number of tables for similar data from different fields. The values of P for each may not be entirely conclusive. The question then arises whether we cannot obtain a value of P for the aggregate, telling us what is the probability of getting, by random sampling, a series of divergences from theory as great as or greater than those observed.

The question is usually answered by pooling the results to form a single table. But, apart from the fact that this is not always possible, we have already seen (Chapter 3) that pooling is likely to introduce fallacies. A better method is to proceed in accordance with the following general rule.

20.25 Suppose we have a number of groups of data, each furnishing a χ^2 and a ν. Add together all the χ^2's to form a single value χ_1^2, and all the ν's to form a single value ν_1. The χ^2 test may then be applied to χ_1^2 and ν_1 as if they came from a single set of cells.

The validity of this rule will be evident when we consider how the χ^2 test was arrived at. The variate x in every cell is normally distributed about a mean m, and χ_1^2 is the sum of the squares of quantities like $\dfrac{x^2}{m}$ just as χ^2 was. This, together with the linearity of the constraints, which remains, was the essential part of the proof of the χ^2 distribution, and hence the test remains true for χ_1^2 and ν_1.

Example 20.9.--In Example 20.4 (inoculation against cholera on a certain tea estate) we saw that the χ^2 test, although suggesting that inoculation had some effect in immunising, did not allow us to place any great confidence in such a conclusion. The following data give χ^2 and P for six estates, including the one we have already discussed—

χ^2	P
9·34	0·0022
6·08	0·014
2·51	0·11
3·27	0·071
5·61	0·018
1·59	0·21

Total 28·40

Here only one value of P is less than 0·01, and we might be inclined to doubt whether the association between inoculation and immunity is real. Let us, however, add the values of χ^2 and of ν. We get $\chi_1^2 = 28\cdot40$ and $\nu_1 = 6$, there being one degree of freedom from each of the six tables.

From Appendix Table 3 we see that this value is well beyond the one per cent. significance point. If we require greater accuracy, from the tables we have—

$$\begin{array}{cc} \chi^2 & P \\ 28 & 0 \cdot 000094 \\ 29 & 0 \cdot 000061 \end{array}$$

Whence by interpolation $P = 0 \cdot 00008$ approximately, i.e. we should expect to get a χ^2 as great as this only 80 times in a million. We can, therefore, regard the results, taken together, as significant with a high degree of confidence.

Estimation of theoretical frequencies from the data

20.26 Our theoretical frequencies m may be calculated partly on the basis of information from the data, partly on *a priori* grounds. Thus, in the dice-throwing data of Example 20.3, our hypothesis that the dice were unbiased enabled us to say that the chance of getting a 5 or a 6 was $\frac{1}{3}$, and hence that the chances with 12 dice were the terms in 26,306 $(\frac{2}{3} + \frac{1}{3})^{12}$. Here we take only the value of N, the total frequency, from the data.

In the association and contingency tables, the values of row and column totals, as well as N, are taken from the data and we assume *a priori* that the attributes are independent.

It may be, however, that we draw further information from the data themselves in fixing the theoretical frequencies. In such cases an important modification is necessary in the previous methods of work, for the number of degrees of freedom is further restricted by each piece of information drawn from the data, as we have already seen for contingency tables.

20.27 Consider, for example, the dice-throwing data of Example 20.3. We have already seen that the dice were probably biased, so that the chance of a success was not $\frac{1}{3}$. What, then, was it ?

To answer this question we can only appeal to the data. The proportion of 5's and 6's in the total number of throws of individual dice $(26,306 \times 12)$ was $0 \cdot 3377$. Let us therefore take this to be an estimate of the true probability. We can be confident that it will be somewhere very close, owing to the large number in the sample. The theoretical frequencies will then be the terms in 26,306 $(0 \cdot 6623 + 0 \cdot 3377)^{12}$.

To take a second case : consider the height distribution of Table 4.7 page 82. We have already had reason to suspect that this is a sample from a normal population. If we suppose this hypothesis to be correct, the question arises. What is the mean and standard deviation of the population ? Here again we must estimate these quantities from the data, in the manner of Chapter 18.

20.28 We shall denote values of the theoretical frequencies which are calculated from parameters estimated from the data by the letter m', and the value of χ^2 calculated from them by χ'^2, so that we have—

$$\chi'^2 = \Sigma \left\{ \frac{(\tilde{m} - m')^2}{m'} \right\}$$

Now, χ'^2 is an estimate of χ^2 and, if the m''s are close to the m's, χ'^2 will be close to χ^2. χ'^2 is made up of two parts, one measuring the divergence between theory and fact, the other due to errors of estimation of χ^2. If the second is small compared with the first, we may expect that the χ^2 test, applied with χ'^2 instead of the unknown χ^2, will continue to reveal significant differences between theory and fact where such exist.

20.29 The question as to the precise conditions under which the test is applicable for such cases has not been completely answered, but it has been shown that, if the cell frequencies are large, the test still applies subject to the following conditions—

(a) The number of degrees of freedom must be reduced by unity for each constant of the population which is estimated from the data.

(b) The estimates must be of the type known as " efficient."

We shall not be able in this Introduction to go into the theory of this important class of estimate, but it will be sufficient if we indicate that the estimates of the mean of a normal population, and the parameter m of the Poisson distribution, are " efficient " if calculated in the ordinary way, i.e. by taking the value of the parameter in the sample to be the value of the parameter in the population.

Example 20.10.—Reverting to the data of Example 20.3, let us estimate the true chance of getting a 5 or a 6 from the data themselves. The frequency of the successful event is $0 \cdot 3377$ of the whole. This is an " efficient " estimate of the chance. The following table gives the observed frequencies and the theoretical frequencies calculated from the formula $26{,}306 \ (0 \cdot 6623 + 0 \cdot 3377)^{12}$—

TABLE 20.5.—12 dice thrown 26,306 times, a throw of 5 or 6 reckoned a success

Number of successes	Observed frequency $(\tilde{m})$	Theoretical frequency (m')	$\tilde{m} - m'$	$\dfrac{(\tilde{m} - m')^2}{m'}$
0	185	187	$-\ 2$	$0 \cdot 021$
1	1,149	1,146	3	$0 \cdot 008$
2	3,265	3,215	50	$0 \cdot 778$
3	5,475	5,465	10	$0 \cdot 018$
4	6,114	6,269	-155	$3 \cdot 832$
5	5,194	5,115	79	$1 \cdot 220$
6	3,067	3,043	24	$0 \cdot 189$
7	1,331	1,330	1	$0 \cdot 001$
8	403	424	$-\ 21$	$1 \cdot 040$
9	105	96	9	$0 \cdot 844$
10 and over	18	16	2	$0 \cdot 250$
Total	26,306	26,306	0	$8 \cdot 201$

Thus $\chi^2 = 8 \cdot 201$. There are 11 cells, with one linear constraint. We have also fitted one constant from the data, and hence we must take $\nu = 9$.

From Appendix Table 3 we then see that P is very close to $0 \cdot 50$. Thus our hypothesis is now, so far as the χ^2 test is concerned, in agreement with experiment.

Experiments on the χ^2 distribution

20.30 Several statisticians have conducted experiments to verify the theory which we have discussed in the foregoing sections. A certain amount of work in this field remains to be done, but generally it may be said that experiment supports the theory. So far as cases where the *m*'s are calculated *a priori* are concerned there is little doubt of its correctness.

In one set of experiments (by Yule) 200 beans were thrown into a revolving circular tray with 16 equal radial compartments and the number of beans falling into each compartment was counted. The 16 frequencies so obtained were arranged (1) in a 4×4 table, and (2) in a 2×8 table. χ^2 was calculated from the independence frequencies, as in Example 20.5.

The experiment and the calculations were repeated 100 times. The following table exhibits the actual and the theoretical distribution of χ^2—

TABLE 20.6.—Theoretical distribution of χ^2, calculated from independence values, in tables with 16 compartments, compared with the actual distributions given by 100 experimental tables

In the first case ν must be taken as 9, in the second as 7

χ^2	4 Rows, 4 Columns		2 Rows, 8 Columns	
	Expectation	Observation	Expectation	Observation
0– 5	16·6	17	34·0	29·5
5–10	48·4	44	47·1	56·5
10–15	26·0	32	15·3	10
15–20	7·3	6	3·0	3
20–	1·8	1	0·6	1
Total	100·1	100	100·0	100

In a second experiment with 2×2 tables 350 experimental tables of 100 observations each were available. Table 20.7 shows the actual and theoretical distributions in this case.

TABLE 20.7.—Theoretical distribution of χ^2 for a table with 2 Rows and 2 Columns, when χ^2 is calculated from the independence values, compared with the actual results for 350 experimental tables

Value of χ^2	Number of tables	
	Expected	Observed
0 −0·25	134·02	122
0·25–0·50	48·15	54
0·50–0·75	32·56	41
0·75–1·00	24·21	24
1 −2	56·00	62
2 −3	25·91	18
3 −4	13·22	13
4 −5	7·05	6
5 −6	3·86	5
6–	5·01	5
Total . .	349·99	350

It is interesting to see what happens if we apply the χ^2 test to these tables.

In Table 20.6, grouping together the frequencies from $\chi^2=15$ upwards, so that $v=3$, χ^2 is found to be $2\cdot27$ for the 4×4 tables and $4\cdot36$ for the 2×8 tables, giving $P=0\cdot52$ in the first case and $0\cdot22$ in the second.

In Table 20.7, $\chi^2=7\cdot53$, $v=9$, $P=0\cdot58$.

Goodness of fit

20.31   The χ^2 distribution, as we have seen, leads to tests of the correspondence between theory and fact, and this and other reasons have led to its being described as a test of the " goodness of fit." This expression may be used in two ways. In the first place, it may describe the " fit " of observed and hypothetical data. In the second, it may be used without reference to a hypothesis merely to provide an objective method of estimating the merits of a particular formula or a particular curve in graduating a set of values or a series of points.

The arithmetic in the second class of cases is exactly the same as in the first. Conventionally, we regard very low values of P as denoting a poor fit, and moderate values as denoting a reasonably good fit. High values show an excellent fit, and in considering them we take no heed of the point discussed in **20.19** (*b*), since we are assessing the closeness of the curve to the data, not the probability that the first represents a population from which the second was derived by random sampling.

SUMMARY

1.
$$\chi^2 = \Sigma \left\{ \frac{(\tilde{m} - m)^2}{m} \right\}$$

$$= \Sigma \left(\frac{\tilde{m}^2}{m} \right) - N$$

where $\tilde{m}$ refers to the observed and m to the theoretical frequencies.

2. The number of degrees of freedom of an aggregate of cells is denoted by ν, and is equal to the number of cells whose frequencies can be determined at will. When ν cell frequencies are determined, the remainder are calculable directly from the conditions to which the cell frequencies are subjected by the nature of the data.

3. The frequency-distribution of χ^2 is given by

$$y = y_0 e^{-\frac{\chi^2}{2}} \chi^{\nu-1}$$

4. From this it is possible to ascertain the probability P that on random sampling we should get a value of χ^2 as great as or greater than a given value. Tables have been constructed for this purpose.

5. The χ^2 distribution may be applied to data grouped in cells provided (a) that the total number N in the sample is large, (b) that no theoretical cell frequency is small, and (c) that the constraints are linear.

6. The value of P for any given case enables us to judge of the correspondence between hypothesis and data.

7. When the theoretical cell frequencies have to be calculated from parameters estimated from the data, the χ^2 test can be applied with

$$\chi'^2 = \Sigma \frac{(\tilde{m} - m')^2}{m'}$$

instead of χ^2, provided that the cell frequencies are large, the estimates are " efficient," and the number of degrees of freedom used in ascertaining P is reduced by unity for every parameter which is estimated.

8. The value of P can also be used to give an objective criterion of the " goodness of fit " of a curve .to a set of points or of a formula to a set of values.

EXERCISES

20.1 The following table (Weldon) gives the results of a dice-throwing experiment :—

12 dice thrown 4,096 times, a throw of 6 reckoned a success

Number of successes	0	1	2	3	4	5	6	7 and over	Total
Frequency	447	1145	1181	796	380	115	24	8	4096

Find χ^2 on the hypothesis that the dice were unbiased and hence show that the data are consistent with this hypothesis so far as the χ^2 test is concerned.

20.2 Perform an experiment by throwing a die 600 times and noting the number of points at each throw. Use these data to inquire whether the die is biased.

20.3 200 digits were chosen at random from a set of tables. The frequencies of the digits were—

Digit . . .	0	1	2	3	4	5	6	7	8	9	Total
Frequency . .	18	19	23	21	16	25	22	20	21	15	200

Use the χ^2 test to assess the correctness of the hypothesis that the digits were distributed in equal numbers in the tables from which these were chosen.

20.4 Perform an experiment on the lines of Exercise 20.3 by taking, say, the last figure in 200 logarithms taken from a set of five-figure logarithm tables.

20.5 (Data: Yule, *Jour. Anthrop. Inst.* 1906, **36**, 325) Sixteen pieces of photographic paper were printed down to different depths of colour from nearly white to a very deep blackish brown. Small scraps were cut from each sheet and pasted on cards, two scraps on each card one above the other, combining scraps from the several sheets in all possible ways, so that there were 256 cards in the pack. Twenty observers then went through the pack independently, each one naming each tint either "light," "medium" or "dark."

The following table shows the name assigned to each of the two pieces of paper—

Name assigned to Lower tint	Name assigned to upper tint			Total
	Light	Medium	Dark	
Light . . .	850	571	580	2001
Medium . .	618	593	455	1666
Dark . . .	540	456	457	1453
Total .	2008	1620	1492	5120

Show that there is a significant association between the name assigned to one piece and the name assigned to the other.

20.6 Apply the χ^2 test to the data of Example 2.8, page 29, and examine the justification for the conclusions there drawn.

20.7 Show that, if ν is large, P is below the 5 per cent level of significance if

$$\sqrt{2\chi^2} - \sqrt{2\nu - 1} > 1 \cdot 65$$

and below the 1 per cent level of significance if

$$\sqrt{2\chi^2} - \sqrt{2\nu - 1} > 2 \cdot 33$$

20.8 Table 3.6, page 64, gives the number of criminals of normal and weak intellect for various ranges of weight.

Assuming this to be a random sample of criminals, do the data support the suggestion that weak-minded criminals are not underweight?

20.9 Show that in a 2×2 contingency table wherein the frequencies are $\begin{array}{c|c} a & b \\ \hline c & d \end{array}$, χ^2 calculated from the "independence" frequencies is

$$\frac{(a+b+c+d)(ad-bc)^2}{(a+b)(c+d)(b+d)(a+c)}$$

20.10 Show similarly that for a $2 \times n$ table

$$\chi^2 = \Sigma_r \left\{ \frac{N_1 N_2 \left(\frac{\mu_{1r}}{N_1} - \frac{\mu_{2r}}{N_2} \right)}{\mu_{1r} + \mu_{2r}} \right\}$$

where μ_{1r}, μ_{2r} are the 2 frequencies in the rth column and N_1, N_2 are the marginal sums of the 2 rows.

20.11 Two investigators draw samples from the same town in order to estimate the number of persons falling in the income groups "poorer," "middle class," "well to do." (The limits of the groups are defined in terms of money and are the same for both investigators.) Their results are as follows—

Investigator	Income group			Totals
	" Poorer "	" Middle Class"	" Well to do "	
A	140	100	15	255
B	140	50	20	210
Totals	280	150	35	465

Show that the sampling technique of at least one of the investigators is suspect.

20.12   Exercise 8.17 gives the number of deaths per day of women over 85 published in *The Times* during 1910–12.   Using the theoretrical frequencies obtained in that exercise on the hypothesis that the numbers are distributed in a Poisson series, employ the χ^2 test to estimate the correctness of this hypothesis.

20.13   Design and execute an experiment involving the χ^2 test to test the randomness of a set of random sampling numbers.

20.14   (Data : G. Mendel's classical paper on " Experiments in Plant-Hybridisation "—quoted in translation in W. Bateson's " *Mendel's Principles of Heredity.*")

In experiments on pea-breeding, Mendel obtained the following frequencies of seeds : 315 round and yellow ; 101 wrinkled and yellow ; 108 round and green ; 32 wrinkled and green.   Total 556.

Theory predicts that the frequencies should be in the proportions 9 : 3 : 3 : 1.

Examine the correspondence between theory and experiment.

20.15   A particular experiment gives, on hypothesis H, $\chi^2=9$, $\nu=8$; when repeated it gives the same result.   Show that the two results taken together do not give the same confidence in H as either taken separately.

20.16   (Data from the Registrar-General's *Statistical Review for England and Wales*, 1941, *Tables, Part II, Civil*).   The following figures show the number of births in England and Wales in 1941 by month of occurrence—

January	50,159	July	49,395
February	45,885	August	50,443
March	50,819	September	51,562
April	49,070	October	50,224
May	50,771	November	47,168
June	46,788	December	50,529
		Total	592,813

Use the χ^2 test to discuss whether there is any seasonality in birth revealed by these data.

THE SAMPLING OF VARIABLES

SMALL SAMPLES

The problem

21.1 We now proceed to examine the theory of samples which are not large enough to warrant the assumptions underlying the work of Chapters 17 to 19.   In particular, it will no longer be open to us to assume (*a*) that the random sampling distribution of a statistic is approximately normal, or even unimodal, or (*b*) that values given by the data are sufficiently close to the population values for us to be able to use them in gauging the precision of our estimates.

The removal of these assumptions imposes severe restriction on our work, and, as we shall see, an entirely new technique is necessary to deal with the problems for which they are not permissible.   The division between the theories of large and small samples is therefore a very real one, though it is not always easy to draw a precise line of demarcation. We should point out, however. that as a rule the methods of the theory of small samples are applicable to large samples, though the reverse is not true.

Estimates

21.2 In the theory of large samples we were able to take as an estimate of a parameter in a population the value calculated from the sample as if it were itself the population.   This procedure, obvious though it seems, is not in general valid for small samples.   We must therefore discuss briefly the basis on which estimates of given parameters are to be made.

A full investigation of this question would take us far beyond the limits of this book.   It involves matters of considerable mathematical and philosophical complexity, some of which still form the subject of dispute among statisticians.   But in the theory of small samples the main parameters of interest are the mean and the standard deviation (or the variance), and we will proceed to consider these two.

Estimates of the arithmetic mean

21.3 We shall take as the estimate of the arithmetic mean the value of the sample mean.   That is to say, if we have n sample values x_1, $x_2, \ldots x_n$, our estimate $\bar{x}$ of the mean in the population is

$$\bar{x} = \frac{1}{n}\Sigma(x) \qquad . \qquad . \qquad . \qquad . \quad (21.1)$$

For estimates of the mean, therefore, the practice is the same for small samples as for large.

It may be shown that for samples from a normal population an estimate obtained in this way is the " best " in the sense that its sampling variance is less than that of any other estimate of the mean.

Estimates of the variance

21.4 Let us denote the variance in the population by σ^2 and the mean by m.

If m is known, we take as an estimate of the variance the mean square deviation of the sample about m; i.e. the estimate, which we write as s^2, is given by

$$s^2 = \frac{1}{n}\Sigma(x-m)^2 \quad . \qquad . \qquad . \qquad . \quad (21.2)$$

In general, however, we do not know the value of m, which will itself have to be estimated.   In this case equation (21.2) is no longer applicable.

21.5 If m is the population mean and $\bar{x}$ is the sample mean, we have—

$$\Sigma(x-m)^2 = \Sigma(x-\bar{x}+\bar{x}-m)^2$$

$$= \Sigma(x-\bar{x})^2+\Sigma(\bar{x}-m)^2$$

$$= \Sigma(x-\bar{x})^2+n(\bar{x}-m)^2$$

Hence,

$$s^2 = \frac{1}{n}\Sigma(x-\bar{x})^2+(\bar{x}-m)^2$$

The term $\frac{1}{n}\Sigma(x-\bar{x})^2$ is the variance of the sample.   We see that it differs from s^2 by the term $(\bar{x}-m)^2$.

Now this term will not, in general, vanish ; nor will it vanish on the average in a large number of cases, for it is essentially positive.   Hence, if we take the variance of the sample to be an estimate of the variance of the population we shall involve ourselves in a systematic error of magnitude $(\bar{x}-m)^2$.

This term is the square of the deviation of the mean of the sample from the mean of the population, and its average value in a large number of samples is the variance of the mean, which we know to be equal to σ^2/n.

It seems reasonable, therefore, instead of ignoring the presence of the term $(\bar{x}-m)^2$, to take it as equal to σ^2/n.   We will attempt, on this basis, a new estimate, which we shall write s'^2.   We have then—

$$s'^2 = \frac{1}{n}\Sigma(x-\bar{x})^2+\frac{\sigma^2}{n}$$

The value of σ is unknown, but we may, as an approximation, write s'^2 instead. If we do so we get—

$$s'^2 = \frac{1}{n}\Sigma(x-\bar{x})^2 + \frac{1}{n}s'^2$$

$$s'^2 = \frac{1}{n-1}\Sigma(x-\bar{x})^2 \quad . \quad . \quad . \quad . \quad (21.3)$$

The effect of taking s'^2 given by equation (21.3), instead of the variance of the sample, will thus be to eliminate the systematic error of estimation to which we have just referred.

21.6 We may look at this in a slightly different way. Suppose we take a large number of estimates of the variance of a population compiled according to equation (21.2), m being assumed known. These estimates will fall into a distribution which is the sampling distribution of the variance in samples of n. If, as will usually be the case, it is of the uni-modal type, we expect it to have a mean located at the true value of the variance in the population.

Now if we take as estimates of the variance the variance of the samples (each about its own sample mean), the above will not be true, owing to the small systematic shift represented by the term $(\bar{x}-m)^2$; but it will be true of the estimates given by equation (21.3), and this is therefore a preferable estimate to take.

21.7 Equation (21.3) was obtained by reasoning which does not depend on the size of n, and strictly speaking we should take it as applicable also to large samples. But if n is large, n and $n-1$ are for all practical purposes equal. With such samples our results are true only within the range of the standard error, which is usually of order $\frac{1}{\sqrt{n}}$, and there is little point in straining after an illusory refinement by taking $n-1$ instead of n in calculating the variance.

From a similar point of view it might be thought that since the term σ^2/n is generally less than the square of the standard error of the variance, it is equally idle to make allowance for it in estimating the variance. This would be true if the term were zero on the average; but in fact it is not, being a biased error, and we are justified in the long run in allowing for it.

Furthermore, we may point out that the use of s'^2, the corrected value obtained by allowing for the term σ^2/n, is only valid *on the average*. If, on random sampling, we get a sample variance greater than the population variance, the correction only makes matters worse, and may even lead to an absurd result.

Degrees of freedom of an estimate

21.8 In discussing the χ^2 test we introduced the notion of *number of* *degrees of freedom,* being the number of cells in an aggregate whose frequency could be assigned at will. We may conveniently extend this nomenclature to estimates of parameters and particularly of variance.

We shall refer to the divisor in the estimates of equations (21.1), (21.2) and (21.3) as the number of degrees of freedom of the estimates, and shall write it as ν. Thus, ν in equation (21.2) is n, and in equation (21.3) is $n-1$.

That this convention conforms to that adopted for the χ^2 test may easily be seen. We saw that ν is the number of cells, that is, the number of terms contributing to the χ^2 sum, less one for each constraint and one for each parameter which had been estimated from the data. In the quantity $\Sigma(x-m)^2$ there are n independent contributions of the type $(x-m)^2$, and hence we may say that n is the number of degrees of freedom of that estimate ; but in the quantity $\Sigma(x-\bar{x})^2$ we have used the data to estimate $\bar{x}$, and hence the number of degrees of freedom is lowered by unity, i.e. equals $n-1$.

Test of significance

21.9 It cannot be over-emphasised that estimates from small samples are of little value in indicating the true value of the parameter which is estimated. Some estimates will be better than others, but no estimate is very reliable. In the present state of our knowledge this is particularly true of samples from populations which are suspected not to be normal.

Nevertheless, circumstances sometimes drive us to base inferences, however tentatively, on scanty data. In such cases we can rarely, if ever, make any confident attempt at locating the value of a parameter within serviceably narrow limits. For this reason we are usually concerned, in the theory of small samples, not with estimating the actual value of a parameter, but in ascertaining whether observed values can have arisen by sampling fluctuations from some value given in advance. For example, if a sample of ten gives a correlation coefficient of $+0 \cdot 1$, we shall inquire, not the value of the correlation in the parent population, but, more generally, whether this value can have arisen from an uncorrelated population, i.e. whether it is *significant* of correlation in the parent.

21.10 The remainder of this chapter will accordingly be devoted to a brief discussion of various *tests of significance*. Within this book we shall not have space to deal with these tests as fully as we should like ; but our account of sampling methods would be incomplete without some reference to sundry results of great intrinsic interest and importance in the field of small samples.

The assumption of normality

21.11 We have already considered one test of significance, that given by the distribution of χ^2. This is one of the simplest and most general tests known ; but the student will recall that it depends on the assumption that the theoretical distribution of cell frequencies in each cell is normal. This is justified under the conditions laid down in **20.18**.

In the tests which we shall now discuss we are similarly compelled to make some assumption about the nature of the parent population, although we shall no longer be able to lay down analogous conditions on the arrangement of the data under which the assumption is justified. We shall specifically assume that the parent population is normal unless otherwise stated.

21.12 Our results will, therefore, be strictly true only for the normal population. Some experiments have been made to throw light on the question whether they are true for other types of population. It appears that, provided the divergence of the parent from normality is not too great, the results which are given below as true for normal populations are true to a large extent for other populations. Theoretical work confirms that the results remain true for populations which do not deviate markedly from normality; but if there is any good reason to suspect that the parent is markedly skew, e.g. **U-** or **J-**shaped, the methods of the succeeding sections cannot be applied with much confidence.

21.13 We may direct attention to one further point on which caution is necessary. In the theory of large samples we recommended the student to base his conclusions on a range of six times the standard error, and pointed out that for normal populations the probability of deviations from the true value outside this range was less than 3 in 1,000. One can feel great confidence in conclusions supported by probabilities of this order. But in the theory of small samples it is, as a rule, necessary to use larger probabilities, say, of one in 20 or one in 100, e.g. the 1 per cent and 5 per cent levels of P in the χ^2 test. The force of inferences based on probabilities of this order is not so great as before, and the student should bear this fact in mind.

21.14 For a known parent population, and in particular for a normal parent, it is not difficult to find expressions for the random sampling distribution of the commoner statistics such as the mean and standard deviation. But these distributions, even when mathematically tractable, will in general contain certain parent values. For instance, the sampling distribution of the means of samples of n from a normal population with mean m and standard deviation σ is also normal with mean m and standard deviation $\sigma/\sqrt{n}$. In the cases which we wish to consider, n is not large enough for us to take estimates of m and σ from the sample to find the sampling distribution to any close degree of approximation.

It is, however, a remarkable fact that we can construct certain statistics whose sampling distributions are either independent of, or dependent on only one of, the constants of the parent. We will proceed to consider two important distributions of this kind, the so-called t-distribution, due to " Student," and the z-distribution, due to R. A. Fisher.

The t-distribution

21.15 Writing, as before,

$$\bar{x} = \frac{1}{n}\Sigma(x)$$

$$s'^2 = \frac{1}{n-1}\Sigma(x-\bar{x})^2$$

let us define a new statistic t by the equation

$$t = \frac{\bar{x}-m}{s'}\sqrt{\nu+1} \qquad . \qquad . \qquad . \qquad . \qquad (21.4)$$

where $\nu = n-1$ and m is the mean of the population.

We shall refer to ν as the number of degrees of freedom of t.

Then it may be shown that, for samples of n from a normal population, the distribution of t is given by

$$y = \frac{y_0}{\left(1+\frac{t^2}{\nu}\right)^{\frac{\nu+1}{2}}} \qquad . \qquad . \qquad . \qquad . \qquad (21.5)$$

21.16 We will imagine y_0 chosen so that the area of the curve given by equation (21.5) is unity. Then, precisely as for the χ^2 distribution, the probability P_s that, on random sampling, we shall get a value of t not greater than some value t_0 is the area of the curve to the left of the ordinate at the point t_0. We may write this

$$P_s = \int_{-\infty}^{t_0} \frac{y_0 dt}{\left(1+\frac{t^2}{\nu}\right)^{\frac{\nu+1}{2}}} \qquad . \qquad . \qquad . \qquad (21.6)$$

Similarly, the probability that we get a value of t between the limits t_1 and t_2 is given by

$$P_s = \int_{t_1}^{t_2} \frac{y_0 dt}{\left(1+\frac{t^2}{\nu}\right)^{\frac{\nu+1}{2}}} \qquad . \qquad . \qquad . \qquad (21.7)$$

Form of " Student's " distribution

21.17 The curves given by equation (21.5) are easy to study. Clearly they are symmetrical about $t=0$, since only even powers of t appear in their equation. Further, since $\dfrac{1}{\left(1+\frac{t^2}{\nu}\right)}$ decreases as t increases, the curves will have a mode (coinciding, of course, with the mean) at $t = 0$, and will tail off to infinity on each side. They will, in fact, be symmetrical single-humped curves rather like the normal curve, only more leptokurtic.

As ν tends to infinity, $\dfrac{1}{\left(1+\dfrac{t^2}{\nu}\right)^{\frac{\nu+1}{2}}}$ tends to $e^{-\frac{t^2}{2}}$, and hence t is distributed normally. This fact enables us to use the tables of the normal integral to evaluate P approximately when ν is large.

21.18 At the end of this book we reproduce by permission tables of the integral (21.6) calculated by " Student " himself (Appendix Table 4). These have been reduced to three places of decimals from the original four.

Tables of rather a different form have been given in the Fisher–Yates *Statistical Tables* and in *Tables for Statisticians and Biometricians, Part I,* and to avoid possible confusion we point out where these tables differ.

Tables for Statisticians, etc., gives the values of

$$P_T = \int_{-\infty}^{z_0} \frac{y_0 \, dz}{(1+z^2)^{\frac{\nu+1}{2}}}$$

where $z = \dfrac{t}{\sqrt{\nu}}$, for ν from 1 to 9. These values (which were also calculated by " Student ") are of the same kind as, but more limited in range than, those of our table.

The Fisher–Yates tables adopt the standpoint we have already noticed in discussing the χ^2 distribution (Chapter 20), and gives values of t corresponding to various values of ν and the 5 per cent and 1 per cent levels of a third probability P_F.

P_s and P_F are simply related. P_s is the probability that an observed value will *not* exceed t_0. P_F is the probability that an observed value of t, *regardless of sign*, will exceed t_0.

Hence,

$P_s =$ Area of curve to the left of ordinate t_0
$P_F =$ Area to right of t_0 + area to left of $-t_0$
$\quad = 2$ (Area to right of t_0) (since the curve is symmetrical)
$\quad = 2 \, (1-P_s)$ . . . . (21.8)

The student should keep these relations in mind, particularly when thinking of levels of significance. In the sense of Fisher and Yates, a value of P_F will fall below the 5 per cent level if P_F is less than $0 \cdot 05$. This implies that P_s is greater than $0 \cdot 975$, not $0 \cdot 95$.[1]

---

[1] A comparison of the tables is not made any easier by the fact that " Student " and Fisher use n to denote the degrees of freedom, whereas *Tables for Statisticians* uses it to denote the number in the sample. It is probable that future editions of *Tables for Statisticians* will give more complete tables for the percentage points of t.

The distinction between P_s and P_F did not arise in Chapter 20 because χ^2 is essentially positive.

Applications of " Student's " distribution

21.19 We proceed to give one or two examples of the way in which the " Student " distribution is generally used to test the significance of various results obtained from small samples.

Example 21.1.—Ten individuals are chosen at random from a population and their heights are found to be, in inches, 63, 63, 66, 67, 68, 69, 70, 70, 71 and 71. In the light of these data, discuss the suggestion that the mean height in the population is 66 inches.

In the first place, let us note that the population is likely to be approximately normal, from our knowledge of height distributions, and the sampling is random.

In the sample we find that

$$\bar{x} = 67 \cdot 8 \text{ inches}$$

and

$$s' = 3 \cdot 011 \text{ inches}$$

Let us now calculate t from equation (21.4), taking m to be 66 inches. We have—

$$t = \frac{67 \cdot 8 - 66}{3 \cdot 011} \sqrt{10} = 1 \cdot 89$$

From the Appendix Table 4 (column $\nu = 9$)—

for $t = 1 \cdot 8$, $P = 0 \cdot 947$

for $t = 1 \cdot 9$, $P = 0 \cdot 955$

Hence,

for $t = 1 \cdot 89$, $P = 0 \cdot 954$

Thus the chance of getting a value of t greater than that observed is $1 - 0 \cdot 954$, i.e. $0 \cdot 046$, or about one in twenty. The probability of getting t greater in *absolute value* is $0 \cdot 092$, or about one in ten. We should hardly regard this as significant ; but if we did, we should argue that as the observed value of t is improbable, the initial assumptions on which we obtained it were incorrect; and this in turn suggests that there is some doubt about the true mean being 66 inches.

Example 21.2.—(Voelcker's data quoted by " Student," *Biometrika*, 1908, **6**, 19.)

Voelcker grew certain crops of potatoes dressed (*a*) with sulphate of potash, and (*b*) with kainite. In four experiments, two of each of 1904 and 1905, the differences in yields per acre (sulphate plot less kainite plot) were—

$$0 \cdot 5464 \text{ ton}$$
$$0 \cdot 3013 \text{ ,,}$$
$$1 \cdot 5241 \text{ ,,}$$
$$0 \cdot 6786 \text{ ,,}$$

This suggests that sulphate of potash is a better manure than kainite. Required to discuss the question.

From our knowledge of crop yields we expect them to be distributed in a unimodal form not very far removed from the normal. Let us suppose that the two manures have the same effect on yield. Then the differences of plots will be distributed in an approximately normal form about zero mean.

The mean of the four differences is $0 \cdot 7626$ ton, and we find $s' = 0 \cdot 5312$. Hence,

$$t = \frac{0 \cdot 7626 - 0}{0 \cdot 5312} \sqrt{4}$$

$$= 2 \cdot 871$$

From the tables, for $\nu = 3$, $P = 0 \cdot 968$ approximately.

Hence the chance P of getting a value of t greater than that observed is about 1 in 33. The chance of getting a value greater *absolutely* than the observed value is $0 \cdot 06$. If we choose to regard this as significant, we are led to suspect our hypothesis that the two manures exert equal influences on yield, and hence to suppose, though with little confidence so far as these data are concerned, that sulphate of potash is the better manure.

21.20 The student who wishes to apply the t-distribution for himself is advised to make a careful study of the logic of the argument underlying the inferences we have drawn in the foregoing two examples.

In Example 21.1 we saw that the chance of getting a value of t less than $1 \cdot 89$ is approximately $0 \cdot 954$. This is not the same thing as saying that the probability of a deviation in the sample mean of $1 \cdot 8$ inches or less is 0.954. In fact, we do not know this probability, and the smallness of the sample prevents us from approximating to it with any closeness. It *might* happen that σ in the population was such that a deviation of $1 \cdot 8$ inches was not at all improbable. The relative improbability of t would then be due to deviations of s' from σ.

Comparison of two samples

21.21 Suppose we have two samples $x_1, x_2 \ldots x_{n_1}$ and $x_1', x_2' \ldots x_{n_2}'$. Let us. as before, define

$$\left.\begin{aligned}
\bar{x}_1 &= \frac{1}{n_1} \Sigma(x) \\[2mm]
\bar{x}_2 &= \frac{1}{n_2} \Sigma(x') \\[2mm]
s_1'^2 &= \frac{1}{n_1 - 1} \Sigma(x - \bar{x}_1)^2 \\[2mm]
s_2'^2 &= \frac{1}{n_2 - 1} \Sigma(x' - \bar{x}_2)^2
\end{aligned}\right\} \qquad . \quad . \quad . \quad (21.9)$$

Let us further define

$$s'^2 = \frac{1}{n_1+n_2-2}\{\Sigma(x-\bar{x}_1)^2+\Sigma(x'-\bar{x}_2)^2\} \qquad . \qquad . \quad (21.10)$$

If the two samples come from the same population, s'^2 will be an estimate of σ^2. It has, as we might expect, n_1+n_2-2 degrees of freedom, since both $\bar{x}_1$ and $\bar{x}_2$ are calculated from the data.

Let us write

$$\nu = n_1+n_2-2 \qquad . \qquad . \qquad . \qquad . \quad (21.11)$$

and define

$$t = \frac{\bar{x}_1-\bar{x}_2}{s'\sqrt{\dfrac{1}{n_1}+\dfrac{1}{n_2}}}$$

$$= \frac{\bar{x}_1-\bar{x}_2}{s'}\sqrt{\frac{n_1 n_2}{n_1+n_2}}. \qquad . \qquad . \qquad . \quad (21.12)$$

Then it may be shown that t, as so defined, is distributed according to the form of equation (21.5) with ν degrees of freedom.

Example 21.3.—(Data from R.A. Fisher, *Metron*, 1925, **5**, 95.)

Eight pots growing three barley plants each were exposed to a high tension discharge, while nine similar pots were enclosed in an earthed wire cage. The numbers of tillers in each pot were as follows—

Caged .	.	.	17, 27, 18, 25, 27, 29, 27, 23, 17
Electrified	.	.	16, 16, 20, 16, 20, 17, 15, 21

We are interested in the question whether electrification exercises any real effect on the tillering.

We find

$$\bar{x}_1 = 23\cdot333 \qquad \bar{x}_2 = 17\cdot625$$

$$\bar{x}_1-\bar{x}_2 = 5\cdot708$$

$$s'^2 = \frac{1}{15}221\cdot875 = 14\cdot7916 \qquad s' = 3\cdot846$$

$$t = \frac{5\cdot708}{3\cdot846}\sqrt{\frac{8\times9}{17}} = 3\cdot05$$

$$\nu = 8+9-2 = 15$$

From the tables we find that $P_{\bar{s}} = 0\cdot996$.

Hence, if the samples came from the same population they furnish a value of t which is improbable—an absolutely greater value would arise only 8 times in a thousand. We therefore suspect that the populations are different, i.e. that electrification does exert some effect on the tillering.

21.22 In applying the t-distribution to two samples as in the preceding example one further point should be borne in mind. It does not follow from a significant value of t that the samples come from populations which have different means. Samples from two populations with the same means and different standard deviations would also furnish significant t's on occasion. We can test whether this is so by the method of **21.27** below.

Significance of regression coefficients

21.23 From (21.4) it is clear that "Student's" t is a ratio, being, apart from constants, the ratio of the estimate of the sample mean (measured from the parent mean) to the estimated standard deviation. The simplicity of its sampling distribution (21.5) arises from the fact (which we state without proof) that in normal samples, and only in normal samples, sampling variations of the mean are completely independent of (and not merely uncorrelated with) those of the variance.

There are other cases in which we find a quantity which is the ratio of two independent variates, the numerator distributed like a mean and the denominator like a standard deviation in normal samples. In such cases, of course, the ratio t follows " Student's " distribution. The most important, perhaps, is that of regression coefficients.

21.24 Consider a linear regression equation—

$$y = \beta x \qquad . \qquad . \qquad . \qquad . \qquad . \quad (21.13)$$

where y, x are measured from their means and β is the parent value of the regression. We will assume that for any fixed x the distribution of y is normal as, for instance, is true if the joint distribution is normal. The corresponding sample regression equation will be—

$$y - \bar{y} = b(x - \bar{x}) \qquad . \qquad . \qquad . \qquad . \qquad . \quad (21.14)$$

Then if $s_1{}^2$, $s_2{}^2$ are the sample variances of x and y respectively it may be shown that—

$$t = \frac{(b-\beta)s_1\sqrt{(n-2)}}{\{s_2{}^2 - b^2 s_1{}^2\}^{\frac{1}{2}}} \qquad . \qquad . \qquad . \qquad . \quad (21.15)$$

is distributed in " Student's " form with $\nu = n-2$ degrees of freedom. The result derives from the fact that $(b-\beta)s_1$ is distributed like a mean in normal samples whereas $(s_2{}^2 - b^2 s_1{}^2)/(n-2)$ is distributed independently like a variance. It is, in fact, an estimate of the variance of the residuals of observed values about the regression line—cf. **9.24**.

The expression for t in (21.15) does not involve any of the parent parameters except β and consequently it may be used to test the significance of β irrespective of the other parameters.

Example 21.4.—In Table 13.1 (page 311) we gave some data for the yields of wheat and potatoes in 48 English counties. The regression of y (potato yield) on x (wheat yield) is found to be —

$$y - 6 \cdot 065 = 0 \cdot 0783 \ (x - 15 \cdot 791)$$

The value of the regression coefficient is small. Could it have arisen by chance in a sample from a population for which $\beta = 0$?
We find—

$$b = 0 \cdot 0783, \qquad \sqrt{(n-2)} = \sqrt{46} = 6 \cdot 7823,$$

$$s_1^2 = 4 \cdot 1749, \qquad s_2^2 = 0 \cdot 5340.$$

Hence, from (21.15)—

$$t = 2 \cdot 06, \qquad \nu = 46$$

Appendix Table 4 does not carry us as far as $\nu = 46$. For large ν, t tends to be distributed normally with zero mean and unit variance and a normal deviate of $2 \cdot 06$ would be significant at the 5 per cent level but not at the 2 per cent level. The regression is of doubtful significance.

More accurately, from the Fisher–Yates Tables we find the following values of t for $P = 0 \cdot 05$—

$$\nu = 40, \qquad t = 2 \cdot 021 ; \qquad \nu = 60 \qquad t = 2 \cdot 000$$

and for $P = 0 \cdot 02$—

$$\nu = 40, \qquad t = 2 \cdot 423 ; \qquad \nu = 60 \qquad t = 2 \cdot 390$$

This confirms our result that the observed t is significant at the 5 per cent but not at the 2 per cent level.

21.25 We have remarked in **19.31** that the significance of a value of Spearman's rank correlation-coefficient can be tested by the use of " Student's " distribution ; and we shall see later (**21.34**) that the product-moment correlation can also be tested in the same way on the hypothesis that there is no parent correlation. These facts are to be regarded as mathematical accidents. They do not depend on the properties of " Student's " t as a ratio, but on the fact that the t- distribution, being a symmetrical unimodal distribution which tends to normality, may be used as an approximation to other distributions of the same kind.

Fisher's distribution

21.26 Suppose that we have two samples, as in **21.21** with variances s_1^2 and s_2^2. Then if the samples come from the same normal population the distribution of the ratio $\xi = s_1 / s_2$ may be shown to be—

$$y = y_0 \ \frac{\xi^{n_1-2}}{(n_1 \xi^2 + n_2)^{\frac{1}{2}(n_1+n_2-2)}} \qquad . \qquad . \ (21.16)$$

where ξ may have any value from 0 to ∞. This may be put in a rather different form. In terms of the *estimated* variances s_1' and s_2', write—

$$z = \log_e \frac{s_1'}{s_2'} = \frac{1}{2} \log_e \frac{s_1'^2}{s_2'^2} \qquad . \qquad . \qquad . \qquad . \quad (21.17)$$

Then it may be shown that in normal samples from the same population z is distributed according to the law

$$y = y_0 \frac{e^{\nu_1 z}}{(\nu_1 e^{2z} + \nu_2)^{\frac{1}{2}(\nu_1 + \nu_2)}} \qquad . \qquad . \quad (21.18)$$

where

$$\left. \begin{aligned} \nu_1 &= n_1 - 1 \\ \nu_2 &= n_2 - 1 \end{aligned} \right\} \qquad . \qquad . \qquad . \quad (21.19)$$

As usual, we take y_0 so that the area of the curve is unity, and the probability that we get a given value z_0 or greater on random sampling will be given by the area to the right of the ordinate at z_0.

21.27 This probability is not easy to tabulate owing to the fact that it depends upon the two numbers ν_1 and ν_2. Fisher has therefore prepared tables showing the 5 per cent and 1 per cent significance points of z, and a further table of the $0 \cdot 1$ per cent points has been given by Colcord and Deming. These tables are reproduced by permission in Appendix Tables 6A, 6B and 6C. For practical purposes they are sufficient to enable the significance of an observed value of z to be gauged. If the exact value of the probability of obtaining a given value of z or greater is required, use may sometimes be made of the tables of the incomplete beta-function. Tables are also available for the values of the variance ratio itself corresponding to specified probability levels. The quantity z of (21.17) was used by Fisher instead of the ratio $s_1'^2 / s_2'^2$ because linear interpolation is more accurate in the z-tables. The 5 per cent, 1 per cent and $0 \cdot 1$ per cent points of the variance-ratio F are given in Appendix Table 5.

Example 21.4.—Consider again the data of Example 21.3.

Here, as always, it is convenient to take the suffix 1 to refer to the larger of the two estimates of variance.

We have—

$$s_1'^2 = \frac{184}{8} = 23$$

$$s_2'^2 = \frac{37 \cdot 875}{7} = 5 \cdot 4107$$

$$z = \tfrac{1}{2} \log_e \frac{23}{5 \cdot 4107}$$

$$= 0 \cdot 724$$

$$\nu_1 = 8, \qquad \nu_2 = 7$$

From Appendix Table 6A we see that for these degrees of freedom the 5 per cent significance value of z is $0 \cdot 6576$. From Table 6B the 1 per cent value is $0 \cdot 9614$.

The observed z lies between these two and is thus of rather doubtful significance.

Alternatively $F = \dfrac{s_1'^2}{s_2'^2} = 4 \cdot 25$ and from Appendix Table 5A and 5B we see that the 5 per cent and 1 per cent points are $3 \cdot 73$ and $6 \cdot 84$, leading to the same conclusion.

21.28 We shall consider this distribution and some of its uses in the next chapter (Analysis of Variance). At this stage we may note that, since it contains no unknown parameters, it provides a significance test for the ratio of any two independent variates each of which is distributed like a variance in normal samples. The distribution of a variance (or equivalently, of course, of a standard deviation) is, in fact that of χ^2, so that z may be regarded as the distribution of the logarithm of the ratio of two independent variates each of which is distributed as χ.

Correlation coefficient in small samples

21.29 Although the distribution of the correlation coefficient in samples from a bivariate normal population tends to the normal form as the size of the sample increases, a fact which justifies the use of the standard error for large n, the distribution diverges very remarkably from the normal when n is small, and even when n is moderately large if the correlation in the parent population is high. Further investigation is therefore necessary before we can assess the significance of correlation coefficients obtained from small samples.

21.30 The distribution of the correlation coefficient in samples from a bivariate normal population was obtained in an exact form by R. A. Fisher in 1915. Ordinates of the frequency-curves which give the distribution have been worked out for various values of n and ρ, the correlation in the population, and are tabulated in F. N. David's *Tables of the Correlation Coefficient*. The general form of these curves is illustrated in fig. 21.1, which shows the curves for $\rho = +0 \cdot 6$ and various values of n.

A glance at this figure will show that even for a moderate value of ρ, such as $+0 \cdot 6$, the distribution of the coefficient is U-shaped for $n=3$, and, although unimodal, distinctly skew to the eye even for $n=20$. For high values of ρ, such as $+0 \cdot 9$, the distribution is skew for higher values of n.

As a result it is safe to say that the values of correlation coefficients calculated from samples of less than five will throw no light on the existence of correlation in the population. For samples of 20 or 30 we cannot apply the standard error with much confidence if the correlation in the population is likely to be very high, whether positive or negative. 50 seems to be the minimum number in the sample for the application of the standard error if ρ is very high, and 100 is safer.

21.31 The equation giving the distribution of the correlation coefficient is very complex, but Prof. David's tables referred to above give the areas under the frequency curves for various values of n, ρ and r. These tables may be used to assess the significance of an observed value of r from a bivariate normal population. For most practical purposes, however, use may be made of a method due to R. A. Fisher, the essence of which is the transformation of the distribution of r into a new distribution which is approximately normal.

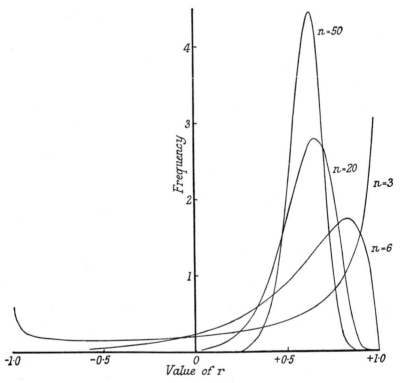

Fig. 21.1.—**Frequency distribution of the correlation coefficient in samples from a normal population with correlation $+0\cdot6$ for various values of the number in the sample n**
In each case the total frequency, i.e. the area under the curve, is unity

21.32 Before we discuss this process, however, it is desirable to point out the degree of applicability of our results.

(1) In the first place, it has been shown that the distribution of partial correlation coefficients in samples of n is of the same form as that of total correlation coefficients in samples of $n-p$, where p is the number of *secondary* subscripts in the partial coefficient.

(2) Secondly, our results are strictly true only for normal populations. There is some experimental evidence to show that they are true for all practical purposes even if the parent is moderately skew but remains of the unimodal type ; but if there is any reason to suppose that the parent is J- or U-shaped according to one or more variates, the student should draw his conclusions with the utmost reserve.

Fisher's transformation

21.33 If r and ρ are the correlations in the sample and the population respectively, let us put

$$r = \tanh z \qquad \rho = \tanh \zeta$$

So that

$$\left. \begin{aligned} z^* &= \tfrac{1}{2} \log_e\frac{1+r}{1-r} \\ \zeta &= \tfrac{1}{2} \log_e\frac{1+\rho}{1-\rho} \end{aligned} \right\} \qquad . \qquad . \qquad . \quad (21.20)$$

Then it may be shown that z is, to a close approximation, distributed normally about mean ζ with standard deviation $\dfrac{1}{\sqrt{n-3}}$.

In fact, the mean of z is given by

$$\bar{z} = \zeta + \frac{\rho}{2(n-1)} + \text{ terms in } \frac{1}{(n-1)^2}, \text{ etc.} \qquad . \qquad . \quad (21.21)$$

and, for the z-distribution

$$\beta_1 = \frac{\rho^6}{(n-1)^3} + \text{terms in } \frac{1}{(n-1)^2}, \text{ etc.} \qquad . \qquad . \quad (21.22)$$

$$\beta_2 = 3 + \frac{2}{(n-1)} + \text{terms in } \frac{1}{(n-1)^2}, \text{ etc.} \qquad . \qquad . \quad (21.23)$$

For $n=11$, say, β_1 is of the order of $0 \cdot 001$ even if ρ is high, which shows how closely the z-distribution lies to the symmetrical ; and β_2-3 is of the order of $0 \cdot 2$, which shows that the distribution has nearly normal kurtosis. In such a case $\bar{z}$ would differ from ζ by $0 \cdot 05$, which is not large, but might be important in some cases. The standard error of z is, however, $\dfrac{1}{\sqrt{n-3}}$, and the factor $\dfrac{\rho}{2(n-1)}$ may, as a rule, be neglected in comparison. This is the basis of the statement above that z is normally distributed about mean ζ.

We now give some examples of the use of the z-transformation in testing the significance of an observed r.

---

* This z is to be distinguished from the z of Fisher's distribution of **21.26**.

Example 21.5.—In Example 9.1, page 223, we found that the correlation between the price indices of animal feeding-stuffs and home-grown oats is 0·68, the sample consisting of 60 members.

This sample is large enough for us to use the standard error. If we do so we get

$$\sigma_r = \frac{1-(0\cdot68)^2}{\sqrt{60}} = 0\cdot07 \text{ approximately}$$

The correlation thus is undoubtedly significant.

We might, alternatively, use the z test, thus, to answer the question, " Could the observed value have arisen from an uncorrelated population? " On this hypothesis

$$\rho = 0 \text{ and } \zeta = 0$$

We have—

$$z = \tfrac{1}{2} \log_e \frac{1\cdot68}{0\cdot32}$$

$$= 0\cdot829$$

The standard error of z is $\dfrac{1}{\sqrt{57}} = 0\cdot13$.

The deviation of z from ζ is more than six times this, and we conclude that our hypothesis was incorrect, i.e. that the population is correlated.

Example 21.6.—Continuing the previous example, could the observed correlation have arisen from a population in which $\rho = +0\cdot8$? Here

$$\zeta = \tfrac{1}{2} \log_e \frac{1+\rho}{1-\rho} = 1\cdot099$$

The deviation of z from ζ is, therefore,

$$1\cdot099 - 0\cdot829 = 0\cdot270$$

This is about twice the standard error of z. It might arise, though rarely, as a sampling fluctuation, and we conclude that ρ is likely to be less than $+ 0\cdot8$.

Example 21.7.—In Example 12.1, page 290, we found a partial correlation of $-0\cdot73$ (38 unions) between earnings of agricultural labourers and the percentage of the population in receipt of relief, when the ratio of numbers in receipt of outdoor relief to those relieved in the workhouse was constant. Is this significant, and can it have arisen from a population in which the real correlation is $-0\cdot667$?

Here

$$z = \tfrac{1}{2} \log_e \frac{0 \cdot 27}{1 \cdot 73}$$

$$= -0 \cdot 929$$

ζ for an uncorrelated population $= 0$

$$\zeta, \text{ if } \rho = -0 \cdot 667 = \tfrac{1}{2} \log_e \frac{0 \cdot 333}{1 \cdot 667}$$

$$= -0 \cdot 805$$

There is one secondary subscript in the partial correlation. Hence, the standard error of $z = \dfrac{1}{\sqrt{38-1-3}} = 0 \cdot 1715.$

If $\zeta = 0$, the deviation is more than five times the standard error and is undoubtedly significant. If $\rho = -0 \cdot 667$, the deviation is less than the standard error and hence may very well have arisen from sampling fluctuations.

Application of " Student's " distribution to correlation coefficients

21.34 The test we have just given is of general application, but it is worth noticing that if $\rho = 0$, the distribution of the correlation coefficient in small samples from a normal population may be tested by the " Student" distribution.

In fact, the distribution of the correlation coefficient assumes a particularly simple form for such uncorrelated populations, namely,

$$y = y_0(1-r^2)^{\frac{n-4}{2}} \qquad . \qquad . \qquad . \qquad . \quad (21.24)$$

If we put

$$t = \frac{r}{\sqrt{1-r^2}}\sqrt{n-2} \qquad . \qquad . \qquad . \quad (21.25)$$

then it may be shown that t is distributed in the " Student " form with $n-2$ degrees of freedom, and its significance may be tested accordingly.

SUMMARY

1. As an estimate of the mean of the population we may take the mean of the sample, whether large or small.

2. If the mean of the population is known, we may take the mean square deviation about that mean as an estimate of the variance of the population ; i.e. the estimate is given by

$$s^2 = \frac{1}{n}\Sigma(x-m)^2$$

3. If the mean of the population is not known, a preferable estimate of the population variance is the " corrected " variance of the sample, given by

$$s'^2 = \frac{1}{n-1}\Sigma(x-\bar{x})^2$$

4. This estimate is said to have $n-1$ degrees of freedom.

5. In samples from a normal population the parameter t, given by

$$t = \frac{\bar{x}-m}{s'}\sqrt{\nu+1}$$

where $\nu=n-1$, is distributed according to the law (due to " Student ")

$$y = \frac{y_0}{\left(1+\dfrac{t^2}{\nu}\right)^{\frac{\nu+1}{2}}}$$

This distribution may be used to give the probability of getting a value of t between specified limits on random sampling.

6. With two samples, $x_1, \ldots x_{n_1}$ and $x_1', \ldots x_{n_2}'$, from the same normal population, the parameter t defined by

$$t = \frac{\bar{x}_1-\bar{x}_2}{s'}\sqrt{\frac{n_1 n_2}{n_1+n_2}}$$

where

$$s'^2 = \frac{1}{n_1+n_2-2}\{\Sigma(x-\bar{x}_1)^2+\Sigma(x'-\bar{x}_2)^2\} \quad \text{and} \quad \nu = n_1+n_2-2$$

is also distributed according to the above law, with ν degrees of freedom.

7. With two samples, as before, with estimated variances

$$s_1'^2 = \frac{1}{n_1-1}\Sigma(x-\bar{x}_1)^2 \qquad s_2'^2 = \frac{1}{n_2-1}\Sigma(x'-\bar{x}_2)^2$$

the parameter

$$z = \log\frac{s_1}{s_2} = \frac{1}{2}\log\frac{s_1^2}{s_2^2}$$

is distributed according to the law (due to R. A. Fisher)

$$y = y_0\frac{e^{\nu_1 z}}{(\nu_1 e^{2z}+\nu_2)^{\frac{\nu_1+\nu_2}{2}}}$$

where

$$\nu_1 = n_1-1, \qquad \nu_2 = n_2-1$$

As usual, this distribution may be used to give the probability of getting a value of z between specified limits on random sampling.

Alternatively tables are available for testing directly the ratio—

$$F = s_1'^2/s_2'^2 = e^{2z}$$

8. The distribution of the correlation coefficient in samples from a normal bivariate population is not normal. However, putting

$$z = \tfrac{1}{2} \log_e \frac{1+r}{1-r}$$

$$\zeta = \tfrac{1}{2} \log_e \frac{1+\rho}{1-\rho}$$

where ρ is the correlation in the population, it may be shown that z is approximately normally distributed about ζ with standard deviation $\frac{1}{\sqrt{n-3}}$, n being the number in the sample.

9. This result remains true of partial correlation coefficients, but in the above formulæ n must be taken to be the number in the sample less the number of secondary subscripts in the coefficient tested.

10. In samples from an uncorrelated normal population the distribution of r is given by

$$y = y_0 (1-r^2)^{\frac{n-4}{2}}$$

The statistic t, defined by

$$t = \frac{r}{\sqrt{1-r^2}} \sqrt{n-2}$$

is distributed in the " Student " form in such cases with $n-2$ degrees of freedom.

EXERCISES

21.1 Find " Student's " t for the following variate values in a sample of 10: $-6, -4, -3, -2, -2, 0, 1, 1, 3, 5$, taking m to be zero, and find from the tables the probability of getting a value of t as great or greater on random sampling from a normal population.

21.2 A farmer grows crops on two fields, A and B. On A he puts £1 worth of manure per acre and on B £2 worth. The net returns per acre, exclusive of the cost of manure, on the two fields in five years are—

Year	Field A, £ per acre	Field B, £ per acre
1	17	18
2	14	16·5
3	21	24
4	18·5	19
5	22	25

Other things being equal, discuss the question whether it is likely to pay the farmer to continue the more expensive dressing. State clearly the assumptions which you make.

21.3   The heights of six randomly chosen sailors are, in inches : **63, 65, 68, 69, 71** and **72**. Those of ten randomly chosen soldiers are : **61, 62, 65, 66, 69, 69, 70, 71, 72** and **73**. Discuss the light that these data throw on the suggestion that soldiers are, on the average, taller than sailors.

21.4   In the data of Exercise 21.3, use the z-distribution to discuss whether the samples can have come from populations which are identical so far as height distribution is concerned.

21.5   In three samples of 50 lines each from Shakespeare's " Romeo and Juliet " (an early play), the following numbers of weak endings were observed : **7, 9, 10**. In three similar samples from " Cymbeline " (late), the numbers of weak endings were **15, 11, 12**. Discuss the suggestion that Shakespeare's prosody, as judged by the number of weak endings, changed with advancing years.

21.6   A random sample of 15 from a normal population gives a correlation coefficient of $-0 \cdot 5$. Is this significant of the existence of correlation in the population?

21.7   Show that in samples of four from an uncorrelated normal population all values of the correlation coefficient are equally probable ; and that for samples of less than four a zero coefficient is the most improbable.

21.8   What is the probability that a correlation coefficient of $+0 \cdot 75$ or less can arise in a sample of 30 from a normal population in which the true correlation is $+0 \cdot 9$? Compare this with the result given by assuming the sampling distribution normal with standard deviation $\dfrac{1-r^2}{\sqrt{n}}$.

21.9   Test the significance of the partial correlation coefficients of Example 12.1, page 290.

21.10   Show that in samples of 25 from an uncorrelated normal population the chance is 1 in 100 that r is greater than about $0 \cdot 43$.

21.11   If two statistics both have the same dimensions show that their ratio must be independent of the scale of the parent population. Hence consider why " Student's " t and Fisher's z (variance-ratio) are independent of σ, the standard deviation of the normal parent.

21.12   By considerations similar to those of the previous exercise show that in normal samples the distribution of the correlation coefficient cannot contain either the parent means or the parent variances, but only the parent correlation.

CHAPTER TWENTY-TWO

THE ANALYSIS OF VARIANCE

22.1 In this chapter we shall consider a technique of analysis which is of wide application whenever samples of variate data can be classified in groups. For instance, we may have a sample which consists of p sub-samples, our interest lying in the question whether the total sample may be regarded as homogeneous or alternatively whether there is some indication that the sub-samples were drawn from different populations. Again, we may have a number of plots of a cereal grown under different manurial treatments. Our interest here is whether the manures exert any differential effect on yields ; and if we classify the yields into groups according to the type of fertiliser applied we have the case, already mentioned, of p sets of data which we require to test for homogeneity, p being the number of different treatments. To take a more complex case, we may have a number of observations taken by p different observers each on a sample affected by q different effects, as for instance, if p laboratory assistants carry out an assay on samples of a drug from q different suppliers. Our classification here is two-fold and we wish to discuss whether there are any significant differences between the q sources of supply and, *independently if possible*, whether there are any differences between the results obtained by the p assistants.

In general we desire to answer the question whether some one variable, treated as dependent variable, does or does not exhibit heterogeneity when classified into " arrays ", " families " or " classes " by one or more independent variables.

A single independent variable

22.2 We shall discuss in the first instance the simplest case of a single classification (i.e. according to one independent variable) and shall proceed to the more complex cases later.

Suppose then that we have a set of variate-values divided into p families, the number in the jth family being n_j. We may array the values thus—

$$
\begin{array}{ll}
\text{First family} & x_{11},\ x_{21},\ \ldots\ x_{n_1 1} \\
\text{Second family} & x_{12},\ x_{22},\ \ldots\ x_{n_2 2} \\
& \quad \cdot \quad \cdot \quad \cdot \quad \cdot \\
p\text{th family} & x_{1p},\ x_{2p},\ \ldots\ x_{n_p p} \qquad \cdot \qquad \cdot \qquad \cdot \quad (22.1)
\end{array}
$$

Let us denote by $x_{..}$ the mean of the whole set and by $x_{.j}$ the mean of the jth family. This is a new notation which will be very convenient for later generalisation, a period replacing any subscript which is averaged. Then, denoting by $\underset{ij}{\Sigma}$ summation over values of i from 1 to n_j and values of j from 1 to p we have the simple algebraic identity

$$\underset{ij}{\Sigma}(x_{ij}-x_{..})^2 = \underset{ij}{\Sigma}(x_{ij}-x_{.j}+x_{.j}-x_{..})^2$$

$$= \underset{ij}{\Sigma}(x_{ij}-x_{.j})^2 + 2\underset{ij}{\Sigma}(x_{ij}-x_{.j})(x_{.j}-x_{..})$$

$$+ \underset{ij}{\Sigma}(x_{.j}-x_{..})^2 \quad . \qquad . \qquad . \qquad . \qquad . \qquad (22.2)$$

Now if we carry out summations over i alone we have

$$\underset{i}{\Sigma}(x_{ij}-x_{.j})(x_{.j}-x_{..}) = (x_{.j}-x_{..})\underset{i}{\Sigma}(x_{ij}-x_{.j}) = 0$$

since, by definition, $x_{.j}$ is the mean of x_{ij} in the jth family. Hence we have, from (22.2)

$$\underset{ij}{\Sigma}(x_{ij}-x_{..})^2 = \underset{ij}{\Sigma}(x_{ij}-x_{.j})^2 + \underset{ij}{\Sigma}(x_{.j}-x_{..})^2$$

$$= \underset{ij}{\Sigma}(x_{ij}-x_{.j})^2 + \underset{j}{\Sigma}n_j(x_{.j}-x_{..})^2 \qquad . \qquad . \quad (22.3)$$

22.3 This is a fundamental identity and we pause to examine its meaning. The expression on the left in (22.3) is the sum of squares of all values taken about their mean, a quantity which we shall call the *deviance*. If the total number of observations $(=\underset{j}{\Sigma}n_j)$ is N, the deviance is N times the variance of the total number of observations, and no confusion will arise if we call it the *total deviance*.

The first term on the right in (22.3) is the sum of the deviances of each family. Regarding the sum of squares of deviations from a mean as a measure of variability, we may regard this term as expressing the variation *within families*. On the other hand the last term on the right in (22.3) is the sum of squares of means of families about the total mean and may be regarded as expressing the variation *between families*. Thus we have analysed the variation of the whole group into two parts, one expressing variation within families, the other expressing variation from family to family.

22.4 Strictly speaking, perhaps, we ought to call this process an analysis of deviance, but it has become known as the *analysis of variance*. In the particular case when all families contain the same number n, (22.3) simplifies in a way which exhibits how this term came into use. For then

$$\underset{ij}{\Sigma}(x_{ij}-x_{..})^2 = N \text{ var } x = np \text{ var } x$$

$$\underset{j}{\Sigma}n_j(x_{.j}-x_{..})^2 = n\underset{j}{\Sigma}(x_{.j}-x_{..})^2$$

and hence, on substitution in (22.3)

$$\text{var } x = \frac{1}{np} \sum_{i,j} (x_{ij} - x_{.j})^2 + \frac{1}{p} \sum_j (x_{.j} - x_{..})^2 \qquad . \qquad . \qquad (22.4)$$

Now if we write s^2 for the variance of the whole, s_m^2 for the variance of the p family means and s_j^2 for the variance within the jth family, we shall have

$$s^2 = \frac{1}{p} \sum_j (s_j^2) + s_m^2 \qquad . \qquad . \qquad . \qquad . \qquad (22.5)$$

Our total variance is then expressed as the sum of two components, a mean of the variances within families and the variance of the means of families.

22.5 Equation (22.5) should be compared with equation (18.13) to which it is formally equivalent. Our discussion of the sampling variation in non-simple sampling was, in fact, a form of variance-analysis. The effect of sampling from the parts of a " patchy " population is to increase the variance by an amount equal to the variation of the means of patches among themselves.

22.6 Now let us suppose that the p families from which our samples were drawn are not different, i.e., that the data are homogeneous. Then the variance of the whole sample will give us an estimate of the (common) parent variance v. If N is large it makes no practical difference whether we use the actual variance of the sample or the alternative estimate of (21.3) obtained by dividing the deviance by $N-1$; but there are practical as well as theoretical reasons for using (21.3) when the sample is small, and we shall use it in all cases ; that is to say, we shall base our estimates of the variance on the appropriate number of degrees of freedom (**21.8**). An estimate of the parent variance v is then given by

$$\frac{1}{N-1} \sum_{ij} (x_{ij} - x_{..})^2 \qquad . \qquad . \qquad . \qquad . \qquad (22.6)$$

But this is not the only estimate we may derive from the data. On our hypothesis as to homogeneity, the deviances within families provide an estimate when divided by the appropriate number of degrees of freedom. Thus a second estimate is given by

$$\frac{1}{N-p} \sum_{ij} (x_{ij} - x_{.j})^2 \qquad . \qquad . \qquad . \qquad . \qquad (22.7)$$

Finally, the means $x_{.j}$ are distributed with variance v/n_j in virtue of (18.8) and it may be shown—we must omit the proof—that a third estimate of v is given by

$$\frac{1}{p-1} \sum_j n_j (x_{.j} - x_{..})^2 \qquad . \qquad . \qquad . \qquad . \qquad (22.8)$$

22.7 Examination of (22.6), (22.7) and (22.8) will show that the various numerators are the items entering into (22.3), while the degrees of freedom forming the denominators are also additive, i.e.—

$$N-1 = (N-p)+(p-1)$$

We may therefore exhibit our estimates of v in the form of a table as follows :

TABLE 22.1.—Form of variance-analysis for a single independent variable

(1) Deviances relating to variation	(2) Degrees of freedom	(3) Deviances	(4) Estimates of v (Column (3) divided by column (2))
Between families .	$p-1$	$\sum_j n_j (x_{.j}-x_{..})^2$	$\dfrac{1}{p-1} \sum_j n_j (x_{.j}-x_{..})^2$
Within families .	$N-p$	$\sum_{ij} (x_{ij}-x_{.j})^2$	$\dfrac{1}{N-p} \sum_{ij} (x_{ij}-x_{.j})^2$
Total	$N-1$	$\sum_{ij} (x_{ij}-x_{..})^2$	$\dfrac{1}{N-1} \sum_{ij} (x_{ij}-x_{..})^2$

This convenient lay-out enables a check to be made in arithmetical examples from the fact that in columns (2) and (3) the value at the foot is the sum of values in the body of the table. This is not, however, true of column (4).

22.8 Now suppose that we have carried out such an analysis for a particular arithmetical case and derive three estimates v_1, v_2 and v_3 of the parent variance v. If these three values are in reasonably close agreement we see no reason to reject the hypothesis that the families all come from the same population, that the data are homogeneous, or that there are no real differences between family means. On the other hand, if the estimates are different (and significantly so in a sense we shall discuss below) we may reject the hypothesis of homogeneity and conclude that there exist real differences between some or all of the families.

22.9 To make the argument satisfactory we require some criterion to decide when the various estimates are significantly different. This brings us to the second fundamental feature of variance-analysis. If the population is normal the two estimates of variance derived from variation within and between families are independent and their ratio is distributed, independently of the actual value of the parent variance, in the form of (21.16) and hence may be tested in Fisher's z-distribution (**21.26**), or the equivalent F- or variance-ratio distribution.

Note that neither estimate of variance can be independent of the estimate derived from the total variance, for the latter incorporates them both. Our significance test must relate to the ratio of variation between classes to variation within classes.

22.10 We shall not present a proof of the results stated in the previous section but the following line of reasoning will indicate how such a proof may be derived. For normal populations as we have stated, the mean is distributed independently of the variance (**19.17**). On the hypothesis of homogeneity, the means of families are therefore independent of the variances within families ; and consequently the estimate between families, which is derived solely from the means, is independent of the estimate within families, which is obtained by pooling the deviances within families. Hence the fact of independence. That the estimates are distributed like variances follows from an elaboration of the consideration that the mean of normal samples is also normally distributed, so that the variance between families is like a variance of a normal sample ; whereas the variation within families is the sum of deviances and, like χ^2, is additive in the sense that its total is distributed like a constant multiple of a variance.

We proceed to consider two examples, one for large and one for small samples.

Example 22.1.—The following table (from the Registrar-General's *Statistical Review of England and Wales for* 1933, Part II) shows the numbers of males married in England in that year classified according to age and district. (Certain small numbers of unspecified age and those under 21 have been omitted). Note the changes of interval at 25– and 35– years.

TABLE 22.2

District	Age (years)						Totals
	21–	25–	30–	35–	45–	55 and upwards	
South-East . .	31,714	43,979	14,995	7,985	3,928	3,717	106,318
North .	31,507	39,849	13,620	7,108	3,362	2,916	98,362
Midland .	17,465	21,496	6,729	3,340	1,624	1,509	52,153
East . .	4,016	5,297	1,820	962	457	386	12,938
South-West .	4,323	6,065	2,218	1,177	514	580	14,877
Totals	89,025	116,676	39,382	20,572	9,885	9,108	284,648

The question we shall discuss is whether the average age at marriage differs significantly between the different districts, i.e. we take " district " as the independent variable. This, apart from its sociological interest, might be an important point for decision if we were about to carry out a sampling inquiry into some quality which was related to age at marriage, such as numbers of children per family.

Taking the centres of the intervals to be 23, 27·5, 32·5, 40, 50 and 57·5 years (the last being an approximation) we find—

TABLE 22.3

District	Mean age (years)	Degrees of freedom	Sum of squares	Quotient, sum of squares divided by degrees of freedom
South-East . .	29·68	106,317	7,092,490	66·71
North . . .	29·31	98,361	6,092,375	61·94
Midland . .	29·01	52,152	3,105,520	59·55
East . . .	29·43	12,937	807,911	62·44
South-West .	29·87	14,876	1,025,284	68·92
Value for the whole area .	29·43	284,643	18,143,921	63·74

This is not a table in the form of Table 22.1. It merely exhibits the means and estimated variances for the different districts and the area as a whole. We note that the differences between districts are not very large but that the mean age at marriage is higher in the south than the north. Is this significant in the sense that it could not be a sampling effect such as would be obtained if the population were homogeneous?

The sum of squares within classes is obtained as the sum of deviances in the fourth column of the above table and is 18,123,580. This is not the sum shown at the foot, which is the deviance for the whole area and is derived from the figures at the foot of the Table 22.2. The difference between the two, 20,341, is the sum of squares between classes $\Sigma n_j (x_{.j} - x_{..})^2$ as can be checked by direct calculation from the means. We then find—

TABLE 22.4

Variation	Degrees of freedom	Sum of squares	Quotient
Between districts	4	20,341	5085·25
Within districts	284,643	18,123,580	63·67
Totals	284,647	18,143,921	

A test of significance is hardly necessary to show that the quotients are in fact significantly different. But if we wish to apply the z-test we proceed as follows—

We have

$$z = \tfrac{1}{2} \log_e \frac{5085 \cdot 25}{63 \cdot 67} = 2 \cdot 19$$

$$\nu_1 = 4, \; \nu_2 = 284{,}643.$$

From Appendix Table 6C we have, for the $0 \cdot 1$ per cent points for $\nu_1 = 4$

$$(\text{for } \nu_2 = 60) \qquad 0 \cdot 8345$$

$$(\text{for } \nu_2 = \infty) \qquad 0 \cdot 7648$$

The observed value is far greater than these and hence is highly significant. Alternatively $F = 5085 \cdot 25 / 63 \cdot 67 = 8 \cdot 0$ which again is beyond the $0 \cdot 1$ per cent point (Appendix Table 5C). We conclude that the differences in the mean ages between districts, though comparatively small, are not accidental.

Example 22.2.—Table 22.5 shows the yields of 30 plots of barley, there being six plots of each of five varieties. In this table the independent variable is the *variety*, so that rows and columns are interchanged as compared with Table 22.2. Moreover the number of plots for each variety is so small that we do not draw up a frequency distribution giving the number of plots with yields between certain limits (on the principle of Table 22.2) but simply the actual yields of the six plots. We are interested in the question whether there is any significant difference in the mean yields of the different varieties.

TABLE 22.5.—Yield of grain in grammes on plots of barley of one square yard, there being five varieties and six plots of each

The tabular arrangement does not represent the physical lay-out of the plots

(Data quoted by Engledow and Yule, "*The principles and practice of Yield Trials,*" 1926)

Plot number	Variety					Mean
	1	2	3	4	5	
1	387	372	350	340	398	369·4
2	420	455	417	360	358	402·0
3	353	375	400	358	334	364·0
4	331	328	325	370	340	338·8
5	358	383	378	395	320	366·8
6	400	308	275	375	430	357·6
Mean	374·8	370·2	357·5	366·3	363·3	366·4

The mean of the whole is $366 \cdot 4$. The deviance is easily found to be 49,934. As in the calculation of a variance, we take some convenient working mean to simplify the calculation. Similarly we find for the contribution between families, from the means of columns

$$\sum_{ij} (x_{.j}-x_{..})^2 = 6\sum_{j} (x_{.j}-x_{..})^2$$

$$= 6\{ (374\cdot8-366\cdot4)^2+ \ . \ . \ .+(363\cdot3-366\cdot4)^2\}$$

$$= 1043$$

For the sum of squares within classes we merely subtract this quantity from the total deviance. Our analysis of variance then becomes—

TABLE 22.6

Variation	Degrees of freedom	Sum of squares	Quotient
Between varieties .	4	1,043	260·75
Within varieties .	25	42,891	1,715·64
Total	29	43,934	

We have here an interesting case in which the variance between varieties is less than that within varieties. If this effect is real there must be some negative intraclass correlation present, a point to which we return below. To test the significance we have

$$z = \tfrac{1}{2} \log_e \frac{1715\cdot64}{260\cdot75} = 0\cdot942$$

$$\nu_1 = 25, \qquad \nu_2 = 4$$

From Appendix Tables 6A and 6B we see that, for these degrees of freedom the 5 per cent point is $0\cdot876$ and the 1 per cent point $1\cdot31$. The observed value lies between them and is just beyond the 5 per cent point. The result thus is barely significant, i.e. the evidence is weak that there is any real difference between the yields of the different varieties.

Some practical points

22.11 We proceed to consider a few practical points in the analysis and interpretation of variance analysis in the case of a single independent variable.

First of all, as regards the arithmetic. There is no difficulty about determining the number of degrees of freedom, and the only arithmetical labour arises from the determination of the sums of squares. The total deviance is determined exactly as in the calculation of variance. We first find the mean, then, with a convenient working mean, determine the sum of squares about that mean, and finally transfer to the real mean by some such formula as

$$\sum_{ij} (x_{ij}-x_{..})^2 = \sum_{ij} (x_{ij}^2)-Nx_{..}^2 \qquad . \qquad . \qquad . \qquad . \qquad (22.9)$$

which is only (6.4) in a different guise.

The next process is to determine the deviance between families. For this we require the family means $x_{.j}$. Again with a working mean if desired (though, as in Example 22.2, it is not always necessary when there are only a few families) we calculate the contribution $\sum_{j} n_j(x_{.j}-x_{..})^2$. A point to watch here is that each contribution to the sum is weighted by the factor n_j. In the case where all the n's are equal we have

$$\sum_{j} n(x_{.j}-x_{..})^2 = n\sum_{j} (x_{.j}-x_{..})^2$$
$$= n\sum_{j} (x_{.j})^2-Nx_{..}'^2 \qquad . \qquad . \qquad (22.10)$$

The direct determination of the sum of squares within families is a tedious business when the numbers in the families are large and ungrouped. The required quantity can, however, be ascertained by subtraction as in Example 22.2. This sacrifices a check on the arithmetic but is the procedure usually followed.

In the light of these comments the reader should verify the arithmetic of Example 22.2.

We might add that the formal analysis of variance does not relieve the student from the necessity of looking at the data in a general way to make a preliminary comparison. In Example 22.1 we tabulated the means and remarked that they were not very different, even if significantly so. Our work may be regarded as the simultaneous testing of the significance of the differences between a set of means. Any pair of means can be compared by the t-test; we have tested all the differences together.

22.12 Consider now the application of the z-test. Strictly speaking, this is valid only when the parent population is normal. There is some evidence that in the contrary case the test remains valid provided that the departure from normality is not great, as for instance, in a great deal of biological material. But when the departure is considerable, special measures may be necessary to deal with the significance test.

22.13 The reader will observe that the values tabulated in Appendix Tables 6 are all positive, which implies (since z is a logarithm) that in working out a variance ratio we always take the larger value for the numerator. In Example 22.1 we examined the ratio given by (variance between families)/(variance within families) whereas in Example 22.2 we took the reciprocal of this ratio. The general rule is always to take the larger figure as the numerator but this raises a point in connection with the significance test on which it is well to be clear. Our significance values attached to a probability level of P per cent are chosen so that there is probability $P/100$ that the values will be attained or exceeded. The probability that a ratio will attain or exceed a given value k, *or that if it is less than unity its reciprocal will fall below* $1/k$, is $2P/100$, twice the value for either contingency alone. When we are interested in either contingency the probability levels given in the Tables should be doubled.

22.14   Appendix Table 6, will probably be sufficient for most purposes but it is worth recording that for large v_1 and v_2, z is distributed approximately normally with mean $-\frac{1}{2}\left(\dfrac{1}{v_1}-\dfrac{1}{v_2}\right)$ and variance $\frac{1}{2}\left(\dfrac{1}{v_1}+\dfrac{1}{v_2}\right)$. In Example 22.1, for instance, v_2 is so large that we may neglect its reciprocal and, since $v_1=4$ the approximate result leads to the conclusion that z is distributed normally with mean $-0\cdot125$ and standard deviation $0\cdot3535$. The actual value of $2\cdot19$ deviates from the mean by more than six times the standard deviation and is therefore highly significant. In our present example the test is rough because v_1 is not large, but for v_1 and v_2 greater than 30 the approximation is quite good ; and even for lower values it is useful to carry in one's head as a rough guide.

Relationship with intra-class correlation

22.15   In **11.38** we considered the intra-class correlation of a number of families. In the notation of the present chapter equation (11.33) can be written

$$\{1+(n-1)r\}\, s^2 = ns_m^2 \qquad . \qquad . \qquad . \qquad . \quad (22.11)$$

or

$$r = \frac{1}{n-1}\left\{\frac{ns_m^2-s^2}{s^2}\right\}$$

$$= \frac{s_m^2}{s^2} - \frac{1}{n-1}\frac{s^2-s_m^2}{s^2} \qquad . \qquad . \qquad . \quad (22.12)$$

Now s^2 is the variance of the total and is equal to S/np where S is the total deviance. Also s_m^2 is S_1/np where S_1 is the sum of squares between families. Writing S_2 for the sum of squares within families $(=S-S_1)$ we find from (22.12)

$$r = \frac{S_1}{S} - \frac{1}{n-1}\frac{S_2}{S} \qquad . \qquad . \qquad . \quad (22.13)$$

This formula exhibits the relation between intra-class r and the constitutent items of the analysis into sums of squares.

22.16   If now we denote by Q_1 and Q_2 the quotients obtained from S_1 and S_2 we have

$$Q_1 = \frac{S_1}{p-1}$$

$$Q_2 = \frac{S_2}{p(n-1)}$$

From (22.13) we see that r is negative if and only if

$$S_2 > (n-1)S_1$$

which is equivalent to

$$pQ_2 > (p-1)Q_1 \qquad . \qquad . \qquad . \qquad . \quad (22.14)$$

This condition was verified in Example 22.2. It is of rather rare occurrence in practical cases.

Two independent variables

22.17 We now proceed to the case when the data are classified by two qualities A and B, p of one and q of the other, making pq sub-classes in all. We shall consider in the first instance the simple case where there is only one member in each sub-class. We shall denote the value of the member in the ith class of A and the jth class of B by x_{ij}. We then have the algebraic identity

$$\sum_{ij} (x_{ij} - x_{..})^2 = \sum_{ij} \{(x_{ij} - x_{i.} - x_{.j} + x_{..}) + (x_{i.} - x_{..}) + (x_{.j} - x_{..})\}^2$$

$$= \sum_{ij} (x_{ij} - x_{i.} - x_{.j} + x_{..})^2 + \sum_{ij} (x_{i.} - x_{..})^2 + \sum_{ij} (x_{.j} - x_{..})^2 . \quad (22.15)$$

The product terms in the expansion vanish as in the case of the single independent variables discussed in **22.2.** This equation presents an analysis of the total sum of squares into three constituent sums. We state without proof that if all the data are drawn from a population with variance v the three items on the right are estimates of $(p-1)(q-1)v$, $(p-1)v$ and $(q-1)\,v$ respectively and they are independent each of the other two. We may then present an analysis of variance in the following form—

TABLE 22.7.— **Form of analysis of variance for two independent variables with one member in each sub-class**

Variation	Degrees of freedom	Sum of squares	Quotient
Between A-classes .	$p-1$	$\sum_{ij} (x_{i.} - x_{..})^2 = S_1$	$S_1/(p-1)$
Between B-classes .	$q-1$	$\sum_{ij} (x_{.j} - x_{..})^2 = S_2$	$S_2/(q-1)$
Residual .	$(p-1)(q-1)$	$\sum_{ij} (x_{ij} - x_{i.} - x_{.j} + x_{..})^2$ $= S_3$	$S_3/(p-1)(q-1)$
Totals	$pq-1$	$\sum_{ij} (x_{ij} - x_{..})^2$	

The first two items are obvious extensions of the variation between families which we encountered in the one-way case of the single independent variable. The item we have called "residual" in this table has no very obvious interpretation but we may regard it as assignable to variation within the sub-class. Each contributory deviation may be looked on as the remainder when the effect of the classes A and B (if any) is removed. For instance $x_{ij}-x_{i.}$ is the deviation of the value from the mean of values in the ith A-class. The mean of $x_{ij}-x_{i.}$ over the B-classes is $x_{.j}-x_{..}$ and thus $x_{ij}-x_{i.}-(x_{.j}-x_{..})$ is the deviation from the average value obtained by taking means for the A- and B-classes separately.

22.18 If the quotient for A is significantly different from the residual quotient we may conclude that there is heterogeneity so far as concerns A ; and similarly for B. We now meet a new point which did not arise in the case of a single independent variable. Suppose that the significance tests show that the data are heterogeneous in A. Can we then proceed to test for heterogeneity in B ?

The answer in general is no, but there is one class of case in which it is affirmative.

Suppose that the value x_{ij} is made up of three independent and additive parts.

(1) the effect of belonging to the class A_i, say a_i.

(2) the effect of belonging to the class B_j, say b_j.

(3) a residual ξ_{ij}, which is normally distributed with zero mean and variance v.

Then we have

$$x_{ij} = a_i+b_j+\xi_{ij} \qquad . \qquad . \qquad . \qquad . \quad (22.16)$$

The reader should consider this hypothesis carefully. It is equivalent to an assumption that the observations are affected by a systematic effect, a_i, which varies from one A-class to another but affects all B-classes alike in the sub-class A_i ; a similar effect for B ; and the residual normal effect.

22.19 If m_{ij} is the population mean of x_{ij}, $a_.$ that of a_j and so on we have from (22.16)

$$\left. \begin{array}{l} m_{ij} = a_i+b_j \\ m_{i.} = a_i+b_. \\ m_{.j} = a_.+b_j \\ m_{..} = a_.+b_. \end{array} \right\} \qquad . \qquad . \qquad . \qquad . \quad (22.17)$$

Then

$$\Sigma(x_{ij}-x_{i.}-x_{.j}+x_{..})^2 = \Sigma(m_{ij}-m_{i.}-m_{.j}+m_{..}+\xi_{ij}-\xi_{i.}-\xi_{.j}+\xi_{..})^2$$
$$= \Sigma(m_{ij}-m_{i.}-m_{.j}+m_{..})^2+\Sigma(\xi_{ij}-\xi_{i.}-\xi_{.j}+\xi_{..})^2, \qquad . \qquad . \quad (22.18)$$

the product term vanishing as usual. Now from (22.17) it is clear that $m_{ij}-m_{i.}-m_{.j}+m_{..}$ vanishes and hence the right-hand side of (22.18) reduces to its last term. Thus the residual quotient is an estimator of the variance which has just the same value as if a_i and b_j were non-existent. That is to say, on the hypothesis represented by (22.16) the residual quotient continues to offer an estimate of v, the variance of ξ.

It follows that, on this type of hypothesis, even if the A-effects are significant we can still test for the B-effects with the aid of the residual quotient. We may also note that, in any case, if the m_{ij}'s are small, the residual variance is not greatly affected so that an approximate test can be carried out.

Example 22.3.—The following is an example in which the dependent variable is or may be subject to the influence of two independent variables. Four varieties of potato are planted each on five plots of ground of the same size and type ; and each variety is treated with five different fertilisers. The yields in tons are as follows—

TABLE 22.8

Variety	Fertiliser				
	1	2	3	4	5
1	1·9	2·2	2·6	1·8	2·1
2	2·5	1·9	2·3	2·6	2·2
3	1·7	1·9	2·2	2·0	2·1
4	2·1	1·8	2·5	2·3	2·4

We require to consider whether there is evidence that (a) any difference exists between the yields of varieties independently of the fertiliser and (b) any differential effect is exerted by the fertiliser independently of the variety.

Before carrying out an analysis let us look at the data generally. Since each variety is treated once and only once with each fertiliser, we may expect that comparisons of totals for the four varieties are permissible ; the total yield of one variety is comparable with that of another because they are both treated by the different fertilisers to the same extent. Similarly, a comparison of fertiliser effects is legitimate because each variety is equally represented in the five fertiliser totals. The data may be said to be balanced.

It will simplify the arithmetic if we measure our yields about mean 2·0 and express them in tenths of a ton. Table 22.8 then becomes, on the insertion of totals—

TABLE 22.9

Variety	Fertiliser					Total
	1	2	3	4	5	
1	−1	2	6	−2	1	6
2	5	−1	3	6	2	15
3	−3	−1	2	0	1	−1
4	1	−2	5	3	4	11
Totals	2	−2	16	7	8	31

The sum of squares of yields (the 20 values in the main body of the table) will be found to be 191. We then have

$$x_{..} = 31/20 = 1\cdot55$$

$$Nx_{..}^2 = 48\cdot05$$

$$\sum_{ij} (x_{ij}-x_{..})^2 = \sum_{ij} (x_{ij}^2) - Nx_{..}^2 = 191 - 48\cdot05$$
$$= 142\cdot95$$

with $(5\times4)-1 = 19$ degrees of freedom.

We may now obtain the sum of squares between varieties direct from the row totals of the table. These totals are, in fact, five time the means. The sum of squares of means is thus $1/25$ of the sum of squares of row totals; but (and here is a slight trap) each square of a mean is to be counted five times in ascertaining the sum of squares between varieties. Thus the latter quantity is given by the sum of squares of row totals, divided by five, less $Nx_{..}^2$. The sum of squares of row totals in Table 22.9 is 383 and thus the sum of squares between varieties is

$$383/5 - 48\cdot05 = 28\cdot55$$

with three degrees of freedom.

Similarly, the sum of squares of column totals is 377 and hence the sum of squares between fertilisers is

$$377/4 - 48\cdot05 = 46\cdot2$$

with four degrees of freedom.

The analysis of variance then becomes—

TABLE 22.10

Variation	Degrees of freedom	Sums of squares	Quotient
Between fertilisers	4	46·2	11·55
Between varieties	3	28·55	9·52
Residual	12	68·2	5·68
Totals	19	142·95	

To test the effect between fertilisers we have

$$z = \tfrac{1}{2} \log_e \frac{11\cdot55}{5\cdot68} = 0\cdot3545, \; \nu_1 = 4, \; \nu_2 = 12$$

This is not significant, being well below the 5 per cent point. Similarly, for the effect between varieties

$$z = \tfrac{1}{2} \log_e \frac{9\cdot52}{5\cdot68} = 0\cdot2609$$

which again is not significant. A test of the variance-ratio direct leads to the same conclusions.

We conclude that for these data there is no evidence of heterogeneity, i.e. that they could have arisen from a population in which there was no difference between the yields of varieties and the fertilisers did not differ in their effect.

Significance of the correlation ratio

22.20 At this point we turn aside from the development of the general theory to show how the analysis of variance provides accurate tests of significance for the correlation ratio, regression coefficients and the multiple correlation coefficient.

The distribution of η^2 in samples from an *uncorrelated* normal population may be derived from Fisher's z-distribution. Hence we may test whether an observed value of η^2 is significant of the existence of correlation in the parent, assumed normal or approximately so.

When considering the correlation ratio in **11.6** we saw that for the array of x's

$$\sigma_x^2 = \sigma_{ax}^2 + \sigma_{mx}^2$$

where

σ_x^2 is the variance of the whole

σ_{ax}^2 is the variance within arrays

σ_{mx}^2 is the variance of array means

If there are p arrays and n_j is the number of members in the jth array, we may write this in the notation of the present chapter.

$$\Sigma(x_{ij}-x_{..})^2 = \Sigma(x_{ij}-x_{.j})^2 + \Sigma n_j(x_{.j}-x_{..})^2 \qquad . \qquad . \qquad (22.19)$$

Now let us regard the arrays as families or classes, and the items of the arrays as class-members. Equation (22.19) is then an analysis of variance in the following form :

TABLE 22.11

Variation	Degrees of freedom	Sums of squares	Quotients
Between classes . .	$p-1$	$\Sigma\limits_{j} n_j\,(x_{.j}-x_{..})^2$	$\dfrac{N\sigma_x^2\,\eta_{xy}^2}{p-1}$
Within classes . .	$N-p$	$\Sigma\limits_{ij}(x_{ij}-x_{.j})^2$	$\dfrac{N\sigma_x^2(1-\eta_{xy}^2)}{N-p}$
Total . .	$N-1$	$\Sigma\limits_{ij}(x_{ij}-x_{..})^2$	

In the last column we have anticipated results which are easily proved as follows—

By definition,

$$\Sigma(x_{ij}-x_{..})^2 = N\sigma_x^2$$
$$\Sigma(x_{ij}-x_{.j})^2 = N\sigma_{ax}^2 = N\sigma_x^2(1-\eta_{xy}^2)$$

Hence, $\Sigma n_j(x_{.j}-x_{..})^2 = N\sigma_x^2\eta_{xy}^2$

Dividing the sums of squares by the appropriate number of degrees of freedom, we get the results of the final column.

Now, if the population is normal and uncorrelated, the two quotients are not significantly different ; for they are independent estimates of the variance of x in the population, all arrays having the same mean and standard deviation.[1] We may test the significance of their difference by the z-distribution. We have—

$$z = \tfrac{1}{2}\log_e \frac{N\sigma_x^2\eta^2}{p-1} \bigg/ \frac{N\sigma_x^2(1-\eta^2)}{N-p}$$

$$= \tfrac{1}{2}\log_e \frac{\eta^2}{1-\eta^2}\cdot\frac{N-p}{p-1} \qquad . \qquad . \qquad . \qquad (22.20)$$

$$\left.\begin{array}{l} \nu_1 = p-1 \\ \nu_2 = N-p \end{array}\right\} \qquad . \qquad . \qquad . \qquad (22.21)$$

---

[1] Strictly speaking, this is only approximately true of arrays of finite width. If the ranges defining the arrays are very broad, the test must be used with reserve.

In equation (22.20) we have omitted the suffix xy in writing η^2. Clearly a similar test may be applied to η_{yx}^2, p in this case referring to the number of y-arrays.

22.21 From the relation (22.20) between z and η^2 it may be shown that the distribution of η^2, corresponding to that of z given by equation (21.18), is

$$y = y_0(\eta^2)^{\frac{p-3}{2}}(1-\eta^2)^{\frac{N-p-2}{2}} \qquad . \qquad . \qquad . \qquad (22.22)$$

It will be seen that this involves the number p, i.e. depends on the number of arrays into which the data are grouped. This fact is important, and reveals that the use of the standard error $\dfrac{1-\eta^2}{\sqrt{n}}$, given in **19.27**, can be no more than an approximation at the best ; for that formula does not contain p.

22.22 It is interesting to note that, since η^2 is positive, its mean value will not be zero. The mean value (which differs from the square of the mean value of η) is given by

$$\overline{(\eta^2)} = \frac{p-1}{N-1} \qquad . \qquad . \qquad . \qquad (22.23)$$

Example 22.4.—Let us consider the data of Table 9.3 (correlation between stature of father and stature of son), in which $\eta_{xy} = \eta_{yx} = 0.52$. We know that the distribution is approximately normal, a fact which is borne out by the approximate equality of the two correlation ratios, and hence we may apply the foregoing theory with considerable confidence.

We have, for η_{yx}—

$$\nu_1 = p-1 = 16$$
$$\nu_2 = N-p = 1078-17 = 1061$$
$$z = \tfrac{1}{2}\log_e\frac{(0.52)^2}{1-(0.52)^2}\cdot\frac{1061}{16} = 1.60$$

From Appendix Table 6C we see that the 0.1 per cent significance points are as follows—

	$\nu_1 = 12$	$\nu_1 = 24$
$\nu_2 = 60$	0.5992	0.4955
$\nu_2 = \infty$	0.5044	0.3786

The observed z is therefore very strongly significant of correlation in the population.

Test of linearity of regression

22.23 In **11.7** we saw that the regression of y on x was linear if, and only if, $\eta_{yx}^2 - r^2 = 0$. An important question to decide is, therefore, can an observed value of $\eta^2 - r^2$ have arisen from a population in which the regression is linear, i.e. the true value is zero ?

This question can be decided by the z–test in a similar manner to that of **22.20** and **22.21**. We consider the analysis of the sums of squares of deviations from the regression line into two parts : (1) deviations within arrays, and (2) deviations of means of arrays from the regression line. In this way it may be shown that the linearity may be tested by taking

$$z = \tfrac{1}{2} \log_e \frac{\eta^2 - r^2}{1 - \eta^2} \cdot \frac{N - p}{p - 2} \qquad \qquad . \qquad (22.24)$$

$$\left. \begin{array}{l} \nu_1 = p - 2 \\ \nu_2 = N - p \end{array} \right\} \qquad . \qquad . \qquad . \qquad (22.25)$$

Example 22.5.—In considering the correlation between old age, pauperism (x) and the proportion of out-relief (y), Yule found (*Economic Journal*, 1896, **6**, 613)

$$N = 235$$

$$r = +0 \cdot 34$$

$$\eta_{xy} = \ 0 \cdot 46$$

$$\eta_{yx} = \ 0 \cdot 39$$

for a grouping of 19 x-arrays and 8 y-arrays. Can the regressions be supposed linear ?

For the x-arrays, $\qquad N - p = 216, \qquad p - 2 = 17$

$$\therefore \quad \frac{\eta^2 - r^2}{1 - \eta^2} = \frac{(0 \cdot 46)^2 - (0 \cdot 34)^2}{1 - (0 \cdot 46)^2} = 0 \cdot 12177$$

$$z = \tfrac{1}{2} \log_e \left(0 \cdot 12177 \times \frac{216}{17} \right)$$

$$= 0 \cdot 218$$

The 5 per cent point for $\nu_1 = 17$, $\nu_2 = \infty$, is about $0 \cdot 25$, and there is thus no reason to suppose from the observed z that the regression is not linear. Alternatively for the variance ratio F we find

$$\frac{(216 \times 0 \cdot 12177)}{17} = 1 \cdot 55$$

For the y-arrays, similarly, $p - 2 = 6$.

$$z = \tfrac{1}{2} \log_e \left(\frac{(0 \cdot 39)^2 - (0 \cdot 34)^2}{1 - (0 \cdot 39)^2} \cdot \frac{227}{6} \right)$$

$$= 0 \cdot 244$$

This also will be found to lie within the sampling limits, and the test therefore does not reject the linearity of either regression.

Significance of the multiple correlation coefficient

22.24 The multiple correlation coefficient is in many ways analogous to the correlation ratio, and we may test its significance by a procedure very similar to that used for the significance of the correlation ratio and regressions.

Consider the regression equation with p variates,

$$x_1 = b_2 x_2 + b_3 x_3 + \ldots + b_p x_p$$

the variates being measured from their means.

We may regard the deviations of observed values of x_1 as composed of two parts : (1) deviations from the values of x_1 given by the regression equation, and (2) deviations of the latter from the mean of x_1. The sum of squares can be analysed accordingly.

The sum of squares of deviations of observed values of x_1 from the mean of $x_1 = N\sigma_1{}^2$, by definition, and has $N-1$ degrees of freedom.

The sum of squares of deviations of observed x_1's from the regression values is $N\sigma_{1.2\ldots p}^2$ which, by the definition of $R_{1(2\ldots p)}$, is equal to $N\sigma_1{}^2(1 - R_{1(2\ldots p)}^2)$. This has $N-p$ degrees of freedom, for $\sigma_1{}^2$ has $N-1$ degrees of freedom, $\sigma_{1.2}^2$ has $N-2$ degrees, and so on. Writing R for $R_{1(2\ldots p)}$, we may express the analysis in the following tabular form :—

TABLE 22.12

Variation	Degrees of freedom	Sums of squares	Quotients
Between classes . . (Regression values from mean.)	$p-1$	$R^2 N\sigma_1{}^2$	$\dfrac{R^2}{p-1} \cdot N\sigma_1{}^2$
Within classes . . (Deviations from regression values.)	$N-p$	$(1-R^2)N\sigma_1{}^2$	$\dfrac{1-R^2}{N-p} \cdot N\sigma_1{}^2$
Total . .	$N-1$	$N\sigma_1{}^2$	

Now if the parent value of R is zero, the quotients should not differ significantly ; for x_1 and $b_2 x_2 + \ldots + b_p x_p$ are then uncorrelated, and hence deviations of x from the regression values are uncorrelated with, and independent of, deviations of the regression values from the mean, the population being normal.

Hence we may test the significance of R by putting

$$z = \tfrac{1}{2} \log_e \frac{R^2}{1-R^2} \cdot \frac{N-p}{p-1} \qquad . \qquad . \qquad . \quad (22.26)$$

$$\left. \begin{array}{l} \nu_1 = p-1 \\ \nu_2 = N-p \end{array} \right\} \qquad . \qquad . \qquad . \quad (22.27)$$

It will be seen that equation (22.24) is of the same form as equation (22.20). The distributions of R^2 and η^2 are formally identical, and we have, for instance, corresponding to equation (22.23),

$$\overline{(R^2)} = \frac{p-1}{N-1} \qquad . \qquad . \qquad . \quad (22.28)$$

Example 22.6.—In Example 12.3, page 299, we found $R_{1(23)}=0\cdot74$. Is this significant ?
We have—

$$p = 3, \qquad N = 38$$

$$\nu_1 = 2, \qquad \nu_2 = 35$$

$$z = \tfrac{1}{2} \log_e \left(\frac{(0\cdot74)^2}{1-(0\cdot74)^2} \cdot \frac{35}{2} \right)$$

$$= 1\cdot53$$

For $\nu_1=2$, the $0\cdot1$ per cent significance points are—

$$\nu_2 = 30 \qquad 1\cdot0859$$

$$\nu_2 = 40 \qquad 1\cdot0552$$

The observed z is well above these values and hence R is significant.

Unequal numbers in classes

22.25 The treatment given in **22.16** to the case of two independent variates was based on the assumption that there was only one member in each sub-class. In the contrary case an accurate treatment is much more difficult and we shall not be able to deal with it here. The following remarks are intended as a preliminary to further reading—

(a) If the number in each sub-class is the same the foregoing theory still applies.

(b) The theory also applies if the numbers in sub-classes are proportionate, that is to say, if the frequency in the sub-class $A_i B_j$ is a constant multiple of $(A_i) (B_j)$ where (A_i) and (B_j) are the frequencies in the classes A_i and B_j respectively.

(c) In other cases the theory does not apply ; but if the numbers in sub-classes are not very different from equality or proportionality, an analysis carried out on the means of sub-classes as if they were the primary data, one to each sub-class, will probably not be misleading, although it sacrifices some information.

(d) In any case a $p \times q$ classification with more than one member in the sub-classes can always be regarded as a one-way classification into pq classes. An analysis on these lines will provide a test of homogeneity but does not distinguish, as it were, whether departures from homogeneity are due to A or B or to a mixture of both.

Non-normal variation

22.26 Some comments are also desirable, though again the matter is too complicated for detailed treatment, on the assumptions of normality which underlie the exact treatment of significance tests in the analysis of variance. When the parent population is not normal estimates of means are not independent of variances, so that the quotients given by the analysis are dependent. Further, the logarithm of the variance-ratio is no longer distributed in the z-form. We have already referred to the fact that sampling and theoretical inquiries suggest that if deviations from normality are only moderate, the theory still applies as an approximation. Sometimes the variate may be transformed so as to bring it nearer to normality or the variances in the different classes nearer to equality. In certain cases, by a process of randomisation before the data are collected, it may be ensured that the z-test remains valid even where the parent is not normal, though this amounts to a change in the nature of the inference. These topics, however, are outside the scope of this book.

The case of three independent variables

22.27 The results appropriate to two independent variables may be extended. The general case of n independent variables is rather complicated and indeed data so completely specified for n greater than three are rare. We shall conclude this chapter by stating without proof the results for three independent variables, commenting on one or two new points, and giving an example.

Consider then the case where there are three classifications into A-, B- and C- classes, one member in each sub-class typified by x_{ijk}. With an obvious generalisation of previous results we have (summation extending over all i, j, k)

$$
\begin{aligned}
\Sigma(x_{ijk}-x_{...})^2 = {} & \Sigma(x_{i..}-x_{...})^2+\Sigma(x_{.j.}-x_{...})^2+\Sigma(x_{..k}-x_{...})^2 \\
& + \Sigma(x_{ij.}-x_{i..}-x_{.j.}+x_{...})^2+\Sigma(x_{i.k}-x_{i..}-x_{..k}+x_{...})^2 \\
& + \Sigma(x_{.jk}-x_{..k}-x_{.j.}+x_{...})^2 \\
& + \Sigma(x_{ijk}-x_{ij.}-x_{i.k}-x_{.jk}+x_{i..}+x_{.j.}+x_{..k}-x_{...})^2
\end{aligned}
\right\} \quad (22.29)
$$

the summations extending over all members of the sample, say pqr in number, where there are p A-classes, q B-classes and r C-classes.

Each item on the right in (22.29) provides an estimate of the parent variance on the hypothesis of homogeneity. The first three items are of the type "between classes" which we have already encountered. The next three are known as *interaction terms*. The last is a residual and may also be regarded as an interaction of second order. We have then an analysis in the following form.

TABLE 22.13.—Form of analysis of variance for three independent variables with one member in each sub-class

Variation	Degrees of freedom	Sums of squares	Residual
Between A-classes .	$p-1$	$\Sigma(x_{i..}-x_{...})^2$	The quotient of the sum of squares by the corresponding number of degrees of freedom
,, B-classes .	$q-1$	$\Sigma(x_{.j.}-x_{...})^2$	
,, C-classes .	$r-1$	$\Sigma(x_{..k}-x_{...})^2$	
Interaction AB	$(p-1)(q-1)$	$\Sigma(x_{ij.}-x_{.j.}-x_{i..}+x_{...})^2$	
,, BC .	$(q-1)(r-1)$	$\Sigma(x_{.jk}-x_{..k}-x_{.j.}+x_{...})^2$	
,, CA .	$(r-1)(p-1)$	$\Sigma(x_{i.k}-x_{..k}-x_{i..}+x_{...})^2$	
Residual .	$(p-1)(q-1)$ $(r-1)$	$\Sigma(x_{ijk}+x_{i..}+x_{.j.}+x_{..k}$ $-x_{ij.}-x_{i.k}-x_{.jk}-x_{...})^2$	
Totals .	$pqr-1$	$\Sigma(x_{ijk}-x_{...})^2$	

22.28 As in **22.18** and **22.19**, if the variate x_{ijk} is regarded as the sum of three class effects a_i, b_j and c_k and a normal residual ξ_{ijk}, the residual quotient continues to provide an estimate of the variance of ξ. It is therefore customary to test the quotients between classes in relation to the residual quotient.

We also have, however, three interaction quotients which, on the hypothesis of homogeneity, should also be equal, within sampling limits, to the residual quotient. If the interaction quotient AB is not equal, within such limits, to the residual we must reject the hypothesis that the variation can be expressed as the sum of the two class effects a_i and b_j. The class effects are, so to speak, entangled, or they "interact." Similarly for the other two interactions.

Example 22.7.—The following example typifies a situation of fairly general occurrence but has been simplified somewhat to reduce the arithmetic. Suppose we have two manurial treatments which we wish to test. We will suppose that they are each applied to five varieties of a cereal, and that, to give the experiment greater generality, it is repeated at four different stations. Our 40 yields are then classified into a $4 \times 5 \times 2$ grouping, four stations, five varieties and two treatments. We will suppose that the yields, measured about some convenient working mean, and expressed in some convenient unit, are as given in Table 22.14, wherein T_1 and T_2 refer to the two treatments.

TABLE 22.14

Stations	Varieties 1		2		3		4		5		Totals	
	T_1	T_2	T_1	T_2	T_1	T_2	T_1	T_2	T_1	T_2	T_1	T_2
1	−6	−4	−4	−2	−10	−7	−3	−5	1	0	−22	−18
2	−2	−1	−5	−1	−3	−4	−4	−1	−2	1	−16	− 6
3	3	2	−2	3	−4	0	4	1	3	3	4	9
4	3	6	3	2	6	3	−1	5	6	8	17	24
Totals	−2	3	−8	2	−11	−8	−4	0	8	12	−17	9

The sum of squares of the 40 values in the main body of the table will be found to be 640. Thus we have

$$
\begin{aligned}
x_{...} &= -8/40 = -0\cdot20 \\
Nx_{...}^2 &= 1\cdot6 \\
\Sigma(x_{ijk}-x_{...})^2 &= 640-1\cdot6 \\
&= 638\cdot4
\end{aligned}
\qquad (a)
$$

Now we find the sum of squares between stations (S), varieties (V), and treatments separately. The yields for the four stations are the totals of the two columns on the right in Table 22.14, namely, -40, -22, 13, 41. The sum of squares of these values is 3934. Now (the first suffix referring to S)

$$
\underset{i,j,k}{\Sigma} (x_{i..} - x_{...})^2 = \underset{i,j,k}{\Sigma} x_{i..}^2 - Nx_{...}^2
\qquad (b)
$$

In the column totals there are $5 \times 2 = 10$ members contributing to the sum; but the summation on the right in (b) takes place over the four stations and the $5 \times 2 = 10$ members for each station. Thus

$$
\begin{aligned}
\underset{i,j,k}{\Sigma} x_{i..}^2 &= 10 \underset{i}{\Sigma} x_{i..}^2 \\
&= \frac{10}{10^2} \underset{i}{\Sigma} y_i^2
\end{aligned}
$$

where the y's are the totals,

$$
= 393\cdot4
$$

Thus

$$
\underset{i,j,k}{\Sigma} (x_{i..} - x_{...})^2 = 393\cdot4-1\cdot6
\qquad (c)
$$
$$
= 391\cdot8
$$

and this gives the sum of squares between stations.

Generally, if we require the sum of squares between p-classes in a $p \times q \times r$ classification we have

$$\sum_{i,j,k} (x_{i..} - x_{...})^2 = \frac{1}{qr} \sum_i (y_i^2) - Nx_{..}^2$$

The five totals of varieties are 1, -6, -19, -4, 20 with a sum of squares equal to 814. Thus for the sum of squares between varieties we have

$$\frac{814}{2 \times 4} - 1 \cdot 6 = 100 \cdot 15 \qquad . \qquad . \qquad . \qquad (d)$$

We leave the student to check as an exercise that the sum of squares between treatments is 16·9. $\qquad . \qquad . \qquad . \qquad . \qquad . \qquad (e)$

Now we have to find the interaction terms. For this purpose it is most convenient to condense the primary Table 22.14 into three others, of which we will write down one. If we add the yields for the two treatments on any particular variety and station, we obtain the following—

Stations	Varieties					Totals
	1	2	3	4	5	
1	-10	-6	-17	-8	1	-40
2	-3	-6	-7	-5	-1	-22
3	5	1	-4	5	6	13
4	9	5	9	4	14	41
Totals	1	-6	-19	-4	20	-8

The sum of squares of values in the main body of the table will be found to be 1112. Each entry is the sum of two values and, with an obvious extension of previous results we have

$$\sum_{i,j,k,} (x_{ij.} - x_{...})^2 = \frac{1112}{2} - 1 \cdot 6 = 554 \cdot 4 \qquad . \qquad . \qquad (f)$$

Now for the interaction $S\,V$ we have

$$\sum (x_{ij.} - x_{i..} - x_{.j.} + x_{...})^2 = \sum (x_{ij.} - x_{...})^2 - \sum (x_{i..} - x_{...})^2 - \sum (x_{.j.} - x_{...})^2$$

Substituting from (f), (c) and (d) we have on the right

$$554 \cdot 4 - 391 \cdot 8 - 100 \cdot 15$$

$$= 62 \cdot 45 \qquad . \qquad . \qquad . \qquad . \qquad (g)$$

which is the required interaction sum of squares for $S\,V$.

Again we leave the student to calculate the other two interactions to obtain that for VT as $3\cdot85$ and that for TS as $2\cdot10$. We have finally (the residual sum of squares being calculated by subtracting the sum of the other terms from the total deviance)—

TABLE 22.15.—Analysis of variance of Table 22.14

Variation	Degrees of freedom	Sum of squares	Quotient
Between stations (S) .	3	391·80	130·60
Between varieties (V) .	4	100·15	25·04
Between treatments (T) .	1	16·90	16·90
Interaction SV . .	12	62·45	5·20
,, VT . .	4	3·85	0·96
,, ST . .	3	2·10	0·70
Residual . . .	12	61·15	5·10
Total .	39	638·40	

Now we first of all test our interactions against the residual term with a quotient of $5\cdot10$ and 12 degrees of freedom. We find in fact that they are not significant to a 5 per cent level. This implies that we may assume that there is no " entanglement " between the factors and that there is support for the hypothesis that the three are affecting yields independently. We can then turn to a consideration of the main effects.

We find that the differences between stations are highly significant, those between varieties are not significant at a 1 per cent level but are so at a 5 per cent level, and that differences between treatments are not significant. We conclude that the variation in yields is due to variation between stations and (perhaps) between varieties, but cannot be ascribed to real differential effects between treatments without further inquiry.

SUMMARY

1. The analysis of variance is essentially a procedure for testing the differences between different groups of data for homogeneity.

2. For a single independent variable (classification into groups according to one quality) an analysis may be carried out to show estimates of the variance between and within classes whether the class-numbers are equal or not. Homogeneity may be tested by comparing the estimates.

3. For small samples and normal parent variation the ratio of between- and within–class variance may be tested in Fisher's z-distribution.

4. For classification according to more than one quality a more elaborate form of analysis may be employed. The method applies only when the numbers in sub-classes are equal (or more generally, proportionate) but is probably a fair approximation when they are near equality.

5. The exact test of significance does not apply to non-normal variation except as an approximation, but where departure from normality is not great, the approximation is probably fair.

6. The analysis of variance provides exact tests of significance (in the case of normal variation) for the correlation ratio, departure from linearity of regression, and the multiple correlation coefficient.

EXERCISES

22.1 The following shows the lives in hours of four batches of electric lamps—

     Batch 1 :   1600, 1610, 1650, 1680, 1700, 1720, 1800

     Batch 2 :   1580, 1640, 1640, 1700, 1750

     Batch 3 :   1460, 1550, 1600, 1620, 1640, 1660, 1740, 1820

     Batch 4 :   1510, 1520, 1530, 1570, 1600, 1680.

Perform an analysis of variance on these data and show that a significance test does not reject their homogeneity.

22.2 Considering two samples as two families of values, derive an explicit form for the ratio of estimated variances between and within families and hence derive the t-test for the difference of means in normal samples with equal variances as given in **21.21**. (The distribution of the variance-ratio for $\nu_1 = 1$ reduces to that of t^2).

22.3 Four experimenters determine the moisture content of samples of a powder, each man taking a sample from each of six consignments. Their assessments are—

Observer	Consignment					
	1	2	3	4	5	6
1	9	10	9	10	11	11
2	12	11	9	11	10	10
3	11	10	10	12	11	10
4	12	13	11	14	12	10

Perform an analysis of variance on these data and discuss whether there is any significant difference between consignments or between observers.

22.4 Verify the arithmetic and the significance tests of Example 22.7.

22.5 Test the significance of the two multiple correlation coefficients of Example 12.3, page 299, other than the one tested in Example 22.6.

22.6 Test the linearity of the regression of the distribution of cows of Table 9.4, page 204 (referring to Exercise 13.1).

22.7 Examine how, in the analysis of variance, sums of squares between classes may be regarded as interactions of zero order and (in the case of three independent variables) the residual may be regarded as an interaction of the second order.

22.8 (Data from Mahalanobis, *J. R. Statist. Soc.*, 1946, **109**, 325). The following table shows estimates of an index of the cost of living in an area of Bengal in 1945 made by five investigators each working in each of five areas.

Investigator	Area				
	1	2	3	4	5
1	270	263	264	263	260
2	280	265	274	274	279
3	275	284	278	271	296
4	271	269	272	297	274
5	279	267	269	263	284

Perform an analysis of variance to see whether there are significant differences between areas and between investigators.

CHAPTER TWENTY-THREE

SOME PROBLEMS OF PRACTICAL SAMPLING

23.1 In the previous seven chapters we have discussed the interpretation of samples and developed various branches of theory which are designed to give precision, in the sense of the theory of probability, to inferences drawn from the sample to the population. At the outset (Chapter 16) we considered briefly the types of sampling to which our theory is applicable, noting in particular the fundamental importance of randomness in the selection of data. We shall now examine in more detail some of the problems arising in the selection of samples to which our theory may apply.

23.2 The complete process of sampling consists in effect of three stages, there being considerable scope for judgment at each stage.

(1) If there is no natural unit, and often even if there is, we have to decide what shall be our unit *for the purposes of sampling*. If our problem is, for example, to determine the mean yield per acre of a certain crop over a certain large area, there is no natural unit of area over which the yield can be measured at each of n points in the large area. We must therefore fall back on practical considerations to decide whether our sampling unit shall be something very small, say a square yard, something a good deal bigger, say 1/10th acre, or something larger still, such as an acre or more. If, on the other hand, the problem is to estimate by way of sampling the proportion of a certain human population possessing a certain characteristic, such as blue eyes, or surname beginning with H, or age under 21, the natural unit is the person ; but this, as we shall see presently, is not necessarily the most convenient unit for sampling purposes.

(2) The unit having been fixed, the next step is to decide what shall be the process of sampling : if it is agreed that the process should be a random one, how is this randomness best secured ? If it appears possible that some departure from unrestricted random sampling may lessen the cost, or may even lower the standard error of estimation, what then shall be the procedure and will this procedure carry with it any countervailing risks ? How are we to treat the cases in which a member that we intended to include cannot be found or, if found, will not provide a reply ?

(3) The sample having been taken, i.e. the specific units to be included in the sample having been determined, the final stage of the work is the measurement, description, or (to use the term in a very general sense)

what we may call the *examination* of the units included in the sample. Properly speaking, this is no part at all of the *sampling* process in the narrower sense ; that was completed when we had determined which specific members of the population were to be included in the sample. Examination of the units is a process of observation such as we would have had to carry out even if we had decided to deal with the entire population and not a mere sample.   But it is a process fundamental to our work and must be considered here, for careless or incompetent " examination " may lead to the most serious, and sometimes astonishing, errors.

We will consider these three stages in the order given, as this will couple the work of the present chapter most closely and logically with that of the preceding chapters.

Size of the sampling unit

Example 23.1.—*Effect of size of unit on bias*

We take, first of all, an example illustrating the importance of the sampling unit in some types of inquiry.   In an investigation into the yield of jute in Bengal in 1940-41 (Mahalanobis, *J. Roy. Stat. Soc.*, 1946, **109**, 325) material was collected for five different sizes of sample-cut from the fields, ranging from one square foot to 256 square feet.   In each field (which was selected at random) an area of 16×16 feet was chosen, also at random, and the crop was harvested in a number of sub-cuts supplying yield rates for the sizes : 1×1, 3×3, 12×4, 12×12 and 16×16 feet, the latter being the whole plot.   The following are the estimates of the yield in lb. per acre based on the various plot sizes—

Size (ft.)	Estimated yield (lb. per acre)	
1×1	27,271	,,
3×3	17,462	,,
12×4	16,080	,,
12×12	16,763	,,
16×16	16,828	,,

Evidently the estimates based on the two smallest sizes of plot are seriously biased.   In this particular case it was easily shown that the differences could not have been sampling effects.

The reason for this effect is not yet beyond doubt, but apparently it is due to unconscious bias on the part of the observer, who, in measuring out the plot, has a tendency to include rather than to exclude plants on land near the boundary.   This effect naturally diminishes in proportion as the plot becomes larger.   The remedy in this case is clear ; it is simply not to use plots which are too small.

23.3   For all practical purposes the case we have just considered may be regarded as one in which the area covered is continuous, so that there is no " unit " indicated by the nature of the data.   We could, it is true, regard the individual plant as the ultimate unit ; but for practical reasons we cannot, in an extensive inquiry, bother ourselves with the selection of plants. We must select fairly large areas, and the question then arises how the size of those areas is to be determined. In Example 23.1 the bias appearing for very small areas dictated a lower limit to the proper size but did not suggest an upper limit.

23.4 Even for discontinuous units the same type of question can arise. Suppose, for example, we are sampling a country for the purpose of determining the size of population or some similar demographic characteristic such as would be given by a census. The ultimate unit is the individual human being, but it may be very troublesome to pick out individuals at random. Shall we lose anything by sampling with families as units, or houses, or streets, or blocks or even whole wards ? Again, in an agricultural inquiry, do we lose anything by taking as our unit the farm instead of the individual field ?

23.5 Such questions rarely admit of a simple answer. In general there will be a group of considerations in favour of choosing as large a unit as possible and another group in favour of choosing a small one. Among those of the first kind we may mention economy (e.g. because less time and travelling are involved if the individuals are grouped and have to be visited, or because information has already been tabulated for the larger units). Among those of the second are the desirability of not clustering sample-members too closely when the population is thought to be " patchy ". Additional complications may arise when our " units " are of different sizes, such as farms, for then there is some intuitive ground for feeling that the different units ought to be given varying weights. When the sizes of the units are known we can sometimes deal with the problem as one of stratification, which we consider below, but there are some rather complicated points arising in this branch of the subject which have not yet been completely solved.

Some sampling procedures

23.6 We shall now consider some sampling procedures which depend for their efficacy on prior knowledge of the population. When nothing is known about the population a purely random selection of members is the best. It avoids bias and can be made to provide information about the standard errors of the quantities under estimate. Only rarely, however, do we embark on an inquiry in complete ignorance about the parent population. Our knowledge may be only vague and general, but even so we can often apply it to improve the precision of our estimates. Moreover, it is often highly inconvenient and expensive to draw a purely random sample from a large existent population (e.g. by the use of random sampling numbers) and practical necessity may dictate a modification of the random process even though no theoretical gain in accuracy or precision may result.

Stratified sampling

23.7   We referred briefly in **16.39** to the process of stratification, in which we divide the population into strata and draw a random sample of specified size from each stratum.   Sometimes our stratification may be a purely geographical basis, as for example if, in sampling farms from England, we decide to draw a certain proportion from each individual county.   Sometimes it may be by reference to a variate-value, as when we decide to draw certain numbers of farms in certain size groups irrespective of their geographical position.   The operation of stratification may be undertaken either to improve the value of an estimate or merely for administrative convenience.   If the strata are determined by some " natural " factor the sampling process by stratification will also facilitate comparison of the strata among themselves, which may be a subsidiary object of the inquiry.

Sampling fractions

23.8   Suppose we have a population stratified into k strata, the number in the ith stratum being N_i and the total number $(\Sigma(N_i))$ being N.   We take a sample of n members such that the number chosen from the ith stratum is n_i.   Suppose that we desire to estimate the mean value α of a variate x in the whole population.   How shall we choose the numbers n_i?

We shall assume that if x_{ij} is the jth member of the sample of n_i, the estimate is of the form

$$t = \sum_{i=1}^{k} \sum_{j=1}^{n_i} (\lambda_{ij} x_{ij}) \qquad . \qquad . \qquad . \qquad . \qquad (23.1)$$

where the λ's are constants to be determined.   This assumption may be expressed by saying that we are looking for a *linear* estimate.   Among all the possible estimating functions of this kind we shall seek the one which has the smallest variance.   There are obvious advantages in an estimate with the minimum of sampling fluctuation.

If the mean value of x_{ij} in the ith stratum is α_i we have

$$\alpha = \frac{1}{N} \sum_{i=1}^{k} N_i \alpha_i \qquad . \qquad . \qquad . \qquad . \qquad (23.2)$$

Thus, writing E to denote the taking of a mean value we have, from (23.1) and (23.2)

$$E\left\{ \sum_{i,j} (\lambda_{ij} x_{ij}) \right\} = \frac{1}{N} \sum_{i=1}^{k} N_i \alpha_i \qquad . \qquad . \qquad . \qquad (23.3)$$

and since, by definition $E(x_{ij}) = \alpha_i$ we have

$$\sum_{i=1}^{k} \left\{ \alpha_i \left(\sum_{j=1}^{n_i} \lambda_{ij} - \frac{N_i}{N} \right) \right\} = 0 \qquad . \qquad . \qquad . \qquad (23.4)$$

If this is to be generally true independently of particular values of α_i we must have

$$\sum_{j=1}^{n_i} \lambda_{ij} = \frac{N_i}{N} \qquad . \qquad . \qquad . \qquad . \qquad (23.5)$$

This provides a first condition on the λ's in order that the estimate may have the true value as its mean value—that it should be unbiased in a sense we define in **23.17**. If $\lambda_{i.}$ is the mean of λ_{ij} in the ith set we may write this as

$$\lambda_{i.} = \frac{N_i}{n_i N} \qquad . \qquad . \qquad . \qquad . \qquad (23.6)$$

Now consider the condition that the variance of t shall be a minimum. Since E denotes a mean value we have for the ith stratum

$$\text{var} \sum_{j=1}^{n_i} (\lambda_{ij} x_{ij}) = E\left[\sum_j \left\{\lambda_{ij}(x_{ij} - \alpha_i)\right\}\right]^2$$

This is equal to

$$E\left[\sum_j \lambda_{ij}^2 (x_{ij} - \alpha_i)^2 + \sum_{j,l}' \lambda_{ij}\lambda_{il}(x_{ij} - \alpha_i)(x_{il} - \alpha_i)\right]$$

where Σ' denotes summation over values of j and l except those for which $j = l$. If the variance of x_{ij} in the ith stratum is σ_i^2 this is equal to

$$\sum_j \lambda_{ij}^2 \sigma_i^2 + \sum_{j,l}' \{\lambda_{ij}\lambda_{il} E(x_{ij} - \alpha_i)(x_{il} - \alpha_i)\} \qquad . \qquad . \qquad . \qquad (23.7)$$

Now since there are $N_i(N_i - 1)$ values for which $j \neq l$

$$E(x_{ij} - \alpha_i)(x_{il} - \alpha_i) = \frac{1}{N_i(N_i - 1)}\left[\left\{\sum_{j=1}^{N_i}(x_{ij} - \alpha_i)\right\}^2 - \sum_{j=1}^{N_i}(x_{ij} - \alpha_i)^2\right]$$

$$= -\frac{1}{N_i(N_i - 1)}\sum_{j=1}^{N_i}(x_{ij} - \alpha_i)^2$$

$$= -\frac{\sigma_i^2}{N_i - 1} \qquad . \qquad . \qquad . \qquad . \qquad (23.8)$$

From (23.7) and (23.8) we then have

$$\text{var } \Sigma_{j}(\lambda_{ij}x_{ij}) = \Sigma_{j}\lambda_{ij}\sigma_{i}^{2} - \Sigma'_{j,l} \lambda_{ij}\lambda_{il}\frac{\sigma_{i}^{2}}{N_{i}-1}$$

$$= \frac{\sigma_{i}^{2}}{N_{i}-1}\left\{N_{i}\Sigma_{j}\lambda_{ij}^{2} - (\Sigma_{j}\lambda_{ij})^{2}\right\}$$

$$= \frac{\sigma_{i}^{2}}{N_{i}-1}\left\{N_{i}\Sigma_{j}(\lambda_{ij}-\lambda_{i.})^{2} + 2N_{i}\Sigma_{j}\lambda_{ij}\lambda_{i.}\right.$$

$$\left. -N_{i}\Sigma_{j}\lambda^{2}_{i.} - n_{i}^{2}\lambda_{i.}^{2}\right\}$$

$$= \frac{\sigma_{i}^{2}}{N_{i}-1}\left\{N_{i}\Sigma_{j}(\lambda_{ij}-\lambda_{i.})^{2}\right.$$

$$\left. +n_{i}(N_{i}-n_{i})\lambda_{i.}^{2}\right\} \qquad . \qquad . \qquad (23.9)$$

Now t is the sum of k items, each of which comes from a different stratum and is therefore independent of the others. Consequently the variance of t is the sum of the constituent variances, i.e. is the sum over i of the expression on the right in (23.9). This is clearly a minimum if, for all i

$$\lambda_{ij}-\lambda_{i.} = 0 \qquad . \qquad . \qquad . \qquad (23.10)$$

This is equivalent to saying that within any substratum the λ's must be equal, which is what we should expect, for there is no reason why one should be greater than another.

We then have

$$\text{var } t = \sum_{i=1}^{k} \frac{\sigma_{i}^{2}(N_{i}-n_{i})}{N_{i}-1}n_{i}\lambda_{i.}^{2}$$

$$= \frac{1}{N^{2}}\Sigma_{i}\frac{\sigma_{i}^{2}(N_{i}-n_{i})}{N_{i}-1}\frac{N_{i}^{2}}{n_{i}}$$

$$= \frac{1}{N^{2}}\Sigma_{i}\frac{N_{i}^{3}\sigma_{i}^{2}}{(N_{i}-1)n_{i}} + \text{constant} \qquad . \qquad (23.11)$$

We have to minimise this for variations in n_i subject to

$$\Sigma\, n_{i} = n = \text{constant} \qquad . \qquad . \qquad . \qquad (23.12)$$

It may easily be shown by the use of differential calculus that the minimal values of n_i are given by

$$n_{i}^{2} \propto \frac{N_{i}^{3}}{N_{i}-1}\sigma_{i}^{2} \qquad . \qquad . \qquad . \qquad (23.13)$$

If now N_i is large we have approximately

$$n_i^2 \propto N_i^2 \sigma_i^2 \quad . \quad . \quad . \quad . \quad . \quad (23.14)$$

or

$$\frac{n_i}{N_i} \propto \sigma_i \quad . \quad . \quad . \quad . \quad (23.15)$$

Thus the ratio which the sample-number n_i bears to the stratum number N_i varies as the standard deviation of the stratum.

23.9   This interesting result has some important applications in stratified sampling.   We need not consider the case in which the σ's are known exactly (for we should rarely have this knowledge without knowing the means, in which case we should not be estimating the mean of the whole from the sample).   There remain, however, two classes of case where the result is useful; when—

(*a*) The standard deviations are known approximately from prior information.   In such a case we can determine the σ's from (23.15) to some degree of approximation.   An estimate based on a sample obtained in this way, though not perhaps as good as it might be, will at least be better than if we had ignored our knowledge of the standard deviations.

(*b*) A pilot inquiry on a small scale can be conducted to determine the standard deviations approximately.   This will bring us back to case (*a*).

Example 23.2.—(Data from Yates, *J. Roy. Stat. Soc.*, 1946, **109**, 12).

The Farm Survey of England and Wales covered all holdings of five acres or more.   Prior information was available as to the size-distribution of these holdings as follows—

Size group (acres)	Number of holdings
5 and less than 25	101,450
25 ,, ,, ,, 100	111,360
100 ,, ,, ,, 300	65,210
300 ,, ,, ,, 700	11,150
700 and over	1,430
	290,600

We wish to take a sample, say, of about one in seven, or about 40,000 holdings, in order to estimate some factor for the population of farms such as the arable acreage.   What fractions of the various size groups should we choose ?

If we have, in the general case, a sample number r_i in the ith stratum, where $\Sigma(r_i) = n$, we shall take as our estimator of the mean of the whole population the statistic

$$\bar{x} = \sum_{i=1}^{k} \frac{N_i}{N} x_i.$$

where $x_{i.}$ denotes the mean of the r_i sample values from the ith stratum. This is an unbiased estimator in the sense of **23.17** for the mean value of $x_{i.}$ is the same as the mean value of x_{ij} over the ith stratum, i.e is α_i.

Furthermore, the variance of $\bar{x}$ will be given by

$$\text{var } \bar{x} = \sum_{i=1}^{k} \left(\frac{N_i}{N}\right)^2 \text{var } x_{i.}$$

$$= \sum_{i=1}^{k} \left(\frac{N_i}{N}\right)^2 \frac{N_i - r_i}{N_i - 1} \frac{\sigma_i^2}{r_i}$$

$$= \frac{1}{N^2} \sum_{i=1}^{k} N_i \sigma_i^2 \left(\frac{N_i}{r_i} - 1\right) \text{ approximately}$$

The reader may verify as an exercise that when r_i is equal to n_i as given by (23.15) this reduces to the minimal variance given by (23.11) to our degree of approximation, which is reached by writing N_i instead if $N_i - 1$ in the denominator.

We do not know the standard deviations of the factor under investigation in the various strata but we may make some very plausible assumptions. There must clearly be some high correlation between arable acreage and farm area. Let us then suppose that the variability of the one is proportional to that of the other, i.e. that our sampling fraction can be taken as proportional to the standard deviations of size of farm. A sketch of the histogram of the data will show that the distribution is approximately J-shaped. If in any stratum the farms were distributed equally frequently with respect to size (i.e. if the histogram were actually the frequency distribution) the variance of a stratum of width h would be $h^2/12$ and hence its standard deviation would be proportional to h. Let us then choose our sampling fractions proportional to the widths of the size groups.

The last group, 700 acres and over, has an unspecified upper limit. We will, therefore, suppose the standard deviation very large and sample 100 per cent. The range of the other groups are 20, 75, 200 and 400 acres and thus our fractions are proportional to these numbers, say $20x$, $75x$, etc. We then have

$$(20x)(101,450) + (75x)(111,360) + (200x)(65,210)$$
$$+ (400x)(11,150) = 39,000, \text{ say, giving}$$
$$x = 0 \cdot 00140$$

The fractions are then approximately $2 \cdot 8$, $10 \cdot 5$, 28 and 56 per cent.

The figures used in actual practice (though not obtained by this method) were 5, 10, 25, 50. As we shall see below, extreme precision in the sampling proportions is unnecessary. It was recognised that the smaller farms were over-represented, this being a deliberate modification introduced for other purposes.

We may form an idea of the relative efficiency of this method of sampling as compared with others which might suggest themselves. With sampling fractions 5, 10, 25, 50 and 100 per cent we have

N_i	$\dfrac{n_i}{N_i}$ (%)	Variance (proportional to)	n_i (Farms sampled)
101,450	5	20^2	5,072
111,360	10	75^2	11,136
65,210	25	200^2	16,302
11,150	50	400^2	5,575
1,430	100	—	1,430
Totals 290,600			39,515

Now from our expression for the variance of $\bar{x}$ we have

$$\text{var } t = \frac{1}{N^2}\Sigma\left\{N_i\sigma_i{}^2\left(\frac{N_i}{n_i}-1\right)\right\}$$

We may now calculate this quantity, or rather a quantity proportional to it (since we are assuming the variances proportional to the squares of the widths of the grouping intervals). For instance the first term in the summation is—

$$101,450\times 400\times (20-1).$$

We find that var t is proportional to $0\cdot1896$. We do not require the variance of the last interval because the factor $\dfrac{N_i}{n_i}-1$ vanishes for it.

It is also of interest to see what happens if we draw the same proportion from each of the five strata, a procedure which has a certain prior plausibility. The total sample number is $39,515/290,600=13\cdot598$ per cent. We shall now require an estimate of the variance in the last class of farm of 700 acres and over, and shall take it to be proportional to 400^2. Denoting the sampling proportion by p we have, for an estimate of the mean w based on this method,

$$\text{var } w = \frac{1}{N^2}\Sigma\left\{N_i\sigma_i{}^2\left(\frac{1}{p}-1\right)\right\}$$
$$= \frac{1}{N^2}\left(\frac{1}{p}-1\right)\Sigma\ (N_i\sigma_i{}^2)$$

This formula gives us var w proportional to $0\cdot3979$, i.e. a variance more than twice as great as that obtained by the first method. ·

23.10 From the determination of the " best " sampling fractions by minimising the variance it follows that fractions near to the optimum will give almost as good results as the best. We may establish the result directly as follows. Let $p_i=n_i/N_i$.

Then

$$\text{var } t = \frac{1}{N^2}\Sigma_i N_i \sigma_i{}^2\left(\frac{1}{p_i}-1\right) \qquad . \qquad . \qquad . \qquad . \quad (23.16)$$

Now suppose that instead of the optimum proportions p_i we choose proportions $p_i+\delta_i$ where the δ's are small and δ^2 may be neglected. Since the sample number is the same in both cases we have

$$\Sigma(N_i p_i) = \Sigma\{N_i(p_i+\delta_i)\}$$

giving

$$\Sigma(N_i\delta_i) = 0 \qquad . \qquad . \qquad . \qquad . \quad (23.17)$$

If u is the alternative estimate

$$\text{var } u = \frac{1}{N^2}\Sigma_i N_i \sigma_i{}^2\left(\frac{1}{p_i+\delta_i}-1\right)$$

and since, to our approximation

$$\frac{1}{p_i+\delta_i} = \frac{1}{p_i\left(1+\frac{\delta_i}{p_i}\right)} = \frac{1}{p_i}\left(1-\frac{\delta_i}{p_i}\right)$$

we have

$$\text{var } u = \frac{1}{N^2}\Sigma N_i \sigma_i{}^2\left(\frac{1}{p_i}-1-\frac{\delta_i}{p_i{}^2}\right)$$

$$= \text{var } t - \frac{1}{N^2}\Sigma\left(\frac{N_i\sigma_i{}^2\delta_i}{p_i{}^2}\right)$$

Now p_i is equal to $a\sigma_i$ where a is a constant and consequently the second term vanishes in virtue of (23.17). Thus var u is practically the same as var t.

The effect of this result is that we need not be too meticulous in determining our sampling fractions. Any values near the optimum will give a sampling variance very near the minimum.

23.11   Various elaborations of ordinary sampling or stratified sampling are possible and are sometimes employed. For example, we may sample in two stages, the second sample being a sub-sample of the members of the first sample; and the method may be extended to further sub-samples. Suppose, for instance, that we require a comparatively small sample from the inhabitants of a certain country. For administrative reasons it may be more convenient to draw first of all a primary sample, consisting of towns and rural districts; then, from each member of the sample, a number of houses; and then, say, one member from each house. At some stage in the process, e.g. in the selection of houses, we might have stratified. There is evidently a very large number of possible combinations of different techniques in general, although in practice a limit is often imposed by cost or convenience.

23.12 The student will inquire whether there is any advantage in these more complicated procedures from the theoretical viewpoint; whether, for example, it is possible to reduce the sampling error by sub-sampling. We shall only have the space for a brief discussion of this question.

If all the sampling is random and the population is homogeneous there is no theoretical advantage in sub-sampling. An ordinary random sampling process gives each member of the population the same chance of being chosen. If we choose groups at random, *and the members of those groups may be regarded as having been allotted at random to the groups,* the more complicated technique also gives each member the same chance of being chosen, and the methods are equivalent.

23.13 In practice, however, the nature of the grouping is often known to be such that the members cannot be regarded as grouped at random, and the effect of stratification or sub-sampling may be to alter the standard errors of estimation quite considerably. To take our former example of sampling from a human population : there may be (and usually there is) a good prior reason to expect that the quantity we are investigating differs between town and country districts, so that the population is patchy and, in any given area, there is a positive correlation between contiguous members of a sample ; or again, if we take only one member from a household we may exclude from occurrence certain coincidences or resemblances which are more likely to occur within a household than between households. This patchiness in the population may, or may not, be an advantage in reducing the standard error. There do not appear to be any very general rules on the subject and a great deal depends on the nature of the patchiness. It is nevertheless possible to make certain assumptions about certain types of population with great confidence, and to base sampling techniques on them.

Example 23.3.—A survey is carried out in a particular town. Certain households are chosen at random and then one member from each household. Suppose the quantity under consideration is some continuous variate x.

Let us suppose that the maximum number of members in a family is k, that there are F_1 families with one member, F_2 with two members and so on. The total number of families we may write as F and the total number of individuals as N. Then we have

$$\sum_{j=1}^{k} F_j = F \qquad . \qquad . \qquad . \qquad . \qquad . \quad (23.18)$$

$$\sum_{j=1}^{k} j F_j = N \qquad . \qquad . \qquad . \qquad . \qquad . \quad (23.19)$$

Let the mean and variance of x in the lth family of the set of F_j families be m_{jl} and v_{jl} respectively. Then if m and v are the mean and variance of the total population of individuals

$$Nm = \sum_{j=1}^{h} \sum_{l=1}^{F_j} jm_{jl} \qquad . \qquad . \qquad . \quad (23.20)$$

$$N(v^2+m^2) = \sum_j \sum_l j(v_{jl}+m_{jl}^2)$$

For an unrestricted random sample of n (small compared with N) from the whole population the variance of the mean is v/n, say v_a so that we have

$$v_a = \frac{1}{n}\left[\frac{1}{N} \sum_j \sum_l j(v_{jl}+m_{jl}^2) - \left\{\frac{1}{N} \sum_j \sum_l jm_{jl}\right\}^2\right] \quad . \qquad . \quad (23.21)$$

Now suppose we take a random sample of n households and choose one member from each household. In such a case we are sampling from a population of F members, one from each member. The variance of such a population is given by V, say, where

$$V + \left(\frac{1}{F}\sum_{j=1}^{k} \sum_{l=1}^{F_j} m_{jl}\right)^2 = \frac{1}{F}\sum_{j=1}^{k} \sum_{l=1}^{F_j} (v_{jl}+m_{jl}^2)$$

and hence the variance of the mean of samples of n, say v_b, is given by

$$v_b = \frac{1}{n}\left[\frac{1}{F} \sum_j \sum_l (v_{jl}+m_{jl}^2) - \left\{\frac{1}{F} \sum_j \sum_l m_{jl}\right\}^2\right] \quad . \qquad . \quad (23.22)$$

The reader will notice that the sampling variance v_b can be exhibited in the form of an analysis of variance. If $\bar{v}$ is the mean of variances within families and v_m is the variance of means (between families) we have

$$v_b = \frac{1}{n}(\bar{v}+v_m) \qquad . \qquad . \qquad . \qquad . \quad (23.23)$$

From (23.21) v_a can be put in a similar form but the mean of v_{jl} is weighted according to the number of members in a family and the sum corresponding to the m_{jl} is similarly weighted.

A comparison of (23.21) and (23.22) will show that if the means and variances increase with size of family, or if the variances increase and the means remain constant, v_a is greater than v_b, for the larger families then contribute relatively more to v_a. The situation might then arise in which we had a smaller sampling variance by choosing one member from each family in the sample. On the other hand we have to be careful not to obtain a biased estimate. In this case, the mean of a sample of n, one from each family, might be biased. For the mean of such a sample (over all possible samples) is the same as the mean of one member over all possible samples consisting of one family, that is to say, is the un-weighted mean

$$\frac{1}{F} \sum_{j=1}^{k} \sum_{l=1}^{F_j} m_{jl}$$

This may differ from the population mean given by (23.20). We must always be careful, therefore, in looking for estimates with minimum variance, not to choose one which may be seriously biased.

23.14 At this point we may mention briefly certain other types of sampling which are sometimes used. In some of these cases the methods have not yet been put on a satisfactory theoretical basis and the reader who proposes to use them should read more widely before doing so.*

(a) *Systematic sampling.* Where the members of a population are arranged in some spatial or temporal order (e.g. persons listed alpha-betically in a telephone directory, price quotations given regularly each week, plants growing in rows in a field) it is sometimes convenient to choose a sample by selecting members at equal intervals along the order. For instance we may select every 100th name on a list, or every fifth plant in a row. We referred in **16.26** to the selection of houses in a street and the dangers of occasional bias which it might introduce. Such methods have been called (not very aptly) *systematic* sampling. Where the population is patchy they have the appearance of avoiding selecting by chance too many members in an unrepresentative area. On the other hand, where there are rhythms present in the population (as, for example, in oscillatory time series or in soil which has been cultivated by machine) the method may give very unreliable results. It can only be recommended when there is good reason to think on prior grounds that the interval between members of the sample has no relation to any possible systematic properties of the population.

(b) *Quota sampling.*—In social surveys involving interviews when the work has, in general, to be divided among a number of investigators it has sometimes been the practice to assign to each a definite sample number which he must attain—he may, for instance, be instructed to secure 200 schedules, and to go on until he has obtained that number. This method would be unobjectionable if the sample were random, but un-fortunately circumstances may arise which vitiate the randomness. The investigator who meets with refusal to complete a schedule or otherwise fails to obtain one from a previously selected individual (e.g. because of his absence), must go on until the quota is full, and may be forced to take his sample where he can get it, not where he would like to get it. Checks and controls throughout are most desirable in this type of sampling.

---

* See F. Yates, *Sampling Methods for Censuses and Surveys*, 1949, Griffin and Co., for an extended account of the subject and a bibliography.

(c) *Sequential sampling.*—This method (which has been put on a satisfactory theoretical basis, although many problems remain unsolved) aims at economising in the size of sample required to reach a prescribed degree of probability in making a correct decision.

In the ordinary sampling process such as we have described it in foregoing chapters, we select a sample of pre-determined size and calculate from it the required estimate together with its standard error (or, for small samples, an equivalent quantity) which sets limits to the values between which the parameter value may be stated to lie to a prescribed degree of probability. In sequential sampling we invert the process to some extent. We decide, on the basis of the prescribed degree of probability, what are the limits within which we can accept the sample estimate as consistent with prescribed parameter values and then sample one by one. If at any stage the sample estimate (or more generally, some suitable statistic calculable from the sample) falls outside the limits appropriate to the size of sample which has been reached up to that point, we reject the hypothesis that the population parameter has the prescribed value or set of values under consideration. An excellent account of the method will be found in A. Wald's *Sequential Analysis.*

Example 23.4.—As an example of an inquiry which was spoilt by violating some of the principles we have proposed, we may take the Lanarkshire nutritional experiment which was undertaken in 1930 at a cost of £7,500. For four months 5,000 children received three quarters of a pint of raw milk per day, 5,000 received the same quantity of pasteurised milk and another 10,000 were chosen as controls. The height and weight of the whole 20,000 were measured at the beginning and end of the experiment.

The main object of the experiment, of course, was to see if the milk-fed groups gained more in height and weight than the controls, but for it to have any value as a basis of generalisation the samples had to be random. The intentions of the planners of the experiment were good. Teachers selected the children either by ballot or by some alphabetical system. But at this point a serious flaw occurred. " In any particular school where there was any group to which these methods had given an undue proportion of well-fed or ill-nourished children, others were substituted in order to gain a more level selection."

It is unfair to be too critical of what was evidently a well-intentioned procedure to improve the representative quality of the data ; but in fact this attempt to balance the samples nearly ruined the experiment. It was found at the end of the inquiry that the controls were both heavier and taller than the fed children by about three months' growth in weight and four months' growth in height. It appears that the substitutive process in what looked like unusual samples resulted in the choice of better nourished children as controls and worse nourished children as feeders. Comparability with controls was thereby invalidated.

A second object of the inquiry was to see whether there was any differential effect between raw and pasteurised milk. Here again a mistake was made. A particular school obtained either one kind of milk or the other, not both. Now in a district which is racially or socially heterogeneous, it is possible that the selection of one half of the schools for one treatment might result in the choice of a set with higher or lower standards than the other half, both in the original measurements and in the rate of growth. It would have been better to select a number for feeding with raw and an equal number for feeding with pasteurised milk *in each school*.

There were other faults in the design of the experiment and the majority of the conclusions which were drawn from it did not, strictly speaking, follow from the data. The student may consult " Student," *Biometrika*, 1931, **23**, 398 for some further criticisms.

Examination of samples

23.15 The liability to error of the result of examination of a sample unit obviously depends to a high degree on the nature of the observation to be made. A simple physical measurement permits of a high degree of accuracy with little chance of bias, but even here care must be exercised, e.g. in taking body-measurements on the human subject to determine correctly the points between which the measurement is to be taken, and to use a constant degree of pressure in adjusting the instrument. If an *estimate* is made, the possibility, indeed the probability, of error is at once greatly increased, as we have seen already in the estimation of shoot-height (**16.21**). The chances of error are widened yet further still if the unit is a human being and makes his own contribution towards misleading the observer, by giving untrue or ambiguous answers to his questions. In such interviewing work a knowledge of and familiarity with psychology may be of far more service to the investigator than a knowledge of statistical method. We will give some examples first of estimation and secondly of interviewing that will serve to illustrate the risks.

Example 23.5.—Corrections for pessimism

Table 23.1 shows the forecasts of yields in potatoes made on various dates as compared with final estimates, for a series of years.

These forecasts and estimates are averages based on figures supplied by a number of estimators scattered over England and Wales. They are not checked against actual yields, although some estimators use known results in their areas for particular farms and fields in arriving at their judgment. The striking thing about the figures is the uniform sign of the difference between the forecasts and the final estimate.

This type of bias is quite different from the one noticed in the Example 23.1. There the investigators measured the yield of definite areas and the bias apparently lay in their enthusiasm in extending those areas a little

TABLE 23.1.—Forecasts of yields of potatoes in England and Wales in tons per acre
From the official agricultural statistics

Year	Sept. 1st		Oct. 1st		Nov. 1st		Final estimate
	Yield	% difference from final	Yield	% difference from final	Yield	% difference from final	
1929	5·7	−17·4	6·2	−10·1	6·5	− 5·8	6·9
1930	6·0	− 7·7	6·1	− 6·2	6·1	− 6·2	6·5
1931	5·5	0·0	5·3	− 3·6	5·3	− 3·6	5·5
1932	6·4	− 3·0	6·2	− 6·1	6·3	− 4·5	6·6
1933	6·4	− 4·5	6·2	− 7·5	6·4	−· 4·5	6·7
1934	6·0	−15·5	6·3	−11·3	6·7	− 5·6	7·1
1935	5·6	− 9·7	5·7	− 5·1	6·0	− 3·2	6·2
1936	6·0	− 3·2	5·9	− 4·8	5·8	− 6·5	6·2

too widely. Here the investigators are not measuring but judging and the bias arises from excessive caution, a kind of chronic pessimism which is well recognised in agricultural circles. The remedy would be either to lay down a series of harvesting experiments on properly chosen sites, or to " correct " forecasts in future by scaling them up proportionately to the average deficiency over a previous series of years. Given time, of course, it might also be possible to educate the observers out of their pessimism, but this would not be without its dangers and might for a time swing the balance the wrong way.

Example 23.6.—When an investigator is sent out into the field to collect results he may, if he is lazy or dishonest, shirk his duties and send in returns which are spurious. Once these faked records have occurred it is difficult to detect them unless the inquiry has been specially designed to be self-checking in this respect, but various methods are available to check the general accuracy of the individual or to restrain his tendency to make entries by guesswork. One useful device is to have a second investigator cover some of the same ground. This results in a certain amount of duplication of effort but is often worth the extra trouble and expense. The two investigators need only have part of their field in common. The knowledge that any particular return is likely to be checked by another investigator is often a sufficient spur to accurate recording in all the records.

Table 23.2 shows a comparison of two recordings by surveyors A and B made on identical fields within a fortnight of each other. The surveyors merely had to record the crop under which each of 332 fields lay and no question of measurement or estimation was involved apart from the identification of the plants.

TABLE 23.2.—Comparison of duplicated complete enumeration in a district of Bengal
(Mahalanobis, *J. Roy. Stat. Soc.*, 1946, **109**, 325.)

A—Survey	B—Survey				
	Jute	Winter rice	Winter rice and jute	No. crop	Totals
Jute. . . .	4	15	4	3	26
Monsoon rice . .	4	12	1	4	21
Monsoon rice and jute	17	66	2	9	94
Jute, monsoon and winter rice . .	—	2	—	—	2
Rice (monsoon and winter) . .	1	—	—	—	1
No crop . . .	37	45	4	102	188
Totals .	63	140	11	118	332

The discrepancies are obviously very large and it is impossible to avoid the conclusion that one of the surveyors at least was not carrying out his duties properly. Errors on this scale can hardly be due to accident or inability. There is a strong presumption that one of the surveyors at least was either not exercising reasonable care or definitely falsifying his records.

23.16 Unintentional errors on the part of investigators can to some extent be eliminated by training and careful instruction, and the magnitude of unconscious bias can often be gauged by letting them undertake a dummy inquiry on material for which the results are known. Where resources permit, however, it is very valuable to replicate the inquiry among different observers to see how far they differ among themselves. This is especially desirable in inquiries which necessarily depend on subjective judgment, such as the assessment of a candidates' qualities in a personal interview, a grading by an inspector of the suitability of a house for habitation or the rating of an employee for promotion.

Example 23.7.—In an inquiry into family budgets in Nagpur (Mahalanobis, *J. Roy. Stat. Soc.*, 1946, **109**, 325) information was collected, *inter alia*, of total income and of monthly expenditure. The area under examination was divided into five zones. Within each zone samples were selected by picking families at random and these were divided into four sub-samples, each of which was random and independent of the others. There were four investigators, each taking one sub-sample at random in each zone. Within each sub-sample about 50 schedules were collected. Thus the total of about 1,000 schedules (actually 997 because of small imperfections in carrying out the design) can be classified into a $5 \times 4 \times 50$ grouping, and the variance-analysis is of the following form.

TABLE 23.3.—Nagpur Family Budget Inquiry
Analysis of Variance
(For ref. see Table 23.2)

Variation	d.f.	Quotient (Income)	Quotient (Monthly expenditure)
Between zones (Z) . .	4	4,439·6	3,707·9
Between investigators (I)	3	85·4	597·1
Interaction (ZI) . .	12	382·5	397·3
Between sub-samples .	19	1,189·7	1,127·1
Within sub-samples . .	977	401·6	384·7
Total	996	424·7	398·9

We have shown only the degrees of freedom and the quotients in the table. If the reader multiplies the two to obtain the sum of squares he will find that the sums " between sub-samples " and " within sub-samples " do not add to the total sum. This, of course, is due to the fact that the numbers in sub-classes are not units but are about 50.

The analysis shows the interaction between zones and investigators. If there were only one schedule in the sub-sample there would only be 19 degrees of freedom altogether ; but as there are about 50 schedules in the sub-samples we can form an estimate of the variance within sub-samples by taking the variance of each set of schedules in a sub-sample and pooling for the 20 sub-samples. It is this " residual " variance (401·6 for income and 384·7 for monthly expenditure) which is to be compared with the other variances to test departure from homogeneity.

Taking income first, we find that the ratios of the residual quotient to the quotients between investigators and the interaction are not significant. This is encouraging and indicates that the investigators are accurate (or at least consistent). The quotients between zones and between sub-samples are significant at a 1 per cent level. This was to be expected from the nature of the inquiry, for the zones were deliberately chosen from differentiated areas.

A similar conclusion is reached in respect of monthly expenditure. The reader can verify the arithmetic of the significance for himself.

23.17 To avoid confusion we refer at this point to a technical meaning of the word " bias " which has recently come into use in advanced theoretical statistics. A statistic t which is used as an estimator of a

TABLE 23.4.—Bengal crop survey

Comparison of two independent estimates of proportion p under winter rice by two parties of investigators

Party A $p(\%)$	Party B												Totals
	0	1–10	11–20	21–30	31–40	41–50	51–60	61–70	71–80	81–90	91–99	100	
0	1,159	84	50	33	30	17	18	15	27	24	28	62	1,547
1–10	74	150	39	22	13	9	11	11	4	14	3	13	363
11–20	31	35	88	14	14	12	10	11	9	3	5	16	248
21–30	26	20	22	65	18	18	16	6	5	7	6	8	217
31–40	15	10	16	25	97	42	15	15	13	16	11	11	286
41–50	17	11	7	14	31	85	32	14	17	12	14	9	263
51–60	17	6	9	8	18	29	71	30	24	11	16	30	269
61–70	22	6	7	6	13	10	27	78	37	31	22	25	284
71–80	24	7	7	8	11	23	17	45	91	45	32	45	355
81–90	28	7	9	11	9	9	25	15	45	129	52	57	396
91–99	29	4	7	6	13	11	12	17	29	48	264	143	583
100	68	13	11	14	13	23	23	31	54	64	152	927	1,393
Totals	1,510	353	272	226	280	288	277	288	355	404	605	1,346	6,204

parameter θ is said to be biased if the mean value of t over all possible samples is not equal to θ. Thus, as we saw in **21.4**, the sample-variance is a biased estimator of the parent variance because the average value of s^2 over all samples is $(n-1)/n$ times μ_2, instead of μ_2 itself. To obtain an unbiased estimator we must use the statistic

$$s'^2 = S(x - \bar{x})^2 / (n-1)$$

The meaning attached to the word "bias" in this chapter is not restricted to departure from the criterion we have just mentioned. In the narrower sense of that criterion "bias" is a quality of the estimator employed and may exist when the sampling is random. In the more general sense bias may be used to connote any effect which distorts the representativeness of the result, whether in the estimating process or in the selection and examination of the sample.

Cumulative effect of bias

23.18 There is a popular belief that even if individuals make mistakes their errors in the aggregate will tend to cancel out, so that an average of a number of instances will be less distorted by bias than any particular single instance. To some extent this is true. If the errors are in the nature of sampling fluctuations we know that the standard error of a mean decreases proportionately to the square root of the number of observations. But it would be a mistake to assume that all types of bias tend to be of the self-cancelling kind. It is not true that if only enough people make enough mistakes the average of their opinions or estimates lies near the real value.

23.19 We have had one example of the cumulative effect of bias in Example 23.5, in which we saw that, in spite of the number of crop estimators concerned, the mean of their forecasts was systematically below the final estimate. Evidently they were all affected more or less by the same tendency which therefore persists in the average of the individual results. How far, in any particular inquiry, we may assume that individual biases tend to cancel in the aggregate depends on the nature of the inquiry. We clearly cannot assume that there is safety in numbers where individuals may be affected by the same kind of bias, e.g. if there is any general tendency to over-estimate for reasons of personal pride, or where some force is at work to remove from the sample individuals of one particular type. On the other hand, cases are known wherein biases (not merely chance fluctuations) do appear to cancel themselves out very largely.

Example 23.8.—(Data from Mahalanobis, *loc. cit.* Example 23.7).

A certain area of 6,204 "grids" of about $2\frac{1}{4}$ acres each was surveyed independently by two parties A and B. Each party recorded for each grid the estimated proportion under winter rice. The results are shown in Table **23.4**.

If the two parties were in complete agreement only diagonal cells would contain non-zero entries. The differences are evidently quite substantial, there being only 51·6 per cent of the cases showing complete agreement.

Nevertheless the mean of p for A (mean of column totals) is 52·0 per cent, whereas that for B (row totals) is 51·9 per cent, an extraordinarily close agreement. Thus, in spite of the differences on individual grids the estimates for the whole are satisfactorily concordant.

Example 23.9.—The " vanity " effect.

The preceding examples have related to defects on the part of the observers. We now consider a different type in which bias is introduced by a distorted response from the members of the samples.

In an inquiry into listeners' preferences for radio programmes subjects were asked by interview for their opinion on broadcast religious services. 52 per cent of the persons indicated by their response, in the interviewer's judgment, that they were enthusiastic or moderately enthusiastic. One might have been tempted to infer that about half the listening public were keen listeners to religious broadcasts. In fact the listening audience seemed to be about 10 per cent of the listening population, another and more direct inquiry into the audition of actual programmes giving proportions ranging from 3 per cent to 18 per cent (See Silvey, *J. Roy. Stat. Soc.*, 1944, **107**, 190 for details).

Without dwelling on questions of standard error we can see at once that the responses in the interviews were strongly biased. There can be little doubt that this was due to the wish on the subject's part not to be classified as indifferent to spiritual influences. The same kind of effect is apt to arise in any inquiry into cultural tastes, few people being willing to admit to a stranger that they do not care for good music, however rarely they go to the trouble of listening to it.

Example 23.10.—The " sympathy " effect.

The Listener is a British weekly journal devoted to broadcasting matters. An inquiry was made to find out how many people read it. Now in this case the circulation of the journal is known and, by making due allowances for the numbers of people who read the same copy in family units, a fair estimate can be obtained of the total number of people who can possibly read one issue. The percentages obtained from sampling inquiries showed that four or five times as many people said they read it as could have done so. (See the remarks by Durant on the paper by Silvey referred to in the previous example.)

It would not be correct to deduce that the majority of the people replying affirmatively to the question whether they read the *Listener* are deliberate liars. There is a natural tendency on the part of many people to give to the questioner the reply which they think would please him. They infer that an affirmative answer would do so (thinking, perhaps, that the questioner is a representative of the publishers) and stretch their consciences to the extent of saying that they read the journal when they may, for instance, only have seen it on a bookstall or in a friend's house, or even if they have merely seen it advertised. This " sympathy " response is all the more difficult to guard against because the interviewer must try to ingratiate himself with his subject in order to obtain a reply at all.

In this particular case there is another possible explanation of the bias. The subject may imagine that if he gives a negative response an attempt will be made to sell him the journal. He therefore anticipates any possible sales pressure by stating that he takes the journal already.

23.20 The lessons to be learnt from such experiences as these are numerous. We will indicate a few methods which the investigator may sometimes be able to use to minimise the risk of the distorted response.

(*a*) If possible the aim of the inquiry should be concealed from the subject. This will prevent him from " co-operating " with the interviewer to get what he may consider the desired result. But it is often impracticable to expect him to answer questions without asking some in return ; and very often the purpose of the inquiry is clear merely from the fact that it is made.

(*b*) The questions should be framed unambiguously so as to elicit a " yes-no " response or a three-way answer customary in opinion inquiries : " yes /no /don't-know ".

(*c*) Independent checks on veracity can sometimes be obtained in a roundabout way. In Example 23.9 we mentioned a case where a direct check was available. An inquiry on a political subject, for example, may well embody some question which permits of checking against known results for the aggregate, such as " Did you vote at the last election ? " The interpretation of the results of these " control " questions is not always very easy, but they provide valuable collateral evidence on the general representative character of the responses.

(*d*) If there is prior reason to suppose that different types of subject will give varying degrees of distortion in response, results for the types may be analysed separately. Suppose we are conducting by personal interview an inquiry which involves recording the subject's age. Knowing that the incentive to lie about age varies from one age-group to another, we may analyse the replies, if they are sufficiently numerous, into age-groups. From known census data or by making certain assumptions about the population under examination based on known facts such as birth-rates and death-rates, we can estimate what the results ought to be if the subjects are telling the truth, and hence gauge the direction and extent of the bias.

SUMMARY

1. The complete sampling process consists of (a) the choice of unit, (b) the selection of the sample of units and (c) the examination of the units.

2. For " continuous " regions there is usually no natural unit ; and for a disconcontinuous population practical considerations may suggest, as size of unit, groups of the individuals comprising the population.

3. By the use of appropriate variable sampling fractions in stratified sampling a considerable reduction may be made in the sampling variance of estimates of the mean. For linear estimates the optimum estimate is given when the numbers taken from the strata are proportional to the standard deviations of the variate under investigation in those strata.

4. Various examples are given of the introduction of bias, due to flaws in the " examination " of the sample.

EXERCISES

23.1 Consider possible sources of bias in replies to the following enquiries :

(a) Persons are asked to state how often they attended a place of entertainment during the previous year ;

(b) Persons are asked to state how many days have elapsed since they last attended a place of entertainment.

Consider how far the answers to (b) may be used as a check on the answers to (a).

23.2 Ten investigators are to be sent to ten traffic centres in a city to record the number of automobiles passing a specified point in a specified time. Two of the investigators are suspected of being unreliable. Design a method of carrying out the inquiry which will exhibit this unreliability, if it exists, and will also provide unbiased results if the other investigators are reliable.

23.3 A number of businesses are asked to provide figures showing stocks of specified goods on hand at a specified date, and the returns are required within a specified and rather short time. Consider what kinds of bias might appear in the answers.

23.4 A random sample is drawn from the records of a fire insurance company with the object of estimating the number of fire " incidents " occurring in a certain period in dwelling houses. Consider how far this sample is likely to be unrepresentative of all fire " incidents " which require the attention of a public fire service.

23.5 If equation (23.10) may be accepted as self-evident, provide a simplified proof of the result of equation (23.11). In the manner of **23.10** derive equation (23.13).

23.6 A population is stratified into four (large) groups for which the number of members and the variances are as follows—

Group	Number	Variance
1	10,000	16
2	20,000	25
3	40,000	36
4	30,000	4

Find the variance of an estimate of the parent-mean based on a sample of 400 from the population

(a) by taking 100 from each stratum ;

(b) by taking a constant proportion $0 \cdot 4$ per cent from each stratum ;

(c) by choosing the sample numbers (to the nearest unit) proportionately to the standard deviations in the strata ;

(d) by taking the sample numbers as the optimum, as given by (23.15).

23.7 A population consists of N members in order, divided into k groups of n. A sample is selected by taking the jth member of each group, so that it is systematic and consists of the members x_j, x_{j+n}, x_{j+2n}, etc. Show that the variance of the mean of the sample, say $\bar{x}$, is given by

$$\text{var } \bar{x} = \frac{v}{k}\left\{1+(k-1)\rho\right\}$$

where v is the variance of the population and ρ is the intraclass correlation coefficient of the n groups of k consisting of jth members ($j=1, \ldots k$). Hence show that var $\bar{x}$ is greater than, equal to, or less than the variance of a random sample according as the intraclass correlation is positive, zero or negative. It may be assumed that N is large compared with k:

23.8 A sample is drawn from an ordered population of $N(=kn)$ members by dividing it into k sets of n and taking a member at random in each of the k sets. Consider generally whether the variance of the mean of such a sample will have a smaller variance than the mean of an unrestricted random sample.

23.9 One of the main difficulties in house-to-house inquiries is to make proper allowance for those houses where there is no one at home when the call is made. It has been suggested that suitable methods of dealing with this problem would be

(a) to call back persistently until an occupant was found to be at home ;

(b) to sub-sample the non-responsive houses by calling back persistently at a proportion of them ;

(c) if possible, to stratify houses beforehand according to the proportion of the day during which somebody was at home, and to sample at random in each stratum, ignoring the non-responders.

Examine the relative merits of these methods.

23.10 Discuss the problems of obtaining estimates of average annual values in the following cases :

(a) Expenditure of persons on holidays by sampling at various dates in the year ;

(b) rainfall at a certain locality by sampling for rainfall on a specified number of days ;

(c) output of a factory product by sampling output on certain dates.

CHAPTER TWENTY-FOUR

INTERPOLATION AND GRADUATION

Simple interpolation

24.1 If the value of a function of a single variable x, say u_x, has been tabulated for equidistant values of the variable x, $x+h$, $x+2h$, etc., we often require to find the value of the function corresponding to an intermediate value of the variable. Functions in very general use, such as common logarithms, have usually been tabulated with intervals so small that even over a range of several intervals the relation between u_x and x may be assumed to be effectively linear, that is of the form

$$u_x = a_0 + a_1 x \qquad . \qquad . \qquad . \qquad . \qquad (24.1)$$

as is shown by the constancy of the differences between successive values of u. For example,

TABLE 24.1

Number	Logarithm	Difference (+)
30597	4·4856788	
		0·0000142
30598	4·4856930	
		0·0000142
30599	4·4857072	
		0·0000142
30600	4·4857214	
		0·0000142
30601	4·4857356	
		0·0000142
30602	4·4857498	

If we then require, say, the value of log 30600·3, it is sufficient to use the familiar process of *simple interpolation*—

$$
\begin{array}{ll}
\text{log } 30600 & 4\cdot4857214 \\
0\cdot3\times0\cdot0000142 & 43 \\
\hline
& 4\cdot4857257
\end{array}
$$

The little multiplication sum, is, in most tables, already done for us in the margin.

Differences

24.2 For any function which has been tabulated to sufficiently fine intervals (within certain limitations) simple interpolation can be used in this way—it is only a question of making the intervals sufficiently small (see below, **24.16**). But many functions have not been tabulated in such detail, successive differences are *not* equal, and consequently simple interpolation cannot give an accurate result. The problem then arises, how are we to interpolate with reasonable precision ? And the answer is given *by proceeding to higher orders of differences*, as they are termed ; i.e. instead of considering only the differences

$$\Delta_0^1 = u_1 - u_0$$
$$\Delta_1^1 = u_2 - u_1$$
$$\Delta_2^1 = u_3 - u_2$$

etc., we also consider the *second differences*

$$\Delta_0^2 = \Delta_1^1 - \Delta_0^1$$
$$\Delta_1^2 = \Delta_2^1 - \Delta_1^1$$
$$\Delta_2^2 = \Delta_3^1 - \Delta_2^1$$

etc., or even the *third differences, fourth differences*, etc.

24.3 To take an actual example, Table 24.2 shows the squares of the first few natural numbers, together with their first and second differences. Following a practice which is convenient for printing and for most purposes of practical work, each difference is printed, not on a line between the two figures to which it relates, as with the logarithms in Table 24.1 above, but on the same line as the upper figure of the two concerned—the line of the figure subtracted ; and as the signs of the differences are constant for each column this sign is simply stated at the top.

TABLE 24.2

Number x	Square u_x	First diff. $\Delta^1(+)$	Second diff. $\Delta^2(+)$	Third diff. Δ^3
0	0	1	2	0
1	1	3	2	0
2	4	5	2	0
3	9	7	2	—
4	16	9	—	—
5	25	—	—	—

Here we see that the *first differences*—the only ones with which we have been concerned hitherto—are no longer constant ; but they follow a simple rule, in that they are an arithmetic series, a linear function of x. As a result, the *second differences* are constant, actually $+2$, and consequently the third differences vanish.

24.4 The figures on the first line of such a table are called the *leading term* (0) and the *leading differences* (+1, +2, 0), and it is evident that, given the leading term and the leading differences, the whole table could be built up by successive addition as far as we pleased, without calculating any square directly except for checking. The series of first differences would be obtained by adding 2 over and over again, starting from the leading difference 1, i.e. $1+2=3$, $3+2=5$, etc. The squares would be given then by adding these differences in succession to the leading term 0 : $0+1=1$; $1+3=4$; $4+5=9$, etc.

Differences of a polynomial

24.5 From these results we may conclude quite generally that the second differences of *any* polynomial of the second degree,

$$u_x = a_0 + a_1 x + a_2 x^2 \quad . \qquad . \qquad . \qquad . \qquad (24.2)$$

are constant and the third differences vanish. For, if we multiply all the squares in Table 24.2 by any factor a_2, we merely multiply all the differences of every order by the same factor ; and the linear part of the function, $a_0 + a_1 x$, cannot contribute to second differences.

Below we give a similar table, Table 24.3, for the *cubes* of the first few natural numbers, and here it will be seen that *third* differences are constant

TABLE 24.3

Number x	Cube u_x	First diff. $\Delta^1(+)$	Second diff. $\Delta^2(+)$	Third diff. $\Delta^3(+)$	Fourth diff. Δ^4
0	0	1	6	6	0
1	1	7	12	6	0
2	8	19	18	6	—
3	27	37	24	—	—
4	64	61	—	—	—
5	125	—	—	—	—

and fourth differences vanish. By similar reasoning we may conclude that the third differences of *any* polynomial of the third degree,

$$u_x = a_0 + a_1 x + a_2 x^2 + a_3 x^3 \qquad . \qquad . \qquad . \qquad (24.3)$$

are constant and the fourth differences vanish. The student will be quite correct if he draws the general conclusion that for a polynomial of the rth degree,

$$u_x = a_0 + a_1 x + a_2 x^2 + \ldots + a_r x^r \qquad . \qquad . \qquad (24.4)$$

the rth differences are constant and the $(r+1)$th differences vanish. To prove this it is only necessary to note that each successive differencing lowers the degree of a polynomial by unity, for the difference of any term x^k is

$$(x+1)^k - x^k = kx^{k-1} + \frac{k(k-1)}{1.2}x^{k-2} + \ldots + 1$$

which is a polynomial of degree $(k-1)$.

Newton's formula

24.6 Evidently these results hold out some possibility of generalising our method of interpolation. If, instead of only considering *two* successive values of u_x, say u_0 and u_1, and using the linear relation between u_x and x that will reproduce these values to give any required intermediate value of u_x, we can use the polynomial of the second degree which will reproduce *three* adjacent values, u_0, u_1, u_2, or that of the third degree which will reproduce *four*, u_0, u_1, u_2, u_3, and evidently we shall be likely to get much more precise results. But to do this we must be able to obtain the required polynomials in terms of the differences. We shall use the notation already introduced, i.e.

x	Function	First diffs.	Second diffs.	Third diffs.	Fourth diffs.
0	u_0	Δ_0^1	Δ_0^2	Δ_0^3	Δ_0^4
1	u_1	Δ_1^1	Δ_1^2	Δ_1^3	—
2	u_2	Δ_2^1	Δ_2^2	—	—
3	u_3	Δ_3^1	—	—	—
4	u_4	—	—	—	—

Further, the common interval for the values of x will be taken as unity, as shown ; in practical work this is always treated as the unit until the end of the work, just as the class-interval is so treated when calculating the moments of a frequency-distribution.

24.7 Now write down the leading term and leading differences at the head of a table with spacious columns, as below, up to the leading fourth difference, and fill in the rest of the table working back from right to left. In column 5 for third differences we can fill in only the second space, $\Delta_0^3 + \Delta_0^4$. In column 4 for second differences the second term will be $\Delta_0^2 + \Delta_0^3$ (always adding from the line *above* to the right) ; the third term will be $\Delta_0^2 + 2\Delta_0^3 + \Delta_0^4$. We leave the student to supply the remainder.

1	2	3	4	5	6
				Third	Fourth
x	u_x	First diffs	Second diffs	diffs	diffs
0	$u_0 = u_0$	Δ_0^1	Δ_0^2	Δ_0^3	Δ_0^4
1	$u_1 = u_0 + \Delta_0^1$	$\Delta_0^1 + \Delta_0^2$	$\Delta_0^2 + \Delta_0^3$	$\Delta_0^3 + \Delta_0^4$	—
2	$u_2 = u_0 + 2\Delta_0^1 + \Delta_0^2$	$\Delta_0^1 + 2\Delta_0^2 + \Delta_0^3$	$\Delta_0^2 + 2\Delta_0^3 + \Delta_0^4$	—	—
3	$u_3 = u_0 + 3\Delta_0^1 + 3\Delta_0^2 + \Delta_0^3$	$\Delta_0^1 + 3\Delta_0^2 + 3\Delta_0^3 + \Delta_0^4$	—	—	—
4	$u_4 = u_0 + 4\Delta_0^1 + 6\Delta_0^2 + 4\Delta_0^3 + \Delta_0^4$	—	—	—	—

Now look at the numerical coefficients in the expressions for u_0, u_1, u_2, etc. ; they run

$$1$$
$$1+1$$
$$1+2+1$$
$$1+3+3+1$$
$$1+4+6+4+1$$

These are familiar figures ; they are the terms in the binomial expansions of $(1+1)^0$, $(1+1)^1$, $(1+1)^2$, $(1+1)^3$, etc. We then have, generally,

$$u_x = u_0 + x\Delta_0{}^1 + \frac{x(x-1)}{1.2}\Delta_0{}^2 + \frac{x(x-1)(x-2)}{1.2.3}\Delta_0{}^3 + \cdots \qquad (24.5)$$

where the series of differences may be continued so far as is necessary to give a result of the precision desired. This important equation is known as *Newton's Rule* or *Newton's Formula*. It may be repeated that in this form of the equation the unit of x is the interval. There are many other formulæ of interpolation, but we propose to limit ourselves to this and illustrate its uses.

24.8 It will be seen that, if the series on the right of (24.5) is terminated at $\Delta_0{}^r$, the expression *is* a polynomial of the rth degree in x, though it is not arranged according to powers of x but according to the successive orders of difference, which is more convenient for our present purpose. This polynomial passes through the $r+1$ successive points $(0, u_0)$, $(1, u_1)$, $(2, u_2)$, . . . (r, u_r). In particular, if the series terminates at $\Delta_0{}^1$, we have simple interpolation and the polynomial reduces to the straight line passing through $(0, u_0)$ and $(1, u_1)$. If it terminates at $\Delta_0{}^2$, the series represents a parabola of the second degree passing through the three points $(0, u_0)$, $(1, u_1)$, $(2, u_2)$. If it terminates at $\Delta_0{}^3$, it represents a polynomial of the third degree passing through the four points $(0, u_0)$, $(1, u_1)$, $(2, u_2)$, $(3, u_3)$; and so on. But the student must remember that even though the polynomial reproduces the values of the function at 0, 1, 2 and 3, it does not *necessarily* closely reproduce the function at intermediate values of x. The whole utility of the formula is dependent on the closeness with which the variable can be represented locally by a polynomial of fairly low degree. Most ordinary functions satisfy this condition when tabulated for small intervals, but occasionally the student may find himself in difficulties. We will give some examples in later sections.

We now proceed to some illustrations, and will give a warning at once : *the student must be very careful as to signs.*

Example 24.1.—Given the cubes below, required to find the cube of 32·4.

We give this first as an example in which the interpolation is *exact*, for the third differences are constant, so that we need not proceed further.

Number	Cube	$\Delta^1(+)$	$\Delta^2(+)$	$\Delta^3(+)$
31	29791	2977	192	6
32	32768	3169	198	6
33	35937	3367	204	—
34	39304	3571	—	—
35	42875	—	—	—

As interpolation is exact, it does not matter which term we take as u_0. Supposing we take an origin at $x=32$. Then for $32\cdot4$, $x=0\cdot4$, and we have—

$$u_{0\cdot4} = u_0 + 0\cdot4\Delta_0{}^1 + \frac{(0\cdot4)(-0\cdot6)}{1.2}\Delta_0{}^2 + \frac{(0\cdot4)(-0\cdot6)(-1\cdot6)}{1.2.3}\Delta_0{}^3$$

$$= 32768 + 0\cdot4(3169) - 0\cdot12(198) + 0\cdot064(6)$$

$$= 32768 + 1267\cdot6 - 23\cdot76 + 0\cdot384$$

$$= 34012\cdot224$$

This may be verified by direct multiplication, or from Barlow's Tables: the student is recommended to carry out a check by taking an origin at $x=31$.

Example 24.2.—Given the following cube roots, find the cube root of $102\cdot5$. The differences have been written, as is frequently done, without the insertion of the decimal point.

Number	Cube Root	$\Delta^1(+)$	$\Delta^2(-)$	$\Delta^3(+)$
101	4·6570095	153192	997	14
102	4·6723287	152195	983	—
103	4·6875482	151212	—	—
104	4·7026694	—	—	—

Here, if we wish to attain the greatest possible precision and include the third difference, we can only take an origin at 101; x is then $1\cdot5$, and

$$u_{1\cdot5} = u_0 + 1\cdot5\Delta_0{}^1 + 0\cdot375\Delta_0{}^2 - 0\cdot0625\Delta_0{}^3$$

$$= 4\cdot6570095 + 0\cdot02297880 - 0\cdot00003739 - 0\cdot00000009$$

$$= 4\cdot67995082$$

Here we have retained an extra place of decimals throughout the arithmetic in order to get the seventh place correct in the final result, and must round this off to 4.6799508. Even so, we cannot avoid the effect of errors in our data, viz. the errors of rounding off, in the seventh place of decimals, the tabulated cube roots : the seventh place in our answer is still liable to an error of ±1 to ±2 for this reason.

It may be noted that, as differences converge so rapidly in this example, simple interpolation would give an error of little more than a unit in the fifth place of decimals.

Example 24.3.—From the table of Ordinates of the Normal Curve (Appendix Table 1) find the value of the ordinate at $x/\sigma = 0\cdot045$.

We give this example partly as a warning to the student to see that his differences are converging so as to be likely to give a good result. The second difference is numerically much larger than the first, viz. 392 against 199 ; he must then look at the third as well ; if this be large also, he may have to go to a high order of differences to get precision. But the third difference is only $+18$ and the fourth difference smaller still, so third differences will suffice for the highest precision attainable with the five-figure table. Note that the first difference is negative, the second negative, the third positive, and since the interval is $0\cdot1$, $x = 0\cdot45$, *not* $0\cdot045$.

In the difference terms we have retained two decimals beyond the five during the work (separated by a comma)—

$$u_{0\cdot45} = u_0 + 0\cdot45\Delta_0{}^1 - 0\cdot12375\Delta_0{}^2 + 0\cdot0639375\Delta_0{}^3$$

$$= 0\cdot39894 - 0\cdot00089{,}55 + 0\cdot00048{,}51 + 0\cdot00001{,}15$$

$$= 0\cdot39854 \text{ rounded off to the fifth place}$$

Interpolating in the seven-figure table, Table II in *Tables for Statisticians and Biometricians*, this is found correct to the last place. It may be noted that, if a calculating machine is used, the products given by successive terms can be cumulated on the machine.

Interpolation of statistical series ·

24.9 So far we have dealt with straightforward interpolation of tabulated mathematical functions. But interpolation may also be employed on statistical series, or series of figures founded on statistics, provided at least that they run tolerably smoothly. No statistical series or series founded on statistics does, however, run absolutely smoothly, like a mathematical function, unless of course it has been deliberately " graduated " to do so. It must be recognised, therefore, in such cases that we are merely using interpolation as a method of *estimating* the truth ; and the truth in all probability would not and could not be given by any process of interpolation.

The following is an illustration of a series based on statistics.

Example 24.4.—In Part II of the Supplement to the 75th Report of the Registrar-General for England and Wales, abridged life-tables were given for a number of counties, etc. The table below shows the expectation of life at ages 25, 35, etc. to 85, based on the mortality of males in Cambridgeshire in 1910-12, i.e. the average number of years that individuals would have lived from the given age onwards, if subjected at each age to the mortality mentioned. Required, to interpolate values for the expectation of life at ages 30, 40, etc.

Age	Expectation of life (Males)	Δ¹	Δ²	Δ³
25	42·21	− 824	+ 20	+ 34
35	33·97	− 804	+ 54	+ 27
45	25·93	− 750	+ 81	+ 76
55	18·43	− 669	+157	− 3
65	11·74	− 512	+154	—
75	6·62	− 358	—	—
85	3·04	—	—	—
Total . . .	—	−3917	+466	+134
Bottom figures less top	−39·17	+ 466	+134	—

Tables of mathematical functions will often give the differences, but in dealing with data of this kind the student will certainly have to form them himself, and should carry out the check shown. Having formed the column of first differences, he should take the total, of course paying attention to signs. In this case the total of first differences is −3917, or inserting the decimal point, −39·17. This obviously must be equal to the difference between the bottom figure and the top figure in the preceding column, as we see is the case. The following columns must be checked similarly.

The second differences are considerably smaller than the first differences. Third differences are also small, but rather irregular; it will be found, however, that the contributions of the third differences affect only the second place of decimals in the function, so we ought to attain a very fair result.

To get the figures for ages 30 and 40 we have not much choice and must use the known values at ages 25 to 55. On general grounds it seems best to keep the value of x for which we require u_x near the centre of the values used for interpolation. So the expectation at 50 was determined from the values at 35 to 65, that at 60 from the values at 45 to 75, and that at 70 from the values at 55 to 85. The expectation at 80 was determined with the use of the second difference only from the values at 65, 75, 85.

The work is quite straightforward and the results were: 30, 38·09; 40, 29·90; 50, 22·10; 60, 14·94; 70, 8·99; 80, 4·64. The student may find it instructive to draw a chart.

But some qualms were felt as to how far the results could be trusted. A polynomial is not a very good function to represent an empirical function of the present kind which is slowly dropping to zero (see below, **24.12**). It might possibly be more appropriate to take logarithms of the expectations, interpolate between the logarithms and then convert back into numbers. The test was carried out as a control. The following are then the data and the differences—

Age	log (Expectation)	Δ^1	Δ^2	Δ^3
25	1·62542	−0·09432	−0·02298	−0·00799
35	1·53110	−0·11730	−0·03097	−0·01662
45	1·41380	−0·14827	−0·04759	−0·00536
55	1·26553	−0·19586	−0·05295	−0·03623
65	1·06967	−0·24881	−0·08918	—
75	0·82086	−0·33799	—	—
85	0·48287	—	—	—
Total . . .	—	−1·14255	−0·24367	−0·06620
Bottom figures less top	−1·14255	−0·24367	−0·06620	—

The work was done exactly as before, except that the expectation at 80 was obtained with three differences from the given values at 55 to 85. The results differed only very slightly from those obtained before, the following table giving a complete comparison—

Age	Interpolation		Difference
	Direct	Logarithmic	
25	42·21	42·21	—
30	38·09	38·07	−0·02
35	33·97	33·97	—
40	29·90	29·91	+0·01
45	25·93	25·93	—
50	22·10	22·11	+0·01
55	18·43	18·43	—
60	14·94	14·92	−0·02
65	11·74	11·74	—
70	8·99	9·00	+0·01
75	6·62	6·62	—
80	4·64	4·63	−0·01
85	3·04	3·04	—

The differences are almost immaterial.

Notes on the practical work

24.10 *Number of differences to use.*—Provided differences converge fairly rapidly and continuously, there is little difficulty in coming to a decision. The student knows to how many digits he desires to be accurate, and it is no use his going on to higher orders of difference which affect only places beyond this ; if he wants four-figure accuracy, it is no good his going on to differences which affect only the sixth and seventh places. To enable him to see more quickly the approximate contribution that a difference of any order will give, the following table of the binomial coefficients may be useful—

TABLE 24.4.—Table of the binomial coefficients in Newton's formula from $x=0$ to $x=2$ by intervals of $0\cdot1$

x	$\dfrac{x(x-1)}{1.2}$	$\dfrac{x(x-1)(x-2)}{1.2.3}$	$\dfrac{x(x-1)(x-2)(x-3)}{1.2.3.4}$
0	0	0	0
0·1	$-0\cdot045$	$+0\cdot0285$	$-0\cdot0206625$
0·2	$-0\cdot08$	$+0\cdot048$	$-0\cdot0336$
0·3	$-0\cdot105$	$+0\cdot0595$	$-0\cdot0401625$
0·4	$-0\cdot12$	$+0\cdot064$	$-0\cdot0416$
0·5	$-0\cdot125$	$+0\cdot0625$	$-0\cdot0390625$
0·6	$-0\cdot12$	$+0\cdot056$	$-0\cdot0336$
0·7	$-0\cdot105$	$+0\cdot0455$	$-0\cdot0261625$
0·8	$-0\cdot08$	$+0\cdot032$	$-0\cdot0176$
0·9	$-0\cdot045$	$+0\cdot0165$	$-0\cdot0086625$
1·0	0	0	0
1·1	$+0\cdot055$	$-0\cdot0165$	$+0\cdot0078375$
1·2	$+0\cdot12$	$-0\cdot032$	$+0\cdot0144$
1·3	$+0\cdot195$	$-0\cdot0455$	$+0\cdot0193375$
1·4	$+0\cdot28$	$-0\cdot056$	$+0\cdot0224$
1·5	$+0\cdot375$	$-0\cdot0625$	$+0\cdot0234375$
1·6	$+0\cdot48$	$-0\cdot064$	$+0\cdot0224$
1·7	$+0\cdot595$	$-0\cdot0595$	$+0\cdot0193375$
1·8	$+0\cdot72$	$-0\cdot048$	$+0\cdot0144$
1·9	$+0\cdot855$	$-0\cdot0285$	$+0\cdot0078375$
2·0	$+1$	0	0

A word of warning may, however, be desirable. Because the use of the $(r+1)$th difference would not affect the result in the kth figure, it does not *necessarily* follow that this polynomial value will agree with the true value of the function to the kth figure.

If differences do not converge rapidly and continuously, this is in itself evidence that a polynomial of moderately high order does not fit the function well and high precision cannot be expected. The student may occasionally find himself faced by cases more difficult than those of the foregoing illustrations. For example, here are the initial values of P for values of χ^2 proceeding by unity, and degrees of freedom $\nu=6$ ($n'=7$), from Table XII in *Tables for Statisticians*, etc., *Part I*—

χ^2	P	χ^2	P
0	$1\cdot000000$	5	$0\cdot543813$
1	$0\cdot985612$	6	$0\cdot423190$
2	$0\cdot919699$	7	$0\cdot320847$
3	$0\cdot808847$	8	$0\cdot238103$
4	$0\cdot676676$	9	$0\cdot173578$

If we wish to find by interpolation the value at, say, $0 \cdot 5$, apparently we have no choice but to take our u_0 at zero, for the table starts there. If the student begins work accordingly, he will find his differences not behaving at all nicely ; the second leading difference is much greater than the first ; the third is a good deal less, but the fourth, fifth and sixth much larger than the third, and it is not until the seventh and higher differences that definite convergence seems to be setting in. If he laboriously works step by step, getting successive approximations to the value of P at $0 \cdot 5$ by using one difference, two differences and so on, he will get a series of *very* slowly converging values—

1.	$0 \cdot 992806$
2.	$0 \cdot 999247$
3.	$0 \cdot 999658$
4.	$0 \cdot 998993$
5.	$0 \cdot 998445$
6.	$0 \cdot 998131$
·7.	$0 \cdot 997973$
8.	$0 \cdot 997899$
9.	$0 \cdot 997865$

The true value is $0 \cdot 997839$, and he could have obtained this much quicker by direct calculation ; even with the nine differences he has got only four-figure accuracy. But he ought not to have expected a good result if he had taken the trouble to look at the run of the differences. The figures give another useful warning. Using three differences, we have a worse result than when using two only. Increasing the number of differences by one step does not *necessarily* increase precision.

Limitation of the number of differences suitable for use, owing to the effect on differences of errors of rounding off, is considered below (**24.14** and **24.15**).

24.11 *Choice of the set of u's.*—To interpolate, say, at $x=2 \cdot 5$, using third differences, one might employ either the u's at 0, 1, 2, 3, or those at 1, 2, 3, 4, or those at 2, 3, 4, 5 ; one would not go outside these limits or one would have to *extrapolate* for the value at $2 \cdot 5$, and that would obviously be unsafe. Which set is it best to choose ? Advice cannot be absolutely definite, but it would seem that usually (but not necessarily) values about equidistant from that sought should be equally valuable as guides, and on this principle we should try and keep the value sought so far as possible central to the set of u's employed.

This suggests that *one* reason for our getting so poor a result above was that we used such a lop-sided set of u's, with the value sought apparently unavoidably near one end. Let us avoid this by a device. Repeat the value of P for $+1$ at -1 on the other side of zero. (It is true that this has no physical meaning, but the function might conceivably run symmetrically on either side of zero, and its graph has clearly high-order contact with a horizontal tangent at zero.) Now take the four values at $-1, 0 +1, +2$ and interpolate, using the resulting three differences only—

x^2	P	Δ^1	Δ^2	Δ^3
-1	0·985612	$+0·014388$	$-0·028776$	$-0·022749$
0	1	$-0·014388$	$-0·051525$	—
$+1$	0·985612	$-0·065913$	—	—
$+2$	0·919699	—	—	—

Interpolating for the value of $u_{1·5}$, we have—

$$u_{1·5} + u_0 = 1·5\Delta_0{}^1 + 0·375\Delta_0{}^2 - 0·0625\Delta_0{}^3$$

$$= 0·997825$$

The true value, as stated above, is $0·997839$, and we have got a closer result by this rearrangement, using third differences only, than we did by using nine differences before.

24.12 *Possible forms of polynomials.*—The student may also get into difficulties if he does not bear in mind the forms that polynomials can, and cannot, take ; and if he attempts to use this method of interpolation where the polynomial is unlikely to represent the function well even over a moderate range. A polynomial (parabola) of the second order can take only the form (*a*) in fig. 24.1. A polynomial of the third order can take the form (*b*), or the form (*c*) with a wave in the centre. A polynomial of the fourth order can take a form very much resembling (*b*), but flatter in the centre, or a form like (*c*), but with three instead of two half-waves in the middle ; and so on. A polynomial *cannot* take the form (1) of a curve tangential or asymptotic to the vertical, like the end near zero of an ideal frequency-curve of the distribution-of-wealth type, or (2) of a curve slowly dropping asymptotically to the horizontal, like a logarithmic curve or the tail of the normal curve—and such functions, mathematical or empirical, are very frequent in statistics. In this latter case it would be more probable that the function could be represented by a function of the form

$$y = e^{a_0 + a_1 x + a_2 x^2 +} \ldots$$

Then taking logs we have—

$$u = \log_e y = a_0 + a_1 x + a_2 x^2 + \ldots$$

that is to say, we come back to the polynomial. Hence, if the function we are dealing with is tailing slowly away to zero, it is probably best to take logarithms and then interpolate on the logarithms. That is why in Example 24.4 we carried out a check in that way. There, as it happened, the direct method did not lead to bad results, but it is quite possible for it to give a completely nonsensical answer. For example, at the extreme end of the χ^2 table for $\nu=28$ ($n'=29$), we are given only the values of P corresponding to the following values of χ^2—

χ^2	P	Δ^1	Δ^2	Δ^3
40	0·066128	−0·059661	+0·053601	−0·047929
50	0·006467	−0·006060	+0·005672	—
60	0·000407	−0·000388	—	—
70	0·000019	—	—	—

Taking differences as shown and interpolating to get an estimate of the value of P for $\chi^2=55$, i.e. $u_{1\cdot5}$, we have—

$$u_{1\cdot5} = u_0 + 1\cdot5\Delta_0{}^1 + 0\cdot375\Delta_0{}^2 - 0\cdot0625\Delta_0{}^3$$

$$= -0\cdot000268$$

But this is nonsense, for P cannot be negative. The polynomial has done its best ; it reproduces the values at 40, 50, 60 and 70—but it can only do this by taking a form like (c) of fig. 24.1 (reversed) with a wave in the centre. It has, as a matter of fact, a minimum at $\chi^2=56\cdot6$ and a maximum at $\chi^2=65\cdot8$, or at $1\cdot66$ and $2\cdot58$ on the scale of u's with 40 as zero and 10 as the unit interval.

If, instead, we take logarithms of the above values of P, interpolate to third differences and then convert back to numbers, as in Example 24.4, we find $0\cdot001699$ for the required value of P—a value which is rational and is probably not far from the truth. For $\chi^2=30$, $P=0\cdot363218$. Even bringing in this much larger value

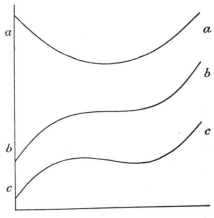

Fig. 24.1.

and using logarithmic interpolation with four differences, we find $0\cdot001746$ for the value of P at $\chi^2=55$. This suggests that at least we may trust the value to two figures as $0\cdot0017$, which would be sufficient for practice ; but the value has not been checked by direct calculation.

Effect of errors in u on the differences

24.13 The student may notice and be troubled by the fact that, in the Normal Curve Tables in the Appendix, second differences appear to get a little irregular towards the tail of the curve ; the phenomenon will become much more evident if he continues the second differences rather further than they have been entered, and still more so in the higher differences if he proceeds to write them out. The irregularities in question are due solely to the errors of rounding off in the last decimal place of the function. Before proceeding to consider the total effect of such a system of errors it may be best to consider the effect of a single error.

24.14 *Effect of an error in a single value of u.*—If $u=v+w$, $\Delta^1 u=\Delta^1 v+\Delta^1 w$, and so on for all orders of differences. Hence, if v represents the true value of u and w represents an error, the differences of the error will simply be superposed on the differences of u, and we may consider the former by themselves. We may then, as below, take the true values of u as zero, and insert an error only at one point, say $+e$.

u	Δ^1	Δ^2	Δ^3	Δ^4	Δ^5	Δ^6
0	0	0	0	0	0	$+\ e$
0	0	0	0	0	$+\ e$	$-\ 6e$
0	0	0	0	$+\ e$	$-\ 5e$	$+15e$
0	0	0	$+\ e$	$-4e$	$+10e$	$-20e$
0	0	$+\ e$	$-3e$	$+6e$	$-10e$	$+15e$
0	$+e$	$-2e$	$+3e$	$-4e$	$+\ 5e$	$-\ 6e$
$+e$	$-e$	$+\ e$	$-\ e$	$+\ e$	$-\ e$	$+\ e$
0	0	0	0	0	0	0

The resulting differences are written down above, up to those of the sixth order, and it is evident that the numerical coefficients of e in the differences of order r are given by the terms of $(1-1)^r$. The effect of the initial error is therefore very rapidly increased as we proceed to higher and higher orders of difference, especially after the first three differences are past. An error of $+e$ in u can produce an error of $+3e$ or $-3e$ in the third differences, of $6e$ in the fourth differences, of $10e$ in the fifth and of $20e$ in the sixth. The maximum numerical coefficient for order r is derived from that for order $r-1$ by multiplying the latter by 2 if r is even, or by $2r/(r+1)$ if r is odd.

This magnification of the error renders differencing a very useful method of checking the calculated table of a function, and it is often employed for that purpose. The matter is not quite simple, for the effects of errors of rounding off in the last decimal place will be superposed on the effects of any actual mistake, but nevertheless the effects of the mistake are likely to show themselves clearly in, say, third or fourth differences. In the following table of square roots, for example, nothing is obviously wrong, but an error of 2 units in the last place has been introduced into the square root of 15, which should read $3 \cdot 87298$ (or more precisely, $3 \cdot 8729833$). When we proceed to take differences, however, a suspicious irregularity shows itself in the third differences, and in the fourth differences it is clear that something is wrong. Since the position of the " peak " rises half a line at each differencing, the peak $+2$ shows that the mistake is in the root of 15. We can even estimate the magnitude of the error. If the fifth differences may be taken as approximately constant, we ought to get a fair estimate of the true fourth difference at the peak $+2$ by adding together that difference and the two on each side of it, the total effect of the error

Number	Square root	$\Delta^1(+)$	$\Delta^2(-)$	$\Delta^3(+)$	Δ^4
10	3·16228	0·15434	686	83	−14
11	3·31662	0·14748	603	69	−12
12	3·46410	0·14145	534	57	−14
13	3·60555	0·13611	477	43	+ 2
14	3·74166	0·13134	434	45	−14
15	3·87300	0·12700	389	31	0
16	4	0·12311	358	31	− 6
1?	4·12311	0·11953	327	25	—
18	4·24264	0·11626	302	—	—
19	4·35890	0·11324	—	—	—
20	4·47214	—	—	—	—

e thus averaging out—compare the scheme showing the effect of the single error given above. This average is −7·6. We then have—

$$6e = +2-(-7\cdot6)$$

$$e = +1\cdot6$$

This is very near the correct value, which, as will be seen from the true value of the root stated, is $300-298\cdot33$ or $1\cdot67$, the unit in the Δ^4 column being the last place of decimals of the function.

24.15 *Effect of a series of random errors in u.*—Suppose these errors to be a, b, c, d, e, as below. Writing down their differences, we have the following results—

Error	Δ^1	Δ^2	Δ^3	Δ^4
a	$b-a$	$c-2b+a$	$d-3c+3b-a$	$e-4d+6c-4b+a$
b	$c-b$	$d-2c+b$	$e-3d+3c-b$	—
c	$d-c$	$e-2d+c$	—	—
d	$e-d$	—	—	—
e	—	—	—	—

The general result is obvious. In differences of the rth order, the resultant error in any one difference is the sum of $r+1$ of the original errors multiplied in succession by the terms in the binomial expansion of $(1-1)^r$, or is of the form

$$e_1-re_2+\frac{r(r-1)}{1.2}e_3-\frac{r(r-1)(r-2)}{1.2.3}e_4+\ldots \qquad . \quad (24.6)$$

If the errors e are distributed in a purely random way, so that e_k is uncorrelated with e_{k+s}, and if it may be assumed that the mean error is zero, then the mean error in the difference of the rth order will also in a long series tend to zero, and the standard deviation, s_r, of the above quantity (24.6) is given by

$$s_r{}^2 = F(r)s_0{}^2 \qquad . \qquad . \qquad . \qquad . \quad (24.7)$$

where s_0 is the s.d. of the original errors e, and $F(r)$ is the sum of the squares of the terms in the binomial expansion of $(1-1)^r$. This may be shown to be equal to $\binom{2r}{r}$.

$F(r)$ increases very rapidly with r. The following table gives the value of $F(r)$ and of its square root from $r=1$ to $r=6$—

r	$F(r)$	$\sqrt{F(r)}$
1	2	1·41
2	6	2·45
3	20	4·47
4	70	8·37
5	252	15·87
6	924	30·40

The standard deviation of errors in the fourth differences is therefore over eight times, and in the sixth differences over thirty times, the s.d. of the errors affecting u.

If the decimal place in u be regarded as following the last figure retained, the errors of rounding off that figure may be regarded as uniformly distributed over a range $\pm 0\cdot5$, and their standard deviation, s_0, is therefore $\sqrt{1/12}$ or $0\cdot288675$. This gives the following figures for the s.d. of errors in the successive orders of difference owing to the errors of rounding off in u—

Order of difference	S.d. of errors
1	0·41
2	0·71
3	1·29
4	2·42
5	4·58
6	8·77

The effect of the errors of rounding off evidently increases very rapidly with the order of difference. With a mathematical function for which the true differences rapidly and continuously converge, the effect of the errors will in fact soon, so to speak, " take charge " ; the *observed* differences will rapidly and steadily diverge, growing larger with each successive differencing. At the same time two other phenomena will show themselves. Looking back at the scheme showing the effect of the errors a, b, c, d, e, it will be seen that in any one *column* the same error enters into successive differences with sign reversed. Also in any one *line* the same error enters into successive differences with sign reversed. Hence, as the effect of errors of rounding off becomes overwhelmingly great, (1) the differences of the same order tend to alternate in sign, (2) differences of successive orders on the same line tend to alternate in sign. If these phenomena start to show themselves, the student may well suspect he has gone too far in his differencing. It is evidently no use proceeding to an order of differences mainly significant of errors.

These results for the effect on differences of a random series of errors have an application, not only to the effect of errors of rounding off in mathematical tables, but also to the theory of the variate-difference method (**26.31**).

Effect on differences of subdividing an interval

24.16 We mentioned early in this chapter (**24.2**) that, in general, it would become possible to use simple interpolation alone on a table of a mathematical function provided intervals were made sufficiently fine, but this was not proved. Let us consider the effect on the differences of subdividing an interval; it will suffice to take the case of halving it, and for brevity let us confine ourselves to the first three differences.

In terms of Newton's formula the values of u at $0, 0\cdot5, 1, 1\cdot5$, are

$$\left.\begin{aligned}
u_0 &= u_0 \\
u_{0\cdot5} &= u_0 + 0\cdot5\Delta_0{}^1 - 0\cdot125\Delta_0{}^2 + 0\cdot0625\Delta_0{}^3 \\
u_1 &= u_0 + \Delta_0{}^1 \\
u_{1\cdot5} &= u_0 + 1\cdot5\Delta_0{}^1 + 0\cdot375\Delta_0{}^2 - 0\cdot0625\Delta_0{}^3
\end{aligned}\right\} \qquad . \qquad . \quad (24.8)$$

If the student will write down these expressions at the left of a sheet of foolscap placed lengthwise, and take the differences in the ordinary way, he will find that the new leading differences for the subdivided series with intervals of half the original interval are given by

$$\left.\begin{aligned}
\delta_0{}^1 &= 0\cdot5\Delta_0{}^1 - 0\cdot125\Delta_0{}^2 + 0\cdot0625\Delta_0{}^3 \\
\delta_0{}^2 &= 0\cdot25\Delta_0{}^2 - 0\cdot125\Delta_0{}^3 \\
\delta_0{}^3 &= 0\cdot125\Delta_0{}^3
\end{aligned}\right\} \qquad . \qquad . \qquad . \quad (24.9)$$

If the Δ's of the original series converge rapidly, an assumption really implied by the fact that we stopped at the third difference, so that we can regard the successive Δ's as of different orders of magnitude, it will be seen that $\delta_0{}^1$ is of the order of magnitude $0\cdot5\Delta_0{}^1$, $\delta_0{}^2$ is of the order of magnitude $0\cdot25\Delta_0{}^2$, and $\delta_0{}^3$ of the order of magnitude $0\cdot125\Delta_0{}^3$. That is to say, the new differences are not only smaller than the original differences, but converge much more rapidly.

If we had divided the original interval into ten instead of only two parts, we could have found the new leading differences in precisely the same way, and would then have obtained the result that $\delta_0{}^1$ was of the order of magnitude $0\cdot1\Delta_0{}^1$, $\delta_0{}^2$ of the order of magnitude $0\cdot01\Delta_0{}^2$, and so on, the general rule being obvious. Hence it is only necessary to subdivide the interval sufficiently in order to render the differences so rapidly convergent that first differences alone can be used.

In works on the method of differences, tables will usually be found giving for various values of the number of subdivisions the formulæ relating the δ's to the Δ's.

We now turn to some statistical problems.

Breaking up a group

24.17 Suppose we are given the numbers living, or the numbers of deaths, in successive ten-year age-groups, we may often desire to estimate the numbers in smaller, e.g. five-year, age-groups, or even at single years of age. The initial difficulty and the method of procedure will best be shown by an illustration.

Example 24.5

The following are the numbers of deaths in four successive ten-year age-groups. Required to estimate the numbers of deaths at 45–50 and 50–55.

Age-group	Deaths
25–	13,229
35–	18,139
45–	24,225
55–	31,496

Now evidently interpolating directly between these figures will not help us. If we interpolated directly between the figure for 35– and the figure for 45– (half-way between), we would only have an estimate of the numbers in the *ten*-year age-group 40–50. We must proceed as follows. Add up the given numbers step by step ; this will give us a new set of figures showing the numbers over 25 but less than 35, over 25 but less than 45, over 25 but less than 55, and over 25 but less than 65. Interpolate in this new series to find the number over 25 but less than 50, and the differences from the numbers next above and below will give the answer desired. The work is as follows—

1	2	3	4	5
Exact age	Sum of deaths from 25 to age stated	Δ^1	Δ^2	Δ^3
25	0	+13,229	+4,910	+1,176
35	13,229	+18,139	+6,086	+1,185
45	31,368	+24,225	+7,271	—
55	55,593	+31,496	—	—
65	87,089	—	—	—

Column 2 gives the numbers from age 25 up to each age stated ; column 3 the first differences, reproducing the numbers in the age-groups ; columns 4 and 5 the second and third differences. Since the two third differences are very nearly equal, working to third differences ought to give us a very fair result. We can accordingly take age 35 as our zero, and age 50 will be 1·5 on the scale with the interval as unit. We have accordingly,

$$u_{1\cdot5} = u_0 + 1\cdot5\Delta_0{}^1 + 0\cdot375\Delta_0{}^2 - 0\cdot0625\Delta_0{}^3$$
$$= 13{,}229 + 1\cdot5(18{,}139) + 0\cdot375(6{,}086) - 0\cdot0625(1{,}185)$$
$$= 42{,}645\cdot7$$

or 42,646 to the nearest unit. Subtracting 31,368 from 42,646, and 42,646 from 55,593, we then have for our estimates of the numbers of deaths—

$$45\text{–}50 \quad 11{,}278$$

$$50\text{–}55 \quad 12{,}947$$

As a matter of fact, the numbers in quinquennial groups were given, and for 45–50, 50–55, were actually 11,404 and 12,821 ; the error of our estimates accordingly is only of the order of 1 per cent.

Example 24.6.—From the same data, estimate the number of deaths in the year of age 50–51.

The limits of this group on our scale of intervals are, with 35 as origin, $1 \cdot 5$ and $1 \cdot 6$. We have already found the number up to $1 \cdot 5$ in Example 24.5, and it remains only to determine the number up to $1 \cdot 6$, the difference between the two figures then giving the answer sought—

$$u_{1 \cdot 6} = u_0 + 1 \cdot 6\Delta_0{}^1 + 0 \cdot 48\Delta_0{}^2 - 0 \cdot 064\Delta_0{}^3$$

$$= 13{,}229 + 1 \cdot 6(18{,}139) + 0 \cdot 48(6{,}086) - 0 \cdot 064(1{,}185)$$

$$= 45{,}096 \cdot 8$$

or 45,097 to the nearest unit. Hence the answer is 45,097 − 42,646, or 2451.

Simple formula for halving a group

24.18 The problem of estimating the numbers in the two five-year groups of which a ten-year group is composed occurs so often, that it is worth while deriving a simple second-difference formula for the purpose. Let u's denote numbers in five-year groups, w's numbers in ten-year groups ; and let δ's and Δ's denote the corresponding differences. For second differences we need only consider three consecutive ten-year groups. From Newton's formula we have—

$$u_0 = u_0$$
$$u_1 = u_0 + \delta_0{}^1$$

$$\overline{}$$

$$w_0 = 2u_0 + \delta_0{}^1$$
$$u_2 = u_0 + 2\delta_0{}^1 + \delta_0{}^2$$
$$u_3 = u_0 + 3\delta_0{}^1 + 3\delta_0{}^2$$

$$\overline{}$$

$$w_1 = 2u_0 + 5\delta_0{}^1 + 4\delta_0{}^2$$
$$u_4 = u_0 + 4\delta_0{}^1 + 6\delta_0{}^2$$
$$u_5 = u_0 + 5\delta_0{}^1 + 10\delta_0{}^2$$

$$\overline{}$$

$$w_2 = 2u_0 + 9\delta_0{}^1 + 16\delta_0{}^2$$

Now write down these values of the w's and difference—

x	w_x	Δ^1	Δ^2
0	$2u_0+\delta_0^1$	$4\delta_0^1+4\delta_0^2$	$8\delta_0^2$
1	$2u_0+5\delta_0^1+4\delta_0^2$	$4\delta_0^1+12\delta_0^2$	
2	$2u_0+9\delta_0^1+16\delta_0^2$		

Whence

$$\Delta_0^1 = 4(\delta_0^1+\delta_0^2)$$
$$\Delta_0^2 = 8\delta_0^2$$

or

$$\delta_0^2 = \tfrac{1}{8}\Delta_0^2$$
$$\delta_0^1 = \tfrac{1}{4}\Delta_0^1-\tfrac{1}{8}\Delta_0^2$$

Hence,

$$u_2 = u_0+2\delta_0^1+\delta_0^2$$
$$= u_0+\tfrac{1}{2}\Delta_0^1-\tfrac{1}{8}\Delta_0^2$$
$$u_2-\tfrac{1}{2}w_1 = -\tfrac{1}{8}\Delta_0^1-\tfrac{1}{16}\Delta_0^2$$
$$= -\tfrac{1}{16}(2\Delta_0^1+\Delta_0^2)$$

It will be convenient for practical work to express this directly in terms of the w's—

$$2\Delta_0^1 \quad = 2w_1-2w_0$$
$$\Delta_0^2 \quad = w_2-2w_1+w_0$$

$$2\Delta_0^1+\Delta_0^2 = \quad w_2-w_0$$

Whence finally,

$$u_2 = \tfrac{1}{2}\{w_1+\tfrac{1}{8}(w_0-w_2)\} \qquad . \qquad . \qquad . \quad (24.10)$$

Thus, taking the figures and problem of Example 24.5 again, we have—

$$w_0 = 18,139$$
$$w_1 = 24,225$$
$$w_2 = 31,496$$
$$\tfrac{1}{8}(w_0-w_2) = -1,669\cdot6$$
$$w_1 = 24,225$$

$$22,555\cdot4$$

and half this gives

$$u_2 = 11,278$$

to the nearest unit, as before. For u_3, of course, we have also, as before, $24,225-11,278=12,947$. Equation (24.10) is really equivalent to the method of Example 24.5, though in that illustration we used three differences. But the third differences of the numbers " aged over 25 but under x " are equivalent to the second differences of the numbers in the successive age-groups.

Graduation

24.19 If a graph is drawn showing the numbers of either sex living at each single year of age, as given in any census which provides data in such detail, it will be found anything but smooth, showing the oddest peaks and hollows which repeat themselves, once adult life is reached, at ages showing the same final digits. Thus, in the Census of England and Wales there are conspicuous peaks at the round-numbered ages 30, 40, 50, etc. (last birthday), and hollows or deficiencies at the ages ending with 1 and, less emphatically, at the ages ending with 7. With returns from less educated populations, the phenomenon may become almost ludicrous, e.g. in a certain Indian census sample-count—

Age last birthday	Number of males
29	927
30	12,294
31	652
32	2,058
33	672
34	892
35	7,723
36	1,437
37	870
38	1,362
39	467
40	10,391
41	460

Now whatever irregularities might occur in the true figures, we may be quite certain that they should *not* show errors that are simply a function of the final digit of the age. We would prefer, therefore, to eliminate these errors. We could do so, somewhat roughly, by drawing a graph as suggested and sweeping a clean curve through the rather scattered and irregular points given by the data, subsequently reading off smoothed or *graduated* figures from the curve. The graphic process has many points to recommend it, but is very dependent on personal skill and judgment. It would be convenient to use a more " mechanical " process that anyone could apply and be sure of obtaining the same results if he used the same process. It would be quite possible to fit polynomials to the data by the methods of Chapter 15, but this would in general entail a great deal of labour and would not necessarily lead to satisfactory results, e.g. with such highly erratic data as those above. More suitable processes can be founded on the method of differences, and the general idea of them all is quite simple, though the details may vary greatly and the practical working of some of them become rather complex. All methods begin by assuming that the *totals* of certain age-groups—five-year or ten-year age-groups as a rule—are reasonably accurate. These totals can then be redistributed over single years of age by the elementary process of Examples 24.5 and 24.6, or the procedure can be in some way elaborated. We shall illustrate only the simple process.

Example 24.7.—The English Census of 1911 gives the following numbers of males in the three age-groups stated. Obtain graduated numbers at single years of age for the decade 40 to 49.

Age-group	Number
30–	2,637,304
40–	2,001,178
50–	1,376,236

As before, we form the sum of these numbers step by step from the top and then take differences.

Exact age	Sum of numbers from 30	$\Delta^1(+)$	$\Delta^2(-)$	$\Delta^3(+)$
30	0	2,637,304	636,126	11,184
40	2,637,304	2,001,178	624,942	—
50	4,638,482	1,376,236	—	—
60	6,014,718	—	—	—

We now, taking 30 as our zero, require to interpolate at $1\cdot1, 1\cdot2, 1\cdot3$, etc. to $1\cdot9$. The coefficients of the several differences in the successive applications of Newton's formula are—

Δ^1	Δ^2	Δ^3
$+1\cdot1$	$+0\cdot055$	$-0\cdot0165$
$+1\cdot2$	$+0\cdot12$	$-0\cdot032$
$+1\cdot3$	$+0\cdot195$	$-0\cdot0455$
$+1\cdot4$	$+0\cdot28$	$-0\cdot056$
$+1\cdot5$	$+0\cdot375$	$-0\cdot0625$
$+1\cdot6$	$+0\cdot48$	$-0\cdot064$
$+1\cdot7$	$+0\cdot595$	$-0\cdot0595$
$+1\cdot8$	$+0\cdot72$	$-0\cdot048$
$+1\cdot9$	$+0\cdot855$	$-0\cdot0285$

The results, with the known numbers to age 40 and to age 50 added, are as given in the second column below, and in the fourth column they are differenced to obtain the graduated numbers at each year of age, the total of which must agree with the observed total in the ten-year group.

1	2	3	4
Exact age	Sum of population from 30 to age stated	Age last birthday	Graduated number
40	2,637,304	40	228,559
41	2,865,863	41	222,209
42	3,088,072	42	215,870
43	3,303,942	43	209,542
44	3,513,484	44	203,226
45	3,716,710	45	196,920
46	3,913,630	46	190,626
47	4,104,256	47	184,344
48	4,288,600	48	178,071
49	4,466,671	49	171,811
50	4,638,482		
Total	—	—	2,001,178

Below, these figures are compared with the actual returns at the single years of age and with two other graduations : (1) A graduation given in the Census report and prepared by Mr. George King, F.I.A., based on certain quinquennial age-groups. (2) A graduation using analogous methods, but based on ten-year age-groups, made at a later date in the Government Actuary's Department, and reproduced by permission. The methods are described in rather more detail below.

1	2	3	4	5
Age last birthday	Census numbers	Graduation above	King's graduation, K_1	Graduation K_2
40	262,690	228,559	231,070	231,397
41	198,344	222,209	223,721	225,456
42	226,889	215,870	216,556	219,233
43	196,204	209,542	209,314	212,785
44	190,949	203,226	202,143	206,169
45	202,458	196,920	195,193	199,442
46	184,881	190,626	188,610	192,661
7	176,713	184,344	182,577	185,883
48	189,271	178,071	176,994	179,165
49	172,779	171,811	171,589	172,564
Total	2,001,178	2,001,178	1,997,767	2,024,755

If we compare the closeness of fit of the several graduations to the Census returns by adding up the differences, observed number less graduated number, without regard to their sign, and expressing this total as a

percentage of the population (2,001,178), it will be found that our graduation gives a percentage deviation of 6·28, King's graduation (K_1) a percentage deviation of 6·09, and the graduation K_2 a percentage deviation of
6·40—figures which do not differ very largely. It will be noticed, however, that both the K graduations give, over the range considered, a small
biased error, the total population over the ten years being too small for
K_1 and too large for K_2. As regards the deviations of the several graduations from one another, the percentage deviation of our graduation from
K_1 is 0·64 and from K_2 1·18, reckoned in each case on the true total population, and the percentage deviation of K_2 from K_1 is 1·35, reckoned on the
K_1 total. At some individual ages the differences run up to nearly 2 per
cent. This is a warning to the student that while it is true that the use
of any one of these methods by different workers must, unlike the use of the
graphic method, lead to the same result, yet the choice of *different* methods
may lead to results almost, if not quite, as divergent as those obtained by
different users of the graphic process. Graduated numbers of hundreds of
thousands carried to the last unit suggest a degree of precision much
higher than exists.

There is evidently a certain imperfection in the elementary method we
have used. If we employed the same method to graduate the numbers at
ages 30 to 39, using the numbers in the three ten-year age-groups 20–, 30–,
40–, there would be a discontinuity at 40, for the two graduated series would
be given by arcs of distinct polynomials. The discontinuity might not
be conspicuous, but it would be there and would probably be brought out
by differencing. To get over this, at least in part, a simple adjustment
can be used. Continue the graduated series for 30 to 39 over the next few
years of age, say to 42. Also continue our series for 40 to 49 backwards to
37. Over the six years 37 to 42 we then have two graduated values at
each age, and these may then be averaged with weights which gradually
throw the weight from the earlier series on to the later—say such simple
weights as 6 to 1, 5 to 2, 4 to 3, 3 to 4, 2 to 5, 1 to 6. We have also paid no
particular attention to the choice of the limits of our ten-year age-group.
Of course it might happen that the numbers were only compiled in ten-
year groups like 20–, 30–, 40–, etc., and then there would be no choice.
But if the figures are given at single years, the choice is at our disposal,
and it may be that we have not chosen wisely. Part of the excess at the
peak figure is probably drawn from lower ages, and it might have been
better to keep the " peak " at the round-number ages well inside the group,
e.g. by compiling totals for the decades 35–, 45–, etc., rather than those
used.

King, in the Census graduation, used five-year age-groups as his
basis, and chose the limits 4–8, 9–13, 14–18, etc., as probably giving the
totals nearest the truth. Taking these five-year totals in successive sets
of three, he used the precise procedure of our Example 24.6 to determine
a graduated figure for the central year of the fifteen—e.g. the three groups

covering ages 4–18 would give a graduated number at age 11, the three covering ages 9 to 23 would give a graduated number at age 16, and so on. But here his process broke away. Taking four consecutive graduated numbers five years apart and determined in this way as " pivotal values," he used the method of differences to determine a polynomial of the third order not passing through the four points u_0, u_1, u_2, u_3, but subjected to the four conditions (1) that it should pass through the *two* points u_1 and u_2, (2) that at u_1 and u_2 it should have a common tangent with the corresponding arc determined from the next (overlapping) set of pivotal values. In this way continuity was assured, but equality of observed and graduated totals for the five-year groups was lost. (The process used was a simplification of the process of *osculatory interpolation*, by which two arcs meeting at a point are given not only a common tangent but also a common radius of curvature. It might be called " tangential interpolation.") The desirability of using five-year groups may be questioned. It is true that ten-year groups are rather large, but the errors that we are trying to eliminate are definitely functions of the ten final digits, and however the limits are chosen there is likely to remain a systematic difference between the adjacent groups of successive pairs if five-year groups are used.

The test of K_2, in which an analogous process was used but based on the ten-year age-groups 5–14, 15–24, etc., was therefore of interest. Over the range of 30–80 years the differences between K_1 and K_2 gave a smoothly running cyclical curve with a tendency towards a period of ten years, as might have been expected.

The simple process given in Example 24.7 is applicable throughout the bulk of life, but not at the two ends of the series, where special tricks of the trade have to be employed. The difficulty of interpolating in a " tail," where the numbers are slowly approaching zero, has already been pointed out. For graduation these difficulties are increased, and it is often best to drop the method of differences altogether and use some special process, such as assuming a law of decrease or fitting the tail of a frequency-distribution.

Inverse interpolation

24.20 By interpolation we determine the value of the function for a given value of the variable. If we are given the value of the function and find the corresponding value of the variable, we are performing *inverse interpolation*. The student has carried out the process, in a form corresponding to simple interpolation, whenever he has determined the number corresponding to a given logarithm by the use of a table of logarithms—not a table of antilogarithms. If we need only take first differences into consideration, the process is, in fact, very simple. From Newton's formula we have

$$u_x = u_0 + x\Delta_0{}^1$$

whence

$$x = \frac{u_x - u_0}{\Delta_0^{1}} \qquad . \qquad . \qquad . \qquad . \quad (24.11)$$

where u_0 will naturally be taken as the tabulated value next below u_x. If we must take second differences also into account, we have

$$u_x = u_0 + x\Delta_0^{1} + \frac{x(x-1)}{1.2}\Delta_0^{2}$$

which gives the quadratic for x

$$\tfrac{1}{2}\Delta_0^{2}x^2 + (\Delta_0^{1} - \tfrac{1}{2}\Delta_0^{2})x - (u_x - u_0) = 0 \qquad . \qquad . \quad (24.12)$$

or, solving,

$$x = -\frac{2\Delta_0^{2} - \Delta_0^{2}}{2\Delta_0^{2}} \pm \sqrt{\frac{2(u_x - u_0)}{\Delta_0^{2}} + \left(\frac{2\Delta_0^{1} - \Delta_0^{2}}{2\Delta_0^{2}}\right)^2} \qquad . \quad (24.13)$$

The sign to be taken for the square root will be evident on carrying out the arithmetic.

This is not always a very convenient expression to use, the solution (compare Example 24.8 below) being given as a comparatively small difference between two large quantities. If x_1 is the approximate solution given by first differences, we can replace x in equation (24.12) by $x_1 + h$ and solve for the correction h on the assumption that h^2 may be neglected. This gives

$$h = \frac{x_1(1 - x_1)\Delta_0^{2}}{2x_1\Delta^2 + 2\Delta_0^{1} - \Delta_0^{2}}$$

$$= \frac{x_1(1 - x_1)\rho}{2 + (2x_1 - 1)\rho} \qquad . \qquad . \qquad . \quad (24.14)$$

where

$$\rho = \frac{\Delta_0^{2}}{\Delta_0^{1}} \qquad . \qquad . \qquad . \quad (24.15)$$

If we may further assume that ρ is small, this reduces to

$$h = \tfrac{1}{2}x_1(1 - x_1)\rho \qquad . \qquad . \qquad . \quad (24.16)$$

Obtaining a first approximation from first differences, we can use (24.16) to get a second approximation, then insert this second approximation in (24.16) and get a third approximation, and so on until the process of approximation makes no further difference. But note the assumption made that ρ is small.

Example 24.8

To find the approximate value of the quartile deviation, i.e. the value of x/σ for which $A = 0.75$, in the normal curve, given that for $x/\sigma = 0.6, 0.7, 0.8$ the values of A are respectively $0.72573, 0.75804, 0.78814$.

The data are—

x/σ	A	Δ_0^1	Δ_0^2
0·6	0·72575	+0·03229	−0·00219

Hence,

$$u_x - u_0 = 0·02425$$

and the first approximation to x by first differences only is

$$x_1 = +\frac{0·02425}{0·03229} = +0·7510 \text{ interval}$$

$$= +0·07510$$

or measured from the zero of the scale, the first approximation to the quartile deviation is 0·67510.

Turning now to the quadratic (24.13), the solution is

$$x = 15·2443 - 14·4997$$

$$= 0·7446 \text{ interval}$$

$$= 0·07446$$

the sign of the root having evidently to be taken as negative. Using second differences, then, our approximation to the quartile deviation is

$$0·67446$$

The true value to five places is

$$0·67449$$

so the use of second differences only has left an error in the last digit.

Let us see how the suggested process of approximation would have worked. From (24.16)—

$$h = -0·0339114 \times 0·751 \times 0·249$$
$$= -0·00634$$
$$x_1 = \quad 0·751$$
$$\overline{}$$
$$x_2 = 0·74466$$

Now taking x_2 as the second approximation—

$$h = -0·0339114 \times 0·74466 \times 0·25534$$
$$= -0·00645$$
$$x_1 = \quad 0·751$$
$$\overline{}$$
$$x_3 = \quad 0·74455$$

If we repeat the same process again, $x_4 = 0·74455$, which is the same as x_3, so it is no use going further, and 0·67446 is as close as we can get.

If third and higher orders of difference are brought into account, we have an equation of higher degree than the second, which can be solved by Newton's method of approximation, but the student will find more direct methods given in advanced works.

Estimation of the position of a maximum

24.21 In this and the following problem an elementary knowledge of the calculus is assumed; the student who does not know the calculus may nevertheless find the results useful.

Suppose we are given three equidistant ordinates u_0, u_1, u_2 at 0, 1 and 2. Required to find the position of the maximum of the parabola passing through the tops of the ordinates. We have—

$$u_x = u_0 + x\Delta_0{}^1 + \frac{x(x-1)}{1.2}\Delta_0{}^2$$

Differentiating with respect to x and equating to zero, the abscissa of the maximum is given by

$$\Delta_0{}^1 + \tfrac{1}{2}(2x-1)\Delta_0{}^2 = 0$$

or

$$x = 0\cdot5 - \frac{\Delta_0{}^1}{\Delta_0{}^2} \qquad . \qquad . \qquad . \qquad . \quad (24.17)$$

Very often, perhaps most frequently, our data are not ordinates but rather areas; e.g. if we want to estimate roughly the position of the mode, our data will be the total frequencies in three successive class-intervals—*not* the central ordinates of those intervals. We should then, as in Example 24.5, form the sum of these data step by step and take the *second* differential of the polynomial passing through the resultant points in order to determine the mode. Thus, calling the sum w—

x	u	x	Sum w
0	u_0	$-0\cdot5$	0
1	$u_0 + \Delta_0{}^1$	$+0\cdot5$	u_0
2	$u_0 + 2\Delta_0{}^1 + \Delta_0{}^2$	$+1.5$	$2u_0 + \Delta_0{}^1$
		$+2\cdot5$	$3u_0 + 3\Delta_0{}^1 + \Delta_0{}^2$

It must be remembered that the sum w starts at half an interval below zero, as shown. Using δ's to denote the differences of w—

$$\delta_0{}^1 = u_0$$
$$\delta_0{}^2 = \Delta_0{}^1$$
$$\delta_0{}^3 = \Delta_0{}^2$$

$$w_x = w_0 + xu_0 + \frac{x(x-1)}{2}\Delta_0{}^1 + \frac{x(x-1)(x-2)}{6}\Delta_0{}^2$$

$$\frac{d^2w_x}{dx^2} = \Delta_0{}^1 + (x-1)\Delta_0{}^2 = 0$$

or

$$x = 1 - \frac{\Delta_0{}^1}{\Delta_0{}^2}$$

Since x is now measured from $-\frac{1}{2}$, this is the same answer as before. If we are concerned only with *second* differences of the data, and not with differences of any higher order, it does not matter whether our data are ordinates or areas.

The method must be used with caution ; obviously it cannot give at all a precise result unless the data run smoothly, and if it be used for determining the mode, may easily give an answer appreciably divergent from that obtained by fitting a frequency-curve. The following illustration will serve as a warning—

Example 24.9.—The following are the frequencies near the mode in a distribution of barometer heights. Estimate the position of the mode, (1) from the first three, (2) from the last three.

Height (inches)	Frequency
29·9	339·5
30·0	382·5
30·1	395·5
30·2	315

Differencing—

Height (inches)	Frequency	Δ^1	Δ^2
29·9	339·5	+43	−30
30·0	382·5	+13	−93·5
30·1	395·5	−80·5	—
30·2	315	—	—

Taking the first three frequencies and their differences—

$$x = 0\cdot5 + \frac{43}{30} = 1\cdot933 \text{ intervals} = 0\cdot193 \text{ inch}$$

$$\therefore \quad \text{Estimated mode} = 30\cdot093$$

Taking the second three frequencies and their differences—

$$x = 0\cdot5 + \frac{13}{93\cdot5} = 0\cdot639 \text{ interval} = 0\cdot064 \text{ inch}$$

$$\therefore \quad \text{Estimated mode} = 30\cdot064$$

Our two answers therefore differ sensibly from each other, and also from the value given by a fitted Pearson curve, viz. $30\cdot039$.

Modifying central ordinates to equivalent areas

24.22 Supposing we fit a theoretical frequency-curve to an actual distribution, and want to determine the "goodness of fit" by the χ^2 method. We would usually proceed by calculating, from the curve determined, the ordinates at the centre of each class-interval and taking these as the frequencies. But this procedure is not exact, for the central ordinates are not precise measures of the areas. In a class-interval centred exactly on the mode, for example, the central (maximum) ordinate obviously gives too large a value for the area. Required, to obtain some simple formula for modifying the central ordinates so as to give the areas.

We have, by Newton's formula,

$$u_x = u_0 + x\Delta_0{}^1 + \tfrac{1}{2}(x^2 - x)\Delta_0{}^2$$
$$= u_0 + (\Delta_0{}^1 - \tfrac{1}{2}\Delta_0{}^2)x + \tfrac{1}{2}\Delta_0{}^2 x^2$$

Integrate this expression for the interval round u_1, i.e. between the limits $0 \cdot 5$ and $1 \cdot 5$, and we will have an expression for the equivalent area, say w_1—

$$w_1 = \int_{0\cdot5}^{1\cdot5} u_x dx = u_0 + \Delta_0{}^1 - \tfrac{1}{2}\Delta_0{}^2 + \tfrac{13}{24}\Delta_0{}^2$$
$$= u_0 + \Delta_0{}^1 + \tfrac{1}{24}\Delta_0{}^2$$
$$w_1 = u_1 + \tfrac{1}{24}\Delta_0{}^2$$
$$= \tfrac{1}{24}(u_0 + 22u_1 + u_2) \left. \right\} \qquad . \qquad . \qquad . \quad (24.18)$$

The first form of the formula is, in general, the more convenient, but the second may be the better if correction is wanted only to a single value of u.

Example 24.10

Table 24.5 (page 585) gives in column 2 the calculated ordinates of a Pearson curve at the centres of the class-intervals. In columns 3 and 4 are given the first and second differences, and in column 5 are given the corrections $\Delta_0{}^2/24$, shifted one line down so as to be on the same line as the ordinate to be corrected. Finally, in column 6 we have the sum of the ordinate and the correction, or the area. The totals given at the foot are simply for the purpose of checking; since columns 2 and 3 both begin and end with zero, the sums of both first and second differences must be zero. Since column 5 is derived from column 4 by dividing by 24, its sum should also be zero, but errors of rounding off have made a very small negative excess. All the corrections are very small; they are necessarily greatest where the curvature is greatest.

24.23 A few words in conclusion. The process of interpolation, and still more that of graduation, is almost as much artistic as scientific. No absolute rules can be laid down, judgment must be used, and it is the experienced craftsman who is likely to get the best results with the least labour. If the student turns up his Latin dictionary he will find that *interpolare* means not only " to polish up " (*polire*, to polish)—so that graduation is really the implication of the word—but hence " to corrupt, to falsify." It will do him no harm to bear this etymological meaning in mind, and keep a look-out accordingly.

TABLE 24.5

1	2	3	4	5	6
Class-interval	Central ordinate	Δ^1	Δ^2	Correction	Area
		0·00	+ 0·08	—	—
0	0·00	+ 0·08	+ 0·70	+0·00	0·00
1	0·08	+ 0·78	+ 3·08	+0·03	0·11
2	0·86	+ 3·86	+ 6·91	+0·13	0·99
3	4·72	+10·77	+ 7·18	+0·29	5·01
4	15·49	+17·95	− 0·55	+0·30	15·79
5	33·44	+17·40	−10·76	−0·02	33·42
6	50·84	+ 6·64	−13·70	−0·45	50·39
7	57·48	− 7·06	− 7·88	−0·57	56·91
8	50·42	−14·94	+ 0·06	−0·33	50·09
9	35·48	−14·88	+ 4·37	+0·00	35·48
10	20·60	−10·51	+ 4·67	+0·18	20·78
11	10·09	− 5·84	+ 3·15	+0·19	10·28
12	4·25	− 2·69	+ 1·64	+0·13	4·38
13	1·56	− 1·05	+ 0·69	+0·07	1·63
14	0·51	− 0·36	+ 0·25	+0·03	0·54
15	0·15	− 0·11	+ 0·08	+0·01	0·16
16	0·04	− 0·03	+ 0·02	+0·00	0·04
17	0·01	− 0·01	+ 0·01	+0·00	0·01
18	0·00	0·00	0·00	+0·00	0·00
Totals	286·02	+57·48 −57·48	+32·89 −32·89	+1·36 −1·37	286·01

SUMMARY

1. The first, second, third, . . . differences of a function u_x are defined by the equations

$$\Delta_0^1 = u_1 - u_0$$
$$\Delta_0^2 = \Delta_1^1 - \Delta_0^1$$
$$\Delta_0^3 = \Delta_1^2 - \Delta_0^2$$

etc.

the intervals between successive values of the variable x being equal

2. By means of Newton's formula,

$$u_x = u_0 + x\Delta_0^1 + \frac{x(x-1)}{1.2}\Delta_0^2 + \frac{x(x-1)(x-2)}{1.2.3}\Delta_0^3 + \cdot \cdot$$

we can interpolate for the value of u_x.

3. Errors in the values of u become of increasing importance as the order of the differences increases.

4. For inverse interpolation

$$x = \frac{u_x - u_0}{\Delta_0{}^1}$$

for first differences;

$$x = -\frac{2\Delta_0{}^1 - \Delta_0{}^2}{2\Delta_0{}^2} \pm \sqrt{\frac{2(u_x - u_0)}{\Delta_0{}^2} - \left(\frac{2\Delta_0{}^1 - \Delta_0{}^2}{2\Delta_0{}^2}\right)^2}$$

for second differences.

We can also proceed by successive approximation. If x_1 is the approximate solution by first differences, a closer approximation is $x_1 + h$, where

$$h = \frac{x_1(1 - x_1)\dfrac{\Delta_0{}^2}{\Delta_0{}^1}}{2 + (2x_1 - 1)\dfrac{\Delta_0{}^2}{\Delta_0{}^1}}$$

EXERCISES

24.1   Given the following values for the normal integral

x/σ	P
1·4	·91924
1·5	·93319
1·6	·94520
1·7	·95543

find the value of A for $x/\sigma = 1·54$, noting the successive approximations up to third differences.   Take u_0 at $1·4$.

24.2   Find as closely as possible the value of P for $\chi^2 = 11·7$ from the following entries in the χ^2 table (*Tables for Statisticians*) : $\nu = 17$ ($n' = 18$). Note the successive approximations and the number of places to which your final answer is probably trustworthy.

χ^2	P
10	0·903610
11	0·856564
12	0·800136
13	0·736186

24.3 From the following entries in the same table for $v=24(n'=25)$, estimate as closely as you can the value of P for $\chi^2=43$. Similarly, estimate the closeness of your approximation.

χ^2	P
30	0·184752
40	0·021387
50	0·001416
60	0·000064

24.4 The following table gives the deaths of males registered in England and Wales during the three years 1930, 1931, 1932, at the ages stated. The figures on the right give the totals of the quinquennial groups which were, on this occasion, held to give the best totals for determining quinquennial " pivotal values." Find graduated numbers for the ages 40 to 44 inclusive.

Age	Numbers	Quinquennial totals
35	3394	
36	3505	
37	3501	
38	3947	
39	3998	18,345
40	4220	
41	4281	
42	5024	
43	4993	
44	5260	23,778
45	5998	
46	6113	
47	6463	
48	6921	
49	7663	33,158

24.5 Let $u_0, u_1, u_2, \ldots u_{14}$ be the numbers in fifteen consecutive years of age, as in Exercise 24.4, and w_0, w_5, w_{10} the totals in the three quinquennial groups. Show that if we want only the graduated figure for u_7 as a " pivotal value," this may be written down at once from the equation

$$u_7 = 0 \cdot 2w_5 - 0 \cdot 008\Delta^2 w_0$$

(King's formula). Verify by comparison with your answer to Exercise 24.4.

24.6 Generalising the above result, show that if w_0, w_r, w_{2r} are three successive age-groups of r years each, we have for the graduated central value

$$w_{\frac{1}{2}(3r-1)} = \frac{w_r}{r} - \frac{r^2-1}{24r^2} \Delta^2 \left(\frac{w_0}{r}\right)$$

and hence if r become indefinitely great, the central ordinate of the middle group of three, with areas w_0, w_1, w_2 and common base c, is given by

$$\frac{w_1}{c} - \frac{1}{24} \Delta^2 \left(\frac{w_0}{c}\right)$$

Verify by finding approximately the central ordinate of the normal curve from the areas between $-0\cdot3$ and $-0\cdot1$, $-0\cdot1$ and $+0\cdot1$, $+0\cdot1$ and $+0\cdot3$ x/σ.

24.7 From the following (abbreviated) entries in the χ^2 table, $\nu=9$ ($n'=10$), estimate the value of χ^2 for which $P=0\cdot25$—

χ^2	P
11	$0\cdot2757$
12	$0\cdot2133$
13	$0\cdot1626$

24.8 The next table shows a frequency-distribution of 1,000 observations, and also gives the frequencies summed from the top. Estimate (1) the median, (2) the first decile, (3) the ninth decile, (a) as usual by simple interpolation, (b) by bringing second differences also into account.

Interval	Frequency	x	Sum of frequencies from 0 to x
0–1	28	1	28
1–2	76	2	104
2–3	114	3	218
3–4	141	4	359
4–5	158	5	517
5–6	142	6	659
6–7	119	7	778
7–8	95	8	873
8–9	63	9	936
9–10	33	10	969
10–11	18	11	987
11–12	8	12	995
12–13	2	13	997
13–14	2	14	999
14–15	—	15	999
15–16	1	16	1000
Total	1000	—	—

24.9   The following are the mean temperatures (Fahrenheit) at Greenwich on three days 30 days apart round the periods of summer maximum and winter minimum.   Estimate the approximate dates and values of the maximum and minimum.

Day	Date	Temp.	Date	Temp.
0	15th June	58·8	16th Dec.	40·7
30	15th July	63·4	15th Jan.	38·1
60	14th Aug.	62·5	14th Feb.	39·3

24.10   Taking the value of the central ordinate of the normal curve from Appendix Table 1, estimate the area between the limits $\pm 0 \cdot 1x/\sigma$, and verify your answer from the area table.

CHAPTER TWENTY-FIVE

INDEX NUMBERS

The general problem

25.1 It often happens, particularly in economic statistics, that a set of similar events moving through time or space gives rise to some general concept expressing variation in their common element. The prices of a number of commodities on sale lead to the notion of a relative " price level " ; the various outputs of manufacturing plants generate the idea of changes in the " volume of industrial production " as a thing-in-itself ; the yields of different crops in a set of agricultural districts suggest a comparison of " agricultural productivity " between different geographical areas. Although there is room for argument about the role of some of these concepts in providing explanations of phenomena, it will not in general be denied that they are useful subjects of inquiry, and in particular that knowledge is advanced when we can measure the properties which they represent, or at least the *relative* values at different times and in different places. In fact, when we leave the domain of philosophical discussion some of these concepts assume a degree of practical importance which is denied to more concrete and less contentious ideas ; whether we agree or not that there is such a thing as the cost-of-living, we must admit that movements in wages and salaries in many countries are influenced (and in some are determined) by a measure of the relative level of the "cost-of-living" expressed in the most definite numerical terms.

25.2 In this chapter we shall be concerned with the measurement of such concepts as relative price-levels and changes in the general price-level by means of *index-numbers*, i.e. numbers which tell us, or at least purport to tell us, that if the price-level in such and such a year be denoted by 100 it is now 127 (or thereabouts) ; or that, if the cost of living of the working classes in London be denoted by 100, in this or that provincial town it is no more than 85 or 90. There are many different types of such quantities and it is not easy to frame a short definition to cover them all which shall be both precise and intelligible. In the majority of cases the index-numbers are calculated over a series of months or years and attention is directed to their variation in *time*, but comparisons also fall to be made in *space*, as in the case of cost of living in different towns above, or, to take illustrations from other fields, if we wish to compare standardised birth-rates in different countries or shipping freight-rates in different sea-routes. From the elementary view-point, it is perhaps easiest to regard an index-number as a measure of central tendency in a group of items ; and many of the index-numbers in common use are nothing more than weighted averages of *relative* numbers for the several component items of the concept in question.

25.3   Table 25.1 shows, in column (2) the average annual price of English wheat, as recorded in the *Official Gazette,* for the years 1930–1945 inclusive. In column (3) we show these prices expressed as a percentage of the price in 1930, and in column (4) the prices are similarly expressed as a percentage of the price in 1945.

TABLE 25.1.—Prices of English wheat

(1) Year	(2) Price (per quarter)	(3) Column (2) as percentage of 1930 price	(4) Column (2) as percentage of 1945 price
	s. d.		
1930	34 3	100	55
1	24 0	70	39
2	25 0	73	40
3	22 10	67	37
4	20 2	59	33
5	22 2	65	36
6	30 9	90	50
7	40 0	117	65
8	28 11	84	47
9	21 5	63	35
1940	42 10	125	69
1	62 10	183	102
2	68 6	200	111
3	69 8	203	113
4	63 11	187	103
5	61 10	181	100

The figures in columns (3) and (4) are very simple cases of index-numbers. The eye cannot very easily follow the variations in price by running down column (2), particularly if it is desired to gauge the magnitude of the variation through time.   By expressing the figures with reference to the basic number of 100 we are, effectively, reducing the data to a convenient common scale.   Such figures are usually called " price-relatives."

25.4   Simple as this example is, it brings out several points of practical importance which are apt to be overlooked in dealing with the theoretical problems arising from more complicated types of index numbers.

(*a*) Arithmetically the series of columns (2), (3) and (4) are equivalent in the sense that they are proportional.   Nevertheless, they may not convey the same impression, particularly to the lay reader.   It is very natural to take the basic figure of 100, not as a purely convenient arithmetical quantity, but as some " norm " or " standard " of what ought to be.   In our example, to say that the price in 1942 was twice as great as in 1930 may convey a different impression from saying that the price in 1930 was half that of 1942 ; in the first case we are taking the earlier year as the standard of comparison, in the second case the later year.   A consumer of bread would probably incline to the former, an arable farmer to the latter.   This kind of point becomes of special importance for economic index-numbers (such as those of wages or cost-of-living) which are likely to be the subject of controversy.   It must always be remembered that the choice of the base-year may have to be exercised on grounds other than those of convenience to the statistician, or those which might appear to him of most importance.

(b) It is common practice to refer to changes in an index-number from one year to another as a movement of so many " points ", e.g. the index in column (3) of Table 25.1 fell by 6 points between 1932 and 1933.   There is no great objection to this phraseology if the basic year is borne in mind, but it is apt to provide a misleading picture of the importance of the movement.   The index also fell 6 points between 1944 and 1945 but clearly the relative fall in the second case was smaller than in the first (in fact, only about a third as great).

Price index-numbers

25.5   To fix the ideas, let us suppose that we require to construct an index for the United Kingdom of wholesale prices over a series of years. We shall first of all have to decide what commodities are to be covered by the index and how to collect the prices.   This leads to a number of practical points which are apt to be troublesome (e.g. how to pick a representative set of commodities, how to treat imported articles, and how to deal with missing price-quotations) but which we shall pass over as not offering any special theoretical problems.   We will suppose that we have m commodities whose prices in the jth year are typified by $p_{1j}, p_{2j} \ldots p_{mj}$. These are *heterogeneous* quantities, each of them representing, it is true, " money per quantity " (for that is what is meant by a price) but the quantity in terms of which the price is stated varying from commodity to commodity.   For pig-iron it is, say, a ton ; for raw cotton it is also a weight, but the weight is only a pound, and for a precious metal only an ounce ; for beer or wine it is not a weight at all but a volume ; for woven textiles perhaps a " piece ", and so on.   In order to apply any of the conceptions or methods of previous chapters, e.g. frequency distributions, averages, measures of dispersion, etc., we require a *homogeneous* set of quantities all of the same dimensions ; as stated in **5.4** an average " is merely a certain value of the variable, and is therefore necessarily of the same *dimensions* as the variable " so that if the data are of differing dimensions the average has no assignable meaning.   As an initial step, therefore, we want to convert the heterogeneous figures of our price-table into a homogeneous set of figures all of the same dimensions.   This can be done in more ways than one, but the simplest is to apply to each column of our prices-table the process used in Table 25.1, i.e. to convert the given prices into price-relatives. As these are simple ratios, they are all pure numbers. Table 25.2 illustrates the procedure ; Col. 2 repeats the wheat prices of Table 25.1 and in Cols. 3 and 4 are added the Gazette-prices of Barley and Oats. In Cols. 5, 6, and 7 these prices are converted into price-relatives with 1930 as base-year.

TABLE 25.2.—Prices and price-relatives of wheat, barley and oats

(1)	Price per quarter			Price relative (1930=100)		
Year	(2) Wheat	(3) Barley	(4) Oats	(5) Wheat	(6) Barley	(7) Oats
	s. d.	s. d.	s. d.			
1930	34 3	28 3	17 2	100	100	100
1	24 0	28 0	17 8	70	99	103
2	25 0	27 1	19 3	73	96	113
3	22 10	28 7	15 10	67	101	92
4	20 2	30 11	17 5	59	109	101
5	22 2	28 7	18 9	65	101	109
6	30 9	29 5	17 8	90	104	103
7	40 0	39 0	23 11	117	138	139
8	28 11	36 4	21 2	84	129	123
9	21 5	31 7	19 3	63	112	113
1940	42 10	64 10	37 2	125	229	217
1	62 10	85 0	40 10	183	303	238
2	68 6	165 5	42 0	200	586	245
3	69 8	113 5	43 8	203	398	254
4	63 11	94 6	45 3	187	335	264
5	61 10	89 2	45 9	181	316	267

25.6 In terms of our symbols then, we replace each price p_{rj} by a price-relative t_{rj}, where, ignoring the factor of 100,

$$t_{rj} = p_{rj}/p_{rs} \qquad \cdot \qquad \cdot \qquad \cdot \qquad \cdot \qquad (25.1)$$

p_{rs} being the price of commodity r in the standard year (or, to put it more generally, the standard price of commodity r, for prices in a single year are subject to casual disturbances and it may be better to take as standard the average price over a five or ten year period). We may now average the relatives (25.1) in any way we please in order to obtain our desired index-number for the " relative general level of prices ". If we take the simple arithmetic mean of the t's, we have, using $_AI_j$ to denote this form of index-number for the year j and Σ to denote summation for all commodities r

$$_AI_j = \frac{1}{m} \Sigma \left(\frac{p_{rj}}{p_{rs}} \right) \qquad \cdot \qquad \cdot \qquad \cdot \qquad \cdot \qquad (25.2)$$

For instance, in the data of Table 25.2, $_AI_{1930}=100$ and $_AI_{1945}=\frac{1}{3}(181+316+267)=255$.

This formula, however, attaches precisely the same 'weight' to each commodity whether little is sold at the specified price or much; a commodity such as wheat is given no more weight than a commodity such as pepper, in spite of the enormous difference between the quantities moving into consumption. We have therefore to consider whether some system of weights can be introduced to allow for this effect.

25.7 Since our price-relatives are all of the same dimensions (pure numbers) our weights should also be all of the same dimensions. They cannot therefore be quantities, for some of the quantities are actual weights, some volumes, and so on. Suppose then we make the weight for each price-relative the *money spent* on that particular commodity in the base year (or the average annual amount in the base period), say $p_{rs} q_{rs}$ where q_{rs} is the quantity in question. Then for form B of the desired index-number we have

$$_B I_j = \frac{\Sigma (t_{rj} \, p_{rs} \, q_{rs})}{\Sigma (p_{rs} \, q_{rs})} \qquad . \qquad . \qquad . \qquad . \qquad (25.3)$$

$$= \frac{\Sigma (p_{rj} \, q_{rs})}{\Sigma (p_{rs} \, q_{rs})} \qquad . \qquad . \qquad . \qquad . \qquad (25.4)$$

This is a remarkable result, for (25.4) is simply the ratio of the cost of the given "basket of goods" (the quantities sold in the base year or on an average in the base period) at the prices of year j to its cost at the prices of the standard year or period. Looking at the matter in another way, we have converted our heterogeneous price-figures, as required, into homogeneous figures by multiplying each price by a quantity expressed in the same units as are used in specifying the price and thus turning them from "money per quantity" into "money."

25.8 Although the index-number $_B I$ has a fairly intelligible meaning, it is still open to some objections. In fact, it depends on the quantities sold in the basic year, and if the actual quantities vary substantially from year to year there is some ground for arguing that such a fact ought to be taken into account. For example, if over a period the proportion of the average household income spent on food drops from 40 per cent in the basic year to 25 per cent, it seems obviously wrong to continue to weight food-prices by a factor of 40 per cent. Our weights, so to speak, ought in some sense to be kept up-to-date.

25.9 Before discussing this problem in generality, let us make four preliminary observations—

(*a*) We noted in **14.15** that errors in weights, if uncorrelated with the prices to which they are attached, will not exert much effect on the index numbers. Thus, if the weights change rather erratically or by small amounts from year to year, the accuracy of the index is not seriously affected. For practical purposes, therefore, $_B I$ should give a reasonable comparison between years which are not far apart in time and may be satisfactory over quite a long period unless there is some systematic movement in weights during that period.

(b) Purely practical difficulties in determining weights from year to year may make some formula of the type (25.4) the only one which can be calculated in time to be of any value.

(c) It is arguable on theoretical grounds that $_BI$ (or some similar formula based on a different type of average) is the correct form to use in estimating price changes. If we make allowance for changing quantities we may be confusing price change with other things. For instance, an index of the form $\Sigma(p_{rj} q_{rj})/\Sigma(p_{rs} q_{rs})$ measures the ratio of the total expenditure in the jth year to that in the basic year, and to that extent is a definite measurable quantity. But when we try to dissect that part of it which is due to price change from the part due to change in quantity, we are in difficulties, for so far as observation goes the two things are really inextricable parts of the same phenomenon. There is, in fact, an element of *convention* in our definition of a price index-number. The statistician will always remember how his index-number is calculated and will know how far he can use it in any particular argument. If he chooses to define his price-index by reference to the " fixed basket of goods " he is perfectly entitled to do so. He may perhaps be challenged on the grounds that his price-index does not possess some desirable properties which might be expected of a perfect price-index. He cannot fairly be accused of doing anything wrong ; only of doing something inexpedient.

25.10 We have attempted to simplify the discussion by speaking of prices and years in the construction of our index-numbers. Evidently similar considerations apply when the periods of comparison are not years, but some other unit of time, except that for short periods, such as months, we may have to pay some attention to seasonal effects. Most of what we are saying about price-indices also applies to other forms of index-numbers although there are certain features of prices which give rise to special difficulties. Broadly speaking, the theory of price-indices covers the general case, and indeed other index-numbers are frequently much easier to construct when they can be freed from measurement in terms of money. We shall refer to the so-called quantum indices below (**25.20**). In the meantime, we continue to discuss price indices on the understanding that our discussion has a somewhat wider application.

Geometric means
25.11 The same kind of considerations which led us in Chapter 6 to express a preference for the arithmetic mean in determining averages also apply to its use for index numbers, except perhaps that the argument from sampling simplicity is not so strong. The use of medians and modes is to be deprecated and only the student of statistical history is likely to encounter them in connection with index-numbers. There is, however,

something to be said in favour of the geometric mean, particularly in connection with price indices. Let us note the formulæ corresponding to $_AI$ and $_BI$.

For the index based on the geometric mean of a set of prices relatives we have

$$_0I_j = \{ \Pi\, p_{rj}/p_{rs} \}^{1/m} \qquad . \qquad . \qquad . \qquad (25.5)$$

where m is the number of prices concerned. For purposes of calculation this is more easily written as

$$\log\, _0I_j = \frac{1}{m} \left\{ \Sigma(\log\, p_{rj}) - \Sigma(\log\, p_{rs}) \right\} \qquad . \qquad . \qquad . \qquad (25.6)$$

Clearly (25.6) can also be written as

$$\log\, _0I_j = \frac{1}{m} \Sigma(\log\, p_{rj}/p_{rs}) \qquad . \qquad . \qquad . \qquad (25.7)$$

It makes no difference whether we take the ratio of the geometric means or the geometric mean of the ratios.

For the corresponding index to $_BI_j$ we have

$$_DI_j = \left\{ \Pi \left(\frac{q_{rs}}{p_{rj}} \middle/ \frac{q_{rs}}{p_{rs}} \right) \right\}^{1/\Sigma(q_{rs})}$$

which is more conveniently written

$$\log\, _DI_j = \frac{1}{\Sigma\,(q_{rs})} \Sigma \left\{ q_{rs} \log\, (p_{rj}/p_{rs}) \right\} \qquad . \qquad . \qquad . \qquad (25.8)$$

Example 25.1.—As an example of a price index-number calculated from the arithmetic mean by reference to a fixed set of weights in a basic period, we consider the British official " interim index of retail prices." This used to be known as the " cost-of-living index," a term which the authorities are attempting to abandon in favour of a more neutral type of wording. A better phrase would be " household budget price-index ", since the object of the index is to measure changes in the average retail prices of the items composing the expenditure in an average household budget. The two main practical questions for decision in constructing the index are ; what commodities are concerned and what is their relative importance in the " average budget " ?

For the index-number, which was first published in 1947, the Ministry of Labour used data collected in 1937/9 by sampling about 10,000 household budgets. The information gave, in considerable detail, the expenditure on all items for four separate weeks in October 1947, January 1938, April 1938 and July 1938, and an arithmetic average of the four was regarded as representative of the proportionate expenditure on each item over the year. Some of the budgets were collected from agricultural households and were separated for the construction of an index relating to agricultural workers.

There are about 90 items involved and they are classified into eight groups—

1. Food
2. Rent and rates
3. Clothing
4. Fuel and light
5. Household durable goods
6. Miscellaneous goods
7. Services
8. Drink and tobacco.

Current prices for the 90 items are collected by the Ministry of Labour from various sources, e.g. by visits of local officers to retailers in regard to food or by inquiries of local authorities and property owners' associations in regard to rent. These prices are related to the corresponding figures for the basic date, namely, 17th June 1947, taken as 100.

It then remains to compound these price relatives into an index for each group, and finally, to compound the eight resultant indices into a single index. The same principles are employed in each case and effectively amount to the use of equation (25.3). They may be exemplified by the method of constructing the final index from the eight component indices.

In calculating the final index, a weighted arithmetic mean is taken of the components, the weights used being as follows

Food	348
Rent and rates . .	88
Clothing . . .	97
Fuel and light . .	65
Household durable goods	71
Miscellaneous goods .	35
Services . . .	79
Drink and tobacco . .	217
Total	1,000

Thus for instance, the index numbers of the eight groups in mid-December 1947 were respectively 103·4, 100·1, 102·4, 107·1, 106·3, 109·2, 102·5, 104·1. Taking our origin as 100 we have for the index for " all items "

$$100 + \{(348 \times 3 \cdot 4) + (88 \times 0 \cdot 1) + \text{etc.}$$
$$+ (217 \times 4 \cdot 1)\} / 1{,}000 = 103 \cdot 7$$

The weights in this case are an attempt to represent the proportional expenditure in 1947 on the eight groups, e.g. it is estimated that 34·8 per cent of household expenditure was devoted to food. As no definite information for 1947 was available, the proportions shown in the budget inquiry of 1937/8 were adjusted to take account of changes in price between 1937/8 and mid-June 1947. The proportion attributable to drink and tobacco was scaled up to take account of 1947 conditions.

Example 25.2.—An illustration of a price-index calculated by the use of geometric means with a fixed set of weights is provided by the British index-number of wholesale prices. This Index purports to measure the movement in the prices of wholesale commodities. It was revised in 1935 on the basis of information obtained from the Census of Production of 1930.

There are 200 commodities composing the Index, the numbers, in eleven groups, being as follows—

Group	Number of Commodities
Cereals	20
Meat, fish and eggs	20
Other food and tobacco	28
Total—Food and tobacco	68
Coal	9
Iron and steel	37
Non-ferrous metals	8
Cotton	10
Wool	11
Other textiles	9
Chemicals and oils	15
Miscellaneous	33
Total—Industrial items	132
Total—All articles	200

These numbers, which are effectively weights for the groups concerned, are based approximately on the relative importance of the various items as indicated by the production figures in the 1930 census and imports in that year, importance for this purpose being measured by the *value* of the gross output.

Prices are obtained from various sources, mostly from trade publications, and relate to certain standard types or specifications. In some cases the prices of two or more qualities are averaged for a particular commodity so as to give a wider coverage.

In the construction of the Index for any particular commodity the price is recorded weekly where possible and an arithmetical average of the weekly quotations provides a figure for the month. This is then related to the price in the corresponding month of the basic year by means of a simple price-relative. A composite index is then constructed for the month for each of the groups specified in the above table by taking a geometric mean (the actual arithmetic process is somewhat different, but this is what it amounts to).

The monthly index for " All Articles " is obtained as a geometric mean of the price-relative for the 200 items in the above table. This is equivalent to taking a weighted average of the eleven groups with weights given by the number of commodities listed above. An annual index is constructed by taking the geometric average of the index numbers for the twelve months.

It will be noticed that in neither of the two examples we have just given—two of the most important industrial indices in the United Kingdom—are the weighting factors actual quantities. For the budgetary index they are based on proportional *expenditure* in a standard period, for the wholesale price index they are based on *value of gross output* in a standard period.

The time-reversal test

25.12 Let us now consider generally some of the properties which we should like to have in an index number. We will not dwell on properties such as ease of calculation, but will discuss some desiderata which arise from our general notion of the functions which an index number ought to perform.

In discussing the price-relative of Table 25.1, we noted that the series of columns (3) and (4) were equivalent in the sense of being proportional. The difference in the base year makes no difference to the index numbers except one of scale. To put it slightly differently, the relative of year a based on year b, say k_{ab}, is the reciprocal of the index of year b based on year a, say k_{ba} (except for the factor of 100 which we may ignore for present purposes). That is to say $k_{ab} k_{ba} = 1$.

The price relative therefore obeys what we may call a *time-reversal* test ; and this is clearly a property which we should welcome in any index number, for then our comparison between two years does not depend on which year we regard as the base year. That is, we should like an index number to obey the relations

$$I_{ab} I_{ba} = 1 \qquad . \qquad . \qquad . \qquad . \qquad (25.9)$$

Of the four indices we have considered earlier in the chapter only one obeys the time reversal test, namely $_cI_j$. When we introduce weights appropriate to a fixed base-year the time-reversal property is destroyed. For instance, with $_BI$ we have

$$_BI_{ab} = \Sigma\,(p_{ra}\ q_{rb})\,/\Sigma\,(p_{rb}\ q_{rb})$$
$$_BI_{ba} = \Sigma\,(p_{rb}\ q_r)\,/\Sigma\,(p_{ra}\ q_{ra})$$

and equation (25.9) is not obeyed unless the q_{ra}'s are equal or proportional to the q_{rb}'s

Nevertheless the test may be approximately obeyed if the changes in weights from q_{ra} to q_{rb} are small or if they are not highly correlated with the prices.   For let

$$q_{ra} = q_{rb} + \delta_r \text{ where } \delta_r \text{ is small.   Then}$$

$$_B I_{ab} \; _B I_{ba} = \frac{\Sigma \, (p_{ra} \; q_{rb}) \; \Sigma \, \{p_{rb}(q_{rb}+\delta_r)\}}{\Sigma \, (p_{rb} \; q_{rb}) \; \Sigma \, \{p_{ra}(q_{rb}+\delta_r)\}}$$

$$= \left\{1+\frac{\Sigma \, (p_{rb} \; \delta_r)}{\Sigma \, (p_{rb} \; q_{rb})}\right\} \left\{1+\frac{\Sigma \, (p_{ra} \; \delta_r)}{\Sigma \, (p_{ra} \; q_{rb})}\right\}^{-1}$$

which is approximately

$$1+\frac{\Sigma \, (p_{rb} \; \delta_r)}{\Sigma \, (p_{rb} \; q_{rb})} - \frac{\Sigma \, (p_{ra} \; \delta_r)}{\Sigma \, (p_{ra} \; q_{rb})} \qquad . \qquad . \quad (25.10)$$

As the quantities δ_r are small the two terms on the right in (25.10) will in general be small; and even if they are moderately large the terms will be small if $\Sigma \, (p_{rb} \; \delta_r)$ and $\Sigma \, (p_{ra} \; \delta_r)$ are small, i.e. if δ_r is only slightly correlated with p_{ra} and p_{rb} ; or if $p_{ra}-p_{rb}$ is small.

Similarly for $_D I$ we have

$$\log \; _D I_{ab} \; _D I_{ba} = \frac{1}{\Sigma \, (q_{rb})} \Sigma \left\{q_{rb} \, \log \, (p_{ra} / p_{rb})\right\}$$

$$+ \frac{1}{\Sigma \, (q_{ra})} \Sigma \left\{q_{ra} \, \log \, (p_{rb} / p_{ra})\right\}$$

We may suppose that $\Sigma \, (q_{ra}) = \Sigma \, (q_{rb})$ for the total " weight " may conventionally be kept constant, and thus we find, after a little reduction,

$$\log \; _D I_{ab} \; _D I_{ba} = \frac{-1}{\Sigma \, (q_{rb})} \Sigma \left\{\delta_r \, \log \, (p_{ra} / p_{rb})\right\}$$

This is nearly zero if the δ's are small or if δ is only slightly correlated with the logarithm of the price changes and again the time-reversal test is obeyed approximately.

25.13   In order to obtain an index number which is certain to obey the time-reversal test we may proceed as follows :

With the base year b, the index $_c I$ for a year a is given by

$$_c I_{ab} = \frac{\Sigma \, (p_{ra} \; q_{rb})}{\Sigma \, (p_{rb} \; q_{rb})}$$

With the weights of the year a, but still with b as base, we have an index number

$$_c I'_{ab} = \frac{\Sigma \, (p_{ra} \; q_{ra})}{\Sigma \, (p_{rb} \; q_{ra})}$$

We then define

$$_E I_{ab} = \sqrt{\left(_c I_{ab} \; _c I'_{ab}\right)}$$

$$= \sqrt{\left\{\frac{\Sigma\,(p_{ra}\ q_{rb})}{\Sigma\,(p_{rb}\ q_{rb})}\ \frac{\Sigma\,(p_{ra}\ q_{ra})}{\Sigma\,(p_{rb}\ q_{ra})}\right\}} \quad . \quad . \quad (25.11)$$

This was called by Irving Fisher the " ideal " index-number. He regarded it as the best possible.

Examination of (25.11) will show that the time-reversal test is obeyed, for the reciprocal of $_E I$ is the product of $_c I_{ba}$ and $_c I'_{ba}$. The principal difficulties in using the " ideal " number are practical ones ; we rarely have data in sufficient detail to allow us to calculate it over a series of years.

The factor-reversal test

25.14 Irving Fisher (*The Making of Index-Numbers*, 1922) also proposed what he called a factor-reversal test for price index-numbers. He argued that if we interchange the symbols for price and quantity we should reach an index of quantity changes which, when multiplied by the index of price changes, should measure the change in total value. Consider, for instance, $_c I_{ab}$. For the price index-number we have

$$_c I_{ab} = \frac{\Sigma\ (p_{ra}\ q_{rb})}{\Sigma\ (p_{rb}\ q_{rb})}$$

Now if we interchange p and q we have an index which we may write

$$_c J_{ab} = \frac{\Sigma\ (q_{ra}\ p_{rb})}{\Sigma\ (q_{rb}\ p_{rb})} \quad . \quad . \quad . \quad . \quad (25.12)$$

This may be regarded as an index of quantity of type $_c I$ weighted according to the prices p_{rb} in the basic year b. Now we have

$$_c I_{ab} \; _c J_{ab} = \frac{\Sigma\ (p_{ra}\ q_{rb})\ \Sigma\ (p_{rb}\ q_{ra})}{\{\Sigma\ (p_{rb}\ q_{rb})\}^2}$$

But this is not equal to the index of total expenditure $\Sigma(p_{ra}\ q_{ra})/\Sigma(p_{rb}\ q_{rb})$ and hence the factor-reversal test is not obeyed.

25.15 Of the indices we have considered in this chapter only the " ideal " index obeys the factor-reversal test. The reader can easily verify that this is so from equation (25.11). This was, to Fisher, a powerful reason in favour of the " ideal " index. It does not appear to us to carry quite so much weight as he attributed to it. There is an element of convention in the construction of an index of quantity such as J, just as in the price index itself and obedience to the factor-reversal test would appear to be most required when indices of price and quantum (**25.19** below) are required together.

The circular test

25.16 If an index is constructed for year a on base-year b, and for year b on base-year c, we may derive an index for a on base-year c. The so-called "circular" test requires that if we do so we ought to get the same result as if we calculated direct an index for a on base-year c without going through b as an intermediary. To put it another way, we require that

$$I_{ab}\, I_{bc}\, I_{ca} = 1 \qquad . \qquad . \qquad . \qquad . \quad (25.13)$$

which presents a kind of extension of the time-reversal test of equation (25.9). We may note in passing that we shall not require to examine more complicated criteria such as

$$I_{ab}\, I_{bc}\, I_{cd}\, I_{da} = 1 \quad . \qquad . \qquad . \qquad . \quad (25.14)$$

for such are always fulfilled if (25.9) and (25.13) are satisfied. For then

$$I_{ab}\, I_{bc} = 1\,/\,I_{ca}, \quad I_{cd}\, I_{da} = 1\,/\,I_{ac}$$

and hence the left-hand side of (25.13) becomes $1\,/\,I_{ca}\, I_{ac} = 1$

25.17 The circular test is obeyed by ${}_0I$ but not by any of the other indices we have considered. Fisher, in fact, for reasons which we do not regard as very cogent, argued that an index-number should not obey the circular test. We need not dwell on the point, since it may be shown, as for the time-reversal test, that the circular test is approximately obeyed if weights do not change very substantially over the period for which comparisons are being made.

Departures from the fulfilment of the circular test are perhaps more important in comparisons in space than in time, for them the weights are likely to differ to a greater extent. For example, index-numbers purporting to compare industrial production, cost-of-living or price levels between different countries may depart from the "circular" criterion very considerably. By the use of an appropriate set of weights it may be possible to compare country A with country B; but to compare either with C new weights may be required. Hence it is quite possible to find that the "production", for example, in A is greater than in B, and in B is greater than in C, whereas a direct comparison can show that A's "production" is less than C's. This inconsistency really implies that we are trying to do too much with our index numbers. There are limits to the amount of information we can compress into single numbers for comparing areas or periods in which conditions are very different. The most workable method of approach is probably the one we noticed in dealing with death-rates (**14.17**) where a standard set of weights is used for each index.

Example 25.3.—*Moving weights*

An interesting attempt to deal with the question of changing weights was made in the official index of agricultural prices introduced by the British Ministry of Agriculture and Fisheries in 1938 (Houghton, *J. Roy. Stat. Soc.*, 1938, **101**, 275). Between the two world wars the pattern of agricultural production changed considerably in the United Kingdom owing to the movement from arable to grassland farming and the introduction of some new crops such as sugar beet. Weights were calculated for each year for the various items entering into the index, based on the proportionate contribution by value to the total output. A five-yearly moving average was taken of these weights and the weighting factors used for any particular year was the value of this average for the five previous years. In an industry such as agriculture, wherein changes from year to year are not very large, this slow and continuous adjustment of weights to current conditions has much to recommend it. Comparisons between years which are fairly close together can be made with confidence.

Linking methods

25.18 Situations sometimes arise in which we may compare each of a series of years with the next, but cannot so easily compare years which are separated in time. This is particularly so when weights are changing rapidly or when new commodities enter the market or disappear from it. In such circumstances it may be possible to construct an index for year 2 based on year 1, for year 3 on year 2 and so on, and hence to construct a continuous series by linking successive years. If, for instance, the index for year 2 on year 1 is i_2 and that for year 3 on year 2 is i_3, etc., we may, taking year 1 as base, regard $i_3 i_2$ as the index for year 3, $i_4 i_3 i_2$ as the index for year 4 and so on. Comparisons for successive years are not invalidated though those for widely separated years may be very unreliable. Index-numbers of this kind are sometimes useful as presenting a general picture of movements over a period ; but they are obviously not so firmly founded from the theoretical viewpoint as those we have described above.

Example 25.4.—*Index number of shipping freight rates* (Isserlis, *J. Roy. Stat. Soc.*, 1938, **101**, 53.)

It was desired to construct an Annual Index representing the course of Tramp Shipping Freights over the period 1869 (when the Suez Canal was opened) and 1936 when the calculations were carried out. From the outset it is clear than any index of this character will require careful interpretation, for the period concerned was one in which sea transport was revolutionized by the change from sail to steam, and later a further partial change to propulsion by Diesel engines. Furthermore, details of the freights for all voyages undertaken in this period were not available, and the actual quantities carried were also not available. In spite of the unpromising conditions of the problem an index was constructed on the following lines—

Quotations of the highest and lowest freights in a particular year were available over the period concerned and the mid-point between the two was taken as representing the average freight for the year. This is a crude form of average necessitated by the paucity of the data, but is probably reasonably accurate except in years such as 1915 when freights trebled as compared with the year before owing to the circumstances of World War I.

These average freights were available for 210 homeward routes to the U.K. and 112 outward routes, but owing to the varying nature of the tramp trade over the period, quotations were not available in respect of each route for each year. Consequently for any particular year there were a number of missing quotations. For each route where quotations in consecutive years were available a price-relative was constructed based on the previous year ; for example, for the route Java/U.K. in Sugar the freight in 1870 was 93 per cent of that in 1869 and the price-relative was therefore 93. In 1919 the freight was 31 per cent of that for 1918, and the price-relative was therefore 31.

For each year the available price-relatives were averaged arithmetically over homeward and outward routes to give an average price-relative for that year as compared with the previous year. For example, the average price relative for 1936 was 117·3.

An index over the 68 years concerned was then constructed on the basis of a chain method. The average price-relative for 1870 was 103, and on the basis of 1869=100 the freight index was also 103. The average price-relative for 1871 was 99 and the index was therefore taken as $(99 \times 103)/100$, namely 102. Similarly, by this chain method, the index was built up from one year to the next. The freight index for 1935 was 88. The price relative for 1936, as noted above, was 117·3 and therefore the index for 1936 was $(88 \times 117·3)/100$, namely 103.

For the purpose of giving a general view over the period, the index is perhaps not unsatisfactory. Although the rates on individual routes cannot be weighted by reference to the quantity of traffic the large number of routes employed ensures some degree of weighting in the index as a whole according to volume of traffic ; and although a comparison between neighbouring years is more reliable than one between two years which are widely separated in time, it is between the closer years that comparisons most frequently fall to be made.

In 1935 there became available detailed information of tramp voyages undertaken in U.K. ships in that year. It was then possible to construct an index of tramp shipping freights weighted according to gross freights earned on cargoes carried in that year. The agreement of this index with the chain index was fairly good.

Quantum indices

25.19 Reduction of the data to homogeneity is a pre-requisite of all index numbers of the type we have considered in this chapter, and we have already noticed that in many instances the only available common unit is money value. Unfortunately, this is precisely the unit which does not remain constant over periods of time. If we measure the industrial production of a country by the value of the gross output of its manufacturing plant and find that the value in 1948 was twice as great as in 1938 we obviously gain a very poor idea of the change in output over the period in any real sense. Our prices have changed in the meantime. Can we then measure in any reasonable way what is the change in output *apart from changes in prices*? Can we obtain some index of production which is related to physical output and is free from changes in prices or money values?

25.20 Suppose that in the basic period the value of the output of a commodity is typified by v_{rs} and the price of some unit by p_{rs}. If the price in the jth year is p_{rj}, and the output is valued at v_{rj}, then the quantity $v_{rj}\, p_{rs}/p_{rj}$ is what the output would have been valued at if the price had been that of the basic year. We may then construct the index-number

$$_{P}I_j = \frac{\Sigma\,(v_{rj}\ p_{rs}/p_{rj})}{\Sigma\,(v_{rs})} \qquad . \qquad . \qquad . \qquad . \quad (25.15)$$

This is the ratio of the value of the output in the jth year, revalued at "basic" prices, to the value of the output in the basic year. It evidently goes a long way to meet our requirements. It bears a kind of inverted relation to the index of equation (25.4). If there exist quantities q such that $v_{rj}=p_{rj}\,q_{rj}$ we have, on substitution for v in (25.15)

$$_{P}I_j = \frac{\Sigma\,(p_{rs}\ q_{rj})}{\Sigma\,(p_{rs}\ q_{rs})} \qquad . \qquad . \qquad . \qquad . \quad (25.16)$$

which exhibits $_{P}I$ as an average of quantities q weighted by prices in the basic period—a similar index to that of equation (25.12). As noted in **25.15**, the factor-reversal test requires that our indices of price and output shall, when multiplied together, measure the change in value of total output—a very reasonable requirement when both indices are used but not necessarily a desideratum when only one of them is to be calculated.

25.21 It is of some importance to note that we can calculate $_{P}I_j$ from (25.15) even when quantities q do not exist. Suppose, for example, we are constructing an index of the price of travel in London, into which there enter expenditures on buses, trams, electric trains and taxis. There is no "quantity" of travel though perhaps we might construct measures on a mileage basis. This, however, is unimportant if we know the expenditures v and the ratios p_{rj}/p_{rs}; if, for instance, we know that in the *j*th year prices of fares on buses, trams and trains are 10 per cent greater than in the basic year, whereas taxi-fares have remained unchanged. So long as the price-relatives are known, the expenditures v_{rj} and v_{rs} are sufficient for the computation of $_rI$ without the intermediate calculation of notionary quantities q.

Index-numbers such as $_rI$ are best known as *quantum* indices. Expressions such as " index of volume " occur but are misleading as the following example shows.

Example 25.5.—The British Board of Trade publishes an index-number of the " volume " of imports and exports. This is obtained by revaluing imports or exports in the given period on the basis of 1938 prices and expressing the results as percentages of the 1938 values. The following are the figures for 1946 and 1949 (1938 = 100)—

	1946	1949
Imports	67	84
Exports (including coal) .	99	151
Exports (excluding coal) .	107	161

Now it so happens in this case that we can estimate the actual weights (in tons of cargo) covered by these import and export figures. For exports (excluding coal) it is estimated that the figures were, in 1946, 98 per cent of 1938 and, in 1949, 120 per cent. Thus, where the quantum index gives 161, the index based on actual weight in tons is only 120. Clearly the quantum index does not measure " volume " in any ordinary sense associated with physical size or weight alone (it may be regarded as an index of this weight weighted by prices). On the other hand, it may be the correct index to use when attention is being directed to the relative contribution of exports to the balance of trade, price changes being eliminated from the comparison with the basic year.

25.22 In conclusion, we may intimate, without being able to pursue the subject, that for certain classes of statistical work it appears to be possible to develop a theory of index-numbers of a rather different kind from that discussed in this chapter. Psychologists have for some time studied techniques for isolating " general factors " from a complex of tests of ability which are capable of application to the isolation of a " general price level " from a complex of price movements. Biometricians, from a different point of view, have considered the problem of forming linear functions of observations which will most closely, in some reasonable sense, summarise the essential properties of classes—the so-called " discriminant functions ". Something has already been done in applying such methods to the formation of index-numbers. The subject has, however, hardly reached the point of practical application in economics, and it is unlikely that the methods described in this chapter will be supplanted for general use.

SUMMARY

1. The price-relative of a commodity for a particular period is the ratio of its price in that period to the price in a basic period. It is usually multiplied by 100 for convenience of expression as a percentage.

2. There is an element of convention in the definition of a price index-number. Simple unweighted numbers are

$$_A I_j = \frac{1}{m} \Sigma \left(p_{rj} / p_{rs} \right)$$

$$_C I_j = \left\{ \Pi \left(p_{rj} / p_{rs} \right) \right\}^{\frac{1}{m}}$$

3. Weighted index-numbers in common use are

$$_B I_j = \Sigma \left(p_{rj} \ q_{rs} \right) / \Sigma \left(p_{rs} \ q_{rs} \right)$$

$$\log \ _D I_j = \frac{1}{\Sigma \left(q_{rs} \right)} \Sigma \left\{ q_{rs} \ \log \left(p_{rj} / p_{rs} \right) \right\}$$

4. The time reversal test requires that

$$I_{ab} \ I_{ba} = 1$$

This is obeyed by $_C I_j$ but not by the weighted indices, though the latter may obey it approximately.

5. The time-reversal test is obeyed by the " ideal " index-number

$$_E I = \sqrt{ \left\{ \frac{\Sigma \left(p_{ra} \ q_{rb} \right) \ \Sigma \left(p_{ra} \ q_{ra} \right)}{\Sigma \left(p_{rb} \ q_{rb} \right) \ \Sigma \left(p_{rb} \ q_{ra} \right)} \right\} }$$

This also obeys a factor-reversal test.

6. The circular test requires that

$$I_{ab} \ I_{bc} \ I_{ca} = 1$$

It is not obeyed by any of the weighted indices unles⌐ the weights are constant, but may be obeyed approximately.

7. Linking methods may give a suitable chain index when data are available to make comparisons possible for adjacent years.

8. Quantum index-numbers purport to measure a " quantity " independently of price change. The principal form in common use is

$$_F I_j = \Sigma \left(v_{rj} \ p_{rs} / p_{rj} \right) / \Sigma \left(v_{rs} \right)$$

Quantum does not necessarily measure physical volume or weight.

EXERCISES

25.1   The following figures show the wholesale prices of refined petroleum per gallon in the U.K. for the years specified.   On the basis of 1923=100 construct a series of price-relatives.

Year	Price per gallon (pence)
1923	13
4	$13\frac{1}{8}$
5	$13\frac{1}{8}$
6	13
7	13
8	$11\frac{11}{16}$
9	$12\frac{3}{4}$
1930	$12\frac{3}{4}$
1	$11\frac{1}{4}$
2	$10\frac{1}{2}$
3	$10\frac{1}{4}$
4	$10\frac{1}{32}$
5	$10\frac{1}{2}$

25.2   Show that the index-number $_cI$ possess the " chain-property " of **25.18,** namely that the index for a year j on base 1 is the product of corresponding indices of j on $j-1$, $j-1$ on $j-2$, . . . , 2 on 1.

25.3   The following figures show for U.K. total imports (a) the declared value and (b) the value on the basis of average values in 1930.   Taking 1930 as a base year construct index-numbers (1) of average values and (2) of quantum for the years 1931–6.

Year	Declared Value £ million	Value on 1930 basis £ million
1930	1,044	1,044
1	861	1,067
2	702	939
3	675	946
4	731	991
5	756	1,012
6	848	1,077

25.4   Using the weights of Example 25.1 calculate the index for all articles if the indices for the constituent groups are as follows : Food 95 ; Rent and rates 90 ; Clothing 110 ; Fuel and light 120 ; Household goods 102 ; Miscellaneous 115 ; Services 98 ; Drink and Tobacco 108.

   Examine the effect of rounding up the weights (a) to the nearest 10 (b) to the nearest 100.

25.5   In the notation of **25.14** consider the index-number

$$_GI = \tfrac{1}{2} \left(_CI_{ab} + _CI_{ba} \right)$$

Show that if the weights in the years a and b differ by a small amount δ_r, the difference between this index and the " ideal " index, is zero to the first order in δ_r.

25.6   The following figures give the annual average prices in the U.K. for beef, mutton and pork.

Year	Beef (prime)	Mutton (prime) pence per 8 lb.	Pork
1935	54	75	62
6	54	73	65
7	61	78	68
8	62	62	69
9	61	68	70
1940	72	85	96
1	72	85	96
2	76	90	101
3	79	96	102

Construct an index of " meat prices " for the period (a) of type $_AI$, (b) of type $_BI$ with weights 4, 2 and 1 for beef, mutton and pork respectively. Take 1935$=$100 in each case.

25.7   Show that the index-number

$$_HI = \frac{\Sigma \left\{ p_{ra} \left(q_{ra} + q_{rb} \right) \right\}}{\Sigma \left\{ p_{rb} \left(q_{ra} + q_{rb} \right) \right\}}$$

obeys the time-reversal test but not the circular test unless the weights in the three years a, b, c are equal.

CHAPTER TWENTY-SIX

TIME-SERIES

Introduction

26.1 When we observe numerical features of an individual or a population at different points of time, the set of observations constitutes a *time-series*. The temperature at a given place over a given period, the population of a country over a number of years, the imports of a country for a series of months, the weight of an animal recorded at various stages of growth, are familiar examples of the kind of phenomena which provide series of values at a succession of points of time. The statistical data which they furnish differ from most of the data which we have discussed hitherto in that we are interested, not merely in the aggregate of values, but in the *order* in which they occur.

26.2 Throughout this and the succeeding chapter we shall consider only series of values given at equidistant intervals of time. By taking the time-interval as unit we can then regard our series as defined at times $t = 1, 2, 3$, etc., and can write the values of the series as u_1, u_2, u_3, etc., the value at time t being u_t. If for any reason we wish to reckon time backwards as well as forwards from time $t = 0$ we can write the series as $u_{-3}, u_{-2}, u_{-1}, u_0, u_1, u_2$, etc.

The restriction as to equidistant intervals is not in practice a serious limitation. Most series which are available in official publications such as economic, demographic, and meteorological series, are in fact given at intervals which are exactly equal, as days, or approximately equal, as years, or more or less roughly equal, as calendar months. Experimental data are usually collected at equidistant intervals as a matter of routine or are recorded (as on barometric graphs) in a continuous form from which equidistant readings may be taken. Our discussion of theoretical questions is greatly simplified by assuming equidistance in the time-intervals.

26.3 Although we shall draw all our illustrations from time-series it should be pointed out that the theory is also capable of application to certain other types of statistical data. For instance, if we put a thread of cotton under the microscope it presents, as we proceed along the thread, a fluctuating profile which bears at least a superficial resemblance to an oscillating time-series ; and we can regard the nitrogen content at various points along a strip of soil as the values of a series in which the time variable is replaced by a space variable. In fact our methods are applicable, and are often appropriate, whenever we have a statistical variable u_t depending on a variable t, whether relating to time or to linear space.

26.4 In general the variable u may be discontinuous or continuous, univariate or multivariate. For example, numbers of human beings are necessarily integral and population-series are therefore discontinuous in the variate ; on the other hand rainfall and temperature are continuous. Again, we may wish to study the movement through time of one variate, such as the price of wheat, or of several, such as wages, employment and volume of industrial output. In the latter case it is usually more convenient to regard each variate as yielding a separate (univariate) series and to study the relations between variates as the joint variation of several series.

26.5 Although our time-values are discontinuous, we must remember that the series itself, of which they form equidistantly spaced observations, may be either continuous or discontinuous in time. Some series are necessarily discontinuous. For example, the final dividends on an industrial security are declared once a year, usually but not always on about the same date, and there are no variate values between those dates. Again, although the act of earning an income may be carried on almost continuously, the remuneration received is usually paid once a week, once a month or once a quarter, namely at discontinuous intervals. Some series are continuous and may be continuously recorded, as for instance, by the instruments which graph on a rotating drum the temperature and barometric pressure in a particular locality. Between the extremes of unambiguous discontinuity and continuity we find numerous cases of a hybrid character. The price of a loaf of bread may be regarded as existing continuously while shops are open and even perhaps while they are shut ; the price of an industrial share can hardly be regarded as existing while the Stock Exchange is closed, and when it is open really varies discontinuously in the sense that on an active market the price may change with each transaction and hence is only determined at particular moments during the day. Certain quantities such as annual income or monthly rainfall are discontinuous in the time-variable in so far as there is only one value for the year or month as the case may be, but continuous in the sense that they are an accumulation over a continuous period of time. Such distinctions will not often cause us difficulty but they provide one more illustration of the maxim, of which perhaps the reader may be growing a little weary by this stage, that one should never forget the nature of one's primary material.

Some examples of time-series

26.6 We now give a few illustrations of the kind of material which we have to study in practice. Some examples have occurred earlier in this

book. Table 15.6 (Fig. 15.6) on page 359, showing the population of
England and Wales at ten-yearly intervals, gives a typical series for the
growth of a large aggregate of human beings. The series is smooth in the
sense that the values lie closely about a continuous curve. On the other
hand, the infantile and general mortality rates of England and Wales
graphed in Figure 13.1 on page 318, though moving downwards over the
period covered by the diagram, do not decline regularly. Table 26.1
and Figure 26.1, showing the sheep population of England and Wales
for certain years, give a picture of a somewhat similar kind, but the
departures from a smooth movement are of longer duration, and it is not
easy to decide from these data whether the increases following the low
point in 1922 are a reversal of the downward movement or only a tem-
porary fluctuation.

TABLE 26.1.—Sheep population of England and Wales for each year from 1867 to 1939

Data from the *Agricultural Statistics*

Year	Population (10,000)	Year	Population (10,000)	Year	Population (10,000)	Year	Population (10,000)
1867	2203	1886	1892	1905	1823	1924	1484
68	2360	87	1919	06	1843	25	1597
69	2254	88	1853	07	1880	26	1686
70	2165	89	1868	08	1968	27	1707
71	2024	90	1991	09	2029	28	1640
72	2078	91	2111	10	1996	29	1611
73	2214	92	2119	11	1933	30	1632
74	2292	93	1991	12	1805	31	1775
75	2207	94	1859	13	1713	32	1850
76	2119	95	1856	14	1726	33	1809
77	2119	96	1924	15	1752	34	1653
78	2137	97	1892	16	1795	35	1648
79	2132	98	1916	17	1717	36	1665
80	1955	99	1968	18	1648	37	1627
81	1785	1900	1928	19	1512	38	1791
82	1747	01	1898	20	1338	39	1797
83	1818	02	1850	21	1383		
84	1909	03	1841	22	1344		
85	1958	04	1824	23	1384		

26.7 The two last examples exhibit not only local variation but a broad
movement over the period, a *trend* as we may call it. In our next three
examples there is no apparent trend but varying degrees of " short-term "
or " local " variation. Table 26.2 and Figure 26.2 show the percentage
losses of British ships per annum (i.e. 100 times the tonnage lost divided
by the tonnage at risk). There is a good deal of variation from year to
year but it is not very regular, at least so far as the eye can judge. In
Table 26.3 (Figure 26.3) showing the crude birth-rates of cattle in Great
Britain on a quarterly basis there is, in contrast, a marked regularity due

to the seasonal character of births of cattle. There may, of course, have been seasonal effects in the data of Table 26.2, but if so they have been obliterated by the use of annual figures. Table 26.4 and Figure 26.4 show a rhythm in numbers of sunspots which is not seasonal. It is not so regular as that of Table 26.3 but there is evidently some degree of regularity present.

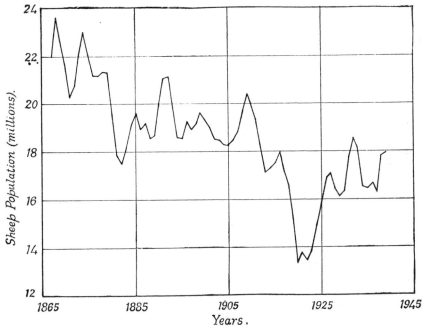

Fig 26.1—Graph of the data of Table 26.1

TABLE 26.2.—U.K. vessels lost as a percentage of the total U.K. fleet in certain years
Vessels of 100 g.r.t. and over

Figures from Lloyds Register *Statistical Summary*

Year	% loss	Year	% loss
1920	0·68	1930	0·49
1	0·34	1	0·17
2	0·62	2	0·30
3	0·73	3	0·39
4	0·57	4	0·42
5	0·32	5	0·41
6	0·58	6	0·24
7	0·34	7	0·46
8	0·59	8	0·50
9	0·56		

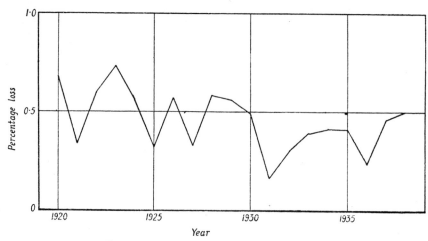

Fig. 26.2.—Graph of the data of Table 26.2

26.8 Examples such as these lead us to regard a time-series as composed of three constituent items, a long-term movement or trend, a short-term systematic movement and an unsystematic or random component. Some series, of course, do not exhibit all three—the movement shown in Figure 15.6 is nearly all trend, that of Fig 26.3 is nearly all systematic oscillation, and that of Figure 26.2 seems on the face of it to contain a good deal of random fluctuation. One of our principal problems is to isolate these components for separate study.

TABLE 26.3.—Crude birth rates (number of births per 100 population) of cattle in Great Britain

Data from Joan Marley, *J. Roy. Stat. Soc.*, **110.**, 187

The figures have been multiplied by a factor of approximately four to make them comparable with annual rates

Year	Birth rate			
	December–February	March–May	June–August	September–November
1940	33·2	45·2	33·2	40·0
1	35·2	44·0	38·8	32·8
2	35·2	46·4	35·6	34·4
3	34·8	44·8	32·0	38·4
4	37·6	41·2	32·8	36·8
5	36·0	42·0	30·0	35·2

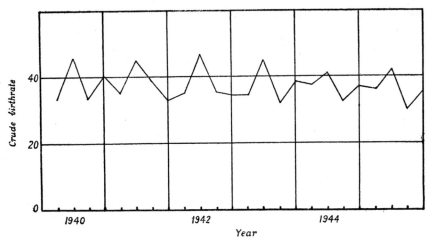

Fig. 26.3.—Graph of the data of Table 26.3

TABLE 26.4.—Wolfer's sunspot numbers for the years 1853-1900
Quoted by G. Udny Yule, *Phil. Trans.* A, **226**, 267

Year	Number	Year	Number	Year	Number	Year	Number
1853	39·0	1865	30·5	1877	12·3	1889	6·3
4	20·6	6	16·3	8	3·4	1890	7·1
5	6·7	7	7·3	9	6·0	1	35·6
6	4·3	8	37·3	1880	32·3	2	73·0
7	22·8	9	73·9	1	54·3	3	84·9
8	54·8	1870	139·1	2	59·7	4	78·0
9	93·8	1	111·2	3	63·7	5	64·0
1860	95·7	2	101·7	4	63·5	6	41·8
1	77·2	3	66·3	5	52·2	7	26·2
2	59·1	4	44·7	6	25·4	8	26·7
3	44·0	5	17·1	7	13·1	9	12·1
4	47·0	6	11·3	8	6·8	1900	9·5

26.9 One initial word of warning is necessary. It is useful to isolate the components of a series for sundry purposes. We may, for instance be interested in the broad movement of a series and hence concentrate attention on the trend to the exclusion of local and casual variation. But this does not necessarily mean that we can in a parallel manner isolate the causal systems underlying these movements. As a pure matter of description we may ignore local variations and consider the trend ; but we must not mislead ourselves by supposing that there is some fundamental cause or set of causes which generates the trend movement and another distinct set which accounts for the local movements. This is sometimes so, but not always so. We shall give later in the chapter (Example 26.4) an example of an artificial series which reproduces most of the features of the so-called trade cycle, namely a series of long swings on which are superposed more erratic short-term movements, but which is not composed of a trend-generator and a short-term generator.

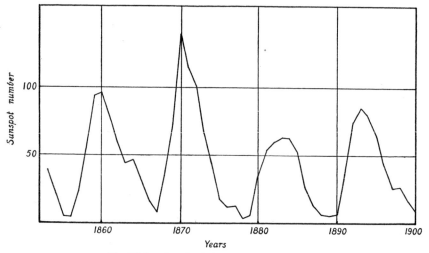

Fig. 26.4.—Graph of the data of Table 26.4

26.10 We may also remark at this stage that the distinction between a long-term and a short-term movement is to some extent arbitrary. The so-called trade-cycle is a long movement for most business purposes, the depressions and peaks occurring about once every ten years on the average. But in considering the recurrence of ice-ages or the growth and decay of civilisations, ten years would be a very short time. What we call a trend in any particular case is a matter of choice. It would be more accurate to speak of long-term or short-term movements and even then it is a convention what length of time we regard as long or short.

Trend
26.11 The general notion of trend as a broad continuous motion of the system leads us to consider the possibility of representing it by a poly-nomial in the time-variable t. The representation of a set of values $u_1, \ldots u_n$ by a parabola of the form

$$u_t = a_0 + a_1 t + a_2 t^2 + \ldots + a_p t^p \qquad . \qquad . \quad . \quad (26.1)$$

has already been considered in Chapter 15 and we need add little to what was said there on the subject. In Example 15.5 we did, in fact, fit cubic parabola to the population data of Table 15.6 and obtained a very fair fit.

26.12 This method of trend determination has some serious drawbacks when, as in Table 26.1, the polynomial required to obtain a good fit is of high order. The arithmetic becomes troublesome ; the higher order terms of the polynomial tend, as we pointed out in **15.22**, to " wag the tail " of the curve ; and if at some stage we add further terms to the series (as frequently happens when new data arise by the passage of time) the work of fitting has to begin afresh. The object of polynomial fitting can be attained by a simpler process known as the method of *moving averages*.

Moving averages

26.13 Consider the first $2m+1$ terms of the series, where m is a number which we can choose at will. We may fit a polynomial of order p to these terms and by convention will take our origin at the $(m+1)$th term, i.e., the middle one. Our polynomial, fitted by the usual method of least squares given in chapter 15, will then be of the type (26.1) and we may determine the constants $a_0 \ldots a_p$ by such equations as

$$\Sigma(u_t\, t^j) - a_0\Sigma(t^j) - a_1\Sigma(t^{j+1}) \ldots -a_p\Sigma(t^{j+p}) = 0 \qquad . \qquad . \quad (26.2)$$

there being $(p+1)$ of these equations corresponding to values of j from 0 to p, and the summations extending over the values of t from $-m$ o $+m$. (Compare equations (15.8) on page 344.)

This polynomial is the best fit, in a least squares sense, to the first $(2m+1)$ terms of the series and we may therefore take it as determining the trend value at the origin, that is to say at the $(m+1)$th point. The trend value is then obtained by putting $t=0$ in (26.1) and reduces simply to a_0. We need therefore only determine a_0 from the equations (26.2). The other constants a are not required.

It should be noted that the sums occurring in (26.2) are simply sums of the integers or their powers from $-m$ to m and hence depend only on m and p, not on the values of u_t, except in the case of the first term $\Sigma(u_t\, t^j)$. It then follows that when we solve the equations for a_0 we shall obtain a linear expression in the values u_t of the type

$$a_0 = b_1 u_1 + b_2 u_2 + \ldots + b_{2m+1}\, u_{2m+1} . \qquad . \quad (26.3)$$

where the b's depend only on m and p. This expression is merely a weighted average of the first $(2m+1)$ values of the series, the weights b being determinate once we have fixed m and p.

We may now repeat the process by moving along the series and fitting a curve to the $(2m+1)$ points from u_2 to u_{2m+2}, determining a trend value corresponding to the point u_{m+2} (the middle one of this set) ; and since our treatment remains the same except for changes in the values of the u's, the trend value will be given by

$$b_1 u_2 + b_2 u_3 + \ldots + b_{2m+1} u_{2m+2}$$

where the b's are the same quantities as were reached in equation (26.3).

We then proceed one step further along the series and repeat the process; and so on.

26.14 The net result of this treatment is that once we have determined the constants b we can ascertain trend values by a weighted average of sets of $(2m+1)$ consecutive terms. We take in fact, a *moving* average along the series. There will be no values corresponding to the first m or the last m terms of the series and we must either resign ourselves to having no trend for these $2m$ terms or adopt special measures to obtain them. Our trend values will " smooth " the series in the sense that they correspond to values of best fit given by polynomials of local application. The process of trend determination is often described as " smoothing."

26.15 Let us consider the simplest case when we fit straight lines to sets of three points, $(m=1, p=1)$. Our polynomial is then simply a_0+a_1t and we have to minimise the sum of squares

$$\sum_{t=-1}^{1} (u_t-a_0-a_1t)^2$$

which leads to the equations

$$\left. \begin{array}{l} \Sigma(u_t)-3a_0-a_1\Sigma(t) = 0 \\ \Sigma(tu_t)-a_0\Sigma(t)-a_1\Sigma(t^2) = 0 \end{array} \right\} \qquad . \qquad . \qquad (26.4)$$

Now $\Sigma(t)=0$ and in general $\Sigma(t^p)=0$ whenever p is odd. We then have simply from the first equation of (26.4)

$$a_0 = \tfrac{1}{3}\Sigma(u_t)$$
$$= \tfrac{1}{3}(u_{-1}+u_0+u_1) \qquad . \qquad . \qquad (26.5)$$

In short, our trend value at any point is simply the arithmetic mean of the three values of u centred at that point.

26.16 Consider next the case when we fit straight lines $(p=1)$ to sets of $2m+1$ points. Corresponding to the first equation of (26.4) we shall have

$$\Sigma(u_t)-(2m+1)a_0 = 0$$

leading to

$$a_0 = \frac{1}{2m+1}(u_{-m}+u_{-m+1}+ \cdots +u_m) \qquad . \qquad . \qquad (26.6)$$

In simple generalisation of the previous case we then have the result that the trend value at any point is the arithmetic mean of the $(2m+1)$ values centred at that point.

26.17 The next case in order of complexity is the fitting of a quadratic parabola to sets of 5 points ($p=2$, $m=2$). We then have to minimise

$$\sum_{t=-2}^{2} (u_t - a_0 - a_1 t - a_2 t^2)^2$$

and remembering that $\Sigma(t^p) = 0$ for odd p we arrive at the equations

$$\begin{aligned}
\Sigma(u_t) \quad -5a_0 \qquad\qquad -a_2\Sigma(t^2) &= 0 \\
\Sigma(tu_t) \qquad\qquad -a_1\Sigma(t^2) \qquad\qquad &= 0 \\
\Sigma(t^2 u_t) \; -a_0\Sigma(t^2) \qquad\qquad -a_2\Sigma(t^4) &= 0
\end{aligned} \right\} \quad . \quad . \quad (26.7)$$

Now $\Sigma(t^2) = 10$ and $\Sigma(t^4) = 34$. The relevant equations are then

$$\Sigma(u_t) \;-\; 5a_0 - 10a_2 = 0$$
$$\Sigma(t^2 u_t) - 10a_0 - 34a_2 = 0$$

leading to

$$\begin{aligned}
a_0 &= \frac{1}{35}\left\{17\Sigma(u_t) - 5\Sigma(t^2 u_t)\right\} \\
&= \frac{1}{35}\left\{-3u_{-2} + 12u_{-1} + 17u_0 + 12u_1 - 3u_2\right\} \quad . \quad . \quad (26.8)
\end{aligned}$$

26.18 Proceeding in this way, we can determine the weights appropriate to any system of m and p. The values of the weights for the cases required in practice, however, have been worked out and the simpler ones are given below. Let us note two properties of any system of weighting given by this method—

(a) The sum of the weights is unity. This follows from the fact that the sum in such an equation as (26.8) is obtained by putting all the u's equal to unity. If we do this in the first equation of (26.7) and equate all the other a's of even order to zero (as we may, since in this case a straight line gives a perfect fit) we see that $a_0 = 1$.

(b) The weights are symmetrical about their middle value. This follows from the fact that we must obtain the same result if we start from the end of the series and work backwards.

We can then write a series of weights such as those of equation (26.8) in the form $\frac{1}{35}$ [−3, 12, **17**, . . .]. Those of (26.5) would similarly be written $\frac{1}{3}$ [1, **1**, . . .]. With this notation we can now write down, without proof, the weights for the simpler cases.

$p = 1$ (straight line)—

$$\frac{1}{2m+1} \; [1, 1, \ldots 1, \ldots] \qquad . \qquad . \quad (26.9)$$

$p = 2$ or 3 (quadratic or cubic)—

Values of m

2	$\dfrac{1}{35} \; [-3, 12, 17, \ldots]$
3	$\dfrac{1}{21} \; [-2, 3, 6, 7, \ldots]$
4	$\dfrac{1}{231} \; [-21, 14, 39, 54, 59 \ldots]$
5	$\dfrac{1}{429} \; [-36, 9, 44, 69, 84, 89, \ldots]$

$$. \; . \; (26.10)$$

$p = 4$ or 5 (quartic or quintic)—

Values of m

3	$\dfrac{1}{231} \; [5, -30, 75, 131, \ldots]$
4	$\dfrac{1}{429} \; [15, -55, 30, 135, 179, \ldots]$
5	$\dfrac{1}{429} \; [18, -45, -10, 60, 120, 143, \ldots]$

$$. \; (26.11)$$

The reader will note that the same formulæ are obtained for $p=2k+1$ as for $p=2k$. We leave it as an exercise for him to examine why this is so.

26.19 It is evident that expressions such as this rapidly become rather cumbrous. We shall consider below how they may be simplified by approximation, but before doing so will give a numerical example.

Example 26.1

To fit a trend line by moving averages to the sheep population data of Table 26.1.

Let us first take a simple average of the type (26.9). We have to decide on the extent of the average, namely the number m. Our process will be sufficiently clear if we fit a curve to the first forty terms of the series only.

There is, at this stage, no golden rule which can be laid down for the determination of the extent of the average. We can only try a few values and see if they give us the kind of trend line we want. Let us then take two values, $m=2$ and $m=4$ (corresponding to extents of 5 and 9 terms respectively).

For the moving average of 5 we have to sum consecutive sets of five terms and divide by 5. The process is illustrated in Table 26.5. It is very simply carried out because in moving on a step we have only to add on one term to the sum of five at the end and take off one at the beginning. A similar process gives us the moving average of nine terms. Figure 26.5 shows the result of fitting the two trend lines.

TABLE 26.5.—Illustration of the arithmetic of fitting a simple moving average of fives to the data of Table 26.1

(1) Number of term, t	(2) Value of series u_t	(3) Sum of consecutive sets of five values of u_t	(4) $\frac{1}{5}$ of column (3)	(5) Deviation, column (2) less column (4)
1	2203			
2	2360			
3	2254	11006	2201	53
4	2165	10881	2176	− 11
5	2024	10735	2147	−123
6	2078	10773	2155	− 77
7	2214	10815	2163	·51
8	2292	10910	2182	110
9	2207	. . .	. . .	. . .
10	2119	. . .	. . .	. . .

Now let us try fitting a quadratic to consecutive sets of 7 points. The appropriate formula is, from (26.10)

$$\frac{1}{21} [-2, 3, 6, 7, \ldots]$$

This is not nearly so easy to apply as in our first case. We shall have, for the initial term corresponding to $t=3$

$$\frac{1}{21} \{(-2 \times 2203) + (3 \times 2360) + (6 \times 2254) + (7 \times 2165)$$
$$+ (6 \times 2024) + (3 \times 2078) - (2 \times 2214)\} = 2157$$

and a new calculation of this kind has to be done for each term of the trend line. The process is straightforward but tedious. It may be facilitated by the construction of a template which leaves only seven consecutive terms exposed to view, so that the eye does not pick out the wrong terms in machine calculations.

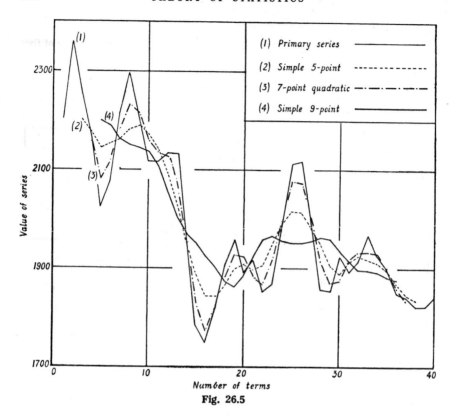

Fig. 26.5

We have shown in Figure 26.5, the result of applying this process to the series of Table 26.1.

An examination of this diagram will reveal the conventional nature of the determination of trend. The 7-point quadratic is not, for most purposes, a good trend line because it follows the primary data too closely and reproduces short term fluctuations. The fit is too good. The same is true, though to a smaller extent, of the moving five-year average. On the other hand the simple nine-year average seems to have the sort of properties we require to describe the general trend. We might have guessed this at the outset by noting that the major fluctuations seem to cover a period of about six years on the average so that a moving average of at least six successive terms is required to smooth them out. See also Example 26.5.

Approximate formula

26.20 By far the simplest kind of moving average to apply is the one in which all weights are equal, and it is possible to simulate the accurate formulæ of (26.10) and (26.11) by repeated simple moving averages. For instance if we apply a simple average of **threes** to a series we have a series typified by $\frac{1}{3}(u_1+u_2+u_3)$; and if we apply a simple average of threes to *this series* we have as a typical term

$$\frac{1}{3}\left\{\frac{1}{3}(u_1+u_2+u_3)+\frac{1}{3}(u_2+u_3+u_4)+\frac{1}{3}(u_3+u_4+u_5)\right\}$$

$$=\frac{1}{9}\{u_1+2u_2+3u_3+2u_4+u_5\}$$

$$=\frac{1}{9}[1,\ 2,\ 3,\ \ldots\ ]\qquad .\qquad .\qquad .\ (26.12)$$

The coefficients here follow more the pattern of (26.9) in that instead of being equal they rise to a maximum at the middle member. We state without proof that for many purposes great accuracy in the weights of a moving average is not necessary, so that formulæ of the kind of (26.12) may be used as substitutes for the accurate formulæ without serious loss of efficiency.

Two formulæ of general use in actuarial work are known as Spencer's 15-point and 21-point formulæ. The weights are as follows—

Spencer's 15-point formula

Writing $\frac{1}{k}[k]$ for a simple moving average of k terms, we have for this formula

$$\frac{1}{320}[4]^2[5]\ [-3,\ 3,\ 4,\ \ldots\ ]$$

$$=\frac{1}{320}[-3,\ -6,\ -5,\ 3,\ 21,\ 46,\ 67,\ 74,\ \ldots\ ]\quad .\ (26.13)$$

Spencer's 21-point formula

$$\frac{1}{350}[5]^2[7]\ [-1,\ 0,\ 1,\ 2,\ \ldots\ ]$$

$$=\frac{1}{350}(-1,\ -3,\ -5,\ -5,\ -2,\ 6,\ 18,\ 33,\ 47,\ 57,\ 60)\qquad .\qquad .\ (26.14)$$

These are accurate as far as third differences, i.e. they reproduce a cubic exactly and will provide a good approximation for higher order curves. The advantage in using them lies in the fact that most of the arithmetic can be carried out by simple summation. For instance, with (26.13) we first of all find a moving sum of fours, then a second moving sum of fours of the result, then a moving sum of fives of that result, and finally apply the moving average of fives $(-3,\ 3,\ 4,\ \ldots\ )$ and divide by 320. This is much more rapid than carrying out the moving average in one stage by the weights given on the right hand side of (26.13).

The statistician will rarely require closer fits than are given by these formulæ and frequently even they are too good in the sense noted in **26.19**. A simple moving average often gives him what he requires if his series fluctuates; if it constantly moves in the same direction so as to remain always concave or convex to the t-axis a simple moving average will systematically under- or over-shoot the mark. Compare Exercise 26.14.

26.21 We have chosen the number of points to which a polynomial is fitted to be odd. This is convenient because in the contrary case either the middle of the fitted range falls between two time-points or we have to fit a polynomial asymmetrically. Where, however, it is essential to fit to an even number of consecutive points we can easily do so by a slight modification of the technique. Consider the case of data given by quarters over a series of years. To eliminate seasonal effects the natural thing to do is to take a moving average of fours, but this gives us a set of values which do not correspond to the time-points of the original data. If, for instance, the information is an average over each quarter, the quarterly figures relate on the average to the *middle* of quarters and a four-point moving average will give values at the *end* of quarters. This may be adequate for our purposes. If not, we can "centralise" the trend values by taking a four-point moving average and then a simple mean (a two-point average) of the result. For instance, with a series starting with the first quarter of 1948, a four-point average will give figures relating to the *end* of June, the *end* of September, the *end* of December, 1948 and so on. A simple average of pairs of the result will give figures relating to the middle of August (the third quarter), the middle of November (the fourth quarter) and so on. In effect, what this process amounts to is the replacement of the scheme $\frac{1}{4}[1, 1, 1, 1]$ by $\frac{1}{8}[1, 2, 2, \ldots]$ as the reader can readily verify. An example is given below (Example 26.2).

Elimination of seasonal effects

26.22 A great many time series, particularly in economics and meteorology, are affected by the seasons. Similarly, other natural rhythms of shorter duration generate periodic effects such as the daily rise and fall in temperature at a given spot or the variation in tides at a port. Man-made periodicities may also appear, as in the change in the nature of road traffic at week-ends, or the rise in current bank balances at the end of the month. For simplicity we may term all such variations "seasonal" where they correspond to indentifiable and strictly periodic rhythms in the causative system even though the period is not one year. The student should beware of regarding an oscillatory movement as "seasonal" (i.e. strictly periodic) merely because it presents some appearance of regularity.

26.23 Our object in considering seasonal effects may be either to get rid of them in order to concentrate on the remaining variation or to isolate them for separate study. Elimination is a simple matter if we are prepared to extend our time-interval to cover a complete period of the seasons. For instance, we can eliminate any seasonal effect in records of sheep population by observing that population at a fixed date each year. The same stage of breeding and slaughtering may not quite be attained on the given date in different years but variations from it will be small *and erratic*. Again, we may eliminate seasonal movements in rainfall by recording only the total occurring in each year, the resulting series of annual figures containing no seasonal effects. Methods like these, of course, " eliminate " seasonal movement only in the sense of choosing a longer time-interval which covers one or more complete seasonal cycles ; they do not record for each part of the year what the value of the series would be if the seasonal part of the movement were abstracted, and to that extent they sacrifice information.

26.24 To fix the ideas, consider a series of monthly prices of a commodity such as eggs. This series has a definite seasonal movement but also may move from year to year independently of the purely seasonal effect. A simple 12-point moving average is often sufficient to smooth out seasonal variation but where enough data are available we may also take the calculations further as in following example.

Example 26.2
The average monthly prices per 120 eggs in England and Wales in 1927 and January 1928 were as follows—

(1927)	Jan.	Feb.	Mar.	Apr.	May	June	July	Aug.	Sept.	Oct.	Nov.	Dec.
Price (pence)	236	232	147	132	131	145	164	200	232	294	327	296

(1928)	Jan.
	286

The average of the prices for the 12 months of 1927 was 211 pence. The monthly prices relate approximately to the middle of the month, (being averages covering the whole month) and this average over the year therefore gives a range centred at the *end* of June. The average for the months Feb. 1927–Jan. 1928 inclusive was 215 pence and this relates to a period centred at the end of July. We therefore take as the appropriate value for the middle of July the mean of 211 and 215, namely 213 pence. This is the 12-month " centred " moving average or " trend-value " for July 1927.

The actual price for July was 164 pence and hence this price, as a percentage of the " trend-value " is $16400/213 = 77.0$. Calculations on these lines for the years 1927–1936 are shown in Table 26.6.

TABLE 26.6.—Percentage relation of actual egg prices to 12-month moving averages and seasonal indices derived therefrom

Data from C.T. Houghton, *J.R. Stat. Soc.*, 101 275.

Month	1927	1928	1929	1930	1931	1932	1933	1934	1935	1936	Seasonal Indices	
											Average 1927-36 Cols. (1) to (9) or (2) to (10)	Figures in Col. (11) adjusted to make their average equal to 100
	(1)	(2)	(3)	(4)	(5)	(6)	(7)	(8)	(9)	(10)	(11)	(12)
January	—	134·9	112·5	104·6	108·7	108·1	98·1	104·7	102·6	110·8	109·4	109·3
February	—	91·1	106·7	100·9	93·4	91·9	107·7	91·3	91·4	101·8	97·4	97·3
March	—	63·1	90·3	66·0	73·2	70·0	70·8	64·4	65·6	68·9	70·3	70·2
April	—	61·7	61·7	64·1	63·6	65·0	59·5	64·2	59·4	60·4	62·2	62·1
May	—	65·0	68·0	63·9	64·2	62·9	63·2	61·7	65·4	66·7	64·6	64·5
June	—	70·6	67·7	70·5	67·1	72·2	74·5	75·0	75·8	73·7	71·9	71·8
July	77·0	78·8	84·7	90·3	87·4	90·4	84·4	81·8	88·7	—	84·8	84·7
August	93·9	100·9	97·4	100·5	99·4	101·3	104·6	112·2	113·0	—	102·6	102·5
September	110·0	105·5	105·4	106·8	111·0	118·5	116·6	105·4	110·4	—	110·0	109·9
October	139·3	131·7	143·2	143·2	138·9	137·2	131·8	134·9	126·2	—	136·3	136·2
November	155·0	150·9	155·7	156·9	168·3	159·0	160·3	164·4	148·5	—	157·7	157·6
December	139·6	130·5	142·9	129·6	122·4	124·4	139·3	137·6	139·8	—	134·0	133·9
Average	—	—	—	—	—	—	—	—	—	—	100·1	100·0

In column (11) of this table is shown the average of the monthly indices for each month ; and column (12) scales these figures down very slightly so as to make them add up to 100·0. The results may be regarded as an index of the purely seasonal part of the egg prices. The January figure, for instance, indicates that on the average over nine years the January price was 109·3 per cent of the trend-value for January, or that seasonally prices are increased by 9·3 per cent in that month.

Let us now return to the prices for January-December 1927 quoted at the beginning of the example. These include an element due to the seasonal effect. Suppose we wish to eliminate seasonality in order to study whether there was any " real " change in the price of eggs over the year. We then divide the January price by 1·093, the February price by 0·973 and so on to obtain—

Corrected price (pence)	Jan.	Feb.	Mar.	Apr.	May.	June	July	Aug.	Sep.	Oct.	Nov.	Dec.
	216	238	209	213	203	202	194	195	211	216	207	212

These may be regarded as the prices " corrected " for seasonality. The movement over the course of the year, apart from seasonal effects, is obviously slight.

Change in price-level

26.25 As we have noted in connection with index-numbers special points arise when our series are expressed in terms of money owing to the change in the value of the unit over a long period. We may, therefore, wish to remove from a series of prices a trend in the general price-level. This is not the same thing as removing a trend in an ordinary series ; there we are concerned with long-term changes in the numbers of units, whereas here we are concerned with changes in the unit itself. The procedure customary in such cases is to divide the actual price by an index of general prices, or the price of gold, or some similar figure expressing the value of money ; alternatively we may revalue on the basis of prices in some standard year when our series relates to a " basket of goods ". We have noticed this latter process in Chapter 25. The former is illustrated in Table 26.7. Column (2) shows the net national income per head of population in the United Kingdom. Column (3) gives an index of prices on the basis of 1900=100. These figures are used to " correct for price changes " or to eliminate trends in prices to give column (4) which thus provides figures for income per head of a more comparable kind.

The effect of trend elimination on other elements

26.26 The success or failure of a method of determining trend is to be judged by results so far as the trend itself is concerned ; that is to say, by whether it gives a sufficiently broad general picture of the movement of the series for our purposes. But if our object is to eliminate trend in order to study short-term movements in the series we have to be most

TABLE 26.7.—Net National Income of the United Kingdom for certain years

Data from A. R. Prest, *Economic Journal*, 1948, **58,** 31

(1) Year	(2) Income per head at current prices £	(3) Price index 1900 = 100	(4) Income per head at 1900 prices col. (2) × 100/ col. (3) £
1900	42·7	100·0	42·7
1930	86·2	172·5	50·0
1	79·5	161·5	49·2
2	77·1	157·1	49·0
3	80·2	153·9	52·1
4	83·1	155·0	53·6
5	87·6	157·1	55·8
6	93·2	161·5	57·7
7	97·6	169·2	57·7
8	98·3	171·4	57·4

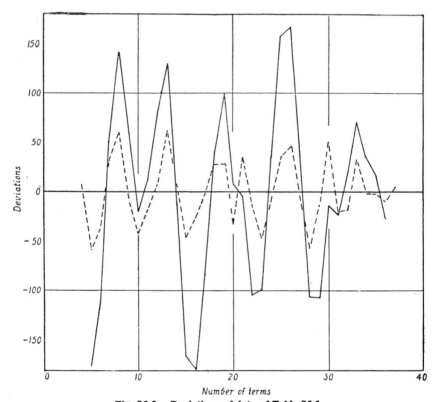

Fig. 26.6.—Deviations of data of Table 26.1

From simple nine-point average (continuous line)
From a seven-point quadratic (broken line)

careful that the residuals do not reflect the nature of the trend fitting rather than any intrinsic property of their own. In no branch of statistics do we have to guard so much against projecting our pre-conceived ideas into the data by the technique of analysis we adopt.

Example 26.3

Figure 26.6 shows the residuals given by two of the three methods of curve fitting derived in Example 26.1, the 9-point simple average and the 7-point quadratic. (By residuals we mean the deviations of the actual series from the trend values). Evidently the magnitudes of the deviations are very different in the two cases so that if we are interested in the size of the residual fluctuation our result depends very much on which method of trend-elimination we use. On the other hand, there seems to be a regularity in the oscillatory movement which is common to both series so that any judgment as to the period of the short-term movement would probably be very much the same whichever method of eliminating trend we had adopted.

26.27 Suppose that a series consists of the sum of three components, a trend, an oscillatory movement and a random element. Our method of trend elimination by moving averages evidently acts separately on these three components; if, therefore, it eliminates the trend perfectly we shall be left with residuals which are the same as if we had applied the method to a series consisting of the sum of an oscillatory and a random component. Let us consider the effect of the method on such components.

26.28 Consider an oscillation which is given by the terms of a sine-series

$$u_t = \sin\left(\alpha + \frac{2\pi}{\lambda}t\right) \qquad . \qquad . \qquad . \qquad . \quad (26.15)$$

where α and λ are constants. Such a series gives a harmonic wave of period λ. In most text-books of trigonometry it is proved that

$$\sum_{t=1}^{k} u_t = \frac{\sin \pi k/\lambda}{\sin \pi/\lambda} \sin\{\alpha + \pi(k+1)/\lambda\} \qquad . \qquad . \quad (26.16)$$

Thus a simple moving average of k terms will result in a sine-series with the same period as the primary series but with amplitude reduced by the factor

$$\frac{1}{k}\frac{\sin \pi k/\lambda}{\sin \pi/\lambda} \qquad . \qquad . \qquad . \qquad . \quad (26.17)$$

If the process is repeated q times the amplitude is reduced by the qth power of this quantity.

If then k is large or $\pi k/\lambda$ is an integral multiple of π, the expression

(26.17) is zero or small. Thus the " trend " determined in the oscillation is small and the residual only slightly affected. But if λ is large and k/λ is small the term (26.17) is nearly unity (since $\sin \theta = \theta$ approximately for small θ) and hence the residual will be very small, most of the primary variation being eliminated as trend.

26.29 This is what we might expect on general grounds. If k/λ is small and λ is large the oscillation has a large period, i.e. is a very slow one and is treated as trend by the moving average. If the period is short compared with k the residuals are only slightly affected.

In general, we may expect from this analysis that a moving average will emphasise the shorter oscillations at the expense of the longer ones. It is interesting to note that in some circumstances (26.17) may be negative so that the oscillation in the residual may be even larger than in the primary series.

26.30 Consider, again, the effect of a moving average on a random series ϵ_t with zero mean. To fix the ideas, consider a moving average of fives. Two consecutive values of the trend would be typified by

$$\tfrac{1}{5}\left(\epsilon_1 + \epsilon_2 + \epsilon_3 + \epsilon_4 + \epsilon_5\right) \text{ and } \tfrac{1}{5}\left(\epsilon_2 + \epsilon_3 + \epsilon_4 + \epsilon_5 + \epsilon_6\right) \quad . \quad (26.18)$$

The variance of this series is $\tfrac{1}{5}$ var ϵ and the covariance (since the residuals are independent) is

$$\tfrac{1}{25} E \left(\epsilon_2{}^2 + \epsilon_3{}^2 + \epsilon_4{}^2 + \epsilon_5{}^2\right) = \tfrac{4}{25} \text{ var } \epsilon$$

Thus the correlation between neighbouring terms is $4/5$. Similarly the correlation between terms 1, 2, 3, 4 members apart is $3/5$, $2/5$, $1/5$, 0. Hence the values of the " trend " will tend to be smooth ; and when we subtract the trend from the original series we shall get a smooth component on which is superposed a random series. The effect of trend elimination is therefore to insert in the residuals a smooth component which, in general, will exhibit oscillations. We have to take care, accordingly, that when we detect " oscillations " in a series from which trend has been eliminated by moving averages, the oscillations are not spurious.

Example 26.4

Figure 26.7 shows the results of a smoothing $\tfrac{1}{15}$ [5][3] on a set of 35 random numbers which could vary from 0 to 19 inclusive. They were obtained from the numbers on page 376 by reading two figure numbers downwards and omitting multiples of 20, e.g. the first numbers are 9, 1, 3, 5, 7. The resemblance to the vague fluctuation of a trade cycle is evident.

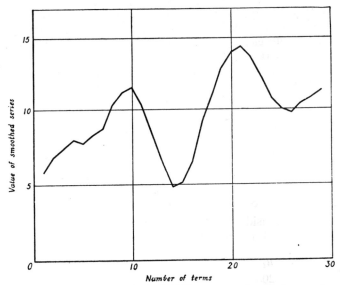

Fig. 26.7.—Smoothing by a $\frac{1}{15}$ [5] [3] average of a random series

Variate-differencing

26.31   As in the case of curve fitting (Chapter 15) the reader may wonder how he is to find out in any particular case what sort of moving average to use.   If he is interested in trend the answer is as indicated in Example 26.1.   But if he is interested in residuals the answer is much more difficult. We will indicate in broad outline a method which has as its object the detection of random variation ϵ and the estimation of its variance and which indicates at any rate an upper limit to the degree of the trend line.

Suppose a series consists of a polynomial of degree r plus a random element.   Then if we take first, second, third differences etc., the resulting series consists of a polynomial of degree $r-1$, $r-2$, etc., plus a residual which increases in variance.   We have, for instance, after the manner of **24.15**

$$E\ (\Delta\epsilon_t) = E\ (\epsilon_{t+1} - \epsilon_t) = 0 \qquad . \qquad . \qquad . \quad (26.19)$$

$$\text{var}\ (\Delta\epsilon_t) = E\ (\epsilon_{t+1} - \epsilon_t)^2$$

$$= 2\ \text{var}\ \epsilon \qquad . \qquad . \qquad . \quad (26.20)$$

Similarly

$$\text{var}\ (\Delta^2\epsilon_t) = 6\ \text{var}\ \epsilon \qquad . \qquad . \qquad . \quad (26.21)$$

and generally

$$\text{var}\ (\Delta^r\epsilon_t) = \binom{2r}{r}\ \text{var}\ \epsilon \ . \qquad . \qquad . \quad (26.22)$$

The effect of differencing is then to enhance the short-term movements at the expense of the long term movements and in particular to multiply the purely random element until it swamps all the others. (There is an exception to this rule if the systematic part of the series has a short period of two or less, for this is not reduced by differencing, as may be seen by considering the series 1, --1, 1, −1, etc.) This gives us a method of estimating the variance of a random element superposed on a series which can be represented (perhaps only locally) by a polynomial. The variances of the first, second, . . . rth difference (or better, the second moments about zero origin) are divided respectively by 2, 6, . . . $\binom{2r}{r}$ and if this quotient seems to be approaching a limit, the limiting value provides an estimate of var ϵ. Further, the degree to which we have had to go is some indication of the degree of the systematic part of the curve.

Example 26.5.—Consider again the sheep data of Table 26.1. A calculation of the differences would proceed as follows—

u_t	Δ^1	Δ^2	Δ^3	etc.
2203				
2360	−157	−263		
2254	106	17	−280	etc.
2165	89	−52	69	
2024	141			

The sums of squares of the differences Δ^r are shown in the following table. Column (3) shows the number N of terms on which they are based, and column (4) the ratio $\Sigma\ (\Delta^r)^2/N\binom{2r}{r}$, that is to say the ratio which we expect to tend to the variance of ϵ.

TABLE 26.8.—Variate-difference analysis of the data of Table 26.1

(1) Order of difference r	(2) Sum of squares of Δ^r	(3) Number of terms in sum N	(4) Column (2) / $N\binom{2r}{r}$
1	499,356	72	3468
2	614,333	71	1442
3	1,195,999	70	854
4	3,037,326	69	629
5	8,883,670	68	518
6	27,735,006	67	448
7	90,957,010	66	402
8	310,670,360	65	371
9	1,110,091,780	64	357
10	4,043,696,988	63	347

We also find, for the original series

$$\Sigma(u_t) = 135,537, \quad \Sigma(u_t{}^2) = 267,800,918.$$

whence we have for its variance

$$\mu_2 = 272,229.$$

A comparison of this figure with the fourth column of Table 26.8 shows that the variation is very substantially reduced by the first two or three differencings. We should be justified in concluding that the data can be represented locally by a polynomial of the third or fourth order, e.g. by a moving cubic or quartic and that the error ϵ (regarded as superposed on this systematic representation) has a variance of about 500.

What we have said above about the adequacy of a trend line is in no way affected by this result. The present example tells us that *if* the data consist of a polynomial plus a random element, there is no need to seek for a polynomial of degree higher than four. It indicates that we should be wasting our time in trying to fit quintic or higher order curves (or in using moving averages based on quintics, etc.). It does *not* say that a quartic is the best trend line for the purposes of a broad description of the trend; a simple curve might be more suitable in particular circumstances.

SUMMARY

1. For descriptive purposes the most general form of univariate time series may be regarded as composed of trend, short-term systematic movement and random or haphazard components.

2. This analysis sometimes corresponds to different causative systems, but not always so.

3. A convenient method of trend determination is to use moving averages. The weights can be determined by least squares and approximations to the exact weights are legitimate and useful.

4. Seasonal effects, i.e. movements occurring in a strictly periodic manner, can be removed or isolated by a special method.

5. Moving averages may distort short-term components and generate spurious oscillatory movements in random components of a time-series.

6. Variate-differencing can be used to estimate the variance of the random component of a series on the assumption that the other components can be represented (at least locally) by a polynomial in time and that no periodic movement is present with a period of two intervals or less.

EXERCISES

26.1 Determine a trend line by a simple moving average of nines in the data of Table 26.1 for the years 1905 to 1939.

26.2   The values of a series $u_1 \ldots u_n$ are plotted on a diagram in the usual way with t as abscissa.   The points corresponding to u_1 and u_2 are joined and the line joining them bisected, giving an ordinate of say, v_1.   The process is repeated by bisecting the line joining u_2 and u_3 to give v_2; and so on along the series.

The procedure is repeated with the series $v_1, v_2, \ldots v_{n-1}$ to give a series $w_1 \ldots w_{n-2}$.   Show that $w_t = \frac{1}{4}(u_t + 2u_{t+1} + u_{t+2})$.   Examine the suitability of this procedure as a method of determining a trend line in the data of Table 26.2.

26.3   The following are the figures for the infantile mortality rate in England and Wales (deaths of infants under one year of age per 1,000 live births)—

Year	Rate	Year	Rate
1922	77	1935	57
3	69	6	59
4	75	7	58
5	75	8	53
6	70	9	51
7	70	1940	57
8	65	1	60
9	74	2	61
1930	60	3	49
1	66	4	45
2	65	5	46
3	64	6	43
4	59		

Fit a simple moving average of fives to this series and apply a further simple moving average of fives to the result.

26.4   The following is the rainfall in inches in England and Wales for certain months—

	Avearge 1881—1915	1943	1944	1945	1946
Jan.	2·99	6·2	3·3	3·4	3·4
Feb.	2·57	1·8	1·7	3·1	3·4
Mar.	2·67	0·9	0·5	1·3	1·5
Apr.	2·12	1·4	2·2	1·7	1·8
May	2·30	3·2	1·5	3·2	3·0
June	2·44	2·3	2·5	3·2	3·4
July	2·87	2·2	2·8	2·6	3·1
Aug	3·35	3·2	3·2	2·8	5·4
Sept.	2·54	3·4	4·2	2·5	4·9
Oct.	3·97	3·4	4·5	4·1	1·5
Nov.	3·49	2·7	6·1	0·8	6·2
Dec.	3·92	2·1	2·8	4·1	4·0
Annual Total	35·23	32·8	35·3	32·8	41·6

Using the average of the period 1881–1915 as a norm derive monthly index numbers, for the period 1943–6 of the rainfall "corrected" for seasonality. Graph your results.

26.5 If the smoothing formula $\frac{1}{21}$ [−2, 3, 6, 7, . . .] is applied to a random series, find the correlations between members of the smoothed series 0, 1, 2, 3, 4, 5, 6 members apart.

26.6 Construct ten terms of the series whose value at time t is $t^2 - 2t + 5$ for $t = 0, 1, . . . 9$. Verify that the formula

$$\frac{1}{35} \ [-3, \ 12, \ 17, \ . . . \ ]$$

gives an exact fit to such a series.

26.7 Take the random digits of **16.30** as random numbers which can vary from 0 to 9 with equal frequency in the long run. Take a simple moving average of threes of the first 50 terms, then a simple moving average of five of the resultant, then another simple moving average of five of that resultant. Note the appearance of smooth series from the repeated averaging.

Write down the coefficients of the smoothing process if carried out in a single stage.

26.8 The following is an index number of the price of lead from 1926 to 1945 together with the " Statist " wholesale price index for the period. Construct an index of lead prices " corrected " for changes in the whole-sale price level.

| Year | Index numbers | | Year | Index numbers | |
	Wholesale prices	Lead		Wholesale prices	Lead
1926	125	157	1936	88	95
7	122	125	7	102	121
8	119	109	8	90	83
9	114	117	9	94	85
1930	96	95	1940	128	127
1	82	71	1	142	129
2	79	63	2	151	129
3	78	65	3	155	129
4	81	61	4	160	129
5	83	78	5	164	142

26.9   For a series in which the values are represented by a cube or lower power of the time variate t show that, if $\frac{1}{k}[k]$ is written in brief for a simple moving average of k terms,

$$\frac{1}{h^2-k^2}\left\{\frac{h^2-1}{k}\,[k]\;-\;\frac{k^2-1}{h}\,[h]\right\}$$

gives an accurate trend line.   Hence show how, by two simple moving averages, we may obtain a trend formula which will be correct to the third degree in the fitted polynomial.

Obtain the formula when $h=5$, $k=3$ in the form

$$\tfrac{1}{10}\,[-1,\ 4,\ 4,\ \ldots\ ]$$

26.10.   By considering the series $(t-2)^3$, $(t-1)^3$, . . . $(t+2)^3$ show that the formula

$$[b,\ -4b,\ 1+6b,\ -4b,\ b]$$

accurately reproduces a cubic curve for any value of b.   Show further that if this formula is applied to a random series the correlation between neighbouring members in the resultant " trend " is

$$-8b(1+7b)\,/(70b^2+12b+1).$$

26.11   The following are the quarterly index numbers of wholesale prices in the U.K. published by *The Statist*.

Year	Quarter			
	1	2	3	4
1928	122	125	118	117
9	119	114	114	109
1930	105	99	93	89
1	86	80	83	84
2	85	80	80	78
3	77	80	81	80
4	82	81	83	82
5	83	84	85	86

By a " centred " moving average of four calculate a quarterly index corrected for seasonal effects.

26.12   If δ is the " central " difference defined by

$$\delta u_t = u_{t+\frac{1}{2}} - u_{t-\frac{1}{2}}$$

show that to third differences,

$$\frac{1}{hk}[h][k]u_0 = u_0 + \frac{1}{24}(h^2 + k^2 - 2)\delta^2 u_0$$

where $\frac{1}{h}$ $[h]$ stands for a simple moving average of h.

26.13   Verify equations (26.10), and show generally that the same formulæ are reached for polynomials of order $2p+1$ as for order $2p$.

26.14   The value u_t at time t is given by $u_t = \sqrt{(t/10)}$.   Sketch the series from $t=0$ to $t=100$ and show that the " trend " determined by a simple moving average is always less than the actual value of the series.

CHAPTER TWENTY-SEVEN

TIME-SERIES—(2)

27.1 In this chapter we shall consider the short-term and random components in time-series, and shall suppose either that our series have no trend present (as in Tables 26.2 and 26.3) or that, if trend was originally present, it has been removed. Our series will then fluctuate more or less irregularly about some central value which we may regard as the mean of the whole series ; and our problems are to detect and to investigate the nature of the components of such fluctuation.

Tests for randomness

27.2 Let us first consider what kind of series we are likely to obtain if the variation is entirely random, i.e. if successive values are independent and the series may be considered as the chance arrangement of a sample from some unknown population. Two features suggest themselves as natural measures of departure from this situation, (*a*) the occurrence of peaks and troughs in the series and (*b*) the correlations between neighbouring members.

27.3 A member of a series u_t is said to be a " peak " if $u_{t-1} < u_t > u_{t+1}$ and it is a " trough " if $u_{t-1} > u_t < u_{t+1}$ In either case it is a " turning-point " and the interval between turning points is called a " phase ". If two or more successive values are the same and are greater than neighbouring values we regard them as determining *one* peak situated in the centre of the range of equal values ; and so for troughs.

It may be shown that in a random series of n terms the mean and variance of the number of turning points p are given by

$$\mu_1'(p) = \tfrac{2}{3}(n-2) \qquad . \qquad . \qquad . \qquad . \qquad . \qquad (27.1)$$

$$\mu_2(p) = \frac{16n-29}{90} \qquad . \qquad . \qquad . \qquad . \qquad . \qquad (27.2)$$

These results are independent of the distribution of the parent population of values of the series and therefore have a considerable generality. As n becomes large the distribution of p tends to normality fairly quickly.

For large n the average number of turning points per unit interval is 2/3 and the average phase (the average distance between such points) is therefore 1·5. Hence the average distance between peaks (or between troughs) is 3, and this is what we expect to find in a random series.

Example 27.1

Consider the data of Table 26.2. If $n=19$ we have, from (27.1) and (27.2), a mean value of 11.3 and a variance $3 \cdot 05$ for p. The actual number of turning points in the table is 9. The deviation from the mean, $2 \cdot 3$, is less than twice the standard deviation of about $1 \cdot 75$ and we conclude that this evidence is not significant of departures of the series from randomness.

On the other hand in Table 26.4 where $n=48$ the mean and variance of p are $30 \cdot 67$ and $8 \cdot 21$. The observed value of p is 14 which differs from the mean by more than six times the standard deviation. We cannot therefore regard the series as random.

Serial correlation

27.4 The coefficient of product-moment correlation between the neighbouring members of a series is called the autocorrelation of order 1 ; and similarly the correlation between members $(k-1)$ apart is called the autocorrelation of order k. Thus

$$\rho_k = \frac{\text{cov}\,(u_t,\,u_{t+k})}{\sqrt{\{\text{var}\,u_t\,\text{var}\,u_{t+k}\}}} \qquad . \qquad . \qquad . \qquad (27.3)$$

These functions are very important in the theory of oscillatory time-series and have applications far beyond the purpose for which we are now going to use them. Where it is important to distinguish between the values derived from a parent series and those from a sample we shall call the latter serial correlations and denote them by r_k. The contrast between *auto* and *serial* (of Greek and Latin origin), as between ρ and r, accords with our usual practice of denoting parent values by Greek and sample values by Latin symbols.

This usage is not universal. Some writers use " autocorrelation " to denote the correlation of members of a series among themselves, whether in population or in sample, and " serial " correlation to denote the correlations between different series.

27.5 In a long series var u_t and var u_{t+k} are practically identical and (27.3) becomes

$$\rho_k = \frac{\text{cov}\,(u_t,\,u_{t+k})}{\text{var}\,u_t} \qquad . \qquad . \qquad . \qquad (27.4)$$

For short observed series it is better to take the variance of the whole series (calculated from n terms) as the estimate of var u although the covariance is based on only $n-k$ terms. Similarly it is better to calculate the deviations of u from the mean of the whole series in determining the product-sum of u_t and u_{t+k}. Then, if the members of the series are measured about the mean of the whole set of terms we then have

$$r_k = \frac{n}{n-k} \frac{\sum\limits_{t=1}^{n-k} (u_t\,u_{t+k})}{\sum\limits_{t=1}^{n} u_t^2} \qquad . \qquad . \qquad (27.5)$$

27.6 Now if a series is random the theoretical value of ρ_k is zero for any k other than $k=0$. We may therefore use the departure of the serial correlations from zero to test departure of the series from randomness. We state without proof that for large n the variance of r_k in a random series is approximately

$$\text{var } r_k = \frac{1}{n-k} \qquad \qquad \qquad (27.6)$$

Example 27.2

Table 27.1 shows the values of the residuals of the sheep series of Table 26.1 when trend has been eliminated by a simple moving average of nines.

The value of r_1 for this series of 65 terms is $0 \cdot 595$. The standard error in a random series, from (27.6) is $1/\sqrt{64}=0 \cdot 125$. The observed value is therefore significant and we conclude that the residual series cannot be regarded as a random one.

TABLE 27.1.—Residual values of the sheep series of Table 26.1 after elimination of trend by a simple nine-point moving average

Year	Residual (10,000)	Year	Residual (10,000)	Year	Residual (10,000)
1871	−176	1893	+ 34	1915	+ 19
72	−112	94	−103	16	+128
73	+ 50	95	−104	17	+ 97
74	+141	96	− 15	18	+ 69
75	+ 60	97	− 23	19	− 29
76	− 20	98	+ 17	20	−174
77	+ 12	99	+ 71	21	−107
78	+ 82	1900	+ 35	22	−142
79	+130	01	+ 16	23	−109
80	− 14	02	− 27	24	− 23
81	−166	03	− 32	25	+ 60
82	−179	04	− 49	26	+121
83	− 84	05	− 61	27	+ 94
84	+ 38	06	− 52	28	− 25
85	+ 97	07	− 24	29	− 90
86	+ 8	08	+ 68	30	− 75
87	− 5	09	+141	31	+ 72
88	−105	10	+119	32	+152
89	− 99	11	+ 66	33	+112
90	+ 35	12	− 52	34	− 64
91	+159	13	−117	35	− 87
92	+167	14	− 61		

The calculation of serial correlation is rather a tedious process but help may be obtained by the following device. The series of n terms is written down vertically on each of two slips of paper, the spacing being equal on the two slips. This can very conveniently be done on a tabulator with a split keyboard. To calculate the first product-sum we pin the slips so that the first term on the right-hand slip is opposite the second on the left-hand slip and so on all the way down. For most series the difference of two terms which are opposite can be obtained mentally by subtraction, squared and set up on an adding machine. The sum of squares of differences is thus determined and the cross product $\Sigma(u_t u_{t+k})$ derived from the simple identity of the type

$$2\Sigma(xy) = \Sigma(x^2) + \Sigma(y^2) - \Sigma(x-y)^2$$

with the aid of $\Sigma(u_t^2)$, which is obtained without difficulty.

27.7 Tests of the randomness of a time-series are often unnecessary because it is obvious from inspection that the series is systematic to some extent. The two tests we have given, however, may be applied when there is any doubt and will usually be sufficient to settle it. Suppose now that we have decided that our series is not random. Some part at least of the oscillatory movement then requires explanation. To set up models which will reproduce the behaviour of oscillatory series is one of the most difficult outstanding problems of current statistical theory and it would be quite beyond the scope of this book to give an account of even what is now known, incomplete though that is. What we shall do is to describe and illustrate two techniques, one classical and one new, which offer the most promise.

Periodogram analysis

27.8 The reader who has an acquaintance with elementary physics is probably familiar with the way in which the motion of many oscillatory physical phenomena (tides, violin strings, pendulums and so forth) can be represented as the sum of a number of " pure " harmonic waves each of which can be represented by a sine or cosine term. The motion of a pure oscillator in time is expressible as a term $A \sin\left(\alpha + \frac{2\pi}{\lambda} t\right)$ where λ is the wavelength and A the amplitude; and oscillatory phenomena can often be represented by a sum of such terms—

$$u_t = A_1 \sin\left(\alpha_1 + \frac{2\pi}{\lambda_1} t\right) + A_2 \sin\left(\alpha_2 + \frac{2\pi}{\lambda_2} t\right) + \ldots + \text{etc.} \qquad (27.7)$$

Light itself is a phenomenon of this kind and Newton's classical experiment with a prism in splitting white light into a spectrum may be regarded as an analysis of a complicated periodic phenomenon into simple terms each with its own " colour " or wavelength.

27.9 Aware that many physical phenomena can be described by series of type (27.7), early investigators of economic and meteorological time-series were led to inquire whether the same methods could be used to describe them. The basic idea was that the series could be regarded as the sum of a number of strictly periodic terms plus, perhaps, an error of observation. This search for strict periodicity has not been very successful. The model on which it is based requires that, apart from casual errors, the peaks and troughs shall recur at equal intervals whereas in economic series at least crises certainly do not recur with strict regularity. Furthermore, the model presupposes that " errors " behave like errors of observation, that is to say, that they occur to disturb the observation at a particular moment but do not affect the subsequent motion of the system. Now in economics and meteorology, at least, it is more plausible to suppose that when something happens to disturb the system, the effect of that disturbance is integrated into the future motion of the system and becomes part of it. The model of superposed harmonics is not therefore a very plausible one. Nevertheless there are branches of our subject where analysis into harmonic components (i.e. sine or cosine terms) is useful and this chapter would be incomplete without some reference to it.

27.10 The process of searching for the periodicities in a time-series by harmonic analysis can be compared to the tuning of a radio set. We correlate a number of series with known wavelengths with the given series and if they are " out of step " with the wavelength of the series the result is a low intensity; but when we come into tune with that wavelength, there is a high intensity of correlation; and hence by considering the various intensities we can discover whereabouts the true wavelength lies.

To put it more accurately we select a trial wavelength μ and form the sums

$$A = \frac{2}{n} \sum_{j=1}^{n} u_j \cos \frac{2\pi j}{\mu} \qquad . \qquad . \qquad . \qquad . \qquad (27.8)$$

$$B = \frac{2}{n} \sum_{j=1}^{n} u_j \sin \frac{2\pi j}{\mu} \qquad . \qquad . \qquad . \qquad . \qquad (27.9)$$

and write

$$S^2 = A^2 + B^2 \qquad . \qquad . \qquad . \qquad . \qquad (27.10)$$

Then S is known as the *intensity*. Apart from constants the numbers A and B are the covariances of the series with the " trial " sine and cosine terms.

Now suppose that the series is in fact given by

$$u_t = a \sin \frac{2\pi t}{\lambda} + b_t \qquad . \qquad . \qquad . \qquad (27.11)$$

where b_t is a term uncorrelated with the trial period. Then

$$A = \frac{2a}{n} \sum_{j=1}^{n} \sin \frac{2\pi j}{\lambda} \cos \frac{2\pi j}{\mu}$$

$$= \frac{2a}{n} \sum \sin \alpha j \cos \beta j$$

where $\alpha = 2\pi/\lambda$, $\beta = 2\pi/\mu$

$$= \frac{a}{n} \Sigma \{ \sin (\alpha-\beta)j + \sin (\alpha+\beta)j \}$$

$$= \frac{a}{n} \left[\frac{\sin \{\tfrac{1}{2}(\alpha-\beta)n\} \sin \{\tfrac{1}{2}(\alpha-\beta)(n+1)\}}{\sin \{\tfrac{1}{2}(\alpha-\beta)\}} \right.$$
$$\left. + \frac{\sin\{\tfrac{1}{2}(\alpha+\beta)n\}\sin\{\tfrac{1}{2}(\alpha+\beta)(n+1)\}}{\sin\{\tfrac{1}{2}(\alpha+\beta)\}} \right] . \quad (27.12)$$

with a similar expression for B in which $\sin \{\tfrac{1}{2} (\alpha-\beta) (n + 1)\}$ is replaced by a cosine. Now for large n this is small unless the term in square brackets is large, that is, unless $\alpha - \beta$ or $\alpha + \beta$ is small. In this case, neglecting the term of order $1/n$ we find

$$A^2 + B^2 = \frac{a^2}{n^2} \cdot \frac{\sin^2 \{\tfrac{1}{2}(\alpha - \beta)n\}}{\sin^2 \{\tfrac{1}{2}(\alpha - \beta)\}}$$

and since, for small θ, $\sin \theta = \theta$ approximately, $\sin \{\tfrac{1}{2} (\alpha - \beta)n\} = \tfrac{1}{2} (\alpha - \beta)n$ and we have

$$A^2 + B^2 + a^2 . \qquad . \qquad . \qquad . \qquad . \qquad . \quad (27.13)$$

Thus S remains small unless α is nearly equal to β (and hence the trial period μ is near to the real period λ) in which case S is equal to the constant a and gives the amplitude of the term.

27.11 To calculate the sums A and B, suppose in the first place that μ is an integer. Write down the series in rows of μ thus :

u_1	u_2	.	.	.	u_μ
$u_{\mu+1}$	$u_{\mu+2}$	.	.	.	$u_{2\mu}$
.	.	.	.	.	
.	.	.	.	.	.
$u_{(\rho-1)\mu+1}$	$u_{(\rho-1)\mu+2}$	.	.	.	$u_{\rho\mu}$

$$\qquad\qquad\qquad\qquad\qquad\qquad . \quad . \quad . \quad (27.14)$$

Totals	m_1	m_2	.	.	.	m_μ

We continue writing down the rows until there are fewer than μ terms left, the extra terms being neglected. The number $\rho\mu$ is then as near as we can get to n in multiples of μ and may be denoted by N.
  The sum

$$\frac{2}{N} \left\{ m_1 \cos \frac{2\pi}{\mu} + m_2 \cos \frac{4\pi}{\mu} + \ldots m_\mu \cos \frac{2\mu\pi}{\mu} \right\} . \qquad . \quad (27.15)$$

is then the sum A of (27.8) for N terms. Similarly we have a formula for B with sines instead of cosines.
  In practice, of course, we do not actually form such a table as (27.14). The sums may be formed direct from the series on an adding machine by adding every μth member, starting in turn at u_1, u_2, and so on.

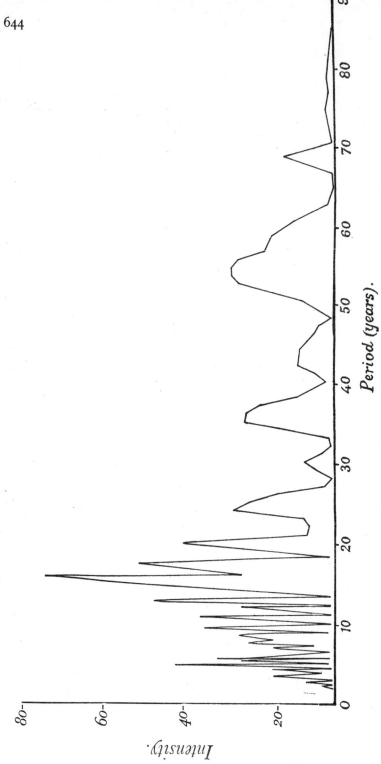

Fig. 27.1.—Periodogram of the Beveridge wheat-price index

27.12 The graph of S as ordinate against μ as abscissa gives us a *periodogram* and the whole process of analysis is known as periodogram analysis.

Example 27.3

Perhaps the most famous (and certainly the most exhaustive) example of a periodogram analysis is the one carried out by Lord (then Sir William) Beveridge on a series of index-numbers of wheat prices constructed by him for a period of about 300 years. Figure 27.1 shows the resulting periodogram.

Beveridge worked out the intensities for many trial periods which are not integral. The method is the same in essence as that of **27.11**. For instance, if $\mu=10/3$ we write down the series in rows of 10 and multiply the sums $m_1, \ldots m_{10}$ by $\cos\dfrac{2\pi}{\mu}$, $\cos\dfrac{4\pi}{\mu}$, $\ldots$ etc., in forming A. There were, in fact, many more trial values for lower values of μ than we have been able to show on the diagram.

The interpretation of a periodogram like this is very difficult. Beveridge himself was inclined to attribute significance to 18 or 19 major peaks, and was only following the practice of the physical sciences in doing so. It has, however, subsequently been shown that three-quarters of the peaks are explainable as sampling effects. In fact, it may be shown that if v is the variance of the series the chance that S^2 exceeds $4v\kappa/n$ in value is $e^{-\kappa}$ and hence if q trial periods are picked out at random the chance that one at least should exceed $4v\kappa/n$ is

$$1-(1-e^{-\kappa})^q$$

On the basis of this criterion, the peak at $\mu=15\cdot25$ is significant and possibly those at $\mu=5\cdot1$, $12\cdot8$, $17\cdot3$ and $20\cdot0$ are significant, but no more. More recent researches on the periodogram for an autoregressive series (**27.13** below) indicate that it may be smoothed and on this basis the peaks at $5\cdot1$ and $15\cdot25$ alone would be significant. But we shall have to make these statements without proof and, indeed without adequate discussion, merely to warn the student to mistrust most of what he finds in the literature on the periodograms of time-series. Different writers have been led to claim the existence of cycles of all kinds in economic and meteorological data. A reconsideration of the data would probably show that none of these cycles exists in the sense of being *strictly periodic*, at least in economics.*

Autoregressive series

27.13 A more modern approach to the subject attempts to take into account the point we noted in **27.9**, namely that when a disturbance occurs it is integrated into the motion of the system. Instead of regarding

---

* For some further discussion and tables to facilitate the performance of a periodogram analysis see Kendall, *Contributions to the Study of Oscillatory Time-Series*, 1946, Cambridge University Press.

our system as oscillating like a pendulum (the only departure from harmonic motion then being in the errors of observation) we shall consider it as swinging like a pendulum subjected to a continual stream of shocks, as for instance if it were pelted by small boys at random with peas. The pendulum will continue to swing backwards and forwards, but not regularly so. The times between its swings will not be constant nor will it always swing out to the same extent. In fact it will behave very much as many oscillatory time-series are seen to behave, which is our main justification for introducing this model for study.

27.14 We shall suppose that the motion of the system is determined by two factors : (*a*) a group of internal properties such as elasticities and constraints which determine how the system moves if left to itself and (*b*) a series of external shocks. We shall further suppose that the existence of factors in the first group can be expressed by saying that the value of the series at time *t* is a linear expression in values at previous points of time. We shall then have equations such as

$$u_{t+1} = \mu u_t + \epsilon_{t+1} \qquad . \qquad . \qquad . \qquad (27.16)$$

where μ is a constant and ϵ represents the external disturbance ; and

$$u_{t+2} = -\alpha u_{t+1} - \beta u_t + \epsilon_{t+2} \qquad . \qquad . \qquad (27.17)$$

where again α and β are constants. Such series are said to be *auto-regressive* because (27.16) and (27.17) may be regarded as regression equations of one term of the series on previous terms. More elaborate systems can, of course, be devised but these two simple cases are all we shall consider.

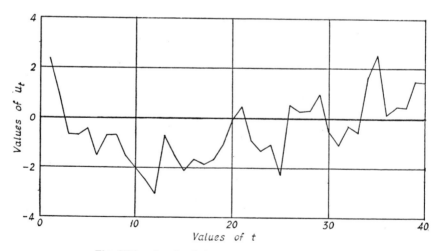

Fig. 27.2.—Graph of the series of Table 27.2

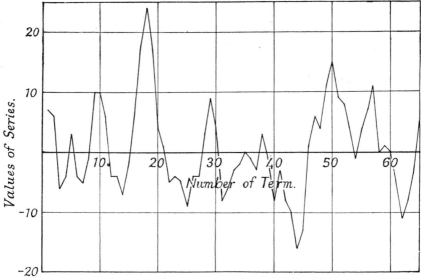

Fig. 27.3.—Graph of the values of Table 27.3

TABLE 27.2.—**Values of series** $u_{t+1} = 0 \cdot 7\, u_t + \epsilon_{t+1}$
Where ϵ_{t+1} is a random normal variable with zero mean
From Kendall, 1949, *Biometrika*, **36**. 267.

Number of term	Value of series	Number of term	Value of series
1	2·390	21	0·546
2	0·985	22	−0·886
3	−0·655	23	−1·321
4	−0·679	24	−1·014
5	−0·044	25	−2·254
6	−1·457	26	0·582
7	−0·731	27	0·272
8	−0·724	28	0·358
9	−1·567	29	0·981
10	−1·654	30	−0·497
11	−2·416	31	−1·078
12	−2·821	32	−0·318
13	−0·701	33	−0·597
14	−1·515	34	1·697
15	−2·112	35	2·585
16	−1·602	36	0·170
17	−1·805	37	0·497
18	−1·624	38	0·437
19	−1·060	39	1·554
20	−0·022	40	1·474

Example 27.4

To show how series of this kind behave, we give in Table 27.2 and Figure 27.2 the graph of a series of type (27.16) with $\mu = 0.7$, the values of ϵ being random numbers chosen from a *normal* population.

In Table 27.3 and Figure 27.3 we show similarly the graph of a series of type (27.17) with $\alpha = -1.1, \beta = 0.5$ where ϵ is a random variable chosen by selecting random numbers from range -9.5 to $+9.5$.

The irregular occurrence of peaks and troughs in such data is quite clear from the diagrams.

TABLE 27.3.—Values of series $u_{t+2} = 1.1\ u_{t+1} - 0.5\ u_t + \epsilon_{t+2}$

Where ϵ_{t+2} is a rectangular random variable with range -9.5 to 9.5, rounded off to nearest unit

From Kendall, 1944, *Biometrika*, **33**, 105.

Number of term	Value of series	Number of term	Value of series	Number of term	Value of series
1	7	23	− 4	45	−13
2	6	24	− 5	46	1
3	− 6	25	− 9	47	6
4	− 4	26	− 4	48	4
5	3	27	− 4	49	11
6	− 4	28	3	50	15
7	− 5	29	9	51	9
8	− 1	30	4	52	8
9	10	31	− 8	53	4
10	10	32	− 6	54	− 1
11	6	33	− 3	55	4
12	− 4	34	− 2	56	7
13	− 4	35	0	57	11
14	− 7	36	− 1	58	0
15	− 2	37	− 3	59	1
16	6	38	3	60	0
17	17	39	− 1	61	− 5
18	24	40	− 8	62	−11
19	17	41	− 3	63	− 8
20	4	42	− 8	64	− 3
21	1	43	−10	65	5
22	− 5	44	−16		

27.15   Consider now the series of (27.16) in the form

$$u_{t+1} - \mu u_t = \epsilon_{t+1} \qquad . \qquad . \qquad . \qquad . \quad (27.18)$$

where ϵ has zero mean (and hence so has u) and successive values of ϵ are independent. It will be clear from the series that u_t involves $\epsilon_t, \epsilon_{t-1}$, etc., but not $\epsilon_{t+1}, \epsilon_{t+2}$, etc. Let us then multiply (27.18) by u_{t-k} and sum over all values of u. Since cov $(u_{t+m}, u_{t-k}) = \rho_{k+m}$ var u where ρ_{k+m} is the $(k+m)$th autocorrelation, we have

$$(\rho_{k+1}-\mu\rho_k) \text{ var } u = \text{cov } (\epsilon_{t+1}, u_{t-k})$$

and since the covariance on the right vanishes for $k>-1$ we have

$$\rho_{k+1}-\mu\rho_k = 0, \ k>-1 \ . \qquad . \qquad . \qquad . \quad (27.19)$$

In particular when $k = 0$

$$\rho_1 = \mu \qquad . \qquad . \qquad . \qquad . \quad (27.20)$$

and hence

$$\rho_k = \mu^k = \rho_1{}^k \qquad . \qquad . \qquad . \quad (27.21)$$

We may note from (27.20) that only values of μ not greater than unity are admissible. If μ were greater than one the series would increase in amplitude and " explode " to infinity.

27.16 In a like manner, for the series of (27.17)

$$u_{t+2}+\alpha u_{t+1}+\beta u_t = \epsilon_{t+2}$$

we have, on multiplying by u_{t-k} and summing over u

$$\rho_{k+2}+\alpha\rho_{k+1}+\beta\rho_k = 0, \ k>-2 \ . \qquad . \qquad . \quad (27.22)$$

In particular, for $k=-1$, $k=0$ we have

$$\rho_1(1+\beta)+ \alpha = 0$$

$$\rho_2+\alpha\rho_1+\beta = 0$$

leading to

$$\alpha = -\frac{\rho_1(1-\rho_2)}{1-\rho_1{}^2} \qquad . \qquad . \qquad . \qquad . \quad (27.23)$$

$$\beta = -1+\frac{1-\rho_2}{1-\rho_1{}^2} \qquad . \qquad . \qquad . \quad (27.24)$$

It may be shown by the theory of finite difference equations (we omit the proof) that the solution of (27.22) is

$$\rho_k = \frac{p^k \sin \ (k\theta+\psi)}{\sin \ \psi} \qquad . \qquad . \qquad . \quad (27.25)$$

TABLE 27.4.—Serial correlations of the sheep data of Table 27.1

Order of correlation k	r_k	k	r_k	k	r_k
1	0·595	11	−0·142	21	−0·381
2	−0·151	12	−0·172	22	−0·118
3	−0·601	13	−0·186	23	0·173
4	−0·537	14	−0·128	24	0·343
5	−0·138	15	0·052	25	0·352
6	0·144	16	0·276	26	0·154
7	0·203	17	0·439	27	−0·203
8	0·118	18	0·293	28	−0·456
9	0·006	19	−0·074	29	−0·415
10	−0·078	20	−0·359	30	−0·184

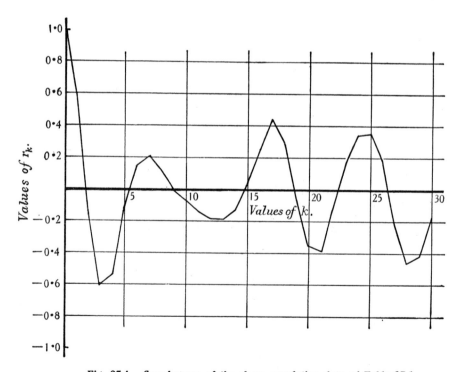

Fig. 27.4.—Correlogram of the sheep population data of Table 27.1

where

$$\begin{aligned}
p &= \sqrt{\beta} \text{ with positive sign} \\
\cos \theta &= -\alpha/(2\sqrt{\beta}) \\
\tan \psi &= \frac{1+\beta}{1-\beta} \tan \theta
\end{aligned} \right\} \qquad (27.26)$$

Here again there are restrictions on the constants α and β. The latter must be positive for p to be real and since $\cos \theta$ is not greater than unity $\alpha^2 \leqslant 4\beta$. Further, since ρ_k cannot exceed unity p cannot do so. Hence β must be positive and not greater than unity and α must be not greater than 2 in absolute value. If these conditions are not obeyed the series will not oscillate within bounds but will diverge to unlimited values.

27.17 The results of **27.15** and **27.16** serve two main purposes. If we know that the series are of the linear autoregressive type, (27.20), (27.23) and (27.24)—and similar equations for more complicated series—enable us to estimate the constants μ, α and β in terms of the autocorrelations which, for large samples at least, we may take to be the observed serial correlations. Secondly, the laws obeyed by successive autocorrelations as exemplified in (27.21) and (27.25) enable us to judge whether given series are of the autoregressive type.

The correlogram

27.18 The graph of the autocorrelation ρ_k as ordinate against k for abscissa is called a *correlogram.* Since $\rho_{-k} = \rho_k$ we draw it only for non-negative values of k. Table 27.4 and Figure 27.4 give the serial correlations and the correlogram of the sheep data of Table 27.1. There is a marked oscillatory movement which may be compared with Figure 27.5, giving the correlogram of the artificial series of Table 27.3.

27.19 Equation (27.21) shows that the theoretical correlogram of a series of the autoregressive type (27.18) will be a simple curve decaying from unity at $k=0$ to zero at $k=\infty$, the ordinate at each point k being ρ_1 times the ordinate at the previous point. On the other hand equation (27.25) shows that the theoretical correlogram of the series (27.17) will not only decay according to the factor p but will also oscillate. This so-called damped harmonic is illustrated in Figure 27.6.

These theoretical forms, however, are reproduced only approximately by series of finite length, as Figure 27.5 illustrates. The correlogram oscillates and its earlier terms damp out, but there comes a point when no further damping appears. This failure to damp must be regarded as a sampling effect.

TABLE 27.5.—Serial correlations of the artificial series of Table 27.3

Order of correlation k	r_k	k	r_k	k	r_k
1	0·70	11	−0·05	21	0·05
2	0·29	12	−0·17	22	−0·12
3	0·01	13	−0·27	23	−0·28
4	−0·17	14	−0·31	24	−0·43
5	−0·27	15	−0·30	25	−0·57
6	−0·25	16	−0·18	26	−0·56
7	−0·13	17	0·12	27	−0·26
8	0·07	18	0·29	28	0·02
9	0·12	19	0·33	29	0·17
10	0·05	20	0·22	30	0·27

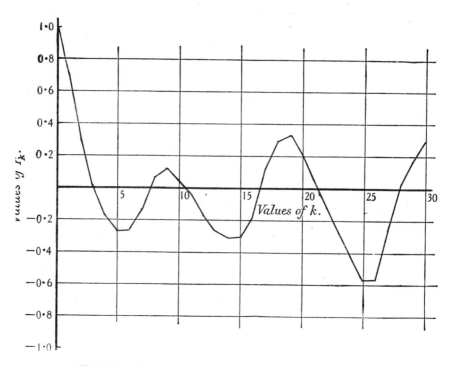

Fig. 27.5.—Correlogram of the artificial series of Table 27.3

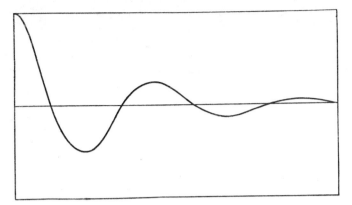

Fig. 27.6.—A damped harmonic curve

27.20 Let us return to the scheme of harmonics represented by (27.7). It may be shown that for the series

$$u_t = \sum_{j=1}^{m} A_j \sin\left(\alpha_j + \frac{2\pi}{\lambda_j}t\right) + \epsilon_t$$

the correlogram is given by

$$\rho_k = \frac{\Sigma\left(A_j^2 \cos\frac{2\pi k}{\lambda_j}\right)}{\Sigma(A_j^2) + 2 \text{ var } \epsilon} \qquad . \qquad . \qquad . \qquad . \qquad (27.27)$$

provided that ϵ is independent of the harmonic terms.

Thus to any term with amplitude A_j in the original series there corresponds a wave of amplitude $A_j^2/(A_j^2 + 2 \text{ var } \epsilon)$ in the correlogram which is undamped.

Theoretically, then, the correlogram should give us a method of discriminating between the scheme of superposed harmonics and the autoregressive scheme. In one case the oscillations in the correlogram do not damp out, in the other case they do. In practice, for short series, the discriminating power of the correlogram is not very high, owing to the failure of autoregressive correlograms to damp out for sampling reasons. Nevertheless an examination of the correlogram is often a very good way to start an investigation into the generating model of a given system.

Example 27.5

Consider again the data of Table 27.4. Taking the observed serial correlations as the parent values we have

$$r_1 = 0 \cdot 595, \ r_2 = -0 \cdot 151.$$

Hence, from (27.23) a (the estimate of α) $= -1 \cdot 060$

and from (27.24) b (,,   ,,   ,, β) $= +0 \cdot 782$

If the series can be represented by the three term linear autoregressive scheme then that scheme is

$$u_{t+2} - 1 \cdot 060 u_{t+1} + 0 \cdot 782 u_t = \epsilon_{t+2}$$

It is natural to wonder whether a three-term scheme is adequate and whether more terms may not be required. The question may be answered by the calculation of partial correlations. The following are the partials of the present series in our usual notation, 13.2, for instance, denoting the correlation between u_t and u_{t+2} when u_{t+1} is constant.

Order of partial correlation	Value of partial	$\Pi(1-r^2)=1-R^2$
12.	$0 \cdot 595$	$0 \cdot 6460$
13.2	$-0 \cdot 782$	$0 \cdot 2509$
14.23	$0 \cdot 097$	$0 \cdot 2485$
15.234	$-0 \cdot 183$	$0 \cdot 2402$
16.2345	$0 \cdot 031$	$0 \cdot 2400$

The product $1 - R^2$ in the last column measures (**12.20**) the closeness of the representation of the series and it is clear that little extra accuracy is gained by taking more than three terms, which will account for 75 per cent of the variation.

27.21 It may be added that for the purposes of detecting oscillatory movements by correlogram analysis " shortness " is a relative term. Even series of 400 terms are sometimes " short " in the sense that the correlogram after the tenth serial correlation or so does not damp out after the manner of Figure 27.6. A consideration of the magnitude of the variance of serial correlations in a random series, $1/(n-k)$, will show why this is so; for $n-k$ of the order of 100 the standard deviation is $0 \cdot 1$ and values of r as great as $0 \cdot 3$ are not impossible. What does appear to be true in practice is that even if the amplitude of the oscillations does not decay quickly, the swings in the correlogram conform to the period of the generating scheme as in Figure 27.4.

27.22 We conclude the chapter with a brief account of some of the properties of the autoregressive schemes of (27.16) and (27.17). Let us note as a preliminary point that such schemes will always give an *approximate* representation of the series in the sense that a regression line will always approximately represent the data to which it is fitted.

From relations such as

$$
\begin{aligned}
u_t &= \mu u_{t-1} + \epsilon_t \\
&= \epsilon_t + \mu(\epsilon_{t-1} + \mu u_{t-2}) \\
&= \epsilon_t + \mu \epsilon_{t-1} + \mu^2(\epsilon_{t-2} + \mu u_{t-3}) \\
&= \epsilon_t + \mu \epsilon_{t-1} + \mu^2 \epsilon_{t-2} + \, .
\end{aligned}
\qquad (27.28)
$$

we see that the series may be regarded as a moving average of infinite extent of the series of ϵ's.* The weights decrease and the contribution to u_t of ϵ_{t-k} is proportional to μ^k, that is, the contribution of the past is less and less important as it becomes more distant, which is what we should expect. We have directly from (27.28), when the ϵ's are independent,

$$\text{var } u_t = (1+\mu^2+\mu^4+ \ldots) \text{ var } \epsilon$$

$$= \frac{1}{1-\mu^2}\text{var } \epsilon, \qquad . \qquad . \qquad . \qquad (27.29)$$

expressing the variance of the series in terms of that of the disturbance function ϵ. If μ is near unity the variance of u may be much larger than that of ϵ.

27.23 In a similar manner it may be shown that for the three-term series (27.17) the solution of u_t, apart from terms which will have damped out of existence if the series was begun a long time ago, is also a moving average of the ϵ's and is given by

$$u_t = \sum_{j=1}^{\infty} \xi_j \epsilon_{t-j+1} \qquad . \qquad . \qquad . \qquad (27.30)$$

where

$$\xi_j = \frac{2}{\sqrt{(4\beta-\alpha^2)}}\rho^j \sin \theta j \qquad . \qquad . \qquad (27.31)$$

These weights are themselves oscillating and damped, like the correlogram. It may also be shown that

$$\frac{\text{var } u}{\text{var } \epsilon} = \frac{1+\beta}{(1-\beta)\{(1+\beta)^2-\alpha^2\}} \qquad . \qquad . \qquad (27.32)$$

which reduces to (27.29) when $\alpha=\mu$, $\beta=0$ as it should.

Example 27.6

In Example 27.5 we found for estimates of α and β the values of $-1\cdot060$ and $+0\cdot782$ respectively. Substitution in (27.32) gives

$$\text{var } u = 3\cdot778 \text{ var } \epsilon$$

Thus of the total variation of the series var ϵ represents about $1/3\cdot778$ or 26 per cent, which agrees with the estimate given by $1-R^2$ in Example $27\cdot5$ within one per cent.

---

*The series of (27.28), to be a complete solution, should have added to it a term $A\mu^t$ where A is an arbitrary constant. We suppose, however, that the series began a long time ago so that this term has damped out of existence, μ being less than unity.

Example 27.7

The sunspot data of Table 26.4 are an extract from a larger series beginning in 1749. An analysis of the series of 176 terms ending in 1924 Yule, *Phil. Trans.*, A, **226**, 267 gave the following—

$$a = -1·342, \quad b = +0·655$$

Partial correlations indicated that this series was adequately represented (about 80 per cent) by a three-term autoregressive scheme and no improvement would be given by further terms. Thus it appears that the series can be regarded as autoregressive with a damping factor $p = \sqrt{0·655}$ $= 0·81$ approximately. The period in the correlogram (θ of equation (27.26) is given by

$$\cos \theta = \frac{1·342}{2\sqrt{0·655}} = 0·829$$

giving 33° approximately. Thus the period of the correlogram is $360/33 = 10·6$ years. The series itself has no single " period " because the interval between successive peaks and troughs varies.

The " period " of an oscillation

27.24 From what we have said above it will be clear that for autoregressive schemes we cannot speak of *the* period of the series. There will be one period in the correlogram for the three-term case of (27.17)— or more with more elaborate schemes—and perhaps we might call this the autoregressive period. But it does not necessarily correspond to the mean-distance between peaks in the series itself and in any case the distances between peaks vary. The same is true of the distances between " upcrosses " or " downcrosses ", namely points where the series (measured from its mean) change sign from negative to positive or vice-versa.

The autoregressive period of (27.17) is given by $2\pi/\theta$ where as in (27.26)

$$\cos \theta = -\alpha/2\sqrt{\beta} \qquad . \qquad . \qquad . \qquad (27.33)$$

Now consider the series of values,

$$\begin{aligned} x_t &= u_{t+1} - u_t \\ y_t &= u_{t+1} - u_{t+2} \end{aligned} \qquad . \qquad . \qquad . \qquad (27.34)$$

We have, since the mean values of x and y are zero

$$\begin{aligned} \text{var } x_t &= \text{var } u_{t+1} + \text{var } u_t - 2 \text{ cov } (u_{t+1}, u_t) \\ &= 2 \text{ var } u (1 - \rho_1) \\ &= \text{var } y_t \end{aligned}$$

and

$$\begin{aligned} \text{cov } (x_t, y_t) &= \text{cov } (u_t, u_{t+2}) + \text{var } u_{t+1} \\ &\quad - \text{cov } (u_{t+1}, u_{t+2}) - \text{cov } (u_{t+1}, u_t) \\ &= \text{var } u (1 - 2\rho_1 + \rho_2) \end{aligned}$$

Hence for τ, say, the correlation between x_t and y_t we have

$$\tau = \frac{1-2\rho_1+\rho_2}{2(1-\rho_1)} \qquad . \qquad . \qquad . \qquad . \qquad (27.35)$$

Now suppose that x and y are normally distributed, as will be the case if u is normal. The relative frequency with which x and y are positive (i.e. $u_{t+1}>u_t$ and $u_{t+1}>u_{t+2}$ so that u_{t+1} is a peak) is then the relative frequency in a bivariate normal distribution in the positive cell among the four into which it is divided by $x=0$ and $y=0$. This, by Sheppard's theorem (Exercise 10.4) is given by f where

$$\tau = \cos (1-2f)\pi$$
$$= -\cos 2\pi f$$

so that

$$1/f = 2\pi /\cos^{-1}(-\tau) \qquad . \qquad . \qquad . \qquad . \qquad (27.36)$$

and this gives us the mean distance between peaks.

27.25 For the autoregressive scheme (27.17) we have in virtue of (27.23) and (27.24)

$$\tau = \tfrac{1}{2}(1+\alpha-\beta) \qquad . \qquad . \qquad . \qquad . \qquad (27.37)$$

and thus

$$\text{mean distance (peaks)} = \frac{2\pi}{\cos^{-1}\{-\tfrac{1}{2}(1+\alpha-\beta)\}} \qquad . \qquad . \qquad (27.38)$$

which is not the same as (27.33).

Example 27.8

Consider a series for which $\alpha=-1\cdot1$, $\beta=0\cdot5$. From (27.38) we find for the mean distance between peaks

$$\tau = \tfrac{1}{2}(1-1\cdot1+0\cdot5)=-0\cdot3$$
$$\cos^{-1}0\cdot3 = 72\cdot54°, \; 1/f = 4\cdot96.$$

In a series of 480 terms constructed according to this formula Kendall (*J. Roy. Statist. Soc.*, 1945, **108**, 93) found an observed value of $5\cdot05$, in excellent agreement.

On the other hand for the autoregressive period, from (27.33)

$$\cos \theta = 1\cdot1 /2\sqrt{0\cdot5} = 0\cdot7778, \; \theta = 38.9°$$

giving for the autoregressive period $360/38\cdot9=9\cdot3$ units.

27.26 Two final comments ;

(*a*) We have emphasised that for certain types of oscillatory series the idea of a single period or set of periods in the strict sense may be inappropriate. The student who is interested in oscillatory movements should accustom himself to think of the *distribution* of distances between peaks or upcrosses as expressing its oscillatory behaviour, in the same way that he thinks about a distribution of frequencies as characterising a population ;

(*b*) For series of such a type the existence of the random variable ϵ means that there is a limit to the accuracy with which we can predict the behaviour of the series. The autoregressive scheme will account, at least approximately, for a certain amount of systematic movement expressible in terms of the constants of the scheme; and hence, given previous members of the series we can predict the next member except for the random element. The latter, though we may estimate its variance, is itself unpredictable and there is thus an *essential* element of uncertainty in any forecast of the future.

SUMMARY

1. Randomness in an oscillatory time series may conveniently be tested by ascertaining the number of turning points which, in a random series of n terms, has a mean value of $\frac{2}{3} (n-2)$ and a variance of $(16n - 29)/90$.

2. Alternatively, a test may be made of the first serial correlation which has a variance of $1/(n-1)$ in random series.

3. The coefficient of product-moment correlation between members of a series $(k-1)$ members apart is called the autocorrelation (for infinite series) or the serial correlation (for observed series) of order k.

4. The graph of the serial correlation as ordinate against the order k as abscissa is called the correlogram of the series.

5. For series which may be regarded as composed of a series of harmonic terms, a technique known as periodogram analysis may be used to isolate the periodic terms.

6. A series in which the value at any point is a function of values at previous points plus a disturbance is said to be autoregressive ; and if the function is linear is linearly autoregressive. The two most important cases are—

$$u_{t+1} = \mu u_t + \epsilon_{t+1}$$
$$u_{t+2} + \alpha u_{t+1} + \beta u_t = \epsilon_{t+2}$$

7. The correlogram offers a means of descriminating between the harmonic series and the autoregressive series.

8. An autoregressive series has no period in the strict sense. The mean-distance between peaks may be quite different from the period of the correlogram.

EXERCISES

27.1   The following table shows the deviations from a moving nine-year average of potato yields in England and Wales for the years 1888-1935 (units are $\frac{1}{10}$th ton)—

Year	Yield	Year	Yield	Year	Yield	Year	Yield
1888	− 6	1900	− 7	1912	−15	1924	− 1
89	+ 2	01	+ 6	13	+ 3	25	+ 2
90	− 4	02	− 3	14	+ 2	26	− 9
91	− 3	03	− 7	15	+ 1	27	− 3
92	− 1	04	+ 2	16	− 2	28	+ 9
93	+ 6	05	0	17	+ 5	29	+ 5
94	− 2	06	+ 1	18	+ 4	30	+ 1
95	+ 7	07	− 7	19	− 4	31	−10
96	+ 3	08	+ 8	20	− 3	32	+ 1
97	− 6	09	+ 4	21	− 9	33	+ 2
98	+ 2	10	+ 3	22	+11	34	+ 5
99	0	11	+ 4	23	− 1	35	− 4

Find the number of turning points and show that it does not differ significantly from what would be expected of a random series.

27.2   From (27.35) derive an expression for the mean-distance between peaks in a series of type (27.16) in the form

$$2\pi / \cos^{-1}\{\tfrac{1}{2}(\mu-1)\}$$

Consider the case when $\mu=0$.

27.3   In an autoregressive series of type (27.17) find the mean-distances between peaks for the following values of α and β.

α	β
−1·5	0·8
−1·0	0·6
−0·8	0·8

Find also the autoregressive periods.

27.4   Show that the kth auto-correlation σ_k of the first difference of a series with autocorrelations ρ_k is given by

$$\sigma_k = -\frac{\Delta^2 \rho_{k-1}}{2(1-\rho_1)}$$

27.5   In a series of type (27.17) the observed r_1 was $0\cdot850$ and the observed $r_2=0\cdot606$. Estimate α and β.

27.6 Two series u and u' are added together so that a new series is formed by $v_t = u_t + u'_t$. If u and u' are independent show that the kth auto-correlation of v is given by

$$\frac{\rho_k \operatorname{var} u + \rho_k' \operatorname{var} u'}{\operatorname{var} u + \operatorname{var} u'}$$

where ρ and ρ' refer to the autocorrelations of u and u' respectively.

27.7 By considering the joint variation of u_t and u_{t+1} show that the mean-distance between upcrosses in a series is $2\pi / \cos^{-1} \rho_1$ where ρ_1 is the first autocorrelation. Find the expression in terms of α and β for series of type (27.17).

27.8 The following are the serial correlations of the Beveridge series referred to in Example 27.3. Draw the correlogram and compare any periods which it suggests to you with the results of that example.

Order of correlation k	r_k	k	r_k	k	r_k	k	r_k
1	0·562	16	0·158	31	0·060	46	−0·036
2	0·103	17	0·109	32	−0·008	47	−0·013
3	−0·075	18	0·002	33	−0·039	48	0·042
4	−0·092	19	−0·075	34	0·007	49	0·062
5	−0·082	20	−0·062	35	0·056	50	0·065
6	−0·136	21	−0·021	36	0·010	51	0·050
7	−0·211	22	−0·062	37	−0·004	52	0·009
8	−0·261	23	−0·088	38	−0·015	53	−0·027
9	−0·192	24	−0·084	39	−0·047	54	−0·053
10	−0·070	25	−0·076	40	−0·047	55	−0·073
11	−0·003	26	−0·091	41	0·008	56	−0·106
12	−0·015	27	−0·052	42	0·034	57	−0·084
13	−0·012	28	−0·032	43	0·065	58	−0·019
14	0·047	29	−0·012	44	0·099	59	0·003
15	0·101	30	0·059	45	0·009	60	0·010

27.9 For the autoregressive series of type (27.17) show that

$$1 - \rho_1 = \frac{1 + \alpha + \beta}{1 + \beta}$$

and hence that $1 + \alpha + \beta$ is not negative.

Show that the variance of the mean of n consecutive terms of the series is

$$\frac{\operatorname{var} u}{n} (1 + \lambda)$$

where, for large n, λ is given by

$$-\frac{2(\alpha + \beta + \beta^2)}{(1 + \beta)(1 + \alpha + \beta)}$$

$$= \frac{2(\rho_1 - \beta)}{1 + \alpha + \beta}$$

Hence show that λ is negative if ρ_1 is less than β, and thus that in some circumstances the mean of n consecutive values can have a smaller variance than the mean of n values chosen at random.

27.10   A Spencer 21-point smoothing formula (26.20) is applied to a random series.   Find the autocorrelations of the resulting series and sketch the correlogram.

27.11   In the autoregressive series of type (27.17) consider the case when $\beta=1$.   Show that the series then becomes undamped and the correlogram reduces to a simple harmonic.

APPENDIX TABLE 1

Normal curve

Ordinates of the Normal Curve $y=\dfrac{1}{\sqrt{(2\pi)}}e^{-\frac{1}{2}x^2}$ with First and Second Differences

x	y	$\Delta^1(-)$	Δ^2	x	y	$\Delta^1(-)$	Δ^2
0·0	0·39894	199	− 392	2·5	0·01753	395	+ 79
0·1	·39695	591	− 374	2·6	·01358	316	+ 66
0·2	·39104	965	− 347	2·7	·01042	250	+ 53
0·3	·38139	1312	− 308	2·8	·00792	197	+ 45
0·4	·36827	1620	− 265	2·9	·00595	152	+ 36
0·5	·35207	1885	− 212	3·0	·00443	116	+ 27
0·6	·33322	2097	− 159	3·1	·00327	89	+ 23
0·7	·31225	2256	− 104	3·2	·00238	66	+ 17
0·8	·28969	2360	− 52	3·3	·00172	49	+ 13
0·9	·26609	2412	0	3·4	·00123	36	+ 10
1·0	·24197	2412	+ 46	3·5	·00087	26	+ 7
1·1	·21785	2366	+ 84	3·6	·00061	19	+ 6
1·2	·19419	2282	+ 118	3·7	·00042	13	+ 4
1·3	·17137	2164	+ 143	3·8	·00029	9	+ 2
1·4	·14973	2021	+ 161	3·9	·00020	7	+ 3
1·5	·12952	1860	+ 173	4·0	·00013	4	—
1·6	·11092	1687	+ 177	4·1	·00009	3	—
1·7	·09405	1510	+ 177	4·2	·00006	2	—
1·8	·07895	1333	+ 170	4·3	·00004	2	—
1·9	·06562	1163	+ 162	4·4	·00002	—	—
2·0	·05399	1001	+ 150	4·5	·00002	—	—
2·1	·04398	851	+ 137	4·6	·00001	—	—
2·2	·03547	714	+ 120	4·7	·00001	—	—
2·3	·02833	594	+ 108	4·8	·00000	—	—
2·4	·02239	486	+ 91				

Precision of Interpolation.—Owing to the magnitude of the second differences, simple interpolation near the beginning of the table may give an error up to 5 in the fourth place ; the use of second differences will bring this down to 1 or 2 in the last place, third differences being small. Where third differences are greatest, in the neighbourhood of $x/\sigma=0·6$, the error may be as large as 3 in the last place unless the third difference is used.

APPENDIX TABLE 2

Areas under the normal curve (Probability function of the normal distribution)

The table shows the area of the curve $y=\dfrac{1}{\sqrt{(2\pi)}}e^{-\frac{1}{2}x^2}$ lying to the left of specified deviates x; e.g. the area corresponding to a deviate $1\cdot86$ $(=1\cdot5+0\cdot36,$ is $0\cdot9686$.

Deviate	0·0+	0·5+	1·0+	1·5+	2·0+	2·5+	3·0+	3·5+
0·00	5000	6915	8413	9332	9772	9^2379	9^2865	9^377
0·01	5040	6950	8438	9345	9778	9^2396	9^2869	9^378
0·02	5080	6985	8461	9357	9783	9^2413	9^2874	9^378
0·03	5120	7019	8485	9370	9788	9^2430	9^2878	9^379
0·04	5160	7054	8508	9382	9793	9^2446	9^2882	9^380
0·05	5199	7088	8531	9394	9798	9^2461	9^2886	9^381
0·06	5239	7123	8554	9406	9803	9^2477	9^2889	9^381
0·07	5279	7157	8577	9418	9808	9^2492	9^2893	9^382
0·08	5319	7190	8599	9429	9812	9^2506	9^2897	9^383
0·09	5359	7224	8621	9441	9817	9^2520	9^2900	9^383
0·10	5398	7257	8643	9452	9821	9^2534	9^303	9^384
0·11	5438	7291	8665	9463	9826	9^2547	9^306	9^385
0·12	5478	7324	8686	9474	9830	9^2560	9^310	9^385
0·13	5517	7357	8708	9484	9834	9^2573	9^313	9^386
0·14	5557	7389	8729	9495	9838	9^2585	9^316	9^386
0·15	5596	7422	8749	9505	9842	9^2598	9^318	9^387
0·16	5636	7454	8770	9515	9846	9^2609	9^321	9^387
0·17	5675	7486	8790	9525	9850	9^2621	9^324	9^388
0·18	5714	7517	8810	9535	9854	9^2632	9^326	9^388
0·19	5753	7549	8830	9545	9857	9^2643	9^329	9^389
0·20	5793	7580	8849	9554	9861	9^2653	9^331	9^389
0·21	5832	7611	8869	9564	9864	9^2664	9^334	9^390
0·22	5871	7642	8888	9573	9868	9^2674	9^336	9^390
0·23	5910	7673	8907	9582	9871	9^2683	9^338	9^404
0·24	5948	7704	8925	9591	9875	9^2693	9^340	9^408
0·25	5987	7738	8944	9599	9878	9^2702	9^342	9^412
0·26	6026	7764	8962	9608	9881	9^2711	9^344	9^415
0·27	6064	7794	8980	9616	9884	9^2720	9^346	9^418
0·28	6103	7823	8997	9625	9887	9^2728	9^348	9^422
0·29	6141	7852	9015	9633	9890	9^2736	9^350	9^425
0·30	6179	7881	9032	9641	9893	9^2744	9^352	9^428
0·31	6217	7910	9049	9649	9896	9^2752	9^353	9^431
0·32	6255	7939	9066	9656	9898	9^2760	9^355	9^433
0·33	6293	7967	9082	9664	9901	9^2767	9^357	9^436
0·34	6331	7995	9099	9671	9904	9^2774	9^358	9^439
0·35	6368	8023	9115	9678	9906	9^2781	9^360	9^441
0·36	6406	8051	9131	9686	9909	9^2788	9^361	9^443
0·37	6443	8078	9147	9693	9911	9^2795	9^362	9^446
0·38	6480	8106	9162	9699	9913	9^2801	9^364	9^448
0·39	6517	8133	9177	9706	9916	9^2807	9^365	9^450
0·40	6554	8159	9192	9713	9918	9^2813	9^366	9^452
0·41	6591	8186	9207	9719	9920	9^2819	9^368	9^454
0·42	6628	8212	9222	9726	9922	9^2825	9^369	9^456
0·43	6664	8238	9236	9732	9925	9^2831	9^370	9^458
0·44	6700	8264	9251	9738	9927	9^2836	9^371	9^459
0·45	6736	8289	9265	9744	9929	9^2841	9^372	9^461
0·46	6772	8315	9279	9750	9931	9^2846	9^373	9^463
0·47	6808	8340	9292	9756	9932	9^2851	9^374	9^464
0·48	6844	8365	9306	9761	9934	9^2856	9^375	9^466
0·49	6879	8389	9319	9767	9936	9^2861	9^376	9^467

Note :—Decimal points in the body of the table are omitted. Repeated 9's are indicated by powers, e.g. 9^371 stands for $0\cdot99971$.

APPENDIX TABLE 3

Significance points of χ^2

Reproduced from Table III of R. A. Fisher's *Statistical Methods for Research Workers*, Oliver & Boyd, Ltd, Edinburgh, by permission of the author and publishers

ν	P=0·99	0·98	0·95	0·90	0·80	0·70	0·50	0·30	0·20	0·10	0·05	0·02	0·01
1	$0·0^3157$	$0·0^3628$	$0·0^3393$	0·0158	0·0642	0·148	0·455	1·074	1·642	2·706	3·841	5·412	6·635
2	0·0201	0·0404	0·103	0·211	0·446	0·713	1·386	2·408	3·219	4·605	5·991	7·824	9·210
3	0·115	0·185	0·352	0·584	1·005	1·424	2·366	3·665	4·642	6·251	7·815	9·837	11·345
4	0·297	0·429	0·711	1·064	1·649	2·195	3·357	4·878	5·989	7·779	9·488	11·668	13·277
5	0·554	0·752	1·145	1·610	2·343	3·000	4·351	6·064	7·289	9·236	11·070	13·388	15·086
6	0·872	1·134	1·635	2·204	3·070	3·828	5·348	7·231	8·558	10·645	12·592	15·033	16·812
7	1·239	1·564	2·167	2·833	3·822	4·671	6·346	8·383	9·803	12·017	14·067	16·622	18·475
8	1·646	2·032	2·733	3·490	4·594	5·527	7·344	9·524	11·030	13·362	15·507	18·168	20·090
9	2·088	2·532	3·325	4·168	5·380	6·393	8·343	10·656	12·242	14·684	16·919	19·679	21·666
10	2·558	3·059	3·940	4·865	6·179	7·267	9·342	11·781	13·442	15·987	18·307	21·161	23·209
11	3·053	3·609	4·575	5·578	6·989	8·148	10·341	12·899	14·631	17·275	19·675	22·618	24·725
12	3·571	4·178	5·226	6·304	7·807	9·034	11·340	14·011	15·812	18·549	21·026	24·054	26·217
13	4·107	4·765	5·892	7·042	8·634	9·926	12·340	15·119	16·985	19·812	22·362	25·472	27·688
14	·660	5·368	6·571	7·790	9·467	10·821	13·339	16·222	18·151	21·064	23·685	26·873	29·141
15	5·229	5·985	7·261	8·547	10·307	11·721	14·339	17·322	19·311	22·307	24·996	28·259	30·578
16	5·812	6·614	7·962	9·312	11·152	12·624	15·338	18·418	20·465	23·542	26·296	29·633	32·000
17	6·408	7·255	8·672	10·085	12·002	13·531	16·338	19·511	21·615	24·769	27·587	30·995	33·409
18	7·015	7·906	9·390	10·865	12·857	14·440	17·338	20·601	22·760	25·989	28·869	32·346	34·805
19	7·633	8·567	10·117	11·651	13·716	15·352	18·338	21·689	23·900	27·204	30·144	33·687	36·191
20	8·260	9·237	10·851	12·443	14·578	16·266	19·337	22·775	25·038	28·412	31·410	35·020	37·566
21	8·897	9·915	11·591	13·240	15·445	17·182	20·337	23·858	26·171	29·615	32·671	36·343	38·932
22	9·542	10·600	12·338	14·041	16·314	18·101	21·337	24·939	27·301	30·813	33·924	37·659	40·289
23	10·196	11·293	13·091	14·848	17·187	19·021	22·337	26·018	28·429	32·007	35·172	38·968	41·638
24	10·856	11·992	13·848	15·659	18·062	19·943	23·337	27·096	29·553	33·196	36·415	40·270	42·980
25	11·524	12·697	14·611	16·473	18·940	20·867	24·337	28·172	30·675	34·382	37·652	41·566	44·314
26	12·198	13·409	15·379	17·292	19·820	21·792	25·336	29·246	31·795	35·563	38·885	42·856	45·642
27	12·879	14·125	16·151	18·114	20·703	22·719	26·336	30·319	32·912	36·741	40·113	44·140	46·963
28	13·565	14·847	16·928	18·939	21·588	23·647	27·336	31·391	34·027	37·916	41·337	45·419	48·278
29	14·256	15·574	17·708	19·768	22·475	24·577	28·336	32·461	35·139	39·087	42·557	46·693	49·588
30	14·953	16·306	18·493	20·599	23·364	25·508	29·336	33·530	36·250	40·256	43·773	47·962	50·892

Note.—For values of ν greater than 30 the quantity $\sqrt{2\chi^2}$ may be taken to be distributed normally about mean $\sqrt{(2\nu-1)}$ with unit variance.

t-Table.—The Proportion of the Area of the Curve $y = \dfrac{y_0}{\left(1 + \dfrac{t^2}{\nu}\right)^{\frac{1}{2}(\nu+1)}}$ of Unit Area lying to

0 to 6, and for values

(Condensed to three figures from the four-figure tables by "Student" in *Metron*, vol. 5, 1925, and published

t	$\nu=1$	2	3	4	5	6	7	8	9	10
0	0·500	0·500	0·500	0·500	0·500	0·500	0·500	0·500	0·500	0·500
0·1	·532	·535	·537	·537	·538	·538	·538	·539	·539	·539
·2	·563	·570	·573	·574	·575	·576	·576	·577	·577	·577
·3	·593	·604	·608	·610	·612	·613	·614	·614	·614⁵	·615
·4	·621	·636	·642	·645	·647	·648⁵	·649⁵	·650	·651	·651
·5	·648	·667	·674	·678	·681	·683	·684	·685	·685⁵	·686
·6	·672	·695	·705	·710	·713	·715	·716	·717	·718	·719
·7	·694	·722	·733	·739	·742	·745	·747	·748	·749	·750
·8	·715	·746	·759	·766	·770	·773	·775	·777	·778	·779
·9	·733	·768	·783	·790⁵	·795	·799	·801	·803	·804	·805
1·0	·750	·789	·804⁵	·813	·818	·822	·825	·827	·828	·830
1·1	·765	·807	·824	·833⁵	·839	·843	·846	·848	·850	·851
1·2	·779	·823⁵	·842	·852	·858	·862	·865	·868	·870	·871
1·3	·791	·838	·858	·868	·875	·879	·883	·885	·887	·889
1·4	·803	·852	·872	·883	·890	·894⁵	·898	·900	·902⁵	·904
1·5	·813	·864	·885	·896	·903	·908	·911	·914	·916	·918
1·6	·822	·875	·896	·908	·915	·920	·923	·926	·928	·930
1·7	·831	·884	·906	·918	·925	·930	·933⁵	·936	·938	·940
1·8	·839	·893	·915	·927	·934	·939	·943	·945	·947	·949
1·9	·846	·901	·923	·935	·942	·947	·950	·953	·955	·957
2·0	·852	·908	·930	·942	·949	·954	·957	·960	·962	·963
2·1	·858⁵	·915	·937	·948	·955	·960	·963	·965⁵	·967	·969
2·2	·864	·921	·942	·954	·960⁵	·965	·968	·970⁵	·972	·974
2·3	·869⁵	·926	·947⁵	·958⁵	·965	·969	·972⁵	·975	·976⁵	·978
2·4	·874	·931	·952	·963	·969	·973	·976	·978	·980	·981
2·5	·879	·935	·956	·967	·973	·977	·979⁵	·981⁵	·983	·984
2·6	·883	·939	·960	·970	·976	·980	·982	·984	·986	·987
2·7	·887	·943	·963	·973	·979	·982	·985	·986⁵	·988	·989
2·8	·891	·946	·966	·976	·981	·984	·987	·988	·990	·991
2·9	·894	·949	·969	·978	·983	·986	·988⁵	·990	·991	·992
3·0	·898	·952	·971	·980	·985	·988	·990	·991⁵	·992⁵	·993
3·1	·901	·955	·973	·982	·987	·989	·991	·993	·994	·994
3·2	·904	·957	·975	·983⁵	·988	·991	·992⁵	·994	·995	·995
3·3	·906	·960	·977	·985	·989	·992	·993	·995	·995	·996
3·4	·909	·962	·979	·986	·990	·993	·994	·995	·996	·997
3·5	·911	·964	·980	·988	·991	·994	·995	·996	·997	·997
3·6	·914	·965	·982	·989	·992	·994	·996	·996⁵	·997	·998
3·7	·916	·967	·983	·990	·993	·995	·996	·997	·997⁵	·998
3·8	·918	·969	·984	·990	·994	·995⁵	·997	·997	·998	·998
3·9	·920	·970	·985	·991	·994	·996	·997	·998	·998	·998⁵
4·0	·922	·971	·986	·992	·995	·996	·997	·998	·998	·999
4·1	·924	·973	·987	·993	·995	·997	·998	·998	·999	·999
4·2	·926	·974	·988	·993	·996	·997	·998	·998⁵	·999	·999
4·3	·927	·975	·988	·994	·996	·997⁵	·998	·999	·999	·999
4·4	·929	·976	·989	·994	·996⁵	·998	·998	·999	·999	·999
4·5	·930	·977	·990	·995	·997	·998	·999	·999	·999	·999
4·6	·932	·978	·990	·995	·997	·998	·999	·999	·999	·999⁵
4·7	·933	·979	·991	·995	·997	·998	·999	·999	·999	1·000
4·8	·935	·980	·991	·996	·998	·998⁵	·999	·999	·999⁵	
4·9	·936	·980	·992	·996	·998	·999	·999	·999	1·000	
5·0	·937	·981	·992	·996	·998	·999	·999	·999⁵		
5·1	·938	·982	·993	·996⁵	·998	·999	·999	·999⁵		
5·2	·939⁵	·982⁵	·993	·997	·998	·999	·999	1·000		
5·3	·941	·983	·993	·997	·998	·999	·999			
5·4	·942	·984	·994	·997	·998⁵	·999	·999⁵			
5·5	·943	·984	·994	·997	·999	·999	·999⁵			
5·6	·944	·985	·994	·997⁵	·999	·999	1·000			
5·7	·945	·985	·995	·998	·999	·999				
5·8	·946	·986	·995	·998	·999	·999				
5·9	·947	·986	·995	·998	·999	·999⁵				
6·0	0·947	0·987	0·995	0·998	0·999	0·999⁵				

TABLE 4

the Left of the Ordinate of Deviation *t*, for values of *t* proceeding by intervals of 0·1 from

of *ν* from 1 to 20.

by permission of *Metron* and the late W. S. Gosset, who supplied a few corrections to the original tables)

t	11	12	13	14	15	16	17	18	19	20
0	0·500	0·500	0·500	0·500	·5000	0·500	0·500	0·500	0·500	0·500
0·1	·539	·539	·539	·539	·539	·539	·539	·539	·539	·539
·2	·577	·578	·578	·578	·578	·578	·578	·578	·578	·578
·3	·615	·615	·615⁵	·616	·616	·616	·616	·616	·616	·616
·4	·652	·652	·652	·652	·653	·653	·653	·653	·653	·653
·5	·686⁵	·687	·687	·688	·688	·688	·688	·688	·689	·689
·6	·720	·720	·721	·721	·721	·721⁵	·722	·722	·722	·722
·7	·751	·751	·752	·752	·753	·753	·753	·754	·754	·754
·8	·780	·780	·781	·781⁵	·782	·782	·783	·783	·783	·783
·9	·806	·807	·808	·808	·809	·809	·810	·810	·810	·811
1·0	·831	·831⁵	·832	·833	·833	·834	·834	·835	·835	·835
1·1	·853	·853⁵	·854	·855	·856	·856	·857	·857	·857⁵	·858
1·2	·872	·873	·874	·875	·876	·876	·877	·877	·878	·878
1·3	·890	·891	·892	·893	·893	·894	·894⁵	·895	·895	·896
1·4	·905⁵	·907	·907⁵	·908	·909	·910	·910	·911	·911	·912
1·5	·919	·920	·921	·922	·923	·923⁵	·924	·924⁵	·925	·925
1·6	·931	·932	·933	·934	·935	·935	·936	·936⁵	·937	·937
1·7	·941	·943	·943⁵	·944	·945	·946	·946	·947	·947	·948
1·8	·950	·951⁵	·952⁵	·953	·954	·955	·955	·956	·956	·956⁵
1·9	·958	·959	·960	·961	·962	·962	·963	·963	·964	·964
2·0	·965	·966	·967	·967	·968	·969	·969	·970	·970	·970
2·1	·970	·971	·972	·973	·973⁵	·974	·974⁵	·975	·975	·976
2·2	·975	·976	·977	·977	·978	·979	·979	·979	·980	·980
2·3	·979	·980	·981	·981	·982	·982	·983	·983	·983⁵	·984
2·4	·982	·983	·984	·985	·985	·985⁵	·986	·986	·987	·987
2·5	·985	·986	·987	·987	·988	·988	·988⁵	·989	·989	·989
2·6	·988	·988	·989	·989⁵	·990	·990	·991	·991	·991	·991
2·7	·990	·990	·991	·991	·992	·992	·992	·993	·993	·993
2·8	·991	·992	·992⁵	·993	·993	·994	·994	·994	·994	·994⁵
2·9	·993	·993	·994	·994	·994⁵	·994⁵	·995	·995	·995	·996
3·0	·994	·994⁵	·995	·995	·995⁵	·996	·996	·996	·996	·996⁵
3·1	·995	·995	·996	·996	·996	·997	·997	·997	·997	·997
3·2	·996	·996	·996⁵	·997	·997	·997	·997	·997⁵	·998	·998
3·3	·996⁵	·997	·997	·997	·998	·998	·998	·998	·998	·998
3·4	·997	·997	·998	·998	·998	·998	·998	·998	·998⁵	·999
3·5	·997⁵	·998	·998	·998	·998	·998⁵	·999	·999	·999	·999
3·6	·998	·998	·998	·999	·999	·999	·999	·999	·999	·999
3·7	·998	·998⁵	·999	·999	·999	·999	·999	·999	·999	·999
3·8	·998⁵	·999	·999	·999	·999	·999	·999	·999	·999	·999
3·9	·999	·999	·999	·999	·999	·999	·999	·999⁵	·999⁵	1·000
4·0	·999	·999	·999	·999	·999	·999⁵	·999⁵	1·000	1·000	
4·1	·999	·999	·999	·999⁵	·999⁵	1·000	1·000			
4·2	·999	·999	·999⁵	1·000	1·000					
4·3	·999	·999⁵	1·000							
4·4	·999⁵	1·000								
4·5	·999⁵									
4·6	1·000									

Note.—The significance points of *t* for values of *ν* greater than 20 can be derived by taking the square-root of *F* (Table 5) for $ν_1 = 1$, $ν = ν_2$, bearing in mind that an *x* per cent point of *F* corresponds to a value of $1 - \frac{1}{2}x/100$ in the above table. In the above table a small terminal ⁵ means that the original four-figure tables from which these were compiled ended in a 5.

APPENDIX TABLE 5—Significance points of the variance-ratio F

A. 5 per cent points

Reproduced from Fisher and Yates: *Statistical Tables for Biological, Medical and Agricultural Research*, Oliver and Boyd Ltd., Edinburgh, by permission of the authors and publishers

ν_2 \ ν_1	1	2	3	4	5	6	8	12	24	∞
1	161·4	199·5	215·7	224·6	230·2	234·0	238·9	243·9	249·0	254·3
2	18·51	19·00	19·16	19·25	19·30	19·33	19·37	19·41	19·45	19·50
3	10·13	9·55	9·28	9·12	9·01	8·94	8·84	8·74	8·64	8·53
4	7·71	6·94	6·59	6·39	6·26	6·16	6·04	5·91	5·77	5·63
5	6·61	5·79	5·41	5·19	5·05	4·95	4·82	4·68	4·53	4·36
6	5·99	5·14	4·76	4·53	4·39	4·28	4·15	4·00	3·84	3·67
7	5·59	4·74	4·35	4·12	3·97	3·87	3·73	3·57	3·41	3·23
8	5·32	4·46	4·07	3·84	3·69	3·58	3·44	3·28	3·12	2·93
9	5·12	4·26	3·86	3·63	3·48	3·37	3·23	3·07	2·90	2·71
10	4·96	4·10	3·71	3·48	3·33	3·22	3·07	2·91	2·74	2·54
11	4·84	3·98	3·59	3·36	3·20	3·09	2·95	2·79	2·61	2·40
12	4·75	3·88	3·49	3·26	3·11	3·00	2·85	2·69	2·50	2·30
13	4·67	3·80	3·41	3·18	3·02	2·92	2·77	2·60	2·42	2·21
14	4·60	3·74	3·34	3·11	2·96	2·85	2·70	2·53	2·35	2·13
15	4·54	3·68	3·29	3·06	2·90	2·79	2·64	2·48	2·29	2·07
16	4·49	3·63	3·24	3·01	2·85	2·74	2·59	2·42	2·24	2·01
17	4·45	3·59	3·20	2·96	2·81	2·70	2·55	2·38	2·19	1·96
18	4·41	3·55	3·16	2·93	2·77	2·66	2·51	2·34	2·15	1·92
19	4·38	3·52	3·13	2·90	2·74	2·63	2·48	2·31	2·11	1·88
20	4·35	3·49	3·10	2·87	2·71	2·60	2·45	2·28	2·08	1·84
21	4·32	3·47	3·07	2·84	2·68	2·57	2·42	2·25	2·05	1·81
22	4·30	3·44	3·05	2·82	2·66	2·55	2·40	2·23	2·03	1·78
23	4·28	3·42	3·03	2·80	2·64	2·53	2·38	2·20	2·00	1·76
24	4·26	3·40	3·01	2·78	2·62	2·51	2·36	2·18	1·98	1·73
25	4·24	3·38	2·99	2·76	2·60	2·49	2·34	2·16	1·96	1·71
26	4·22	3·37	2·98	2·74	2·59	2·47	2·32	2·15	1·95	1·69
27	4·21	3·35	2·96	2·73	2·57	2·46	2·30	2·13	1·93	1·67
28	4·20	3·34	2·95	2·71	2·56	2·44	2·29	2·12	1·91	1·65
29	4·18	3·33	2·93	2·70	2·54	2·43	2·28	2·10	1·90	1·64
30	4·17	3·32	2·92	2·69	2·53	2·42	2·27	2·09	1·89	1·62
40	4·08	3·23	2·84	2·61	2·45	2·34	2·18	2·00	1·79	1·51
60	4·00	3·15	2·76	2·52	2·37	2·25	2·10	1·92	1·70	1·39
120	3·92	3·07	2·68	2·45	2·29	2·17	2·02	1·83	1·61	1·25
∞	3·84	2·99	2·60	2·37	2·21	2·09	1·94	1·75	1·52	1·00

Lower 5 per cent points are found by interchange of ν_1 and ν_2, i.e. ν_1 must always correspond with the greater mean square

APPENDIX TABLE 5—*(continued)*—Significance points of the variance-ratio F

B. 1 per cent points

Reproduced from Fisher and Yates: *Statistical Tables for Biological, Medical and Agricultural Research*, Oliver and Boyd Ltd., Edinburgh, by permission of the authors and publishers

v_2 \ v_1	1	2	3	4	5	6	8	12	24	∞
1	4052	4999	5403	5625	5764	5859	5981	6106	6234	6366
2	98·49	99·00	99·17	99·25	99·30	99·33	99·36	99·42	99·46	99·50
3	34·12	30.81	29·46	28·71	28·24	27·91	27·49	27·05	26·60	26·12
4	21·20	18·00	16·69	15·98	15·52	15·21	14·80	14·37	13·93	13·46
5	16·26	13·27	12·06	11·39	10·97	10·67	10·27	9·89	9·47	9·02
6	13·74	10·92	9·78	9·15	8·75	8·47	8·10	7·72	7·31	6·88
7	12·25	9·55	8·45	7·85	7·46	7·19	6·84	6·47	6·07	5·65
8	11·26	8·65	7·59	7·01	6·63	6·37	6·03	5·67	5·28	4·86
9	10·56	8·02	6·99	6·42	6·06	5·80	5·47	5·11	4·73	4·31
10	10·04	7·56	6·55	5·99	5·64	5·39	5·06	4·71	4·33	3·91
11	9·65	7·20	6·22	5·67	5·32	5·07	4·74	4·40	4·02	3·60
12	9·33	6·93	5·95	5·41	5·06	4·82	4·50	4·16	3·78	3·36
13	9·07	6·70	5·74	5·20	4·86	4·62	4·30	3·96	3·59	3·16
14	8·86	6·51	5·56	5·03	4·69	4·46	4·14	3·80	3·43	3·00
15	8·68	6·36	5·42	4·89	4·56	4·32	4·00	3·67	3·29	2·87
16	8·53	6·23	5·29	4·77	4·44	4·20	3·89	3·55	3·18	2·75
17	8·40	6·11	5·18	4·67	4·34	4·10	3·79	3·45	3·08	2·65
18	8·28	6·01	5·09	4·58	4·25	4·01	3·71	3·37	3·00	2·57
19	8·18	5·93	5·01	4·50	4·17	3·94	3·63	3·30	2·92	2·49
20	8·10	5·85	4·94	4·43	4·10	3·87	3·56	3·23	2·86	2·42
21	8·02	5·78	4·87	4·37	4·04	3·81	3·51	3·17	2·80	2·36
22	7·94	5·72	4·82	4·31	3·99	3·76	3·45	3·12	2·75	2·31
23	7·88	5·66	4·76	4·26	3·94	3·71	3·41	3·07	2·70	2·26
24	7·82	5·61	4·72	4·22	3·90	3·67	3·36	3·03	2·66	2·21
25	7·77	5·57	4·68	4·18	3·86	3·63	3·32	2·99	2·62	2·17
26	7·72	5·53	4·64	4·14	3·82	3·59	3·29	2·96	2·58	2·13
27	7·68	5·49	4·60	4·11	3·78	3·56	3·26	2·93	2·55	2·10
28	7·64	5·45	4·57	4·07	3·75	3·53	3·23	2·90	2·52	2·06
29	7·60	5·42	4·54	4·04	3·73	3·50	3·20	2·87	2·49	2·03
30	7·56	5·39	4·51	4·02	3·70	3·47	3·17	2·84	2·47	2·01
40	7·31	5·18	4·31	3·83	3·51	3·29	2·99	2·66	2·29	1·80
60	7·08	4·98	4·13	3·65	3·34	3·12	2·82	2·50	2·12	1·60
120	6·85	4·79	3·95	3·48	3·17	2·96	2·66	2·34	1·95	1·38
∞	6·64	4·60	3·78	3·32	3·02	2·80	2·51	2·18	1·79	1·00

Lower 1 per cent points are found by interchange of v_1 and v_2, i.e. v_1 must always correspond with the greater mean square

APPENDIX TABLE 5—(continued)—Significance points of the variance-ratio F

C. 0·1 per cent points

Reproduced from Fisher and Yates: *Statistical Tables for Biological, Medical and Agricultural Research*, Oliver and Boyd Ltd., Edinburgh, by permission of the authors and publishers

ν_2 \ ν_1	1	2	3	4	5	6	8	12	24	∞
1	405284	500000	540379	562500	576405	585937	598144	610667	623497	636619
2	998·5	999·0	999·2	999·2	999·3	999·3	999·4	999·4	999·5	999·5
3	167·5	148·5	141·1	137·1	134·6	132·8	130·6	128·3	125·9	123·5
4	74·14	61·25	56·18	53·44	51·71	50·53	49·00	47·41	45·77	44·05
5	47·04	36·61	33·20	31·09	29·75	28·84	27·64	26·42	25·14	23·78
6	35·51	27·00	23·70	21·90	20·81	20·03	19·03	17·99	16·89	15·75
7	29·22	21·69	18·77	17·19	16·21	15·52	14·63	13·71	12·73	11·69
8	25·42	18·49	15·83	14·39	13·49	12·86	12·04	11·19	10·30	9·34
9	22·86	16·39	13·90	12·56	11·71	11·13	10·37	9·57	8·72	7·81
10	21·04	14·91	12·55	11·28	10·48	9·92	9·20	8·45	7·64	6·76
11	19·69	13·81	11·56	10·35	9·58	9·05	8·35	7·63	6·85	6·00
12	18·64	12·97	10·80	9·63	8·89	8·38	7·71	7·00	6·25	5·42
13	17·81	12·31	10·21	9·07	8·35	7·86	7·21	6·52	5·78	4·97
14	17·14	11·78	9·73	8·62	7·92	7·43	6·80	6·13	5·41	4·60
15	16·59	11·34	9·34	8·25	7·57	7·09	6·47	5·81	5·10	4·31
16	16·12	10·97	9·00	7·94	7·27	6·81	6·19	5·55	4·85	4·06
17	15·72	10·66	8·73	7·68	7·02	6·56	5·96	5·32	4·63	3·85
18	15·38	10·39	8·49	7·46	6·81	6·35	5·76	5·13	4·45	3·67
19	15·08	10·16	8·28	7·26	6·61	6·18	5·59	4·97	4·29	3·52
20	14·82	9·95	8·10	7·10	6·46	6·02	5·44	4·82	4·15	3·38
21	14·59	9·77	7·94	6·95	6·32	5·88	5·31	4·70	4·03	3·26
22	14·38	9·61	7·80	6·81	6·19	5·76	5·19	4·58	3·92	3·15
23	14·19	9·47	7·67	6·69	6·08	5·65	5·09	4·48	3·82	3·05
24	14·03	9·34	7·55	6·59	5·98	5·55	4·99	4·39	3·74	2·97
25	13·88	9·22	7·45	6·49	5·88	5·46	4·91	4·31	3·66	2·89
26	13·74	9·12	7·36	6·41	5·80	5·38	4·83	4·24	3·59	2·82
27	13·61	9·02	7·27	6·33	5·73	5·31	4·76	4·17	3·52	2·75
28	13·50	8·93	7·19	6·25	5·66	5·24	4·69	4·11	3·46	2·70
29	13·39	8·85	7·12	6·19	5·59	5·18	4·64	4·05	3·41	2·64
30	13·29	8·77	7·05	6·12	5·53	5·12	4·58	4·00	3·36	2·59
40	12·61	8·25	6·60	5·70	5·13	4·73	4·21	3·64	3·01	2·23
60	11·97	7·76	6·17	5·31	4·76	4·37	3·87	3·31	2·69	1·90
120	11·38	7·31	5·79	4·95	4·42	4·04	3·55	3·02	2·40	1·56
∞	10·83	6·91	5·42	4·62	4·10	3·74	3·27	2·74	2·13	1·00

Lower 0·1 per cent points are found by interchange of ν_1 and ν_2, i.e. ν_1 must always correspond with the greater mean square

APPENDIX TABLE 6.—Significance points of the distribution of z

A. 5 per cent points

Reproduced by kind permission of Professor R. A. Fisher and Messrs. Oliver and Boyd from the former's
Statistical Methods for Research Workers

ν_2 \ ν_1	1	2	3	4	5	6	8	12	24	∞
1	2·5421	2·6479	2·6870	2·7071	2·7194	2·7276	2·7380	2·7484	2·7588	2·7693
2	1·4592	1·4722	1·4765	1·4787	1·4800	1·4808	1·4819	1·4830	1·4840	1·4851
3	1·1577	1·1284	1·1137	1·1051	1·0994	1·0953	1·0899	1·0842	1·0781	1·0716
4	1·0212	·9690	·9429	·9272	·9168	·9093	·8993	·8885	·8767	·8639
5	·9441	·8777	·8441	·8236	·8097	·7997	·7862	·7714	·7550	·7368
6	·8948	·8188	·7798	·7558	·7394	·7274	·7112	·6931	·6729	·6499
7	·8606	·7777	·7347	·7080	·6896	·6761	·6576	·6369	·6134	·5862
8	·8355	·7475	·7014	·6725	·6525	·6378	·6175	·5945	·5682	·5371
9	·8163	·7242	·6757	·6450	·6238	·6080	·5862	·5613	·5324	·4979
10	·8012	·7058	·6553	·6232	·6009	·5843	·5611	·5346	·5035	·4657
11	·7889	·6909	·6387	·6055	·5822	·5648	·5406	·5126	·4795	·4387
12	·7788	·6786	·6250	·5907	·5666	·5487	·5234	·4941	·4592	·4156
13	·7703	·6682	·6134	·5783	·5535	·5350	·5089	·4785	·4419	·3957
14	·7630	·6594	·6036	·5677	·5423	·5233	·4964	·4649	·4269	·3782
15	·7568	·6518	·5950	·5585	·5326	·5131	·4855	·4532	·4138	·3628
16	·7514	·6451	·5876	·5505	·5241	·5042	·4760	·4428	·4022	·3490
17	·7466	·6393	·5811	·5434	·5166	·4964	·4676	·4337	·3919	·3366
18	·7424	·6341	·5753	·5371	·5099	·4894	·4602	·4255	·3827	·3253
19	·7386	·6295	·5701	·5315	·5040	·4832	·4535	·4182	·3743	·3151
20	·7352	·6254	·5654	·5265	·4986	·4776	·4474	·4116	·3668	·3057
21	·7322	·6216	·5612	·5219	·4938	·4725	·4420	·4055	·3599	·2971
22	·7294	·6182	·5574	·5178	·4894	·4679	·4370	·4001	·3536	·2892
23	·7269	·6151	·5540	·5140	·4854	·4636	·4325	·3950	·3478	·2818
24	·7246	·6123	·5508	·5106	·4817	·4598	·4283	·3904	·3425	·2749
25	·7225	·6097	·5478	·5074	·4783	·4562	·4244	·3862	·3376	·2685
26	·7205	·6073	·5451	·5045	·4752	·4529	·4209	·3823	·3330	·2625
27	·7187	·6051	·5427	·5017	·4723	·4499	·4176	·3786	·3287	·2569
28	·7171	·6030	·5403	·4992	·4696	·4471	·4146	·3752	·3248	·2516
29	·7155	·6011	·5382	·4969	·4671	·4444	·4117	·3720	·3211	·2466
30	·7141	·5994	·5362	·4947	·4648	·4420	·4090	·3691	·3176	·2419
60	·6933	·5738	·5073	·4632	·4311	·4064	·3702	·3255	·2654	·1644
8	·6729	·5486	·4787	·4319	·3974	·3706	·3309	·2804	·2085	0·000

APPENDIX TABLE 6—(contd.)—Significance points of the distribution of z

B.   1 per cent points

Reproduced by kind permission of Professor R. A. Fisher and Messrs. Oliver and Boyd from the former's
Statistical Methods for Research Workers

ν_2 \ ν_1	1	2	3	4	5	6	8	12	24	∞
1	4·1535	4·2585	4·2974	4·3175	4·3297	4·3379	4·3482	4·3585	4·3689	4·3794
2	2·2950	2·2976	2·2984	2·2988	2·2991	2·2992	2·2994	2·2997	2·2999	2·3001
3	1·7649	1·7140	1·6915	1·6786	1·6703	1·6645	1·6569	1·6489	1·6404	1·6314
4	1·5270	1·4452	1·4075	1·3856	1·3711	1·3609	1·3473	1·3327	1·3170	1·3000
5	1·3943	1·2929	1·2449	1·2164	1·1974	1·1838	1·1656	1·1457	1·1239	1·0997
6	1·3103	1·1955	1·1401	1·1068	1·0843	1·0680	1·0460	1·0218	·9948	·9643
7	1·2526	1·1281	1·0672	1·0300	1·0048	·9864	·9614	·9335	·9020	·8658
8	1·2106	1·0787	1·0135	·9734	·9459	·9259	·8983	·8673	·8319	·7904
9	1·1786	1·0411	·9724	·9299	·9006	·8791	·8494	·8157	·7769	·7305
10	1·1535	1·0114	·9399	·8954	·8646	·8419	·8104	·7744	·7324	·6816
11	1·1333	·9874	·9136	·8674	·8354	·8116	·7785	·7405	·6958	·6408
12	1·1166	·9677	·8919	·8443	·8111	·7864	·7520	·7122	·6649	·6061
13	1·1027	·9511	·8737	·8248	·7907	·7652	·7295	·6882	·6386	·5761
14	1·0909	·9370	·8581	·8082	·7732	·7471	·7103	·6675	·6159	·5500
15	1·0807	·9249	·8448	·7939	·7582	·7314	·6937	·6496	·5961	·5269
16	1·0719	·9144	·8331	·7814	·7450	·7177	·6791	·6339	·5786	·5064
17	1·0641	·9051	·8229	·7705	·7335	·7057	·6663	·6199	·5630	·4879
18	1·0572	·8970	·8138	·7607	·7232	·6950	·6549	·6075	·5491	·4712
19	1·0511	·8897	·8057	·7521	·7140	·6854	·6447	·5964	·5366	·4560
20	1·0457	·8831	·7985	·7443	·7058	·6768	·6355	·5864	·5253	·4421
21	1·0408	·8772	·7920	·7372	·6984	·6690	·6272	·5773	·5150	·4294
22	1·0363	·8719	·7860	·7309	·6916	·6620	·6196	·5691	·5056	·4176
23	1·0322	·8670	·7806	·7251	·6855	·6555	·6127	·5615	·4969	·4068
24	1·0285	·8626	·7757	·7197	·6799	·6496	·6064	·5545	·4890	·3967
25	1·0251	·8585	·7712	·7148	·6747	·6442	·6006	·5481	·4816	·3872
26	1·0220	·8548	·7670	·7103	·6699	·6392	·5952	·5422	·4748	·3784
27	1·0191	·8513	·7631	·7062	·6655	·6346	·5902	·5367	·4685	·3701
28	1·0164	·8481	·7595	·7023	·6614	·6303	·5856	·5316	·4626	·3624
29	1·0139	·8451	·7562	·6987	·6576	·6263	·5813	·5269	·4570	·3550
30	1·0116	·8423	·7531	·6954	·6540	·6226	·5773	·5224	·4519	·3481
60	·9784	·8025	·7086	·6472	·6028	·5687	·5189	·4574	·3746	·2352
∞	·9462	·7636	·6651	·5999	·5522	·5152	·4604	·3908	·2913	0·0000

APPENDIX TABLE 6—(*contd.*)—**Significance points of the distribution of** *z*

C. 0·1 per cent points

Reproduced by kind permission of Professor R. A. Fisher, Dr. W. E. Deming and Messrs. Oliver and Boyd
from Prof. Fisher's *Statistical Methods for Research Workers*

ν_2 \ ν_1	1	2	3	4	5	6	8	12	24	∞
1	6·4562	6·5612	6·5966	6·6201	6·6323	6·6405	6·6508	6·6611	6·6715	6·6819
2	3·4531	3·4534	3·4535	3·4535	3·4535	3·4535	3·4536	3·4537	3·4536	3·4536
3	2·5604	2·5003	2·4748	2·4603	2·4511	2·4446	2·4361	2·4272	2·4179	2·4081
4	2·1529	2·0574	2·0143	1·9892	1·9728	1·9612	1·9459	1·9294	1·9118	1·8927
5	1·9255	1·8002	1·7513	1·7184	1·6964	1·6808	1·6596	1·6370	1·6123	1·5845
6	1·7849	1·6479	1·5828	1·5433	1·5177	1·4986	1·4730	1·4449	1·4134	1·3783
7	1·6874	1·5384	1·4662	1·4221	1·3927	1·3711	1·3417	1·3090	1·2721	1·2296
8	1·6177	1·4587	1·3809	1·3332	1·3008	1··2770	1·2443	1·2077	1·1662	1·1169
9	1·5646	1·3982	1·3160	1·2653	1·2304	1·2047	1·1694	1·1293	1·0830	1·0279
10	1·5232	1·3509	1·2650	1·2116	1·1748	1·1475	1·1098	1·0668	1·0165	·9557
11	1·4900	1·3128	1·2238	1·1683	1·1297	1·1012	1·0614	1·0157	·9619	·8957
12	1·4627	1·2814	1·1900	1·1326	1·0926	1·0628	1·0213	·9733	·9162	·8450
13	1·4400	1·2553	1·1616	1·1026	1·0614	1·0306	·9875	·9374	·8774	·8014
14	1·4208	1·2332	1·1376	1·0772	1·0348	1·0031	·9586	·9066	·8439	·7635
15	1·4043	1·2141	1·1169	1·0553	1·0119	·9795	·9336	·8800	·8147	·7301
16	1·3900	1·1976	1·0989	1·0362	·9920	·9588	·9119	·8567	·7891	·7005
17	1·3775	1·1832	1·0832	1·0195	·9745	·9407	·8927	·8361	·7664	·6740
18	1·3665	1·1704	1·0693	1·0047	·9590	·9246	·8757	·8178	·7462	·6502
19	1·3567	1·1591	1·0569	·9915	·9442	·9103	·8605	·8014	·7277	·6285
20	1·3480	1·1489	1·0458	·9798	·9329	·8974	·8469	·7867	·7115	·6086
21	1·3401	1·1398	1·0358	·9691	·9217	·8858	·8346	·7735	·6964	·5904
22	1·3329	1·1315	1·0268	·9595	·9116	·8753	·8234	·7612	·6828	·5738
23	1·3264	1·1240	1·0186	·9507	·9024	·8657	·8132	·7501	·6704	·5583
24	1·3205	1·1171	1·0111	·9427	·8939	·8569	·8038	·7400	·6589	·5440
25	1·3151	1·1108	1·0041	·9354	·8862	·8489	·7953	·7306	·6483	·5307
26	1·3101	1·1050	·9978	·9286	·8791	·8415	·7873	·7220	·6385	·5183
27	1·3055	1·0997	·9920	·9223	·8725	·8346	·7800	·7140	·6294	·5066
28	1·3013	1·0947	·9866	·9165	·8664	·8282	·7732	·7066	·6209	·4957
29	1·2973	1·0903	·9815	·9112	·8607	·8223	·7679	·6997	·6129	·4853
30	1·2936	1·0859	·9768	·9061	·8554	·8168	·7610	·6932	·6056	·4756
40	1·2674	1·0552	·9435	·8701	·8174	·7771	·7184	·6463	·5513	·4016
60	1·2413	1·0248	·9100	·8345	·7798	·7377	·6760	·5992	·4955	·3198
∞	1·1910	·9663	·8453	·7648	·7059	·6599	·5917	·5044	·3786	0·0000

xv

ANSWERS TO THE EXERCISES

AND HINTS ON THEIR SOLUTION

CHAPTER 1

1.1.	N	26,287	(AB)	887
	(A)	2,308	(AC)	374
	(B)	2,853	(BC)	353
	(C)	749	(ABC)	149

1.2.	(ABC)	156	(αBC)	179
	$(AB\gamma)$	431	$(\alpha B\gamma)$	1,249
	$(A\beta C)$	272	$(\alpha\beta C)$	163
	$(A\beta\gamma)$	759	$(\alpha\beta\gamma)$	20,504

1.3. The frequencies not given in the question itself are—
(a) (AB) 107 (AC) 405 (BC) 525.
(b) $(A\beta\gamma)$ 22,980 $(\alpha B\gamma)$ 13,585 $(\alpha\beta C)$ 96,478 $(\alpha\beta\gamma)$ 28,868,495.

1.4. $$\frac{(AB)}{(A\beta)} > \frac{(B)}{(\beta)} \quad \therefore \quad \frac{(AB)}{(AB)+(A\beta)} > \frac{(B)}{(B)+(\beta)}$$

that is $$\frac{(AB)}{(B)} > \frac{(A)}{N}, \text{ that is } \frac{(AB)}{(B)-(AB)} > \frac{(A)}{N-(A)}$$

that is $$\frac{(AB)}{(\alpha B)} > \frac{(A)}{(\alpha)}$$

1.7. 160. Take $A=$husband exceeding wife in first measurement, $B=$husband exceeding wife in second measurement, and find $(\alpha\beta)$.

1.8. 38. If A, B, C denote passing first, second and third examinations, (C), $(\alpha\beta C)$ and $(AB\gamma)$ are all that is necessary to answer the question. The other five frequencies (including N) are redundant.
Further, $N-(\alpha\beta C)-(\alpha\beta\gamma)=(A)+(B)-(ABC)-(AB\gamma)$, i.e. there is a linear relation between the given frequencies and the ultimate frequencies are therefore indeterminate.

1.9. 10 per cent.

1.11. Denoting government, voting for the motion and English membership by A, B, C, we have $(ABC)=300$, $(\alpha BC)=53$, $(A\beta C)=10$, $(\alpha\beta C)=102$, $(AB\gamma)=30$, $(\alpha B\gamma)=72$, $(A\beta\gamma)=8$, $(\alpha\beta\gamma)=25$.

1.13. 80/263 or 304 per thousand.

1.14. 55/85 or 65 per cent.

1.15. 32 per cent and 30 per cent.

1.16. 117.

1.17. 108.

1.20. $p \leqslant \frac{1}{4}(1-2q)$, $p \geqslant \frac{1}{4}(1+2q)$, i.e. p must lie between 0 and $\frac{1}{4}(1-2q)$ or between $\frac{1}{4}(1+2q)$ and $\frac{1}{2}$.

1.21. As a hint, remember the condition that—
$$(BC) \geqslant (B)+(C)-N$$

1.22 If A, B, C denote liking chocolates, toffee or boiled sweets, $(\alpha\beta\gamma)$ is negative.

CHAPTER 2

2.1. Deaf-mutes from childhood per million among males 222 ; among females 183 ; there is therefore positive association between deaf-mutism and male sex ; if there had been no association between deaf-mutism and sex, there would have been 3,176 male and 3,393 female deaf-mutes.

2.2. (a) Positive association, since $(AB)_0 = 1,457$.
(b) Negative association, since $294/490 = 3/5$, $380/570 = 2/3$.
(c) Independence, since $256/768 = 1/3$, $48/144 = 1/3$.

2.3.

	Percentage of Plants above the Average Height	
	Parentage Crossed	Self-fertilised
Ipomæa purpurea . .	86 per cent	25 per cent
Petunia violacia . .	79 ,,	17 ,,
Reseda lutea . . .	78 ,,	34 ,,
Reseda odorata . . .	71 ,,	45 ,,
Lobelia fulgens . . .	50 ,,	35 ,,

The association is much less for the species at the end than for those at the beginning of the list.

2.4. Percentage of dark-eyed amongst the sons of dark-eyed fathers 39 per cent. Percentage of dark-eyed amongst the sons of not dark-eyed fathers 10 per cent. If there had been no heredity, the frequencies to the nearest unit would have been $(AB)_0$ 18, $(A\beta)_0$ 111, $(\alpha B)_0$ 121, $(\alpha\beta)_0$ 750.

2.5. Percentage of light-eyed amongst the wives of light-eyed husbands 59 per cent. Percentage of light-eyed amongst the wives of not light-eyed husbands 53 per cent. If there had been no association : $(AB)_0 = 298$, $(A\beta)_0 = 225$, $(\alpha B)_0 = 143$, $(\alpha\beta)_0 = 108$.

2.6. The following are the proportions of the insane per thousand in successive age-groups—

In general population : 0·9, 2·3, 4·1, 5·7, 6·9, 7·5, 7·7, 6·8
Amongst the blind : 20·1, 16·0, 16·3, 20·7, 18·3, 17·8, 11·4, 5·3

Note the diminishing association, which is especially clear in the age-group 65–, and the negative association in the last age-group. The association coefficient gives the values below, which decrease continuously—

Association coefficient : $+0·92$, $+0·75$, $+0·61$, $+0·57$, $+0·46$, $+0·41$, $+0·20$, $-0·13$.

2.10. $+0·90$.

2.11. $+0·70$.

2.13. The frequencies are, for association—

(1)	(AB)	0	
	(αB)	$(\alpha\beta)$	
(2)	(AB)	$(A\beta)$	
	0	$(\alpha\beta)$	
(3)	(AB)	0	
	0	$(\alpha\beta)$	

and for disassociation—

(1)	0	$(A\beta)$	
	(αB)	$(\alpha\beta)$	
(2)	(AB)	$(A\beta)$	
	(αB)	0	
(3)	0	$(A\beta)$	
	(αB)		

2.14.

$(D)/N$	$= 6·9$ per cent		$(A)/N$	$= 6·8$ per cent
$(AD)/(A)$	$= 45·0$,,		$(AD)/(D)$	$= 44·6$,,
$(\beta D)/(\beta)$	$= 3·6$,,		$(A\beta)/(\beta)$	$= 4·7$,,
$(A\beta D)/(A\beta)$	$= 41·2$,,		$(A\beta D)/(\beta D)$	$= 54·9$,,
$(BD)/(B)$	$= 42·7$,,		$(AB)/(B)$	$= 29·2$,,
$(ABD)/(AB)$	$= 51·6$,,		$(ABD)/(BD)$	$= 35·3$,,

The above give two legitimate comparisons. The general results are the same as for the boys, i.e. a very small association between development defects and dulness amongst those exhibiting nerve signs, as compared with those who do not exhibit nerve signs, or with the girls in general. As the association amongst those who do not exhibit nerve signs is quite as high as for the girls in general, the " conclusion " quoted does not seem valid.

2.15.

	(1) Per thousand	(2) Per thousand		(1) Per thousand	(2) Per thousand
$(B)/N$	3·2	7·5	$(A)/N$	0·9	4·0
$(AB)/(A)$	14·9	11·7	$(AB)/(B)$	4·0	6·3
$(BC)/(C)$	38·8	63·0	$(AC)/(C)$	6·6	18·8
$(ABC)/(AC)$	216	214	$(ABC)/(BC)$	36·8	63·8

The above give the two simplest comparisons, either of which is sufficient to show that there is a high association between blindness and mental derangement amongst the deaf-mutes as well as association in the general population ; amongst the old, the association is, in fact, small for the general population, but well-marked for deaf-mutes. This result stands in direct contrast with that of Exercise 2.14, where the association between the two defects A and D was much smaller in the defective population β than in the population at large. As previously stated, no great reliance can be placed on the census data as to these infirmities.

2.16. If the cancer death-rates for farmers over 45 and under 45 respectively were the same as for the population at large, the rate for all farmers over 16 would be 2·726. This is *slightly* greater than the actual value 2·633 but the difference would not justify any statement that " farmers were peculiarly liable to cancer," or not.

2.17. 15 per cent.

2.19. If A and B were independent in both C and γ populations, we should have (AB) equal to

$$\frac{471 \times 419}{617} + \frac{151 \times 139}{383} = 374 \cdot 7$$

Actually (AB) is only 358. Therefore A and B must be disassociated in one partial population or both.

2.22. (1) 68·1 per cent. (2) 42·5 per cent. The possible fallacy that a total association between " spending more than one's opponent " and " winning " only meant that Conservatives spent more and that Conservative principles carried the day is now avoided, and there seems no reason for declining to consider this as evidence of the effect of expenditure on election results.

2.23. The limits to y are

$$y < \tfrac{1}{2}(3x - x^2 - 1) \\ > \tfrac{1}{2}(x + x^2)$$

subject to the conditions $y \leqslant x$, $y \geqslant 0$, $y \geqslant 2x - 1$. No inference of a positive association from two negatives is possible unless x lies between the limits $0 \cdot 382 \ldots , 0 \cdot 618 \ldots$

2.24. The limits to y are

(1)
$$y < \tfrac{1}{2}(6x - 6x^2 - 1) \\ > \tfrac{1}{2}(x + 6x^2)$$

subject to conditions $y \geqslant 0$, $\geqslant 4x - 1$, $\leqslant x$.
An inference is only possible from positive associations of AB and AC if $x \leqslant \tfrac{1}{6}$; an inference is only possible from two negative associations if x lie between $0 \cdot 211 \ldots$ and $0 \cdot 274 \ldots$ Note that x cannot exceed $\tfrac{1}{3}$.

(2)
$$y < \tfrac{1}{2}(6x - 3x^2 - 1) \\ > \tfrac{1}{2}(2x + 3x^2)$$

subject to conditions $y \geqslant 0$, $\geqslant 5x - 1$, $\leqslant x$.
No inference is possible from positive associations of AB and BC.
An inference is only possible from negative associations if x lie between $0 \cdot 183 \ldots$ and $0 \cdot 215 \ldots$ Note that x cannot exceed $\tfrac{1}{4}$.

(3)
$$y < \tfrac{1}{2}(6x - 2x^2 - 1) \\ > \tfrac{1}{2}(3x + 2x^2)$$

subject to the conditions $y \geqslant 0$, $\geqslant 5x - 1$, $\leqslant x$.
As in (2), no inference is possible from positive associations of AC and BC ; an inference is possible from negative associations if x lie between $0 \cdot 177 \ldots$ and $0 \cdot 224 \ldots$ Note that x cannot exceed $\tfrac{1}{4}$.

CHAPTER 3

3.1. A, $0 \cdot 68$; B, $0 \cdot 36$.

3.2. $C = 0 \cdot 02$, $T = 0 \cdot 01$.

3.4. The table is not isotropic as it stands. It becomes positively so if the columns are arranged in the order A_1, A_3, A_5, A_4, A_2, and the rows in order (from top to bottom) B_3, B_2, B_1.

3.5. $C = 0 \cdot 05$, $T = 0 \cdot 03$.

3.7. $C = 0 \cdot 40$. For a large number such as 1,000 this is probably significant, i.e. not due to fluctuations of sampling. From inspection of the tables the contingency is positive, i.e. this evidence would suggest that persons tended on the whole to prefer music of their own nationality. But there are exceptions, e.g. the English.

In any case these data are purely imaginary, and it is not suggested that they reflect in any way the true state of affairs.

3.8. $C = 0 \cdot 23$, $T = 0 \cdot 17$ suggestive of slight association.

3.10. $C = 0 \cdot 10$.

CHAPTER 4

4.1. 1200, 200.

4.2. 270, 40.

4.3. $92 \cdot 375$.

4.4. $216 \cdot 5$

4.5. (a) J-shaped ; (b) U-shaped ; (c) single-humped moderately asymmetrical; (d) J-shaped in all three cases.

CHAPTER 5

5.2. $14 \cdot 58$.

5.3. Mean, $156 \cdot 73$ lb. Median, $154 \cdot 67$ lb. Mode (approx.), $150 \cdot 6$ lb. (Note that the mean and the median should be taken to a place of decimals further than is desired for the mode ; the true mode, found by fitting a theoretical frequency curve, is $151 \cdot 1$ lb.)

5.4. Mean, $0 \cdot 6330$. Median, $0 \cdot 6391$. Mode (approx.), $0 \cdot 651$. (True mode is $0 \cdot 653$.)

5.5. About £3,250.

5.6. Mean $= \dfrac{n+1}{2}$.

5.7. (1) $82 \cdot 75$, (2) $81 \cdot 78$, (3) $80 \cdot 25$, (4) $80 \cdot 25$.

5.8. Arithmetic mean $= \dfrac{1}{n+1}(2^{n+1} - 1)$.

Geometric mean $= 2^{\frac{n}{2}}$.

Harmonic mean $= \dfrac{n+1}{2\left(1 - \dfrac{1}{2^{n+1}}\right)}$.

5.9. Mean $= np$. If the terms of the given binomial series are multiplied by 0, 1, 2, . . ., note that the resulting series is also a binomial when a common factor is removed. (A full proof is given in Chapter 10.)

5.11. (1) 921,507, (2) 916,963.

5.12. For N.M. specials, 15s. 1d. per 120 ; for ordinaries, 12s. 9d. per 120.

CHAPTER 6

6.2. Standard deviation 21·3 lb. Mean deviation 16·4 lb. Lower quartile 142·5, upper quartile 168·4; whence $Q=12·95$. Ratios: m.d./s.d.$=0·77$, Q/s.d.$=0·61$.

6.3. Median$=£3,250$, upper quartile$=£5,000$, 9th decile$=£8,600$ approximately.

6.4. $Q_1=24·13$ years. Median$=27·29$ years. $Q_3=32·19$ years. $Q=4·03$ years.

6.5. $2·872$.

6.6. This proposition is equivalent to the one that the square of the mean of a set of positive numbers is less than the mean of the squares. This is proved in most textbooks on Algebra.

6.8. (1) $M=73·2$, $\sigma=17·3$; (2) $M=73·2$, $\sigma=17·5$; (3) $M=73·2$, $\sigma=18·0$. (Note that while the mean is unaffected in the first place of decimals, the standard deviation is higher the coarser the grouping.)

6.9. England, $\sigma=2·55$; Scotland, $\sigma=2·48$; Wales, $\sigma=2·33$; Ireland, $\sigma=2·15$ inches. For the weight distribution $\sigma=21·14$ lb.

6.10. $\sqrt{npq}$. The proof is given in Chapter 8.

6.11. The assumption that observations are evenly distributed over the intervals does not affect the sum of deviations, except for the interval in which the mean or median lies; for that interval the sum is $n_2(0·25+d^2)$, hence the entire correction is

$$d(n_1-n_3)+n_2(0·25+d^2)$$

In this expression d is, of course, expressed as a fraction of the class-interval, and is given its proper sign.

6.14. $3·80$, $3·65$, $3·53$, $3·20$.

CHAPTER 7

7.1. In class-intervals of 10 lb.
$\mu_2=4·470$, $\mu_3=6·927$, $\mu_4=89·119$; $\beta_1=0·537$, $\beta_2=4·461$.
Curve leptokurtic.

7.2. $0·06$, $0·29$, $0·27$.

7.3. $\mu_2=11·375$, $\mu_3=12·705$, $\mu_4=428·708$, in class-intervals of 1 gallon.
$\beta_1=0·110$, $\beta_2=3·313$.
Measures of skewness are $0·027$, $0·14$, $0·15$. The second is obtained by approximating to the mode in the manner of **5.26**.

7.4. Before corrections, $\mu_2=7·301$, $\mu_3=0·166$, $\mu_4=163·465$;
After corrections, $\mu_2=6·551$, $\mu_3=0·166$, $\mu_4=132·975$.
Note that the small negative μ_3 in the finer grouping becomes positive in the coarser grouping.

7.5. $\mu_3=npq(q-p)$.
$\mu_4=3p^2q^2n^2+pqn(1-6pq)$.

7.6. About the mean, $\mu_2=14·75$, $\mu_3=39·75$, $\mu_4=142·3125$.
About the origin, $\mu_2'=21$, $\mu_3'=166$, $\mu_4'=1132$.

7.8. This proposition is equivalent to that of Exercise 6.6. For U-shaped populations $\beta_2<2$.

7.9. $\kappa_2=7·057$, $\kappa_3=36·152$, $\kappa_4=259·335$.

CHAPTER 8

8.1. $27·31$ per cent.

8.2. Expected frequencies are: 1, 12, 66, 220, 495, 792, 924, 792, 495, 220, 66, 12, 1.
Expected mean$=6$; expected $\sigma=1·732$.
Actual mean $=6·139$; actual $\sigma=1·712$.

8.3. $y=\dfrac{4096}{1\cdot712\sqrt{2\pi}}e^{-\frac{1}{2(1\cdot712)^2}(x-6\cdot139)^2}$

Expected frequencies, to nearest units, are : 2, 11, 51, 178, 438, 765, 951, 841, 529, 236, 75, 17, 3, totalling 4097 ; (these are obtained by simple interpolation in Appendix Table 1).

8.4. 17.

8.5. If p is the expectation of getting an even number,
$$^{10}C_5p^5q^5=2\times{}^{10}C_4p^4q^6$$
Hence, $p=\frac{5}{8}$, and the number of times is $10,000(\frac{3}{8})^{10}=$ once.

8.8. The frequency of r successes is greater than that of $r-1$ so long as $r<np+p$; if np is an integer, $r=np$ gives the greatest term and also the mean.

8.9. This follows at once from a consideration of the Galton-Pearson apparatus.

8.10.

Binomial	Normal curve
1	1·7
10	10·5
45	42·7
120	116·1
210	211·5
252	258·4
210	211·5
etc.	etc.

8.11. Mean 74·3, standard deviation 3·23.

8.12. About zero mean the deciles are : 0, 0·2533, 0·5244, 0·8416, 1·2816, and the corresponding negative values.

8.13. $y=\dfrac{8585}{2\cdot57\sqrt{2\pi}}e^{-\frac{1}{2(2\cdot57)^2}(x-67\cdot46)^2}$

Calculated mean and quartile deviations, 2·05 and 1·73 (observed, 2·02 and 1·75) These figures are in units of one inch.

8.14. Calculated mean and quartile deviations (years), 6·37 and 5·38 (observed 5·44 and 4·03).

8.15. 18.

8.16. $\sigma=2\cdot267$ (uncorrected).
Theoretical frequencies, 2, 5, 11, 20, 29, 35, 35, etc.

8.17. Theoretical frequencies, 336·5, 397·1, 234·6, 92·5, 27·3, 6·5, 1·3, 0·2.

8.18. $\kappa_2=1\cdot362$, $\kappa_3=1\cdot766$, $\kappa_4=2\cdot510$.

CHAPTER 9

9.1. $\sigma_x=1\cdot414$, $\sigma_y=2\cdot280$, $r=+0\cdot81$.
$X=0\cdot5Y+0\cdot5$, $Y=1\cdot3X+1\cdot1$.

9.2. r (between X and Y)$=-0\cdot66$; between Y and $Z=0\cdot60$; between Z and $X=-0\cdot13$.

9.4. $r=+0\cdot96$.

9.5. (1) $-0\cdot41$, (2) $+0\cdot40$.

CHAPTER 10

10.3. From equations (10.11) and (10.12) replace σ_1 and σ_2 by S_1 and S_2 in equation (10.10). Regarding this as an equation for r, note that r^2 is a maximum when tan 2θ is infinite, or $\theta=45°$.

10.4. In fig. 10.1 suppose every horizontal array to be given a slide to the right until its mean lies on the vertical axis through the mean of the whole distribution :

then suppose the ellipses to be squeezed in the direction of this vertical axis until they become circles. The original quadrant has now become a sector with an angle between one and two right angles, and the question is solved on determining its magnitude.

10.5. The ellipse is a horizontal section of the surface. Its equation is

$$\frac{x^2}{\sigma_1^2} - \frac{2rxy}{\sigma_1\sigma_2} + \frac{y^2}{\sigma_2^2} = 1 - r^2$$

and the standard deviations of sections are the square roots of the lengths of radii vectors of the ellipse.

10.6. The maximum and minimum s.d.'s are given by the principal axes, which leads to equations (10.11) and (10.12).

For an intermediate value there are two radii vectors and hence two sections.

10.8. a and b must be negative, and $ab - h^2 \geqslant 0$.

$$\sigma_1^2 = -\frac{1}{2}\frac{b}{ab - h^2}, \qquad \sigma_2^2 = -\frac{1}{2}\frac{a}{ab - h^2}$$

$$r = \frac{h}{\sqrt{ab}}$$

10.9. The sum of the pth powers of the first n natural numbers is $n^{p+1}/(p+1)$ plus terms of lower order in n.

10.10. Use equation (9.11).

CHAPTER 11

11.1. $\eta_{xy} = 0.242$, $\eta_{yx} = 0.266$.

11.2. $\eta_{xy} = 0.82$, $\eta_{yx} = 0.80$.

11.3. $\rho = +0.79$.

11.4. If the judges be denoted by 1, 2, 3,

$$\rho_{12} = -0.21, \qquad \rho_{23} = -0.30, \qquad \rho_{13} = +0.64$$

This suggests that judges 1 and 3 have tastes in common, but neither has much in common with judge 2.

11.5. $Q = 2/3$.

11.6. $Q = 0.77$.

11.10. $r = +0.83$.

11.11. $r = +0.22$, 11,868 entries.

CHAPTER 12

12.1. $r_{12.3} = +0.759$, $r_{13.2} = +0.097$, $r_{23.1} = -0.436$.

$\sigma_{1.23} = 2.64$, $\sigma_{2.13} = 0.594$, $\sigma_{3.12} = 70.1$.

$X_1 = 9.31 + 3.37X_2 + 0.00364X_3$.

12.2. $R_{1(23)} = 0.80$, $R_{2(31)} = 0.84$, $R_{3(12)} = 0.57$.

12.3. $r_{12.34} = +0.680$, $r_{13.24} = +0.803$, $r_{14.23} = +0.397$.

$r_{23.14} = -0.433$, $r_{24.13} = -0.553$, $r_{34.12} = -0.149$.

$\sigma_{1.234} = 9.17$, $\sigma_{2.134} = 49.2$, $\sigma_{3.124} = 12.5$, $\sigma_{4.123} = 105.4$.

$X_1 = 53 + 0.127X_2 + 0.587X_3 + 0.0345X_4$.

12.4. $R_{1(23)} = 0.87$, $R_{1(234)} = 0.89$.

12.5. $(X_1 - 19.9) = 4.51(X_2 - 49.2) - 0.88(X_3 - 30.2)$
$$-0.072(X_4 - 4814) + 0.63(X_5 - 41.6)$$

$r_{15.3} = -0.03$.

$r_{15.4} = +0.25$.

$r_{15.34} = +0.23$.

$R_{1(2345)} = 0.77$.

12.7. Number of order $s = n \times {}^{n-1}C_s$

Total number $= n \{2^{n-1} - 1\}$

This includes coefficients of type $R_{1(2)}$ and counts $R_{1(2)}$ as different from $R_{2(1)}$.

12.8. The correlation of the pth order is $r/(1+pr)$. Hence if r be negative, the correlation of order $n-2$ cannot be numerically greater than unity and r cannot exceed (numerically) $1/(n-1)$.

12.9. $r_{12.3} = -1$, $r_{13.2} = r_{23.1} = +1$.

12.10. $r_{12.3} = r_{13.2} = r_{23.1} = -1$.

CHAPTER 13

13.1. In Table 9.5 the unit, being a weekly figure, is not modifiable to the extent that it relates to the situation at a given point of time. The choice of different intervals between the points (e.g. months) might, perhaps, give a somewhat different picture. In Table 9.6 the unit is a registration district and is modifiable by the amalgamation of districts.

13.2. For this series $r = -0.87$. This is to be regarded as a nonsense-correlation, although a very profound analysis might suggest that the falling infantile mortality was due to technical progress which also made increases in population possible.

13.3. During the period steam vessels were replaced by diesel oil burners to some extent and horse-drawn vehicles by oil-propelled vehicles. From this point of view the correlation is hardly nonsense, though the relationship is very remote.

CHAPTER 14

14.1. Estimated true standard deviation 6.91; standard deviation of fluctuations of sampling 9.38. (The latter, which can be independently calculated, is too low, and the former consequently probably too high. Cf. **17.30**.)

14.2. 0.43.

14.3. 58 per cent.

14.4. $\sigma_2{}^2 / \sqrt{(\sigma_1{}^2 + \sigma_2{}^2)(\sigma_2{}^2 + \sigma_3{}^2)}$

14.5. $\dfrac{a\sigma_1}{\sqrt{a^2\sigma_1{}^2 + b^2\sigma_2{}^2}}$

14.6. 0.29

14.7. $r_{12} = \dfrac{1}{2ab\sigma_1\sigma_2}(-a^2\sigma_1{}^2 - b^2\sigma_2{}^2 + c^2\sigma_3{}^2)$

The others may be written down from symmetry.

14.8. (1) No effect at all. (2) If the mean value of the errors in variables is d, and in the weights e, the value found for the weighted mean is—

$$\text{The true value} + d - r.\sigma_x.\sigma_w \frac{e}{\overline{w}(\overline{w}+e)}$$

If r is small, d is the important term, and hence errors in the quantities are usually of more importance than errors in the weights. If r become considerable, errors in the weights may be of consequence, but it does not seem probable that the second term would become the most important in practical cases.

14.9. $r = +0.036$.

14.10. $\dfrac{\text{var B}}{\sqrt{\{(\text{var A} + \text{var B})(\text{var B} + \text{var C})\}}}$

CHAPTER 15

15.1. Line : $\qquad Y = 2 \cdot 58 + 1 \cdot 13(X-2)$
$\quad$ Quadratic : $\quad Y = 1 \cdot 48 + 1 \cdot 13(X-2) + 0 \cdot 55(X-2)^2$
$\quad$ Cubic : $\qquad Y = 1 \cdot 48 + 0 \cdot 025(X-2) + 0 \cdot 55(X-2)^2 + 0 \cdot 325(X-2)^3$
$\quad$ Sums of squares of residuals : $5 \cdot 819,\ 1 \cdot 584,\ 0 \cdot 063.$

15.2. If Y is the average number of children for the duration X to $X+1$ years—

$\quad$ Line : $\qquad Y = 3 \cdot 814 + 0 \cdot 887\left(\dfrac{X}{5} - 3\right)$

$\quad$ Quadratic : $\quad Y = 4 \cdot 351 + 0 \cdot 887\left(\dfrac{X}{5} - 3\right) - 0 \cdot 134\left(\dfrac{X}{5} - 3\right)^2$

$\quad$ Cubic : $\qquad Y = 4 \cdot 351 + 0 \cdot 912\left(\dfrac{X}{5} - 3\right) - 0 \cdot 134\left(\dfrac{X}{5} - 3\right)^2 - 0 \cdot 00361\left(\dfrac{X}{5} - 3\right)^2$

For $X = 17$ the three values are $4 \cdot 17,\ 4 \cdot 68,\ 4 \cdot 69.$

15.3. $\gamma = 1 \cdot 42$

15.4. $X = $ Gross output per £100 labour, $Y = $ gross output.
$\quad Y = 48 \cdot 33 + 0 \cdot 2375X - 0 \cdot 00005546X^2.$

CHAPTER 17

17.1. Theo. $M = 6,\ \sigma = 1 \cdot 732$: Actual $M = 6 \cdot 116,\ \sigma = 1 \cdot 732.$

17.2. (a) Theo. $M = 2 \cdot 5,\ \sigma = 1 \cdot 118$: Actual $M = 2 \cdot 48,\ \sigma = 1 \cdot 14.$
$\quad$ (b) $\quad,, \qquad M = 3, \quad\ \ \sigma = 1 \cdot 225$: $\quad,, \qquad M = 2 \cdot 97,\ \sigma = 1 \cdot 26.$
$\quad$ (c) $\quad,, \qquad M = 3 \cdot 5,\ \sigma = 1 \cdot 323$: $\quad,, \qquad M = 3 \cdot 47,\ \sigma = 1 \cdot 40.$

17.3. The standard deviation of the proportion is $0 \cdot 00179$, and the actual divergence is $5 \cdot 4$ times this, and therefore almost certainly significant.

17.4. The standard deviation of the number drawn is 32, and the actual difference from expectation 18. There is no significance.

17.5. Difference from expectation $7 \cdot 5$; standard error $10 \cdot 0$. The difference might therefore occur frequently as a fluctuation of sampling.

17.6. Standard error of proportion of bad eggs $= 1 \cdot 6536$ per cent. A range of three times this gives range of $7 \cdot 5$ per cent to $17 \cdot 5$ per cent approximately.

17.7. The test can be applied either by the formulæ of Case 2 (**17.28**) or those of Case 3 (**17.29**). Case 2 is taken as the simplest.
$\qquad (AB)/(B) = 70 \cdot 1$ per cent. ; $(A\beta)/(\beta) = 64 \cdot 3$ per cent.
Difference $5 \cdot 8$ per cent. $(A)/N = 67 \cdot 6$ per cent and thence $\epsilon_{12} = 3 \cdot 40$ per cent. The actual difference is $1 \cdot 7$ times this and might, rather infrequently, occur as a fluctuation of sampling.

17.9. Difference of proportions $= \frac{1}{10}$, $\epsilon_{12} = 0 \cdot 033$. Difference significant. Similar conclusions follow if the formulæ of Case 3 (**17.29**) are applied.

17.10. Proportion $= 36$ per cent. Limits $32 \cdot 4 - 39 \cdot 6$ per cent. The sampling is almost certainly not simple. Possible causes are : (a) nature of subject-matter might require words of certain type, e.g. scientific words probably would not be Anglo-Saxon ; (b) the occurrence of one word influences the occurrence of the next.

17.11. If there are f_1 samples of n_1 individuals each, f_2 of n_2, etc.,

$$Ns^2 = pq\left(\frac{f_1}{n_1} + \frac{f_2}{n_2} + \ldots\right)$$

$$s^2 = \frac{pq}{H}$$

17.12. Standard error of expected proportion=23·05 per cent.
Standard deviation of actual distribution=23·09 per cent.

17.13. Standard deviation of simple sampling 23·0 per cent. The actual standard deviation does not, therefore, seem to indicate any real variation, but only fluctuations of sampling.

17.14. $\sigma^2=npq$ as if the chance of success were p in all cases (but the mean is $n/2$, not pn).

17.17. Mean number of deaths per annum$=\sigma_0^2=680$,
$$\sigma^2=566{,}582 \qquad r=0\cdot000029.$$

CHAPTER 18

18.1. $P=0\cdot1773$.

18.2. $P=0\cdot9595$.

18.3. Median : Estimated frequency$=1554$. Standard error $0\cdot28$ lb.
Lower Q : frequency 1472. Standard error $0\cdot26$ lb.
Upper Q : frequency 1116. Standard error $0\cdot34$ lb.

18.4. $0\cdot18$ lb.

18.5. $0\cdot24$ lb., 14 per cent less than the s.e. of the median.

18.6. Estimated frequencies : $Q_1=67{,}548$, $Mi=63{,}152$, $Q_3=30{,}488$.
Standard errors (years) $0\cdot011$, $0\cdot013$, $0\cdot023$.

18.7. Standard error of mean$=0\cdot015$ years.

18.8. Standard error of quartiles $0\cdot020$ years.

18.9. $\dfrac{\sigma}{\sqrt{n}}\times1\cdot34270$.

18.10. $\epsilon_{12}=1\cdot36$ shillings. Difference of means 2 shillings. Difference hardly suggestive of real effect.

18.12. Yes, one might, because the results on farms in successive years are correlated.

18.13. Mean $=5\cdot613$; s.e. of mean $0\cdot10$.
Median $=8\cdot128$; s.e. of median $0\cdot21$.

18.14. $P=0\cdot309$.

18.15. £450,000 ; £1,350,000.

18.16. $0\cdot12$ inch.

CHAPTER 19

19.1. Standard error$=0\cdot223$ lb.
On basis of normal distribution$=0\cdot170$ lb.

19.2. $0\cdot011$, $0\cdot014$.

19.3. S.e. of s.d.$=0\cdot707\dfrac{\sigma}{\sqrt{n}}$

S.e. of Q. $=0\cdot787\dfrac{\sigma}{\sqrt{n}}$

19.4. Difference of s.d.'s $0\cdot2$. On the assumption of normality $\epsilon_{12}=0\cdot088$. Difference might therefore arise, rather infrequently, as sampling fluctuation.

19.5. $r=-0\cdot008$ for height distribution, $r=+0\cdot71$ for marriage distribution.

19.6. var $\lambda_1 = \dfrac{\sigma^2}{n}$

var $\lambda_2 = \dfrac{\mu_4 - \mu_2}{n} = \dfrac{2\sigma^4}{n}$ for normal curve.

var $\lambda_3 = \dfrac{\mu_4 - \mu_3{}^2 - 6\mu_4\mu_2 + 9\mu_2{}^3}{n} = \dfrac{6\sigma^6}{n}$ for normal curve.

var $\lambda_4 = \dfrac{1}{n}\{36\mu_2{}^2(\mu_4 - \mu_2{}^2) + (\mu_8 - \mu_4{}^2 - 8\mu_5\mu_3)$

$$+ 16\mu_2\mu_3{}^2 - 12\mu_2(\mu_6 - \mu_2\mu_4 - 4\mu_3{}^2)\}$$

$= \dfrac{24\sigma^8}{n}$ for normal curve.

19.7. For the 6th and lower moments.

19.9. Standard errors are $0\cdot0176$, $0\cdot0158$, $0\cdot0263$, and results might all have arisen from an uncorrelated population ; if the population were actually uncorrelated, the standard errors would be the same to the number of places given, owing to the smallness of r.

19.10. Standard errors $0\cdot0758$, $0\cdot1308$, $0\cdot0850$, and the correlations are all significant.

CHAPTER 20

20.1. $\chi^2 = 5\cdot811$, $\nu = 7$, $P = 0\cdot56$.

20.3. $\chi^2 = 4\cdot3$, $\nu = 9$, $P = 0\cdot89$. The hypothesis seems reasonable.

20.5. $\chi^2 = 27\cdot94$, $\nu = 4$, $P = 0\cdot000012$. The association is significant.

20.6. $\chi^2 = 0\cdot7080$, $\nu = 1$, $P = 0\cdot400$. The divergences from expectation may well have arisen by sampling fluctuations.

20.7. Use the result that for large n, χ^2 is distributed approximately normally.

20.8. $\chi^2 = 27\cdot68$, $\nu = 4$, $P = 0\cdot00001$. The data are very suggestive of association.

20.11. $\chi^2 = 13\cdot15$, $\nu = 2$, $P = 0\cdot0014$. This is rather low and we suspect the sampling to be non-random.

20.12. $\chi^2 = 9\cdot993$, $\nu = 3$, $P = 0\cdot018$. Not a very good fit. (In this Exercise the last four frequencies have been grouped together and ν reduced by unity to allow for the estimation of the mean of the Poisson distribution.)

20.14. $\chi^2 = 0\cdot4700$, $\nu = 3$, $P = 0\cdot943$ (by direct calculation).

20.16. If the total number of births is spread over the period evenly (on the basis of number of days in the various months) the theoretical frequencies are 50,349, for a month of 31 days, 48,724 for a month of 30 days and 45,476 for February. $\chi^2 = 333\cdot9$ and deviations cannot be due to chance.

CHAPTER 21

21.1. $t = -0\cdot664$, $\nu = 9$, $P = 0\cdot738$.
The probability that we should get a value of t greater *in absolute value* is $0\cdot524$.

21.2. The differences in the returns, including cost of manure, have mean$=1$, $s'^2 = 1\cdot375$, $t = 1\cdot907$, $\nu = 4$, $P = 0\cdot935$. Assuming that distribution of differences is normal, a greater value would arise about 65 times in 1,000. There is some reason for supposing that the increased returns on the better manured plot are real, and that it would therefore pay to continue the more expensive dressing.

21.3. Applying the t test for two samples,

$$t = 0\cdot0991, \qquad \nu = 14, \qquad P = 0\cdot54$$

There is nothing in this test to suggest that populations were unlike as regards height,

21.4. $z=0.1761$, $\nu_1=9$, $\nu_2=5$. The difference of standard deviations is not significant. Coupled with Exercise 21.3, we conclude that there is no ground for supposing the two populations different as regards height.

21.5. Applying the t test for two samples,

$$t=2.683, \qquad \nu=4, \qquad P=0.972$$

The difference of means is likely to be significant, which supports the suggestion.

21.6. $z=\tfrac{1}{2}\log_e\dfrac{1+r}{1-r}=-0.549 \qquad \sigma=\dfrac{1}{\sqrt{12}}=0.2887$

The observed deviation is suggestive, but not decisive.

21.8. $P=0.0048$. For the standard error formula $P=0.0000078$.

21.9. All significant.

CHAPTER 22

22.1. The analysis is

	Sum of squares	d.f.	Quotient
Between batches . .	44,360	3	14,787
Residual . .	151,351	22	6,880
Total . .	195,711	25	7,828

$z=0.383$ which is not significant.

22.3. The analysis is

	Sum of squares	d.f.	Quotient
Between consignments .	9.71	5	1.94
Between observers .	13.13	3	4.38
Residual . .	13.12	15	0.87
Total . .	35.96	23	

Differences between observers are significant at the 5% level.

22.5. All significant.

22.6. Significantly non-linear.

22.8. The analysis is

	Sum of squares	d.f.
Between investigators	775	4
Between areas . .	239	4
Residual . .	1,175	16
Total . .	2,190	24

Differences are not significant.

CHAPTER 23

23.6. (a) 0.0726, (b) 0.0553, (c) 0.0661, (d) 0.0482.

CHAPTER 24

24.1. 0.93877, 0.93823, 0.93822.

24.2. 0.823632, 0.818050, 0.817939. The inclusion of the third difference affects only the fourth place by a single unit, so we can probably trust the answer to four figures.

24.3. Using logarithmic interpolation, the successive approximations are : 0·11200, 0·10044, 0·09963. Second difference interpolation using the last three data only gives 0·09859. It looks as if we could trust the figure as about 0·100 or 0·099.

24.4 4195, 4443, 4724, 5036, 5380.

24.7. 11·388 approximately.

24.8. Median 4·8924, 4·8869. First decile 1·9474, 1·9572. Ninth decile 8·4286, 8·3733. As we would probably state such figures only to two decimal places, the median would not be appreciably affected by taking second differences into account, but the deciles would be slightly corrected.

24.9. Maximum at 1·336, or day 40, 25th July, value 63·7.
Minimum at 1·184, or day 35·5, 20th-21st January, value 38·0.
These estimates are very poor. The maximum is actually 63·4 on 15th-17th July, and the minimum 37·9 on 8th-12th January.

CHAPTER 25

25.1. Index numbers are

1923	100	1927	100	1931	87
4	101	8	90	2	81
5	101	9	98	3	79
6	100	1930	98	4	77
				5	81

25.3. Index numbers are

	(1)	(2)
1930	100	100
1	81	102
2	75	90
3	71	91
4	74	95
5	75	97
6	79	103

25.4. To nearest unit, index is 102 in all cases.

25.6. Index numbers are

	(1)	(2)
1935	100	100
6	101	100
7	109	110
8	103	105
9	106	107
1940	134	131
1	134	131
2	141	138
3	146	144

CHAPTER 26

26.1. The figures are given in Table 27.1, page 640.

26.3. To the nearest unit the first average gives—
73 (1924), 72, 71, 71, 68, 67, 66, 66, 63, 62, 61, 59, 57, 56, 56, 56, 56, 56, 54, 52, 49 (1944).
A second average of these figures gives—
71 (1926), 70, 69, 68, 66, 65, 64, 62, 60, 59, 58, 57, 56, 56, 55, 55, 53 (1942).

26.4. Expressed as a percentage of the average monthly rainfall the figures are—

		1943	1944	1945	1946
Jan.	. .	207	110	114	114
Feb.	. .	70	66	121	132
Mar.	. .	34	19	49	' 56
April	. .	66	104	80	85
May	. .	139	65	139	130
June	. .	94	102	131	139
July	. .	77	98	91	108
Aug.	. .	96	96	84	161
Sept.	. .	134	165	98	193
Oct.	. .	86	113	103	38
Nov.	. .	77	175	23	178
Dec.	. .	54	71	105	102

26.5. $r_1 = +0.735$, $r_2 = +0.367$, $r_3 = +0.054$, $r_4 = -0.102$, $r_5 = -0.082$, $r_6 = +0.027$.

26.7. The weights of the process are

$$\frac{1}{75} [1, 3, 6, 9, 12, 13, \ldots]$$

26.8. The index-numbers are—

1926	126	1936	108
7	102	7	119
8	92	8	92
9	103	9	90
30	99	40	99
1	87	1	91
2	80	2	85
3	83	3	83
4	75	4	81
5	94	5	87

26.9. As a preliminary show that for a cubic curve (third differences constant)

$$\frac{1}{k} [k] u_t = u_t + \frac{k^2 - 1}{24} (u_{t+1} - 2u_t + u_{t-1})$$

26.10. The index-numbers are—

	Quarter			
	1	2	3	4
1928			120	118
9	117	115	112	109
30	104	99	94	89
1	86	84	83	83
2	83	82	80	79
3	79	79	80	81
4	81	82	82	83
5	83	84		

26.12 See the hint on Exercise 26.9.

CHAPTER 27

27.1. The number of turning points is 31, almost exactly the expected number 30.67.

27.2. When $\mu = 0$, the mean-distance is 3, the known result for random series.

27.3. The mean distances are $7 \cdot 28$, $4 \cdot 96$ and $4 \cdot 96$ and the autoregressive periods are $10 \cdot 90$, $7 \cdot 24$ and $5 \cdot 68$, respectively.

27.5. $a = -1 \cdot 206$, $b = +0 \cdot 420$.

27.10. The autocorrelations are as follows—

k	r_k	k	r_k
1	0·957	11	−0·053
2	0·836	12	−0·030
3	0·660	13	−0·012
4	0·461	14	−0·002
5	0·269	15	0·003
6	0·111	16	0·003
7	0·000	17	0·002
8	−0·061	18	0·001
9	−0·082	19	0·000
10	−0·074	20	0·000

INDEX

[The references are to pages. References to Greek letters follow those for Roman letters.]

nical definition, 547-9 ; cumulative effect of, 549

—, in scale reading, 74

Biehl, K., data cited from, 315

Bielfeld, Baron, J. F. von, use of word " statistics ", xvi

Binomial distribution, 169-195 ; genesis of, 169-171 ; form of, 172-174 ; contents of, 174-6 ; mechanical representation of, 176 ; limiting form, 177-181 ; Poisson distribution, 189-191 ; in sampling of attributes, 386-394, *see* Sampling of Attributes

Birth-rate, in local government areas, 70 ; correlation with number of births, 206, constants of distribution (Exercise 9.3) 234 ; standardisation of, 333-7

—, of cattle, (Table 26.3), 614

Bivariate distribution, 201 ; normal surface, 237-250 ; *see also* Correlation

Blackman, V. H., data on duckweed, 350

Bortkiewicz, L. von, Poisson distribution, 193

Breaking-up a group, in interpolation, 571-3

British Association, data cited from, (stature, Table 4.7) 82 ; (weight, Table to Exercise 4.6), 100

CAMBRIDGESHIRE, mortality in, 561

Cards, punched, for recording of data, 62 ; for sampling, 375

Carroll, Lewis (pseudonym), (Exercise 1.9) 16

Cells, in χ^2-test, 459

Census data, *see* Registrar-General

Centred averages, 624

Chance, *see* Randomness, Probability

Charlier, C. V. L., in sampling theory, 407

Chi-square, chi-squared, *see* χ^2.

Cholera and inoculation, 25, 27, 467, 473

Chrysomelidae, *see* Beetles

Circular test, in index-numbers, 602

Clark, R. D., data from, 194

Class, in theory of attributes, 2-4 ; class-frequency, 3 ; ultimate classes, 5-7 ; positive and negative classes, 3

Class-interval, definition, 70 ; choice of magnitude and position, 72-4 ; *see also* Sheppard's Corrections

Classification, generally, 1-2 ; by dichotomy, 2-3 ; manifold, 49 ; homogeneous 59-61 ; as series of dichotomies, 61 ; by punched cards, 62

Closeness of fit, *see* χ^2

Cloudiness at Greenwich, (Fig. 4.15), 93, (Table 4,14) 96 ;

Coefficients of association etc, *see* under Association etc.

Complex frequency-distributions, 92

Confluence analysis, 323

Consistence, of class-frequencies, 9-11 ; of correlation coefficients, 301-2.

Constraints, in Lexis' sense, 408 ; in χ^2, 461

Contingency, coefficient of (Pearson's) 53, (Tschuprow's) 54 ; isotropy in, 57-9 ; relation with normal correlation, 250 ; standard error of, 454

—, tables, definition, 50 ; association in, 51-2 ; isotropy in, 57-9, 248 ; independence in, 59 ; degrees of freedom in, 462 ; tests of divergence from independence, 467-8

Corrections, for grouping, *see* Sheppard's Corrections

—, of correlations for errors of observation, 328 ; of death-rates, 335-7

Correlation, generally, 199-339 ; construction of tables, 199-201 ; representation of tables by diagrammatic methods, 203-212 ; treatment as contingency, 212 ; for illustrations *see* Frequency-distributions, Illustrations

Product-moment coefficient, definition, 218 ; lines of regression 214-8 ; calculation of, 222-230 ; corrections for grouping, 231 ; estimation of, 253-5 ; modifiable unit, 310-2 ; attenuation of, 313-5 ; nonsense correlations, 315-7 ; errors of observation in, 328 ; between indices, 330-1 ; heterogeneity of material, 331 ; standard error of, 451-2; significance in small samples, 495-9

Rank-correlation, 258-268, *see* Rank-correlation ; grade-correlation, 268-9 ; tetrachoric correlation, 270-1 ; intraclass correlation, 272-7

—, normal, 237-252 ; linearity of regression in, 240-1 ; homoscedasticity in, 241 ; isotropy in, 248-250 ; relation with contingency, 250 ; multivariate, 303-6

—, partial, 281-306 ; generalised regressions, 282 ; notation, 284 ; expression in terms of lower order coefficients, 290 ; calculation, of, 290-7 ; expression in terms of higher order coefficients, 300-1; fallacies in interpretation, 302-3 ; test of significance, 451, 495-9

—, multiple, 281, 361 ; coefficient of, 298-300 ; significance of, 453, 521-2

—, ratios, 256-8 ; relation with goodness of fit, 361 ; significance of, 453, 517-9

—, serial, in time-series, 639

Correlogram, definition, 651 ; of autoregressive and harmonic series, 651-4

Cosin, value of estates in 1715 (Table 4.12), 94

Cost of living index, 596

—, of electricity, *see* Electricity

Covariance, definition, 222

Coutts, J. R. H., data cited from (Table 15.5), 356.

GRIFFIN'S STATISTICAL MONOGRAPHS AND COURSES:

Descriptive brochure available from Charles Griffin & Co. Ltd.